INTERNATIONAL HANDBOOK OF JEWISH EDUCATION

International Handbooks of Religion and Education

VOLUME 5

Aims & Scope

The *International Handbooks of Religion and Education* series aims to provide easily accessible, practical, yet scholarly, sources of information about a broad range of topics and issues in religion and education. Each Handbook presents the research and professional practice of scholars who are daily engaged in the consideration of these religious dimensions in education. The accessible style and the consistent illumination of theory by practice make the series very valuable to a broad spectrum of users. Its scale and scope bring a substantive contribution to our understanding of the discipline and, in so doing, provide an agenda for the future.

For further volumes:
http://www.springer.com/series/7477

International Handbook of Jewish Education

Part Two

Edited by

Helena Miller
UJIA, London, UK

Lisa D. Grant
Hebrew Union College-Jewish Institute of Religion, New York, NY, USA

and

Alex Pomson
Hebrew University, Jerusalem, Israel

Editors
Helena Miller
United Jewish Israel Appeal (UJIA)
37 Kentish Town Road
NW1 8NX London
United Kingdom
helena.miller@ujia.org

Prof. Lisa D. Grant
Hebrew Union College
Jewish Institute of Religion
Brookdale Center
1 West 4th St.
10012 New York
NY
USA
lgrant54@gmail.com

Prof. Alex Pomson
Hebrew University of Jerusalem
Melton Centre for Jewish Education
Mount Scopus
Jerusalem
Israel
apomson@mscc.huji.ac.il

ISSN 1874-0049 e-ISSN 1874-0057
Printed in 2 parts
ISBN 978-94-007-0353-7 e-ISBN 978-94-007-0354-4
DOI 10.1007/978-94-007-0354-4
Springer Dordrecht Heidelberg London New York

Library of Congress Control Number: 2011922526

© Springer Science+Business Media B.V. 2011
No part of this work may be reproduced, stored in a retrieval system, or transmitted in any form or by any means, electronic, mechanical, photocopying, microfilming, recording or otherwise, without written permission from the Publisher, with the exception of any material supplied specifically for the purpose of being entered and executed on a computer system, for exclusive use by the purchaser of the work.

Printed on acid-free paper

Springer is part of Springer Science+Business Media (www.springer.com)

Contents of Part Two

Section Three: Applications

Academic Jewish Studies in North America 657
Judith R. Baskin

Adult Jewish Learning: The Landscape 669
Lisa D. Grant and Diane Tickton Schuster

Congregational Schools 691
Isa Aron

**Day Schools in the Liberal Sector: Challenges and Opportunities
at the Intersection of Two Traditions of Jewish Schooling** 713
Alex Pomson

Day Schools in the Orthodox Sector – A Shifting Landscape 729
Shani Bechhofer

Early Childhood Education 749
Michael Ben-Avie, Ilene Vogelstein, Roberta Louis Goodman,
Eli Schaap, and Pat Bidol-Padva

Experiential Jewish Education: Reaching the Tipping Point 767
David Bryfman

**Gender: Shifting from "Evading" to "Engaging"—Gender
Issues and Jewish Adolescents** 785
Shira D. Epstein

**Informal Education: The Decisive Decade – How Informal
Jewish Education Was Transformed in Its Relationship
with Jewish Philanthropy** 805
Joseph Reimer

Intermarriage: Connection, Commitment, and Community 825
Evie Levy Rotstein

Learning Organisations: Learning to Learn – The Learning
Organisation in Theory and Practice 843
Susan L. Shevitz

Limmud: A Unique Model of Transformative Jewish Learning 861
Raymond Simonson

Mentoring: Ideological Encounters – Mentoring Teachers
in Jewish Education 879
Michal Muszkat-Barkan

Parents and Jewish Educational Settings 901
Jeffrey S. Kress

Practitioner Enquiry and Its Role in Jewish Education 917
Alex Sinclair

Preparing Teachers for Jewish Schools: Enduring Issues
in Changing Contexts 937
Sharon Feiman-Nemser

Professional Development of Teachers in Jewish Education 959
Gail Zaiman Dorph

Professional Development: *Vini, Vidi, Vici*? Short-Term Jewish
Educators Trips to Israel as Professional-Development Programs 981
Shelley Kedar

Rabbis as Educators: Their Professional Training
and Identity Formation 1001
Lisa D. Grant and Michal Muszkat-Barkan

Special Education: "And You Shall Do That Which Is Right
and Good . . ." Jewish Special Education in North America:
From Exclusion to Inclusion 1021
Rona Milch Novick and Jeffrey Glanz

Teacher Education: Ensuring a Cadre of Well-Qualified
Educational Personnel for Jewish Schools 1041
Leora Isaacs, Kate O'Brien, and Shira Rosenblatt

Ultra-Orthodox/Haredi Education 1063
Yoel Finkelman

Section Four: Geographical

American-Jewish Education in an Age of Choice and Pluralism 1087
Jack Wertheimer

Anglo-Jewish Education: Day Schools, State Funding
and Religious Education in State Schools 1105
David Mendelsson

Contents of Part Two

Australia: The Jewel in the Crown of Jewish Education 1125
Paul Forgasz and Miriam Munz

Canada: Jewish Education in Canada 1141
Michael Brown

**Europe: Education of Adult Jewish Leaders
in a Pan-European Perspective** 1155
Barbara Lerner Spectre

**Europe: Something from (Almost) Nothing – The Challenges
of Education in European Communities – A Personal Perspective** . . . 1167
Steve Israel

Former Soviet Union: Jewish Education 1183
Olga Markus and Michael Farbman

France: Jewish Education in France 1203
Ami Bouganim

Israel: State Religious Education in Israel 1219
Zehavit Gross

Israel: Innovations in Secular Schooling in Israel 1235
Yehuda Bar Shalom and Tamar Ascher Shai

**Latin America – Jewish Education in Latin America:
Challenges, Trends and Processes** 1253
Yossi Goldstein and Drori Ganiel

Netherlands – Social Integration and Religious Identity 1271
Henny van het Hoofd

Author Index 1289

Subject Index 1295

Contents of Part One

Introduction 1
Helena Miller, Lisa D. Grant, and Alex Pomson

Section One: Vision and Practice

**Analytic Philosophy of Education and Jewish Education:
The Road Not Taken** 11
Barry Chazan

**Community Engagement: The Challenge of Connecting Jewish
Schools to the Wider Community** 29
Helena Miller

Culture: Restoring Culture to Jewish Cultural Education 47
Zvi Bekerman and Sue Rosenfeld

**Curriculum Development: What We Can Learn
from International Curricula** 63
Roberta Louis Goodman and Jan Katzew

**Curriculum Integration in Jewish Day Schools: The Search
for Coherence** 83
Mitchel Malkus

Gender and Jewish Education: "Why Doesn't This Feel So Good?" . . 99
Tova Hartman and Tamar Miller

**Historiography of American Jewish Education:
A Case for Guarded Optimism** 117
Jonathan Krasner

Janush Korczak's Life and Legacy for Jewish Education 143
Marc Silverman

Jewish Identities: Educating for Multiple and Moving Targets 163
Stuart Charmé and Tali Zelkowicz

Jewish Identity and Jewish Education: The Jewish Identity Space and Its Contribution to Research and Practice 183
Gabriel Horenczyk and Hagit Hacohen Wolf

Jewish Identity: Who You Knew Affects How You Jew—The Impact of Jewish Networks in Childhood upon Adult Jewish Identity 203
Steven M. Cohen and Judith Veinstein

Jewish Thought for Jewish Education: Sources and Resources 219
Jonathan A. Cohen

Philosophy of Jewish Education: Some Thoughts 237
Michael Rosenak

Planning for Jewish Education in the Twenty-First Century: Toward a New Praxis 247
Jonathan S. Woocher

Pluralism in Jewish Education 267
Bryan Conyer

Post Modernism Paradoxes: After Enlightenment – Jewish Education and the Paradoxes of Post Modernism 285
Hanan Alexander

Spirituality: The Spiritual Child and Jewish Childhood 301
Michael J. Shire

Visions in Jewish Education 319
Daniel Pekarsky

Section Two: Teaching and Learning

Art: Educating with Art Without Ruining It 339
Robbie Gringras

Arts and Jewish Day School Education in North America 355
Ofra A. Backenroth

Bible: Teaching the Bible in Our Times 373
Barry W. Holtz

Environment: Jewish Education as if the Planet Mattered 389
Eilon Schwartz

Havruta: What Do We Know and What Can We Hope to Learn from Studying in Havruta? 407
Elie Holzer and Orit Kent

Hebrew Language in Israel and the Diaspora 419
Nava Nevo

Contents of Part One

History: Issues in the Teaching and Learning of Jewish History 441
Benjamin M. Jacobs and Yona Shem-Tov

Holocaust Education 461
Simone Schweber

Israel Education: Purposes and Practices 479
Alick Isaacs

Israel Travel Education 497
Scott Copeland

Jewish Peoplehood Education 515
David Mittelberg

Life Cycle Education: The Power of Tradition, Ritual, and Transition 541
Howard Deitcher

Other Religions in Jewish Education 561
Michael Gillis

Talmud: Making a Case for Talmud Pedagogy—The Talmud as an Educational Model 581
Marjorie Lehman and Jane Kanarek

Technology: The Digital Revolution That Is Shaping Twenty-First-Century Jewish Education—A Fleeting Snapshot from the First Decade 597
Brian Amkraut

Travel as a Jewish Educational Tool 615
Erik H. Cohen

Travel: 'Location Location Location' – A Practitioner's Perspectives on Diaspora Jewish Travel 633
Jeremy Leigh

Section Three: Applications

Introduction

This section of the International Handbook focuses on applications, the ways that Jewish Education is transmitted in particular contexts. The 22 chapters in this section can be divided into three sub-sections that address the settings and audiences served through Jewish education, and the trends in the professional development of the educators who serve them.

Despite David Bryfman's lingering questions about whether it is a sub-discipline itself, ideas about experiential learning are infused throughout many of these chapters, including those of Isa Aron on congregational education, Susan Shevitz on congregations as learning organizations, Alex Pomson on liberal day schools, Lisa Grant and Diane Schuster on adult learning as an activity of community-building, and Shelley Kedar on teacher trips to Israel. Experiential learning also seems to be a popular focus of Jewish philanthropists who fund a wide range of initiatives designed to deliver high-quality Jewish experiences and/or professionalize the field, as noted by Joe Reimer.

Another through-line in these chapters is about how organizations learn. We find this theme first framed by Shevitz and again appearing in chapters about congregational education (Aron), and in many of those concerning teacher development and professional learning (Dorph, Feiman-Nemser, Isaacs, and Sinclair).

A final recurring theme in this section is the significant role of parents as decision makers, as supporters of their children's Jewish learning and as Jewish learners themselves, themes we find in chapters by Aron, Ben Avie et al, Grant and Schuster, Kress, Novick and Glanz, Pomson, and Rotstein.

The first sub-section includes nine chapters that describe a wide range of formal and informal settings for Jewish education. The overall question of how the concept of a learning organization has taken hold in and shaped Jewish educational settings is the central focus of the chapter by Susan Shevitz. She employs the example of Jewish family education to explore the shift from narrow programmatic change to the wider lens of organizational learning. As she notes, learning organization theory is no longer a "transmission of knowledge model" but rather an experiential learning model where the learner encounters the world.

Organizations that continuously learn are also central to Isa Aron's chapter on congregational education. Aron articulates core principles that contribute to a shift from an old paradigm that focused on children and age-graded instruction, to a new paradigm of enculturation, bringing students and their families into a rich Jewish cultural milieu. These principles include more direct involvement of parents in Jewish education both as learners and teachers, and strengthening the connection between Jewish learning and living where learning is done in context. They also focus more on the underlying vision and values of the school where it sees its primary goal as creating community for students and their families, and its primary tasks as creating powerful memories that will implant strong Jewish values and commitments.

Three different authors investigate the world of Jewish day schools and the various audiences they serve. Alex Pomson focuses on how the historical tensions between survivalist and integrationist impulses in Jewish day school development account for some of the most intense contemporary debates surrounding liberal day school education worldwide. As with Aron's findings in congregational education, Pomson points to a shift in the aims of liberal day school education from a paradigm of instruction (concerned with helping children acquire knowledge of the ideas and skills that society values) to one of enculturation (the more broadly conceived task of initiating children into a culture to which they may not already be committed).

A different challenge exists in Orthodox day schools as described by Shani Bechhofer who presents a rich description of the changing landscape of Orthodox education in America. She argues that the decentralized nature of the Orthodox sector, combined with the cultural–reproductive aspirations of a number of ideological movements and strands within contemporary Orthodoxy, produces a variety of institutional and educational pressures upon schools that ultimately result in schools that are more diverse, more competitive, more ideologically differentiated, and also more innovative than ever before.

The Ultra-Orthodox/Haredi world is the focus of our third chapter on day schools in this section. Here, Yoel Finkelman describes trends and challenges in Haredi education both in Israel and the Diaspora, noting how prescribed gender roles require dramatically different kinds of education and different kinds of schools for males and females. Finkelman also points out how isolationist impulses in the Haredi world make it difficult for the academic community to investigate topics that might be most useful for Haredi educators such as effective and ineffective pedagogic methods, best practices, student achievement, knowledge of the curriculum, and effective teacher training.

Two complementary chapters explore the sub-field of informal and experiential education from very different perspectives. First, by means of two case studies Joseph Reimer describes the potentially profound impact that creative collaborative partnerships between business-oriented philanthropists and Jewish educational leaders can have on the field of informal Jewish education. David Bryfman then explores both the theoretical and practical aspects of experiential education and how it has shaped the field of Jewish education in general. He suggests that experiential education is poised to reach a "tipping point" in the Jewish communal landscape and offers both a language and strategies for helping experiential education to further impact the Jewish identity development of Jewish youth and young adults.

The robust growth of Jewish studies in North American universities is the focus of the chapter by Judith Baskin. She reports that over 230 endowed chairs of Jewish studies exist at 80 colleges and universities with many other positions and programs in Jewish studies present at other North American institutions that are funded internally without outside support. As Baskin reports, while most Jewish studies academics would agree that the teaching of Jewish subject matter in secular universities cannot be considered Jewish education in the traditional sense, it appears that many students are looking for personal affirmation and a strengthening of their Jewish identities when they enroll in Jewish studies courses in higher education.

The final chapter in this sub-section about settings for Jewish learning examines the powerful and potentially transformative impact retreat-based learning can have on adults. In this chapter, Raymond Simonson provides an extensive analysis of Limmud, a cross-communal, multi-generational, volunteer-led Jewish learning experience that began in Britain in the 1980s that now attracts upward of 7,000 people a year and has been emulated by dozens of other communities across the globe. Simonson describes how Limmud's commitment to pluralism, voluntarism, and high-quality Jewish learning account for its success in the UK and beyond.

The second sub-section of the Applications section includes six chapters that explore research about a variety of audiences for Jewish education. These chapters include specific age and/or stage groups as well as focused populations with particular needs.

The very youngest learners are the focus of the chapter by Michael Ben-Avie and his co-authors. They chronicle many of the key initiatives taking place in North America in recent years to enrich early childhood education with more Jewish content and purpose. A key finding of significant import for policymakers is that promoting Jewish identity formation is not an important criterion for parents when choosing a Jewish early childhood education. However, if they perceive and experience the programs as excellent in quality, they do become more engaged in Jewish activities.

The relatively new field of Jewish special education is the topic of the chapter by Rona Novick and Jeffry Glanz. Their research shows that the move toward greater inclusion of learners with special needs has been propelled by parents and secular forces far more than it has by Jewish understandings of disability and difference. The authors explore the factors that have delayed the move to inclusionary practices in Jewish schools and document the need for further research to inform the field.

Shira Epstein's chapter focuses on gender issues, another relatively new area in Jewish education. Epstein documents how formerly evaded topics such as body image, sexuality, healthy relationship building, and sexual violence have become normative parts of many North American Jewish educational programs and professional development initiatives. She also describes how participatory action research between Jewish educators and cohorts of adolescents can transform the landscape of gender in Jewish education.

A different perspective on adolescents is explored by Evie Levy Rotstein in her chapter on children of intermarried parents. Rotstein's research reveals a variety of factors that motivate such teens to continue their Jewish education into their high school years, including family life, parental commitment to Jewish education, a positive religious school experience, and the students' own involvement in the decision to continue. Her case is supported by drawing on a broader literature relating to "resilient youth."

Just as parental involvement is key in the decision of adolescent children of intermarried parents to continue their education, so too is it central to virtually all aspects of Jewish educational engagement, as documented by Jeff Kress. In his chapter, Kress shows how North American parents today are much more active in choosing educational settings for their children than in past generations. Indeed, individualization results in a range of educational choices within the same family. As Kress shows, the ways in which parents relate to other Jewish organizations, particularly synagogues, impact their experiences and expectations of Jewish education regardless of setting.

Choice also appears as a key theme in the chapter on adult Jewish learning by Lisa Grant and Diane Tickton Schuster. Here they present how contemporary social forces have led to new developments in the field and what changes and priorities appear to be shaping the vision and decisions of adult education planners and policymakers today. They provide a conceptual framework moving away from a primary focus on literacy-based learning to a more diversified niche-marketing approach for situating the "where, when and what" of different types of learners and the learning programs and experiences that will meet their interests and needs.

The final sub-section of the Applications section includes seven chapters that offer different lenses on pre-service teacher preparation and professional development from close-up views, to more global perspectives such as an analysis of innovations in professional learning as well as of trends in recruitment and retention.

Michal Muszkat-Barkan examines the personal one-on-one approach of mentoring in her chapter, focusing on how the ideology of teacher-mentors informs their practice. Her research suggests that the professional discussion between teacher and mentor in Jewish studies is strongly tied to personal attitudes. Thus, she claims that goals of teacher mentoring in Jewish education should include enhancing awareness of the ideological–cultural components of personal attitudes toward Jewish practice.

Alex Sinclair focuses on the emerging field of practitioner enquiry. He reports on practitioner research as a form of professional learning, what Schön labeled reflection *on* action. A small body of work in Jewish education already demonstrates how practitioner enquiry can serve as a valuable resource to aid teachers in their thinking and action in professional practice.

Shelley Kedar's chapter on the purposes and practices of Jewish educators' trips to Israel as a professional development experience also connects teacher learning to action. Building on a modest body of research, this chapter introduces a conceptual model for thinking about the purposes and design of professional development trips for teachers and describes how an educator's Israel trip could serve as a professional development program within three interacting fields: tourism, religion, and education.

Another emerging field of study is addressed by Lisa Grant and Michal Muszkat-Barkan in their chapter on the professional identity formation of rabbi-educators working in a variety of settings. This cross-cultural research explores how Conservative and Reform rabbi-educators in Israel and North America describe their roles and goals based on their rabbinic and education training. This small study urges further investigation to determine whether the professional identity of rabbi-educators is indeed distinct from that of educators or rabbis who perform similar functions.

A broader view of professional development of Jewish educators is taken by Gail Dorph in her chapter. Dorph's exploration of this topic centers on key questions about the principles and challenges in creating and sustaining effective professional development. She then offers three case studies that provide images of effective professional learning that can impact the capacity of teachers to enhance student learning in Jewish schools.

Sharon Feiman-Nemser's chapter presents what she describes as two "experiments" in Jewish teacher preparation, one historical and one contemporary. She examines the development of the Teachers Institute at the Jewish Theological Seminary in New York as an example of the early twentieth-century emergence of Hebrew Teachers colleges to provide qualified teachers for communal Talmud Torahs. She then turns to DeLeT, a contemporary initiative for liberal day school teacher preparation. In each case, she describes how trends both in general education and the emergence of a new kind of Jewish school influenced the creation of these programs of Jewish teacher development.

This sub-section closes with a chapter by Leora Isaacs, Kate O'Brien, and Shira Rosenblatt on the challenges, successes, and potential facing the field of Jewish education as it moves to recruit, retain, and provide excellent professional development for Jewish educators. The authors assert the need for a systemic approach in linking excellence in teaching and student outcomes. They explore levers for change that directly impact the complex environment that influences teaching and learning in Jewish day and congregational school settings.

As a compilation, these 22 chapters provide us with a broad and rich portrait of the wide range of applications for Jewish education by setting, context, mode, and audience. They emphasize the need for depth and breadth in professional and organizational learning across all settings and offer us a sophisticated research agenda to further our knowledge and growth in all of these varied domains.

Helena Miller
Lisa D. Grant
Alex Pomson

Academic Jewish Studies in North America

Judith R. Baskin

History of Jewish Studies

The significant expansion of Jewish studies in American universities is a relatively recent phenomenon. Although the Hebrew language was included in the curriculum of several of the earliest colleges to be established on the North American continent in the seventeenth and eighteenth centuries, it was taught as part of a theologically oriented curriculum designed to assist potential Christian clergymen in understanding their own religious heritage. Some instructors of Hebrew, such as Judah Monis who taught at Harvard University between 1722 and 1760, were Jews or of Jewish heritage.

Jewish studies at American universities were truly established in the 1890s under the influence of German–Jewish scholarship, specifically the *Wissenschaft des Judentums* (Scientific Study of Judaism), a post-Enlightenment European Jewish movement dedicated to promoting the rational, scientific, and critical study of Jewish religion, history, and culture. *Wissenschaft des Judentums* reshaped Jewish learning into an academic endeavor that was compatible with the scientific methodologies of the German university while arguing that the Jewish experience had a place in higher education and scholarship. Although pervasive anti-Semitism tended to deny Jewish studies a secure place in the European university curriculum, the *Wissenschaft* approach, furthered by nineteenth-century scholars like Leopold Zunz, Abraham Geiger, and Heinrich Graetz, found an institutional home in the academic rabbinic seminaries of Central Europe (Ritterband & Wechsler, 1994).

In the late nineteenth-century United States, academic Jewish learning was established at secular universities, most often with the active communal and financial support of members of the American Jewish community. In the early twentieth century at least 16 subsidized positions in Semitic studies at major universities were held by Jewish scholars. Many of the donors for these positions hoped that recognition of the centrality of Jewish knowledge and scholarship in the development of Western thought would also hasten acceptance and appreciation of Jews in the

---

J.R. Baskin (✉)
University of Oregon, Eugene, OR, USA
e-mail: jbaskin@uoregon.edu

United States. Certainly, the establishment of positions in Semitic languages and literatures played a role in legitimizing the Jewish and Judaic presence in the American university at a time when being a Jew could still disqualify a candidate for an academic post. Most of the courses in Semitics that these scholars offered appealed to advanced students in biblical and related subjects, both Jewish and non-Jewish; they were generally beyond the interests and ability levels of most undergraduates. Still, their very existence delivered the message that the Jewish literary and cultural heritage belonged in the university curriculum (Ritterband & Wechsler, 1994).

In the second decade of the twentieth century, communal support for university positions diminished as Jewish philanthropists focused on the multiple needs of the large hosts of immigrants from Eastern Europe. In the period between the world wars, American academic Jewish studies took a new direction as the focus on Semitics was replaced with an emphasis on the breadth and diversity of the Jewish experience. This "cultural pluralism" movement, as Ritterband and Wechsler call it, argued that the focus on Hebrew and the Hebrew Bible, and related languages and literatures, was only a small part of Jewish religion, history, thought, and culture. During this era several elite institutions, again with the financial support of generous endowments from American Jews and Jewish communities, established positions in such areas as Jewish history and Modern Hebrew language and literature. These institutions integrated the faculty members holding these positions into appropriate university departments, whether History, English, Near Eastern Languages, or Religious Studies, where their courses became part of the mainstream undergraduate academic curriculum. Such scholars include the historian Dr. Salo Baron at Columbia University. Ritterband and Wechsler write, "Baron studied and taught in both universities and seminaries; communicated with academics and communal audiences; and successfully related Jewish history to general historical themes, while focusing on Jews and Judaism" (Ritterband & Wechsler, 1994, p. 171).

A third phase in the development of academic Jewish studies in North American colleges and universities began in the last third of the twentieth century. The impact of the 6-Day War in 1967 and the Yom Kippur War of 1973, as well as increasing discussion of the Holocaust, inspired many Jewish young people to learn more about their identities and heritage on the university level. The unprecedented number of Jewish "baby boomers" who descended on college campuses beginning in the mid-1960s, particularly in the Northeast, played a role, as did the expanding number of Jews in the professoriate.

Another central factor in the establishment of separate academic entities devoted to Jewish studies was the assertiveness of other ethnic groups on the American campus, including African Americans and Latinos, in advocating academic courses that explored and analyzed their particular historical and cultural backgrounds. Jewish students and faculty, who were rediscovering the richness of their own tradition, also encouraged universities to offer academic courses on the Jewish experience. When these were established, it was generally due to concentrated pressure from Jewish faculty members from a variety of academic disciplines, with the support of Jewish students, and often with significant backup from local Jewish communities

(Ritterband & Wechsler, 1994). Most of the programs founded in this era were financially supported by the college or university, rather than directly by Jewish donors, although often community groups undertook to raise funds for library resources and other program enhancements such as endowed lectureships and scholarship funds.

The emphasis in the 1960s and 1970s on concentrating Jewish learning in one academic program that transcended disciplinary agendas was a decisive move away from the earlier "cultural pluralism" approach that had encouraged the location of Jewish studies scholars within larger departments. The arguments for establishing separate Jewish studies units were similar to those for other particularistic area studies, such as African-American studies and women's studies. For one thing, such academic endeavors were essentially interdisciplinary. For another, without dedicated outside funding it was unlikely that more traditional disciplines would allocate limited and highly contested resources to what many faculty members regarded as marginal and intellectually problematic areas of discourse. Such professional concerns were also a factor in the 1969 founding of the Association for Jewish Studies, discussed below (Ritterband & Wechsler, 1994).

There is no absolute data as to the precise number of positions, programs, and departments in Jewish studies. However, in February 2009, the website of the Association of Jewish Studies listed over 230 endowed chairs in Jewish studies at 80 colleges and universities, including several in Israel, Canada, and Australia (AJS website: Resources: Directory of Endowed Chairs in Jewish Studies). Many other positions and programs in Jewish studies at North American institutions of higher learning and elsewhere are not dependent on outside funding.

Women and Academic Jewish Studies

The contemporaneous growth of the field of women's studies also helped establish the importance of studying marginalized social groups, including the Jews. The conflation of both concerns led to increased interest in the roles and experience of Jewish women. Prior to the 1970s most scholars and teachers of Jewish studies were men; many had moved into the academic world after completing rabbinic training. Jewish historical and textual studies were long seen as a male endeavor and women's lives and contributions were virtually ignored in histories and analyses of the Jewish experience.

A major change in Jewish studies in North America in the decades between 1975 and 2010 is the number of women who have entered the field and climbed the academic ladder from graduate students to professors in every area of Jewish studies scholarship. This sudden appearance of females in the world of academic Jewish scholarship is, of course, the result of the overwhelming changes in the domestic, religious, and communal roles of Jewish women in recent decades as a result of the social, educational, economic, and technological transformations that have characterized life since the end of World War II. The presence of women has transformed the content and methodological approaches of Jewish studies teaching and research.

At the end of the first decade of the twenty-first century, most female and male academics involved in Jewish studies teaching and scholarship take for granted the importance of gender as an intellectual category of analysis and consider the constructions and consequences of gender in explicating the many facets of the Jewish experience (Davidman & Tenenbaum, 1994).

Association for Jewish Studies

The 1969 establishment of the Association for Jewish Studies (AJS) was a signal indication of the growth of academic Jewish studies in late twentieth century North America. Initially founded to facilitate communication among a relative handful of Jewish studies scholars, by 2009 the AJS had over 1,800 members, many of whom were PhDs teaching in an institution of higher education. A fifth of the membership consisted of graduate students, representing the future of Jewish studies in North America. The Women's Caucus of the AJS was founded in 1986; in 2009, more than 47% of AJS members were women as compared to just over 10% in the late 1970s (AJS website: Resources: 2007–2008 Membership Survey).

In 1985, the AJS became a constituent member of the American Council of Learned Societies. This acceptance, after several unsuccessful applications, served as final validation that the academic world recognized Jewish studies as "an important and well-populated field of study" with a "unique intellectual focus and interdisciplinary concerns" (ACLS, 1977); it legitimized the field in the larger scholarly arena and it was also significant for the organization's continued professionalization. With offices at the Center for Jewish History in New York City, the AJS convenes an annual conference, administers several book prizes, publishing subsidies, and travel grants, and publishes an academic journal, *The AJS Review*, and a twice-yearly magazine, *AJS Perspectives* (Loveland, 2008; AJS website).

In recent decades, several regional professional organizations have also been formed in North America and hold annual meetings. These include the Midwestern Jewish Studies Association, the Western Jewish Studies Association, and the Canadian Association for Jewish Studies.

Other Professional Organizations

In addition to the Association for Jewish Studies, there are several other professional organizations that focus on disciplines related to Jewish studies. These include the National Association for Professors of Hebrew (NAPH) which holds an international annual conference on Hebrew language, literature, and culture, and publishes the journals *Hebrew Studies, Hebrew Higher Education*, and an annual newsletter, *Iggeret* (NAPH website). The Association for Israel Studies (AIS), established in 1985, is an affiliated member organization of the Middle Eastern Studies Association of North America (MESA). AIS, an international society with offices in Israel, meets annually and also sponsors sessions at the annual MESA meeting (AIS website). The American Academy for Jewish Research, founded in 1920, is a fellowship of senior scholars who are admitted through nomination and election. The AAJR sponsors sessions at the annual meeting of the AJS and awards the Baron Book Prize (AAJR website).

Jewish Studies Instruction

As Jewish studies expanded and programs and departments were established across the United States and Canada, several central questions were raised by established scholars. These included the appropriate qualifications for faculty members in Jewish studies at a time when few universities specifically trained PhDs in that area. They also addressed the necessary components of Jewish studies courses and curriculum for undergraduate and for graduate students. Similarly, Jewish studies faculty debated whether Hebrew language should be a requirement for an undergraduate degree and, if so, at what level of proficiency. Should the focus be on Modern or Classical Hebrew? A non-curricular issue, but one that was of great concern, was the extent to which university-based Jewish studies could or should be expected to address and strengthen the Jewish identity of students (Jick, 1970). Many of these topics continue to be of concern among practitioners in the field at the beginning of the twenty-first century (Lewis, 2006; Meyer, 2004).

The framework for academic Jewish studies varies from institution to institution. In some instances Jewish studies are taught in a separate designated department; in other cases, interdepartmental concentrations or programs in Jewish studies are organized and administered by committees of faculty members holding appointments in a variety of scholarly disciplines. The freestanding Jewish or Judaic studies program or department that awards undergraduate degrees in Jewish/Judaic studies is increasingly common in the early twenty-first century. Often donor endowments support the hiring of a faculty director and in some cases subsidize additional faculty lines and the administrative costs of the program.

Many but not all Jewish studies programs require several years of Hebrew language and literature study for undergraduate majors and for graduate students. In some colleges and universities students must study Classical Hebrew language and texts; in others Modern Hebrew is required; some offer a choice. The result has been a proliferation of Hebrew language study across North American institutions of higher education to a degree that would certainly not have occurred without the linkage of Hebrew to Jewish studies. Several Jewish studies programs also offer instruction in Yiddish language and literature while those with graduate programs may teach Aramaic, Judaeo-Arabic, and Ladino, among other languages important for access to Jewish texts from various places and eras. Some programs and departments allow students to complete degree requirements by substituting Yiddish or another "Jewish" language for Hebrew.

The diversity of organizational and structural approaches, as well as academic emphases and requirements, remains a characteristic and somewhat problematic aspect of academic Jewish studies. This lack of consensus on the essential components necessary for a degree in Jewish studies is likely to remain the *status quo* given the broad range of institutions of higher education that offer Jewish studies, the diverse audiences they are serving, and the varying qualifications and interests of faculty who identify themselves with the field. Over the decades a continuing interest in defining the parameters of Jewish studies is evident in the production of textbooks and anthologies of primary texts intended for college and university courses. Collections of course syllabi that offer models of how to approach a range of topics from introductory courses on Jewish history and civilization, Judaism as a religious tradition, Jewish thought, the Holocaust, Israel, women in Judaism, to Jewish Art, aspects of Jewish popular culture, and much more, have been published from time to time so that instructors can have a sense of how their colleagues tackle particular subject matters (Baskin & Tenenbaum, 1994; Garber, 2000). A course syllabus archive is a feature of the AJS website (Resources: AJS Directory of Course Syllabi) and some sessions at the AJS annual meeting address pedagogical issues.

Links with Jewish Students and Jewish Organizations

Most Jewish studies academics at the beginning of the twenty-first century would agree that the teaching of Jewish subject matter in secular universities cannot be considered "Jewish education" in any traditional sense. Their courses are not intended to persuade students of the truth of Jewish beliefs and values nor do they provide guidance on how to perform Jewish rituals. There is no assumption in any academic Jewish studies course at a secular institution that any of the enrolled students are Jews. As rabbi and educator Alfred Jospe once wrote, "the purpose of Jewish studies in the university is the study of Judaism and the Jewish people and not the Judaization of young Jews, the stimulation of their Jewish commitment, or the strengthening of their Jewish identification" (Jospe and Jospe, 2000, p. 78). Similarly, in a 1969 colloquium on academic Jewish studies at Brandeis University that led to the founding of the AJS, Irving Greenberg argued that if the field and the AJS wished to achieve academic respectability, they should not attain "too close an identification with the concerns of the Jewish community and the Jewish civilization." He went on to say that "The teacher cannot serve in good conscience as a spokesman for any one version of the entire tradition or for the Jewish community as it sees itself" (Greenberg, 1970).

Nevertheless, when Jewish studies programs of various kinds were undergoing significant expansion in the 1960s and 1970s, data indicates that a large proportion of undergraduates taking these courses were Jewish. In fact, the presence of Jewish studies courses on any given campus, and the enrollments in these courses, were strongly associated with the number of Jewish students (Ritterband & Wechsler, 1994). Despite efforts by faculty to dissociate themselves from modeling Jewishness, it is clear that many students were looking for personal affirmation and a strengthening of their Jewish identities when they enrolled in Jewish studies courses.

In 2009, this personal expectation is less frequent, although Jewish studies faculty report that they often teach students of Jewish background who have had no previous Jewish education (Cattan, 2004). Many Jewish studies courses and programs have been established at institutions that do not have significant numbers of Jews in the student body, including Roman Catholic institutions. Moreover, as a 2004 article in *The New York Times* reported, a large number of students enrolled in Jewish studies courses are not Jews. Of 250 students enrolled in Jewish studies classes at City College in New York City, including 26 majors and over 150 minors, some 95% were not Jewish (Freedman, 2004). The reasons for this phenomenon are complex but there is no doubt that in an era when Jewish demographics are shrinking, the diversity of students and faculty in Jewish studies will be an increasing reality that further distances academic Jewish studies from other forms of Jewish education.

Nevertheless, academic Jewish studies continue to be perceived as having special ties with the Jewish community, in part because of communal funding support. Most Jewish studies academics are aware of the need to maintain boundaries between their programs and Jewish campus and community advocacy and religious groups. However, they must frequently deal with inappropriate expectations. These can come from some Jewish students, who don't always understand the distinction between academic Jewish studies and their previous Jewish educations; from student leaders and adult professionals associated with campus Jewish organizations who believe Jewish studies should share their parochial missions; and from members of local Jewish communities who suppose that Jewish studies academics will support Jewish causes and concerns, especially when the community or individuals are providing financial resources.

The dilemmas caused by such misunderstandings can be difficult but most Jewish studies academics learn to negotiate working relationships with the different Jewish advocacy constituencies on their campuses and in their larger communities. Positive collaborations may include co-sponsoring events with academic content with Jewish student groups; working with community professionals to construct credit-earning internships in local Jewish schools and agencies for motivated students; and being available to speak to Jewish student and community groups about new developments in Jewish studies research. Many Jewish studies programs on college and university campuses schedule a range of interesting speakers and events that are open to the general public without charge. In these and other valuable ways, academic Jewish studies programs have provided a significant non-denominational source of education about Judaism and the Jewish experience for the larger community, both Jewish and Gentile.

It should be noted that some Jewish studies professors believe that an involved communal role is not only desirable but imperative for the Jewish studies academic. Hal M. Lewis of Spertus College suggests that "Scholarship has much to contribute to the Jewish world outside the portals of the academy as well as inside. The congregations, federations, and Jewish organizations in our communities ought to look upon Jewish studies professors as communal leaders – not merely programmatic opportunities . . . no Jewish community should deliberate its significant issues, absent the leadership of credible scholars working side-by-side with influential rabbis and respected communal executives" (Lewis, 2006, pp. 131–132). Michael A. Meyer of Hebrew Union College-Jewish Institute of Religion is among other scholars who have recently addressed this dilemma (Meyer, 2004).

Donors and Endowments

Since the 1980s, the establishment and expansion of Jewish/Judaic studies in a variety of North American institutions of higher learning has been made possible by the philanthropy of individual donors. The growth of personal wealth in this era, together with increasing communal concern about strengthening of Jewish identity at a formative period in young people's lives, has led to a proliferation of endowed faculty positions, programs, and Jewish/Judaic studies centers, both at public and private research universities offering graduate degrees and at institutions with a primary focus on undergraduate education. Data from the 2000–2001 National Jewish Population Survey indicating that as many as 41% of Jewish students in North America take at least one course in Jewish studies during their undergraduate or graduate careers has added further impetus to such initiatives (National Jewish Population Survey).

There is no doubt that the investment of philanthropic resources to fund Jewish studies has been a wonderful boon for North American colleges and universities and for the field itself. With the economic downturn at the end of the first decade of the twenty-first century, it is unclear if such philanthropy will continue to be forthcoming. The continuation of programs that are wholly or even significantly donor-dependent may be called into question in a time of declining portfolios and/or shrinking endowments.

Dependence on donor generosity has also raised challenging issues of academic objectivity versus parochial communal agendas; questions of undue emphasis placed on donors' particular interests and propensities; and concern over the increasing amounts of faculty time and effort devoted to fundraising activities. Moreover, additional donor-driven funding for lecture series, visiting scholars, student scholarships, etc., has often placed Jewish studies programs in a privileged and sometimes uncomfortable position in relation to other older and larger academic departments as well as to newer and still struggling academic entities, particularly those with a focus on gender and ethnic studies (Horowitz, 1998). In the best circumstances, Jewish studies directors have found ways to create intellectual and interdisciplinary partnerships with less well-endowed academic departments and programs in endeavors of mutual interest.

While many donors to Jewish studies programs at colleges and universities with significant Jewish student bodies have expressed particularistic concerns about educating Jewish students as a way to strengthen Jewish identity formation, others have chosen to endow Jewish studies positions and programs at institutions, both public and private, that do not have a critical mass of Jewish students, including colleges and universities in parts of North America with small Jewish populations and at institutions linked to the Roman Catholic Church and various Protestant denominations. These donors, some of whom wished to support local institutions, argued that Jewish studies should be integrated into the academic curriculum of all institutions of higher education; they hoped, as well, that exposing diverse groups of students to academic study of aspects of the Jewish experience would increase understanding and tolerance in the larger North American society.

Communal funding of positions in Israel studies is one area which has proved particularly contentious when scholars who are supported by endowment funds voice views that do not accord with some local opinions about Israeli history, society, and politics. One case that generated significant publicity and played a significant role in a faculty member's decision to leave Jewish studies academics entirely took place at San Francisco State University in 1995 (Mahler, 1997).

International Links

Increasingly, the world of academic Jewish studies is a vibrant international community of students and scholars who meet at conferences and collaborate on scholarly projects across the world. Unlike North America and Israel, where the preponderance of Jewish studies academics are of Jewish background, this is not necessarily the case in Europe, where Jewish studies are attracting many serious students at the graduate level. Recent decades have seen the growth of academic Jewish studies and of Jewish studies professional organizations in Western Europe, in Eastern Europe, and the former Soviet Union, as well as in Latin America and in China. Among these are the European Association for Jewish Studies (EAJS), founded in 1981, with offices in Oxford, UK, which encourages and supports the teaching of Jewish studies at the university level in Europe and furthers an understanding of the importance of Jewish culture and civilization and of the impact it has had on European cultures over many centuries. In Russia, SEFER, housed at the Moscow Center for the University Teaching of Jewish Civilization, is an umbrella organization for university Jewish studies in the CIS (Commonwealth of Independent States) and the Baltic States.

Many North American programs welcome academic colleagues from Europe, Israel, and elsewhere as speakers and visiting scholars. These international ties have been strengthened for many North American scholars by participation in the World Union of Jewish Studies (the Israeli professional society for academic Jewish studies centered at Hebrew University), which holds conferences every 4 years in Jerusalem.

Jewish studies programs and departments in North America have consistently encouraged their students, undergraduate and graduate, to study abroad for a summer, term, or academic year. Study at an Israeli university is one desirable possibility, since this provides an optimal way to improve Hebrew language skills and to take detailed courses on a range of topics from archeology of various eras, Jewish art and architecture, anthropological approaches to Jewish practice and ritual, to the sociology and politics of Israel, that might not be available at the home institution. Study abroad with a focus on Jewish studies is also available at universities in numerous other countries, including the United Kingdom, Italy, Germany, the Czech Republic, Hungary, and Lithuania.

Since the Second Intifada of 2000, a significant number of North American colleges and universities have placed limitations on Israel study and research options for students and faculty due to security fears and insurance implications. In a number of cases, longstanding programs with various universities in Israel have been suspended. Some institutions permit students to petition to attend study-abroad programs in Israel on the condition that students and their parents sign waivers absolving the college or university from responsibility in case of injury or death. However, students who choose to study at Israeli universities under these circumstances generally lose financial aid while they are abroad and have to negotiate with their institutions for acceptance of credits earned in Israel. While the ease of arranging study in Israel that will be credited at the home institution varies from place to place, the details reported above are accurate for the University of Oregon in 2010.

Future Challenges

Changing demographics in the early twenty-first century indicate clearly that the absolute numbers of Jews in the larger population, including student populations, is in steady decline. The future of Jewish studies in North American universities will depend on the field's continuing appeal to a larger constituency. Most Jewish studies programs design their curriculum and courses to appeal to the broadest possible student audiences; in part this is accomplished by ensuring that their courses fulfill university "general education" and "diversity" requirements. At the beginning of the twenty-first century, more and more students who take courses and choose undergraduate majors and graduate training in Jewish studies are non-Jews who have come to the field out of intellectual curiosity, not out of interest in their own religious or ethnic heritage (Freedman, 2004). Similarly, many scholars and faculty members who work in Jewish studies in North America and abroad are not themselves Jews. This phenomenon is indicative of the increasing integration of Jewish studies into higher education as the field has moved beyond being an academic venture "about Jews, by Jews, and for Jews" (Freedman, 2004). While this "normalization" of Jewish studies within the university is desirable from a scholarly point of view, it also points to potential future conflicts between academic Jewish studies programs and the concerns of the Jewish communities and donors who have thus far been essential to the presence and success of Jewish studies at many North American institutions.

Research Desiderata

Very little systematic and comprehensive academic research on the phenomenon of Jewish studies in North America is currently underway. The last book-length study appeared in 1994 (Ritterband and Wechsler). Given the enormous changes in the field since that time, new scholarly work on academic Jewish studies units and their varying formation histories, academic structures, components, requirements, and funding sources, as well as the ethnic, religious, and gender identifications of participating faculty and students, is highly desirable. Similarly welcome would be systematic comparative research on relationships among academic Jewish studies entities and Jewish student, faculty, and lay communities (both on and off campus); analyses of the varying roles of donors; and studies of how Jewish studies programs, both endowed and supported institutionally, interact with academic administrators and other interdisciplinary academic units. Comparisons of North American Jewish studies and programs abroad in all of the areas mentioned above would also be extremely useful.

References

American Academy for Jewish Research. http://www.aajr.org/. Accessed January 10, 2011.
American Council of Learned Societies (1977). Policy statement on admission of new constituent societies, adopted at the Annual Meeting, May 13.
Association for Israel Studies. http://www.aisisraelstudies.org/. Accessed January 10, 2011.
Association for Jewish Studies. http://www.ajsnet.org/. Accessed January 10, 2011.
Baskin, J., & Tenenbaum, S. (Eds.). (1994). *Gender and Jewish studies: A curriculum guide*. New York: Biblio Press.
Cattan, N. (2004). Judaic studies classes see enrollment boom. *The Jewish daily forward*, January 23.
Davidman, L., & Tenenbaum, S. (Eds.). (1994). *Feminist perspectives on Jewish studies*. New Haven, CT: Yale University Press.
Freedman, S. G. (2004). Classes in Judaic studies, drawing a non-Jewish class. *The New York times*, November 3.
Garber, Z. (Ed.). (2000). *Academic approaches to teaching Jewish studies*. Lanham, MD: University Press of America.
Greenberg, I. (1970). Scholarship and continuity: Dilemma and dialectic. In L. Jick (Ed.), *The teaching of Judaica in American universities: The proceedings of a colloquium* (p. 116). New York: Ktav Publishing House, Inc.
Horowitz, S. (1998). The paradox of Jewish studies in the new academy. In D. Biale, M. Galchinsky, & S. Heschel (Eds.), *Insider/outsider: American Jews and multiculturalism*. Berkeley, CA: University of California Press.
Jick, L. (Ed.). (1970). *The teaching of Judaica in American universities: The proceedings of a colloquium*. New York: Ktav Publishing House, Inc.
Jospe, A. (2000). Academic Jewish studies: Objectivity or advocacy. In E. Jospe & R. Jospe (Eds.), *To leave your mark: Selections from the writings of Alfred Jospe* (p. 78). New York: Ktav Publishing House, Inc.
Lewis, H. M. (2006). The Jewish studies professor as communal leader. *Shofar: An Interdisciplinary Journal of Jewish Studies*, 24(3), 127–135.
Loveland, K. (2008). The association for Jewish studies: A brief history. Association for Jewish studies resource document. http://www.ajsnet.org/resources.htm.

Mahler, J. (1997). Howard's end: Why a leading Jewish studies scholar gave up his academic career. *Lingua Franca*, 7(3), 51–57.

Meyer, M. A. (2004). The persistent tensions within *Wissenschaft des Judentums*. *Modern Judaism*, 24(2), 105–119.

National Association for Professors of Hebrew. http://polyglot.lss.wisc.edu/naph/. Accessed January 10, 2011.

Ritterband, P. & Wechsler, H. S. (1994). *Jewish learning in American universities: The first century*. Bloomington, IN: Indiana University Press.

Adult Jewish Learning: The Landscape

Lisa D. Grant and Diane Tickton Schuster

In the first decade of the twenty-first century, adult Jewish learning has become a normative aspect of the North American Jewish communal landscape. This was an evolutionary process that began in the 1980s, when Jewish communal attention perceived a connection between rising rates of intermarriage and low levels of Jewish literacy. As the "continuity crisis" became the clarion call of the Jewish community in the early 1990s, communal leaders despaired that a lack of Jewish literacy would contribute to the deterioration of Jewish identity in future generations. The community's educational responses to this challenge were rich and diverse, resulting in the creation of a wide array of initiatives to support the development of Jewish day schools, summer camps, Israel trips, and other educational programs for children and adolescents.

Around the same time, various groups of adults recognized that they lacked adequate Jewish education to make informed decisions about Jewish life in adulthood. For some – particularly parents in Conservative and Reform households whose children participated in the new initiatives – there was the uncomfortable discovery that they themselves were ill equipped to support their children's learning or to integrate the lessons of Jewish education into family life. For others – such as women who had been deprived of Jewish education and individuals exploring midlife spiritual concerns – there was a hunger for learning that would enrich personal meaning making. By the early 2000s, younger generations of college-educated, "postmodern" Jews entered adulthood, asking questions about Jewish identity, seeking new types of Jewish social networks, and responding to new modalities of access for relevant Jewish learning experiences.

Throughout these years, Jewish educational leaders recognized the potential benefits of reaching more learners about more topics in more locations using a greater range of instructional strategies. As a result, across North America a variety of serious and substantive adult Jewish learning programs were created. Highly differentiated from one another in terms of target audiences, content, rigor, venue, length, and mode of delivery, these programs were offered by synagogues,

---

L.D. Grant (✉)
Hebrew Union College, New York, NY, USA
e-mail: lgrant54@gmail.com

federations, Jewish community centers, retreat centers, independent organizations, and consortia.

In 2005, we described the evolution of the field of adult Jewish learning in a retrospective review of the research literature, situating the blossoming of adult Jewish learning in the historical and social contexts of the late twentieth century (Schuster & Grant, 2005). In this chapter, we assess how social forces have led to new developments, updating our understanding of the changes and priorities that are shaping the vision and decisions of planners and policy makers today. Our focus is primarily on programs and experiences of liberal Jews in adult Jewish learning. While Jewish study has been a consistent and integral component of Orthodox Jewish life, Jewish learning in the Orthodox sector has grown significantly as well in recent years, particularly, though not exclusively, among women. However, the engagement in Jewish learning among the liberal strands of American Judaism follows a more cyclical pattern (Sarna, 2005). For most of the twentieth century, adult study was a low priority on the communal agenda that was more focused on rescue and resettlement of immigrants and refugees, supporting Israel, and other "civic" expressions of Jewish belonging. Starting in the 1980s and increasing at a dramatic rate after the "wake-up" call of the 1990 National Jewish Population Study, adult Jewish learning emerged at the center of the religious and communal agenda for the revitalization of contemporary American Jewry. Many Jewish communal leaders believed that increasing Jewish literacy and learning would lead to more meaningful involvement in Jewish practices, philanthropy, and communal life. After the economic downturn that began in 2008 and has seriously impacted American Jewish community, it will be interesting to see whether and how this commitment to adult learning remains. Indeed, there were signs even before the financial crisis that adult Jewish learning had waned as a communal priority.

In the earlier paper, we also noted that over the years, very little communal conversation had taken place at the national level about the *purposes* of adult Jewish learning. When providers of such literacy-focused programs as the Florence Melton Adult Mini-Schools created their curricula, they emphasized that the learning was for its own sake rather than to promote specific behavioral changes or to advocate deeper involvement in the Jewish community (Grant, Schuster, Woocher, & Cohen, 2004). Such objectives might have been a tacit goal or part of a hidden curriculum in emerging adult Jewish learning programs, but they were not articulated publicly.

With the maturation of the field and a more financially constrained world, it now appears that adult educators are thinking more strategically about whom to serve, how to serve them, and to what purpose. Today, program providers are beginning to articulate a much more purposeful link between adult Jewish learning, leadership development, and Jewish community building. Alongside these developments, we note the emergence of an increasingly differentiated structure for adult Jewish learning programming that responds to the diverse motivations and needs of the adults who participate in such activities.

The landscape we depict is a North American one. However, adult Jewish learning is not exclusively a North American phenomenon. Indeed, there are flourishing initiatives across Western and Eastern Europe, in Israel, and across the Jewish world, some of which are described elsewhere in this handbook. In addition, some of the programs we mention, such as the Florence Melton Adult Mini-School, are international in scope. Others, such as Limmud New York and the Skirball Center for Adult Jewish Learning, were inspired in whole or in part by successful initiatives in the UK and Israel.

Using Schwab's four commonplaces as an organizing frame, we describe who today's adult Jewish learners are, the venues in which they learn, the content of their learning, and the characteristics of their teachers. Accordingly, we begin with a description of the increasingly diverse constituencies who now participate in adult Jewish learning activities and consider how various contemporary social and historical factors have affected these groups' learning needs and responses. Next we offer a new conceptual framework for situating the "where, when, and what" of different types of learners and the learning programs that attract them. Then follows a discussion of the evolving roles of adult educators and implications for professional development. Finally, we conclude with suggestions for future research.

The data for this chapter are drawn from a number of qualitative and quantitative studies about North American Jewish adults and their learning experiences. In addition, we supplement our analysis with findings from over a dozen interviews conducted in 2008 about the changing field of adult Jewish learning in the United States. Our interviewees included a geographically diverse group of educational program directors at independent institutions and retreat centers, representatives from various movement and nationally based learning programs, and academics and lay leaders involved in Jewish community programming.[1]

Who Are the Learners?

Over the past 25 years, the expansion of the field of adult Jewish learning has resulted in the growth and diversification of adult learning populations throughout the Jewish community, with the greatest changes occurring in the more liberal sectors. In the 1950s–1970s, learners outside the Orthodox world typically were highly homogeneous midlife adults, either synagogue-going women who sought out daytime enrichment classes taught by male rabbis or post-retirement couples who

---

[1] Adam Berman, Executive Director, The Isabella Freedman Jewish Retreat Center; Rabbi Joan Glazer Farber, Director of Adult Learning, Union for Reform Judaism; Dr. Sherry Israel, Board Chair, National Havurah Institute; Dr. Betsy Dolgin Katz, North American Director (retired), Florence Melton Adult Mini-School; Lisa Kogen, Director of Education, Women's League for Conservative Judaism; Rabbi Alvin Mars, Director (retired), Mandel Center for Jewish Education, Jewish Community Centers Association; Rabbi Leon Morris, Director, Skirball Center for Adult Jewish Learning; Rabbi Jeremy Morrison, Director, Riverway Project, Temple Israel, Boston; Rabbi Jay Moses, Director, Wexner Heritage Program; Rabbi Kerry Olitzky, Director, Jewish Outreach Institute; Professor Jeffrey Schein, Siegal College of Jewish Studies and former Education Director, Jewish Reconstructionist Federation; Daniel Sieradski, Director of Digital Media, Jewish Telegraphic Agency; Dr. David Starr, Vice President for Community Education and Dean, Me'ah, Hebrew College.

attended public lectures by high-profile speakers. Today, however, diverse new constituencies of learners have emerged. Distinctive in their motivations and learning needs, these newcomers include

- Young adults, age 21–35, many of whom have participated in university-level Jewish studies classes, Israel trips, and Jewish social networking events. This group is marrying later than their parents and having children later and tend to seek informal, personal, and "open source" Jewish experiences (Kirshenblatt-Gimblett, 2005, Greenberg, 2006) that are not institutionally bound.
- Parents of preschoolers who, though themselves "older" and accomplished in professional roles, feel unprepared to make Jewish educational or lifestyle choices for their families. Parker (2006) reports that Jewish parents are especially receptive to educational programs that help them "take home" Jewish practices and values.
- Parents of school-age children who feel ill-prepared to support their children's learning due to their own inadequate or far-distant Jewish education. Katz and Parker (2008) note that as some Jewish parents "realize that Jewish learning is not just for kids," family educators have broadened and diversified family programming, recognizing that adult-level Jewish learning is an important (and sometimes distinct) component.
- Intermarried Jews and their non-Jewish spouses who have chosen to raise their children as Jews. Olitzky and Golin (2008) describe a variety of "outreach" programs that provide intermarried adults with education that can help them to feel less remote from the established Jewish community and to enrich their Jewish home life.
- Grandparents who feel motivated to function as "interpreters" and "autobiographers" for the next generation and thus benefit from educational programs that help them to explain and model the Jewish legacy they hope will be carried into the future (Sonnheim, 2004; Olitzky and Golin, 2006).
- Spiritual seekers who have turned or returned to Judaism at times of life transition or personal soul searching. Amann (2007) and Thal (2008) describe the experiences of Jewish adults who have engaged in new meaning making, showing how they used diverse adult-educational resources in their quest for spiritual integration.
- Advanced learners. Many Jewish adults who become involved in ongoing study continually strive to expand their knowledge base (Grant et al., 2004). As these adults become Jewishly knowledgeable, they pursue alumni classes offered by the Melton Mini-Schools and Boston's Me'ah initiative, courses at the Hartman Institute and other adult education centers in Israel, and other intensive learning opportunities whether in classrooms or via the Internet.
- Independent and "do-it-yourself" learners who cultivate learning opportunities outside of "traditional" communal organizations, preferring to find and develop their own study resources and learning partnerships. Such learners gravitate to the rapidly multiplying online Jewish learning opportunities, as well as the "emergent

spiritual communities" that encourage egalitarian and democratic participation in the teaching-learning process.
- Jewish professionals who strive to serve the Jewish community by becoming more effective as Jewish adult educators. These include Jewish community center program directors, camp senior staff, Federation community education coordinators, interfaith program organizers, book group conveners, and others who find themselves in situations in which they need to function as adult educators but lack frameworks for planning programs responsive to their learners' needs. In addition, there are advanced learners who aspire to share their knowledge with others, but are unprepared to move from lay to paraprofessional teaching roles (Schuster, 2003b).

Adult Jewish Learners in Context

To put the emergence of new populations of adult Jewish learners in perspective, it is useful to consider several phenomena that have shaped the social and historical contexts of contemporary adult Jewish education. First, since the "wake-up call" of the 1990 National Jewish Population Study, adult Jewish learning has become a central part of the religious and communal agenda for the revitalization of contemporary American Jewish life. Consistent with views expressed by Jewish communal spokespersons such as Barry Shrage (1996), executive director of the Council of Jewish Philanthropies in Boston, and Rabbi Eric Yoffie (1997), president of the Union for Reform Judaism, today there is widespread belief among community leaders that Jewish literacy and learning leads to more meaningful involvement in Jewish practices, philanthropy, and communal participation.

Then, too, with the aging of the Baby Boomer population (and the first wave of Gen Xers who were born in the late 1960s), increasing numbers of Jewish adults are reaching midlife and older adulthood and thus confronting life-stage-related questions – about personal meaning, health, mortality, and legacy – that compel many to look to Jewish spiritual and intellectual sources and resources for guidance and support (Roof, 1993; Schuster, 2003a). As these adults move into their post-parenting and retirement years, they have increased discretionary time to pursue Jewish learning that will enhance personal well-being and enrich intergenerational family life. Moreover, given longer life spans, the post-60 population has many more years in which to explore various Jewish learning modalities. The continuing popularity of Jewish retreat centers, travel programs with Jewish themes, programs for Jewish grandparents, and community-based lifelong learning institutes points to a trend in contemporary Jewish education that is unlikely to diminish in the decades ahead.

The changing role of Israel in American life is a further influence on the design and direction of adult Jewish learning initiatives. For the thousands of young adults who have participated in Birthright Israel trips to Israel, the opportunity to continue dialogue about their relationship to Israel and Judaism is of immediate interest; as part of the "emerging adult" population, these 20–30-year-olds are part of a cohort that questions – and seeks education about – Mideast politics and Jewish identity with post-modern sensibilities quite distinct from earlier generations (Kelner, 2002; Saxe & Chazan, 2008). Education about Israel may be especially important for a generation of midlife Jewish adults who grew up with no memory of the struggle for the formation of the State; the majority of this group have little firsthand contact with the country, its people, or the concept of Klal Yisrael, and thus may benefit from educational opportunities to learn about the relevance of Israel and its survival to the future of the Jewish people.

A changing social climate over the past several decades has resulted in a Jewish communal *zeitgeist* dominated by individualism, self-determination, and a resistance to authority structures. Cohen and Eisen (2000) reported that increasing numbers of Jewish adults have turned "inward" and look to "the sovereign self" rather than normative Jewish tradition for determining how they regard Judaism, its practice and meaning. Correspondingly, Horowitz (2000) found that over the life cycle many contemporary Jewish adults move in and out of their attachment to Jewish life and observance, with the consequence that Jewish identity frequently is perceived as "voluntary" and considered a choice among diverse alternatives. Given the fluidity of Jewish identity formation and the privileging of independent decision making about Judaism and Jewish life, many Jewish adults are "in flux" and can benefit from educational experiences that can help them to articulate their beliefs and make informed choices. Adult Jewish learning programs that encourage learners to gain a broad understanding of Jewish texts, history, philosophy, law, and values help such individuals to make responsible and personally meaningful decisions about their Jewish lives today and in the future.

Finally, given the rapid dissemination and exchange of ideas afforded by the "information age," there are increasingly diverse numbers of Jewish adults who have access to ever-expanding sources of knowledge about all aspects of Judaism. As more and more adults turn to electronic platforms for education and discourse, the potential for reaching wider constituencies of Jewish learners grows exponentially. At the same time, with the increased self-authorship afforded by Web 2.0 and other media, the risks associated with ungrounded, do-it-yourself Jewish adult education are ever present. Moreover, given the pace of modern life, many adults find that their "extracurricular" learning must be fit into busy schedules that are already burdened and over-extended with work- and family-life demands. Accordingly, even serious adult Jewish learners find themselves hard-pressed to commit to studying Judaism on a regular basis. Although some learners take on the obligation to meet regularly for study programs, the majority of Jewish adults prefer short-term, time-limited learning activities.

Adult Jewish Learning Programs: Changing Communal Responses

When the late twentieth century renaissance of adult Jewish learning first began, the stated purpose was to enhance Jewish literacy and enrich Jewish identity in the North American Jewish community. This commitment to fostering Jewish literacy was seen in programs such as the Florence Melton Adult Jewish Mini-School, Hebrew College's 2-year Me'ah program, the Union for Reform Judaism's (URJ) Kallah (an annual 5-day adult study retreat), the Wexner Heritage Program (a 2-year leadership development program), and independent institutes (e.g., The Skirball Center for Adult Jewish Learning in New York; Lehrhaus Judaica in the San Francisco Bay Area; and Kolel: The Adult Centre for Liberal Jewish Learning in Toronto).

Around the time that these programs were established, a large number of North American synagogues embarked on a process of strategic reflection about the place of learning in their overall vision and mission (Aron, 2000; Dashefsky, Grant, Miller, & Koteen, 2002; Herring, 2003; Koteen, 2005). Through these deliberative change processes, synagogues created or expanded their adult Jewish learning repertoires, featuring a broad array of classes, workshops, book groups, film series, retreat opportunities, and other modalities designed to attract new and diverse audiences. A telling byproduct of these "cafeteria style" offerings was the opportunity they afforded Jewish adults who had never been part of any organized Jewish learning experience to meet like-minded peers and develop new social networks.

Despite the rapid growth of adult Jewish learning programs, it also became clear during the past decade that only a relatively small percentage of the North American Jewish community was engaged in any kind of systematic adult Jewish learning. Moreover, even when there was interest, the participants tended to be the same people over and over again. Indeed, the 2000–2001 National Jewish Population study revealed that less than one-quarter of Jewish adults reported attending a Jewish education class or other adult Jewish learning program in the year prior to the survey. Similarly, in a national survey of adult Jewish learning patterns of participation and interests, Cohen and Davidson (2001) found that only 22% of respondents indicated they had attended a lecture on a Jewish theme in the past year, while an even smaller number (16%) indicated they had taken a class on a Jewish topic in the same time period.

Studies of Jewish adults engaged in learning revealed that the most dedicated learners typically were part of the "committed core" in the organized Jewish community. This was true both of those who enrolled in long-term programs such as the Me'ah and the Melton Mini-School, as well as those who participated in retreat settings that are more likely to combine Jewish learning with culture, worship, and other Jewish experiences (Cohen & Veinstein, 2008; Grant & Schuster, 2006; Grant et al., 2004). Compared to the general Jewish community, these learners were more motivated to learn new skills, to become more knowledgeable Jews, to have an intellectual experience, and to increase their sense of connection to the Jewish community. They were also more interested in the study of sacred texts, Jewish history, theology, and other topics that are traditionally associated with Jewish study.

To attract new learners, many community-based program providers began by offering Jewish literacy programs. Over time, however, they found it important to diversify offerings and to become more learner-centered in their planning. Recognizing that relatively few learners are attracted to traditional text study or literacy-based programs, they began to identify other, potentially "serious" learners who are motivated to learn because they want to feel informed as lay leaders in Jewish organizations or because they want to strengthen their leadership skills. While not interested in conventional literacy programs per se, these learners often seek ways to engage in and enrich their Jewish communal lives through study.

Indeed, in the past decade, more and more program providers have explicitly linked adult Jewish learning, the life experience of the learner, and the dynamic relationship that exists (or could exist) between the learner and his or her Jewish community. Our interviews with adult Jewish learning leaders revealed a significant shift in attitude toward a more differentiated and holistic understanding of the scope and potential of adult learning in Jewish life *writ large*. Our informants' responses reflected their insight into the realities of contemporary Jewish life – a milieu where Jewish identity is voluntary and self-constructed – and their recognition of the need to offer customized programs that can meet individualized needs. They pointed out the limitations of the old model of "casting a broad net" to see how many learners could be "captured," as compared to designing programs for specific learners with specific interests and needs.

The experience of moving from a "one size fits all" approach to "niche marketing" required these educational leaders to rethink how they defined adult Jewish learning and the nature of the populations they endeavored to serve. As Daniel Sieradski, Director of Digital Media for the Jewish Telegraphic Agency, commented, "Everyone has different interests. Do you want to reach the Hasidic *ba'al teshuvas* – or the Kahanist fundamentalists – or the organic hippie eco-Jews? You can program for each of those segments."

Moreover, as Dr. Betsy Dolgin Katz, who served as the North American Director of the Melton Mini-Schools from 1989 to 2008, pointed out, this new direction was reinforced by funding decisions by major Jewish foundations. For example, in recent years the Steinhardt Foundation has supported adult-education programs specifically for parents of preschoolers, and the Wexner Heritage Foundation has invested significantly in intensive Jewish literacy seminars for communal leaders under age 45. In talking about emerging trends in the field, Katz opined that "separate from the federation and its institutions, and separate from the synagogues" individual funders and foundations may shape the future of adult learning by prioritizing the kinds of programs to be offered and populations to be served.

Our informants spoke of the importance of program planning and design that provides diverse entry points and anticipates the variegated learning modalities that will serve the wide array of adults who are (or could be) engaged in adult Jewish learning activities. Their insights helped to clarify that today there are at least four broad categories of adult learners, characterized by distinctive needs, expectations, and orientations, who need to be served by the contemporary North American Jewish community. These are (1) learners on the periphery of Jewish communal life, for whom learning is primarily about helping them to engage in Jewish life; (2) learners in the "committed core," for whom learning serves to enrich their Jewish life experience; (3) Jewish lay leaders who need to become more Jewishly informed; and (4) Jewish educators and rabbis who seek to become more effective teachers of adults. Table 1 presents a conceptual framing of the types of programs and methodologies that seem to attract these different groups.

Table 1 Jewish identity and Jewish community building through adult Jewish learning: A sampling of programs and methodologies placed in a contextual framework

A. Engagement	B. Enrichment		C. Leadership development	D. Cultivation of adult educators
	B-1. Literacy focused	B-2. Experiential		
Mothers Circle (Jewish Outreach Institute)	Melton Mini-School	Jewish calendar	Wexner Heritage	Melton and Me'ah's faculty development programs
	Me'ah	Jewish life cycle	Hadassah Leadership Institute	
PEP (Melton)	Skirball	Jewish cooking	UJC Limudim	Educators' track at URJ Adult Study Retreat
Journeys (JCC) Torah yoga	Women's league institutes Torah and Talmud study	Adamah (Jewish environmental fellowship program (Isabella Freedman)	Local federation programs for community leaders	National Havurah Institute
Big name speakers/ scholars-in-residence	Hebrew	Choir practice	Davening Leadership Training Institute (Isabella Freedman)	Temple Israel Lifelong Learning Institute (TILLI)
	Community-wide Days of Learning	Cantillation classes		
Cultural programs (film festivals, book festivals, concerts, etc.)	Women's League study materials	Shabbatonim		Synagogue-based adult educator training programs
		Torah yoga	Service leading workshops	

Table 1 (continued)

A. Engagement	B. Enrichment	C. Leadership development	D. Cultivation of adult educators
	E-learning (URJ Ten Minutes of Torah, Myjewishlearning.com, Maqom.com)	Bibliodrama Purim shpiels	
	The Women's Torah commentary study guide		
	Synagogue classes		
	B-3. Hybrid		
	Adult bat mitzvah		
	Israel trips		
	Field trips (e.g., Ellis Island)		
	National Havurah Institute		
	North American Jewish Choral Festival		
	Limmud New York		
	Skirball's Artists' Beit Midrash		
	Advanced Torah Academy (Temple Chai)		
	Rosh Chodesh groups		

To clarify the layout of Table 1, note that across the top of the table we denote the types of the learning experiences that appeal to adults who are at different levels of involvement in Jewish life. Column A lists learning activities that focus on *engaging* individuals, such as programs that are targeted at particular developmental needs (e.g., Melton's Parent Education Program); cultural events; and scholar-in-residence programs that feature well-known speakers.

Engagement programs typically appeal to both more minimally involved Jewish adults *and* also to highly affiliated individuals. However, more Jewishly involved individuals are more likely to go beyond activities at the engagement level and pursue the kinds of "enrichment" activities listed in Column B. Within this latter category, we differentiate three types of activities that attract adults who are seeking to deepen their connection to Judaism through learning: literacy-focused programs such as Melton, Me'ah, and text-based study groups (Column B-1); experiential education programs that are designed to enrich some aspect of Jewish living, such as holiday observance, synagogue skills, and home practices (Column B-2); and "hybrid" programs that blend the experiential with the intellectual (Column B-3).[2]

Column C presents Jewish communal initiatives that specifically link Jewish learning with the cultivation of lay leaders. In some cases, such programs focus on Jewish learning to promote deeper Jewish knowledge and commitments among board and committee members of Jewish communal organizations; in other cases, they are geared toward developing skills in leading worship or other aspects of ritual life.

Column D lists programs that link learning and educational leadership development; such activities are designed to enhance the professional and avocational development of adult Jewish educators.

Table 1 identifies a representative sample of the types of programs and modalities that fit within the different categories. Although incomplete (to date, there is no national data base that gathers or updates information about extant adult Jewish learning programs), what seems apparent even with this partial list is that the scope and range of the literacy-based *enrichment* programs listed in Column B are more robust than those listed in the other columns. This trend was articulated by many of our interviewees who described their own recent decisions to expand engagement and experiential programs in order to attract more learners and be more responsive to different learners' interests and needs.

The New Adult Jewish Learning Marketplace

Table 1 provides a graphic representation of the changing "marketplace" of adult Jewish learning and has implications for future planning and policy across the

---

[2]Hybrid program opportunities often occur through trips and programs in retreat settings. In addition, "intentional communities" such as independent minyanim and certain synagogue-based groups (e.g., adult *b'nei mitzvah* cohorts and Rosh Chodesh groups) may also fit within this category of programs that integrate serious Jewish learning with Jewish living and celebration.

contemporary North American Jewish community. Insights from our interviewees – all individuals involved in thriving national and local adult Jewish learning initiatives – provided a more nuanced explanation of the emergent trends and needs identified in the table.

Engagement Programs: Reaching Jews on the Periphery

Engaging the unengaged in Jewish learning is certainly no easy task. Our informants indicated that, even when targeted to specific audiences such as parents of young children or adults in their 20s and 30s, even the most basic text study and other literacy-type programs have limited appeal. Indeed, these anecdotal reports are borne out by the research. The relatively few studies of adult Jewish learning patterns consistently show a strong relationship between levels of affiliation and participation rates in adult Jewish learning (Chertok, Saxe, & Silvera-Sasson, 2005; Cohen & Davidson, 2001; Cohen, 2008; Grant & Schuster, 2006; Grant et al., 2004; NJPS, 2000/2001). The richer and more in-depth the program, the more likely the participant is to be highly engaged in Jewish communal life.

Reaching the unengaged is further complicated by the reality that, faced with the multiple "mental demands of modern life" (Kegan, 1998), Jewish adults *selectively* participate in Jewish activities that not only fit into their busy schedules but also are responsive to their individualized learning needs. Rabbi Kerry Olitzky of the Jewish Outreach Institute observed that today's adults seek experiences that are "customized," perceiving the process as similar to contracting with a personal trainer at the gym: "People's time is much more precious... What I see happening is what I would call the personal trainer modality. [People] want the convenience of learning at their own schedule when they want."

Similarly, the URJ's Rabbi Joan Glazer Farber noted that people are interested in finding points of intersection between Judaism and the rest of their lives:

> People are concerned more with how things touch their lives—spirituality, understanding of God; how and why do I connect with Israel? Yes, the Holocaust happened, we need Israel, but what does it mean to me? Not that our learners are self-centered. It's more that, if they are going to take the time to enter a conversation, it has to have an impact.

Farber and others commented that people are seeking meaning and relevance through a variety of ways other than Jewish learning programs and experiences. Enticing or encouraging people to discover the possibility that Judaism may enrich their lives requires offering alternate topics and venues for Jewish learning.

Rabbi Alvin Mars, recently retired Director of the Mandel Center for Jewish Education of the Jewish Community Centers (JCC) Association, noted that his primary constituency – adults who look to JCCs for connection to Jewish communal life – are not people who would sign up for 2-year programs: "We have people who walk through the place; if they're lucky, they'll read a Jewish sign that might turn them on to ask questions." Hoping to "elevate all JCC experiences," Mars developed a 12-session engagement program called Journeys that has "circular entry with no one place to begin or end." Built around highly engaging themes (e.g., wine tasting,

Jewish humor, Israel arts), Journeys sessions are often structured to attract particular age cohorts and emphasize experiential learning. Indeed, Mars indicated that experiential learning is a crucial strategy for successfully engaging adults in Jewish education.

Professor Jeffrey Schein of Siegal College pointed to "public space" Judaism as another approach to make Jewish learning more accessible and inviting, as well as more connected to other aspects of people's daily lives. The URJ's Farber provided some specific examples of this type of program:

> We need to take learning out of the classroom, into the marketplace. We should be holding Jewish book groups at Starbucks, offering Jewish cooking classes at Whole Foods. If there are synagogue groups making chemo caps, they can be studying healing texts at the same time.

The public spaces where this type of Jewish engagement can take place are both real and virtual. The electronic marketplace has particular appeal for young adults and other geographically mobile Jewish populations. Jewish groups on Facebook.com, as well as venue- and community-specific online information resources such as OyBay.com and Jewandthecarrot.com, are all making Jewish learning opportunities more accessible to otherwise hard-to-reach audiences.

Several of those interviewed noted that parent education is another underdeveloped area for potential growth. In many communities, there are Jewish learning programs that target parents of preschool-aged children. Likewise, family education programming is a standard feature of most synagogues today. However, these programs rarely take up issues of Jewish parenting. Outreach programs such as Shalom Baby[3] and Jewish early-childhood education programs have had some success in building social networks for new Jewish parents (Kelner, 2007; Rosen, 2006) but have yet to link their community-building outcomes to education about parenting or Jewish family life. Likewise, Olitzsky reported that the Jewish Outreach Institute has had some success with developing programs for both parents and grandparents of children in interfaith families, but he, too, mentioned that the press of busy lives often constrains participation. As Schein observed, "I'm not sure that it's reasonable to expect people in the prime of their parenting years to participate in a lot of adult learning. [But we can do more to] offer it at the best time and to make it relevant to parenting."

Engagement experiences have the potential to spark interest in deeper and more consistent learning. Accordingly, some programs are now offering a range of learning activities to encourage participants to "start small" and add on later. For example, since 2001, The Riverway Project has used study and ritual experiences to "connect adults in their 20s and 30s to each other, to Judaism and to Temple Israel

---

[3] Shalom Baby is a program adopted by many Jewish federations designed to welcome and integrate new parents into the Jewish community. It begins with gift baskets but often extends to include a wide range of programs and services designed to support and connect new parents to the Jewish community. For examples, see http://www.jewishphilly.org/page.aspx?id=71620, http://www.ujannj.org/page.aspx?ID=140109, http://boulderjcc.org/index.php?id=19

of Boston."[4] Riverway events first engage unaffiliated Jews by encouraging them to bring to Torah study the kind of critical thinking they acquired as college students. As Riverway's director, Rabbi Jeremy Morrison, explained, as the learners become more involved, there are "stratified learning opportunities":

> Riverway begins with a nice easy approach of "Torah and Tonics" which stresses a critical approach to text. Then we have something called "Mining for Meaning," which takes text study to a more intensive level but is also pragmatic because we study text and history and ritual. In that group, we ask how ritual comes to be around a certain holiday and what the meaning of the holiday is based on text from a critical historical perspective. This past year we launched a 2-year Me'ah course just for people in their twenties and thirties. We wouldn't have had people to [commit to] that more intensive program if they hadn't first gone through the other steps.

Another model of stratified adult Jewish learning has recently emerged on Long Island, where the UJA-Federation of New York's J Learn program has diversified its offerings to target distinct niche markets based on geographic location and learner interests and needs. Originally conceptualized as a Jewish literacy initiative offering 2-year Melton Mini-School and Me'ah courses in various sites across Long Island, J Learn has evolved to a more nuanced set of learning opportunities designed both for engagement and enrichment of audiences, including short-term classes, leadership-development programs, seminars for clergy, and cross-community study events (Grant & Schuster, 2008).

Enrichment Programs for the Committed Core

Table 1 shows three different types of enrichment learning experiences that seem to appeal mostly to groups of learners who are seeking ways to deepen and strengthen their engagement in Jewish life. Our informants indicated that these types of programs have the most potential for fruitful growth in Jewish learning. As Rabbi Jay Moses, Director of the Wexner Heritage Program, remarked, "Generally, the core is getting more energized, more interested, more involved… while the fringes are drifting farther and father away." However, even among the core of actively affiliated Jews, the pool of learners who seem to be attracted to formal classroom-based learning is limited. This subgroup consists of a small but significant cadre of advanced Jewish learners who are drawn to the intellectual dimensions of Jewish study. This is the audience for whom most literacy-based classes, community-wide Days of Learning, electronic learning opportunities, and ongoing Torah and Talmud study groups seem to be designed. Some of these learners are already active as lay leaders in their congregations and elsewhere in the Jewish community; others become active as a result of or concurrent with their engagement with Jewish study. Others still are simply *lishma* learners who find personal meaning in serious engagement with Jewish texts.

---

[4]http://www.riverwayproject.org/about_us/index.php

Echoing Franz Rosenzweig's (1955) admonition that at all levels of participation in the Jewish community people feel a degree of alienation, many adults still need support for finding their way "from the periphery back to the center; from the outside in." Two of our interviewees noted that even the most involved learners may feel that they, too, are on the periphery. As Professor Schein said, "We have to help people to see that we're *all* moving from the 'periphery to the center' and that you don't have to sacrifice who you are to learn." And the Skirball Center's Rabbi Leon Morris explained that most of today's adult learners come to Jewish education from their own particular vantage point:

> Today there are more students who have their area of interest and it's this little niche of a larger Jewish portrait that they are focused on: history, art, philosophy, literature, etc. Given that we are all on the periphery anyway, it doesn't really matter that one's entree into Jewish studies is located in a specific area of interest. In the end, through that specific area they will come to encounter many other topics and vital areas worthy of study.

An exponentially expanding domain for literacy-based learning is the worldwide web, extending from basic learning sites such as www.myjewishlearing.com and www.Jewishvirtuallibrary.com, to online opportunities for formal and informal text study, to the endless universe of the blogosphere. The latter ranges from straightforward dissemination of information to edgier approaches (such as David Plotz's "The Complete Blogging the Bible," so far at http://www.slate.com/id/2150150) that combine Jewish study with discussions of culture, politics, and social activism. According to JTA's Sieradski, the potential impact of new electronic technology for Jewish adult education is unlimited. He cited a few examples in the following remark:

> You have the National Havurah Committee that has a group writing new Torah commentaries online. You have Wikipedia articles for Jewish content. Now there is a service called Wikibooks: people are typing the entire Mishna and the entire Tanakh in the original Hebrew and Aramaic into Wikipedia. Anyone can annotate, comment, and hyperlink this text. Likewise JPS is doing a project called "the Tag Tanach," where they're taking the entire Tanakh and putting it online and people can keyword and tag different parshiot.

Sieradski particularly noted that e-learning cuts across all age and social groups, affording diverse learners with differing needs and capabilities opportunities to participate in meaningful study:

> There are different people whose needs are suited by different things. Some people may enjoy myjewishlearning.com or interfaithfamily.com or g-dcast.com. You can use the Web to learn to *layn* your bar mitzvah portion or learn Gemara online. You can learn to read Hebrew online or your basic Bible lessons or more advanced halachic reasoning. It's all up to you.

Further opportunities for expanding adult learning options for adults within the committed core may take place through experiential programming that links Jewish experience with Jewish learning and more deliberately contributes to a sense of Jewish community. While some who are drawn to these types of activities may also be interested in more intellectual pursuits of text study and formal classes, others are looking for more holistic education where formal learning is secondary to a firsthand experience of Jewish community, spiritual growth, and/or Jewish culture. These may include one-off events such as the Women's League "Vashti's Banquet" (a day-long event that combined spa treatments, belly dancing, Persian cuisine and music, and study of midrashim on the Book of Esther), to ongoing programs such as adult Bat Mitzvah. Rosh Chodesh groups and programs that focus on spirituality and prayer, music, holiday and life cycle observance, and/or other aspects of Jewish living fit within this type of blend of learning and living. Within this domain are retreat programs, such as Limmud NY, the National Havurah Institute, Camp Isabella Freedman, and the URJ's Adult Study Retreat, that combine Jewish learning, cultural programming, worship, and celebration. Also included here is a range of niche programs for individuals who want to link particular interests with Jewish life such as Jewish environmentalism, Jewish choral festivals, spirituality institutes, and gourmet Jewish cooking classes.

Programs that Cultivate Jewish Leaders Through Learning

Jewish communal leadership development is another dimension of adult Jewish education. As noted above, some people become lay leaders as a result of their participation in serious literacy-based text study; others begin as leaders and then may seek out even deeper learning opportunities; and yet others are encouraged to study by virtue of their roles as leaders in the Jewish world. Regardless of how these leaders arrive at the study table, they are increasingly being offered opportunities to enrich their Jewish knowledge base and to become Jewishly informed as communal decision makers. As Wexner Heritage's Rabbi Moses noted, "There is a normalization of the idea that a serious Jewish learning experience is helpful if you want to be taken seriously as a leader in the Jewish community... there is an increased cachet associated with it."

The Wexner Heritage program is the pioneer among this type of initiative, but we now see other leadership development programs emerging through federations, Hadassah, synagogues, and retreat centers. Some of these programs are designed to help Jewish lay leaders become more Jewishly knowledgeable; others focus on specific skill development such as courses that teach people how to lead worship, chant Torah, or speak Hebrew. According to Adam Berman, executive director of the Isabella Freedman Jewish Retreat Center that houses a number of specialized adult Jewish learning activities, participants in these programs take seriously the opportunity to receive certificates that "formally" acknowledge that they have studied systematically to acquire a particular skill set or to take on leadership roles. Moreover, Berman said learners will commit to long-term study – indeed are "hungry for longer commitment" – if it means they will "get something for it... something that can actually be put on their resume."

Leadership development appears to be another domain ripe for innovation and program expansion in adult Jewish learning. Presently, little has been published that documents the process or impact of existing programs. Moses commented that beyond the immediate value of leadership development, participants in the Wexner

Heritage program especially treasure the opportunity to be with peers who share common values about service to the Jewish community. The social context of the learning community has been described heretofore (Grant et al., 2004), but the need for a more nuanced analysis of how learning affects leadership development per se is certainly pressing.

Developing Adult Educators

To date, the literature on adult Jewish learning has focused primarily on the experience of the learner, with some attention paid to the setting of adult Jewish education programs. Relatively little research has been conducted about the experience of the teacher or about the preparation and professional development of Jewish educators who work with adults (Grant et al., 2004; Schuster & Grant, 2003; Schuster, 2003b). Our informants mentioned the issue of faculty development with some frequency, indicating that this is a topic that needs to be more systematically addressed in discussions about advancing the field. Presently, the Melton Mini-Schools, Me'ah, and the Skirball Center systematically involve their teachers in professional development activities, drawing on staff resources to assist faculty members in thinking about adult learners, curricular issues, and their own instructional practice. According to Dr. Betsy Katz, the Melton Mini-School's faculty has thrived due to the organization's sustained commitment to faculty conferences, consultations, and online dissemination of instructional materials. Dr. David Starr, Dean of Me'ah, opined that in addition to the program's tremendous success with learners, Me'ah has had "a huge impact on teachers... both in terms of the impact on their thinking about the boundaries between critical and engaged learning, and their connection to the community." Starr reported that Me'ah has "created a conversation" about faculty members' relationship to the materials they are teaching and has provided personal mentoring that "gets them to think about issues." Watching how excited faculty have become about teaching for his program, Starr concluded, "If we had vibrant communities that could promise a job that would be half-time academic and half-time serious adult education in the community, a lot of people would jump at that! If we had the resources, I think that would happen."

The Skirball Center's Morris also reported that his faculty benefits from their experiences as adult educators and from opportunities to systematically reflect on their roles and responsibilities:

> We spend a lot of time at faculty retreats discussing the differences in teaching adults versus teaching in an academic setting. The faculty are encouraged to bring themselves in more and to think about the reality that this isn't learning with the "objectivity" that academia strives for. We are invested in the Jewish lives of the people we are teaching, so the folks coming from universities are thinking about what that means.

Siegal College's Schein has long worked with college faculty who teach in adult Jewish learning programs in the Cleveland area. He finds that some faculty are not comfortable interacting in the non-hierarchical, informal ways that befit much of adult Jewish study. He speculated, however, that, to make the content of their teaching more accessible to a wider range of adults in the community, faculty members need to re-equip themselves, to come "off the stage."

Schein also mentioned that some Siegal professors now team-teach with members of the college's board of trustees, in an effort to build partnerships across the campus community. A byproduct of this experiment is that board members are now recognizing their own proclivities for teaching – which points to a different issue we found in our interviews: the question of who might be included in the pool of individuals considered suitable to teach Jewish adults. There are many ways this question can be answered. In some communities, adult education is the exclusive domain of the clergy, while in others there is a more level playing field that embraces lay teachers of all ages and ability levels.[5] Presently there are no certification procedures or standards for adult Jewish educators. Professional development of teaching staff for adult education is only rarely considered part of a Jewish organization's agenda. Consequently, the field of adult Jewish learning is still "in formation," and future policies likely will be derived from the many lessons being learned by the current generation of program administrators, adult educators, and adult students.

Some Jewish organizations are experimenting with new models of cultivating adult educators and enlarging the pool of potential teachers. For example, Temple Israel of Boston recently launched an Institute of Lifelong Learning (TILLI), in which synagogue members develop and teach courses based on their own areas of expertise. The idea of developing lay teachers has been supported, as well, by the Reform Movement. One of the criteria by which the URJ evaluates the bi-annual Congregation of Learners awards[6] is the extent to which a broad mix of faculty, including lay people, teach in adult education programs. The URJ also has offered an "educators' track" at its Adult Study Retreat for participants who want to build on their own Jewish knowledge and offer effective adult education courses in their home communities. In the view of Glazer Farber, there is a pressing need for an "institute for teachers of Jewish adults" that can help clergy, lay people, and general educators to improve their practice in Jewish settings. This perspective was echoed by Lisa Kogen of the Women's League of Conservative Judaism, who said that rabbis would greatly benefit by taking courses on adult education and community building.

The issue of how and where to develop quality adult educators is only beginning to be part of conversations in the larger Jewish community. One of our informants expressed concern that because many adult learners want to share what they

---

[5] An example of an egalitarian teaching-learning community was provided by Dr. Sherry Israel, Executive Committee Chair of the National Havurah Institute. Dr. Israel described the Institute's longstanding philosophy as "Everyone is a teacher, everyone is a learner, there are no gurus." At the Institute's annual study retreat, the policy is that "No one gets paid and you teach a class, then take a class." A similar situation exists at Limmud New York and its many regional offshoots. Here too, faculty are not paid and are expected to fully participate in the life of the community throughout the retreat.

[6] http://urj.org/_kd/Items/actions.cfm?action=Show&item_id=16777&destination=ShowItem

have learned with others, there is a risk of encouraging people who lack sufficient grounding in Jewish studies to become part of the "community of commentators" and to take on teaching roles beyond their reach. As our interviews showed, in looking forward, program planners and communal leaders must keep issues of teacher preparation and professional development firmly planted on the policy agenda.

Future Research

The maturation of the field of adult Jewish learning is reflected not only in the rich array of program options, settings, and orientations to content and learners, but also in the amount of knowledge that we now have about the field. An array of studies provides us with a sense of who the learners are and what they get out of their learning experiences in the short term. However, we do not yet have a clear picture of the long-term impact of Jewish learning on students' behaviors and attitudes, and ultimately on their communities. Longitudinal studies to track these trends would be most useful in terms of designing programs that best fit learners' needs.

While we do not have a comprehensive map of all adult Jewish learning programs and offerings, the conceptual framework presented herein provides a useful way to categorize adult learning for learners with different motivations, interests, and needs. Further development of this organizational structure should be helpful in guiding program planners and design of appropriate curricula and instruction for the various contexts and target audiences of learners.

Our interviews with a sampling of program leaders suggest that North American providers of adult Jewish learning experiences are much more sensitive now to the possibility of diverse entry points for Jewish learning than they were two or three decades ago. Perhaps the most significant finding from these interviews, however, is that adult educators and program designers are much more explicitly articulating a connection between adult Jewish learning and the need to build stronger, more dynamic communities, and to develop Jewish leaders who are better informed and guided by Jewish learning in their leadership roles. Further research is needed to explore how widespread this articulation of purpose is, as well as to measure its impact on the broader community across the different sectors of contemporary Jewish life.

Further research also would be useful to better understand how evaluation studies that are commissioned by program funders are utilized in planning adult Jewish education. As noted here and in our earlier research as well, we do not yet have a solid body of research that analyzes how Jewish educators are being prepared to work with the burgeoning adult Jewish learning population or that explores what constitutes excellent teaching of Jewish adults. Indeed, inquiry into all of these domains to explore the dynamic relationship between learners, teachers, content, and contexts would greatly assist communal leaders and educators in developing a strategic vision for adult Jewish learning for the next quarter century and beyond.

References

Amann, P. (2007). *Journeys to a Jewish life: Inspiring stories from the spiritual journeys of American Jews*. Woodstock, VT: Jewish Lights.

Aron, I. (2000). *Becoming a congregation of learners*. Woodstock, VT: Jewish Lights.

Chertok, F., Saxe, L., & Silvera-Sasson, R. (2005). *Exploring the impact of the Wexner Heritage program on a development of leadership capital in the Jewish community*. New Albany, OH: Wexner Foundations.

Cohen, S. M. (2008). Identity and Jewish education. In R. L. Goodman, P. A. Flexner, & L. D. Bloomberg (Eds.), *What we now know about Jewish education* (pp. 75–86). Los Angeles: Torah Aura.

Cohen, S. M., & Davidson, A. (2001). *Adult Jewish learning in America: Current patterns and prospects for growth*. New York: Heller/JCCA Research Center.

Cohen, S. M., & Eisen, A. (2000). *The Jew within: Self, family, and community in America*. Bloomington, IN: Indiana University Press.

Cohen, S. M., & Veinstein, J. (2008). *A diverse community of leaders learning: The Limmud NY experience* (unpublished internal report). New York: UJA-Federation of New York.

Dashefsky, S., Grant, L., Miller, R., & Koteen, L. (2002, Winter). La'atid: Synagogues for the future – An experiment in synagogue revitalization. *Jewish Education News, 23*(1), 50–53.

Grant, L., & Schuster, D. T. (2006). *The impact of J Learn on the Long Island Jewish community: Baseline year findings 2005-2006* (unpublished internal document). New York: UJA-Federation of New York.

Grant, L., & Schuster, D. T. (2008). *J Learn on Long Island and in a broader context* (unpublished internal document). New York: UJA-Federation of New York.

Grant, L., Schuster, D. T., Woocher, M., & Cohen, S. M. (2004). *A Journey of heart and mind: Transformative Jewish learning in adulthood*. New York: JTS Press.

Greenberg, A. (2006). *Grand soy vanilla latte with cinnamon, no foam: Jewish identity and community in a time of unlimited choices*.

Herring, H. (2003, Spring). Peering into the future: Considerations for restructuring the synagogue. *The Reconstructionist*, 35–47.

Horowitz, B. (2000). *Connections and journeys: Assessing critical opportunities for enhancing Jewish identity*. New York: UJA-Federation.

Katz, B., & Parker, M. (2008). The Jewish education of parents. In R. L. Goodman, P. A. Flexner, & L. D. Bloomberg (Eds.), *What we now know about Jewish education* (pp. 151–160). Los Angeles: Torah Aura.

Kegan, R. (1998). *In over our heads: The mental demands of modern life*. Cambridge, MA: Harvard University Press.

Kelner, S. (2002). *Almost pilgrims: Authenticity, identity and the extra-ordinary on a Jewish tour of Israel* (unpublished doctoral dissertation). New York: City University of New York.

Kelner, S. (2007). Who is being taught? Early childhood education's adult-centered approach. In J. Wertheimer (Ed.), *Family matters: Jewish education in an age of choice* (pp. 59–79). Waltham, MA: Brandeis University Press.

Kirshenblatt-Gimblett, B. (2005). *The "New Jews": Reflections on emerging cultural practices*. http://www.nyu.edu/classes/bkg/web/yeshiva.pdf.

Koteen, L. (2005). *What every synagogue should know about organizational transformation before taking step one*. (Unpublished paper).

NJPS 2000-2001. *Strength, challenge, and diversity in the American Jewish population: A United Jewish Communities report*. http://www.jewishdatabank.org/default.asp

Olitzky, K. M., & Golin, P. (2006). *Twenty things for grandparents of interfaith grandchildren to do (and not do) to nurture Jewish identity in their grandchildren*. Los Angeles. CA: Torah Aura.

Olitzky, K., & Golin, P. (2008). Outreach and Jewish education. In R. L. Goodman, P. A. Flexner, & L. D. Bloomberg (Eds.), *What we now know about Jewish education* (pp. 87–98). Los Angeles: Torah Aura.

Parker, M. (2006). Creating new transmission lines: Teachers to parents to children. A case study of Jewish education for the parents of young children. *Jewish Education News, 27*(1), 42–44.

Roof, W. C. (1993). *A generation of seekers: The spiritual journeys of the Baby Boom generation*. New York: HarperCollins.

Rosen, M. (2006). *Jewish Engagement from Birth: A Blueprint for Outreach to New Jewish Parents* (Executive Summary). http://www.cmjs.org/Publication.cfm?IDResearch=127

Rosenzweig, F. (1955). Towards a renaissance of Jewish learning. In N. Glatzer (Ed.), *On Jewish learning* (pp. 55–71). New York: Schocken.

Sarna, J. (2005). The cyclical history of adult Jewish learning in the United States: Peers' law and it implications. In M. Nisan & O. Schremer (Eds.), *Educational deliberations: Studies in education dedicated to Shlomo (Seymour) Fox* (pp. 207–222). Jerusalem: Keter.

Saxe, L., & Chazan, B. (2008). *Ten days of Birthright Israel: A journey in young adult identity*. Waltham, MA: Brandeis University Press.

Schuster, D. T. (2003a). *Jewish lives, Jewish learning: Adult Jewish learning in theory and practice*. New York: URJ Press.

Schuster, D. T. (2003b). Placing adult Jewish learning at the center. *Agenda: Jewish Education 16*, 2–6.

Schuster, D. T., & Grant, L. (2003). Teaching Jewish adults. In N. S. Moscowitz (Ed.), *The ultimate Jewish teachers handbook*. Denver, CO: A.R.E.

Schuster, D. T., & Grant, L. D. (2005). Adult Jewish learning: What do we know? What do we need to know? *Journal of Jewish Education, 7*, 179–200.

Shrage, B. (1996). *Building a community of Torah and tzedek: A new paradigm for the Jewish community of the 21st century*. Boston: Combined Jewish Philanthropies.

Sonnheim, M. (2004). *Welcome to the club: The art of Jewish grandparenting*. New York: Devorah.

Thal, L. (2008). Jewish spirituality and adult spiritual development. In R. L. Goodman, P. A. Flexner, & L. D. Bloomberg (Eds.), *What we now know about Jewish education* (pp. 173–186). Los Angeles: Torah Aura.

Yoffie, E. (1997, October). Presidential sermon. Paper Presented at the meeting of the UAHC 64th Biennial Convention, Dallas, TX.

Congregational Schools

Isa Aron

The congregational school, perhaps the most maligned form of Jewish education, is still the most popular.[1] This chapter reviews the predicaments the congregational school has faced in the past, and offers a guardedly optimistic appraisal of its prospects for the future.

A Brief History of the Congregational School

The percentage of Jewish children enrolled in congregational schools in the United States has varied greatly over time. During the Colonial era, families of means hired tutors for their children, with only the poorest being tutored under synagogue auspices (Gartner, 1969, p. 5); by the time of the American Revolution, these private arrangements began to be superseded by congregational and communal schools (Graff, 2008). A study conducted in New York City in 1909 (Kaplan & Cronson, 1909/1969) found an assortment of Jewish educational venues, including privately run *chedorim* (one-room schools) and institutional schools (run by orphanages and settlement houses), in addition to congregational schools. The authors of the survey (one of whom was Mordecai Kaplan) recommended that the community invest in a nascent institution, the communal Talmud Torah. Promoted by newly established Bureaus of Jewish Education in many major cities, Talmud Torahs flourished in the 1920s and 1930s. But as Jews moved, first to the outer rings of settlement in cities, then to the suburbs, the Talmud Torah, whose staffing model was based on the enrollment of a large number of neighborhood children, was no longer economically viable. Thus, in the 1940s and 1950s, the congregational school became the predominant form of Jewish education.[2] Since then, however, the number of day

---

I. Aron (✉)
Hebrew Union College, Los Angels, CA, USA
e-mail: Iaron@huc.edu

[1]This is only in the United States, which differs from Canada and many European and Latin American countries, where day schools receive public funding.
[2]Over the past few decades, communal Talmud Torahs have largely disappeared from the scene.

Table 1 School affiliation[3]

Affiliation	Schools	Percent of total
Chabad/Lubovitch	222	12.91
Community/Pluralistic	52	3.02
Conservative	511	29.71
Modern orthodox	54	3.14
Reconstructionist	65	3.78
Reform	676	39.30
Other or no affiliation	140	8.14
Total	1,720	100.0

schools has grown steadily, and both the popularity and the status of congregational schools have declined, explained below.

A comprehensive census of supplementary schools[4] in the United States (Wertheimer, 2008) identified 1,720 schools and a total enrollment of 212,566.[5] Table 1 shows the affiliation of these schools by denominations, and Table 2 the enrollment, by denomination. Wertheimer estimated student enrollment (grades 1–12) in all supplementary schools at 230,000. A comparable census of day schools conducted several years earlier found 172,447 students in grades 1–12 (Schick, 2004). Thus, despite the fact that day schools have eroded their "market share," supplementary schools still enroll the majority (57%) of students.

Table 2 Enrollment by denomination[6]

Affiliation	Schools	Total enrollment	Percent of total enrollment	Average school size
Chabad/Lubovitch	222	8,468	3.98	38.14
Community/Pluralistic	52	7,750	3.65	151.13
Conservative	511	55,915	26.30	109.42
Modern orthodox	54	2,481	1.17	45.94
Reconstructionist	65	6,166	2.9	94.86
Reform	676	121,380	57.10	179.56
Other or no affiliation	140	10,406	4.90	74.33
Total	1,720	212,566	100	123.66

---

[3] Source: Wertheimer (2008).

[4] "Supplementary schools" is the general category for all schools that meet after school hours or on weekends. In the United States over 90% of these schools operate under congregational auspices. In this chapter the terms "congregational school" and "religious school" are used interchangeably.

[5] Information of this sort had never been collected before, and it proved extremely difficult to identify all the schools, and even to elicit a response from all those that were identified. Wertheimer estimates that 10% of the schools were not reached, though he assumes that these schools are very small.

[6] Source: Wertheimer (2008).

A Beleaguered Institution

The 1950s and 1960s are generally considered the heyday of the congregational school, "an era of growth, expansion and legitimization," in which "synagogue schools became respectable institutions, which engendered excitement, dynamism and hope" (Chazan, 1987, p. 170). Whether or not most congregational schools were as successful as this quote suggests, a significant number are remembered as being so. A number of factors accounted for the success of these institutions, especially in comparison with their counterparts today. The hope and enthusiasm attendant upon the founding of the State of Israel lent a sense of purpose and excitement to studying Hebrew. There existed a cadre of American-born teachers, largely women, who approached their work, part-time though it was, with a strong sense of professionalism. As day schools were still a relatively new phenomenon, congregational schools retained a core of committed, knowledgeable parents. The rates of intermarriage and divorce were lower, as were the number of working mothers. Perhaps most importantly, American society validated attendance at "Sunday" school as part of wholesome, middle-class life (Gans, 1951, p. 333). But even in the 1950s, there were problems with this model, and these problems accelerated with each successive decade.

The Congregational School as "Bar/Bat Mitzvah Factory"

Perhaps the biggest problem facing the congregational school is that a significant plurality, if not the majority, of American Jewish parents are not interested in *torah lishma* (learning for its own sake); rather, they send their children to congregational schools to prepare them for their *bar* or *bat mitzvah*. This instrumental view of Jewish learning fits with the conventional wisdom of an earlier era (and perhaps this era as well) that one's education ends with the acquisition of a diploma. In the minds of parents, religious school is the equivalent of public school, and bar or bat mitzvah is the equivalent of graduation.

The Jewish educational establishment unwittingly lent credence to this view in the 1930s and 1940s when bureaus of Jewish education throughout the United States worked with the Conservative and the Reform movements to link the celebration of *b'nei* mitzvah (there were no *b'not* mitzvah in those days) to formal Jewish study (Schoenfeld, 1988). They set standards that required a minimum of a certain number of years of study, a number of times a week. The exact calculus of years and hours varied, but the principle remained the same. The result was a Faustian bargain: religious schooling became inextricably linked (in the minds of parents, synagogue leaders, and even some synagogue professionals) with preparation for *bar* (and later *bat*) mitzvah. While this assured a steady stream of students in grades 4–7, it made it more likely that these children would drop out after 7th grade; and it reinforced the notion that adult learning was unnecessary and irrelevant. A 1989 study quotes a synagogue board member as saying, "Does the congregation really want quality education? Maybe we just want kids to make it through their *Bar Mitzvah*" (Schoem, 1989, p. 71).

The problem persists to this day, though it is difficult to gauge its extent. Parents interviewed in a recent study (Kress, 2007) mentioned a range of goals for their children's religious school education in addition to preparation for *b'nei mitzvah*, including carrying on the tradition, participating in a range of home and synagogue rituals, and developing strong moral values. Statistics, on the other hand, tell a different story. Wertheimer's census found dropout rates ranging from 35% in 8th grade and 55% by 9th grade, to 80–85% by 11th and 12th grades. And sociologist Steven M. Cohen notes that surveys of congregational membership consistently find that the distribution of families with children peaks at the age of 13 in Reform Movement, but is relatively constant in the Conservative movement.[7]

A Shortage of Qualified Teachers

The congregational school has been plagued by other problems as well. Shevitz (1988) documented the chronic shortage of teachers, which began as early as the 1930s. Teaching loads in communal in the Talmud Torahs could, if the teacher wished, come close to those in public schools, because these schools operated on double or even triple shifts, and offered teachers additional duties. This created a profession that attracted a cadre of dedicated and well-trained young people; but this newly established profession began to decline with the demise of the Talmud Torah. By the 1960s, only the largest congregational schools ran on double sessions, and even these rarely hired teachers for more than 12 hours a week. A 1998 study of Jewish teachers conducted by the Council for Initiatives in Jewish Education found that 64% of supplementary school teachers taught 1–4 hours a week, and 32% taught 5–12 hours; only 4% taught 13 hours or more (Gamoran, Goldring, Robinson, Tammivaara, & Goodman, 1998, p. 12).[8] Under these circumstances, it is difficult to attract qualified teachers, and the study revealed just how unqualified these teachers were. Fifty-five percent of supplementary school teachers worked in general education, presumably having some sort of formal training in education, but only 12% had a degree in Jewish studies, while 18% had a certificate in Jewish studies; and 29% had no pre-collegiate Jewish education at all (not even once a week) after the age of 13. As one might guess from these figures, only 19% had any professional training in both Jewish studies and general education.

A Flawed Paradigm

Elsewhere (Aron, 1989) I have argued that the fundamental problem of the congregational school is that it adheres to the "schooling/instructional paradigm." Instruction is the deliberate, formalized process of handing over elements of a

---

[7] Steven M. Cohen, personal communication, April 30, 2009.

[8] Teachers from three communities were surveyed: Atlanta, Baltimore, and Milwaukee.

culture by those designated as "teachers" to those designated as "students." The schooling/instructional paradigm works best when it is buttressed by a number of incentives: laws which mandate attendance; societal expectations (and empirical evidence) that schooling correlates positively with one's earning potential; and competition for entrance to elite colleges. Lacking these motivators, the Jewish school has suffered by comparison; Judaic studies, even in day schools, continue to be seen as less important than general studies.

I find most persuasive John Westerhoff's (1976) argument that it is a mistake for congregational schools to adhere to the instructional model. Rather, they ought to conceive of their educational task as that of enculturation, the welcoming of newcomers into a culture. This view of culture is very broad, encompassing knowledge, skills, attitudes, practices, and values. A culture is strong when newcomers have daily encounters with well-enculturated veterans. Under these circumstances, the transmission of attitudes, practices, and values does not require any deliberate, self-conscious processes, and the newcomer simply "absorbs" them. Anyone and everyone is a "teacher," and no particular learning sequence is better than any other. For example a community which values reading, and in which everyone over a certain age reads for pleasure, will, in most cases, transmit a love of reading to its children, making it easier for them to learn the knowledge and skills taught in school. Conversely, when a culture is weak, the transmission of attitudes, practices, and values is not automatic, and there is a much thinner context to situate and support new knowledge and skills.

Data from the 1990 National Jewish Population Study suggests that the Jewish culture of religious-school families tends to be weak. The survey divided parents who send their children to religious school into two groups: those who attend only once a week, and those who attend more than once a week. Table 3 shows that fewer than half of those in the first group, and only half of those in the second, light Shabbat candles, to take just one example.

Other data are more positive, with over 95% of both groups attending a Passover seder; over 98% lighting Hanukkah candles; and over 70% having read a book with Jewish content in the past year. It would be difficult to argue, however, that the majority of religious-school children grow up in a strong Jewish culture.

Table 3 Jewish activities in which religious-school parents engage[9]

Activity	Parents whose children attend 1x/wk (%)	Parents whose children attend more than 1x/wk (%)
"Usually" light Shabbat candles	34	50
Attend synagogue more than once a month	35	37
Agree that "Being Jewish is very important to me"	48	72

---

[9]Steven M. Cohen, personal communication, December 30, 2008.

Enculturation and instruction are not antithetical. Enculturation is the broadest framework; but within this framework, certain knowledge and skills must be taught through instruction. But the knowledge and skills transmitted through instruction will only "stick" when they are appreciated and utilized on a regular basis. The Talmud Torah, for example, saw its goal as providing instruction for a group of students who were presumed to be well on their way to enculturation. While this assumption might have been a reasonable one in the 1920s and 1930s, the progressive assimilation of American Jews since that time has made it increasingly dubious.

For strongly identified, well-educated Jews, instruction and enculturation still function as complementary processes. The family, synagogue, and neighborhood combine to inculcate basic attitudes, practices, and values, one of which is the importance of Judaic learning. Instruction, layered onto ongoing enculturation, proceeds smoothly and successfully. In contrast, for most students attending congregational schools, enculturation is episodic and fragmentary.

The Persistent Grammar of Congregational Schooling

Despite all of its problems, the congregational school remained relatively unchanged during the last half of the twentieth century. New programs in teacher training came and went, as did experiments with alternative settings, like retreats and day camps. The idea with the most traction, family education, was too often reduced to a series of one-shot stand-alone programs (Shevitz & Karpel, 1995).

To many, it seems perplexing that American Jewry, which has mobilized itself to support any number of causes, could not muster the resources to address the fundamental problems of the majority of its schools. But this would not surprise sociologists of education, who find a comparable situation in public education. Tyack and Cuban (1995) attribute the failure of public school reform to the persistence of a "grammar of schooling," a set of underlying assumptions about how schools should function:

> The basic grammar of schooling, like the shape of the classroom, has remained remarkably stable over decades. Little has changed in the ways that schools divide time and space, classify students and allocate them to classrooms, splinter knowledge into "subjects," and award grades and "credits" as evidence of learning. . . . [This] has puzzled and frustrated generations of reformers who have sought to change these standardized organizational forms. (p. 85)

With the vast majority of students attending schools that were organized in similar fashion, it is no wonder that "the public. . . came to assume that the grammar embodied the necessary features of a 'real school'" (p. 107).

Michelle Lynn-Sachs argues that the grammar of religious schooling, remarkably similar in the Catholic, Protestant, and Jewish Sunday schools she studied, is doubly intractable. Not only do parents and administrators expect *schools* to adhere to a conventional pattern, there is a "grammar of congregations" that exerts a strong, conservative pull on *congregations* as well. Like other organizations, congregations "tend to seek legitimacy within their field by conforming to ritualized, expected ways of operating, rather than organizing their work according to purely rational, goal-oriented demands" (2007, p. 63).

With the grammar of religious schooling taken as a given throughout the twentieth century, the education departments of the Conservative and Reform (and later Reconstructionist) movements saw their role as developing new curricula, which they did periodically. But the "system" of Jewish education is "loosely coupled" (Shevitz, 1995) at best, and the channels for distributing these materials were poorly developed; the curricula were utilized in half of the possible schools at best. The Los Angeles Bureau of Jewish Education Teacher Census (Aron & Phillips, 1989) found that fewer than 45% of teachers in congregational schools were given a curriculum by their education directors; a recent study by the Union for Reform Judaism (URJ) (Shevitz, 2008) found that 50% of the teachers in Reform congregations use the Movement's Chai Curriculum. Moreover, the absence of qualified teachers who could bring these curricula to life in the classroom continues to be problematic. The URJ study found that fewer than half of the teachers utilizing the Chai Curriculum felt prepared to meet the following stated goals of the curriculum: making Torah real in the students' lives; feeling connected to Israel; becoming more comfortable with *t'filot* (prayers); and developing a personal understanding of *k'dushah* (holiness) (p. 23). To its credit, the URJ has offered a series of local and national workshops for teachers; it sees the curriculum and the workshops as resources for an important group of adult learners.[10]

An Attitude of "Benign Neglect"

Perhaps the most intractable problem of all is the poor reputation of the congregational school, and, hence, the low set of expectations shared by a range of its stakeholders. A 1977 task force convened by the American Jewish Committee observed that supplementary schools

> produce graduates who are functionally illiterate in Judaism and not clearly positive in their attitudinal identification.... [M]ost graduates look back without joy on their educational experience. (p. i)

Many researchers and communal leaders continue to share this dismal view today. Kress (2007) reports that

> [in speaking with] colleagues and Jewish communal professionals, the very mention of religious schools would often provoke a Pavlovian smirk or rolling of the eyes. When I asked about these reactions, I was regaled with countless narratives about negative experiences in religious school or about frustrations encountered as professionals working with religious schools. (p. 143)

---

[10]Dr. Jan Katzew, Director, Department of Lifelong Learning, URJ, personal communication, February 27, 2009.

Given the poor reputation of the congregational school, it is no wonder that central agencies, federations and foundations turned their attention to day schools, Israel trips, and summer camps, maintaining an attitude of "benign neglect" toward congregational schools.

The Tide Begins to Turn

Fortunately, the news is not all bad. In the past two decades, congregational schools have begun to change, due to the confluence of a number of factors: increased interest in adult learning; increased attention to Jewish education in general, coupled with an acceptance of the fact that a majority of Jewish children will, for the foreseeable future, receive their formal Jewish education in congregational schools; and the rise of a number of projects whose goal is to transform the congregational school.

The Revival of Adult Learning[11]

For most of the twentieth century, relatively few Jewish adults engaged in ongoing Jewish learning. Synagogues typically had a Torah study group, an "Introduction to Judaism" course, and little else. During the 1980s this began to change. "Lifelong learning" became a buzzword in the secular world. In particular, Jewish feminism prompted women who had not celebrated a *bat mitzvah* as children to do so as adults. In response, synagogues developed the adult *b'nei mitzvah* class, a 1- or 2-year course of study that, to this day, is popular among women, and continues to attract some men, as well (Grant, 2007; Schoenfeld, 1989).

Concurrently, the 1980s and 1990s saw the rise of a number of programs devoted to high-level, ongoing, text-based Jewish learning, including the Wexner Heritage Program, the Florence Melton Adult Mini School, and the Boston Federation's *Me'ah* program (which offered 100 hours of study with Judaic studies professors over a period of 2 years). Having partaken of serious adult study, graduates of these and comparable programs became avid learners, turning to their congregations for more (Grant, Schuster, Woocher, & Cohen, 2004). Synagogues responded with varying degrees of alacrity. Though some developed an impressive array of classes, workshops, and retreats, most concentrated their efforts—and allotted the bulk of their funding—to stand-alone scholar-in-residence programs.

Even when synagogues increased their adult learning opportunities dramatically, they did not always pay comparable attention to the religious school. Because adult education was accorded more status, it was often viewed as a separate undertaking,

---

[11] This section focuses on the effects of the revival of adult learning on congregational schools. For a much more extensive discussion of adult learning, see Chapter "Adult Jewish Learning: The Landscape" in this handbook.

under the aegis of the rabbi, rather than the educator. Rarely was there much coordination between adult and children's education, nor was there an overall vision for congregational learning as a whole.

Nonetheless, some synagogue schools benefited from a "trickle down" effect. For example, a mother who spent several years in an ongoing Torah study group observes

> The adult learning that a lot of us were engaged in put pressure on the religious school, because suddenly we had an experience that was positive and phenomenal.... We realized that what our kids were getting was so old school,... and that there was another way to go about this. (Aron, 2009b)

When opportunities to improve the religious school came along, parents like this were ready to participate.

The "Continuity Commissions"

The 1990 National Jewish Population Study (NJPS) was not the first report to raise concerns about the future of the American Jewry, but it managed to create a sense of urgency that prior reports had not. Not only did it find that the rate of intermarriage was 52%,[12] it also found that only 32% of respondents were members of synagogues, fewer than 20% lit Shabbat candles on a regular basis, and only 40% gave to a Jewish cause. (Kosmin, Goldstein, Waksberg, & Lerer, 1991).

One hopeful finding among all of the gloom was that higher levels of Jewish education were correlated with more active participation in Jewish life. The more intensive the Jewish education of NJPS respondents, the more likely they were to join a Jewish organization, give to a Jewish cause, marry a Jewish partner, and practice Jewish rituals (Fishman and Goldstein, 1993, p. 7). As leaders of the Jewish community searched for positive steps they could take in response to this study, they saw Jewish education as an important weapon in the "battle" for Jewish survival. In the words of a 1991 report, "The responsibility for developing Jewish identity and instilling a commitment to Judaism... now rests primarily with education" (Commission on Jewish Education, p. 15).

Initially, most of the attention and funding coming out of the various "continuity commissions" of the 1990s was bestowed on pre-schools, day schools, and Israel trips. Over time, however, federations, foundations, and funders have come to see that neglecting congregational schools might mean neglecting as many as half of American Jewish children. A recent JESNA (Jewish Education Services of North America)[13] report put this more positively, focusing on the potential of the synagogue:

---

[12] This finding was later challenged by other demographers, but it certainly captured the attention of the public.

[13] JESNA is national resource center for Jewish education and serves as the umbrella organization for local and regional Central Agencies of Jewish Education.

The synagogue is, in principle, if not yet in practice, an ideal setting in which... Jewish education [as a life-long endeavor] can take root and flourish. For more individuals and families than any other single institution, the synagogue is the embodiment of Jewish community. It is also, at least potentially, a gateway into the full variety and richness of Jewish life, not only within its own walls, but in the larger Jewish community. (2008, p. 1)

New Vision and New Experimentation

The JESNA report listed 11 initiatives undertaken to "improve and renew" congregational education. These are summarized in Table 4.

These initiatives (whose full names are spelled out in the table) are sponsored by a range of organizations. Three are under the auspices of the Conservative, Reform, and Reconstructionist movements; three (The Goldring/Woldenberg Institute, STAR, and Synagogue 3000) are independent entities; two (La'atid and NESS) are sponsored by Central Agencies; one (ECE) is affiliated with a school of education; one (Legacy Heritage) is a foundation; and one (PELIE) is a consortium of funders.

The goals of these initiatives may be arrayed on a continuum from *improvement* to *transformation*. Advocates of improvement assume that the structure of the congregational school will remain the same for the foreseeable future, and that the greatest need is for new curricular materials, teacher training, and/or more family education. The case for transformation follows the argument made for enculturation offered earlier in this chapter: Given the relatively impoverished culture of liberal American Jews, the overriding aim of congregational education should be enculturation, rather than merely instruction. This calls for a radical change in how the school should be structured, in ways that are discussed in the next section.

While four of the initiatives (those of the denominations and the Goldring/Woldenberg Institute) fall squarely at the improvement end of the continuum, the others are not so easily categorized. NESS, while concentrating mostly on improvement, also engages the education committee and the board, which is a step toward transformation. Legacy Heritage and PELIE support both types of efforts, though Legacy Heritage tends to favor transformational projects. ECE's RE-IMAGINE and La'atid encourage transformation, but also support congregations that do not end up re-structuring their school. And STAR, Synagogue 3000, and ECE's Congregation of Learners project concentrate their efforts on the congregation as a whole.

Transforming the Congregational School

Earlier I argued that the congregational school is doomed to have limited results if it conceives of its task as largely one of instruction, since its students lack the cultural background to appreciate and utilize this instruction. If one accepts this argument, it follows that the century-old paradigm of the congregational school, which focuses primarily on children and takes place in age-graded classrooms, needs to be re-thought. Since 2003, ECE's RE-IMAGINE Project has worked with

Table 4 Initiatives devoted to improving and/or transforming congregational schools

Name of initiative	Sponsoring organization	Primary focus
Experiment in congregational education (ECE) ■ The RE-IMAGINE project www.eceonline.org	Rhea Hirsch School of Education, HUC-JIR	Has worked with over 70 congregations in the United States to ■ Transform them into congregations of learners ■ Re-imagine the religious school
Goldring/Woldenberg Institute of Southern Jewish Life education program www.isjl.org/education	Goldring/Woldenberg Institute of Southern Jewish Life	Serves southern Jewish communities through ■ Creating a common curriculum ■ Traveling educational fellows ■ Annual conference
"Next generation"	Jewish Reconstructionist Federation www.jrf.org	Builds connections among all educational settings serving members of the Reconstructionist movement
La'atid: Synagogues for the future	Jewish Federation of Hartford, CT hartford.ctujcfedweb.org	Works with local congregations and schools by engaging them in an individualized change process
Legacy Heritage innovation project www.legacyheritage.org	An independent foundation	Gives grants to synagogues that are creating new paradigms of congregational education
NESS (nurturing excellence in Synagogue schools)	Auerbach Central Agency for Jewish Education, Philadelphia www.acaje.org	Works with local schools on ■ Assessment of assets and limitations ■ Training for teachers, educators, and lay leaders
PELIE (Partnership for effective learning and innovative education) www.pelie.org	An independent consortium of funders	Works toward substantially improving "complementary" Jewish education and transforming the reality, perception, and funding of the field
STAR (Synagogue transformation and renewal) www.starsynagogue.org	An independent organization	Designs and delivers synagogue-based initiatives and continuing educational opportunities for rabbis

Table 4 (continued)

Name of initiative	Sponsoring organization	Primary focus
Synagogue 2000/3000 www.synagogue3000.org	An independent organization	Sponsors ■ A leadership network ■ A synagogue studies research initiative
Chai curriculum www.urj.org/chai	Union for Reform Judaism	This curriculum is designed to be used with students in grades 2–7, families with children aged 7–14, teachers, education directors, and synagogue boards
■ Framework for excellence ■ Project Etgar	United Synagogue of Conservative Judaism www.uscj.org	■ Provides benchmarks for the congregation and the school. ■ Project Etgar is a curriculum for grades 6–8

Adapted from JESNA (2008, pp. 2–4).

over 50 congregations to re-envision and re-structure their schools. In addition, at least a dozen congregations have launched their own efforts at transformation, either adapting the models highlighted and profiled by the ECE or devising their own alternative models (Langer, 2002; Margolius & Weissman, 2002; Weissman & Margolius, 2002; Aron, 2009b).

In both RE-IMAGINE and the individual change efforts, the engine for transformation has been a task force, which functions as a "temporary parallel learning system" (Schein, 1999, pp. 130–132). The advantage of a task force, Schein explains, is the synergy that results when stakeholders who don't ordinarily have sustained contact with one another have an opportunity to exchange experiences and ideas. The most reflective and cooperative representatives of each stakeholder group are asked to join the task force. Because the work of the task force does not include quotidian tasks like oversight or budgeting, its members are freed to think in new ways.

The following is a brief overview of a few of the alternative models that congregations (either on their own or through the ECE) have introduced.

The Shabbat Community

One of the oldest and most popular of the alternative models is the Shabbat Community, in which parents attend school along with their children, on either Shabbat morning or Shabbat afternoon (Langer, 2002; Margolius & Weissman, 2002; Weissman & Margolius, 2002). The programs generally include a family worship service, an opportunity to learn as a family, and an opportunity to learn in age cohorts, either weekly or biweekly.[14] A few programs of this type meet on Sunday mornings, and thus may not have a worship component, but adhere to the same basic structure otherwise.

By attending along with their children, parents in these programs demonstrate that Jewish learning is a lifelong pursuit. This model takes family education to its logical extension and can have a profound effect on families. Susan Wolfe, a parent in *Shabbaton* at Congregation Beth Am in Los Altos Hills, CA, one of the earliest of these programs, writes

> After 5 years, how has *Shabbaton* affected our family? For one thing, it has demonstrated to our children that Jewish learning is not only for children; we are involved in their learning, and in our own. When they go to religious school, we go to religious school. When we come back together, we each have an experience to share on a common Jewish topic. Additionally, we are practicing what we preach: We tell our children that Shabbat is a time for relaxation and study; each Shabbat, we relax and study with other Jewish families at our synagogue....
>
> But perhaps the most meaningful outcomes have been personal. As much as anything I have learned at Shabbaton, I have learned how very much I have yet to learn. I discovered the depth of my hunger to further my understanding and appreciation of our Jewish heritage. (Aron, 2000, p. 19)

---

[14]Students in grades 3–7 generally continue studying Hebrew during the week, alongside their former Sunday-school classmates.

Thinking back on 15 years of *Shabbaton*, its first coordinator, Lisa Langer, comments

> A huge number of adults who had never ever done Jewish learning before became engaged in Jewish learning. It built friendships and community because people saw each other week after week. These family groups became *chavurot* (fellowship groups) for many families. For a lot of people it became their connection to the synagogue.... *Shabbaton* transformed the leadership; at one point, at least 90% of the board had participated in the *Shabbaton* at some point. (Aron, 2009a)

Of course, not all parents are willing or able to spend so much time learning with their children, which is why larger congregations generally offer these family schools as alternatives to the traditional religious school, rather than the only possible option. In these synagogues the percentage of parents participating in the family school alternative ranges from 20 to 60%. This creates a natural experiment, with students who attend the normative school serving as a "control group." While no hard data exists to date,[15] educators in these congregations report that students in the family school are more engaged than their Sunday-school counterparts. Rabbi/Cantor Angela Warnick Buchdal, who led the Sharing Shabbat program at Westchester Reform Temple, notes that despite the fact that families joined the program for a variety of reasons, the effect on the children was nearly always the same:

> At the end of the day, virtually everyone comes out of the experience feeling, "I am a super involved Reform Jew. I am literate with the liturgy, I'm a regular Shabbat goer. Shabbat has become a real part of my week and my family's week. This has become a sanctuary and time for my family." (Aron, 2009a)

Combining Religious School with Day Care

The idea of combining after-school day care with after-school religious school has an obvious appeal for both dual-career and single-parent Jewish families. Kesher, an independent school that has two sites in the Boston area, pioneered this model in 1991.[16] In Kesher's early years, many children attended 4 or 5 days a week. But because of the school's commitment to maintaining a small size and a small student/teacher ratio, it has priced itself out of the after-school market, and the majority of children now attend only 2 days a week. Nonetheless, the essence of Kesher's approach remains the same. Children come straight from school, and spend nearly 2 hours playing and interacting informally with the teachers (who use what they call "incidental Hebrew" for small talk like greetings and directions). Another 20 minutes at the end are spent singing, often with parents participating. In between are

---

[15] The ECE is conducting such a study and has collected its "baseline" data, before many of these models were launched; it will take a number of years with this model (and others) running, before data for comparisons can be collected.

[16] The two sites are incorporated separately, but share their curricula, and maintain close ties.

two 50-minute teaching blocks, one devoted to *Yahadut* (Judaism), the other to *Ivrit* (Hebrew). Kesher's leaders believe that the informal time blocs are as important as the formal ones. To quote the website,

> To think of Kesher as only a Hebrew school/after-school misses the essence of what makes Kesher special. Though Hebrew school and after school are still at the core of what Kesher does, since its beginning, Kesher has become a community.[17]

Essential to this model is the ongoing presence of the teachers, who are available to be with the students from the moment they arrive, 4 days a week.[18] In fact, teachers are on site 2 hours prior to the arrival of the students, in order to plan their lessons and meet with their supervisors.

The director of a school that adheres to this model takes care to impress upon new teachers that the informal part of the day is just as important as formal class time:

> Teaching here isn't just teaching *Yahadut* (Judaism), just teaching *Ivrit* (Hebrew). We talk about this all the time that teaching begins from the moment the kids get off the bus or the moment they are dropped off from their car pool. (Aron, 2009b)

Teachers find that this emphasis on enculturation, as well as instruction, gives them a great advantage in relating to the children:

> These are all things that I didn't have in my prior religious school teaching experience: Really taking the time to talk about kids, what their needs are, who their friends are, who is more sociable, who needs a different kind of help. We try to really focus on not just the outstanding and most troublesome kids but also the kids who could, in other systems, kind of fall through the cracks. (Aron, 2009b)

This model includes relatively few family education programs. There are annual family dinners for each grade, and *havdalah* (the ceremony marking the end of Shabbat) get-togethers for everyone approximately every 6 weeks, along with a variety of packets that are sent home. Nonetheless, parents in these schools feel very connected, perhaps because the school is so small and relations between parents and staff are so close. One father notes

> Kesher is not only the kids' educational resource, but also their Jewish community.... I think that for people who are either not Jewish but married into interfaith marriages, or people who are very secular in their orientation, or just ambivalent, who haven't gotten around to joining a synagogue, this is a central focal point for their Jewish life. (Aron, 2009b)

Given how many Jewish families have a need for some sort of after-school care, it is surprising that this model has not been adopted in any congregational school. To date, the model has been exported to two additional sites (one in a JCC, the other independent), in New York City. This replication was facilitated by PELIE, which has plans to promote it in other locations as well.

---

[17] http://www.kesherweb.org/about.php

[18] At one branch there is an abbreviated program on Fridays, to accommodate families that need day care on that day.

Deconstructing and Reconstructing the Religious School

The most recent attempts to re-structure the religious school take an expanded view of learning, and situate it in new settings and/or new time frames. The oldest of these experiments was piloted in 2002; the newest are, as of this writing, still in the planning stages; by the time this book is published, there will undoubtedly be new examples around. Here is a sample of these new configurations:

- The Beit Midrash program at Temple Beth Elohim, in Wellesley, Massachusetts, situates most of the learning in the home. Students in grades 3–5 read books and do a variety of projects with their parents, coming to the synagogue on Sunday afternoons every 6 weeks to discuss the reading and do joint activities. Families in this program also get together regularly for Shabbat dinners and *tzedakah* (social justice) projects; 6th and 7th graders in the Ma'asim Tovim program at Beth Elohim are involved in ongoing *tzedakah* projects, combined with short text-study sessions, in lieu of Sunday classes. High school students in the synagogue's Havaya program attend weekend retreats, and meet in *Havurot* (fellowship groups) that combine an activity like drama, hiking, or social justice work, with text study.[19]
- The MASA program at Temple Shaaray Tefila, in New York City, plans to take families on a variety of "journeys," with different themes each year. The first of these, Celebrations, focuses on the Jewish holidays. Families come for 3-hour preparatory sessions, and then celebrate holidays together.[20] At least one Los Angeles congregation is planning a similar model.
- The Nisayon program at Temple Judea in Tarzana, California, substitutes day camp for religious school. Campers attend for 2 weeks in the summer and a week during winter break. In addition to t'fillot, singing, Israeli dancing, and the usual camp activities, there are two 90-minute classes each day. During the school year, students in grades 4–6 are tutored in Hebrew at their homes. In addition, there are 11 family events throughout the year.[21]
- Students and parents in Limmud Mishpacha at Congregation Beth Simchat Torah in New York City meet once a week in small groups at people's homes, and twice a month all together on Shabbat morning.[22]
- The Morei Derech Project at Temple Beth Sholom in Roslyn, New York, pairs families who are looking for greater Jewish involvement with *Morei Derech* (literally guides), "Jewish Life Coaches" who will help these families make the connection between the synagogue and their homes and navigate their Jewish journeys.[23]

---

[19] http://www.bethelohim-wellesley.org/learning/index.php
[20] http://www.shaaraytefilanyc.org/school/masa.php
[21] http://www.templejudea.com/news.php?bridge_id=91
[22] http://cbst.org/children.shtml
[23] http://209.85.173.132/custom?q=cache:kOujOAaR2n4J:www.tbsroslyn.org/bulletin/2008–06.pdf+More+Derech&hl=en&ct=clnk&cd=1&gl=us, p. 12.

Common Principles

All of these alternative models, whether relatively established like the "Shabbat Community" or a more recent experiment, like MASA, share a commitment to at least two of the following four principles of enculturation:

(1) Rather than delegating Jewish education to the synagogue, parents are directly involved as either learners or teachers.
(2) It is not assumed that the connection between Jewish learning and Jewish living will happen automatically. Learning is done in context—*t'fillah* as part of a service; *tzedakah* among those who need it; celebration on the holidays; and so on.
(3) The school sees one of its primary tasks as creating powerful, memorable moments, which will implant strong Jewish values and commitments.
(4) The school sees one of its primary goals as creating community for students and their families.

Challenges that Remain

The opening paragraph of this chapter promised a "potentially optimistic" appraisal of the state of the congregational school today. The oldest of the alternative models, the Shabbat Community and the combined after-care/supplementary school, are permanent fixtures in the landscape; their replication/adaptation is proceeding slowly but steadily. The fate of the newer experiments is as yet unknown. Undoubtedly, some of these new approaches will catch on, while others will not.

An estimated 30–50 synagogues have restructured all or part of their schools in the ways described above; and many others have focused more on enculturation, through all-school "happenings," project-based learning, and more frequent and concerted family education. But while there is justification for cautious optimism, a great deal of work remains to be done. In this section I will highlight some of the issues the congregational schools face today. These include inertia, the continual pressure from parents to reduce the number of hours of instruction; the challenges of teaching Hebrew; the paucity of new models for post-bar/bat mitzvah education; and the shortage of both educators and teachers.

Can Synagogues Overcome Their Inertia?

To paraphrase the proverb made popular by Hillary Clinton, it takes a community to improve (or transform) a congregational school. For too many decades, the task of improving the congregational school was left to the educators, education committees, and central agencies of education; too few rabbis, synagogue boards, or federations, and too few leaders of the Jewish community at large saw this as their responsibility. This situation has begun to change, in *some* synagogues. The success of ECE, L'atid, and NESS is due, in no small part, to the fact that they have recruited congregational leaders who are more prominent and have more influence than those who typically sit on the synagogues' education committees. Too many schools, in contrast, seem to be mired in the status quo.

Only certain types of congregations are poised to take a close and candid look at their religious school, and work to either improve or transform it. A forthcoming study (Aron et al., 2009, 2010) analyzes the accomplishments of eight synagogues that had participated in either ECE or Synagogue 2000 (S2K) and were able to make and sustain significant changes. These congregations were compared to eight others that also participated in these projects, but were unable to either make changes at all, or to sustain the changes they had introduced. All of the former synagogues shared, to a greater or lesser degree, a set of characteristics: they had a sense of sacred purpose; they viewed their activities holistically; they were highly participatory; they attempted to engage people in meaningful ways; they were reflective; and they were innovative. The study's authors called these congregations "visionary," in contrast to the other eight congregations, which they termed "functional." These other congregations are well run, but they are more limited: their congregants have a "fee for service" mentality; they are segmented in their functioning; they expect passivity, rather than active participation; they evoke a feeling of detachment; their leaders are not particularly reflective. Not surprisingly, these synagogues resist transformation, and they often resist improvement, as well.

And there is yet a third set of congregations that this study did not look at— the dysfunctional ones. These are congregations whose day-to-day operations are fraught with problems: they might be unable to balance their budgets; there might be ongoing battles between members of the staff, or between the clergy and the lay leaders; and so on. It is difficult to know just how many synagogues fall into this third category, but anecdotal evidence suggests that there are many. Before these synagogues can begin to even improve their schools, they must at least become functional. The denominations do their best to advise and support these congregations, but helping them overcome their inertia is a major challenge.

Pressure to Reduce Even Further the Number of Days of Instruction

The story of the congregational school might be told as that of a series of battles between parents and educators over the number of days of instruction. The Talmud Torah often met five times a week; the congregational schools of the 1950s met three or even four times a week. In the 1990s and the first half of this decade, many schools faced (and lost) the battle to maintain 3 days, rather than two (Aron, 2007; Reimer, 1992, 1997). Today, the pressure is mounting for schools to meet only 1 day a week, and a number have already succumbed.

As argued earlier in this chapter, instruction should not be the primary task of the religious school. When days of instruction are replaced by family get-togethers, projects done at home, *tzedakah* projects, and the like, the gain in enculturation may far outweigh the loss in instruction. But many of the schools that have severely reduced instructional time have not added family time or service learning.

Creating Attractive Alternatives for Post-bar/bat mitzvah Education

Whatever the cause of the high dropout rate after *bar/bat mitzvah* (be it the assumption that "graduation" is at age 13, or the increased academic pressures on high school students), a contributing factor is the dearth of creative, engaging programs for adolescents. Synagogues that have devoted their efforts to creating a flexible array of options that appeal to teens with different interests, such as Temple Beth Elohim (described above) have stemmed the dropout rate; 70% of their high school students are enrolled in some form of Jewish education. The "village" that rallied to create and promulgate alternative models for younger children must now help congregations devise equally attractive programs for the post-*b'nei mitzvah* students.

What Kind of Hebrew Should Be Taught and What Can Be Accomplished?

Because attendance at religious school is linked to preparation for bar/bat mitzvah, most schools teach *siddur* (prayer book) Hebrew. But the Hebrew of the *siddur* is grammatically complex and largely removed from the students' day-to-day experience, with concepts that are difficult to grasp, especially when one does not have a "prayer life." Realizing how difficult it is for students to retain the vocabulary of the *siddur*, most schools concentrate on making sure that the students can decode or recite the prayers, rather than understanding the basic vocabulary or grappling with the concepts. However, there are other choices that might make more sense. Kesher, for example, focuses on Modern Hebrew; the school Reimer studied taught Biblical Hebrew; and Hebrew Literacy or a technique like TPR (Total Physical Response) (Asher, 1993) might serve as useful complements to a *siddur* Hebrew program (Aron, 2004b). None of these alternatives are ready-made, which is why it will take the proverbial "village" (publishing houses, central agencies, etc.), to make them available and accessible. There are still champions of the Hebrew language in our midst; hopefully some of them will take up this challenge.

The Shortage of Teachers and Educators

To reach their full potential, religious schools must be led by at least one highly qualified professional and staffed by well-trained teachers. The good news is that congregational educators can earn relatively high salaries. The bad news is that the shortage of qualified personnel persists. The Wexner, Davidson, Mandel, and Jim Joseph Foundations have made generous fellowships available to those studying to be Jewish educators. It is hoped that this will attract a much larger pool of students.

The shortage of religious school teachers, on the other hand, appears to be chronic. With over half of the teachers teaching less than 10 hours a week and nearly a third teaching less than 4 hours a week (Aron & Phillips, 1989), teaching in religious school can only be a part-time job for all but a few. Central Synagogue in New York has employed full-time professional educators to teach in the religious school for a number of years. When not teaching children, these educators write curriculum, meet with families, and run other programs within the synagogue (Kaiserman, 2007). While a number of other congregations are attempting to replicate this teaching arrangement, only the most affluent synagogues will be able to raise the necessary funds. The pool of potential teachers includes college students, under-employed young adults, day school and public school teachers, and congregants who see teaching as an avocation. Some of these teachers have weak Judaic backgrounds; others may lack teaching skills. Much can be done to work with these teachers to help maximize their potential (Aron, 2004a), but only with communal help will most synagogues be able to bear this burden.

An Agenda for Future Research: Studying Experimentation and Success

The spirit of experimentation has been accompanied by a new and welcome trend in scholarship, with research that focuses on success, rather than failure. Two earlier ethnographic studies (Heilman, 1992; Schoem, 1989) highlighted the insufficiencies and internal contradictions of the congregational school. In contrast, Joseph Reimer (1997) set out to find a school "with the reputation for maintaining broad educational excellence." As its title, *Succeeding at Jewish Education,* suggests the resultant book presents a more positive picture, though it does not shy away from the problems of congregational education. The book portrays classroom sessions that vary from excellent to troubling, and probes both the enthusiasm and the ambivalence of parents and the professional staff. Another work, *Best Practices in the Supplementary School* (Holtz, 1993), collects short essays highlighting some of the best features of supplementary schools throughout North America.

Two upcoming works continue this line of research. A book on synagogue transformation (Aron 2009a) contains a chapter on three synagogues that transformed themselves into Congregations of Learners in the past two decades, a process that involved both improving the traditional religious school and creating parallel alternative models. Most ambitious of all is a study commissioned by the Avichai foundation (Wertheimer, 2009), which yielded 10 case studies of supplementary schools, six of which are under the auspices of congregations. While not all of these sites proved to be equally excellent, among them were some outstanding examples of what can be accomplished in a synagogue school, when a combination of community resources, national projects, foundation grants, and, most importantly, visionary educators and rabbis, and committed lay leaders come together.

As efforts aimed at both improvement and transformation continue, the need for additional research is clear. A full research program would include, but not be limited to portraits (such as those in the Avichai study) and ethnographies (such as Reimer's) of alternative models; studies of the impact of these programs on children, their parents, and the congregation as a whole; an exploration of the motivations and competencies of both actual and potential pools of teachers; and deeper inquiries into the pedagogic content knowledge needed to teach Torah, Hebrew, and other subjects.

References

American Jewish Committee. (1977). *Does Jewish schooling matter?* New York: AJC.
Aron, I. (1989). The malaise of Jewish education. *Tikkun, 4*, 32–34.
Aron, I. (2000). *Becoming a congregation of learners: Learning as a key to revitalizing congregational life*. Woodstock, VT: Jewish lights publishing.
Aron, I. (2004a). Realism as the key to excellence in congregational education. *Agenda: Jewish Education* (17), 9–12.
Aron, I. (2004b) Teaching Hebrew in the congregational school. Unpublished report commissioned by the Memorial Foundation for Jewish Culture, NYC.
Aron, I. (2007). The longest running social drama, now coming to a congregation (of learners) near you. *Journal of Jewish Education, 77*, 25–50.
Aron, I. (2009a). Kehillah. In J. Wertheimer (Ed.), *Supplementary schools that work*. Waltham, MA: Brandeis University Press.
Aron, I. (2009b). Beit Knesset Hazon: A visionary congregation. In J. Wertheimer (Ed.), *Supplementary schools that work*. Waltham, MA: Brandeis University Press.
Aron, I., Cohen, S. M., Hoffman, L., & Kelman, A. Y. (2010) *Sacred Strategies: Becoming a Visionary Congregation*. Herndon, VA: Alban Institute.
Aron, I., Cohen, S. M., Hoffman, L., & Kelman, A. Y. (2009) Functional and visionary congregations. *CCAR Journal* Winter: 10–25.
Aron, I., & Phillips, B. (1989) Findings of the Los Angeles BJE Teacher Census. Unpublished report, Los Angeles.
Asher, J.. (1993) The Total Physical Response. Invited presentation to the California Education Association.
Chazan, B. (1987). Education in the synagogue: The transformation of the supplementary school. In J. Wertheimer (Ed.), *The American Synagogue*. Cambridge: Cambridge University Press.
Commission on Jewish Education in North America. (1991). *A Time To Act*. Lanham, MD: University Press of America.
Fishman, S. & Goldstein, A. (1993, March). *When they are grown they will not depart: Jewish education and the behavior of American adults*. Research report #8. Cohen center for modern Jewish studies, Brandeis University, Waltham, MA.
Gamoran, A., Goldring, E., Robinson, B., Tammivaara, J., & Goodman, R. (1998). *The teachers report*. New York: Council for Initiatives in Jewish Education.
Gans, H.. (1951) Park Forest: Birth of a Jewish community. *Commentary* April, 1951.
Gartner, L. (Ed.) (1969). *Jewish education in the United States: A documentary history*. New York: Teachers College Press.
Graff, G. (2008). *And you shall teach them diligently: A concise history of Jewish education in the United States 1776-2000*. New York: Jewish Theological Seminary.
Grant, L. (2007). Finding her right place in the synagogue: The rite of adult bat mitzvah. In R. Prell (Ed.), *Women remaking American Judaism*. Detroit, MI: Wayne State University Press.
Grant, L., Schuster, D. T., Woocher, M., & Cohen, S. M. (2004). *Journey of heart and mind: Transformative Jewish learning in adulthood*. New York: Jewish Theological Seminary.
Heilman, S. (1992). Inside the Jewish school. In S. Kelman (Ed.), *What we know about Jewish education*. Los Angeles: Torah Aura Productions.
Holtz, B. (Ed.) (1993). *Best practices project: The supplementary school*. Cleveland, OH: Council for Initiatives in Jewish Education.

JESNA (2008) *Transforming Congregational Education: Lessons Learned and Questions for the Future.* NY: Jewish Education Services of North America. http://www.jesna.org/jesna-publications/cat_view/41-jesna-publications/74-lippman-kanfer-institute-publications/75-lippman-kanfer-institute-working-papers

Kaiserman, S. (2007). Teaching in a religious school as a full-time job. *Contact, 10,* 6–7.

Kaplan, M., & Cronson, B. (1909/1969). A survey of Jewish education in New York City (1909). In L. Gartner (Ed.), *Jewish education in the United States: A documentary history.* New York: Teachers College Press.

Kosmin, B., Goldstein, S., Waksberg, J., & Lerer, N. (1991). *Highlights of the CJF 1990 Jewish population survey.* New York: Council of Jewish Federations.

Kress, J. (2007). Expectations, perceptions, and preconceptions: How Jewish parents talk about "supplementary" religious education. In J. Wertheimer (Ed.), *Family matters: Jewish education in an age of choice.* Waltham, MA: Brandeis University Press.

Langer, L. (2002) Shabbaton. *Sh'ma,* March, 2002.

Lynn-Sachs, M. (2007) Inside Sunday school: Cultural and religious logics at work at the intersection of religion and education. Unpublished doctoral dissertation, NYU.

Margolius, M., & Weissman, C. (2002) Creating a Shabbat-centered community. *Sh'ma,* March, 2002.

Reimer, J. (1992). Between parents and principal: Social drama in a synagogue school. *Contemporary Jewry, 13,* 60–73.

Reimer, J. (1997). *Succeeding at Jewish education.* Philadelphia: Jewish Publication Society.

Schein, E. (1999). *Organizational culture and leadership.* San Francisco: Jossey Bass.

Schick, M.. (2004) *A Census of Jewish Day Schools in the United States.* New York: Avichai Foundation. www.avichai.org

Schoem, D. (1989). *Ethnic survival in America: An ethnography of a Jewish afternoon school.* Atlanta, GA: Scholar's Press.

Schoenfeld, S. (1988). Folk Judaism, elite Judaism and the role of the bar mitzvah in the development of the synagogue and Jewish school in America. *Contemporary Jewry, 9,* 67–85.

Schoenfeld, S. (1989) Ritual and role transition: Adult Bat Mitzvah as a successful rite of passage. Paper presented at the Conference of the Network for Research in Jewish Education, Chicago, June, 1989.

Shevitz, S. (1988). Communal responses to the teacher shortage in the North American supplementary School. In J. Aviad (Ed.), *Studies in jewish education* (Vol. 3). Jerusalem: Magnes Press.

Shevitz, S. (1995). An organizational perspective on changing congregational education: What the literature reveals. In I. Aron, S. Lee, & S. Rossel (Eds.), *A congregation of learners: Transforming the congregation into a learning community.* New York: UAHC Press.

Shevitz, S. (2008) Report on the CHAI teacher survey. Unpublished report, Union of Reform Judaism.

Shevitz, S., & Karpel, D. (1995). *Sh'arim family educator initiative: An interim report of programs and populations.* Boston: Bureau of Jewish Education.

Tyack, D., & Cuban, L. (1995). *Tinkering toward Utopia: A century of public school reform.* Cambridge, MA: Harvard University Press.

Weissman, C., & Margolius, M. (2002, Summer). A systems approach to school and synagogue change. *Agenda: Jewish Education* (15), 41–44.

Wertheimer, J. (1999). Jewish education in the United States: Recent trends and issues. *American Jewish Year Book, 99,* 3–115.

Wertheimer, J. (2008). *A census of Jewish supplementary schools in the United States.* New York: Avichai Foundation, Available online a at www.avichai.org.

Wertheimer, J. (Ed.) (2009). *Learning and community: Jewish supplementary schools in the 21st century.* Boston: University Press of New England.

Westerhoff, J. (1976). *Will our children have faith?* New York: Seabury Press.

Day Schools in the Liberal Sector: Challenges and Opportunities at the Intersection of Two Traditions of Jewish Schooling

Alex Pomson

The contemporary Diaspora liberal Jewish day school (a religiously non-orthodox or non-denominational all-day school that provides both Jewish and general education) has its origins in two distinct traditions: one integrationist, one survivalist. The first tradition, with its origins in the lofty goals of not-yet-emancipated eighteenth-century German Jewry, saw the Jewish school as a bridge to participation in civic and national life (Eliav, 1960). The second tradition, forged in the early part of the twentieth century by a generation of Jewish immigrants to the United States fearful for the survival of Judaism, saw the day school as a fortress to prevent Judaism being overwhelmed by contemporary society (Schiff, 1966).[1]

Over the last 200 years the fortunes of these traditions have waxed and waned. As Jews achieved emancipation and gained relatively equal access to public education, the first, integrationist, tradition lost much of its raison d'être. The all-day Jewish school seemed not only an anomaly, but an unpatriotic impediment to upward social mobility (Syme, 1983). However, with an almost global movement "to expand and equalize educational opportunities for all classes of citizens [having] brought about a perceived deterioration in the standards and quality of public education" all over the world (Himelfarb, 1989), Jews, over the last quarter of a century, have once more begun to conceive of private all-day Jewish day schools as a preferred route to social and educational success much as the *Haskallah* [Jewish Enlightenment] pioneers once did.

The survivalist tradition, a direct descendent of the traditional *Heder* with its curriculum of intensive Jewish study, appealed, at the start of the twentieth century,

---

A. Pomson (✉)
Hebrew University, Jerusalem, Israel
e-mail: apomson@mscc.huji.ac.il

[1] A third Hebraist/Socialist tradition flourished during the middle years of the twentieth century, first in Central Europe and then, after the Shoah, in survivor outposts in Latin America, Canada, and Australia (Frost, 1998). Conceived as "the instrument of an ideology rather than an instrument for the education of children in terms appropriate to them" (Adar & Chazan, 1977), the schools inspired by this "revolutionary" tradition survive only in Israel, or in the Diaspora, in an almost unrecognizable form.

only to a small and often impoverished minority in Europe and North America. Yet, over the last half century, as orthodox Jewry has experienced a demographic and ideological revival, and as non-orthodox Jews have exhibited increased concern about whether their "grandchildren will be Jewish," many parents and policy makers have come to see the Jewish day school with its core curriculum of Jewish study and experience as the most effective means for guaranteeing the survival of Jews and Judaism in open societies.

Below I sketch the particular features of these two day school traditions since, as I suggest, outside Haredi (ultra-orthodox) communities, they no longer exist as alternatives, but are increasingly seen as complementary if not always compatible models for Jewish schooling. I argue that the challenges in reconciling these traditions account for some of the most intense contemporary debates surrounding liberal day school education, in relation to educational goals, curriculum content, marketing, and recruitment. I survey these debates as well as other central trends in liberal day school education. Finally, I review the questions and concerns that have been of most interest to researchers of day schools in general (and of liberal day schools in particular), and finish by proposing a research agenda for the next decades of day school research. Throughout, I use the label "liberal" to refer to a range of schools that Schick (2005) identified in his census of North American Jewish day schools as Conservative, Reform, or Community. Although it may be more precise to define these schools as non-orthodox and/or non-denominational, it is clumsy to describe them in terms of what they are not (that is, as neither orthodox nor denominational); it would also be misleading to convey a sense of them as lesser or non-normative.

Origins

The first modern all-day Jewish schools were opened under the influence of Jewish Enlightenment thinkers in the late eighteenth century, in Berlin and then in other German cities (Katz, 1978, pp. 126–7). These schools differed from previously existing institutions for the provision of Jewish education by delivering a curriculum that included both Jewish and secular studies, not just study of traditional Jewish texts, and by their being open to all Jewish children, not just the offspring of the wealthy or the learned. The intent of such schools was, in the words of Naphtali Herz Wessely, one of their earliest ideologues, to ensure that "the Children of Israel will also be men who accomplish worthy things, assisting the king's country in their actions, labor and wisdom" (Wessely, 1995). In the case of the Berlin school, in fact, non-Jewish students were also admitted since it was assumed that social and academic contact between Jewish and non-Jewish children would facilitate integration and cooperation between them as adults (Eliav, 1960, pp. 76–77).

As I have argued elsewhere (Pomson, 2009), the most fully realized institutional expression of this educational vision was seen at the end of the nineteenth century in England, where by 1899, the Jews Free School (JFS), with more than 4,000 students, had become the largest school in Europe. According to one historian of the school, the JFS was conceived by its founders so as "to refashion the young by taking them off the streets and putting them in a modern Jewish school where they would learn artisan skills and English manners" (Black, 1998, p. 33). The student body was almost entirely made up of the children of poor immigrants, and the school was widely admired for gathering "within its walls...the children of those who are driven here by persecution, making of them good and desirable citizens of our beloved England" (Quoted by Black (1998) from an article in *The Sphere* subtitled, "Where Russian Jews are made in to good British subjects"). In the words of Louis Abrahams, headmaster at the start of the twentieth century, the school sought to "wipe away all evidences of foreign birth and foreign proclivities, so that children shall be so identified with everything that is English in thought and deed, that no shadow of anti-Semitism might exist,...[and] they may take a worthy part in the growth of this great Empire" (Black, 1988). This outcome – known by admirers and critics as "Anglicization" – was forged, it was claimed, on a bedrock of Jewish religious values, but it is notable that although the school was conceived as a religiously orthodox institution, rarely was more than one hour a day devoted to instruction in Jewish values and associated Jewish texts. The remaining five or six hours of daily instruction were devoted to a broad curriculum of general studies as well as to preparation for various artisan trades.

The rhetoric of the Berlin *Maskilim* and the JFS patriots may be alien today, but in functional terms their view of what the Jewish day school promises is not so different from what is proposed by those who currently promote day school education. The Day School Advocacy Forum, a community-based network in Boston, advises, for example, that "day school marketing and advocacy should focus on the quality of math, science and English" (Lieberman Research Worldwide, 2004). Adopting a more scholarly stance, researchers commissioned to explore the question, "what difference does day school make?" found that "day schools provide top-notch preparation for a broad range of colleges and universities, including those that are the most selective" (Chertok et al., 2007). In both these cases, the day school's appeal to liberal Jews is assumed to be contingent on its capacity to serve (and to be seen to serve) as a portal to academic and material success in the wider society.

This view of the day school's purpose is quite different from that inscribed in, what I called above, the survivalist tradition. When all-day Jewish schools were established in the United States in the years between World War I and World War II, following a short-lived experiment in day school education by Reform Jewish educators in the nineteenth century, they were animated by a different impulse (Zeldin, 1988). While Jewish immigrants widely regarded the nation's public schools as gateways to the opportunities promised by America, Jewish day schools were regarded by their founders as "fortresses" or "bulwarks" to protect Judaism from being overwhelmed in America. While public schools were, in the words of one Cincinnati leader, "temples of liberty [where] children of the high and low, rich and poor, Protestants, Catholics and Jews mingle together, play together and are taught that we are a free people" (Gartner quoted by Sarna, 1998), day schools were seen as training grounds for the future leadership of the Jewish community; its priesthood, as Dushkin (1948) put it. In the words of one prominent school leader writing at mid-century, these schools, with a curriculum that devoted at least the first half of every day to the study of traditional Jewish texts, provided "the safest assurance for the continuation of Jewish life and the survival of Jewish culture" (Lookstein, 1945).

In their early years, this conception drew a chorus of disapproval, most famously from the proponents of "Americanization," in what Dr Samson Benderley coined the "double school system," "a system of Hebrew schools which our children can attend *after* their daily attendance in public schools" ((Sarna, 1998, pp. 16–17) emphasis in original). From the perspective of those who criticized the day school, its undoubted promise of "Jewish group survival" came at too high a price, what one opponent called, "the price of segregation." The schools' establishment pointed towards "narrow intellectual and social horizons, to a sect-divided society, and to an isolated Jewish group" (Grossman, 1945). And yet, in recent years as rates of intermarriage have soared and as levels of Jewish literacy have plummeted, segregated schooling has no longer seemed too high a price to pay for nurturing a Jewish renaissance among liberal Jews (Shrage, 2007), or at least for improving the odds that young Jews will choose to raise their own children as Jews (JESNA, 1999).

The confluence of these two traditions (the days school's promise of both superior academic outcomes *and* of lasting Jewish engagement), along with other social forces such as, what one might call, Jewish *embourgoisement* (the inclination and capacity of middle-class Jews to pay private school fees), and the confluence of multiculturalism and "school choice" politics (each of which legitimate the withdrawal of minorities from an often deteriorating public education system) have fueled both demand for and supply of day school education, in North America especially, but also in other countries such as England and France (Cohen, 2007; Pomson, 2004). By 2007, a majority of all Jewish children in Britain, aged 4–18, attended Jewish day schools, up from 20% in 1975; in the United States more than a quarter of Jewish children attended day schools compared to 10% in 1975; and in France close to 40% attended day schools compared to 16% in 1986 (JPPPI, 2007; Schick, 2005). While much of day school growth over the last 50 years – in Europe as well as North America – can be attributed to natural population growth among ultra-orthodox Jews (still, the great majority of those enrolled in the schools), the increased numbers of liberal day schools and the enrollment of an unprecedented number of students in such schools has been remarkable. The first non-orthodox day school in North America opened in 1951, some 50 years after the first orthodox day school. Today, there are approximately 165 day schools either affiliated with non-orthodox denominations or organized as pluralistic or non-denominational institutions, with their enrollment estimated to be just under one-fifth of the total day school population (Schick, 2009). Growth on this scale has attracted popular comment and scholarly inquiry (Beinart, 1999; Miller, 2001; Murphy, 2001; Prager, 2000; Wertheimer, 1999). It has also led to speculation, especially since the acute financial downturn of 2008, as to whether such rates of growth can be sustained in changed economic circumstances (Rosenblatt, 2009; Sarna, 2009; Schick, 2003).

Issues

If the Jewish day school's appeal to liberal Jews has been fueled by the confluence of integrationist and survivalist traditions, this confluence also accounts for some of the most intense debates that surround schools. Scholars and practitioners debate whether such historically distinct goals can be fully compatible, or whether, as one influential educational magazine put it, parents will inevitably find schools to be either "too Jewish or not Jewish enough" (Davis, 2007). Theorists for liberal day school education have argued otherwise. Walter Ackerman, a day school headteacher at an early stage of his career, writing three years before the Conservative Solomon Schechter Day School Association was founded, made an argument that has been repeated down the years: "The public school is concerned with the child as an American; the afternoon religious school is concerned with him as a Jew; the Conservative day school is concerned with the child who is heir to two traditions, and addresses itself to the synthesis of this dual heritage within the embracive framework of Torah" (Ackerman, 1961, p. 47). A generation later, following the creation of the first Reform day schools in 1970, Michael Zeldin, the most prolific theorist of Reform day school education, again contended that liberal schools were fully able to serve multiple goals. "They provide a holistic environment for transmitting Jewish culture, embody a commitment to the core values of Reform Judaism, meet the demands of today's social realities by providing excellence in secular education with an emphasis on ethnic identity, and concretize the mandate to invite Jews to participate in Jewish life" (Zeldin, 1992, p. 75). While, latterly, the philosophical tensions or "dissonance" between the different purposes served by liberal schools have been more fully explored, in relation to Reform schools by Zeldin himself (1998) and by Ellenson (2008), and in relation to community (non-denominational or pluralistic schools) by Grumet (2003), the overwhelming impression created by the theoretical literature on liberal day school education is that these schools do indeed promise their students the best of all worlds: a relatively strong general education, and an immersion in core Jewish literacies and behaviors.

Empirical research reveals, however, that the combination of integrationist and survivalist conceptions within a single school has been less seamless than the pioneers of liberal day schooling might have hoped. Ingall (1998), studying the same Reform school over a number of years, found its leadership wrestling between nurturing progressive Jewish values among students and satisfying parental pressure for more academics and more competition. Hyman (2008), conducting intensive doctoral research in a Reform Jewish high school, found a confused set of educational purposes reflected in a disconnect between what she called the intellectually vigorous "jungle gym" atmosphere in general studies classes and the fearful or apologetic "china shop" sensibilities in Judaic studies. Marom (2003), in a case study of vision-driven leadership in a non-denominational community day school, revealed how without deliberative leadership, the community day school with its multiple purposes can easily become "a cacophony of voices, a melee of pedagogical stimuli, and a marketplace for the transmission of skills" (p. 329).

Perhaps the richest vein within which the competing/multiple purposes of the liberal day school have been explored is in relation to its curriculum, that is, in how its purposes are, and might be, translated into a program of learning planned and guided by the school. As seen above, the theorists of day school education had hoped that liberal schools would provide students with a holistic experience, and with equal access to a dual heritage. Over the years, a number of theoretical models and examples have been developed for how this might be done. Lukinsky, a pioneer in this respect, proposed a set of concepts for the integration of curriculum across Jewish and general studies (Brown & Lukinsky, 1979), as well as within the disciplines of Jewish studies (Lukinsky, 1978). Holtz (1980) mined his experience teaching both Talmud and English Literature in a liberal day school to propose the "thematic integration" of subject matter that "draws on the best thinking of both Jewish and non-Jewish minds." Solomon, as the principal of a liberal day school committed to "creating integrative experiences" for his students, provided a case study drawn from his own experience (1989), and also a more theoretically grounded map of what integration promised (1984).

Despite the best intentions of curriculum designers, the organization of schools, the preparation of teachers, the disposition of students, and what Tyak and Tobin (1994) call, the "grammar of schooling" have all militated against such outcomes. As Ingall and Malkus (2001) show, the terrain that connects Jewish learning with the rest of the curriculum is a "border-land" that requires careful negotiation between powerful interest groups, who tend to pull in different directions. As a result, there is often a disconnect between practices in the Jewish and general studies classroom, or what Bekerman and Kopelowitz (2008), in a study of the teaching of Jewish texts in liberal schools, call a secular/religious dichotomy. In her research on moral education in a range of school settings, Simon was surprised to find that in a liberal day school with a school mission statement that highlights "the idea of the integration of 'secular knowledge' and 'Jewish ideals'," "serious discussion of moral and spiritual matters are primarily relegated to religion classes" (Simon, 1998, p. 42). Tanchel (2008) and Hyman (2008) show that even in liberal day schools, Judaic studies teachers often seem reticent to challenge students to engage in the kind of critical thinking that is the hallmark of the general studies curriculum, although Tanchel shows how this might be done by taking up her own experiences teaching Biblical criticism in a community day school. It seems, as Zeldin (1998) indicated in an influential programmatic piece, that successful "integration and interaction in Jewish day schools" calls (challengingly) for schools to pay attention to all four of what Bolman and Deal (2003), in their influential sociology of organizational change, identify as the frames of school (actually, all organizational) life: human resources (concerned with the needs of individuals in an organization), structure (concerned with organizational efficiency), politics (where members of an organization compete for power), and symbol (where members find meaning and inspiration).

One last realm where the tensions created by the confluence of integrationist and survivalist conceptions have been evident is in relation to the marketing of schools. During the early decades of the liberal day school, it was widely assumed that many if not most parents were attracted to non-orthodox schools *in spite of* their Jewish curriculum, seeing them as superior alternatives to a decaying public system. These assumptions were confirmed by research conducted by Kapel (1972) and Kelman (1979) and they continue to be highlighted by advocates for Jewish day schools who strongly emphasize the capacity of schools to serve as outstanding providers of general education. More recent research suggests a more complex picture: of parents wrestling with commitments both to public education and to Jewish engagement (Shapiro, 1996), of "students and parents navigating among [multiple] worlds" (Goldberg, 1999), of liberal parents looking for and finding meaning for themselves in their children's Jewish school (Pomson & Schnoor, 2008), or of the day school satisfying deep values that liberal parents discover they want for their children (Prell, 2007). What more recent research shares with earlier studies of the liberal day school is recognition that a majority of those parents whose children attend liberal day schools today did not attend such schools themselves. This not only makes the marketing of schools more challenging, it also places a strain on schools to generate a shared and reasonable set of expectations among those they serve.

Trends

As the mission of the liberal day school has evolved to include both an integrationist and a survivalist agenda, and as its clientele has changed, so schools have been asked to assume an accumulating burden of social tasks. Jewish children were once expected to acquire knowledge of Judaism, develop attitudes about the Jewish world, and learn Jewish behaviors from people and places in their immediate surroundings – in the family, at the synagogue, even on the street (Dash Moore, 1987; Kanarfogel, 1992; Marcus, 1996). Today, responsibility for the emotional, moral, and interpersonal development of Jewish children has been increasingly devolved to schools (Himelfarb, 1989). In many ways, the challenges posed by these changes are similar to those that face public school educators who have also been called upon by governments to take up roles once performed by families, religious institutions, and workplaces. In recent times, schools have been asked, among other things, to instruct children in how to drink sensibly, eat healthily, vote conscientiously, and have sex responsibly (see Crowson, 2001; Driscoll & Kerchner, 1999; Dryfoos, 1994).

For Jewish day schools, one of the most surprising ramifications of these developments is that schools have become some of the major providers of informal Jewish education, a field once considered the preserve of youth movements and summer camps. Faculty trained to teach academic subjects in classroom settings are now asked to provide Jewish experiences such as religious holyday celebrations, residential Shabbat retreats, and trips to Israel that were once the responsibility of synagogues, families, or youth groups. These changes are challenging schools as is seen in professional journals for Jewish teachers that discuss, for example, how to nurture spirituality in day schools (*Jewish Educational Leadership* 5:2 (2007)); how to make the most of "educational travel and student exchange" (*HaYediyon* (Passover 2006)); and how to respond to the demands of "The evolving day school" (*Jewish Education News, 24*: 2 (Spring 2003)).

Inevitably, perhaps, research literature has only slowly emerged to capture and examine aspects of these changing roles. Kress and Reimer (2009) have studied how students experience *Shabbatonim*, school-organized Shabbat residential retreats. Aviv (1999) looked at the messages conveyed to the students who participate in school Israel trips, and Pomson and Deitcher (2009) researched the experiences that schools provide outside the classroom to connect their students with Israel. One expects that more research will follow as schools cultivate these newly acquired responsibilities. For the moment, the professional literature on day schools suggests that liberal schools in particular may have undergone a shift from a paradigm of instruction (concerned with helping children acquire knowledge of the ideas and skills that society values) to one of enculturation (the more broadly conceived task of initiating children into a culture to which they may not already be committed). This is much like the shift called for a generation ago in Jewish supplementary schools by Aron (1989) and others.

Another concern to emerge from the evolving profile and purposes of schools relates to their capacity to serve an increasingly diverse student body. For most of the twentieth century, day school families were, typically, synagogue members, residents of Jewish neighborhoods, and had been recipients of a relatively intensive Jewish education themselves (Ackerman, 1989). With few exceptions, day school parents were Jewish by birth, orthodox in denominational orientation, and married to other Jews. Paying for all-day Jewish schooling constituted therefore the most complete expression of an intensely engaged Jewish identity. Today, in many countries, Jewish day schools have successfully recruited increasing numbers of families with diverse religious commitments. Many of the families being drawn to Jewish elementary schools lack an intensive Jewish education of their own and, as seen above, depend on schools to teach their families Jewish practices and ideas that extended Jewish families had previously been able to provide from their own social and cultural resources (Pomson & Schnoor, 2008). At the high-school level this phenomenon takes on an even more challenging aspect, with liberal high schools in recent years enrolling a significant minority of students who had not previously received an intensive Jewish elementary school education. Schools must figure out how to meet the needs of an increasingly diverse group of students sitting in their classrooms (Kashti, 2007).

Most of the literature to focus on this issue relates not to the question of pedagogic differentiation (how to teach a single class of students whose knowledge base is very different from one another) but, rather, is concerned with matters of religious pluralism, that is, how classrooms and schools can enable students with diverse religious commitments to feel comfortable and secure. Kramer (2003), for example, has outlined what special tasks are called for from those teaching in these circumstances. Conyer (2009), too, clarifies what in conceptual and educational terms a commitment to pluralism demands of a liberal Jewish school. Baker (2008), writing as the head of what he calls "an intentionally pluralist" high school, details the "core pillars of Jewish identity…the broadly defined norms of practice and belief" with which such a school expects students to engage. Lastly, Wasserfall and Shevitz, as part of a longitudinal research project, have explored the language that the teachers and administrators in a pluralistic high school use to talk about pluralism (2006), and how students come to understand what pluralism and Jewish community mean (Shevitz & Wasserfall, 2009).

There is one more concern that has increasingly surfaced with the evolution of the liberal day school's profile and mission – one that relates to the financing and cost of day school education. Of course, the heavy burden of day school finance has never been limited to schools of one denomination or another. But as day schools have started to appeal to a greater diversity of Jewish families, speculation has increased about the extent to which the high cost of private day school education (rather than issues of principle) has been a deterrent to the wider enrollment of liberal Jews. At the same time, it is commonly assumed that while highly affiliated and highly orthodox Jews are less sensitive to increases in the cost of day school education because of their a priori commitment to parochial Jewish schools, moderately affiliated families will be much more likely to withdraw from schools if their fees continue to rise.

There have been very few studies to examine or test these assumptions. The exceptions include a study by Cohen (1999) of the school-choice preferences of conservative Jews in relation to income. He found that cost sensitivity was "a key obstacle to expanding day school enrollments among those who are already sympathetic to day schools." In similar fashion, by running a theoretical econometric model derived from what was known about the families in Toronto already enrolled in day schools, Abba (2002) also predicted that a relatively limited reduction in school fees would result in significantly increased enrollments. Some communities and national foundations have run local experiments to test the sensitivity of families to changes in day school costs, but these exercises have not generally resulted in published research or publicly available reports (see Continental Council for Jewish Education (2003) for a summary of such experiments). Mainly, then, the literature that debates these issues tends to be cautionary, speculative or, in the worst cases, alarmist (Baker, 2006; Lauer, 2001; Prager, 2005; Schick, 2003; Wertheimer, 2001).

Day School Research: The Larger Context

While most of the literature discussed above focuses on issues provoked by or integral to the development of liberal day school education, a great deal of day school research is not limited to schools of one denomination or another, but is concerned with the day school as a genus, distinct from state/public schools (Valins, 2003), from other kinds of parochial or ethnically constituted schools (Feinberg, 2006), and/or from other private schools (Herman, 2006). In a chapter of this length, it is not possible to survey all of the themes that have emerged in this research; some have recently been surveyed by Elkin and Hausman (2008) and by Pomson (2009). In the space that remains here, I argue that despite its recent proliferation, empirical research concerned with Jewish day school education tends to remain focused around two primary themes, and as a consequence I suggest where the most significant lacunae continue to exist in this field.

Empirical research into all-day Jewish schooling has tended to be concerned with inputs and outputs; it is interested primarily in those who teach in or lead schools, and in those who graduate from them.[2] As a consequence, this has produced an ever-thickening appreciation of the motivations, dispositions, beliefs, experiences, and satisfactions of those who teach and work in day schools in general and also in liberal schools. A number of doctoral studies have focused, for example, on the identities and characteristics of teachers and principals in liberal schools (Dorph, 1993; Kramer, 2000; Markose, 1998; Reiss Medwed, 2005). While Ingall's (2006) study of the short-lived careers of three idealistic and well-qualified day school teachers remains the only book-length study in this field, there is an accumulating body of peer-reviewed work that thickens our understanding of those who choose to become day school teachers (Backenroth, 2004; Pomson, 2005; Shkedi, 1993). Finally, although sometimes harder to access, in recent years there have been a number of important commissioned reports concerning day school educators that compare them with other personnel working in other sectors of Jewish education (Ben-Avie & Kress, 2007; Gamoran, Goldring, Robinson, Tamivaara, & Goodman, 1998; Schaap & Goodman, 2006).

Research on the outputs of day school education has been no less prolific, constituting a kind post-mortem obsession with the lasting effects of day school education on the Jewish identities and behaviors of graduates. Although, one might have expected that, to have validity, studies of this kind would need to be of a scale that goes beyond the efforts of individual doctoral candidates, a number of doctoral dissertations have examined different outcomes of day school education (see, for example, Charytan, 1996, and Shapiro, 1988). More commonly, these matters have been explored as part of larger projects that seek to compare the impact of day schools with other vehicles for Jewish education (for example, Fishman & Goldtsein, 1993; Chertok et al., 2007; Cohen & Kotler-Berkowitz, 2004). There have also been a small number of case studies focused on the impact of individual schools on their alumni (Dickson, 2004; Jacobs, 2003). The combined "message" of these studies is that day schools do have a superior impact on measures of Jewish identification when compared with other forms of Jewish education. But, then, as Chertok et al. (2007) caution, because of the relatively recent development of liberal day school education, there is currently a lack of data systematically gathered on the long-term impact of this educational option.

---

[2]Of course, there has also been no lack of theoretical work on day schools. This has concentrated around the questions of, first, what are the distinctive goals and outcomes of day school education and how might these be extended or transformed; and second, what is the place of the different disciplines of Jewish studies in the day school curriculum, and what are the relationships of these disciplines to one another and to the general studies curriculum. I do not discuss them here, since this work is well reviewed by Malkus elsewhere in this volume.

A Day School Research Agenda

Research on the liberal day school continues to proliferate. This intellectual activity reflects the fact that the emergence of the liberal day school – and its integration of what I have called survivalist and integrationist conceptions of Jewish schooling – represents nothing less than a reassessment of what it means to be Jewish in the world (Sarna, 1998). Nevertheless, there are two significant lacunae in the field's research literature whose redress would serve its further development. First, while it is generally agreed, as the last section showed, that all-day Jewish schooling has a positive effect on measures of Jewish identification that no other educational vehicle can match, little is known about why Jewish day schools produce the effects they do. We don't know, for example, to what extent these positive effects are a consequence of what children learn and experience in school, or are a banal outcome of the fact that Jewish children spend so much time together in these settings. The Jewish school remains a black box, what happens inside hidden from view. A first task in the development of day school research is analogous to the cognitive revolution in the study of teaching that moved from the investigation of the inputs and outputs of teaching to an examination of what goes on inside the teacher's head. We need to know what goes on inside schools.

Of course, literature of this kind exists in abundance in the field of general education, where it is as likely to be produced by sociologists, ethnographers, and historians as by practitioners writing in an autobiographical or confessional vein. There is no shortage of evocative accounts of life in schools and classrooms that in turn both shape and are shaped by theories of schooling. Such literature is rare, however, when it comes to Jewish day schools (The careful studies of classroom life in day schools by Lehmann (2007), Krakwoski (2008), and Hyman (2008) are, however, recent promising exceptions that demonstrate how nuanced doctoral work can contribute to the field).

A second task for research is that of developing a crosscultural mode of inquiry. The Jewish day school has emerged as a popular and frequently normative option for the education of Jewish children in almost every community where there are at least 1,000 Jewish households. The day school is an international phenomenon, and there have been studies in a wide variety of international settings (such as the Czech Republic (Foltynova, 2007); Denmark (Anderson, 2008); and Argentina (Goldstein, 2009)). There are sharp differences between the ways schools are funded, governed, and educationally organized in different countries, yet there has never been an attempt to compare the commonalities and differences between schools in a systematic and theoretically grounded fashion. In the same way that studying the insides of schools would open up something of a black box, so studying the outsides of schools – their contexts – in relation to their particular cultural settings would clear a good deal of the mystery that surrounds them.

The emergence of the liberal day school has been one of the most unexpected developments of Jewish social life since World War II; it may prove one of the most significant. Few sectors of Diaspora Jewish education provide so many opportunities for research. As the bibliography below demonstrates, a great deal has been written about this phenomenon over the last 50 years. Looking out on this field while it wrestles with challenges posed by the post-2008 "great recession," one suspects that there are still many twists and turns to come whose story is yet to be told.

References

Abba, S. (2002). *Forecasting the demand for enrolment in Toronto Jewish day schools*. Toronto, ON, UJA Federation of Great Toronto: Board of Jewish Education.
Ackerman, W. (1961). The day school in the Conservative movement. *Conservative Judaism, 15*(2), 46–57.
Ackerman, W. (1989). Strangers to tradition: Idea and constraint in American Jewish education. In H. S. Himelfarb & S. DellaPergola (Eds.), *Jewish education worldwide: Cross-cultural perspectives*. Lanham, MS: University Press of America.
Adar, Z., & Chazan, B. I. (1977). *Jewish education in Israel and in the United States*. Jerusalem: Samuel Mendel Melton Center for Jewish Education in the Diaspora.
Anderson, S. (2008). The competition, the rabbi, and the prize: Anger, guilt, and inclusion in a pluralistic Jewish day school. Paper presented at the American Anthropological Association, November 11, 2008.
Aron, I. (1989). The malaise of Jewish education. *Tikkun, 4*, 32–34.
Aviv, D. (1999). *Aliyah for two weeks: Moderate affiliation and the Israel experience in an American community day school*. Jerusalem: Melton Centre for Jewish Education.
Backenroth, O. A. (2004). Art and Rashi: A portrait of a Bible teacher. *Religious Education, 99*(2), 151–166.
Baker, J. (2006). The falling crown? The future of Jewish day schools in Australia. In M. Fagenblat, M. Landau, & N. Wolski (Eds.), *New under the sun: Jewish Australians on religion, politics and culture* (pp. 346–356). Melbourne: Black Inc.
Baker, M. (2008). Jewish identities in process: Religious purposefulness in a pluralistic day school. *HaYidion*, Autumn, 20–21, 30–31.
Beinart, P. (1999). The rise of the Jewish school. *Atlantic Monthly, 284*, 21–23.
Bekerman, Z., & Kopelowitz, E. (2008). The unintended consequences of liberal Jewish schooling: A comparative study of the teaching of Jewish texts for the purpose of cultural sustainability. In Z. Bekerman & E. Kopelowitz (Eds.), *Cultural education-cultural sustainability* (pp. 323–342). New York: Routledge.
Ben-Avie, M., & Kress, J. S. (2007). A North American study of educators in Jewish day and congregational schools. Technical report of the Educators in Jewish Schools Study (EJSS). Jewish Educational Change.
Black, E. C. (1988). *The social politics of Anglo-Jewry, 1880–1920*. Oxford: Blackwell.
Black, G. (1998). *JFS: The history of the Jews' Free School, London, since 1732*. Trowbridge: Redwood Books.
Bolman, L. G., & Deal, T. E. (2003). *Reframing organizations: Artistry, choice and leadership*. San Francisco: Jossey-Bass.
Brown, S. I., & Lukinsky, J. S. (1979). Integration of religious studies and mathematics in the day school. *Jewish Education, 47*(3), 28–35.
Charytan, M. (1996) The impact of religious day school education: A study of changes in seven modern Orthodox day schools and the impact on religious transmission to students and their families. Graduate Faculty of Sociology. City University of New York. Doctor of Philosophy.
Chertok, F., Saxe, L., Kadushin, C., Wright, G., Klein, A., & Koren, A. (2007). *What difference does day school make?* Boston: Maurice and Marilyn Cohen Center for Modern Jewish Studies, Brandeis University.
Cohen, S. M. (1999). Money matters: Incentives and obstacles to Jewish day school enrollment in the United States. In Y. Rich & M. Rosenak (Eds.), *Abiding challenges: Research perspectives on Jewish education* (pp. 251–274). London: Freund Publishing House.

Cohen, E. H. (2007). *Heureux comme Juifs en France? Etude sociologique.* Jerusalem-Paris: Akadem.
Cohen, S. M., & Kotler-Berkowitz, L. (2004). The impact of childhood Jewish education on adults' Jewish identity: Schooling, Israel travel, camping and youth groups. United Jewish Communities Report Series on the National Jewish Population Survey 2000–2001. New York: United Jewish Communities.
Continental Council for Jewish Education. (2003). *Day school tuition subvention, reduction and scholarship programs.* New York: Jewish Educational Services of North America.
Conyer, B. (2009). Pluralism and its purposeful introduction to a Jewish day school. *Religious Education, 104*(5), 463–478.
Crowson, R. L. (2001). Community development and school reform: An overview. In R. L. Crowson (Ed.), *Community development and school reform* (pp. 1–18). Oxford: Elsevier Science.
Dash Moore, D. (1987). The construction of community: Jewish migration and ethnicity in the United States. In M. Rischin (Ed.), *The Jews of North America* (pp. 105–117). Detroit, MI: Wayne State University Press.
Davis, B. (2007). Balancing "too Jewish" with "not Jewish enough". *HeYidiyon, Summer, 6*.
Dickson, S. (2004). Kadimah: The pursuit of scholastic excellence and religious commitment. *Journal of Jewish Education, 69*(3), 15–47.
Dorph, G. Z. (1993). *Conceptions and preconceptions: A study of prospective Jewish educators' knowledge and beliefs about Torah.* New York: Jewish Theological Seminary of America. Doctor of Philosophy.
Driscoll, M. E., & Kerchner, C. (1999). The implications of social capital for schools, communities and cities: Educational administration as if a sense of place mattered. In J. Murphy & K. Louis (Eds.), *Handbook of research on educational administration* (pp. 385–404). San Francisco: Jossey-Bass.
Dryfoos, J. (1994). *Full-service schools: A revolution in health and social services for children, youth and families.* San Francisco: Jossey-Bass.
Dushkin, A. (1948). Jewish education in New York city, 1918. *Jewish Education, 20*(1), 15.
Eliav, M. (1960). Ha'hinukh ha-yehudi be-Germanyah. Jerusalem: Jewish Agency for Israel.
Elkin, J., & Hausman, B. (2008). The Jewish day school. In R. L. Goodman, P. A. Flexner, & L. D. Bloomberg (Eds.), *What we now know about Jewish education: Perspectives on research for practice* (pp. 397–406). Los Angeles: Torah Aura Productions.
Ellenson, D. (2008). An ideology for the liberal Jewish school: A philosophical-sociological investigation. *Journal of Jewish Education, 74*(3), 245–263.
Feinberg, W. (2006). *For goodness sake: Religious schools and education for democratic citizenry.* New York: Routledge.
Fishman, S. B., & Goldstein, A. (1993). *When they are grown up they will not depart.* Waltham, MA: Cohen Center for Modern Jewish Studies, Brandeis University.
Foltynova, T. (2007) Jewish education in the Czech Republic: A case study of the Lauder schools in Prague. Rappaport Center for Assimilation Research and Strengthening Jewish Vitality, Bar Ilan University.
Frost, S. (1998). *Schooling as a socio-political expression.* Jerusalem: Magnes.
Gamoran, A., Goldring, E. B., Robinson, B., Tamivaara, J., & Goodman, R. L. (1998). *The teachers' report: A portrait of teachers in Jewish schools.* New York: Council for Initiatives in Jewish Education.
Goldberg, H. E. (1999). A tradition of invention: Family and educational institutions among contemporary traditionalizing Jews. In S. M. Cohen & G. Horencyzk (Eds.), *National variations in Jewish identity: Implications for Jewish identity* (pp. 85–106). Albany, NY: State University of New York Press.

Goldstein, Y. (2009). Community school versus school as community: The case of the Bet El community in Buenos Aires. In A. Pomson & H. Deitcher (Eds.), *Jewish day schools, Jewish communities: A reconsideration* (pp. 172–192). Oxford: Littman Library of Jewish Civilization.

Grossman, M. (1945). Parochial schools for Jewish children – An adverse view. *Jewish Education, 16*(3), 20–25.

Grumet, Z. (2003). *The community school: Proceedings from an online discussion.* Ramat Gan: Lookstein Center for Jewish Education.

Herman, C. (2006). Managerialism, fundamentalism, and the restructuring of faith-based community schools. *Educational Theory, 56*(2), 137–156.

Himelfarb, H. S. (1989). A cross-cultural view of Jewish education. In H. S. Himelfarb & S. DellaPergola (Eds.), *Jewish education worldwide: Cross-cultural perspectives* (pp. 3–41). Lanham, MD: University Press of America.

Holtz, B. (1980). Towards an integrated curriculum for the Jewish school. *Religious Education, 75*(5), 546–557.

Hyman, T. (2008). The liberal Jewish day school as laboratory for dissonance in American-Jewish identity formation. Steinhardt School of Culture, Education, and Human Development. New York, New York University. Doctor of Philosophy.

Ingall, C. K. (1998). The Nachshon School: Portrait of a caring community. *Religious Education, 93*(3), 227–240.

Ingall, C. K. (2006). *Down the up staircase: Tales of teaching in Jewish day schools.* New York: Jewish Theological Seminary of America.

Ingall, C. K., & Malkus, M. (2001). Negotiating the borderlands: Implementing an integrated curricular unit in a Jewish day high school. *Journal of Jewish Education, 67*(1/2), 36–47.

Jacobs, M. R. (2003). The Jewish Academy of Metropolitan Detroit: The experience of the pioneering graduating class. Unpublished report submitted to the Partnership for Excellence in Jewish Education. Retrieved November 22, 2009 from http://peje.org/docs/DetroitHSgraduates.pdf

JESNA. (1999). *Task force on Jewish day school viability and vitality.* New York: Jewish Educational Services for North America.

JPPPI. (2007). *Background policy documents.* Jerusalem: Jewish People's Policy Planning Institute.

Kanarfogel, E. (1992). *Jewish education and society in the high middle ages.* Detroit, MI: Wayne State University Press.

Kapel, D. E. (1972). Parental views of a Jewish day school. *Jewish Education, 41*(3), 23–38.

Kashti, O. (2007). Viva la Pluralism. Haartez, June 25. Retrieved July 26, 2009, from http://www.haaretz.com/hasen/spages/862398.html.

Katz, J. (1978). *Out of the ghetto: The social background of Jewish emancipation, 1770–1870.* New York: Schocken Books.

Kelman, S. L. (1979). Why parents send their children to non-orthodox Jewish day schools. In M. Rosenak (Ed.), *Studies in Jewish education* (Vol. 2, pp. 289–298). Jerusalem: Magnes Press.

Krakowski, M. (2008). *Isolation and integration: Education and worldview formation in ultra-Orthodox Jewish schools.* Evanston, Il: Northwestern University. Doctor of Philosophy.

Kramer, M. N. (2000). *The pathways for preparation: A study of heads of Jewish community day schools affiliated with the Jewish community day school network, 1998–1999.* New York: Columbia University. Doctor of Education.

Kramer, M. N. (2003). Teaching in a Jewish community school. In N. S. Moskowitz (Ed.), *The ultimate Jewish teacher's handbook* (pp. 66–73). New York: Behrman House.

Kress, J. S., & Reimer, J. (2009). Shabbatonim as experiential education in the North American community day high school. In A. Pomson & H. Deitcher (Eds.), *Jewish day schools, Jewish communities: A reconsideration* (pp. 342–361). Oxford: The Littman Library of Jewish Civilization.

Lauer, C. (2001). Thoughts on tuition reduction, fundraising and education. *Agenda: Jewish Education, 14*, 21–23.

Lehmann, D. (2007). *Literacies and discourses in the two worlds of a modern Orthodox Jewish high school*. New York: Columbia University. Doctor of Philosophy.

Lieberman Research Worldwide. (2004). Understanding the needs of Jewish parents in the Greater Boston to more effectively market day schools. Retrieved December 12, 2008, from http://www.peje.org/docs/DAFStudy.pdf.

Lookstein, J. H. (1945). The modern American Yeshivah. *Jewish Education, 16*(3), 12–16.

Lukinsky, J. S. (1978). Integration within Jewish studies. *Jewish Education, 46*(4), 39–41.

Marcus, I. G. (1996). *Rituals of childhood: Jewish acculturation in Medieval Europe*. New Haven, CT: Yale University Press.

Markose, J. O. (1998). *Individualism and community: A study of teachers in a Canadian Jewish day school*, Ontario Institute for Studies in Education. Toronto, ON: University of Toronto. Doctor of Education.

Marom, D. (2003). Before the gates of the school: An experiment in developing educational vision from practice. In S. Fox, I. Scheffler, & D. Marom (Eds.), *Visions of Jewish education* (pp. 296–331). Cambridge: Cambridge University Press.

Miller, H. (2001). Meeting the challenge: The Jewish schooling phenomenon in the UK. *Oxford Review of Education, 27*(4), 501–513.

Murphy, C. (2001). *Longing to deepen identity, more families turn to Jewish day school* (p. B1). Washington Post. Washington, DC.

Pomson, A. (2004). Jewish day school growth in Toronto: Freeing policy and research from the constraints of conventional sociological wisdom. *Canadian Journal of Education, 27*(3), 321–340.

Pomson, A. (2005). Parochial school satisfactions: What research in private Jewish day schools reveals about satisfactions and dissatisfactions in teachers' work. *Educational Research, 47*(2), 163–174.

Pomson, A. (2009). Introduction. In A. Pomson & H. Deitcher (Eds.), *Jewish day schools, Jewish communities: A reconsideration* (pp. 1–28). Oxford: The Littman Library of Jewish Civilization.

Pomson, A., & Deitcher, H. (2009). Much ado about something: Clarifying goals and methods of Israel education. *HaYediyon* (Spring), 32–34.

Pomson, A., & Schnoor, R. F. (2008). *Back to school: Jewish day school in the lives of adult Jews*. Detroit, MI: Wayne State University Press.

Prager, Y. (2000). All things to all people? *Sh'ma, 31*, 6–7.

Prager, Y. (2005). The tuition squeeze: Paying the price of Jewish education. *Jewish Action, 66*, 13–18.

Prell, R. E. (2007). Family formation, educational choices, and American Jewish identity. In J. Wertheimer (Ed.), *Family matters: Jewish education in an age of choice* (pp. 3–33). Waltham, MA: Brandeis University Press.

Reiss Medwed, K. G. (2005). Three women teachers of Talmud and rabbinics in Jewish non-orthodox day high schools: Their stories and experiences. Humanities and Social Sciences in the Professions. New York: New York University. Doctor of Philosophy.

Rosenblatt, G. (2009) Jewish day school model may now be thing of past. The Jewish Week, June 5, Retrieved July 22, 2009, from http://www.thejewishweek.com/viewArticle/c52_a15707/Editorial__Opinion/Gary_Rosenblatt.html.

Sarna, J. (1998). American Jewish education in historical perspective. *Journal of Jewish Education, 61*(1–2), 8–21.

Sarna, J. (2009) Lesson from the past. EJewishPhilanthropy.Com, February 22. Retrieved July 22, 2009, from http://ejewishphilanthropy.com/lessons-from-the-past/

Schaap, E., & Goodman, R. L. (2006). *Recruitment of college students into the field of Jewish education: A study of the CAJE Schusterman college program alumni (1990–2003)*. New York: CAJE.

Schick, M. (2003). *The impact of the economic downturn on Jewish day schools.* New York: AVI CHAI Foundation.

Schick, M. (2005). *A census of Jewish day schools in the United States, 2003–2004.* New York: AVI CHAI Foundation.

Schick, M. (2009). Summary of key findings: A census of Jewish day schools in the United States, 2008–2009. http://www.avi-chai.org/Static/Binaries/Publications/Key_Findings_of_2008_09_Day_School_Census_Final.pdf

Schiff, A. I. (1966). *The Jewish day school in America.* New York: Jewish Education Committee Press.

Shapiro, S. (1996). A parent's dilemma: Public vs. Jewish education. *Tikkun, 17,* 13–16.

Shapiro, Z. (1988). From generation to generation: Does Jewish schooling affect Jewish identification? New York, New York University. Doctor of Philosophy.

Shevitz, S. L., & Wasserfall, R. (2009). Building community in a pluralist high school. In A. Pomson & H. Deitcher (Eds.), *Jewish day schools, Jewish communities: A reconsideration* (pp. 376–395). Oxford: Littman Library of Jewish Civilization.

Shkedi, A. (1993). Teachers' workshops encounters with Jewish moral texts. *Journal of Moral Education, 22*(1), 19–30.

Shrage, B. (2007). Jewish renaissance: A broad vision for the next decade. In S. Berrin (Ed.), *Ten years of believing in Jewish day school education* (pp. 9–14). Boston: Partnership for Excellence in Jewish Education.

Simon, K. G. (1998). Bring it up with the Rabbi: The specialization of moral and spiritual education in a Jewish high school. *Journal of Jewish Education, 64*(1&2), 33–43.

Solomon, B. I. (1984). Curricular integration in the Jewish all-day school in the United States. In M. Rosenak (Ed.), *Studies in Jewish Education* (Vol. 2, pp. 150–174). Jerusalem: Magnes Press.

Solomon, B. I. (1989). Curriculum innovation: What Jewish education must learn from educational research. In J. Aviad (Ed.), *Studies in Jewish Education* (Vol. 4, pp. 63–82). Jerusalem: Magnes Press.

Syme, D. B. (1983). Reform Judaism and day schools: The great historical dilemma. *Religious Education, 78*(2), 153–181.

Tanchel, S. (2008). "A Judaism that does not hide": Teaching the documentary hypothesis in a pluralistic Jewish high school. *Journal of Jewish Education, 74*(1), 29–52.

Tyack, D., & Tobin, W. (1994). The "grammar" of schooling: Why has it been so hard to change? *American Educational Research Journal, 31*(3), 453–479.

Valins, O. (2003). Defending identities or segregating communities? Faith-based schooling and the UK Jewish community. *Geoforum, 34*(2), 235–247.

Wasserfall, R., & Shevitz, S. L. (2006). *The language of pluralism in a Jewish day school.* Waltham, MA: Brandeis University.

Wertheimer, J. (1999). Who's afraid of Jewish day schools? *Commentary, 108,* 49–54.

Wertheimer, J. (2001). *Talking dollars and sense about Jewish education.* New York: AVI CHAI Foundation.

Wessely, N. H. (1995). Words of peace and truth. In P. Mendes-Flohr & J. Reinharz (Eds.), *The Jew in the modern world* (pp. 70–74). New York: Oxford University Press.

Zeldin, M. (1988). The promise of historical inquiry: Nineteenth-century Jewish day schools and twentieth-century policy. *Religious Education, 83*(3), 438–452.

Zeldin, M. (1992). What makes the reform day school distinctive? A question of purpose and practice. In D. J. Margolis, E. S. Schoenberg (Eds.), *Curriculum, community, commitment: Views on the American Jewish day school in memory of Bennett I. Solomon* (pp. 67–77). West Orange, NJ: Behrman House.

Zeldin, M. (1998). Integration and interaction in the Jewish day school. In R. E. Tornberg (Ed.), *The Jewish educational leader's handbook* (pp. 579–590). Denver, CO: A.R.E.

Day Schools in the Orthodox Sector – A Shifting Landscape

Shani Bechhofer

Composition of the Field of Orthodox Schools

Although Orthodox Jews constitute only 7–9% of the total Jewish population in America, roughly 79% of all Jewish day schools are Orthodox and an estimated 99% of Orthodox children attend day schools (Wertheimer, 1999). Reflecting these numbers, it is estimated that soon, a quarter of a million children will be enrolled in Orthodox K-12 schools in North America.[1] Today's field of Orthodox Jewish schools in America (the geographic focus for this chapter) includes approximately 466 elementary schools and 361 high schools spread across Orthodox communities of various sizes in 34 states (Torah Umesorah, 1993, 2002, 2007).[2]

About 45% of Orthodox schools are located in the Orthodox geographical core, namely New York and New Jersey, and in particular Brooklyn, Rockland County NY, Lakewood NJ, and Bergen County NJ. The remaining 55% are almost evenly split between large Orthodox communities (such as Los Angeles, Chicago, Miami, Baltimore, Cleveland, and Detroit) and small Orthodox communities.

Table 1[3] shows the approximate distribution of schools across categories of identification. For purposes of this overview, schools are divided into Hasidic[4], Haredi,

---

S. Bechhofer (✉)
Yeshiva University, New York, NY, USA
e-mail: sbechhof@yu.edu

[1] Conversation with Rabbi Dovid Bernstein of Torah Umesorah.

[2] Any attempt to count schools must grapple with the problem of the diverse organizations and structures characterizing Orthodox schools. Given the market orientation of this chapter and the need to create comparable numbers across categories, each division was counted as a school. Thus if a community had one boys' elementary school, one boys' high school, and one boys' K-12 school, it was counted as two boys' elementary and two boys' high schools. Similarly, a school with separate girls' and boys' divisions in different buildings and with different principals was counted as two schools.

[3] All numbers in this section are based on publicly available documents. Even in these documents, details such as founding dates, identification, and educational structure are not available for each school.

[4] The largest American Hasidic groups are Belz, Bobov, Satmar, Skverr, and Vishnitz.

Table 1 Current identification distribution of schools

Haredi	305 (37%)
Modern Orthodox	194 (23%)
Hasidic	147 (18%)
Lubavitch	108 (13%)
Sephardic	44 (5%)
Specialty	37 (4%)

Table 2 Current distribution of level and gender options

Elementary school options	466	166 boys
		155 co-educational
		145 girls
High school options	361	198 boys
		32 co-educational
		131 girls

Table 3 Current geographic distribution by school identification

	Core Orthodox communities	Large Orthodox communities	Small Orthodox communities
Haredi	145	124	30
Modern Orthodox	27	65	88
Hasidic	130	9	9
Lubavitch	11	25	53
Sephardic	27	15	1
Specialty	32	6	2

Modern Orthodox, Lubavitch[5], Sephardic, and specialty[6] schools.[7] Table 2 shows the approximate distribution of schools across levels and gender. Table 3 shows the approximate geographic distribution of schools across categories of identification. These numbers do not reflect the demographic distribution of *children* in these school categories. For example, Hasidic schools tend to be much larger, on average, than either Haredi or Modern Orthodox schools (Schick, 2005).

---

[5] Information based on list provided by The Merkos Chinuch Office run by Rabbi Nochem Kaplan, Director. See www.chinuchoffice.org.

[6] Such as schools for outreach to new immigrants from the former Soviet Union or to unaffiliated Jews.

[7] Schick (2009) devised six ideological identifications for Orthodox schools; I have chosen to refer to all Religious Zionist schools, whether modern or centrist, as Modern Orthodox to reduce the interpretive nature of these categories. All of these categories aim to capture the most salient dividing lines among Orthodox day schools, but it should be recognized that the boundaries between even these categories are blurry, and that within each category there exist distinct subgroups. Additionally, many schools have shifted in emphasis over the years, which is why these categories are broad.

Table 4 Number of new American Orthodox schools founded

1960s	84
1970s	117
1980s	148
1990s	155
2000s	Numbers not yet available

Table 5 Year of founding by school identification

	Before 1960	1960–1984	1985–present
Haredi	55	85	141
Modern Orthodox	74	61	38
Hasidic	35	66	41
Lubavitch	20	31	38
Sephardic		20	14
Specialty	1	13	25

Aside from outposts in upstate New York, virtually all Hasidic, Sephardic, and Specialty schools are located in core communities. Almost half of Haredi schools are located in core communities, a third are in large communities, and the remaining 15% are in small communities. The opposite is true for Modern Orthodox schools. Half are located in small communities, about a third in the large communities, and only 15% in core communities. Lubavitch schools are even more likely to be found in small communities.

The rate of growth in the number of Orthodox day schools in America has increased over time, as displayed in Table 4.[8] Indeed, these numbers may open questions about the oft-quoted truism that by the 1990s, non-Orthodox day schools were the fastest growing phenomenon in the American Jewish community. The founding rates across school identification are displayed in Table 5.

Not all categories have experienced the same pattern and pacing of growth. For instance, Haredi schools are the largest and institutionally fastest-growing sector of the field with over 300 schools. More than half of today's Haredi schools were founded after 1985. The Modern Orthodox schools are an older group; more than half of today's Modern Orthodox schools were founded before 1965. Hasidic schools have increased at a fairly regular rate. In the next sections of this chapter, larger developments in American Orthodoxy are explored in order to understand the story behind the numbers presented above.

---

[8]This analysis is necessarily limited by its reliance on schools' self-reports of dates of founding to Torah Umesorah; by lack of information from at least 28 schools that were not included in the directories; by missing data on location, gender composition, identification, and dates of founding among some of the schools in the directories; and by the lack of information on schools that closed before 1993.

Ideological Diversity and Competition

Unlike other denominational day schools, Orthodox schools do not have institutional ties to a central movement-affiliated seminary. This is not a new development. Over 60 years ago, Nardi (1944) expressed frustration that, "Despite the growth in the number of Jewish all-day schools, no national or communal organization has succeeded in gaining control of any of the already existing schools. The fact is that very few [schools] of any kind are willing to accept authority from any quarter, either from an educational bureau or even from an Orthodox organization. Each [school] board is intent upon meeting its own problem and upon going its own way without outside advice or direction" (Nardi p. 19).

This reflects a broader reality. As Waxman (2003) notes, "Although ...Orthodoxy is the smallest of the major American Jewish denominations...it is also the most diverse. Orthodoxy has neither a single seminary nor a single rabbinic organization. It is comprised of a variety of philosophies and movements" (p. 409). These philosophies and movements generally have no one institutional home, however, and their identities are often contested or interpreted differently by different groups. The primary strands within American Orthodoxy are typically referred to as Haredi and Modern Orthodox, although these labels are problematic. Using the term Haredi for Americans, for example, obscures the "vast differences" (Waxman, 2003, p. 410) between Haredi institutions and social organization in Israel and America. Additionally, in some popular discourse "Modern Orthodox" is a label distinct from "Centrist Orthodox."

The larger strands are to some extent represented by national umbrella lay organizations. These include Agudath Israel for Haredim, both Hasidic and non-Hasidic, and the Orthodox Union for Modern and Centrist Orthodoxy.[9] But these organizations exercise no formal authority over individuals or institutions, and the people who identify with them are in no way monolithic in viewpoint.

Blurring Boundaries and Nuances of Difference

In fact, some current sociologists of Orthodoxy have presented a compelling case that the Modern Orthodox/Haredi divide, at least in the United States, is no longer as salient in the real world as it may be to sociologists or ideologues, a conclusion that Waxman (2007b) suggests is "perhaps the most significant development in contemporary American Orthodoxy" (p. 169). Ferziger (2007) agrees that the spectrum of Orthodox beliefs and practices is much more nuanced than this bifurcation would imply.

The stereotypical depiction of Haredim as secularly uneducated, economically dependent, isolationist historical revisionists tends to implode under the scrutiny

---

[9]Some would list Chabad-Lubavitch as a third strand, as they are not identified with Agudath Israel or the Orthodox Union and have a separate international organization.

of empirical research. Many American Haredim attend college, work as professionals, and enjoy aspects of American high or popular culture. Gonen (2001), for example, found a high representation of non-Hasidic Haredi men in occupations requiring "highly qualified personnel" (p. 24) and noted the "common practice" of combining *yeshiva* and college study. He attributed this to the flexibility generated by the coexistence of norms of religious study and breadwinning among American Haredi men. American Haredim exercise, listen to popular Jewish music, and read self-help literature, none of which would be considered acceptable among Israeli Haredim (Waxman, 2007b). Despite scholarly and popular interest in deconstructing Artscroll and other Haredi publications to discover historical inaccuracies and inconsistencies, Caplan's (2005) analysis suggests that Modern Orthodox historiographers are actually quite similar to Haredi historiographers in their approach to "the meaning of history and how the past should be studied and evaluated, certainly on the level of popular religion" (p. 361). Israel has great significance to American Haredim. "Contrary to popular mythology, they are overwhelmingly not anti-Zionist and certainly not anti-Israel" (Waxman, p. 148).

Similarly, a monolithic depiction of the Modern Orthodox as acculturative, cosmopolitan, lax in observance of *Halacha* (Jewish law), committed to coeducation, and unwaveringly supportive of the Israeli government, does not do justice to the variety of styles of American Orthodox lived experience outside of Haredi Orthodoxy. Neither does the depiction of a society tilted rightward, its members slipping into the Haredi abyss.

To understand American Orthodox schooling without resorting to stereotypes requires insight into these trends. The blurring of boundaries is clearly evident, for example, when examining the changing norms regarding gender in Modern Orthodox schools. The practice of educating boys and girls together (coeducation) has historically represented a dividing line between Hasidic and Haredi schools on the one hand, and Modern Orthodox schools on the other. Torah Umesorah, the organization dedicated to founding Orthodox day schools since 1944, deemed it acceptable to create coeducational elementary schools in smaller communities due to economic necessity. Coeducational high schools, however, were not considered acceptable, and parents were encouraged by Torah Umesorah to send their children to separate gender high schools in nearby large Orthodox communities. In contrast, coeducational high schools were founded by Modern Orthodox communities. Even today, 60% of coeducational schools are located in small Orthodox communities, with only 27% of single-gender schools located in those small communities. There are far fewer coeducational high schools than elementary schools (see Table 2).

In recent years, however, coeducation has become less valid as a distinctive marker of Modern Orthodoxy. Since 1975, one-third of the new Modern Orthodox schools founded have been gender separated. Numerous coeducational schools[10] have instituted some form of gender separation. Today's Modern Orthodox schools

---

[10]Based on observational and anecdotal evidence; the numbers are not available.

Table 6 Gender and education in American Modern Orthodox schools today

Boys only – 11 schools		Elementary	2
		High school	9
Girls only – 13 schools		Elementary	2
		High school	11
Boys and girls separate –17 schools	Different sections of building, all learning gender separated	Elementary High school	10 7
Fully coeducational – 89 schools		Elementary	77
		High school	12
Modified coeducational – 56 schools	Early grades coeducational, older grades[a] separate gender	Elementary	21
	Early grades separate gender for Judaic studies only; older grades completely separate gender	Elementary	22
	Judaic studies separate gender, general studies coeducational	Elementary High school	1 12

[a] The cut-off points vary among schools.

practice both coeducation and gender separation in various formats and formulas, as depicted in Table 6.

Just as Modern Orthodox schools are shifting in regard to gender separation, Ferziger and Waxman both argue that there is a change in the sectarianism which had characterized Haredi Orthodoxy. While this sector has not become pluralistic, they argue, it has developed new models that involve Haredim in inter-communal activity. Agudath Israel is politically active, engaging in extensive lobbying on a variety of issues on local and national levels. Ferziger (2007) documents the rise of the community *kollel* beginning in 1987,[11] "a new concept in Jewish education and collective activity... [that] emphasizes inclusiveness, communal involvement, and working with a broad range of Jews" (p. 119). He contrasts this move toward "promoting unity among Jews of all orientations" to the Modern Orthodox *kollelim* that have been founded since 1994, which have drafted graduates of Israeli *yeshivot* and Yeshiva University "primarily to buttress Modern Orthodox educational institutions" (p. 122).

Both Ferziger and Waxman claim that the sectarianism of Haredi Orthodoxy and contrasting openness of Modern Orthodoxy do not, in fact, reflect deep ideological

---

[11] A *kollel* is an institution in which men may continue their Talmud study for several years after marriage. Ferziger describes three stages in the development of Haredi *kollelim* in America, which at first existed almost exclusively in the core communities of New York/New Jersey; the second stage beginning in the 1970s with the establishment of somewhat traditional *kollelim* in smaller communities; and the third stage beginning in 1987 with a distinct focus on outreach beyond the Orthodox community.

convictions but are rather a product of each group's self-confidence and sense of security as a force on the American Jewish scene. The Haredi community feels secure, religiously autonomous, and confident that their style of Orthodoxy will survive. In contrast, the Modern Orthodox feel "beleaguered and defensive," and are therefore "much more likely to engage in intellectual discussions among themselves rather than to actively reach out beyond their border" (Waxman, 2007b, p. 149).

Continuity Challenges: Preserving Modern Orthodox Ideology

Concerned observers have argued that American Orthodoxy has become "Haredized" and that Modern Orthodoxy has been "in crisis" and even "under siege" (see for example Heilman, 2006; Helmreich & Shinar, 1998; Sacks, 1984). The organization Edah, with its tagline "the courage to be modern and Orthodox," was formed in 1996 partially out of this concern. In 2000, Rabbi Avi Weiss established Yeshivat Chovevei Torah, a rabbinical school which advocates for a more "open" Orthodox rabbinate than that presumably being fostered at Yeshiva University, historically the intellectual home of Modern Orthodoxy.

Some contemporary researchers, however, have taken issue with this alarmist analysis. Waxman (2007b) claims that most of those who identify as Modern Orthodox have done so "behaviorally rather than philosophically" (p. 139). It is the less rigorous practice of *halachic* minutiae, rather than a religious philosophical stance towards the State of Israel or an ideological commitment to worldly knowledge, that defines Modern Orthodoxy, at least for the laity. Ferziger (2007) argues that even if it is true that the Modern Orthodox have become more stringent in ritual observance, it is because of the significant increase in Jewish learning among both children and adults, rather than the abandonment of Modern Orthodox ideals. Waxman (2007b) cites Galinsky (2008),[12] who found that the opening of *yeshivot* and the expansion of Jewish knowledge that took place in late thirteenth and early fourteenth century Spain also resulted in increases in piety and more rigorous observance of *mitzvot* and *halakhah*, because of increased awareness in the general population about many domains of *halakhah*.

These researchers acknowledge the difficulties facing Modern Orthodoxy as a movement. Waxman (2007b) argues that it is hard for K-12 schools to socialize children into Modern Orthodoxy because of its emphasis on personal autonomy, and because of the "distant intellectual coolness of the philosophical modern Orthodox" (p. 142). But it seems that there are other challenges to perpetuating Modern Orthodox ideology as well.

One of the key elements differentiating Modern Orthodox schools from the varied forms of Haredi schools is the centrality of the State of Israel to their school's identity. In fact, this ideological commitment is considered essential to the very definition of Modern Orthodoxy (Liebman, 1965; Heilman, 2005; 2006; Schick, 2005). Modern Orthodox schools struggle, however, with defining and unpacking

---

[12] At the time the manuscript had not yet been published.

the nature of this commitment and its implications for educational practice. Schools seem eager for guidance; this is one of the few domains in which curricula have been developed externally and adopted by schools enthusiastically.

Pomson and Deitcher (2009) posit that both Modern Orthodox and non-Orthodox schools are "engaged in enculturative work...seeking to cultivate commitments and inculcate values by providing students with formative experiences" (p. 34). The challenge, in their analysis, is that schools are "uncertain about how best to translate their commitments into practice" (p. 34). Issacs (2009), on the other hand, argues that the fundamental challenge of Israel education is not the problem of how to successfully transmit Zionist values and commitments, but rather of what those values and commitments ought to be.

Modern Orthodox schools have indeed, for the most part, avoided articulating definitive statements of their particular Religious Zionist ideology in favor of adopting bland, non-committal slogans. An explicit written commitment in the mission statement to a particular understanding of Religious Zionism is highly unusual. In fact, the mission statements of dozens of Modern Orthodox schools (along with those of many Conservative and pluralistic Jewish day and high schools) utilize, verbatim, language developed by the Avi Chai Foundation as their sole articulation of the school's stance toward Israel and Zionism.[13] Because of its intended use by the Foundation as a minimum standard of support for Israel in order to qualify for funding, it is abstract and vague enough not to commit schools to a particular interpretation or stance on Israel, or to specific educational practices. It also contains no reference whatsoever to religion, spirituality, or even Zionism. It is striking that so many Modern Orthodox schools adopt such an abstract, secular articulation of a central element of their mission and distinctive religious identity, especially those schools that seem to have invested a great deal of thought into the articulation of other elements of their mission statements.

The Israel education curriculum in Modern Orthodox schools, when it exists, is commonly enacted as Israel advocacy training (Pomson & Deitcher, 2009). Two popular curricula, "Eyes on Israel" and "The David Project" (2009), function essentially as training programs for Israel advocacy and activism.[14] Both teach students to recognize distortions in the media's reportage of Israel, supply facts to provide students with a counter-narrative, and emphasize their focus on developing students' critical thinking skills.

These curricula are in line with Modern Orthodoxy's typically strong support for the right-wing stances of the Israeli Religious Zionist Orthodox (Waxman, 2007a). In Spring 2009, Jewish Action magazine, the official publication of the Orthodox

---

[13] The statement reads, "The creation of the State of Israel is one of the seminal events in Jewish history. Recognizing the significance of the State and its national institutions, we seek to instil in our students an attachment to the State of Israel and its people as well as a sense of responsibility for their welfare" (www.avi-chai.org).

[14] "Eyes on Israel" is a free curriculum for middle-school and high-school students created by CAMERA (the Committee for Accuracy in Middle East Reporting in America) to help students develop a critical approach toward what they see, read, and hear about Israel in the media.

Union, published a review of Libby Kahane's book *Rabbi Meir Kahane: His Life and Thought (Volume One: 1932–1975)*. The reviewer (Rakeffet-Rothkoff, 2009) pens an enthusiastic personal tribute to the late Rabbi Kahane, the man he "met and adored" as a youth in the Bnei Akiva youth group. The magazine's editors chose to highlight the following quote from the review: "If ever a human being felt the pain and anguish of his brothers, it was Meir Kahane." That this piece was printed in the official publication of a prominent national Modern Orthodox organization, without contextual commentary or response and without recognition that the political party founded by Kahane is outlawed in the State of Israel, underscores his enduring legacy and warrants attention in any serious exploration of American Modern Orthodoxy.

Regardless of the "what" of their Religious Zionist vision, Modern Orthodox schools also struggle to determine the way they ought to nurture these commitments in practice. Religious Zionism is typically implemented as an extension of Hebrew language instruction, or at special event celebrations of *Yom Ha'atzma'ut* (Israel Independence Day) and *Yom Yerushalayim* (Jerusalem Day), and for schools in or near New York, participation in the annual Israel Day Parade. Israel education is still often seen as the responsibility of the Hebrew teacher in high schools. Yet as it becomes clearer that most Modern Orthodox schools are failing to create literate Hebrew readers and speakers despite instruction in Hebrew language and *"Ivrit b'Ivrit"* (teaching Judaic subjects in Hebrew) systems (Safran, 1990; Stadtmauer, 1990; Wolowelsky, 1990), the role and prestige of the Hebrew department and the rigorous enforcement of *"Ivrit b'Ivrit"* practices in schools have taken a major hit.

Whatever its antecedents, and they are hotly debated, this sense of failure in Hebrew instruction, in practice, relegates Religious Zionist education to the low end of the prestige continuum in many schools. As Modern Orthodox schools wrestle with the issues of cheating, drugs, promiscuity, religious apathy, and the challenges of infusing *Tefillah* with meaning or spirituality (Eliovison, 2008; Fluk, 1987; Goldberg, 1981; Kessler, 2007; Margolese, 2005; Soloveichik, 1972; Unterman, 2000), educating for an unclearly defined Religious Zionism appears to be a less compelling imperative. This creates the ironic reality of schools that claim Religious Zionism to be at the core of their mission, and yet relegate actual Religious Zionist education to the edges of their attention, or to certain days of the year.

For schools that claim a Religious Zionist orientation, the task ahead remains the articulation of an ideology of Religious Zionism in the Diaspora that resonates with today's educators and students. This task calls for working out how actually to convey this ideology to students in a way that will be likely to generate an enduring commitment to Religious Zionist ideals.

These issues present a real challenge to the continuity of Modern Orthodoxy. For years, Modern Orthodox parents and educators experienced concern and disappointment as they noticed alumni of their schools becoming more religiously stringent, and rejecting Modern Orthodoxy in favor of a Haredi lifestyle, during their year or two in Israel, where 90% of graduates go after completing high school (Berger, 2007). This transformation became such a high profile, universally acknowledged pattern that a slang term for it developed: *flipping out*. This process "manifests itself in a change of outward appearances (including a change of dress and hairstyle), college and professional choices, and a changed attitude toward secular society and culture" (Berger p. 71).

The search for a cause and a remedy for this phenomenon has led to the floating of both a number of hypotheses and proposed solutions among Modern Orthodox educators and leaders. One approach has been to psychologically contextualize and normalize the phenomenon as part of normal adolescent development (Fowler, 1981; Jacobson, 2007). It is said that during the year in Israel the typical student is in the period of identity formation and role moratorium, in which the developmentally appropriate task is "solidifying an identity independent of one's parents" (Jacobson, p. 138).

A second approach has focused on the deliberate design and orchestration of the "year in Israel" experience to create the ideal environment for identity transformation. Finkelman (2003), for example, finds that Israeli *yeshivot* (and presumably seminaries) structure students' experiences during that year in order to maximize the likelihood that they will be able to "transform the students into more ideal, Haredi laymen. These programs aim to resocialize students out of 'flawed Modern Orthodox values'" (p. 2). He deconstructs the Talmud *shiur* (pedagogy) format, the charisma of the Talmud instructors, and the total environment created by the year in Israel, to reveal the latent goals enacted through them.

A third approach, not always explicitly linked to the issue of flipping out, emphasizes the fact that many teachers in K-12 Modern Orthodox schools are personally from a Haredi background (Gonen, 2001). Educational leaders and parents fear that these teachers exert a subtle influence on their young charges, undermining the ideology and religious stance of the school. Helmreich and Shinar (1998), for example, have suggested that the shortage of Modern Orthodox teachers is a significant factor in the "slide to the right" in American Orthodoxy. The Haredi teachers, referred to as "agent provocateurs," enter Modern Orthodox schools and serve to undermine their message, replacing it with a more Haredi one (see also Wertheimer, 1989 and Spolter, 2004).

The argument that the year in Israel undermines 12 years of effort invested by Modern Orthodox schools (Fowler, 1981; Heilman, 2005; Helmreich & Shinar, 1998) rings somewhat hollow when one examines the reality of the weak and diffuse form of Religious Zionist education many schools have actually provided. Rather than focus blame outward on the role of Haredim in undermining Modern Orthodox values, some critical reflection and serious research on the values and practices of Modern Orthodoxy as lived experience, especially in schools, could yield important insight for those to whom the continuity of Modern Orthodox values is important.

If Berger (2007) is correct in his analysis, the social construction of the *flipping out* phenomenon as a crisis has been somewhat out of proportion, possibly in an effort to connect it to arguments about the rightward swing of American Orthodoxy. Berger found that almost all of his study participants ended their year(s) in Israel with their commitments to completing their college education and to their career plans intact. In the final analysis, what is possibly most noteworthy about the prominence of this issue in the Modern Orthodox sensibility is the underlying anxiety it reflects about the viability of Modern Orthodoxy as an enduring set of behavioral norms and as a compelling *weltanschauung*. As described next, Haredi society is experiencing its own version of this continuity anxiety.

Continuity Challenges: Perpetuating the Haredi Society Through Schooling

If the late 1980s was a time of increased Haredi confidence as it faced outward, it was also a time of developing Haredi concern facing inward. Orthodox mental health professionals and educators expressed concern over a growing trend of drug abuse and promiscuity among a subculture of teenagers from Haredi families.[15] These children were going "off the Derech (path)." Some educators who had been involved in outreach to non-observant Jews began to redirect their efforts to reaching inward to draw alienated young people back onto the path.

Nefesh International, The International Network of Orthodox Mental Health Professionals, was founded in 1992, its published mission to bring Orthodox Jewish mental health professionals, educators, and rabbis together to network and collaborate on issues affecting the Orthodox community. According to its website, Nefesh today has 560 members worldwide, and an annual conference that draws 300–400 people. Nefesh, with its Haredi rabbinic advisory council, created a legitimate forum for surfacing and discussing Haredi societal problems. Psychologists, social workers, and other mental health professionals were catapulted into the center of Haredi communal discourse and as advisors to its highest levels of rabbinic leadership.

In the mid-1990s, the "crisis" of the Jewish family and teenage dropouts was the topic of sessions at the national conventions of Agudath Israel and Torah Umesorah, and articles in The Jewish Observer (Wolpin,1996a, 1996b, 1999). In 1996, Agudath Israel itself founded Project YES (Youth Enrichment Services), which created hotlines, school and job placements, teen mentoring programs, and other interventions to support disengaged youth.

By 1999, the Metropolitan New York Coordinating Council on Jewish Poverty estimated that 3,500 Jewish teens in Brooklyn alone were engaged in at-risk behavior. But it was the November 1999 "special issue" of The Jewish Observer devoted entirely to "Children on the Fringe…and Beyond," that served as a watershed, powerfully moving the problem out of the backrooms and into the public discourse. A second issue of The Jewish Observer was published shortly thereafter on the same topic, the editor explaining that they had decided to extend the conversation due to the unprecedented number of responses and letters elicited. These publications opened a public conversation at the national level that has not yet abated. The subsequent explosion of programs for teens, parent support groups, teacher training

---

[15] For example see: www.timessquarerabbi.com, www.rabbihorowitz.com, www.abrahamtwerski.com.

sessions, and telephone hotlines further attested to the resonance of the issue within the Haredi community.

The communal search for causes and remedies continues, although unfortunately, and perhaps unsurprisingly, no large-scale, rigorous social science research study was ever launched; so the dimensions, contributing factors, and consequences of this crisis are not known empirically. While more careful study of the written and oral communal discourse around this subject is needed, as pioneered by Finkelman (2009) for example, anecdotal evidence points to blame being attributed alternately to parents, teachers, school systems, secular western culture, the community's spiritual failings, and Divine decree. While parents blame schools and schools blame poor parenting, communal leaders and publications have generated a more circumspect discourse. Children are easily tempted, they say, and some teenagers, such as those with learning or attention disabilities or difficult family circumstances, are especially vulnerable to the dangerous influence of the secular world and its values (Russell & Blumenthal, 2000). Like their Modern Orthodox counterparts, these Haredi leaders accept blame for having allowed these bad influences into their community's midst (in this case through technology), and resolve to repair the breaches in the ideological wall. On the other hand, a popular book titled *Off the Derech: Why Observant Jews Leave Judaism* (Margolese, 2005) summarizes the popular positions on this issue after conducting key informant interviews, and then argues that troubled teens are not as much attracted to the outside world as they are seeking to escape their own.

One concrete Haredi response has been the attempt to shield children from harm by banning the Internet or significantly limiting its use. The primary concerns in this regard are that through the Internet children will access immodest images and will socially network with strangers, with the opposite gender, with members of the "off-the-Derech" subculture, and with non-Jews. Many schools in the core communities now have policies that require parents and children to attest to the child's lack of access to Internet in the home. Unlike other segments of the Jewish community, there are a significant number of Haredi families who do not utilize the Internet at all, personally or professionally. It remains to be seen whether strict avoidance of the Internet will come to serve as a defining feature of a subgroup of Haredim, or whether the ruling will ultimately prove to be unsustainable. Meanwhile, researchers have to be aware that computer-use patterns are currently very different in the Haredi sector than elsewhere in the Jewish community, which has implications for everything from survey administration to cultural interpretation.

It is arguable that the impact on Haredi education of the November 1999 Jewish Observer issue is analogous to the impact of the 1990 National Jewish Population Study on the larger Jewish education field. Both served as wake-up calls warning of a breakdown in the system; both spawned a large number of interventions, programs, and agencies, of variable quality but all well meaning; and in their rush to fix both crises, funders and educators alike have tended to work independently of one another, sometimes duplicating efforts, and often failing to learn systematically from their own or one another's experiences. Perhaps more significantly, however, both have released tremendous energy and creativity on the part of professional educators and lay leaders. It is doubtful whether so many Haredi schools would feature resource rooms, parenting workshops, Orthodox school counsellors, remedial reading programs, even teacher training programs, were it not for the heightened awareness of their potential role in keeping vulnerable children "on the *Derech*."

Institutional Diversity and Competition

A sense of creative urgency among educators and parents has been engendered by this heightened awareness in the Orthodox public of the impact of school on children's religious identification or alienation. In the Modern Orthodox community, the perception of a slide to the right led many to conclude that a stronger ideological foundation in Modern Orthodoxy was needed at the K-12 level. In the Haredi community, concern over an increase in children "off the *Derech*" led to advocacy for new approaches: a kinder, gentler, more child-focused and positive environment; a more sheltered, selective, safe environment to prevent exposure to negative cultural influences; schools that would embrace children's individuality; or schools that were professional enough to deal effectively with learning differences (Grossman, 2002; 2007).

Some established schools have adapted, shifted, and generally been responsive to these parental and communal concerns. They have managed to change in deep ways so as to fit new religious sensibilities and concerns, new ideological trends, new economic conditions, and new educational ideas. These changes come at a cost, however, engendering either alienation of some factions of school communities, turnover in key educational personnel, or reduced confidence in the school's stability, all of which can adversely affect recruitment and fundraising, and thus institutional survival, at least in the short term.

As often as not, however, the response to the continuity concerns has been the establishment of new schools that would presumably be more successful than the existing institutions at preventing negative outcomes. There is much scepticism among Orthodox parents and lay leaders that changing existing school cultures is possible. At the periphery of the educational field, in fact, the phenomenon of Orthodox families homeschooling has been gathering momentum for years, although the number of these families is not known and the antecedents of these decisions have not been rigorously studied (Siegel, 2004).

Shift from Community to Ideological Loyalty

The institutions of advanced Talmud study in which most Orthodox school and synagogue leaders receive their training are numerous and varied. Rich yet subtle ideological diversity exists among students and instructors even within those institutions solidly identified with a primary strand in American Orthodoxy, such as Beth Medrash Govoha in Lakewood, NJ, with its 4,300 adult Talmud students, and

Rabbi Isaac Elchanan Theological Seminary at Yeshiva University, with over 300 rabbinical students.

Graduates of these and other institutions have founded new schools of their own, each with its own specific interpretive vision of Jewish life and learning. This cycle of ideological elaboration and institutionalization has helped to generate a host of niche markets and related educational institutions that identify more or less with umbrella groups and established ideologies. By positioning themselves as more authentic representatives of particular ideological communities, or more responsive to particular concerns, than the larger, older schools, they have successfully created cultural understandings of their identities that protect their specialist niches (Carroll & Swaminathan, 2000).[16]

Many of the older schools in large and small communities were founded as community-serving institutions in the early years of their local Orthodox community's development. Parents and school supporters were often involved in building other community organizations as well. The challenges of diversity were seen as surmountable because of shared values of unity and community.

Over time, however, new priorities have altered the hierarchy of values among many educators, lay leaders, philanthropists, and parents. The trend to open new schools has been enabled by the concurrent shift from community to ideological loyalty.[17] Today's parents want to send their children to schools that reinforce their values and religious identification, and that do not flinch from taking stands on issues of importance to them, whether that be the celebration of *Yom Ha'atzma'ut* [Israel Independence Day] or protection from the Internet. Not only has American Orthodoxy continued to splinter into ideological communities based on ever-finer-grained differences, but the salience of these differences has concurrently risen in the identity definition of individuals and institutions. Ideological loyalty has intensified and risen in the hierarchy of values, over loyalty to local community.

In a common scenario, an Orthodox school that has served a community over the course of a decade or more finds itself facing a breakaway school; the strategies for holding the school community together are no longer effective. While at one time, one constituency may have acceded to the demands or needs of another constituency for the sake of "keeping the school together" or maintaining communal harmony, that constituency is no longer willing to compromise on its own needs and demands. This can be an expression of a new, more militantly ideological generation of lay leadership emboldened by the rhetoric of its national spokespersons and publications; or this could come about because of the accumulated frustrations

---

[16] See Carroll's theory of resource partitioning (1985) and a fascinating study of resource partitioning in the microbrewery movement (Carroll & Swaminathan, 2000).

[17] This chapter does not explore the role of economic prosperity in the 1980s and 1990s in the explosion of founding of new schools . While increased wealth was certainly necessary to this development, it is not sufficient in itself to explain spending choices, although see Diamond's (2000) argument to the contrary.

and disappointments of decades, set off by an incident and/or somehow reaching the breaking point.[18]

In a world of increasingly splintered Orthodox identities and thus, narrow niches, the "generalist" schools with the mission of serving their local Orthodox communities, which at one time dominated the Orthodox day-school field, are losing ground to the specialist schools serving niche markets (Carroll, 1985).

Implications of the Competitive Marketplace

As would be predicted by a typical organizational density-dependence model (Hannan & Freeman, 1989; Hannan, 2005), once the Orthodox day school achieved legitimization as an institutional form, it has continued to spread and diversify, and only market forces can slow the field's growth. Indeed, a diverse and competitive market exists. The Orthodox consumer in most communities can now select from among a variety of identifications and multiple interpretations of each identification. Schools in small Orthodox communities tend to have fewer resources but greater flexibility in interpreting ideological identifications. Schools in large communities with several schools of a variety of identifications tend to face intensive competition for market share to remain viable. In the core communities there is a population scale to support a wide variety of schools serving specific populations or niches.

The shifting of market share from the large, established community schools to an increased number of smaller niche schools has its own consequences. On the one hand, schools targeting narrow segments cannot grow very large and will never have scale advantages of the larger and usually older schools. Thus the communal cost of supporting the burgeoning field involves not only the support of a greater number of schools, but that of funding many small schools that appeal to a limited number of supporters and that are not cost efficient (Schick, 2009, p. 18). On the other hand, the reduced market share of the large, established community schools has allowed for the flourishing of diversity. This has enriched the field and increased options for parents choosing schools for their children.

In the core and large communities, where there is a robust competitive environment, Orthodox schools are to a great extent market driven, and thus particularly vulnerable to the expectations of their audiences (Polos, Hannan, & Carroll, 2002), which may include potential parents, potential teachers, community leaders, local philanthropists, and national organizations, networks, and leaders. Against the backdrop of shifting priorities and ideological boundaries, and anxieties over continuity, these expectations are ambiguous and often unstated.

In this environment, a school's competitive advantage may depend on perceptions of legitimacy and prestige. Legitimacy and prestige are hard to win, easy to

---

[18] There ought to be considerable research on the causes and history of breakaway schools because of their tremendous economic impact; but it does not appear that this phenomenon has been the subject of any scholarly inquiry.

lose, and difficult to restore. Thus, claims of greater ideological legitimacy have become convenient and potent tactics for attracting students in this competitive market. Efforts to build or maintain prestige require focus on positioning the school in the field's status structure (Podolny, 1993). These pressures are dangerous in that they can draw the energy and attention of lay and professional school leaders away from the substantive issues of education, and can distort decision making to the detriment of school quality.

The danger is exacerbated by the longstanding challenge of funding, which the current recession has brought to a head. Despite its growth and differentiation over the years, from a financial perspective Orthodox schooling is based on a model whose sustainability rests on expectations of heroic self-sacrifice on the part of parents, lay leaders, and educational professionals. The pervasive informal, familial culture among both lay and professional members of Orthodox schools creates the perfect environment for conflict avoidance, lack of accountability and transparency, unclear standards, improvisation rather than planning, and relationship games (Bechhofer, 2004). These organizational habits make it unlikely that schools and communities will face uncomfortable truths about the quality of their offerings and of their lay leadership structures, and re-examine the values, premises, and market assumptions upon which they were founded (Litman, 2007; Dym & Hutson, 2005; Heifetz & Linsky, 2002; Heifetz, 1994). Yet these dispositions will be needed if schools are to maintain a continued commitment to educational quality and substance in a financial model that pits quality, financial viability, accessibility, and ideological fidelity against one another.

Conclusion

The decentralized nature of the field of Orthodox schooling and the evolving relationship between the various segments of Orthodoxy have led to a dramatic increase in the number of Orthodox day schools over the last three decades, under the predominant paradigms of ideology and specialization. Increasingly finer-grained differences in religious beliefs have developed and become more salient. Additionally, members of both Modern and Haredi Orthodoxy have become publicly concerned about dilemmas and challenges to their ideological continuity. For these and other reasons, the community-inclusive Orthodox school model has been challenged, and in an increasing number of communities displaced, by smaller schools with fidelity to specific visions of religious life or alternative educational approaches.

The Orthodox day-school field is large and diversified enough for ecological analysis of field dynamics to yield insights into both the market conditions in which individual schools operate and the larger communal dynamics in which American Orthodox schooling is situated. This chapter has introduced some fruits of this analysis, demonstrating that the field has grown more diverse, more competitive, and more innovative.

References

Bechhofer, S. (2004). Change in Jewish day schools: Organizational capacity and barriers. *Journal of Jewish Education*, *70*(3), 74–87.
Berger, S. Z. (2007). Engaging the ultimate: The impact of post-high school study in Israel. In S. Z. Berger (Ed.), *Flipping out: Myth or fact* (pp. 5–68). Brooklyn, NY: Yashar Books.
Caplan, K. (2005). Absolutely intellectually honest: A case-study of American Jewish Modern Orthodox historiography. In R. Elior & P. Schafer (Eds.), *Creation and re-creation in Jewish thought: Feastschrift in honor of Joseph Dan on the occasion of his seventieth birthday* (pp. 339–362). Tubingen, Germany: Mohr Siebeck.
Carroll, G. R. (1985). Concentration and specialization: Dynamics of niche width in populations of organizations. *American Journal of Sociology*, *90*(6), 1262–1283.
Carroll, G. R., & Swaminathan, A. (2000). Why the microbrewery movement? Organizational dynamics of resource partitioning in the US brewing industry. *American Journal of Sociology*, *106*(3), 715–762.
Diamond, E. (2000). *And I will dwell in their midst: Orthodox Jews in suburbia*. Chapel Hill, NC: University of North Carolina Press.
Dym, B., & Hutson, H. (2005). *Leadership in nonprofit organizations*. Thousand Oaks, CA: Sage Publications.
Eliovison, Y. (2008). In their own words. *Jewish Educational Leadership*, *6*(2), 20–21.
Ferziger, A. S. (2007). Church/sect theory and American Orthodoxy reconsidered. In S. Cohen & B. Susser (Eds.), *Ambivalent Jews: Charles Liebman in memoriam*. New York: Jewish Theological Seminary.
Finkelman, Y. (2003). Virtual Volozhin: Social vs. textual aspects of the Talmud curriculum in contemporary one-year yeshiva programs. In J. Saks & S. Handelman (Eds.), *Wisdom from all my teachers: Challenges and initiatives in contemporary torah education* (pp. 360–381). Jerusalem: Urim Publications.
Finkelman, Y. (2009). Relationships between schools and parents in Haredi popular literature in the United States. In A. Pomson & H. Deitcher (Eds.), *Jewish schools, Jewish communities: A reconsideration*. Oxford: Littman Library of Jewish Civilization, pp. 237–254.
Fluk, G. H. (1987). The ethics of cheating: The Jewish view. *Ten Da'at*, *1*(1), 9–11.
Fowler, J. (1981). *Stages of faith: The psychology of human development and the quest for meaning*. New York: Harper Collins.
Galinsky, J. D. (2008). On popular Halakhic literature and the Jewish reading audience in fourteenth-century Spain. *Jewish Quarterly Review*, *98*(3), 305–327.
Goldberg, H. (1981). Critique of the American Jewish day school. *Tradition*, *19*(4), 290–296.
Gonen, A. (2001). *From yeshiva to work: The American experience and lessons for Israel*. Jerusalem: The Floersheimer Institute for Policy Studies.
Grossman, L. (2002). Jewish communal affairs. In L. Grossman & D. Singer (Eds.), *American Jewish yearbook: The annual record of Jewish civilization* (pp. 221–245). New York: American Jewish Committee.
Grossman, L. (2007). Jewish communal affairs. In L. Grossman & D. Singer (Eds.), *American Jewish yearbook: The annual record of Jewish civilization* (pp. 111–132). New York: American Jewish Committee.
Hannan, M. T. (2005). Ecologies of organizations: Diversity and identity. *The Journal of Economic Perspectives*, *19*(1), 51–70.
Hannan, M. T., & Freeman, J. (1989). *Organizational ecology*. Cambridge, MA: Harvard University Press.
Heifetz, R. A. (1994). *Leadership without easy answers*. Cambridge, MA: Belknap Press of Harvard University Press.
Heifetz, R. A., & Linsky, M. (2002). *Leadership on the line: Staying alive through dangers of leading*. Cambridge, MA: Harvard University Press.

Heilman, S. C. (2005). Jews and fundamentalism. *Jewish Political Studies*, *17*(1-2), 75-113.
Heilman, S. C. (2006). *Sliding to the right: The contest for the future of American Jewish Orthodoxy*. Berkeley, CA: University of California Press.
Helmreich, W. B., & Shinar, R. (1998, June 1). Modern Orthodoxy in America: Possibilities for a movement under siege. *The Jerusalem Letter*. Retrieved from http://www.jcpa.org/cjc/jl-383-helmreich.htm
Issacs, A. (2009, Spring). Putting the ideology back in Israel education. *Hayidion*, 16-17.
Jacobson, D. (2007). In search of self: Psychological perspectives on change during the year in Israel. In S. Berger (Ed), *Flipping out: Myth of fact* (pp. 79-143). Brooklyn, NY: Yashar Books.
Kessler, R. (2007). Inviting soul into the classroom. *Jewish Educational Leadership*, *5*(2), 4-9.
Liebman, C. S. (1965). Aspects of the religious behavior of American Jews. *American Jewish Yearbook*, *66*, 21-98.
Litman, S. (2007). *Jewish day school peer yardstick: Multiyear retroactive report 2003-2007*. Retrieved from Partnership for Excellence in Jewish Education (PEJE) website: http://www.peje.org/docs/20071129_yardstick_generic_hs.pdf
Margolese, F. (2005). *Off the derech: Why observant Jews leave Judaism*. Jerusalem: Devora publishing.
Nardi, J. (1944). A survey of Jewish day schools in America. *Journal of Jewish Education*, *16*(1), 12-26.
Podolny, J. (1993). A status-based model of market competition. *The American Journal of Sociology*, *98*(4), 8229-8872.
Polos, L., Hannan, M. T., & Carroll, G. R. (2002). Foundations of a theory of social forms. *Industrial and Corporate Change*, *11*(1), 85-115.
Pomson, A., & Deitcher, H. (2009). Much ado about something: Clarifying goals and methods of Israel education. *Hayidion, Spring*, 32-34.
Rakeffet-Rothkoff, A. (2009). A review of Rabbi Meir Kahana: His life and thought, Volume I: 1932-1975. *Jewish Action*, *69*(3), 83-86.
Russell, S., & Blumenthal, N. (2000). *Children in crisis: Detection and intervention: A practical guide for parents, educators and mental health professionals*. Teaneck, NJ: Nefesh.
Sacks, J. (1984). Modern Orthodoxy in crisis. *Le'eyla*, *17*, 20-25.
Safran, E. (1990). Response Ivrit, b'Ivrit. *Ten Da'at*, *5*(1), 49-50.
Schick, M. (2005). *A census of Jewish day schools in the United States*. Retrieved from Avi Chai Foundation website: http://www.avi-chai.org/Static/Binaries/Publications/Second%20Census%202003-04_0.pdf
Schick, M. (2009) A census of Jewish day schools in the United States. Retrieved from Avi Chai Foundation website: http://www.avi-chai.org/census.pdf
Siegel, J. (2004, August 13). Turning living rooms into schoolrooms: Long a domain of religious Christians: Home schools make Jewish inroads. *Jewish Daily Forward*, Retrieved from http://www.forward.com/articles/5137/
Soloveichik, A. (1972). Torah tzniut versus new morality and drugs. *Tradition*, *13*(2), 52-58.
Spolter, R. (2004). In search of leaders. *Jewish Action*, *64*(3), 38-44.
Stadtmauer, A. (1990). Response to Ivrit b'Ivrit. *Ten Da'at*, *5*(1), 50.
The David Project. (2009). Curriculum initiative for Jewish high schools: The Arab Israeli conflict. *The David Project: Educating Voices for Israel*. Retrieved January 28, 2010, from http://www.thedavidproject.org/resources/curricula/UAIC-TOC.pdf
Torah Umesorah: The National Society for Hebrew Day Schools. (1993). *Directory of day schools in the United States and Canada*. New York: Author.
Torah Umesorah: The National Society for Hebrew Day Schools. (2002). *Directory of day schools in the United States and Canada*. New York: Author.
Umesorah, T. (2007). The National Society for Hebrew Day Schools. *Directory of day schools in the United States and Canada*. New York: Author.
Unterman, J. (2000). A day (school) dream. *Ten Da'at*, *8*, 12-14.

Waxman, C. (2003). From institutional decay to primary day: American Orthodox Jewry since World War II. *American Jewish History, 91*(3–4), 405–421.
Waxman, C. (2007a). American Orthodoxy, Zionism and Israel. In S. Berger (Ed.), *Flipping out: Myth of fact* (pp. 145–197). Brooklyn, NY: Yashar Books.
Waxman, C. (2007b). Needed: New typologies, the complexity of American Orthodoxy in the 21st century. In S. Cohen & B. Susser (Eds.), *Ambivalent Jew: Charles Liebman in memoriam*. New York: Jewish Theological Seminary of America.
Wertheimer, J. (1989). Recent trends in American Judaism. In D. Singer (Ed.), *American Jewish yearbook* (pp. 63–164). New York: American Jewish Committee. Philadelphia, PA: Jewish Publication Society.
Wertheimer, J. (1999). Jewish education in the United States: Recent trends and issues. In D. Singer (Ed.), *American Jewish yearbook* (pp. 3–118). New York: American Jewish Committee.
Wolowelsky, J. (1990). Ivrit b'Ivrit. *Ten Da'at, 4*(2), 39–41.
Wolpin, N. (Ed.) (1996, October). Preventing teenage dropouts. *The Jewish Observer.*
Wolpin, N. (Ed.) (1996, May). The Jewish family in its glory and in crisis. *The Jewish Observer*
Wolpin, N. (Ed.) (1999, November). Children on the fringe . . . and beyond. *The Jewish Observer.*

Early Childhood Education

Michael Ben-Avie, Ilene Vogelstein, Roberta Louis Goodman, Eli Schaap, and Pat Bidol-Padva

> *It was an exciting day in the lives of the four-year-old class. They had planned and prepared for this event for months. It was time for 24 children to leave their safe, secure and serene environment and move on to the next step in their lives. Parents, grandparents, siblings, and friends were entering the building with cameras, flowers and presents. The energy was palpable. The teachers were in the classrooms with the children sharing their last minute instructions. The children could hardly contain themselves.*
>
> *Behind the scenes that same morning, I had the privilege of working with Jake who was distributing the programs. After the programs were placed on approximately 90 chairs, Jake realized we were ten programs short. He came to me with a very specific directive. "Joanie, we need ten more programs, go upstairs and make ten more copies, okay?" Realizing, after all, that Jake was just turning five, I asked him if he thought we should make more than ten copies, in case other visitors showed up for the celebration. He looked at me in such a way that I will never forget, and repeated his directive, but this time used his hands and all ten fingers to emphatically state, "I counted the chairs, we are ten short, and we need only ten." I reluctantly said, "Okay, I will be right back with the copies." As I stood at the copier for what seemed like an hour trying to decide if I should respect Jake's decision and make ten more copies, knowing I would probably have to go back upstairs to make more when more people arrived, I pressed the number ten on the copier machine. As I watched Jake proudly and competently place each program on the remaining ten chairs, I realized how empowered and capable this young boy felt.*
>
> Joanie Smeltz, Director of Early Childhood Programs, Ohr Kodesh Congregation. Orh Kodesh is affiliated with the Jewish Early Childhood Education Initiative (JECEI)

M. Ben-Avie (✉)
Yale University, New Haven, CT, USA
e-mail: michael.ben-avie@yale.edu

Jake's story is about quality in Jewish Early Childhood Education (JECE). The research that we present for the first time in this chapter demonstrates that JECE impacts the engagement of families in Jewish life. The analysis also reveals that this is a far more complex process than simply intensifying the Judaic content of the educational program. The key factor is the level of excellence of the JECE program's underlying "operating system." It is worth considering that the parents who rate that their children's JECE programs operate at a superb level are more open to enhancing their lives with Jewish connections. Thus, for many parents the promotion of children's Jewish identity is not an important criterion when choosing a JECE program. However, if they perceive and experience the JECE programs as excellent and well-run, they will become more engaged in Jewish actions after they enroll their children as a "side effect." While Joanie Smeltz's finger was suspended over the copy button, she was making a cross-roads decision. The decision that she made to listen to children, respect them, and provide them with opportunities to make decisions for themselves exemplifies the level of excellence essential to influencing the lifepaths of the children and their families' formation of a strong relationship to the Jewish people.

In JECE, there are many talented directors and teachers, beautiful buildings, sparkling curriculum, small classes in safe surroundings, and educators willing to personally change in order to promote children's learning and development. The problem is that the ground is shifting. Haynes, Ben-Avie, and Gilliam (2000), of the Yale Child Study Center, explain the roots of what is known today as Universal Pre-Kindergarten. At the Yale Child Study Center, a collegial debate raged between Edward Zigler and James P. Comer that was to span decades—until the two decided to collaborate. Associated in the public mind with Head Start was Edward Zigler, Director of the Office of Child Development and Chief of the Children's Bureau in Washington, DC. He was later to join the Yale Child Study Center. James P. Comer, associate dean of the Yale School of Medicine and founder of the Yale Child Study Center's School Development Program, was well aware of Zigler's work and the newly established Head Start.

At the heart of the matter were children walking through the doors of elementary schools who were not "ready" for school, according to the school staff. In response, Zigler took the lead in establishing a new national infrastructure to "immunize" the children against the negative developmental experiences that they were likely to encounter in schools. This infrastructure became known as "Head Start." If it is possible to "awaken" or "spark" young children's development, and thus accelerate the developmental process, should not early childhood programs organize themselves in a way that would make this happen? This was the central premise of Head Start. The US government could have taken the approach to wait until the children reach kindergarten and address the achievement gap at that educational level. Instead, the US Economic Opportunities Act of 1964 launched Head Start, a program for 3- and 4-year-old children that was designed to help children overcome the deprivation caused by poverty. By way of contrast, Comer took the stance that if the problem inheres in the elementary schools, then the best solution was to fix the "bad" schools. In his approach, the aim of early childhood education is to provide underprepared *children* with positive developmental experiences—not to solve the problem that the *teachers* in elementary schools were underprepared to educate all children.

A renewed interest in early childhood education emerged with the launching of the Goals 2000 education initiative by President Clinton in 1994 which stated that by the year 2000 "all children will start school ready to learn." The statement admitted that not all children were ready. The mood at the time was captured by Hayes, Ben-Avie, and Gilliam (2000): "Labeling a child unready for school may serve to release the school from the responsibility of promoting that child's development. Given the potential of schools' early intervention programs to act as positive catalysts in the lives of children, we ask *Are schools ready to promote development among all the children?*" (p. 93). The results of model preschool programs and large-scale preschool programs that were newly published at that time provided solid evidence of the long-term impact of early childhood education. Consistent with the theme of this chapter, the most relevant finding was: "High quality programs clearly have the potential of improving the school readiness of these children and can often lead to remarkable long-term effects in terms of improved functioning in school, work, and life" (p. 99).

Today's universal pre-kindergarten is designed to provide all preschool-aged children with an opportunity to learn in a supportive, high-quality, literacy-rich educational environment prior to entering kindergarten; as a state-funded initiative, all families have access to this free program. It is free—and here inheres the challenge to Jewish early childhood education (JECE). Consider the school choice decision that many Jewish parents face when weighing free public school versus expensive Jewish day school education. Until the introduction of universal pre-kindergarten, we, the authors, could have thought that we were very close to actualizing the hopes that we had when we were voices in the wilderness calling for attention to be paid to early childhood within the Jewish community. Up until recently, we could have expected natural growth to occur in JECE as more and more school communities learned about the learning and developmental outcomes among young children like Jake in Jewish early childhood education (the latest estimate of the number of children in JECE is 123,000 in total, of which about 104,000 are Jewish. This estimate is based on Schaap & Goodman, 2004). With the introduction of universal pre-k, this natural growth is not as assured. Now that families have an absolutely free option for early childhood education, JECE programs will increasingly need to demonstrate excellence in order to recruit and retain families.

Despite the introduction of universal pre-k, Jewish early childhood education has the potential to thrive. At this crossroad, the next best step is to consider anew the premises underlying Jewish early childhood education. Fortunately, this work of reflection and action has already started. In 2007, the Coalition for the Advancement of Jewish Education (CAJE) convened a session for Jewish early childhood professionals at the national conference (authors of this chapter who were affiliated with CAJE include Eli Schaap, Ilene Vogelstein, and Pat Bidol-Padva). The result of that discussion was a draft statement on *Key Elements for Creating a Jewish Early Childhood Education Program* (http://www.caje.org/earlychildhood/JewishEC-DraftStatement.asp). The aim of Jewish early childhood education is addressed in the opening section of the "Key Elements" document. This opening section is noteworthy because of the dual focus on children and on families. The statement also articulates engagement in Jewish life as the outcome.

> The purpose of Jewish early childhood education (JECE) is to lay the foundation for lifelong Jewish engagement by supporting the development and enhancement of the Jewish identity of children and their families through Jewish knowledge, Jewish values, and Jewish experiences.

Key Elements for Creating a Jewish Early Childhood Education Program concludes with a section on excellence. The focus of this chapter, therefore, is on excellence in Jewish early childhood education, specifically within a North American context.

Voices in the Wilderness

Influenced by *From Neurons to Neighborhoods: The Science of Early Childhood Development* (National Research Council & Institute of Medicine, 2000), a partnership was established in 2002 to begin the development of a set of quality indicators, anchored in relevant theory and research, for describing excellence in Jewish early childhood education. The partnership with the Center for Applied Child Development (CACD) at Tufts University's Eliot-Pearson Department of Child Development was initiated by one of us (Ilene Vogelstein). The seeds of this partnership were sown in 1979 when a group of six women met at the conference of the National Association for the Education of Young Children (NAEYC) at what was to become the first meeting of the Jewish Caucus of NAEYC (later renamed the National Jewish Early Childhood Network). These "matriarchs" were the early childhood professionals in Baltimore, Washington, DC, Los Angeles, New York, and Chicago.

In 1998, the Mandel Foundation published *The Teachers Report: A Portrait of Teachers in Jewish Schools*. Among the findings, the report noted that 55% of the early childhood teachers had received no Jewish education after the age of 13, 22% had received no Jewish education before the age of 13 and only 15% had received a day school education before the age of 13. The report surveyed teachers in three communities (Baltimore, Milwaukee, and Atlanta). When the report was shared with the Baltimore leadership, the family of The Children of the Harvey and Lyn Meyerhoff Philanthropic Foundation decided to invest in Jewish early childhood education and established Machon L'Morim: Bereshit.

In June 2000, The Children of the Harvey and Lyn Meyerhoff Philanthropic Foundation convened a regional conference on Jewish early childhood education. At the conclusion of the conference, the attendees agreed to contribute funds to obtain more information regarding the Jewish early childhood education profession. In this way, the Jewish Early Childhood Education Partnership, a partnership of six philanthropists, was launched. The funders later contributed to the establishment of a permanent national home where advocacy, research, and services could be offered to this emerging field. The home was the Early Childhood Department at the Coalition for the Advancement of Jewish Education (CAJE).

CAJE partnered with the Center for Applied Child Development (CACD) at Tufts University's Eliot-Pearson Department of Child Development. This research, coupled with the demographic research on Jewish early childhood programs (Vogelstein & Kaplan, 2002) and the impact of a Jewish early childhood education on families (Beck, 2002), was a catalyst for intensifying the discussions identifying the issues facing Jewish early childhood education.

In developing the quality indicators for Jewish early childhood education, the Tufts researchers (2004) rejected using "developmentally appropriate practices" as the standard. All of the accreditation guides that were reviewed and critiqued referred to standards of excellence that were developed by the National Association for the Education of Youth Children (NAEYC), the leading (non-Jewish) accrediting agency in the country for early childhood programs. These standards emphasize the importance of "developmentally appropriate practices" (DAP). The researchers from Tufts commented on this term: "This somewhat overused term for excellence in early childhood education is rarely defined in detail; as a result, the phrase *developmentally appropriate* is subject to multiple interpretations. For example, some early childhood educators believe developmentally appropriate means that children are using hands-on materials. This simplistic definition may lead them to over-emphasize the importance of activities, even if those activities have no clear learning goals" (p. 2). Thus, the quality indicators were listed under six categories: (1) Program development and leadership; (2) Curriculum, instruction, and assessment; (3) School and classroom environment; (4) Interactions with children; (5) Partnerships with parents and families; and (6) Partnerships with host institutions.

From the work of the partnership between CAJE and Tufts emerged such initiatives as The Alliance for Jewish Early Education, the Jewish Early Childhood Education Initiative (JECEI), the development of a new Jewish Child Development Associates (CDA) degree, and the partnership among seven institutions of higher learning to develop an initiation course for educators in Jewish early childhood education. JECEI was funded by several Jewish philanthropic institutions in 2004. According to JECEI's logic model, the initiative increases the capacity of lay and professional leaders to effect change in schools and communities. In December 2005, The Alliance for Jewish Early Education was established. The Alliance is open to any international, national, or communal organization addressing Jewish early childhood education. In this way, professionals holding a national, international, or communal portfolio in Jewish early childhood education have an opportunity to learn, grow, and support each other while they collectively advocate, network, and collaborate to advance the field of Jewish early childhood education. The examples used in this chapter draw on our experiences in these organizations and the research we conducted in our professional capacity.

Development as the Aim of Early Childhood Education

While there are over 1,300 Jewish early childhood programs in the United States (CAJE Early Childhood Department and JECEI, 2003), there is not consensus regarding the aims of Jewish early childhood education. What should JECE promote? Coleman and Hoffer (1987) in their description of the basis for private schools write that the "school is an extension of the family, reinforcing the family's values. The school is *in loco parentis*, vested with the authority of the parent to carry out the parent's will" (p. 3). According to this approach, the aim of JECE is to help create the next generation in the "image of the preceding one" (p. 4). By way of contrast, an alternative approach builds on the families' hopes and aspirations for their children. Education is seen as a way to improve society by promoting developmental outcomes that will result in the second generation becoming *different* than their parents (for example, more engaged in Jewish life). Thus, it is enticing for Jewish organizations to see JECE as a way of promoting Jewish continuity. The second approach also opens the door for educative institutions to promote the learning and development of both generations at the same time.

Both of these approaches have to wrestle with the transmission of Judaism's very large sociocultural inheritance (*m'dor l'dor*). On one side of the equation is an inheritance that is comprised of all the group life-events of Jews as well as the accumulated wisdom of thousands of years. On the other side of the equation are very small children.

Young children may not understand, yet, the knowledge of past generations encased within concepts embedded within the sacred texts. Through guided play, however, they will encounter language, behavior, attitudes, and practices associated with these concepts. Vygotsky (1978) maintained that it is possible to "awaken" or "spark" child development. As a Jew, it is not surprising that Vygotsky dealt with the psychological mechanism through which a large sociocultural inheritance is transferred to young children. This psychological mechanism is concept formation, because embedded within concepts are ideas, values, and historical events from past generations. Consider the concept of the "the presence of G-d in the world." Other concepts are the "world to come," "divine providence," and "tzedekah" (charity). Vygotsky explained that thought and language are intertwined. In this way, young children develop the ability to think conceptually. Initially, young children develop pseudo-concepts, verbal labels that are initially without content. For example, a child may know the verbal label of "covenant" or "Tikkun Olam" (responsibility to change one's self and thereby the world). Vygotsky considered the development of pseudo-concepts as a critical step in the process of developing actual concepts. Thus, young children may engage in Shabbat activities at their JECE programs, even if they do not have yet a fully developed grasp of the essence of Shabbat as a "sanctuary in time," to quote Heschel (1951, p. 29). Without the verbal label, actual concepts will not emerge later in time. Through which activity do children form everyday concepts? Play!

This approach stands in contrast to the "academic-oriented" preschools that seek to give children a "head start" through direct instruction. For example, Haynes et al. (2002) observed educators in early childhood centers compelling 3-year olds to "write" their names before permitting them to play. Play was considered an activity on the periphery of the core mission of academic learning— "recess," as it were. The approach of the Jewish Early Childhood Education Initiative (JECEI) is to draw out the competencies of children through play to inquire, explore, wonder in order that they actively process everyday experiences under Judaism's framework of thoughts, emotions, actions, and ways of partaking in community.

At the Yale Child Study Center, the study group on play investigates the mental actions involved in children's fantasy play. For example, Mayes and Cohen (2006) observe that *"just pretending* provides a world where the child is able to try out relationships, identifications, and solutions" (p. 130). For 3–5-year-old children, imagination represents a special mode of mental functioning that motivates them toward increasingly complex relationships with others. Mayes and Cohen (2006) explain:

> With a capacity for imagination, relationships with others are colored both by the child's previous experiences and by his imagined wishes and beliefs. The capacity for sustained imaginary play emerges in parallel with the child's acquisition of an understanding of how the actions and words of others reflect and are motivated by their feelings, beliefs, wishes, and memories, each actions of mind. Such an understanding allows the child to imbue the persons in his imaginary play with complex feelings and desires towards others, and to create the stories, or an inner world, by which he defines himself and through which he will continue to view and define his external world. (p. 145)

Unfortunately, early childhood programs have become increasingly "academic-oriented." To illustrate, *The Brown University Child and Adolescent Behavior Letter* ran an article under the following headline: "Play: The New Dirty Word." In the article, Mary Mindess (2001) wrote: "Play is extremely important. It's part of being human. It shouldn't get lost in the push toward higher standards. It is, in fact, one of the factors that contributes to higher standards, as well as to psychological and social well-being. When we discourage free time for play, a great deal of creative energy is lost to the individual, and ultimately, society becomes the loser" (p. 7). Unfortunately, children are playing less these days as academic lessons are introduced as early as preschool. Mindess describes the prevalent attitude: "We've got to give children the right start." She translates this phrase to mean, "We've got to give children the best chance to get the highest test scores" (ibid).

Similar to Dewey (1938), Comer recognized that activities had to be meaningful to the children in the here-and-now, and not only in service of a far-away goal. Thus, the first curriculum that he designed addressed the children's social skills, and not their test scores. He is steadfast in that it is all about relationships. The relations that children form in early childhood education could serve as a template for all future healthy relationships. This is especially important because children at this age "strive always to learn how to be, how to act, how to cope, how to adapt, how to solve problems" (Noshpitz & King, 1991, p. 319). It is for this reason that an excellent JECE program builds into the schedule of the day time for children to explore relationships with others—and with themselves. Time for self-discovery, time for self-expression through such means as music and art, time for experiencing the ways of partaking in community, time for engaging in group play, time for engaging in fantasy—all these are characteristics of excellent JECE programs. James Fowler (1986) made a similar point in his description of the stage of faith that is relevant to young children (pp. 236–232): Stage I Intuitive-Projective faith is the fantasy-filled, imitative phase in which the child can be powerfully and permanently influenced by examples, moods, actions, and stories of the visible faith of the adults who are meaningful to the child.

The Jewish Early Childhood Education Initiative (JECEI), as an approach that incorporates Fowler's key teachings about faith development, falls into the constructivist and progressive educational "camps." Constructivism focuses on the knowledge and meaning that learners make from their experiences. Learners are active participants, not just recipients of knowledge. Learners participate fully in the educational process including setting direction of what is learned, how it is learned, and evaluating or reflecting on the educational experience. Progressivism similarly focuses on the importance of experience, but adds to the conversation the larger significance of education to a people, society, culture, or nation. Dewey's (1938) emphasis on the need for educating citizens for democracy to survive and thrive greatly influenced modern education in the United States for both children and adults. The schools of Reggio Emelia have embraced him as a major thinker in formulating their philosophy and approach.

The schools of Reggio Emilia offer an education based on the theories of Dewey and Vygotsky among others, but elevated to a new level of practice. For example, the schools of Reggio have developed the practice of documentation of children's work to a level unforeseen beforehand. In general, early childhood programs tend to be oral cultures and, therefore, activity-based learning activities soon fade from memory. Documentation makes the process of learning visible to children, educators, families, and community members. In this way, the documentation sparks reflection and growth. However, the approach of Reggio Emilia cannot be simply replicated, despite the claims of numerous schools billing themselves as "Reggio schools" who have only copied specific methods and tools. At the foundation of the holistic approach of Reggio Emilia is an historical and culturally specific vision of what it means to live a full life as a citizen in an Italian democracy (Edwards, Gandini, & Forman, 1998). This represents both the goal of education and the values that are embodied in the educational practices of the schools. Thus, to develop a Reggio-inspired JECE program entails understanding and articulating an historical and culturally specific vision of what it means to live a full Jewish life in contemporary society.

Other types of schools are constructivist and/or progressive without being Reggio-inspired. Montessori early childhood programs of which there are some Jewish early childhood programs share many of the same foundational ideas about children and their capabilities and importance to society as do Reggio-inspired schools. Yet, Montessori schools have their own distinctive approach to early childhood education. Play theory is a popular approach that many Jewish schools have embraced either for their school as a whole or as an educational strategy (e.g., play with blocks). Informed by Piaget's understanding of development among others, play theory supports the notion that children learn and grow not just cognitively, but in terms of social and emotional growth, through playing with their peers. Play allows children to discover lessons about life.

The greatest intersection between JECEI and the Yale Child Study Center's Comer Process is the use of child development as a framework for decision making.

In professional development academies of both initiatives, educators learn to see children's everyday experiences from a developmental perspective. To illustrate this point, consider the case of the boy and circle time. The teacher sang a song to signal the transition to announce that it was to circle time. All the children ran to the mat—except for Jacques. He continued playing in the block area. The teacher finally went over to him and asked, "Did you not hear the song we sing to announce circle time?" He replied, "I heard the song." She said, "When we sing the song, everyone is to stop what they are doing and come to the circle." He then asked, "What's with you teachers?" It's not hard to understand why a teacher might view the interaction through the "lens" of order and discipline. Thus, her response was to punish the child. Was there another "lens" she could have used to interpret the interaction? For example, JECEI, uses seven lenses, big ideas about Jewish living and learning to inform the educational process. If she had viewed the situation through the lens of *b'tzelem elokim* (the image of God) which JECEI associates with cultivating the potential of each child, then perhaps she would have cheerfully clapped her hands together and remarked, "What a great question! Let's go to the circle area and talk about why do we feel that it is necessary several times a day to gather all the children together for circle time? Would you like to start the discussion?" In this scenario, she "listened" to what the child really wanted to ask—and not to how he phrased his question. Through showing educators how an interaction may be considered from different perspectives, they learn that children's behavior is a form of communication, and an opportunity for individual children and the whole community to grow.

The lenses that JECEI uses are concepts that are embedded with ideas, values, and historical events form past generations (http://jecei.org/lenses.html). Consider the lens of *Hit'orerut* which alludes to the mystical concept of G-d awakening those who slumber. JECEI took this concept and applied it to early childhood education: Awaking (Amazement and Gratitude). From the outer reaches of the universe to the smallest atoms, there is much in the world to fill us with amazement and respect. Wonder fuels a culture of inquiry and reflection. By way of contrast, educators who view children through the lens of order and discipline are likely to see children "getting into things," making "messes," and "excessively mischievous."

JECEI today uses the lenses as a framework for decision making as well as a set of guiding principles: Ideally, the lenses are manifest daily in JECEI early childhood centers in the ways they structure their time; curricula and classrooms; the quality of relationships with the children, educators, and host institutions; and the partnerships JECEI forges with the families. The lenses are a response to the ambivalence of what is "Jewish" in Jewish early childhood education.

When the educators learn the different concepts ("lenses") through which to interpret everyday occurrences in classrooms, then a "mindfulness" emerges, to use Ellen Langer's (1994) term. As a result, children's cognitive structures develop "which select and categorize information, and serve as reference frames for thinking and acting" (Pepitone & Triandis, 1987, p. 481). In this way, a mindfulness to these concepts emerges both among the educators and the children, and the process of transmitting a very large cultural inheritance to the children is initiated.

With development as the aim of Jewish early childhood education, the focus is on the intersection between Judaism's sociocultural inheritance and children. As mentioned above, this intersection is facilitated through concept formation. While young children may form only *verbal labels* in their minds of certain concepts, the groundwork is set for them to fill in these verbal labels with rich content through play and direct instruction later in school.

For the home and school to create a "conspiracy on behalf of children," to use a common expression within the Yale Child Study Center's School Development Program (Comer, Haynes, Joyner, & Ben-Avie, 1996), both the educators and family members need to learn not only the ideational content of these concepts. Educators and parents also need to learn how these concepts provide a rhythm to the week, month, and year. They also need to experience, along with the children, how everyday activities commonly considered to be secular may become laden with meaning when viewed through the lens of Jewish thought; hence the importance of professional development for educators and parent education.

The key difference between Jewish early childhood education and Universal Pre-K is the implication of the educative process for the families. Even from the beginning of the rapid growth in early childhood programs in the United States following the close of World War I, children's play was not the only educational purpose of early childhood programs. During this period at the Yale Child Study Center, Arnold Gesell established a program that was to serve as a model. Gesell's articulation that children's behavior develops in a patterned way, through predictable stages (e.g., the "terrible twos") still resonates with many parents today. In 1924, Gesell wrote, "Should the nursery school become a thinly disguised day nursery for the custody of children, its future is doubtful." Rather, Gesell advocated that early childhood education should become "an educational adjunct to the home for the instruction and guidance of parents and ultimately for pre-parental training" (Ames, 1989, p. 134). The US Economic Opportunities Act of 1964, which launched Head Start, was designed to help children overcome the deprivation caused by poverty. Josh Kagan (2002), New York University School of Law, explains that "Civil rights activists and academics united behind Head Start, both hoping that it would lead to some kind of reform of public education and involve parents more productively than typical public schools" (p. 517). For some schools, parents are important to the extent that their involvement strengthens the education of the child. Parents are asked to help out in the classroom, serve on a Parent-Teacher Organization, or are consulted when a problem arises with a child. While these can be warm and welcoming communities, their explicit agenda and approach does not focus on meeting the needs of parents. Other schools are family-centered where the families, and not just the child, are viewed as part of the educational vision and goals. For example, a family-centered school might provide to parents: learning and support on areas of interest or need and opportunities for building relationships and community with peers. Thus, the Jewish community, primarily due to concerns regarding Jewish continuity, views JECE as an effective lever for involving parents in the life of the JECE program and thereby for impacting their engagement in Jewish life. For this reason,

JECE schools may intentionally engage and facilitate the learning and growth of parents both as parents and as adults.

JECEI's work in the field demonstrates the importance of providing families with rich Jewish learning that challenges them intellectually and connects to their emotional lives as parents. Moreover, families benefit when JECE provides them with a sense that they are part of a community of Jewish families that learn and celebrate together and support each other in times of need. To this list, the Yale Child Study Center and JECEI would advocate that parents become partners in education. This is most effectively accomplished by developing governance and management structures that function well when family involvement is seen as far more than "something nice to do." Rather, parents-as-partners is at the core of the school enterprise. With effective governance and management structures, families become engaged in promoting the well-being of all the children in the school, and not just that of their own children. One such structure is the School Planning and Management Team—an umbrella committee that coordinates all the initiatives bombarding the school, often with mutually exclusive goals. The School Planning and Management Team is comprised of families, school administrators, educators, community representatives, and all those who have a stake in the life success of the children. The School Planning and Management Team and other school structures are described in Comer, Joyner, and Ben-Avie (2004).

Research and experience in educational and organizational change point toward several key factors that are characteristic of successful change efforts. Through setting up governance and management structures to anticipate and manage change, the collective energies of JECE will not be diffused by putting out one fire after another. To make these governance and management structures function well, learning and development cannot be limited to only the children. Administrators, educators, and families need to change the way that they work and interact with one another. The governance and management structures will thereby change the underlying "operating system" of the JECE.

In this manner, the educators in Jewish early childhood programs build school communities characterized by healthy relationships, increased capacity to successfully promote children's learning and development, and passion for Jewish life. The natural outcome of the commitment to creating community through healthy relationships is that families and educators collaborate to influence the lifepaths of the young children.

Outcomes

Goodman, Schaap and Bidol-Padva (2008) administered an inventory to parents who enrolled their children in JECE programs that were affiliated with either the JECEI or Project *Kavod* II, which focused on the work conditions of Jewish early childhood educators. The two initiatives have different goals: JECEI is a long-term initiative that seeks to achieve excellence over a period of 3 or more years in a school and in a community; Project *Kavod* II was an innovative 1-year initiative in the Greater Palm Beach area that engaged the hearts and minds of lay and professional leaders in a joint exploration of Jewish early childhood education. Both initiatives sought to better understand the identity, perceptions, and characteristics of the parents of the children enrolled in the early childhood programs.

The online parent inventory was administered at 7 JECEI Jewish early childhood programs (which had a response rate representing 79% of the families) and at 7 Project *Kavod* II JECE programs (which had a response rate representing 69% of the families). In total, 1,159 completed the parent inventory. On the inventory, the parents were provided with a list of possible reasons why families may enroll their children in JECE programs; they were asked to list their three most important criteria that they used when they selected their children's programs. One would assume that families who are not interested in transmitting the faith culture of the institution would not send their children to an institution that is incompatible with their beliefs. However, location, convenience, and cost are more frequently stated than faith-based beliefs. Hence, the importance of exploring the reasons why parents enroll their children in Jewish early childhood education. On a 5-point scale, ranging from "Not at all important" to "Very important," the most important factor was the quality of the staff and educators (4.88). This criterion was closely followed by the quality of the child development program (4.77). Thus, the original selection criteria were driven by the families' search for an excellent early childhood education for their children.

To discern the Jewish-related criteria of the parents' selection criteria, they were provided with a list of "characteristics" they desired that their children would acquire as a result of enrolling their children in the programs. Jewish areas of learning and development were included in the list of criteria. The two top criteria were related to child development, and not Jewish life. They were the children's development of a strong sense of competence in their abilities as well as the development of strong social skills.

The parents' original selection criteria represented the families' priorities prior to enrolling their children in Jewish early childhood education. Also on the parent inventory there was a section in which the parents were presented with a list of Jewish actions (e.g., attend adult Jewish classes, celebrate Shabbat). They were asked to indicate how often their family participated in the following before and after enrolling their children in a Jewish early childhood program. The average rate of change was computed by averaging the differences of the scores observed over time (that is, the pre-test score was subtracted from the post-test score). The following two items had the greatest rate of change: "Read Jewish books or sing Jewish songs" (0.69); and "Celebrate Shabbat" (0.63). Among the Jewish parents in JECEI educational programs, there was a 28% increase in their participation in parent education programs after enrolling their children.

Does Jewish early childhood education impact the engagement of families in Jewish life? An analysis of the data indicates that this is indeed the case. The analyses also revealed that this is a far more complex process than simply intensifying the Judaic content of the educational program. The key factor is the level of excellence of the JECE program's underlying "operating system." These statements are based on a series of data analyses (e.g., principal component factor analysis, internal consistency reliability analysis, regression). The factor that measures excellence is comprised of the quality rating that the families assign to different aspects of the programs' operation (e.g., "The program is well planned and efficiently run.").

In summary, for many parents the promotion of their children's Jewish identity is not an important criterion when choosing a JECE program. However, if they perceive and experience the JECE programs as excellent and well-run, they will become more engaged in Jewish actions after they enroll their children as a "side effect." This finding has important consequences for how the Jewish community considers its investment and planning for these JECE programs. This finding aligns well with JECEI's premise that a long-term transformative change effort to improve early childhood programs in schools and communities will lead to the families' Jewish connectedness. It is worth considering that the parents who rate that their children's JECE programs operate at a superb level are more open to enhancing their lives with Jewish connections. It is this willingness of families to expose themselves to unaccustomed experiences that marks the initiation of Jewish journeys.

To confirm the finding that the families' ratings of the JECE programs' level of excellence predict, in part, their engagement in Jewish life after enrolling their children in JECE, the scores of the JECEI parents were compared with those of the Project *Kavod* II parents. JECEI's change model focuses on improving the underlying operating system of Jewish early childhood education in a way that Project *Kavod* II did not. The JECEI parents had higher ratings that were not due to chance on the extent to which the program influenced the Jewish part of themselves, the school climate, and the knowledge and skills of the teachers.

Moreover, when comparing the scores of the JECEI families both in-married (two Jews) and intermarried with the scores of the Project *Kavod* II families, the JECEI families had statistically significant higher scores on the likelihood of furthering their children's Jewish education through enrollment in an Israel experience and/or Jewish camp. They also showed greater interest in the possibility of enrolling their children in a Jewish day school. Also, an increase was noted in the engagement in Jewish life of non-Jewish spouses after enrolling their children in JECEI early childhood education. JECEI has a way of reaching out to intermarried families, and it is effective.

Throughout our lives, our understanding about how the world works and our place in the world entwine with our sense of our own emotional and behavioral capacity and habits, as well as with our sense of community (Ben-Avie, 2008). Developmental outcomes of the process of forging a strong relationship with a religious community are framed in terms of thoughts, emotions, actions, and partaking of community (especially through language). A first analysis that was conducted predicted the families' thoughts, emotions, and ways of partaking of community—but especially their actions. The second also predicted the families' thoughts, emotions, and actions—but especially the ways of partaking in the Jewish community. In both cases, the most important predictor dealt with how well the JECE programs function. These findings validate JECEI's approach to change: The most effective leverage for enhancing families' engagement in Jewish life is improving the underlying operating system of Jewish early childhood education.

Creating Excellence in Jewish Early Childhood Education: Standards for the Preparation of Qualified Educators

The most important criterion that parents had when selecting their children's early childhood program was the quality of the staff and educators. One of the concerns from the Tufts study mentioned at the beginning of this chapter was the impact of the large number of educators with limited Jewish knowledge employed in Jewish early childhood education. Studies on educators in JECE (Holtz, 1993; Vogelstein & Kaplan, 2002; Gamoran, Goldring, Goodman, Robinson, & Tammivaara, 1998) noted the lack of professional training in education and/or Judaica. In-service training, while available to most early childhood professionals, was inadequate for addressing sustained change initiatives; the training focused on either Jewish content or early childhood pedagogy. Finding qualified, skilled early childhood educators is difficult considering the low status and the low level of compensation. Finding professionals who are trained in early childhood development, skilled in current best practice, and who are knowledgeable about Jewish customs, practices, and traditions, is extremely difficult—especially in smaller Jewish communities.

The aims of The Alliance for Jewish Early Education include the articulation of a global vision of excellent Jewish early childhood early childhood education and advocacy to establish professional and program standards of excellence (the Alliance is open to any international, national, or communal organization addressing Jewish early childhood education). The Alliance raised the question of what knowledge, skills, and attitudes professionals entering the field of Jewish early childhood education should have. In order to address that problem, the Alliance invited representatives from all the Jewish institutions of higher learning to discuss the feasibility of developing a common course for all professionals entering the field. The goal of the Alliance was to work collaboratively to ensure more early childhood professionals obtained a basic licensing requirement. It is important to note that in 2006 only two Jewish institutions of higher learning were offering courses that integrated Jewish content and values with early childhood development and pedagogy. For non-Jewish educators, in particular, this was a glaring need. So, too, among Jewish educators without a solid background in Judaism.

The representatives from the seven institutions of higher learning developed an initiation course. The course was designed to explore the connection between early childhood settings and the broader Jewish community and the relationship between effective practice and one's own connection to Judaism. By consensus, the following learning objectives were agreed upon:

- Be familiar with current trends and practices regarding the integration of Judaic and General educational practices in Jewish early childhood programs ("blending").

- Understand the principles behind high-quality Jewish early childhood education and reflect on models of high-quality Jewish early childhood programs.
- Identify and understand the network of relationships within the Jewish community that early childhood programs are a part of and brainstorm strategies for developing those relationships.
- Design educationally purposeful environments and experiences that integrate Jewish concepts and content in routine activities that are commonly considered to be secular.

The course was conceived as a stepping stone to entering a degree program at an institution of higher education. In the fall of 2008, the Board of Jewish Education of New York City offered the initiation course to new professionals. In the spring of 2009, the first Jewish CDA graduates received their certificates.

At the same time, as the group was working on the common course, a parallel group was working on the standards for the number and type of credentials expected of early childhood Jewish educators. Up until that point, there was not a national organization that was recognized by all Jewish communities as being responsible for licensing Jewish early childhood professionals. Moreover, there were not standards for the preparation of qualified educators in Jewish early childhood education.

The standards group created five levels to advocate for pay scales that reflect the educators' credential level. For example, Level 1 consists of two courses in Jewish Studies plus a Child Development Associates (CDA) degree or a Jewish CDA. Level 5 is a Masters in Jewish early childhood education or an MA in early childhood education with four graduate level courses in Jewish topics and four graduate level courses in early childhood education.

When we started, in 2001, there were approximately four national organizations or institutions addressing Jewish early childhood education (JECE). Today, there are 23 organizations in North America and Israel that address JECE in some way.

Conclusion

Jewish early childhood education in the United States is at crossroads. JECE could either succumb to market forces in the face of free Universal Pre-Kindergarten or expand. Given that JECE impacts the lifepaths of families as well as the children, an effective leverage for influencing families would be diminished if JECE does not thrive. And to thrive, the quality of JECE's operating systems will need to rise. When a school is constantly operating in a crisis mode, the school community does not have the wherewithal to engage in the type of long-term, global planning that leads to improved learning and developmental outcomes for students and their families. By way of contrast, well-functioning schools focus the full attention of the school community on the learning and development of children and their families.

What is the most effective intervention? Schools revise the curriculum, try to reshape schooling along the lines of the business sector, bring in motivational speakers for drive-by professional development workshops, and implement family education programs. Without governance and management teams that create community, all these different initiatives lead to program fragmentation, duplication, conflict, and the waste of psychological energy. Mandating change—without creating the conditions that would make change possible—is not useful at all, even counterproductive (Comer, 2004). Promoting excellence in JECE takes changing the way people interact with one another in behalf of the children and their families. It is all about relationships.

References

Ames, L. B. (1989). *Arnold Gesell: Themes of his work*. New York: Human Sciences Press, Inc.
Beck, P. (2002). Jewish preschools as gateways to Jewish life: A survey of Jewish preschool parents in three cities. http://www.caje.org/files/PearlBeckHighlights.pdf
Ben-Avie, M. (2008). A moment of developmental triumph! Adolescents in Jewish education. In R. L. Goodman, P. A. Flexner, & L. D. Bloomberg (Eds.), *What we now know about Jewish education: Perspectives on research for practice* (pp. 113–122). Los Angeles: Torah Aura Productions.
Coleman, J. S. & Hoffer, T. (1987). *Public and private high schools: The impact of communities*. New York: Basic Books, Inc.
Comer, J. P. (2004). *Leave no child behind: Preparing today's youth for tomorrow's world*. New Haven, CT: Yale University Press.
Comer, J. P., Haynes, N. M., Joyner, E., & Ben-Avie, M. (1996). *Rallying the whole village. The Comer process for reforming education*. New York: Teachers College Press.
Comer, J. P., Joyner, E. T., & Ben-Avie, M. (2004). *Six pathways to healthy child development and academic success*. Thousand Oaks, CA: Corwin Press.
Dewey, J. (1938). *Experience and education*. New York: Collier Books, Macmillan Publishing Company.
Edwards, C., Gandini, L., & Forman, A. (1998). *The hundred languages of children. The Reggio Emilia approach to early childhood education*. Norwood, NJ: Ablex Publishing.
Fowler, J. (1986). Stages of faith. http://faculty.plts.edu/gpence/html/fowler.htm
Gamoran, A., Goldring, E., Goodman, R. L., Robinson, B., & Tammivaara, J. (1998). *The teachers report: A portrait of teachers in Jewish schools*. Cleveland, OH: Mandel Foundation.
Goodman, R. L., Schaap, E., & Bidol-Padva, P. (2008). *Parent inventory*. New York: The Steinhdardt Foundation.
Haynes, N. M., Ben-Avie, M., & Gilliam, W. (2000). School readiness: Implications for daycare and early childhood education. In C. C. Yeakey (Ed.), *Edmund W. Gordon: Producing knowledge; pursuing understanding* (pp. 91–105). Stamford, CT: JAI Press.
Haynes, N. M., Ben-Avie, M., Ihuegbu, N., Doepper, K., Bukowski, D., & Cavanaugh, T., et al. (2002). *Evaluation of Connecticut's implementation of the U.S. Department of Education's Early Childhood Educators Professional Development Initiative (Project STARS)*. New Haven, CT: Center for Community and School Action Research.
Heschel, A. J. (1951). *The Sabbath: Its meaning for modern man*. New York: Farrar, Straus, and Giroux.
Holtz, B. W. (1993). *Jewish early childhood education*. Cleveland, OH: Mandel Foundation.
Kagan, J. (2002). Empowerment and education: Civil rights, expert advocates, and parent politics in Head Start, 1964–1980. *Teachers College Record, 104*(3), 516–562.
Langer, E. (1994, July). The mindful education. Keynote Address at The Sixth International Conference on Thinking, Massachusetts Institute of Technology.
Mayes, L., & Cohen, D. (2006). The development of a capacity for imagination in early childhood. In A. Martin & R. King (Eds.), *Donald Cohen: Life is with others* (pp. 142–158). New Haven, CT: Yale University Press.

Mindess, M. (2001, August). *Play: The new dirty word. The Brown University child and adolescent behavior letter* (pp. 1–7). Hoboken, NJ: Wiley.
National Research Council & Institute of Medicine (2000). From neurons to neighborhoods: The science of early childhood development. In J. P. Shonkoff & D. A. Phillips (Eds.), *Board on children, youth, and families, commission of behavioral and social sciences and education*. Washington, DC: National Academy Press.
Noshpitz, J. D., & King, R. (1991). *Pathways of growth: Essentials of child psychiatry* (Vol. 1). New York: Wiley.
Pepitone, A., & Triandis, H. C. (1987). On the universality of social psychological theories. *The Journal of Cross-Cultural Psychology, 18*, 471–498.
Schaap, E., & Goodman, R. (2004). *Early childhood Jewish education and profiles of its educators. The number of students and teachers within Jewish education in the United States*. http://www.caje.org/earlychildhood/ec-survey04.pdf
Vogelstein, I., & Kaplan, D. (2002). *Untapped potential: The status of Jewish early childhood education in America*. Baltimore: Jewish Early Childhood Education Partnership.
Vygotsky, L. S. (1978). *Mind in society*. Cambridge: Harvard University Press.

Experiential Jewish Education: Reaching the Tipping Point

David Bryfman

At 8 years I attended my first sleepaway camp. Mixed with the emotions of leaving home for the first time are also the memories of the singing, playing games, having late night discussions, and my first simulation activity—involving a lot of running around at night and stealing flags off the British or some other dastardly enemy of the Jewish people. Ten years later I boarded my first international flight, to spend a year in Israel with the members of my youth movement, some of whom had been there with me at that first summer camp. From a journal entry 1 month into my journey I recounted that "nothing could prepare me for my first time in Israel. There is something about being here, overlooking Jerusalem alongside Agnon, Shemer and Amichai, none of who are unfamiliar to me, that is now bringing out emotions and connections that I never really understood." Jump forward almost two decades and amid conducting my own research, I witness many of the similar learnings, emotions, and connections, but this time in the experiences of hundreds of Jewish youth on yet another continent and in a new millennium.

What I am describing is hardly the unique path of an individual. In many ways it is the ubiquity of my journey that is significant. Experiences like these have provided the most profound moments of Jewish experience and learning for tens, if not hundreds of thousands of Jewish youth. Although the impact of informal Jewish education has seldom been questioned, it has only been relatively recently that some of these key Jewish educational experiences have garnered communal attention and resources on par with other more formal institutions of Jewish learning.

The purpose of this chapter is not to further accentuate the somewhat artificial divide between informal and formal settings of Jewish learning. What I am describing in this chapter, whether it occurs in these formal or informal contexts, is a philosophical and pedagogical approach that bridges both of these settings and is united under the banner of experiential Jewish education. The focus on the group, the role of educator as facilitator, the implicit nature of challenge within these activities, the framing of the experience within a Jewish context, the active engagement of learners in their own learning, and the role of reflection by individuals upon these

---

D. Bryfman (✉)
The Jewish Education Project, New York, NY, USA
e-mail: bryfman@nyu.edu

experiences are just some of the major characteristics which constitute experiential Jewish education. In articulating what it is, and what it can strive to become, it is hoped that this chapter will further elevate the field of experiential Jewish education as one of the most powerful and viable strategies to develop and maintain the positive individual and collective identity of Jewish youth and young adults.[1]

This chapter is written at an important juncture in the development of the field of experiential Jewish education. Depending on one's vantage point, the world of experiential Jewish education has never looked brighter; more communal and media attention, more philanthropic and communal dollars, and more participating numbers all serve as high indicators of success. An alternate view acknowledges that despite the successes of relatively few larger entities, many more grassroots, long-established organizations, along with many emergent informal Jewish educational initiatives, are struggling to find their place in the Jewish communal landscape of the twenty-first century. Regardless of whether one regards the glass of experiential Jewish education to be half-full or half-empty, almost all would agree that despite all that has been achieved more is certainly possible. But unlike many other previous calls to see this type of Jewish education succeed and flourish, the onus within this chapter is placed firmly on the field of experiential Jewish education to take the necessary next steps to reach its Tipping Point, its "moment of critical mass, the threshold, the boiling point" (Gladwell, 2000, p. 12).

Why Informal Jewish Education

Informal Jewish education is pervasive, in terms of both the numbers participating in its various forms and the significant impact that these experiences are having on people. Even so, at the outset of a chapter such as this it remains necessary to articulate precisely what it is that we are discussing. The work of Barry Chazan to define informal Jewish education remains the reference point for all discussions about this topic:

> Informal Jewish education is aimed at the personal growth of Jews of all ages. It happens through the individual's actively experiencing a diversity of Jewish moments and values that are regarded as worthwhile. It works by creating venues, by developing a total educational culture, and by co-opting the social context. It is based on a curriculum of Jewish values and experiences that is presented in a dynamic and flexible manner. As an activity, it does not call for any one venue but may happen in a variety of settings. It evokes pleasurable feelings and memories. It requires Jewishly literate educators with a "teaching" style that is highly interactive and participatory, who are willing to make maximal use of self and personal lifestyle in their educational work. (Chazan, 2003)[2]

---

[1] Although I do believe that experiential Jewish education can and should also be offered to adults, the arguments in this chapter, although applicable to an adult audience (as well as to younger children), are based primarily on my research and experiences with the youth and young adult population.

[2] For a further analysis of the evolution of the term, including the eight characteristics that he considers essential to informal Jewish education, see Joseph Reimer's chapter in this handbook.

Despite the work of a few to discuss the field as whole (Reimer & Bryfman, 2008; Reimer, 2001, 2003a, 2003b, 2007; Reisman & Reisman, 2002; Reisman, 1979), most studies have opted to treat the individual settings where informal Jewish education takes place as discrete entities. Although differing in their levels of short- and long-term impact, almost all research in this domain has found that Jewish summer camps (for example, S. M. Cohen, 1999; Farago, 1972; Fox & Novak, 1997; Joselit Weisman & Mittelman, 1993; Keysar & Kosmin, 2001, 2004b; Lorge & Zola, 2006; Sales & Saxe, 2002, 2004), Jewish youth groups (for example, Ben-Avie & Goodman, 2009), and Jewish travel programs (especially those to Israel) (Chazan, 1994, 1997, 2002; E. H. Cohen & E. Cohen, 2000; Israel & Mittelberg, 1998; Saxe & Chazan, 2008; Saxe et al., 2004; Shapiro, 2006) all contribute significantly to the development of individual and collective identity among Jewish youth and young adults.

In citing these references I fall into the some of the very traps that I am trying to avoid. First, although experiential Jewish education does exist in Jewish summer camps, travel programs and youth groups, it can, and does also exist in a much larger array of Jewish settings, including schools, congregations, and universities. Second, much of the research cited above fails to capture the essence of what these experiences look and feel like, and often assumes that uninitiated readers know of the "magic" or the "wonder" that occurs in many such environments. The scarcity of qualitative research in Jewish education, in general, means thick descriptions of environments where Jewish learning influences the affective, behavioral, as well as the cognitive dimensions of individuals are rare. Where researchers have embarked on more ethnographic portrayals of these environments, especially of Israel trips (Frank, 1996; Goldberg, Heilman, & Kirshenblatt-Gimblett, 2002; Kelner, 2002; Shapiro, 2006), the understanding of these phenomena has been greatly enriched. And third, by drawing attention to specific settings where experiential Jewish education takes place, I further accentuate the fact there is an absence of large-scale meta-analyses that would help us better understand what constitutes the field of experiential Jewish education, what it looks like, and why it should be considered an essential sub-field of Jewish education.

Recently, I joined a virtual Jewish community in cyberspace. There I was able to learn and experience Jewish life in a way that is presumably foreign to many. My avatar can light Shabbat candles, float on the Dead Sea, and participate in a Passover Seder. As more iterations of experiential Jewish education continue to evolve, the adage of "you know it when you see it," if it was ever adequate, is an increasingly insufficient starting point for many related discussions. In providing an analysis of the field of experiential Jewish education today and what remains its greatest challenges, I hope to show that experiential Jewish education exists in many different types of settings, that its powerful essence can be conveyed, and that it justifies the stature which it has achieved to date in certain domains and will continue to develop more broadly in the future. To do so, this chapter begins by providing a comprehensive definitional approach to what experiential Jewish education is and what it is not.

Reaching the Tipping Point

Almost 10 years after Malcolm Gladwell's (2000) "The Tipping Point" was first released and found its way onto many Jewish bookshelves and conference schedules, it is my contention that despite some major inroads, the development of considerable momentum and even achieving some major accomplishments, experiential Jewish education has yet to reach its point of peak success. For this to occur a few major things need to occur, none of which are insurmountable for a Jewish community whose agenda continues to be dominated by a determination to promote and preserve Jewish identity.

I come to this conclusion largely because of some Jewish educational experiences; specifically, I refer to Birthright Israel (Saxe & Chazan, 2008) and Jewish summer camping (Sales & Saxe, 2002) that have already blazed a trail which the field should be primed to follow. Some might argue that it is because these relatively few larger institutions have attracted unprecedented philanthropic, media, and communal attention, that other smaller organizations have been unable to assert themselves on the communal landscape. However, these signals, along with a mixture of hope and optimism, lead me to suggest that the Tipping Point for what is often referred to as informal Jewish education is not only attainable, but achievable, in the not-too-distant future.

To its detriment, the world of experiential Jewish education is a disparate and decentralized one. Further complicating matters, as intimated above, there is no broad consensus about what the term means and there is disagreement whether or not it even constitutes a field. Nevertheless, my experiences working and interacting with many of the key practitioners, thinkers, and institutions in this domain have led me to the conclusion that, regardless of any technical definition of what constitutes a field, the phenomenon of informal Jewish education does exist and, more importantly, it must be considered an extremely significant force within efforts to promote Jewish identity in the contemporary world.

In order for this growth and acceptance to take place, a radical shift in the way informal Jewish education represents itself needs to occur. A re-claiming of terminology might first appear to be semantic but ultimately is integral as an initial step in this struggle. The term informal Jewish education was initially bestowed upon those Jewish educational organizations that were not schools. Even though some proponents of informal education have attempted to define this term (Chazan, 2003) *informal Jewish education*, by its very label it still describes what it is *not* instead of what it *is*. Re-labeling this enterprise as *experiential Jewish education* better describes the type of learning that is at the essence of this pedagogy: learning that occurs when the mind meets the heart and is translated into actions, whereby learner experience something, reflect upon the experience, and learn from the experience for themselves. As will be articulated throughout this chapter, the terms *formal* and *informal* are relevant in that they describe the settings where Jewish education is taking place, however, it is the term *experiential Jewish education* that best describes the type of learning that is occurring within them—and the term that I will use throughout this chapter to more accurately reflect what it is that is being described.

The bulk of my research and practice over the last 5 years has taken place in youth organizations in North America and Israel, and this is largely reflected in the research and examples upon which this chapter draws. With the addition of the United Kingdom, a region that has contributed somewhat to the literature of informal Jewish education (Rose, 2005), and more significantly to that of informal education in general (Smith & Jeffs, 1990), the examples that I cite largely mirror the global development of the field. While I can certainly attest to the idiosyncratic nature of the various communities and organizations where I have lived and worked, I believe that this chapter reflects the current state of experiential Jewish education, regardless of geographic or institutional boundaries.

As well as outlining the current state of experiential Jewish education, primarily through redefining the "field," this chapter will describe three major strategies that experiential Jewish education must undertake in order both to consolidate its place in the Jewish educational landscape and excel by moving even closer toward its Tipping Point: (1) Developing robust and compelling instruments to measure its success; (2) Creating systematic and comprehensive professional development programs; and (3) Building and maintaining a comprehensive unifying structure (or structures). These are the three major strategies that I believe are necessary for experiential Jewish education to become entrenched as a valued commodity within Jewish communal life. While at face value there may seem to be nothing new about these three strategies, combined they signify major changes taking place both in the Jewish community and in the rapidly changing word in which we live.

Formal, Nonformal, Informal, and Experiential Jewish Education

At the heart of the struggles facing experiential Jewish education has always been the inability to adequately define the phenomenon. It, therefore, remains necessary in a chapter such as this to articulate a meaningful definition and understanding of experiential Jewish education. To assist with these definitions, it is important to look first at how "formal," "nonformal," "informal," and "experiential" are defined in general education.

Formal Education: Within general education, the term *formal education* refers to learning that occurs in a structured system that includes chronological assessment, specific teacher qualifications, and is often government regulated. Formal education has been described as the learning that takes place in "the form of age-graded and bureaucratic modern school systems or elders initiating youths into traditional bodies of knowledge" (Livingstone, 2006, p. 204). Jewish schools, with their core practice often being the transmission of Jewish knowledge and skills, and often characterized by the physical presence of classrooms, trained teachers, and assessment tools, are the paradigmatic examples of formal Jewish education. There is little question that Jewish schools are also sites of Jewish socialization, but until relatively recently their dominant modus operandi was the transmission of a cognitive-based knowledge and skills set. As will be seen later, those formal Jewish institutions that have adopted a more experiential approach to Jewish education and socialization have been able to embrace a more holistic approach to their students' Jewish journey.

Nonformal Education: *Nonformal education* is the deliberate and systematic learning, often with an emphasis on skills, that takes place in less traditional educational institutions (Husén & Postlethwaite, 1994). In a Jewish context these nonformal structures traditionally included Jewish summer camps, youth groups and travel programs. Increasingly several other Jewish institutions, including congregational schools, community supplementary schools and certain aspects of some Jewish day schools, could be classified as nonformal.

Informal Education: The term *informal education* describes the incidental transmission of attitudes, knowledge, and skills (often with an emphasis on attitudes) that occurs through daily lived experiences (Husén & Postlethwaite, 1994; Smith, 1996). In a Jewish sense, this is the learning that a person often undergoes, for example, by participating in Jewish rituals or communal life. It can also refer to the moments of Jewish learning that occur in everyday life outside of the parameters of what are generally considered specifically Jewish contexts or settings.

Nicholas Burbules, in a compendium of articles about informal education, distinguishes between nonformal and informal learning on the basis of the degree of *structure* and the degree of *intentionality*.

> Nonformal education is characterized by some kinds of structure (though different ones from formal educational institutions and processes), and includes some level of conscious intent to achieve learning, whether by overt teaching or other means. Informal education, as I understand it, is more continuous with the activities of everyday life, in which some teaching and learning might occur, but largely in an unintentional and tacit way. (Burbules, 2006, p. 282)

Experiential Education: As will be analyzed further, *experiential education* focuses on the transactive process between teacher and student that takes place within the learning environment and content (Itin, 1999), and that allows learners to directly experience, and reflect upon these experiences, in order to increase their knowledge, develop skills, and clarify personal values (Kolb, 1984). In a Jewish sense, experiential education, as it is described here, is known to take place in summer camps, on trips, in retreat settings, as well as in many day schools. Recognition of this broad scope of possibilities is essential for better understanding experiential education as a philosophy and pedagogy that can occur in multiple institutions rather than in any specific setting.

With these definitions in mind, it is important to recognize that what Jewish education has traditionally referred to as informal Jewish education, is more precisely what the general education world refers to as nonformal education. Specifically, in his seminal piece on the topic, the eight characteristics that Barry Chazan identifies as being essential to informal Jewish education resemble elements that would often be present in many nonformal learning environments (Chazan, 1991, 2003).[3]

---

[3] The eight characteristics that Chazan defined as part of his philosophy of informal Jewish education—person-centered Jewish education; the centrality of experience; a curriculum of Jewish

Experiential Jewish Education

This language is essential as we transfer the discussion to a Jewish context. Informal education refers to the incidental Jewish learning that takes place in everyday life. Formal and nonformal describe the different types of settings where Jewish education takes place. As my colleague Joseph Reimer and I have argued in recent articles, "experiential Jewish education," a term first used by Bernard Reisman (Reisman & Reisman, 2002; Reisman, 1979), is a more accurate and compelling depiction of the educational processes taking place within many different types of Jewish educational institutions today (Reimer & Bryfman, 2008) and it is this *experiential Jewish education* that should also be of greater interest to researchers and educators alike.

To further understand these distinctions and what constitutes *experiential Jewish education*, it is also necessary to examine what is meant by both "experiential learning" and "experiential education."

Experiential Learning: According to Aristotle, "For the things we have to learn before we can do them, we learn by doing them," (Aristotle, 1998). This principle encapsulates much of what the term experiential learning has come to mean especially in contrast to didactic or traditional learning. However, it is important to recognize that not all experiences lead to learning. As David Kolb suggests, four conditions need to be met for genuine knowledge to be gained from an experience:

1. The learner must be willing to be actively involved in the experience;
2. The learner must be able to reflect on the experience;
3. The learner must possess and use analytical skills to conceptualize the experience;
4. The learner must possess decision-making and problem-solving skills in order to use the new ideas gained from the experience (Kolb, 1984).

As mentioned in the description of informal education, experiential learning takes place all the time in the Jewish world. Jews are constantly engaged in unstructured, incidental activities that cause them to analyze, reflect, and learn from their experiences within the broader context of their Jewish identities.

Experiential Education: In contrast to experiential learning where an educator is not necessarily present, *experiential education* necessarily focuses on the transactive process between the teacher and students who are directly experiencing the learning environment and content (Itin, 1999). Experiential Jewish education explicitly refers to the purposeful learning that occurs when an educator and learner interact, and that causes learners to experience something for themselves. To adapt a definition from the Association for Experiential Education, experiential Jewish education can be defined as:

---

experiences and values; an interactive process; the group experience; the "culture" of Jewish education; an education that engages; and informal Jewish education's holistic educator—are still clearly present when experiential Jewish education is done well.

> A philosophy and methodology in which educators purposefully engage with learners in direct experience and focused reflection in order to increase their Jewish knowledge, develop skills and clarify values. (The Association for Experiential Education in Gilbertson, 2006, p. 9)

The key elements of this definition include its focus on the direct experience of the learners and their subsequent focused reflection in order for growth to occur (Dewey, 1938). This type of learning can be considered as diametrically opposed to what Dewey refers to as traditional education or what Paulo Freire vividly describes as the scholar depositing knowledge into the assumed-empty bank accounts of their students (Freire, 1970).

The work of Mihaly Csikszentmihalyi about achieving a state of flow is useful to consider in the context of good experiential Jewish education. According to Csikszentmihalyi, flow describes a person's mental state when he or she is fully immersed in what he or she is doing. In a state of flow, a person's full energy is dedicated to contributing toward the success of the process that the activity offers (Csikszentmihalyi, 1997). When an individual is climbing down a rock face or kayaking down a river, evidence of flow within an individual might be obvious. The challenge for experiential Jewish educators is to create sophisticated programming that can engage learners at such a level of intensity within meaningful Jewish experiences. As Reimer and I have described, it is this element of challenge that often distinguishes education from socialization, primarily because it enables individuals to achieve the state of flow necessary for meaningful and enduring learning to take place (Reimer & Bryfman, 2008).

This lengthy theoretical introduction has considerable implications for the practice of many Jewish organizations. Central to these practical implications is the realization that the false dichotomy between what has been incorrectly labeled *formal* and *informal* Jewish education has largely disregarded the reality of Jewish education today. It is this *process* of experiential Jewish education that should most concern us, rather than the various settings in which Jewish learning takes place.

What We Know About Experiential Jewish Education

Largely focusing on discrete informal settings and programs, there have been very few attempts to synthesize our cumulative knowledge about experiential Jewish education. While some could claim that this proves that the field is not a unified one, or even that there is no field at all, I suggest that this is more a feature of individual researchers being drawn to specific experiences, or of specific philanthropic foundations selecting specific organizations or programs to research. Where meta-analyses have taken place they often highlight many of the common features that exist across settings and institutions and subsequently consolidate these experiences within the broader field of experiential Jewish education (Chazan, 1991; Reimer & Bryfman, 2008; Reimer, 2007).

Perhaps, suggesting that experiential Jewish education is being taken more seriously, there has been an upsurge in the number of research studies that have focused on the impact that specific settings of experiential Jewish education have on individuals. These studies have examined a variety of settings including summer camp (Keysar & Kosmin, 2001; Sales & Saxe, 2002, 2004), the Israel experience (Saxe & Chazan, 2008; Saxe et al., 2004), Jewish youth groups (Ben-Avie & Goodman, 2009; Fishman, 2007; Teenage Research Unlimited, 2006, 2009), and Jewish Community Centers (S. M. Cohen & Blitzer, 2008). Interestingly, there are also some studies that have focused on more typically formal settings, including supplementary schools (Wertheimer, 2009), that have also paid attention to the experiential learning taking place within these environments. A handful of studies have also looked at the relationship between the education taking place within a variety of different settings including one study that looked at the interaction between summer camp, congregational school, and youth group in the lives of Jewish youth in the Conservative Movement (Kosmin & Keysar, 2000).

The variety of research methodologies that these studies have employed is beginning to supply us with an accumulating body of knowledge. Whereas once the dominant research form was survey-based, with many quantitative studies reporting on how many Jews were involved in which programs, a new generation of qualitative studies has elucidated the experiential learning process taking place within these environments. Such methodologies have included ethnographies, open-ended interviews, and focus groups all of which have better contributed to our understanding of what is taking place in these settings rather than who is attending them (examples include Bryfman, 2009; Kelner, 2002; Shapiro, 2006). The ambitious longitudinal study on which Ramah has embarked (Keysar & Kosmin, 2004a; Kosmin & Keysar, 2000) is one of the few studies in the Jewish community that has looked at the long-term impact of experiential Jewish education in such a systematic and focused manner.

Perhaps most significant among all of these studies, especially in terms of research methodology, are those conducted on Birthright Israel. Birthright Israel studies offer the unusual possibility to employ an experimental design that includes a control group. Whereas many other studies are unable to isolate the impact of multiple variables, these studies are designed to identify the impact of a single experience on the identity development of individuals, by comparing those young adults who were accepted on the 10-day journey to Israel with those who were not. While such a design is highly desirable and valuable, it is extremely rare (Saxe et al., 2004; Saxe et al., 2009).

In most instances, when such experimental designs are not possible, studies that have looked at the whole experience of individuals, not just their Jewish influences, are extremely important (Kadushin, Kelner, & Saxe, 2000). Designs that have adopted an ecological systems approach have been able to look at the multiple variables that influence the identity development of individuals (Kress & Elias, 1998; Kress, 1998).

This new generation of studies also highlights the willingness of Jewish Federations and foundations to invest in studies of experiential Jewish education.

While there could always be more research, foundations such as the Avi Chai Foundation (Sales & Saxe, 2002) and the Jim Joseph Foundation (Sales, 2006a, 2006b) have highlighted the important connection between research, philanthropy, and experiential Jewish education in the twenty-first century. Whereas, once, the agendas of these various organizations were disconnected from one another, current economic times, as well as common sense, demand that they work more closely together.

Earlier I claimed that experiential Jewish education has not reached its full potential and that as a field it continues to struggle to gain legitimacy as a powerful and desirable tool to develop positive Jewish identity. Nonetheless, several studies have shown that when experiential Jewish education is successful, there is little doubt that it has tremendous positive impact on the identity development of Jews. However, in the field of experiential Jewish education the gap between successful and less successful educational experiences is large, and therefore it might be more accurate to say that as a whole experiential Jewish education has been unable to assert itself as the equal of formal education that generally demands higher standards of excellence.

The Challenges Before Experiential Jewish Education

The research conducted to date highlights what I consider to be three great challenges that lie before experiential Jewish education: (1) Developing robust and compelling instruments to measure its success; (2) Creating systematic and comprehensive professional development programs; and (3) Building and maintaining a comprehensive unifying structure (or structures) to organize the field of experiential Jewish education. All three of these elements are essential if experiential Jewish education is to reach its Tipping Point.

Developing Robust and Compelling Instruments to Measure the Success of Experiential Jewish Education

> *I am so grateful for being able to do March of the Living. It has been the most meaningful time of my life. The contrast of the tainted Poland with the beauty that is Israel has changed my life.* (Anonymous, March of the Living participant)

Phrases like "I had the time of my life" or "life-changing experience" resonate for many who have been part of powerful Jewish learning experiences, especially immersive experiences including pilgrimages to Poland, trips to Israel, and Jewish summer camps. While educators may beam with pride when they hear such reactions, for researchers such comments are insufficient measures of success. The adage that "we know good experiential Jewish education when we see it" may ring true for many educators within the field, but such measures are increasingly seen as an inadequate measures of success. While there always will be a place for anecdotal evidence, there is also a need to develop more comprehensive mechanisms to evaluate experiential Jewish education.

Better evaluation of experiential Jewish education only will become possible when institutions are better able to articulate not only *what* it is they are trying to achieve, but *why* it is that they are trying to achieve these things. Vision statements must be vivid idealized descriptions of a desired outcome that inspires, energizes, and helps create a mental picture of what each organization ultimately aspires to achieve. It is in relation to these vision statements that the success of organizations must be measured.

I contend that it is largely because of the lack of compelling visions that experiential Jewish educational institutions lack adequate measures of success. Instead of asking if they are moving closer to their ultimate objectives and real purpose, they have focused on measuring whether consumers were satisfied with the services provided or how many people participated in specific programs and activities. Often fueled by funders (foundations and federations alike), these measures seldom reflect what really matters—the learning outcomes and impact of these experiences on the development of identity within individuals.

I am involved in some recent initiatives that are beginning to articulate learner outcomes in experiential Jewish education. Initially, these discussions were based around trying to identify specific behaviors, attitudes, skills, and knowledge that were considered important for learners to achieve in various settings where experiential Jewish education takes place. As these discussions progressed, it was realized that assessing the success of these experiences based on learner outcomes was of secondary importance, compared to the ability to identify what were the major goals and purposes of such education. For example, while knowledge of Hebrew language was considered important as a skill to be able to converse with other Jews, or partake in Jewish ritual life, it was considered more important as illustrative of a learner's connection to fellow Jews and Jewish tradition. While identifying specific learner outcomes (possibly in the domains of behaviors, attitudes, skills, and knowledge) and developing indices within these domains that can be measured remain important, further attention must also be paid to the meta questions of what it is that experiential Jewish education wants to achieve, and why it is uniquely poised to do so.

To be fair, this is neither a critique of individual institutions nor of experiential Jewish education alone, but of the broader field of education in general, and of Jewish education in particular, that has rarely looked seriously into questions such as these, and struggled to address adequately the question of what success in Jewish education should and could look like.

Professional Development of Experiential Jewish Educators

One of the primary obstacles for experiential Jewish education is the inadequate credentials of educators in the field. Without intensive, quality professional development opportunities, experiential Jewish education will remain the domain of energetic and passionate young Jewish women and men whose primary motivation is often to offer today's youth opportunities similar to ones they were able to experience in their younger years. While their enthusiasm is critical, the inability of these educators to adapt their own experiences to contemporary times ultimately ensures that much of Jewish education remains dated and irrelevant for the youth of today. This limited capacity to conceive of new programs and structures is intensified by the fact that most experiential Jewish educators lack the theoretical, philosophical, and pedagogical base that is mandated for many of their counterparts in formal Jewish educational settings.

In many regards the term professional development is a misnomer. Many of the educators in this domain are anything but professional educators, often committing to this work as a summer job, for supplemental income and frequently with little or even no financial remuneration.

However, these realities do not mean that experiential Jewish educators could not and should not undergo intensive and extensive training and development. Some may rightly argue that the success of experiential Jewish education is due to the fact that it has, by and large, been facilitated by young adults who in many instances are not much older than the participants themselves. I would argue that the reliance on youth and enthusiasm, instead of training and professional development, is ultimately damaging to the field as it furthers the argument of critics who look upon experiential Jewish education as being less serious and less significant in the lives of young Jews than those institutions that employ more credentialed educators. I also argue that youthfulness and enthusiasm, and training and professional development, are not mutually exclusive and that a balance needs to be met between these two artificial constructs. Whether we call it professional development, training, hadracha, or capacity building, the suggestion that young people cannot receive ongoing professional development is something that the field of experiential Jewish education must reject. Where organizations have invested in this type of training, the limited data available indicate that a more qualified cadre of experiential Jewish educators has emerged (Sales, Samuel, Koren, Gribetz, & Reimer, 1997). Many key aspects of experiential education can be learned in education schools. Concepts such as constructivist, project-based, and discovery learning all resonate within the framework of experiential Jewish education. The emergence of several academic courses, classes, and programs focusing specifically on experiential/informal Jewish education at various academic institutions—including American Jewish University, Hebrew College, Hebrew Union College, Hebrew University, Jewish Theological Seminary, and less academic programs including the Institute of Informal Jewish Education at Brandeis University, the Machon Le Madrichei Chutz L'Aretz (Institute for Youth Leaders from Abroad), and Melitz— all signal promising changes for the field. But these institutions seldom, if ever, meet together, rarely talk with one another, almost never exchange ideas, and have little consistence in terminology when talking about their work. For the field of experiential Jewish education to advance, these institutions must begin to work together to establish a common discourse surrounding the theory of experience within experiential Jewish education. Not only will this aid in the creation of sophisticated professional development for experiential Jewish educators, but it will also catapult the field to greater heights.

In reality most training that experiential Jewish educators undergo does not occur in university settings or in long-term immersive programs. These programs are lengthy, expensive, and require a commitment far greater than most experiential Jewish youth educators are willing or able to make. As a result, the vast majority of professional training and development that experiential Jewish educators receive is conducted by the organizations within which they work and takes the form of seminars, retreats, and conferences. While undoubtedly better than nothing, these programs are often rushed, poorly resourced, lack expertise and fail to address the fundamentals required to excel in this field. What would be ideal is a combination of long-term professional development programs, internships, followed by ongoing training in the various forms described above.

While many of the elements of such an overall experience might exist they do so in isolation from one another. What would an ideal program to train and develop experiential Jewish educators look like? What knowledge would they need to have and what skills would they need to learn? It is precisely because pieces of this equation exist within various organizations, and have never been brought together, that I am led to a third major challenge that I believe experiential Jewish education needs to confront in order for it to advance—the unification of the field.

Unifying the Field of Experiential Jewish Education

Experience has taught me that just because the field as a whole has not achieved its full potential, this does not indicate a lack of success within the field. In fact the very opposite might be the case, with successful organizations able to grow and develop at the expense of other institutions. Accordingly, I prefer to adopt the paradigm that ultimately the sum of the parts will indeed lead to a greater whole.

The current global economic crisis has brought about several significant changes in the Jewish non-profit world that were perhaps inevitable and even necessary. In order better to advocate for the field of experiential Jewish education, a more collaborative venture needs to be launched.

However, juxtapose this belief with the reality that North American Jewry is seeing the decline of several national organizations—specifically those related to Jewish education—and the thought of more umbrella-type organizations may seem far from reality.[4] Nevertheless, networking and collaboration remains essential as processes that can only take place within forums that work together to advance the field as a whole.

The unification of the field of experiential Jewish education today will necessarily look very different to how it was previously conceived. A few central elements necessary for the field to advance could include—the establishment of a national (or international) body, credentialed status to become a member of the field, a

---

[4]Specifically, I refer to the demise of JEXNET, the Network for Experiential Jewish Youth Education (formerly the NAA (the National American Alliance for Jewish Youth), an organization that existed solely to advance the cause of experiential Jewish education. I also point to the collapse of CAJE (Coalition for the Advancement of Jewish Education) and recent media reports that point to the struggles of many other national Jewish organizations.

recognized conference that brings together practitioners and researchers, and a journal (academic or otherwise) that serves to promote both research and practice. Other elements would also emerge, some consistent with other sub-fields of Jewish education and others unique to experiential Jewish education.

Unlike other models of national organizations in their first iteration, this new unifying model for experiential Jewish education will be one that shares, develops, and cultivates expertise. It will necessarily utilize the principles of the Web 2.0 society in which we live, both as an organizing principle and as a means of interaction. Although initially conceived as a web-design principle, the concept of a Web 2.0 world now refers to a broader understanding of the way people live and interact with one another, both as consumers and generators of information in a collaborative and democratized fashion. As an organizing principle, a unifying body designed with Web 2.0 principles in mind will harness the wisdom of hundreds, if not thousands of experiential Jewish educators to advance the field (Surowiecki, 2005). The conventional wisdom that a few experts will be able to promote and advocate for the field is a relic of the past. This new model elevates the role of practitioner to expert— or at least as one of many experts—whose accumulated knowledge will be utilized to promote, advance, and advocate for the field of experiential Jewish education. In this way, those in the field, together with researchers and academicians, would be able to generate what it would take toward better understanding both evaluation and professional development within the field of experiential Jewish education.

Such a body will rely almost certainly on new technologies, especially those that utilize social networking capabilities to advance its cause. As Clay Shirky, a consultant on the impact of interactive media in society, indicates, this new technology will both serve to gather information and also enable new kinds of groups, like the one I am suggesting, to form (Shirky, 2009). Currently, this technology is fairly dispersed and unmonitored, but I am suggesting that a unified body would be able to utilize the technologies of today and tomorrow, and with vision and direction, be able to harness the collective power to advance the field of experiential Jewish education and achieve the force necessary for the field to climb to its summit. Without such a unified effort, it is difficult to conceive of a time whereby experiential Jewish education will be able to forge ahead as a field. Without such efforts, the result will be multiple institutions, across various informal Jewish settings, doing their own thing, resembling the status quo, and unable to grow and develop the field of experiential Jewish education to its full potential.

Reaching the Tipping Point of Experiential Jewish Education

In the introduction to this chapter I posited that experiential Jewish education was at a crossroads. Despite my personal optimism, I do not believe it contradictory or alarmist to suggest that the very existence of many experiential Jewish educational programs and institutions might also be at risk. To avoid such doomsday scenarios, those within the field must take proactive measures by implementing the three key strategies I articulated as necessary for the field to reach its Tipping

Point: (1) Developing robust and compelling instruments to measure its success; (2) Creating systematic and comprehensive professional development programs; and (3) Building and maintaining a comprehensive unifying structure (or structures). All of these must become key features that will demonstrate that further investment in experiential Jewish education is warranted.

In this chapter we have seen that the efforts to define *experiential Jewish education* are far greater than a semantic endeavor. By better understanding what experiential Jewish education is, we move a lot closer to realizing why it is such a powerful force within the Jewish community, specifically in the development of positive Jewish identity. That being said, it is also important to suggest that another key indicator of its success will be realized when experiential Jewish education has become so entrenched within the fabric Jewish life that articles and chapters defining and explaining the field will become obsolete.

As educators we anticipate that better quality experiences will have a greater stickiness factor—in that they will be successful because they have an enduring impact (Heath & Heath, 2007). Furthermore, we believe that participation in more meaningful Jewish activities will have a greater positive impact on identities and will lead to greater rates of participation and engagement in Jewish life. While these assumptions are difficult to prove they remain ingrained among those who consider experiential Jewish education to be one of the most powerful, if not the most powerful tool available today—to foster positive personal Jewish identity, to develop a collective sense of belonging to the Jewish people, and to enhance a deep-rooted commitment to making the world a better place in which to live. The struggle to convey this core message remains one of the greatest challenges confronting the field of experiential Jewish education today.

Future Research Agenda

This chapter does not attempt to provide a meta-analysis of experiential Jewish education. However, highlighting some of the recent studies conducted within this field, it focuses attention on several of the issues in experiential Jewish education that require further research and analysis. I suggest the following research projects as being important steps in both uniting and advancing the field of experiential Jewish education:

(a) A compendium of case studies of experiential Jewish education.
(b) Development of instruments capable of evaluating the outcomes, impact, and success of experiential Jewish education.
(c) Compilation of theoretical research that constitutes the literature necessary to understand experiential Jewish education.
(d) An analysis of current professional development programs and opportunities for experiential Jewish educators that enables the field to identify what gaps exist in this arena. Such a study should also focus on those professional development programs that exist in the general field of experiential education and

related fields. In doing so, such an analysis would also enable the formulation of appropriate opportunities that are currently not being offered to experiential Jewish educators.
(e) Investigation of what creativity and innovation look like in the field of experiential Jewish education, so that organizations can remain relevant.
(f) Conducting more longitudinal studies that look at the long-term impact of experiential Jewish education, even though it will be difficult to isolate the impact of specific experiences on the identity development of individuals.
(g) For the sake of unifying the field, more meta-analyses need to be carried out, bringing together disparate organizations and programs so that a more comprehensive discourse surrounding the field can emerge.

A great deal of what we can learn about experiential Jewish education already exists in other fields—whether it be general education, business, sociology, or psychology, to name but a few. Certainly, much can also be learned by looking at examples outside of Jewish contexts. It also goes without saying (especially in an *International Handbook of Jewish Education*) that this research should not be restricted to North America or Israel. Experiential Jewish education should know no geographic boundaries; and the broader the insights, the richer the field will become.

References

Aristotle. (c.350 B.C.E/1998). *Nicomachean ethics* (D. Ross, Trans.). London: Oxford University Press.
Ben-Avie, M., & Goodman, R. L. (2009). Learning About Youth Development from the NFTY Survey.
Bryfman, D. (2009). *Giving Voice to a Generation: The Role of the Peer Group in the Identity Development of Jewish Adolescents in the United States.* Unpublished Ph.D thesis, New York University, New York.
Burbules, N. C. (2006). Self-educating communities: Collaboration and learning through the internet. In Z. Bekerman, N. C. Burbules, & D. Silberman-Keller (Eds.), *Learning in places: The informal education reader*. New York: Peter Lang Publishing.
Chazan, B. (1991). What is informal Jewish education? *Journal of Jewish Communal Service, 67*(4), 300–308.
Chazan, B. (1994). *The Israel trip: A new form of American Jewish education in Youth trips to Israel*. New York: Jewish Educational Services of North America (JESNA).
Chazan, B. (1997). *Does the Teen Israel experience make a difference?* New York: Israel Experience Inc.
Chazan, B. (2003). The Philosophy of Informal Education. *The Encyclopedia of Informal Education* Retrieved September 1, 2006, from www.infed.org/informaleducation/informal_jewish_education.htm
Chazan, B. (Ed.). (2002). *The Israel experience: Studies in Jewish Identity and youth culture*. Jerusalem: Andrea and Charles Bronfman Philanthropies.
Cohen, E. H., & Cohen, E. (2000). *The Israel experience*. Jerusalem: Jerusalem Institute for Israel Studies.
Cohen, S. M. (1999). Camp Ramah and adult Jewish identity. In S. Dorph (Ed.), *In Ramah: Reflections at fifty: Visions for a new century*. New York: National Ramah Commission.
Cohen, S. M., & Blitzer, L. (2008). *Jewish teenagers and their engagement with JCCs*. New York: Florence G. Heller-JCC Association Research Center.

Csikszentmihalyi, M. (1997). *Finding flow: The psychology of engagement with every day life* (1st ed.). New York: Basic Books.

Dewey, J. (1938/1998). *Experience and education.* New York: The Macmillan Company.

Farago, U. (1972). *The Influence of a Jewish Summer Camp's Social Climate on the Campers' Identity* Unpublished doctoral dissertation, Brandeis University, Waltham, MA.

Fishman, S. B. (2007). Generating Jewish connections: Conversations with Jewish teenagers, their parents, and Jewish educators and thinkers. In J. Wertheimer (Ed.), *Family matters: Jewish education in an age of choice.* Waltham, MA: Brandeis University Press.

Fox, S., & Novak, W. (1997). *Vision at the heart: Lessons from Camp Ramah on the power of ideas in shaping educational institutions.* Jerusalem: The Mandel Institute and The Council for Initiatives in Jewish Education.

Frank, N. L. (1996). *Adolescent Constructions of Jewishness: The Nesiya 1988 Summer-Trip to Israel.* Unpublished Ed.D Thesis, Harvard University.

Freire, P. (1970). *Pedagogy of the oppressed.* New York: Seabury Press.

Gilbertson, K. (2006). *Outdoor Education: Methods and Strategies.* Champaign, IL: Human Kinetics.

Gladwell, M. (2000). *The tipping point how little things can make a big difference* (1st ed.). Boston: Little, Brown.

Goldberg, H., Heilman, S., & Kirshenblatt-Gimblett, B. (2002). *The Israel experience: Studies in Jewish identity and youth culture.* New York: The Andrea and Charles Bronfman Philanthropies.

Heath, C., & Heath, D. (2007). *Made to stick: Why some ideas survive and others die.* New York: Random House.

Husén, T., & Postlethwaite, T. N. (1994). *The international encyclopedia of education* (2nd ed.). Oxford, New York: Pergamon.

Israel, S., & Mittelberg, D. (1998). *The Israel Visit— Not Just for Teens: The Characteristics and Impact of College-age Travel to Israel*: Waltham, MA: The Maurice and Marilyn Cohen Center for Modern Jewish Studies, Brandeis University.

Itin, C. M. (1999). Reasserting the philosophy of experiential education as a vehicle for change in the 21st century. *The Journal of Experiential Education, 22*(2), 91–98.

Joselit Weisman, J., & Mittelman, K. S. (1993). *A Worthy use of summer: Jewish summer camping in America.* Philadelphia: National Museum of American Jewish History.

Kadushin, C., Kelner, S., & Saxe, L. (2000). *Being a Jewish teenager in America: Trying to make it.* Waltham, MA: The Maurice and Marilyn Cohen Center for Modern Jewish Studies, Brandeis University.

Kelner, S. (2002). *Almost Pilgrims: Authenticity, Identity and the Extra-Ordinary on a Jewish Tour of Israel.* Unpublished Dissertation, City University, New York.

Keysar, A., & Kosmin, B. A. (2001). *The camping experience, 19995–1999: The impact of Jewish summer camping on the conservative high school seniors of the "Four up study".* New York: National Ramah Commission, Inc. of The Jewish Theological Seminary.

Keysar, A., & Kosmin, B. A. (2004a). *"Eight up": The college years.* New York: Ratner Center for the Study of Conservative Judaism, The Jewish Theological Seminary.

Keysar, A., & Kosmin, B. A. (2004b). *Research findings on the impact of Camp Ramah.* New York: National Ramah Commission, Inc. of The Jewish Theological Seminary.

Kolb, D. A. (1984). *Experiential learning: experience as the source of learning and development.* Englewood Cliffs, NJ: Prentice-Hall.

Kosmin, B. A., & Keysar, A. (2000). *"Four up": The high school years, 1995–1999.* New York: The Jewish Theological Seminary.

Kress, J. S. (1998). *An Ecological Approach to Understanding Jewish Identity Development in Adolescence.* Unpublished Ph.D thesis, Rutgers, The State University of New Jersey.

Kress, J. S., & Elias, M. J. (1998, Summer). It takes a Kehilla to make a Mensch: Building Jewish identity as part of overall identity. *Jewish Education News, 19*, 20–24.

Livingstone, D. W. (2006). Informal learning: Conceptual distinctions and preliminary findings. In Z. Bekerman, N. C. Burbules, & D. Silberman-Keller (Eds.), *Learning in places: The informal education reader.* New York: Peter Lang Publishing.

Lorge, M. M., & Zola, G. P. (Eds.). (2006). *A place of our own: The rise of reform Jewish Camping*. Tuscaloosa, AL: University of Alabama Press.

Reimer, J. (2001). Jumping into the currents: The art of informal Jewish education. *Shma, 31*, 582.

Reimer, J. (2003a). A Response to Barry Chazan: The Philosophy of informal Jewish Education [Electronic Version]. Retrieved August, 13, 2004, from http://www/jafi.org.il/edcuation/moriya/newpdf/Chazan.pdf

Reimer, J. (2003b). *Getting From Good to Excellent in Informal Jewish Education*. Retrieved October, from http://www.brandeis.edu/ije/pdfs/papers/GettingfromGood.pdf

Reimer, J. (2007). Beyond more Jews doing Jewish: Clarifying the goals of informal Jewish education. *Journal of Jewish Education, 73*(1), 5–24.

Reimer, J., & Bryfman, D. (2008). What we know about experiential Jewish education. In R. Goodman, P. Flexner, & L. Bloomberg (Eds.), *What we now know about Jewish education*. Los Angeles: Torah Aura.

Reisman, B. (1979). *The Jewish experiential book: The quest for Jewish identity*. New York: Ktav Pub. House.

Reisman, B., & Reisman, J. I. (2002). *The new Jewish experiential book* (2nd ed.). Jersey City, NJ: KTAV Pub. House.

Rose, D. (2005). The World of the Jewish Youth Movement [Electronic Version]. Retrieved June 12, 2008, from www.infed.org/informaljewisheducation/jewish_youth_movements.htm

Sales, A. L. (2006a). *Mapping Jewish education: The national picture*. San Francisco: Jim Joseph Foundation.

Sales, A. L. (2006b). *Philanthropic lessons from mapping Jewish education*. San Francisco: Jim Joseph Foundation.

Sales, A. L., Samuel, N., Koren, A., Gribetz, M., & Reimer, J. (1997). *Mapping professional development for Jewish educators*. Waltham, MA: The Fisher-Bernstein Institute for Jewish Philanthropy and Leadership at Brandeis University.

Sales, A. L., & Saxe, L. (2002). *Limmud by the lake: Fulfilling the educational potential of Jewish Summer camps*. New York: The Avi Chai Foundation.

Sales, A. L., & Saxe, L. (2004). *How goodly are thy tents: Summer camps as Jewish socializing experiences*. Lebanon, NH: Brandeis University Press in association with The Avi Chai Foundation, published by University Press of New England.

Saxe, L., & Chazan, B. (2008). *Ten days of birthright Israel: A journey in young adult identity*. Waltham, MA: Brandeis University Press.

Saxe, L., Kadushin, C., Hecht, S., Rosen, M., Phillips, B., & Kelner, S. (2004). *Evaluating birthright Israel: Long- term impact and recent findings*. Waltham, MA: The Maurice and Marilyn Cohen Center for Modern Jewish Studies, Brandeis University.

Saxe, L., Phillips, B., Sasson, T., Hecht, S., Shain, M., & Wright, G., et al. (2009). *Generation birthright Israel: The impact of an Israel experience on Jewish identity and choices*. Waltham, MA: Maurice & Marilyn Cohen Center for Modern Jewish Studies.

Shapiro, F. L. (2006). *Building Jewish roots: The Israel experience*. Montreal and Kingston: McGill-Queen's University Press.

Shirky, C. (2009). *Here comes everybody: The power of organizing without organizations*. New York: Penguin.

Smith, M. K. (1996). Non-formal education [Electronic Version]. Retrieved January 20, 2009, from http://www.infed.org/biblio/b-nonfor.htm

Smith, M. K., & Jeffs, T. (1990). *Using informal education: An alternative to casework, teaching, and control?* Milton Keynes, England; Philadelphia: Open University Press.

Surowiecki, J. (2005). *The wisdom of crowds*. Harpswell, ME: Anchor.

Teenage Research Unlimited. (2006). New Survey [Electronic Version]. Retrieved July 10, 2008, from http://bbyo.org/index.php?c=529&kat=Press+Release

Teenage Research Unlimited. (2009). BBYO Program Impact: Jewish Connection Among Alumni.

Wertheimer, J. (2009). *Schools that work: What can we learn from good Jewish supplementary schools 2009*. New York: AVI CHAI Foundation.

Gender: Shifting from "Evading" to "Engaging"—Gender Issues and Jewish Adolescents

Shira D. Epstein

Introduction: Gender as a "Hot Topic" in Jewish Education

In recent years, "gender" has emerged as a prism through which Jewish educators discuss adolescents and Jewish identity, communal participation, and programming. Several Jewish organizations and journals have recently spotlighted this area of focus: the Union for Reform Judaism sponsored a symposium on gender and Jewish education as a pre-conference to its 2007 Biennial Convention and dedicated an issue of *Torah at the Center* to this topic, and The Lookstein Center's Spring 2008 issue of *Jewish Educational Leadership* and the February 2009 issue of *Sh'ma: A Journal of Jewish Responsibility* have each utilized gender and Jewish education as its theme. The category of gender and Jewish education has a wide scope that spans a spectrum of topics. Some practitioners and researchers focus on implications for schooling, such as learning differences between boys and girls (Goldberg & Gurian, 2007; Tannenbaum, 2008), gendered reading of Jewish text (Reimer, 2007), and assumptions about adolescent male learners (Baker, 2009). Others have championed educational initiatives on gender and sexual identity (Brill, 2007), sexuality, and healthy relationship building (Epstein, 2007; Grumet, 2008; Seidler-Feller, 2009), as well as staff development and training for Jewish youth practitioners (Benjamin, 2007; Epstein, 2008a). The diversity of topics indicates an emergent desire to address the concerns of teen participants within both formal and informal learning settings.

Gender issues also serve in educational circles as a lens through which adults express anxieties about disruption in teens' active participation in Jewish life. Many have underscored a crisis in male adolescent Jewish communal involvement (Fishman & Parmer, 2008; Saxe & Kelner, 2001; Saxe, Kelner, Kadushin, & Brodsky, 2000) and disconnection to formal and informal Jewish education (Kuriloff & Reichert, 2009; Meyer, 2009; Pollack, 2007; Sax, 2007). Others have used the phrase *at risk* to describe Jewish girls, accentuating the prevalence of destructive

S.D. Epstein (✉)
Jewish Theological Seminary, New York, NY, USA
e-mail: shepstein@jtsa.edu

experiences such as disordered eating or sexual violence and the potential impact of such experiences on girls' desire to engage in intimate relationships (Altmann, 2008; Shalom Bayit, 2007). In response, there has been a heightened interest in utilizing Jewish content as a means for discussing gender issues (e.g., Adelman, Feldman, & Reinharz, 2005) and fostering adolescent resiliency (Goldfein, 2005; Steiner-Adair & Sjostrom, 2008).

This chapter will discuss the various initiatives that have stemmed from recent attention to the topic of Gender and North American Jewish Education, highlighting curricula, professional development and educator training programs, and research studies. The discussion begins with further consideration of why gender has become a topic of focus in Jewish adolescent education.

A Social Constructivist Approach to Gender

Although practitioners often utilize the terms "gender" and "sex" interchangeably, they are not transposable terms (Glasser & Smith, 2008). In contrast to "sex," which connotes the biological definition ("male" or "female"), "genders" are actively constructed, and continuously reconstructed, through interactions in context–specific surroundings (Crawford & Unger, 2000; Mac an Ghaill, 1994; Phoenix, Frosh, & Pattman, 2003). Gender rules and behavioral norms are discursively developed and accepted in social institutions (Biklen & Pollard, 2001; Butler, 1999). Gender is viewed as an "ongoing process" (Thorne, 2005, p. 61), through which young people continuously learn how to perform socially defined expectations. For example, the gendered norms for dressing like a "girl" are vastly different in an ultra-Orthodox school than in a public school setting, and attitudes toward what qualifies in a Jewish youth group as a male-specific prayer ritual will vary according to denominational context. In both these examples, adult-developed policies shape what institutions accept as "male" or "female" behavior.

Adolescents and Gender Roles

A social constructivist perspective toward adolescence and gender makes visible the ways in which educators have attempted to correct perceived deviations from predefined expectations. "Gender" serves as a trope for adult anxieties about preparation of youth for future familial duties, and educational policies become conduits for maintenance of traditional roles. For example, during the early twentieth century psychologist G. Stanley Hall successfully advocated innovative initiatives such as all boys' school sports programs and male-run student government as a means to countering the fear that increased female presence in public schooling was depleting boys' virility. Engagement in physical and civic pursuits would conserve male sexual energy, and activities for girls such as domestic science classes and cheerleading would counterbalance intellectual activity, which he believed diluted reproductive organ functions (Hall, 1904). Hall and his supporters asserted that these school reforms would solve the problem of "at-risk" adolescents, who were being led astray by their libidos, "sexually charged beings who needed...focus" (Lesko, 2001, p. 49). The reforms would ensure that teens' sexual energy would be conserved for procreation.

While the initial purpose behind cheerleading, school sports, student government, and domestic science has transformed, their genesis highlights how educational interventions can be impacted by concerns regarding teens' ability to fulfill expected family roles (Epstein, 2009a). Curricula that favor discussion of puberty solely as a process of preparing the body for procreation can delimit honest discussion about adolescent experience of emerging sexuality and desire.

Views of Adolescent Sexuality, Gender Identity, and Sex Education

Current discourse of sexually "at-risk" youth reflects a desire to contain and control adolescents' discussions about intimacy. In recent years, popular American media has reported what has been perceived as an epidemic of meaningless teen sex and in Jewish circles, of promiscuity at *b'nei mitzvah* parties (Flanagan, 2006). This perspective positions teens as a bundle of out-of-control hormones (Lesko, 2001) that need to be reigned in through educational initiatives that preach against premarital sex, such as the popular American sexual education response of teaching abstinence only until marriage (AOUM) (Fine & McClelland, 2006). However some maintain that an AOUM response serves to uphold an unfounded myth of "lost innocence" (Bogle, 2008; Parker-Pope, 2009; Warner, 2009), as statistics demonstrate that teen sex has declined 6–8% in the past few decades (Eaton, 2008). Others oppose AOUM interventions' confinement of conversations about sexuality to the risks of pregnancy and sexually transmitted diseases (STDs), their omission of discussions about love, friendship, power and sexual violence, and gender identity (Fine & McClelland, 2006; Gilbert, 2004; Rofes, 2004), and censorship of dialogue about resources for teens. Bruckner Bearman's (2005) findings that 88% of those who took "virginity pledges" ultimately engaged in premarital sex and that incidences of unprotected sex were 30% higher than their non-pledging peers call into question the effectiveness of AOUM sexuality education.

Adult labeling of adolescents as "at risk" impacts the range and scale of institutional and curricular initiatives on sexuality (Talburt, Rofes, & Rasmussen, 2004). Educators construct interventions and define solutions *for* teens, rather than viewing teens as having agency to co-create programming and self-reflect (Lesko, 2001; Rasmussen, 2004). Fine and McClelland (2006) found that teens desired sexuality education that allowed for conversation "where we're asked what we think, what we want to know" (p. 326). This perspective can extend to the way educators engage youth on varied gender issues, as opportunities to "imbue both youth and institutions with agency" (Talburt et al., 2004, p. 3) and offer a discourse of empowerment and student voice. It suggests the possibility of creating programming that includes critical discussions about the choices and dilemmas that Jewish teens face. As described below, Jewish institutions have developed initiatives to help teens dialogue about their experiences and utilize Jewish values as a lens through which to discuss gender issues.

Gender Initiatives in Jewish Adolescent Education

Until recently, Jewish educational gender initiatives consisted of a mere handful of formal curricula (Gorsetman, Ament, Hurwitz, & Svirsky, 2005; Novick, 1994). In the past 7 years, organizations have developed a range of youth and professional development initiatives; many of the programs were driven by research advocating programming that encourages teens to talk openly about experiences of and attitudes toward friendship, intimate relationships, power dynamics, sexuality, and their bodies (eg; Brown, 2003; Tolman, 2002). They emphasize the importance of dialogue with Jewish teens, recognizing that young people value "the critical role of caring and supportive adults" (Fine & McClelland, 2006, p. 315) and are based on the premise that behavioral change can occur as discussions take place within a Jewish framework. Below, I highlight current significant contributions to the field of gender and Jewish education.

Curricula as an Educational Response

Scripted curricula's roadmaps of clearly delineated goals and objectives (Doll, 1993; Kliebard, 1986) offer standardized ways for Jewish educators to talk about sensitive subjects. Several Jewish organizations have developed curricula to address "evaded" topics (AAUW, 1992, p. 75): body-image issues, sexuality, healthy relationship building, gender identity, and sexual violence. The curricula interweave skill-building activities and conversations about self-concept, relationships with others, and prevalent "social codes," perceptions of the gender-acceptable ways of behaving in peer groups (Finders, 1997). Scripted curricula offer open-ended questions for the facilitator, e.g., "Are there ever times when you feel pressured by friends to be in a relationship or 'get more experience?'" (Epstein, 2006, p. 28). Many include introductory sections that emphasize the ways in which resources and materials link Jewish content to adolescent concerns; the developers offer ready-made connections for educators between socio-emotional issues and Jewish values (Adelman et al., 2005). Several curricula share common Jewish themes (the initiatives listed below are described in detail later in this section):

- *B'zelem Elokim*: We are created in the image of the divine, are mirrors of the divine, and have a Jewish obligation to treat all with respect (*Beyond Miriam, Foundation for Jewish Camp; Life Values, Yeshiva University's Center for the Jewish Future; Love Shouldn't Hurt, Shalom Bayit; Sacred Choices, Union for Reform Judaism; Yad B'Yad, Faithtrust Institute;*
- *Tzni'ut: Tzni'ut*, the Hebrew word for modesty, is "being confident in your innermost core and wanting to live from that core" (Adelman et al., 2005, p. 86). It

offers a lens for deciding what information to keep private and what to share with others (*Life Values, Sacred Choices*);
- *Supporting Friends:* It is a Jewish obligation to support others in times of need (*Strong Girls, Jewish Women International*). "You shall not stand idly by the blood of your neighbor"—Leviticus 19:16 (*Love Shouldn't Hurt*).

As these three categorizations demonstrate, curriculum developers have utilized Jewish texts and themes as frames for exploration of gender issues within formal and informal Jewish educational programming. I highlight below both coeducational and single-sex programming initiatives that aim to address healthy relationship building with Jewish adolescents, and further describe Jewish values and texts that are incorporated into curricula.

Learning Together: Coeducational Curricular Programming

The proliferation of programming has precipitated a divide on the most effective structure for honest dialogue. Curricula on dating abuse and relationships that foster cross-sex conversation (Orenstein, 1994) are built upon a deep-seated educational view that coeducation can lead to positive changes in power dynamics (Tyack & Hansot, 1992). Three Jewish coeducational programs have taken up the call for sexuality education that teaches about partnership and positive models of relationships (Fine & McClelland, 2006; Phillips, 2000): *Yad B'Yad* (Eliav, 2005), developed by the Faith Trust Institute with the goal of offering a Jewish response to teen dating violence; Shalom Bayit's *Love Shouldn't Hurt* (2007), self-described as the only Jewish dating violence prevention curriculum designed for middle school, high school, and college learners; Jewish Women International (JWI)'s *When Push Comes to Shove...It's No Longer Love* (Arts Engine, Inc (Producer), & Mandel, E. (Director) 2005), launched in 2005 as the centerpiece of its healthy relationships initiative for high school and college students.

The three curricula share the common goal of utilizing Judaism as a lens for discussing healthy relationships and dating abuse. The curriculum designers desire to teach skills for building loving relationships such as communication techniques and methods for respectful disagreement. All three initiatives integrate Jewish texts and themes into activities. *Yad B'Yad* incorporates the Jewish values of *Kavod* ("respect"), *Shalom Bayit* ("peace in the home"), and *Ahavat HaBriot* ("love for all God's creatures") (Eliav, 2005, pp. 7–8), and draws upon biblical narratives (eg., Isaac/Rebecca) and liturgical texts (e.g., *Eshet Chayil*, "A Woman of Valour") to open conversations about power dynamics in relationships and proscribed gender roles. *Love Shouldn't Hurt* (2007) draws upon Jewish values such as *G'milut Chasadim* ("acts of loving kindness") and *Kedushah* ("holiness, related to being created in the image of God"). *Push*'s Discussion Guide (JWI, 2007) suggests text study of the *Purim* narrative to guide discussion on status and power in relationships, and utilizes the Tamar/Amnon (Samuel II) narrative to help participants discuss the prevalence of "victim blaming" in instances of sexual, physical, and emotional violence and abuse.

While data on implementation does not exist, impact of the initiatives is evidenced in partnerships between organizations. For example, in 2008–2009 the Greater Houston National Council of Jewish Women (NCJW) partnered with *Love Shouldn't Hurt* to implement the curriculum in area synagogue schools, and United Synagogue Youth has collaborated with JWI to develop training sessions and a study sourcebook on healthy relationships for its 2009 international convention (Stein, 2009). Such partnerships have elevated discussions and awareness of dating abuse and violence in the Jewish community.

Strong Girls and Good Guys: Single-Sex Curricular Programming on Healthy Relationships

Jewish Women International (JWI) developed three initiatives to help teens discuss relationships and gender roles in single-sex contexts, with the intention of creating safe space for discussion and of tailoring activities to distinct engagement styles and socio-emotional needs of boys and girls (Kindlon & Thompson, 1999; Tyack & Hansot, 1992). Each of the curricula is designed to help Jewish teens explore themes of power dynamics, status, and equality within friendships and intimate relationships (Brown, 2003; Phillips, 2000).

Strong Girls, Healthy Relationships: A Conversation on Dating, Friendship, and Self-Esteem (Epstein, 2006) is a 12-h curriculum for 13–15-year-old Jewish girls that weaves together discussion of intimate relationships and friendships. As the author, I crafted the curriculum upon the premise that "self-esteem stems from self-knowledge" (p. 3), and that empowerment emerges from the ability to express feelings within a supportive relationship. Participants discuss the elements of healthy relationship building, the role of compromise and negotiation within friendships and intimate relationships, and how to support friends who have experienced abuse. Biblical texts (e.g., Hagar/Sarai narrative) are utilized to open up conversations about power and control. I modified the initial curriculum into a 4-1/2-h version for 12–15-year-old girls: *Strong Girls!: Friendships, Relationships, and Self-esteem* (Epstein, 2008b). Participants discuss contemporary definitions of "dating" and explore methods for connecting with their intuition, or "inner voice." The condensed curriculum complements JWI's initiative for 12–14-year-old boys, *Good Guys!: Partnership and Positive Masculinity* (Kaplowitz, 2008), which aims to help participants "understand how to be a positive force and make healthy relationship decisions" (p. 6). Like *Strong Girls, Good Guys* explores issues of power, control, and self-esteem. Participants utilize biblical texts (e.g., Joseph and his Brothers) to consider messages they receive within Judaism around "being a man." The curriculum is contextualized within a framework of "positive masculinity": that "Healthy power is power used to do good; not to dominate or destroy..." (p. 5). As the titles suggest, the curricula address tacit assumptions that "aggressiveness" is a male role, "goodness" is a feminine trait, and that females should adopt responsibility for creating and maintaining healthy relationships within heterosexual partnering (Brown, 2003).

Judaism as a Lens for Making "Holy" Choices

Three initiatives encompass the view that Jewish ethics, values, and traditional texts can promote discussions about sexual choices and desires (Ruttenberg, 2009). Though each originates from differing ideological and theological stances, they share the common message that Jewish tradition can aid adolescents in making challenging decisions about their bodies, sexuality, and relationships. *Sacred Choices* (Novak-Winer, 2007) was designed specifically for Reform congregational schools and camps. In 2008, Tzelem, an initiative of Yeshiva University's Center for the Jewish Future introduced *Life Values and Intimacy Education* (Debow, 2008), which self-describes as the only comprehensive sex education curriculum for Modern Orthodox day schools in grades 3–8. The goal of *Life Values* is to offer a "Torah-framed" (p. 23) discussion of intimacy, sexuality, and love. For example, the curriculum presents puberty in the context of *Hashem's* (God's) way of preparing bodies to be able to have children, and as a pathway to learning self-restraint and control. Likewise, the curriculum teaches that because the physical body houses the soul, pleasure is not an end-goal; *mitzvot* (commandments) are vehicles for elevating sexual experiences to spiritual acts. Sessions include discussion of the centrality of marriage and family to Judaism, *tzni'ut* (modesty) as a concept that guides dress, speech, and restraint in exposure to sexual information and images, and reproduction and infertility.

Like *Life Values* (Debow, 2008), *Sacred Choices* (Novak-Winer, 2007) celebrates the ways in which Judaism can serve as an "antidote"(p. 4) to popular messages and media regarding the immediacy of sexual pleasure; it teaches that our bodies and souls are gifts from God, and that Judaism values mutuality and *kavod* (respect) as core elements in any healthy relationship. The middle and high school curricula utilize Jewish texts to guide discussions about decision making and sexual ethics within friendships and relationships (www.urj.org/sacredchoices). The middle-school modules address the balance between respectful communication and healthy assertiveness, and reflect the Reform movement's stance that middle-school students should not be engaging in sexual relationships. High-school modules explore gender roles and Jewish definitions of masculinity and femininity, and use biblical and philosophical texts to discuss the difference between love and lust.

Educators' widespread implementation of *Sacred Choices* and *Life Values* within their respective denominations' formal and informal youth programs and summer camps has enabled discussions that otherwise might have been evaded. Non-denominational efforts have also utilized Judaism as a catalyst for self-reflection about sexuality. For example, the *JGirl's Guide*'s (Adelman et al., 2005) chapter on "Becoming a Woman" acknowledges Jewish girls' sexual feelings and desires (Tolman, 2002), stating that "The way you feel about sex and sexuality is unique to you...You may begin to have sexual fantasies and desires now...It's all part of experiencing your new womanly body" (pp. 99–100). Resources such as the *JGirl's Guide* provide further entry points for connecting adolescents to Jewish views on gender and sexuality.

Including Adolescent Voices

Prepackaged materials and programs provide valuable resources for Jewish educators. However, curricular interventions can offer a false sense that the few brief sessions have fully explored and changed participants' ingrained behaviors and beliefs. Additionally, the above-described curricula and training programs are premised upon adult-defined understandings of what young people both need and want to know. Recently, however, three Jewish organizations have placed primacy on dialogue with teens about their lived experiences (Darder, Baltodano, & Torres, 2003), asking them to co-imagine and participate in the creation of programming that explores Judaism, relationships, and self-identity. The 14th Street Y, Ma'yan: The Jewish Woman's Project, and Moving Traditions have launched initiatives that emphasize adolescent voice and agency, the latter two shaping programmatic and research agendas.

The 14th Street Y's (http://www.14streety.org) *Girls Theater Project* (GTP) is a developing model for utilizing the arts to facilitate Jewish adolescent girls' exploration of the common issues they face. During its pilot year (2008–2009), a select group of girls participated in weekly workshops with playwright/educator Joyce Klein to explore topics that the girls had suggested, including friends, college, boys, the body, Judaism, and family. Through writing exercises, structured conversations, and dramatic improvisations, the girls shared their views, concerns, and dreams for the future. Klein then incorporated the girls' recorded comments into an original theater piece, titled *Becoming*. Evaluative data (Epstein, 2009b) demonstrate that the girls' discussions included diverse opinions about their connections with religion, interactions with boys, and experiences of competition within friendships. An expanded pedagogy might allow a shift from generating material for adult-written script (Wolf, 1993, 1994, 1995) to teen engagement in joint decision making and co-facilitation of youth theater activities, which Heath (1999, 2001) suggests can help adolescents develop leadership qualities. The 14th Street Y is developing pre- and post-performance workshops to cultivate "exploratory talk" (Barnes, 1992, p. 28) with female audiences about beliefs, experiences, and identity, and deepen the potential for utilizing drama to help girls imagine their "possible selves" (Knox, 2006; Markus, 2006).

Ma'yan and Moving Traditions are developing models through which Jewish adolescents might become agents of change (Gore, 2003). When Ma'yan (www.mayan.org) launched *Koach Banot* (Girl Power) to support Jewish communities seeking to strengthen existing girls' programming, its staff felt that they needed to know more about the ways that girls themselves describe the key issues in their lives. They developed *The Ma'yan Research Training Internship* (RTI), which includes girls in the framing, designing, executing, and reporting of research on Jewish American adolescent girls' experiences and attitudes (Benjamin, 2009). Participatory Action Research (PAR) is used as a means to hear directly from teen girls and "creat[e] a space of shared power and trust, in order to spark dialogue around issues relevant to their lives" (Ma'yan, 2008a), as well as engage the interns in practices of critical reflection, power sharing, and perspective taking. Staff explain that the *RTI* invests authority and power in the interns, "disrupting the usual hierarchical structure of youth programming" and the common practice of "representing girls exclusively through our own lens as concerned adults" (Ma'yan, 2008b).

During its inaugural year of 2007, teen interns and Ma'yan staff designed a study that included the following research questions: *What do we know (or think we know) about American Jewish teen girls? What do we want to learn about them?* (Ma'yan, 2008a). The team designed two original surveys that were distributed to self-identifying Jewish American teenage girls between ages 13–19. The interns analyzed 227 longer survey responses and 85 short-answer survey responses, with the vast majority of respondents 15–17 years of age (Benjamin, 2009). Data suggest that Jewish girls experience intense pressure to meet adults' and friends' expectations to juggle school demands, social life, and extracurricular activities (Ma'yan, 2008a). An unanticipated finding was that surveyed girls are actively engaged in Jewish life and in exploring their Jewish identities, and are committed to taking on leadership roles. The findings suggest several implications for Jewish educators' interactions with adolescent girls. Jewish youth professionals have the potential to interact and engage with Jewish girls (Benjamin, 2009) and "provide a sort of oasis, away from the pressure [of daily life]" (Ma'yan, 2008b). In addition, Jewish girls' desire for leadership roles suggests that adults need to foster opportunities to both explore and practise roles that require power and authority. An intern reported that one survey respondent's note that "We are the next world leaders; if we don't try to help, who will?" suggests the desire for girls to develop leadership capacities through Jewish youth programming (Ma'yan, 2008b).

Ma'yan's initiative demonstrates a paradigm for power sharing with adolescents. According to Ma'yan staff, joint research promotes possibility for "establishing new models for leadership and participation in Jewish youth programs" as "the process was, ultimately, just as important as the finished product" (Ma'yan 2008b). One intern shared, "Other programs, they're basically telling you things. While here, we're like figuring out all these things, find out all the information for ourselves" (Ma'yan, 2008b). Another stated, "We really got to talk about what we wanted to talk about and discuss what we wanted to discuss" Ma'yan, 2008b). A third intern offered an endorsement for adults jointly developing projects that engage adolescents in opportunities to critically reflect: "By focusing on ourselves, and being a little introspective, for a little while, will really help us learn more about ourselves and will make us more effective in trying to apply what we know to the greater world" (Ma'yan, 2008b).

Like Ma'yan, Moving Traditions is offering a new structure for including teens in gender-in-Jewish education research and program development. Moving Traditions launched the *Campaign for Jewish Boys: Where have all the Young Men Gone?* in the fall of 2007 with the goal of better understanding why boys are dropping out of organized Jewish life after Bar Mitzvah age, and examining how to strengthen boys' Jewish identity and encourage connection and commitment to the Jewish community at large (www.movingtraditions.org). Moving Traditions convened the Round Table on Jewish Life and the Development of Adolescent Boys with the University of Pennsylvania Graduate School of Education and the Center for the Study of Boys' and Girls' Lives. A cross-disciplinary group of 26 leaders raised key themes for future exploration. One adult-defined theme, that boys should be involved in the creation of their own programming, was confirmed and reasserted in follow-up research with Jewish boys.

Moving Traditions organized semi-structured focus group interviews (November-December 2007) in Denver with 41 Jewish boys predominantly affiliated to the Jewish community through involvement in their synagogues, Jewish camps, and Jewish youth organizations, as well as 20 parents, and 4 day school teachers (Reichert & Ravitch, 2008). Researchers found that while boys expressed their desire for meaningful Jewish exploration, they were dissatisfied with the offerings available to them. The researchers suggest the need to develop opportunities for boys' agency within the Jewish community: "Jewish boys must be permitted to access opportunities for religious education and cultural connection based on their own determination of their needs" (p. 38). The researchers further suggest that rather than defining for Jewish boys who they *should* be, adults need to create spaces where the boys can feel comfortable exploring who *they themselves* want to become. In addition, the findings suggest that boys desire to collaborate in design, development, and implementation of innovative programming. Findings are being tested in Moving Tradition's current action research and will be reported on in the forthcoming Framework for Working with Jewish Boys. The framework will include research on adolescent male development, a toolkit of effective techniques for working with Jewish boys, including marketing strategies, and a program for 8th and 9th grade boys with six meeting plans, including activities and resources for use across settings and denominations. The program content will enable boys to discuss topics of masculinity and their identities within a Jewish context.

Successful implementation of the types of power-sharing models that are summarized above requires partnering with seasoned adult facilitators. The next section describes professional development and teacher education initiatives designed to foster adult comfort level in addressing socio-emotional issues within both formal and informal Jewish educational settings.

Systemic Change Through Professional Development and Teacher Education

Previous academic discussions about Jewish educators' teaching on relationships, gender stereotypes in Jewish texts, and gendered perceptions of Jewish rituals (Kaplan & Reinharz, 1997) are now resurfacing, as professional development and teacher education initiatives have proliferated to support educators in identifying gaps in knowledge (Epstein & Less, 2009), resistances to addressing difficult subjects in teaching (Fine & McClelland, 2006), discomfort in discussing specific issues (e.g., Tolman, 2002), and resources for expanding pedagogy (Epstein & Less, 2008; Leone-Perkins, 2008). Several organizations have developed training initiatives to support educators in understanding that changes in adolescent practice and growth in understanding are recursive (Lesko, 2001; McLaren, 2003), and require continual discussions that are responsive to learners' needs. The professional development and teacher education projects described below offer space for Jewish educators to examine their practice of facilitating dialogue and learning opportunities with teens on gender and sexual identity, body image, and Jewish identity.

Educator-Training Initiatives to Promote Systemic Change

Recent training initiatives offer possibility for systemic change in the ways that Jewish institutions develop a culture of inclusion and in which youth practitioners build practices of active listening, mentorship and non-judgmental dialogue (Brown, 2003). Their designers acknowledge that deep-seated gender inequities and violent behaviors such as sexual harassment, bullying, self-harm, and abuse cannot be stemmed through institutional policies and penalties alone (Orenstein, 1994). Rather, systemic change can occur through shifts in the ways that schools, camps, youth groups, and synagogue programs mindfully address power dynamics, and cultivate connections between learners as well as between adults and teens. They share messages of empowering educators to take a proactive role in dialoguing with teens, and recognize that the act of "naming" gender-related concerns can lead to deeper conversation (Brown, 2003, p. 223). The five initiatives below offer frameworks for educators to examine their practice of addressing overarching teen issues of body image, self-image and esteem, gender identity, and friendship and relationships, and offer means for reflection on how they respond to gender-related moments that arise in teaching.

Long-term change in teaching practice can emerge from opportunities for educators to "self-audit" and reflect upon how they do or do not facilitate dialogue with learners about the "evaded curriculum" (AAUW, 1992), the delicate subject areas related to gender that are sometimes avoided (Epstein, 2008a). As project director of the Jewish Theological Seminary's initiative *Evaded Issues in Jewish Education*, I co-developed *Educational Jewish Moments* (Epstein & Less, 2009; jtsa.edu/evadedissues). An *Educational Jewish Moment* (EJM) is an "off the page" moment that can arise as Jewish educators hear student remarks, questions, or conversations related to gender issues (e.g., pressure to "hook up"; use of derogatory language such as "slut," "fag," or "bitch"). The *EJM* methodology offers a schema for educators to engage learners in dialogue and make connections to Jewish values and resources, through a four-part methodology:

(1) NAMEing: Identifying key gender issues by asking clarifying questions such as, "What did you mean when you said...?"
(2) SELECTing: Choosing a type of response, such as pausing a formal lesson to talk about what just occurred
(3) CONNECTing: Integrating resources, such as referring to Jewish values or textual sources
(4) INTERJECTing: Considering how to craft the response in a way that feels authentic to the educator

The *EJM* training sessions teach educators to identify moments when they might name aloud connections between Judaism and a wide variety of gender issues with which learners grapple. Other professional development initiatives have focused on educating practitioners on specific issues. The Foundation for Jewish Camp's *Beyond Miriam* (Goldfein, 2005) resource guide for camp directors and the Orthodox Union's *Hungry to be Heard* (Diamond, 2008) documentary-style DVD were developed on the premise that issues such as body image can be systemically addressed when educators are more educated and aware of the prevalence of eating disorders and destructive behaviors such as self-mutilation (i.e., "cutting"). In turn, leaders can develop support systems for adolescents. The guide and DVD both suggest opportunities for demonstrating Judaism's emphasis on *Bezlem Elokim,* that we are all "Godlike." For example, *Beyond Miriam* instructs camp counselors to "create a bunk poster with pictures of each girl and nice things written below describing the many Godlike attributes that each girl possesses" (Goldfein, 2005, p. 35). The two resources emphasize the role that positive messaging can play in shifting the culture and attitude of Jewish institutions around body image-related concerns.

Like *Beyond Miriam* (Goldfein, 2005) and *Hungry to be Heard* (Diamond, 2008), *Kyriya Leshenuyi – A Call to Action for Raising Strong Healthy Jewish Girls* (http://www.bishviliforme.com/index.html) was developed with the goal of initiating systemic change in the ways that adults talk with adolescent girls about their bodies. Jewish educators are familiarized with the resources of *Bishvili: For Me* (Steiner-Adair & Sjostrom, 2008) a Jewish companion guide to *Full of Ourselves* (Steiner-Adair & Sjostrom, 2006). *Full of Ourselves* (FOO) self-describes as effecting positive changes in "girls' body image, body satisfaction, and body esteem, and girls' knowledge about health, nutrition, weightism, and puberty" (xi). *Bishvili* aims to strengthen Jewish girls' body and self-esteem and offer resiliency skills through connection to Jewish values, rituals, and texts. For example, the *Bishvili* compendium asks facilitators to insert the following prayer into an *FOO*-suggested "body appreciation relaxing" guided meditation (2006, pp. 15–16): "We praise you....with divine wisdom You have made our bodies...I will praise you, God, for I am awesomely and wondrously made" (2008, p. 11). Facilitators then ask, "How does connecting your body to God change how you think about and live in your body?" During another exercise, *Bishvili* instructs facilitators to ask girls questions such as, "What are some ways Judaism transforms eating into a holy process?" (2008, p. 4).

Initiatives such as these just described can impact the ways that Jewish practitioners incorporate dialogue about body image; a small-scale study of *Bishvili* revealed its success in increasing girls' connections to Jewish values (http://www.bishviliforme.com/index.html). However, one is not required to participate in training in order to facilitate the *FOO* or *Bishvili* activities. In contrast, Moving Traditions has developed a model for centralized training of all adult group facilitators for *Rosh Hodesh: It's a Girl Thing!* (www.movingtraditions.org) monthly programming for middle- and high-school girls. Leaders of the local groups connect issues such as body image, family dynamics, popularity, and friendships to Jewish values, themes, narratives, and holidays. Since the program's national launch in 2002, it has trained over 650 educators. In a survey of 2007–2008 *Rosh Hodesh* participants, 75% of respondents either agreed or strongly agreed with the statement, "Compared to when I began *Rosh Hodesh* I now…feel more connected to other Jewish girls." Of the respondents, 77% agreed or strongly agreed with the statement, "I feel close to the group leaders" (Goldsmith, 2008). Survey results suggest the key role that group leaders play in fostering a sense of community and belonging within an all-girl setting, offering a contrasting model to what Brown (2003) describes as the stereotype of the aggressive, "mean girl" presented in recent literature (e.g., Wiseman, 2002).

While programs such as *Rosh Hodesh* focus on training practitioners to foster community building, others encourage educators to examine the culture within their institutions. Recognizing that teen sexuality is an uncomfortable and often taboo subject, Keshet Boston (www.keshetboston.org) has launched the *Shalem Education Project* to prepare Jewish educators and youth professionals to be change agents in their institutions, as they learn how to develop and implement action plans for fostering Gay Lesbian Bisexual Transgender Queer (GLBTQ) inclusion and identify resources for support. Educators discuss how the documentary film *Hineini: (Fayngold & Keshet, 2005). Coming Out in a Jewish High School* (2005) can be used as a catalyst for conversation with teens about the boundaries of inclusivity within their own community. They learn how to utilize the film's story of a female student's fight to establish a gay-straight alliance at a Jewish high school in the Boston area to spark dialogue on the possibilities and challenges of embracing pluralism and diversity. The accompanying *Curriculum Resource Guide* (Hammer, Westheimer, & Jacobs, 2008) provides lesson plans, Jewish text study, and resources on GLBTQ issues. Participants explore how to facilitate discussions on the Jewish obligation to stand up for others in times of need and support, what it means to be a "straight ally," and the Jewish value of creating a community that embraces difference.

Impact of Academic Teacher Education Programs

Systemic change in gender and Jewish education can occur when educators are engaged in ongoing reflection on their roles as "responsive educators"—responsive to the questions, concerns, and connections that adolescent learners offer. Research has explored the ways in which Jewish academic preservice programs prepare novice teachers to engage in continuous inquiry about their own teaching and response to gender-related concerns (Barth, 2004). As emerging Jewish educators reflect upon their practice within a community of learners, they consider what Orenstein (1994) refers to as the "hidden curriculum" that often impedes systemic change in addressing subjects such as harassment, bullying, and sexuality in schools: "All the things that teachers don't say, but that you learn in class anyway" (p. 270). What are the cultural messages that they convey through the curricula they teach, the books they assign, the pedagogical choices that they make, and the comments they offer? In addition, they raise questions about the possibilities and limitations of their roles in cultivating student empowerment (Darder et al., 2003).

I have developed Participatory Action Research (PAR) in order to simultaneously inquire into my practice as a teacher educator and support four novice Jewish educators' inquiry into their practice of addressing gender issues with their own learners. The four participants were former students in the course *Perspectives on Gender and Education* (taught at The William Davidson Graduate School of Jewish Education of the Jewish Theological Seminary). Research questions emerged directly from our joint engagement in the praxis cycle of reflection and action on our teaching (Brydon-Miller, 2001; Cammarota & Fine, 2008; Lather, 1991; Weis & Fine, 2000): *What is the role of teacher education in developing the field of gender and Jewish education? How do former graduate students view their developing roles as Jewish educators who address gender issues in their teaching settings?*

I have crafted case studies of the four former graduate students: Kayla, a day-school teacher, discussed the ways in which her desire to launch a Girls Advisory Group for her middle-school female learners was an outgrowth of preservice emphasis on self-inquiry on the ways in which she addresses gender issues (Epstein, 2008a); first-year teacher Adena dialogued about her decision to organize a series of girls-only and boys-only lunches as "interventions" to heightened relational aggression between her second-grade learners; second-year teacher Keren shared the dilemmas she faced in engaging middle-school boys in learning activities; Gabe, a graduating college student, reflected on how our course discussions on dating abuse lead to his integration of conversations about the elements of healthy relationships into his Jewish fraternity's Big Brother-Little Brother program. The study suggests that engagement with "gender and education" in preservice learning helps novice formal and informal educators consider their roles potential roles as change agents in the ways their Jewish institutions address adolescent gender issues (Cochran-Smith & Lytle, 1999; Zeichner, 1994). This is best achieved by simultaneously exploring scholarly work around issues of gender and education and applications to teaching. It is this participation in praxis that leads to tangible changes in the ways gender issues are addressed.

The research suggests that reconstructed approaches to practice (Johnston, 1994) emerge from ongoing professional development on gender and education. Early career educators balance numerous competing pressures and demands and are more apt to address complex issues connected to socio-emotional health and well-being when perceived as imperative, relevant, and inherent to teaching (Boler, 1999; Ellsworth, 1997). In addition, educators need opportunities to examine the broader discourses that tacitly inform their work with adolescents (Thorne, 2005). Structured opportunities to pose questions, seek advice, and engage in collaborative dialogue can enable shifts in the ways that Jewish educators view their role in addressing sexuality, harassment, and body-image issues with adolescents, as well as consider connections to Jewish content. Engagement in praxis enables educators to become change agents in the ways that their Jewish sites respond to the needs of their learners.

Conclusion: Advancement of Praxis-Based Research

The curricula and initiatives described above offer varied lenses for discussing gender and Jewish education, each sharing a common goal of preparing youth to fully engage within the Jewish communal structures of school, synagogue, and informal learning and relationships of family, friendships, and intimate partnership. Many offer occasions for dialogue and reflection, and several cultivate adolescent leadership. Communities of Jewish educators can partner with cohorts of adolescents to develop Participatory Action Research models for researching their institution-based gender practices (Ma'yan, 2008). PAR-oriented studies offer the possibility of continuing to engage both educators and learners in examining established policies and pedagogy, and conduct scans of current support systems and resources for learners. Future studies can continue to investigate what teens want to discuss and the programming they seek to design. Potential adolescent-adult partnership can transform the landscape of gender in education. Within the PAR model, "research findings become launching pads for ideas, actions, plans, and strategies to initiate social change" (Cammarota & Fine, 2008, p. 6). Further research that focuses on praxis can offer an empowerment that, as Gore (2003) suggests is done "with" rather than "for" others.

While this chapter evidences the breadth of Jewish programming and curricula available, scant empirical research exists on the impact of these initiatives on institutional culture. An agenda for future research will advance initiatives that encourage and enable learners and educators, alike, to become critical analyzers of their communities' policies and norms, and how they can become enactors of change. As this agenda further develops, researchers can further investigate the efficacy of praxis-based models and the ways in which they might support reflection on approaches to teaching. Systemic solutions can continue to take hold as educators deepen and expand their pedagogy, and actively progress communal discourse from language of crisis to language of opportunity and possibility for teen programming.

References

AAUW Educational Foundation (1992). *How schools shortchange girls: A study of major findings on girls and education.* Washington, DC: Wellesley College Center for Research on Women.

Adelman, P., Feldman, A., & Reinharz, S. (2005). *The JGirl's guide: The young Jewish woman's handbook for coming of age.* Woodstock, VT: Jewish Lights.

Altmann, E. (2008, Winter). Adolescent girls at risk for eating disorders: How educators can help. *Jewish Educational Leadership, 6*(2), Retrieved January, 2009, from http://www.lookstein.org/online_journal.php?id=178.

Arts Engine, Inc. (Producer), & Mandel, E. (Director). (2005). *When push comes to shove...It's no longer love!: Young perspectives on healthy & unhealthy relationships* [Motion picture]. USA: JWI.

Baker, M. (February 2009). All systems go: Masculinity in a Jewish high school. *Sh'ma, 39*(656), 4–5.

Barnes, D. (1992). *From communication to curriculum*. Portsmouth, NH: Heinemann.
Barth, R. (2004). *Learning by heart*. San Francisco: Jossey-Bass.
Bayit, S. (2007). *Love shouldn't hurt: Building healthy relationships for Jewish youth*. Oakland, CA: The Tides Center.
Benjamin, B. C. (Fall 2007). Putting gender on the agenda for supervisors of Jewish youth professionals. *Torah at the Center*, 2(1), 19.
Benjamin, B. C. (2009). *'Pretty soon we'll be taking over:' Voices and perspectives from the Ma'yan surveys of American Jewish Teen Girls*. New York: Ma'yan.
Biklen, S. K., & Pollard, D. (2001). Feminist perspectives on gender in classrooms. In V. Richardson (Ed.), *Handbook of research on teaching* (4th ed., pp. 723–748). Washington, DC: American Educational Research Association.
Bruckner, H., Bearman, P. (April 2005). After the promise: the STD consequences of adolescent virginity pledges. *Journal of Adolescent Health*, 36(4), 271–278.
Bogle, K. A. (2008). *Hooking up: Sex, dating and relationships on campus*. New York: NYU Press.
Boler, M. (1999). *Feeling power: Emotions and education*. New York: Routledge.
Brill, S. (Fall 2007). Gender, transgender, gender variance and Jewish educators. *Torah at the Center*, 2(1), 11.
Brown, L. M. (2003). *Girlfighting: Betrayal and rejection among girls*. New York: New York University Press.
Brydon-Miller, M. (2001). Education, research, and action: Theory and methods of participatory action research. In D. L. Tolman, & M. Brydon-Miller (Eds.), *From subjects to subjectivities: A handbook of interpretive and participatory methods* (pp. 76–89). New York: New York University Press.
Butler, J. (1999). *Gender trouble: Feminism and the subversion of identity* (10th anniversary ed.). New York: Routledge.
Cammarota, J., & Fine, M. (2008). Youth participatory action research: A pedagogy for transformational resistance. In J. Cammatota, & M. Fine (Eds.), *Revolutionizing education: Youth participatory action research in motion* (pp. 1–11). New York: Routledge.
Cochran-Smith, M. & Lytle, S. (1999). The teacher research movement: A decade later. *Educational Researcher*, 28(7), 15–25.
Crawford, M. & Unger, R. (2000). *Women and gender: A feminist psychology* (3rd ed.). Boston: McGraw-Hill.
Darder, A., Baltodano, M., & Torres, R. (2003). Critical pedagogy: An introduction. In A. Darder, M. Baltodano, & R. D. Torres (Eds.), *The critical pedagogy reader* (pp. 69–96). NewYork: RoutledgeFalmer.
Debow, Y. (2008). *Life values and intimacy education: Health education for the Jewish school*. New York: Ktav.
Diamond, E., & Better World Productions Inc. (Producers). (2008). *Hungry to be heard: Addressing eating disorders in the Orthodox Jewish community* [Motion picture]. USA: Young Leadership Cabinet of the Orthodox Union.
Doll, W. (1993). *A post-moderns perspective on curriculum*. New York: Teachers College Press.
Eaton, D. K. (2008, June 6). *Youth risk behavior surveillance*. Retrieved January, 2009, from CDC Web site: http://www.cdc.gov/mmwr/preview/mmwrhtml/ss5704a1.htm
Eliav, I. (2005). *Yad B'Yad: Working hand in hand to create healthy relationships*. Seattle, WA: FaithTrust Institute.
Ellsworth, E. (1997). *Teaching positions: Difference, pedagogy, and the power of address*. New York: Teachers College Press.
Epstein, S. D. (2006). *Strong girls, healthy relationships: A conversation on dating, friendship, and self esteem*. Washington, DC: JWI.
Epstein, S. D. (2007). From 'queen' to 'nobody': A language for discussing healthy relationships. *Torah at the Center*, 2(1), 17.
Epstein, S. D. (2008a). From reflection to action: Professional development as springboard to gender education. *Jewish Educational Leadership*, 6(3), 10–14.

Epstein, S. D. (2008b). *Strong girls! Friendships, relationships, and self-esteem.* Washington, DC: JWI.

Epstein, S. D. (February 2009a). Moments of opportunity. *Sh'ma, 39*(656), 2.

Epstein, S. D. (2009b, June). *The Pedagogy and Practice of Jewish Communal Artistic Engagement: LABA and the 14th Street Y.* New York: The 14th Street Y.

S. D. Epstein, & N. Less (Eds.) (2008, June). *Evaded issues in Jewish education: A resource guide for Jewish educators.* Retrieved from http://www.jtsa.edu/William_Davidson_Graduate_School_of_Jewish_Education/Addressing_Evaded_Issues_in_Jewish_Education/Resource_Guide.xml

Epstein, S. D., & Less, N. (2009). *Educational Jewish Moments: The training.* A publication of *Evaded Issues in Jewish Education* at the Jewish Theological Seminary.

Fayngold, I., & Keshet (Producers), & Fayngold, I. (Director). (2005). *Hineini: Coming out in a Jewish high school* [Motion picture]. USA: Keshet.

Finders, M. J. (1997). *Just girls: Hidden literacies and life in junior high.* New York: Teachers College Press.

Fine, M., & McClelland, S. I. (Fall, 2006). Sexuality education and desire: Still missing after all these years. *Harvard Educational Review, 76*(3), 297–338.

Fishman, S., & Parmer, D. (2008). *Matrilineal Ascent/ Patrilineal Descent: The growing gender imbalance in contemporary Jewish life.* Waltham, MA: Cohen Center for Modern Jewish Studies, Brandeis University.

Flanagan, C. (2006, January/February). Are you there God? It's me, Monica. *The Atlantic Online.* Retrieved from http://www.theatlantic.com/doc/200601/oral-sex/6

Gilbert, J. (2004). Between sexuality and narrative: On the language of sex education. In M. L. Rasmussen, E. Rofes, & S. Talburt (Eds.), *Youth and sexualities: Pleasure, subversion, and insubordination in and out of schools* (pp. 109–130). New York: Palgrave Macmillan.

Glasser, H. M., & Smith, J. P., III (August/September 2008). On the vague meaning of 'gender' in education research: The problem, its sources, and recommendations for practice. *Educational Researcher, 37*(6), 343–350.

Goldberg, A., & Gurian, M. (Fall 2007). Teach girls and boys diligently and differently. *Torah at the Center, 2*(1), 22.

Goldfein, N. (2005). *Beyond Miriam: A resource guide for camp directors on girl's issues of body image, eating disorders, and cutting.* New York: Foundation for Jewish Camping.

Goldsmith, M. B. (2008, October). *Report to Moving Traditions: Analysis of survey of Rosh Hodesh: It's a Girls Thing! participants.*

Gore, J. (2003). What we can do for you! What can "we" do for "you"? In A. Darder, M. Baltodano, & R. D. Torres (Eds.), *The critical pedagogy reader* (pp. 331–350). New York: RoutledgeFalmer.

Gorsetman, C. R., Ament, A., Hurwitz, S., & Svirsky, A. J. (2005). *Bereishit: A new beginning.* New York: JOFA.

Grumet, N. M. (Spring 2008). Gender differences in messages about sexuality in religious education. *Jewish Educational Leadership, 6*(3), 15–17.

Hall, G. S. (1904). *Adolescence: Its psychology and its relations to physiology, anthropology, sociology, sex, crime, religion, and education* (2 Vols.). New York: Appleton.

Hammer, J., Westheimer, K., & Jacobs, A. (2008). *Hineini curriculum resource guide.* Jamaica Plain, MA: Keshet.

Heath, S. B. (1999). Imaginative actuality: Learning in the arts during the nonschool hours. In *Champions of change: The impact of the arts on learning.* Washington, DC: Arts Educational Partnership and The President's Committee on the Arts and the Humanities.

Heath, S. B. (2001). *Making learning work* [on-line]. Retrieved from: www.shirleybriceheath.com

Johnston, S. (1994). Conversations with student teachers: Enhancing the dialogue of learning to teach. *Teaching and Teacher Education, 10*(1), 71–82.

JWI (2007). *When push comes to shove…it's no longer love!: Discussion guide* (2nd ed.). Washington, DC: JWI.

Kaplan, J., Reinharz, S. (Eds.). (1997). *Gender issues in Jewish day schools*. Waltham, MA: Brandeis University.
Kaplowitz, R. (Ed.). (2008). *Good guys! Partnership and positive masculinity*. Washington: DC: JWI.
Kindlon, D., & Thompson, M. (1999). *Raising Cain*. New York: Ballantine.
Kliebard, H. (1986). *The struggle for the American curriculum, 1893–1958*. Boston: Routledge.
Knox, M. (2006). Gender and possible selves. In C. Dunkel, & J. Kerpelman (Eds.), *Possible selves: Theory, research and application* (pp. 61–77). New York: Nova Science Publishers, Inc.
Kuriloff, P., & Reichert, M. (February 2009). Restrictive masculinities: Programming and Jewish boys. *Sh'ma, 39*(656), 6–7.
Lather, P. (1991). *Getting smart: Feminist research and pedagogy with/in the postmodern*. New York: Routledge.
Leone-Perkins, M. (2008, October). *Jewish Women International survey of destructive behaviors in Jewish girls. Love shouldn't hurt: Building healthy relationships for Jewish youth*. (2007). Oakland, CA: Shalom Bayit.
Lesko, N. (2001). *Act your age! A cultural construction of adolescence*. New York: Routledge Falmer.
Mac an Ghaill, M. (1994). *The making of men: Masculinities, sexualities, and schooling*. Buckingham, UK: Open University Press.
Markus, H. (2006). Introduction, In: *Possible Selves: Theory, Research and Application*. Eds: C.
Ma'yan (Ed.). (2008a). *A model for participatory action research: Based on the Ma'yan Research Training Intern Program*. Ma'yan.
Ma'yan (Producer). (2008b). *Untitled Ma'yan Research Training Internship film* [Motion picture]. (Available from Ma'yan, 334 Amsterdam Avenue, New York, NY 10023)
McLaren, P. (2003). Critical pedagogy: A look at the major concepts. In A. Darder, M. Baltodano, & R. D. Torres (Eds.), *The critical pedagogy reader* (pp. 69–96). NewYork: RoutledgeFalmer.
Meyer, D. (February 2009). Teens, gender, and identity. *Sh'ma, 39*(656), 1.
Novak-Winer, L. (2007). *Sacred choices: Adolescent relationships and sexual ethics (middle school module)*. New York: URJ Press.
Novak-Winer, L. *Sacred choices: Adolescent relationships and sexual ethics (high school module)*. (n.d.). New York: URJ Press. Retrieved September, 2008, from http://urj.org/youth/sacredchoices/highschool/
Novick, B. (1994). *In God's image: Making Jewish decisions about the body*. New York: United Synagogue of Conservative Judaism, Department of Youth Activities.
Orenstein, P. (1994). *Schoolgirls: Young women, self-esteem, and the confidence gap*. New York: Anchor Books.
Parker-Pope, T. (2009, January 26). *The myth of rampant teenage promiscuity*. The New York Times. Retrieved from http://www.nytimes.com/2009/01/27/health/27well.html
Phillips, L. M. (2000). *Flirting with danger: Young women's reflections on sexuality and domination*. New York: New York University Press.
Phoenix, A., Frosh, S., & Pattman, R. (2003). Producing contradictory masculine subject positions: Producing narratives of threat, homophobia and bullying in 11–14 year old boys. *Journal of Social Issues, 59*, 179–195.
Pollack, W. S. (Fall 2007). Jewish boys-A spiritual crisis of disconnection: Healing the rift within Jewish educational and organizational life. *Torah at the Center, 2*(1), 4–5.
Rasmussen, M. L. (2004). Safety and subversion: The production of sexualities and genders in school spaces. In M. L. Rasmussen, E. Rofes, & S. Talburt (Eds.), *Youth and sexualities: Pleasure, subversion, and insubordination in and out of schools* (pp. 131–152). NewYork: Palgrave Macmillan.
Reichert, M. C., & Ravitch, S. (2008, March). *Wishing for more: Jewish boyhood, identity, and community*. Jenkintown: Moving Traditions.

Reimer, G. T. (2007, Fall). Midrashic clues for a gendered reading of Matan Torah. *Torah at the Center*, 2(1), 6.
Rofes, E. (2004). Martyr-target-victim: Interrogating narratives of persecution and suffering among queer youth. In M. L. Rasmussen, E. Rofes, & S. Talburt (Eds.), *Youth and sexualities: Pleasure, subversion, and insubordination in and out of schools* (pp. 41–62). New York: Palgrave Macmillan.
Ruttenberg, D. (2009). *The passionate Torah: Sex and Judaism*. New York: New York University.
Sax, L. (2007, Fall). Boys adrift: The five factors driving the growing epidemic of unmotivated boys and underachieving young men. *Torah at the Center*, 2(1), 12.
Saxe, L., & Kelner, S. (2001, May). Teenage boys and girls: A Jewish world apart. *Shma, 31*(582), 12–13.
Saxe, L., Kelner, S., Kadushin, C., & Brodsky, A. (2000, Summer). Jewish adolescents: American teenagers trying to `make it`. *Agenda, 13*, 3–7.
Seidler-Feller, D. (2009, February). Approaching sexual discovery. *Sh'ma, 39*(656), 9.
Stein, K. (Ed.). (2009). *Love your neighbor, love yourself:* Building healthy relationships. New York: United Synagogue Youth.
Steiner-Adair, C., & Sjostrom, L. (2006). *Full of ourselves: A wellness program to advance girl power, health, and leadership*. New York: Teachers College Press.
Steiner-Adair, C., & Sjostrom, L. (2008). *Bishvili, for me: A Jewish implementation guide to Full of Ourselves*. New York: Hadassah Foundation. Retrieved from http://www.bishviliforme.com/curriculum.html
Steiner-Adair, C., & Sjostrom, L. (2008). *Research summary, Full of ourselves: Advancing girl power, health, and leadership*. (n.d.). Abstract retrieved September, 2008, from http://www.midcoast.com/~megirls/Full%20of%20Ourselves%20Research%20Summary.htm
Talburt, S., Rofes, E., & Rasmussen, M. L. (2004). Introduction: Transforming discourses of queer youth and educational practices surrounding gender, sexuality, and youth. In M. L. Rasmussen, E. Rofes, & S. Talburt (Eds.), *Youth and sexualities: Pleasure, subversion, and insubordination in and out of schools* (pp. 131–152). New York: Palgrave Macmillan.
Tannenbaum, C. (2008, Spring). Jewish women as learning different. *Jewish Educational Leadership, 6*(3), 15–17.
Thorne, B. (2005). *Gender play: Girls and boys in school*. New Brunswick, NJ: Rutgers University Press.
Tolman, D. L. (2002). *Dilemmas of desire: Teenage girls talk about sexuality*. Cambridge, MA: Harvard University Press.
Tyack, D., & Hansot, E. (1992). *Learning together: A history of coeducation in American public schools*. New York: Russell Sage Foundation.
Warner, J. (2009, January 29). *The myth of lost innocence* [Editorial]. The New York Times. Retrieved from http://warner.blogs.nytimes.com/2009/01/29/at-a-journalism-conference-a-c/
Weis, L. & Fine, M. (2000). *Speed bumps: A student-friendly guide to qualitative research*. New York: Teachers College Press.
Wiseman, R. (2002). *Queen bees & wannabes: Helping your daughter survive cliques, gossip, boyfriends & other realities of adolescence*. New York: Three Rivers Press.
Wolf, S. A. (1993). What's in a name? Labels and literacy in readers theatre. *The Reading Teacher, 46*(7), 540–545.
Wolf, S. A. (1994). Learning to act/Acting to learn: Children as actors, critics, and characters in classroom theatre. *Research in the teaching of English, 28*(1), 7–44.
Wolf, S. A. (1995). Language in and around the dramatic curriculum. *Journal of Curriculum Studies, 27*(2), 117–137.
Zeichner, K. M. (1994). Personal renewal and social construction through teacher research. In S. Hollingsworth & H. Sockett (Eds.), *Teacher research and educational reform* (pp. 66–84). Chicago, IL: University of Chicago Press.

Informal Education: The Decisive Decade – How Informal Jewish Education Was Transformed in Its Relationship with Jewish Philanthropy

Joseph Reimer

Introduction

Informal Jewish Education in North America was transformed by its interaction with Jewish philanthropy during the decade from 1997 to 2007. As an active participant in that interaction, I have a story to tell about how that partnership developed. In this chapter, I have also drawn on the available literature to tell that story. I have highlighted two cases – that of Birthright Israel and the Executive Leadership Institute of the Foundation of Jewish Camp – to raise questions about this developing partnership. The key question is: How can powerful philanthropists and change-minded Jewish educational leaders learn to better understand one another's perspectives to productively partner to create lasting positive change for Jewish life in North America?

Jewish Philanthropy and Jewish Education

> Amid all the changes that have taken place within the American Jewish community during the past 15 years, few are as striking and significant as those in the fields of Jewish philanthropy and Jewish education. These two areas have experienced fundamental shifts, independently and in relation to each other.

Thus Cardin and Prager (2008) open their examination of how these two fields have deeply influenced one another over the past 15 years. Their insights lay the groundwork for my more detailed examination of the interaction between Jewish philanthropy and the sub-field of informal Jewish education.

They tell a familiar story of the rise of the Jewish private foundations. The 1990 NJPS, with its alarming news of the sharp rise in the intermarriages between Jews and non-Jews, set off a deeply felt alarm that perhaps the Jewish enterprise in North America was endangered by the forces of assimilation. Jews would become the next disappearing minority group unless the leaders of the community took wise action to

J. Reimer (✉)
Brandeis University, Boston, MA, USA
e-mail: reimer@brandeis.edu

counteract these demographic trends. Jewish education – broadly understood – was viewed as the best available 'medicine' for this 'condition.' It was widely assumed that the federation movement would take the lead.

> For years the Jewish federation system was widely and justifiably recognized as a fundraising juggernaut. It was the self-proclaimed 'central address' of Jewish giving; the largest federations collected and allocated tens of millions of dollars each year through a well-choreographed, consensus-driven, and deliberative process in which volunteer leadership worked very closely with their professional counterparts. (ibid., p. 537)

But the federation system proved slow-footed and uncertain in responding to this internal crisis of continuity. Federations largely did not have the expertise to parse the subtle strategies needed to creatively engage the next generation of increasingly uninvolved Jewish youth.

> At the same time as the federation system began to grapple with these challenges, a significant number of existing and potential donors with substantial personal wealth and influence began to take a greater interest in the future of the American Jewish community. Many of these philanthropists and foundations turned to the federation system for guidance and partnership…With a few notable exceptions, what these philanthropists discovered about the federation world did not impress them. They found a system responding to the situation in a slow, bureaucratic fashion, failing to recognize the true extent of the problem at hand. (ibid., p. 538)

The 1990s witnessed a sharp rise in the number of private foundations (Fleishman, 2007; Tobin, 2001). Among these were those whose mission focused on building a more viable future for the Jewish community. These foundations began to develop "programs they believed would be more effective in the struggle to reverse the troubling trends" (ibid.). Jewish philanthropists invested widely within Jewish education. But the investment in informal Jewish education – particularly in the Israel experience and in Jewish camping – was extraordinary. I will explore how that philanthropic investment has transformed this sector, and will raise questions about how philanthropists and educators have negotiated their working relationships.

What Is Informal Jewish Education?

No one has worked harder to define informal Jewish education than Barry Chazan. Chazan (1991, 2003) has offered clear conceptual parameters for this sector, advocated for its importance, and combated common misunderstandings that persist.

Chazan argues that it is *not* helpful to think of informal education as all the Jewish education that takes place outside of schools. For that defines informal education by *what it is not*: it is not what takes place in schools. This reduces informal education to the "not-formal" and underestimates the complexity of what takes place at school. Jewish education is too broad and complex to be divided into two domains: formal and informal education.

Chazan argues that while many identify 'education' with their school experience, they overlook that cooking with grandma in her kitchen was also educational as was singing and dancing on Shabbat at their summer camp. *Education* – as Cremin (1977) taught – is a broad term that describes the varied ways that we learn from significant models important cultural content and values. We should focus on informal education to capture the richness of the *experiential learning* that takes place at many times and in many settings in our lives.

Chazan contends it would be a strategic error for the North American Jewish community to invest all its resources in schools, for we need to be educating a wide variety of Jews at multiple moments in their lives. Schools are primarily for the young. Many Jews are seeking meaningful communal participation not easily found in a classroom. We have to become experts in bringing people together to celebrate their Jewishness, share their Jewish meanings, and learn their traditions. Learning how to provide Jews with those meaningful experiences is the business of informal Jewish education.

Chazan views informal Jewish education as an approach to bringing Jews together to learn about their Judaism. This approach has clear characteristics. To be fully realized, informal Jewish education is characterized by:

1. Beginning with the needs of the individual participants
2. Creating group contexts in which individual and group learning is promoted
3. Developing a trusting atmosphere
4. Encouraging participants to explore and clarify their own Jewish values and commitments
5. Learning from their own experiences
6. in a curriculum of Jewish experiences and values
7. that create a culture of Jewish involvement
8. and is facilitated by a holistic Jewish educator.

At heart is the commitment to *learning from experience*; not isolated experiences, but a variety of Jewish experiences as part of a well-articulated Jewish educational program. These planned experiences will take place in a supportive educational environment in which the very culture of the place educates. Participants will have as their role models holistic Jewish educators who will teach by example and help shape the experience of others. Their genuine interest in the participants' lives and openness to sharing their commitments form the foundation for this educational approach.

Chazan teaches that informal Jewish education is an approach that requires professional skill, imagination, and planning. His is a call to the Jewish community to take seriously the potential of this approach for transforming Jewish lives. But the history of this sector tells a different story.

A Historical Background

Sarna (2006) records that Jewish summer camps – the earliest form of informal Jewish education – began over a century ago. Jews were not the first to start summer camps, but quickly followed the example of their Christian neighbors and began their camps by the turn of the twentieth century. Summer in the city posed threats to the well-being of children and communities provided funds to take Jewish children out to the 'fresh air' of the country.

By 1936, there were 88 communally run Jewish camps in North America with astounding variety. Camps were run by federations, JCCs, Zionist organizations, Yiddishists, and others. There were philanthropic camps for the poor and private camps for the affluent. There was a Jewish camp to reflect almost any shade of Jewish life (Isaacman, 1976).

Camps came up first to meet a necessity, but soon Jewish educators discovered their educational potential. There were early private camps whose founders were deliberate in using camp as 'a laboratory for religious education' (Sarna, 2006, p. 31). A more sophisticated effort was initiated at Camp Cejwin in 1922 (Stern, 2007). Many others were to follow and camps became a primary setting for informal Jewish education.

Following closely behind was the creation of Jewish youth movements. The first was Young Judaea. With the rise of Zionism in the early twentieth century came the formation of Zionist youth societies. In 1909, "a special conference was held to create a movement dedicated to advancing the cause of Zionism, furthering the mental, moral, and physical development of Jewish youth and promoting Jewish culture and ideals" (YJ website). Young Judaea as a national youth movement was born.

A similar pathway led to the formation of BBYO. In 1922 in Omaha, Nebraska, a few Jewish boys got together to form a Jewish fraternity which they call AZA – Aleph Zadik Aleph. Their fraternity was a mix of a social club and study group. A year later, they attracted the attention of Sam Beber who had big aspirations and saw in this local club the seeds of a national movement (Baer, 1983).

Beber was active in Bnai Brith and dreamed of forming a national youth organization. He threw himself into the task of writing a constitution for this national organization, helping to start clubs in other cities, and sponsoring a national convention. Beber was successful in attaining sponsorship from Bnai Brith and funding from local chapters (ibid.). AZA clubs for young men sprung up primarily in the Midwest.

In California, the women of Bnai Brith began to sponsor clubs for their teenage daughters. By the 1930s, there were a growing number of Bnai Brith Girls' clubs (BBG). The spread of girls' clubs was by word of mouth on very modest budgets. When the membership in BBG rose sharply, the women formed a national organization to oversee the growth. In 1943–1944, AZA and BBG were united into a single organization called BBYO (ibid.).

For all their differences, Young Judaea and BBYO had these similarities. They began as local initiatives by youth to organize themselves in social clubs. The youth sought help from adult organizations that responded with financial and organizational support. That adult structure became essential for the growth of the movement. But neither movement was identified with a religious denomination.

As Sarna (2006) notes, after the end of the Second World War, American Jews began to more decisively affiliate with the main religious denominations. The Conservative movement was the first to begin organizing youth in the 1920s in an organization that did not last. The Reform movement began its youth movement in the 1939 and NFTY persisted and grew. The Conservative movement tried again successfully when beginning USY in 1951. While there were many ways that Orthodox youth organized themselves, in 1954, NCSY – with its ties to Yeshiva University – began to develop. Thus from the mid-1950s, these Jewish youth organizations developed – with clubs opening throughout North America.

The world of informal Jewish education was broader than described in this short history. But the main points are as follows: (1) These were organizations focused on serving Jewish youth, particularly teens, which were (2) complementary to – not substitutes for – formal Jewish education. (3) They relied heavily on adult volunteers and part-time advisors as well as (4) a few Jewish professionals who provided national and regional leadership. (5) All the youth organizations were 'ideological' in that they represented a particular set of articulated values that the adult organization hoped to transmit. (6) All realized that American teens sought enjoyable leisure-time activities that were as crucial to sustaining membership as was the Jewish value system they espoused.

A View from 1990

In 1988, Mort Mandel, a prominent Jewish lay leader from Cleveland, working in close collaboration with Professor Seymour Fox and Annette Hochstein, convened the Commission on Jewish Education in North America. This 2-year gathering brought together a broad-based group of prominent North American Jewish leaders – both lay and professional – to consider the big questions facing the community. Most particularly, they discussed how Jewish education could be deployed more effectively to insure the future of the Jewish enterprise in North America. This commission can be seen as the launching event in which the newly emerging private Jewish foundations claimed leadership for the future direction of Jewish education.

In 1990, the Mandel Associated Foundations commissioned Professor Bernard Reisman to write a report on the state of Informal Jewish Education. This was one of several reports by scholars to help inform the members of the Commission on various sectors of Jewish education and how that sector could best contribute toward Jewish continuity.

Reisman (1990) wrote a report that covered the principles of informal Jewish education as well as the many settings of informal Jewish education. Reisman offered a set of recommendations "to optimize for the American Jewish community the potential inherent in this process [of informal Jewish education]." They included:

- to upgrade the professional status of those working in this field
- to help synagogues become more responsive to the needs of their congregants
- to upgrade the summer camps – both staff and facilities
- to invest in more effective research to investigate best practices in this field (pp. 60–64).

The Commission, however, did not adopt any of these recommendations in its final report (1991). By reading that report, one would barely find any references to informal Jewish education. In retrospect, Reisman and Chazan were the two voices calling for the community to create a field out of what in 1990 remained a disparate set of organizations that each operated on its own. There was as yet no field of informal Jewish education, and as such, it was not surprising that the Commission passed over Reisman's recommendations.

Turning a Corner in the 1990s

For all the effort invested in the Commission, it was not its report that galvanized the North American Jewish community, but rather a much drier document that had little to do with the Jewish education – the National Jewish Population Survey 1990 (Kosmin, Goldstein, & Waksberg, 1991). Suddenly, a much broader circle of Jewish leaders and philanthropists was actively concerned with the very questions that the members of the Commission had been considering.

> In particular the leadership came to believe that substantial numbers of their children and grandchildren were at risk of losing their connection to Judaism. Their response took the form of enhancing support for intensive Jewish educational environments such as day schools, Jewish summer camps, campus programs, university-based Jewish studies programs and Israel educational experiences. Funding for all of these from Jewish philanthropic agencies and individuals increased. (Saxe and Chazan, pp. 27–280)

By the 1990s, almost all the national youth organizations had long been sponsoring Israel educational experiences (Chazan, 1994). They also had close relationships with their movement's summer camps. After decades of laboring alone in the fields of informal Jewish education, they found themselves potentially more in the eye of the Jewish community and its private foundations. But how could these disparate organizations present their youth programs to a community poised to increase its funding for Jewish continuity? One response was to create an umbrella for all the national Jewish youth organizations that could speak for this sector in a coherent voice.

Forming the NAA

The move toward greater cooperation resulted in the formation of a new umbrella organization called the North American Alliance for Jewish Youth (NAA). The first act of this newly formed umbrella was to organize a conference for Jewish youth professionals from across the spectrum of the community.

That conference was announced in the fall of 1996 in a letter that heralded the formation of the NAA and listed 16 member organizations. These included both denominational and Zionist youth organizations, summer camps, and providers of Israel experiences.

The letter announced that the NAA conference "will bring together approximately 400 Jewish Youth Professionals." The authors noted that "informal education is now taking its deserved place in the world of Jewish identity building, continuity, and education."

Three individuals would be honored at the conference. Two were informal Jewish educators and the third was Charles Bronfman. His inclusion was significant. Bronfman stood virtually alone among the major Jewish philanthropists in championing this cause. By the mid-1990s, Bronfman was actively working with others to create Israel Experience, Inc., an advocacy agency for travel to Israel. It was widely recognized that the youth organizations that sponsored Israel experiences could be recipients of support from this new initiative. Charles Bronfman was a key player and the NAA wished to play on his court.

The conference in March 1997 took place and was followed by annual conferences for the next decade that drew hundreds of youth professionals from these varied organizations. This annual gathering represented an important step forward for this field which had never before brought together youth professionals in those numbers or offered the workshops and presentations that defined what a Jewish youth professional across organizational lines needs to know.

But the NAA never accomplished much more than sponsor that annual conference. The NAA was largely run by volunteers who were doing this work on top of their regular demanding jobs. Those volunteers never succeeded in connecting with philanthropists like Charles Bronfman. The NAA represented an old world of informal Jewish education. As the twentieth century was nearing the end and with the Jewish world rapidly changing, these organizations were not well positioned to partner with the emerging Jewish philanthropists. Perhaps as a result, the NAA – after a decade in existence – first reorganized as JEXNET, briefly attracted foundation funding, and then went out of business (Bryfman, 2009).

Charles Bronfman

We do not know why Charles Bronfman did not connect with the NAA, but that he did not is central to our story. For Bronfman, scion of the famous Bronfman family of Montreal, had by 1997 emerged as the leading philanthropist supporting both the Israel experience for teens and more broadly, informal Jewish education as a way of engaging greater numbers of Jewish youth. After having founded the CRB Foundation in Montreal, he and his wife moved to New York to begin a new foundation with broader ambitions to be called the Andrea and Charles Bronfman Philanthropies (ACBP).

Bronfman was passionate about Israel. He could see that the two largest Jewish communities, Israel and North America, were moving apart from each another. His passion was to bring together young Israeli and North American Jews to form common bonds as Jews. He also believed that no other experience could enliven the hearts of North American Jewish youth as a significant visit to Israel (Saxe and Chazan, pp. 4–5). Never a great student himself, Bronfman believed that the most significant learning came through direct interaction with other people, places, and events. He was close to Chazan and learned that this kind of learning was called "informal education." Bronfman emerged as its champion.

Starting Israel Experience, Inc. was an initial attempt to bring a business perspective to the field of informal Jewish education. While the Jewish youth organizations had been running well-regarded Israel trips, the number of Jewish teens who went on these trips was still quite limited. Bronfman knew from his business experience that if one wished to attract significantly larger numbers of people to buy a product, that product needed to be marketed to attract their attention and interest. Yet Jewish youth organizations were primarily offering these Israel trips to their own members and not marketing them to the majority of Jewish teens. Bronfman felt it was precisely these less affiliated youth who could benefit most from an Israel experience (ibid., pp. 9–10).

Who was the intended audience for informal Jewish educational programs? This key question stood as a potential divider between Bronfman and the NAA Jewish educators. I remember a gathering of informal educators convened by the Bronfman initiative. One of the leading educators – passionate about the Israel experience – explained his perspective on increasing the numbers of youth in that organization's Israel experience. He said that these trips were designed primarily for youth who had been active in their movement. Those teens, he added, were familiar with the rules and norms of that movement and could be trusted to behave in Israel. To recruit a whole new group of youth would open their educators to the risks of handling teens whose behavior might be completely unacceptable.

That perspective was antithetical to Bronfman's vision to reach the majority of less affiliated Jewish youth. As a proud Jew who himself never affiliated with these movements, Bronfman identified with these other youth and was certain that they could be trusted – under appropriate supervision – to have a meaningful Israel experience.

Yet Israel Experience, Inc. was to serve the existing youth organizations by providing new tools to attract greater numbers of teens to their Israel trips. But this initiative would be short-lived. Jeffrey Solomon, President of ACBP, in retrospect has called this initiative "a failure" – a $19 million dollar investment "which produced no additional kids going to Israel" (Ruskay & Solomon, 2009, p. 7). This significant initiative – which might have connected the existing youth organizations to the emerging philanthropic world – did not work for reasons that will need to be explored in greater depth.

The Institute for Informal Jewish Education at Brandeis University

In a 1998 conversation with Jeffrey Solomon, I learned that ACBP might support a university-based institute dedicated to creating a more professionalized field of informal Jewish education. I leaped at this opportunity. Soon, the Institute for Informal Jewish Education (IJE) was established with a generous 5-year grant to

Brandeis University. This would be the first institute based at a research university in North America to sponsor academic research on Jewish teens, create a professional leadership institute for this field, and initiate new programs to engage under-engaged youth.

As its first act, the IJE commissioned an empirical study of the Jewish teen population of the Greater Boston area. This study confirmed in detail what was commonly known: Jewish teens after their bar or bat mitzvahs begin to disengage from Jewish education. There is a big drop-off at age 13 and then a gradual drop-off year by year until the end of high school (Kadushin, Kelner, & December, 2000). These findings raised the question that would guide the subsequent work. What could the IJE do to slow this process of disengagement and help shape a field that would be more responsive to the needs of today's teens?

The IJE claimed that informal Jewish educators need to rethink their traditional approaches and learn to aim their arrows more precisely to hit the targets of contemporary teen interest and availability. The IJE aspired to recreate experiential Jewish modalities for teens by taking these steps:

- Create a Professional Leadership Seminar for promising young professionals from across the field to take on future leadership;
- Create a grants program to fund a few innovative programs most likely to attract under-engaged Jewish teens;
- Work with communities across North America ready to bring innovative youth programs to their teens (Reimer & Shavelson, 2004, p. 4).

These years (1999–2004) proved to be both exciting and humbling: exciting because we were able to implement the three primary strategies for change. They were humbling because even so we made little progress in the largest challenge: engaging under-engaged Jewish youth.

Two moments stand out in our struggle to achieve our primary mission. The first came when we were working with our first group of young leaders who were intensely devoted to the cause of informal Jewish education. When they were to devise new projects to reflect all that they were learning at the Leadership Seminar, we, the staff, assumed their projects would be aimed at engaging under-engaged teens. But many members of the seminar balked at that suggestion. Those teens were too hard to reach. They believed they had their hands full working with teens that were still engaged. They wanted to rev up the base of the committed kids; our notion of reaching further out in the community to the disengaged seemed too academic to be taken seriously.

Respecting practitioner wisdom, I thought perhaps we were asking for too much. There would be a better opportunity when the next year we launched our grants for innovative practice. These grants were designed precisely for those organizations that were experimenting with programs to engage Jewish teens who had fallen away from active involvement.

I was very encouraged to receive 86 grant applications. Choosing just four grantees seemed daunting, but surely these select few would share our goals.

However, I was in for another surprise. When we first met with the four grantees, a crucial misunderstanding surfaced. "While we saw the grantees as pioneering new approaches, they saw themselves launching new programs for their organizations that would work in their accustomed ways. While we wanted them to place special emphasis on recruiting under-engaged youth, they were primarily interested in marketing the program to whichever teens would be most interested" (Reimer & Shavelson, 2004, p. 26).

We worked out with each grantee a definition of "under-engaged youth" that worked for their context. Together we learned that to work successfully to attract these less enthused youth, an organization had to make that a priority and limit the more involved teens from filling all the program slots. It takes more ingenuity and flexibility to engage teens for whom the Jewish component is not the best hook. But all this could be done and the results were that teens that were once indifferent could develop interest and involvement.

But we also learned that had the IJE not insisted on this extra effort, even these Jewish organizations would probably fall back on the accustomed path of serving primarily youth who show the greatest interest. This field primarily serves the teens that line up to gain Jewish experience, and those teens unintentionally block access for the less engaged kids. Clearly, the IJE did not have the clout to change that well-established pattern.

Birthright Israel

Even had the IJE met with greater success, we would not have attracted much notice. For within a year of our beginning, ACBP undertook with its partners a much more ambitious initiative: launching Birthright Israel (BRI). The story of this launch and its growth has been told elsewhere (Saxe & Chazan, 2008). The focus here is on how that growth illustrates the emerging intersection between Jewish philanthropy and informal Jewish education.

When philanthropist Michael Steinhardt approached Bronfman to partner to launch Birthright Israel, Bronfman brought to the table much more than money. He and his team had learned a great deal of what *not* to do and what *could be* done from the years in which they had experimented with the Israel Experience, Inc. (ibid.).

BRI emerged from the new philanthropic environment that Cardin and Prager (2008) describe. Within that environment some foundations choose to work alone and some to work in partnership with others (Fleishman, 2007). These two venture philanthropists – Steinhardt and Bronfman – had a big dream which they spearheaded. But they never worked alone. They sought partnership with existing Jewish organizations – especially the federation system and the State of Israel – as well as other philanthropists.

BRI marks both true innovation and a bridge with much that came before – especially in the Israel experience. It is vital to understand both where BRI broke with past practice and where it built upon that practice. I begin with three features of BRI that differed sharply from previous Israel experiences.

(1) *The gift of a free trip.* That was the attention-grabber. While most previous Israel experiences came with a hefty price tag, Steinhardt and Bronfman insisted that to grab the attention of young people who had shown no previous interest, BRI had to give the gift of a free trip. "In focus groups on college campuses we learned that young Jews were neither connected to Israel nor inspirationally moved by their own Jewish connection... The gift was designed to confront those realities" (Solomon, Cardin, & Gedzelman, 2009, p. 75).

(2) *The 10-day trip for college students and young adults.* Equally audacious was the decision to market this trip to college students and young adults. For 40 years, the Israel experience had been designed primarily for high-school students and had usually run for 4–6 weeks. There was little track record of attracting 18–26-year-olds to this experience. Yet the founders reasoned correctly that a free 10-day trip would have special appeal to this older group.

(3) *Those who had been on an educational trip to Israel were not eligible.* The founders were clear who their audience was: not those who were most committed, but those who had shown little previous interest. BRI had a singular mission: to reach and influence the majority of Jewish youth who have been in danger of losing any connection to Jewish commitments (Saxe and Chazan, pp. 14, 98).

In these pivotal decisions, we can see how these philanthropists thought differently about the Israel experience than had the Jewish educators who had designed the traditional Israel experiences.

Coming from the business world, these philanthropists brought a marketing perspective. They were comfortable playing a numbers game. What they most cared about was finding a way to make a difference in the lives of young adult Jews who had not been hooked on Judaism. They believed that a quality experience in Israel could light their Jewish fires, and aimed for *much larger* numbers to come to Israel. Their message to this group was: "If it takes a free trip to get you to Israel, here is the gift. If you only have 10 days, we can do it in ten. If you want to bring friends, just have them sign up. If you want winter, fine; if summer is better, we have those trips too. Just sign up and come."

Calling this program 'birthright' means that it is yours for the asking. It does not matter what kind of Jew you are, if you ever received a Jewish education or had a bar mitzvah. One Jewish parent is all it takes. No one before had made *that* offer in these numbers. Nothing represents a sharper break with Jewish communal tradition than this offer: *we take you as you are and ask in return only that you take this trip seriously – however you define that.* To these philanthropists, the important question is not what kind of Jew you will be, but whether you will choose to be Jewish in any meaningful sense. If the answer is yes, all else is mere commentary (Solomon et al., 2009).

By contrast, for most Jewish educators, all else is *not mere commentary*. Most Jewish educators begin from a particular Jewish value system. We became educators because we have a values-message to communicate and a wish to influence young

Jews to develop in certain directions. When seeking work, educators choose to work where we feel most identified with the values of that organization.

Most Jewish organizations sponsor an Israel experience with two goals in mind. They primarily want their youth to experience Israel and develop a close relationship with the Jewish homeland. But they also want those youth to experience Israel from a particular angle. They want this trip to solidify both the tie to Israel and to their movement. They place the Israel experience so that it will culminate earlier experiences in that movement and serve as a powerful bonding experience with peers and educators. They want the participants to feel "We all cried at the *kotel* together and love Israel and now feel even more committed to working for our movement."

From that educational perspective, numbers matter, but only to a point. Educators try to convince a maximal number of their charges to come on their movement's Israel experience. They raise money to subsidize those trips. But they are not primarily looking to provide an Israel experience for Jewish teens that dropped out at bar mitzvah.

Those kids would not feel at home on these movement trips that serve as culminating experiences; for they have not been part of the earlier socializing experiences.

Education and marketing often do *not* lead to the same conclusions. Informal Jewish education has aimed to exert a deep influence over those youth who have pursued this interest over time. A marketing approach seeks to attract those who had little previous interest to try something new (Reimer, 2006). Following a marketing strategy, BRI chose to break from the traditional Israel experience that developed from the 1950s through the 1990s (Chazan, 1997). The question of interest is how these two different languages – marketing and informal Jewish education – can productively communicate with one another.

Having emphasized the break in tradition, we need also note that these philanthropists and their partners did not seek to erase the history of informal educational experience, but rather to build upon it.

> The founders realized that to make BRI 'work' they would need professional guidance from those who knew the mind-set of their target audience and understood education. The program would have to be more than a tour; it would need to have rich emotional and intellectual content, yet be attractive enough to tens of thousands of young adult participants... Perhaps the key development that made BRI feasible was collaboration between the philanthropists and educational trip organizers. Unlike prior efforts, BRI was conceived as a partnership – not only among funders, but also between BRI and organizations that had the ability to recruit and provide educational programming for young adults. (Saxe and Chazan, p. 12)

Bronfman, Steinhardt, and these professionals knew that to be an effective instrument for promoting Jewish identity, BRI would have to embody the characteristics of a good Israel experience that incorporate an informal Jewish educational approach. That realization led to their partnering with providers whose educational staffs were trained in that approach and who were also open to trying new practices for a new clientele.

A Partnership Between Marketing and Informal Education

To create a 'transformative' program, the BRI founders took some unprecedented steps. First, they decided that the BRI organization would not itself be running Israel trips, but would hire providers to design and implement those Israel experiences. Second, they decided not to limit the providers to the traditional Jewish youth organizations, but to open the competition to for-profit touring companies that might offer the less traditional youth more attractive options. Third, they decided that the BRI organization would exercise its control over the quality of these experiences by being very clear to the providers about the goals of the BRI curriculum and the expectations of what each BRI experience must contain. At the same time, they would be flexible in allowing each provider to implement those goals and expectations as they thought best within the BRI paradigm (Saxe and Chazan, pp. 12–13, 124–25).

How has this balancing act worked out? Providers know they only have 10 days to accomplish a broad set of educational goals. Their challenge is to use those 10 days to the fullest – to engage the minds, hearts, and hands of the participants. Their relationship with these young adults will be short-term. Their primary educational goal is to open minds and initiate a dialogue about being Jewish that hopefully others will continue back in North America. That entails designing a program that raises a lot questions and possibilities, but leaves the participants feeling excited and thinking "I want to know more and seek further engagement."

BRI is an instance where a marketing perspective and an educational perspective *can* share a common goal. In this case, a satisfied customer is an eager learner, and an engaged learner will be a future customer for more Jewish experiences. When the participants emerge both as well-satisfied customers who truly enjoyed their trip and as more engaged Jews who are open to further Jewish exploration, the program works well on both fronts. That can only happen – I would contend – when both perspectives are built into the planning and implementation process and when both sides – philanthropists and educators – respect each other's agenda as legitimate and helpful.

The Foundation for Jewish Camp

One organization that has taken to heart the lessons of BRI is the Foundation for Jewish Camp (FJC). Jewish summer camps have stood at the heart of informal Jewish education from the beginning. But there was no single organization devoted to furthering the larger enterprise of Jewish camping until the formation of FJC in 1998. (It was originally named the Foundation for Jewish Camping and later changed its name.)

FJC was initiated by a pair of Jewish philanthropists, a married couple, Rob and Elisa Spungen Bildner. The Bildners had been participants in the Wexner Heritage Program and felt inspired to give back. As parents of school-aged children who were not attending Jewish day schools, the Bildners were concerned to find other contexts for their children to form Jewish friendships and build a Jewish identity. Both remembered fondly the summers they had spent at summer camps and wondered why Jewish summer camps were not receiving the kind of philanthropic support that Jewish day schools had. That was when the idea of starting a foundation that would support Jewish camps began to form. Their interest was with residential (and not day) camps and the majority of these camps are run as non-profit organizations. They decided that their newly minted public foundation would have at its mission enhancing non-profit residential Jewish mission camps (Bildner, 2009).

The Bildners had entrepreneurial business experience and sought as their professional partner a well-regarded informal Jewish educator. They selected Rabbi Ramie Arian to be the first executive director. Together, they sought to convince the larger community that Jewish camps could be a powerful address for providing large numbers of young Jews with a powerful Jewish living experience (Bildner, 2009).

It proved at first a hard sell. While most had been to Israel many times, few Jewish philanthropists had ever attended Jewish camps or sent their children to one. Over the years, Jewish mission camps had done little to change their image in the community and had little attraction to Jewish philanthropists. This situation prompted Elisa Bildner to write: "The sad and ridiculous irony is that non-profit Jewish overnight camps, one of our community's most effective resources for transmitting identity and fighting assimilation, are among our least supported" (Bildner, 2002, p. 4).

Arian put forward a clear program for what the Jewish philanthropic community could do to maximize the effectiveness of Jewish camping.

> We need to create many more camps in the Jewish community to accommodate the many children who want to attend but are closed out. But more than additional space, we need to upgrade our camps to match or exceed the state of the art in the secular camp world. Many of our camps suffer from years of 'deferred maintenance' and need significant upgrades to their buildings and grounds. (Arian, 2002, p. 3)

In addition, he argued, Jewish camps need better programming, higher pay for staff, more money for scholarships, and incentive programs to encourage Jewish families to choose Jewish camps. It was a well-conceived analysis of what it would take to turn Jewish camping from an educational system that served only a very small percentage of Jewish children to one that served many more.

Yet that message did not take off. After a few hard years, the Bildners began to feel that the philanthropic community was becoming more receptive to the message that informal Jewish education could be a powerful tool for Jewish continuity (Bildner, 2009). But the program of investment in Jewish camps that Arian outlined would cost many millions of dollars and FJC was only slowly raising the needed funds. Raising those larger sums would call for new leadership (Vichness, 2008).

The FJC board turned for new leadership in 2004 to Jerry Silverman, a successful corporate leader who also had been an active lay leader in the Ramah movement. The Bildners believed Ramie Arian had built credibility for FJC; but now was the time to raise much larger sums. With Silverman's appointment FJC underwent a transformation. Silverman saw the success that BRI enjoyed and understood that for Jewish camps to fulfill their mission, they would have to attract and retain a much higher percentage of Jewish families. Jewish camps had been serving around 5% of available Jewish youth. To become a credible answer to philanthropists' concerns about Jewish continuity, camps would have to demonstrate that they had appeal beyond these most committed Jewish families.

Like Steinhardt and Bronfman, Silverman is primarily a marketer. That low percentage of market penetration is for him totally unacceptable. Jewish camps may be serving the educational needs of their committed clientele, but how can one be satisfied knowing that 95% of all Jewish children in North America will never spend a summer – or even a week – at a Jewish residential camp? If you believe in the power of Jewish camping, he contends, you have to be committed to increasing its market penetration (Silverman, 2008).

That was not a new idea for FJC, but Silverman made those numbers the primary focus of FJC. The board set as a goal that in 5 years FJC will double the number of children attending Jewish camps. They agreed that Jewish camps had many other needs, but in meeting those other needs, FJC would also seek to attract and retain far larger numbers of Jewish families to Jewish camping.

Silverman (2008) never saw raising the numbers of Jewish campers as simply a matter of better marketing for the existing programs. For unless Jewish camp leaders offer their potential market an excellent camp program, they will not compete with both private camps and other growing summer program options for the attention of Jewish families. Attaining excellence is a pre-requisite to attracting more market share. Excellence in camping is a complex matter. For a Jewish camp to be competitive, it has to display excellence in many of its features.

Silverman was convinced that leadership matters crucially in determining the future of these camps. Private camps have an advantage of being led by directors who often remain at the leadership helm for several decades (given their financial stake in the camp's success). But Jewish non-profit camps hire camp directors who often have little direct training for this complex role and less of a personal stake in the future of the camp. As a result, many Jewish camps have suffered from unsteady leadership and a lack of long-term strategic planning and development. Silverman knew from his experience in the corporate sector that a well-crafted leadership program can make a significant difference in an executive's capacity to lead with vision and more skill.

In the fall of 2004, Silverman invited me and Richard Levin, a corporate coach and business consultant, to join him in developing a new executive leadership program for Jewish camp directors. He saw a tremendous need to invest in camp directors and thereby raise the bar in the pursuit of excellence. He wanted all three perspectives represented in this effort: his business-marketing outlook, Levin's expertise in developing executive presence and communication, and my expertise in integrating Jewish educational and value perspectives. When we developed an initial conception of the curriculum for ELI – the Executive Leadership Institute – he and Elisa Bildner secured initial funding from the Marcus Foundation.

Focusing on the many conversations we had in planning and implementing ELI, I will reflect on what it meant to be part of an active collaboration in which I represented the perspective of informal Jewish education while they represented the perspectives of corporate marketing and developing executive talent. This is a brief case study of a dialogue-in-action in preparing a leadership institute for Jewish camp directors.

Developing and Implementing ELI

In trying to decide how I could play a constructive role within ELI, I spoke with Alvin Mars who was initiating *Lechu Lechem*, a leadership program for camp directors from the JCC movement supported by the AVI CHAI Foundation. In that initiative, the goal was to provide those camp directors with a deepening Jewish experience through which they would grow as Jewish learners and provide more knowledgeable Jewish leadership for their camps. That was not the premise of ELI, and I had to decide: Could I join an effort that would primarily focus on developing business-oriented skills like marketing, customer service, and fund-raising? I could agree only if I came to believe what is a cardinal principle for Silverman: increasing the numbers of Jewish children going to Jewish camps is itself holy work. I did decide that getting many more children to Jewish camps for several summers is the best chance of their having an intensely meaningful Jewish experience, and that was worthy of my time and effort.

Once I joined this team, what would my contribution be? What is the role of a Jewish educational leader on this team? The obvious answer is to provide a set of experiences through which the participants can engage in Jewish learning and develop ideas about Jewish leadership at camp. It remains important that the discourse within a leadership program not be entirely captured by the lingo of corporate culture and that participants be reminded that as much as the program asks them to stretch to become more competent executive leaders, those skills work in the service of bringing more children to a rich Jewish experience. Their role is to be the Jewish host of this enlarging Jewish tent called camp.

But there is a role beyond the obvious. I found that business-oriented people – even when sympathetic to the goals of Jewish education – do not understand the perspectives of Jewish educators. For example, take the question of camp size. Silverman and I were discussing a particular Jewish camp that is considered to be top quality and has been full with a waiting list. From Jerry's perspective that camp is ripe to grow and should consider opening a second camp. He said private camp owners would seize that growth opportunity. But this director – a good Jewish educator – believes that this camp is of an ideal size, and its relatively small size presents educational advantages she would be loathe to give up. Indeed for many Jewish educators creating an intimate community is an educational ideal. But that line of reasoning baffles Silverman. Why is this educator reluctant to grow this camp when that opportunity is to be seized?

My role got to be to mediate between these two perspectives. I could explain to the educator that Jerry is not criticizing her for preferring the small camp, but he is passionate about bringing that experience to more children. I could also suggest that there are ways to grow, which need not destroy that feeling of intimacy. I could explain that this educator is not simply risk-aversive, but takes genuine pride in the camp community she has helped to create. If she were to grow her camp, it will have to be while still preserving that feeling of intimate community.

Why is this mediating role important? I fear that business-oriented leaders with access to philanthropic funds will simply not understand the perspectives of many Jewish educators. In parallel, I fear that many Jewish educators will outwardly agree to go along with the wishes of such funders, but inwardly resist those funder's ambitious change strategies. When these two sides talk past each other, it creates the conditions for maximal misunderstanding which could result in undermining serious efforts at changing Jewish education in North America.

In the early years of BRI, Jewish educational leaders like Barry Chazan and Irving Greenberg played crucial roles in mediating between the philanthropists and the providers of the Israel experience (Chazan, 2008). At ELI, Richard Levin and I played that role. One feature of the ELI program has been the opportunity for camp directors and FJC leaders like Jerry Silverman and Skip Vichness to talk and understand one another's perspectives. I believe that ELI has worked hard to create the kind of dialogue that the broader sector of informal Jewish education urgently needs.

Beyond ELI, FJC has created many opportunities to increase the numbers of campers attending Jewish camps. But thinking ahead, it will be up to the camp directors and their lay partners to keep up the momentum that FJC and other funders – like the Grinspoon Foundation – have now initiated. Foundations can only launch initiatives; the fate of those initiatives is in the hands of educational leaders who will either embrace this mission or allow it to fade. I believe, the more that camp directors are brought into this conversation, the more likely they will be to embrace these goals over time.

Conclusion: The Need for Greater Dialogue

> There is no single answer to the challenges of strengthening Jewish identity in a highly open society... Family foundations have a great role to play, but if they become absolutist, they can undermine the whole community and over time weaken it. (Ruskay & Solomon, 2009, pp. 6–7)

The annals of educational reform in North America are replete with well-intentioned initiatives that were launched with great hope, but over time produced little substantive change (Fullan, 2007). Current Jewish philanthropists might miss the primary lesson of these past efforts: *it takes more than money, intelligence, and good will to bring about lasting change*. It takes as well a truly collaborative effort by funders, educators, and families to come to an understanding of what they all want to change and what realistically they need to do together to make that change happen over time (Sarason, 1971).

I have presented two cases – BRI and FJC – in which there have been interesting efforts at collaboration and dialogue between the perspectives of business-oriented philanthropists and Jewish educational leaders. This partnership has been integral to the initial success of these programs and there is much more to learn about how philanthropists and educators can productively work together to bring about enduring change. I am not arguing that these cases present an ideal scenario of partnership, but that philanthropic efforts to make change in Jewish education is less likely to succeed over time if one side of this partnership dominates the other and does not attempt to reach mutual understanding and agreement.

The danger of domination is much greater for philanthropists who have the money and the power. There is a danger when philanthropists – based on what they have learned through their business experiences – assume those lessons apply directly to the world of education. There is no question that business perspectives have much to contribute to improving the reach and effectiveness of Jewish education. But in the long run, education is about creating a cultural change – a change in how North American Jews value their Judaism and view themselves as Jews. That adaptive change cannot be accomplished by technical or marketing means alone. It will take a deeper, more visionary effort that perhaps only the most gifted leaders can imagine and effect (Heifitz, 1994).

In the immediate future, I see no more promising path than that of partnership and dialogue between Jewish philanthropists and educators. Philanthropists, anxious to see quicker changes and more measurable outcomes, need to also think more long-term. When their initial funding is over, what will sustain the changes that they are hoping to initiate? What will their funding leave in place over time that will insure that their fondest hopes will outlast their last dollar invested (Fleishman, 2007)?

Many Jewish educators need a crash course in adapting to these changing times. When the Bildners became passionate about Jewish camps, they could articulate what few Jewish educators could: that no matter how well individual camps or camp movements might be doing at any given time, if the larger world of non-profit Jewish camping does not change its mode of operation, these camps are in danger of losing their small slice of the summer market. No camp or movement stands alone. They are all part of an industry – summer leisure for children – that is rapidly changing. Jewish summer camps can either step up on the balcony to see those changes coming or face being washed away as almost happened to companies like Chrysler and General Motors.

There is no turning back the clock on the decade when Jewish philanthropy and informal Jewish education became deeply intertwined. Philanthropists now see the promise of informal Jewish education. The institutions of informal Jewish education have become dependent on the support of philanthropists. But beyond this mutual interdependence, what have these two sides learned from one another? To what extent have they come to better understand their partner? To what degree are they learning to work more effectively as partners? My assumption is that much of the Jewish future in North America hinges on answers to these questions.

References

Arian, R. (2002). Summer camps: Jewish joy, Jewish identity. *Contact*, 4(4), 3.
Baer, M. F. (1983). *Dealing in futures: The story of a Jewish youth movement*. Washington, DC: Bnai Brith International Publication.
Bildner, E. S. (2002). Why I support Jewish camping. *Contact*, 4(4), 4–5.

Bildner, E. S. (2009, January). Telephone interview.
Bryfman, D. (2009, July). Personal Communications.
Cardin, S., & Prager, Y. (2008). Philanthropic funding for Jewish education: Unlimited potential, questionable will. In R. L. Goodman, P. A. Flexner, & L. D. Bloomberg (Eds.), *What we now know about Jewish education* (pp. 537–551). Los Angeles: Torah Aura.
Chazan, B. (1991). What is informal Jewish education? *Journal of Jewish Communal Service, 67*(4), 300–308.
Chazan, B. (1994). The Israel trip: A new form of Jewish education. In *Youth trips to Israel: Rationale and rationalization.* New York: JESNA.
Chazan, B. (1997). *Does the teen Israel trip make a difference?* New York: Israel Experience.
Chazan, B. 2003. The Philosophy of informal Jewish education. *Encyclopedia of Informal Education.* http://www.infed.org/informaljewisheducation/informal-jewish-education.htm.
Chazan, B. (2008, December). Interview.
Commission on Jewish Education in North America. (1991). *A time to act.* New York: University Press of America.
Fleishman, J. L. (2007). *The foundation: A great American secret.* New York: Public Affairs.
Fullan, M. (2007). Understanding change. In *Educational leadership* (2nd ed., pp. 169–182). San Francisco: Jossey-Bass.
Heifitz, R. (1994). *Leadership without easy answers.* Cambridge: Harvard University Press.
Isaacman, D. (1976). The development of Jewish camping in the United States. *Gratz College Annual of Jewish Studies, 5*, 111–120.
Kadushin, C., Kelner, S., & Saxe, L. (2000, December). *Being a Jewish teenager in America.* Waltham, MA: Cohen Center for Modern Jewish Studies.
Kosmin, B., Goldstein, S., & Waksberg, J. (1991). *Highlights of the CJF 1990 national jewish population survey.* New York: Council of Jewish Federations.
Reimer, J. (2006). Beyond more Jews doing Jewish: Clarifying the goals of informal Jewish education. *Journal of Jewish Education, 73*(1), 5–24.
Reimer, J., & Shavelson, S. 2004. Strengthening the field of informal Jewish education: Five years of the Institute for informal Jewish education. Final report to the Andrea and Charles Bronfman Philanthropies.
Reisman, B. (1990, December). *Informal Jewish education in North America.* Cleveland, OH: The Commission on Jewish Education in North America.
Ruskay, J., & Solomon, J. (2009). Organized philanthropy's relationship to independent Jewish philanthropy. *Journal of Jewish Communal Service, 84*(1/2), 4–19.
Sarason, S. B. (1971). *The culture of school and the problem of change.* Boston: Allyn and Bacon.
Sarna, J. (2006). The crucial decade in Jewish camping. In M. M. Lorge & G. P. Zola (Eds.), *A place of our own: The rise of reform Jewish camping* (pp. 27–51). Tuscaloosa, AL: University of Alabama Press.
Saxe, L., & Chazan, B. (2008). *Ten days of birthright Israel.* Waltham, MA: Brandeis University Press.
Silverman, J. (2008, November). Interview.
Solomon, J., Cardin, S., & Gedzelman, D. (2009). The 'gift' as a new paradigm. *Journal of Jewish Communal Service, 84*(1/2), 74–75.
Stern, M. H., 2007. Your children, will they be yours? Educational strategies for Jewish survival, The Central Jewish Institute, 1916–1944. Ph.D. Dissertation, Stanford University.
Tobin., G. A. (2001). *The transition of communal values and behavior in Jewish philanthropy.* San Francisco: Institute for Jewish and Community Research.
Vichness, S. (2008, December). Phone Interview.
Young Judaea Website. March, 2009. www.youngjudaea.org/history.

Intermarriage: Connection, Commitment, and Community

Jewish Education and Teenagers from Interfaith Families

Evie Levy Rotstein

Introduction

While the phenomenon of intermarriage represents one of the most important challenges facing American Jewry today, it is interesting to note that few academic researchers have examined the lives of the adolescents from interfaith families. This chapter provides much-needed insight into the lives of these adolescents and considers the role of Jewish education in developing a sense of Jewish commitment and continuity for this population.

According to National Jewish Population Survey data, 32% of children from interfaith families are being raised as Jewish (Phillips & Chertok, 2004 based on NJPS 2000–2001). The survey findings indicate that 33% of children are being raised as Christian, and 25% as both Jewish and Christian (Phillips, 1997, p. 49). The subject of intermarriage evokes considerable response in the Jewish community because it arouses basic fears about group survival. There are two aspects of concern. The first is the sheer matter of numbers. How many children of interfaith families will remain Jewish? The second consideration is one of identity and commitment. What will be the quality of affiliation of the interfaith family?

There are those researchers who believe that children from interfaith homes are lost to Judaism (Bayme, Greenwood, & Block, 1998; Wertheimer, Liebman, & Cohen, 1996), and there are others who argue that this does not have to happen. Phillips and Chertok (2004) remind us that we cannot dismiss children of intermarriages: "Intermarried households are diverse, and those raising children exclusively as Jews are far from a lost cause" (p. 10).

With the rising numbers of interfaith marriages and community concern about the decrease in Jewish population, the question of teen involvement in both formal and informal education is becoming significant. The American Jewish community has been struggling with the fact that there is a relatively large number of students (68%) who do not continue their Jewish education post-bar/bat mitzvah into the middle teen years (Kadushin, Kelner, & Saxe, 2000). The impact of this attrition rate

E.L. Rotstein (✉)
Hebrew Union College, New York, NY, USA
e-mail: ERotstein@huc.edu

has far-reaching effects in light of the reality that the adolescent years are the developmentally appropriate years for identity formation. "By default, today's Jewish school whether afternoon, Sunday, or day school, carries a bigger proportion of the burden of Jewish identity training than in the past" (London & Frank, 1987, p. 11). The Jewish community has taken modest measures to develop awareness of this issue and to create programming that will reach out to teenagers to increase religious affiliation and participation in Jewish activities. Programs such as Israel teen tours, leadership training summer institutes, and various social action mitzvah corps, are some examples. One of the major contributions of the Reform movement to the continuation of Jewish education through high school has been the emphasis it gives to the life-cycle ceremony of confirmation.

The relationship between adolescent Jewish education and adult commitment to Jewish life has been explored in a number of research studies in the last 30 years (Cohen, 1974; Fishman & Goldstein, 1993; Mayer 1983; Fishman, 2007a; Phillips, 1997, 2000). Findings indicate that Jewish education into adolescent years is a significant predictor for Jewish engagement as adults, and yet it is common knowledge that the American Jewish community is faced with great attrition rates for post-bar/bat mitzvah Jewish teens involved in formal and informal Jewish educational programs (Kadushin et al., 2000).

A study conducted by the Union for Reform Judaism in 2008, entitled *Portraits of Learning*, found that the retention rate in Reform congregations for post-bar/bat mitzvah is 47% and 32% after confirmation in the 10th grade. Rabbi Jan Katzew, the director of the Department of Lifelong Jewish Learning, states: "We need to stop the teen recessional out of synagogues and out of the Jewish community. Teens are too precious to lose. We need them to succeed us and to exceed us as adult leaders and members of the Jewish community, as teachers and students of Torah and as lovers of Israel and of God" (Katzew, 2008).

These data challenge Jewish educators to better understand what they might do to actively engage teenagers in the Jewish community, particularly those from interfaith families. The goal of this chapter is to add to our understanding of what motivates these young adults to continue their Jewish education throughout their high-school years.

Adolescence, Retention, and Intermarriage

Research about the role of Jewish education specifically in the lives of teenagers is minimal. Some recent studies offer insight into the adolescent Jewish world and highlight a number of significant points. The Jewish Adolescent Study (JAS) (2000) conducted by Kadushin et al. explored the various influences on Jewish affiliation in adolescence such as family, school, peer group, and neighborhood. The study investigated the lives of teens from diverse levels of Jewish commitment and from many different communities. In an effort to deepen understanding of the American Jewish adolescent experience, the study examined attitudes and behaviors in all aspects of teenagers' lives. One of the more challenging findings for Jewish educators concerned the widespread negative attitude toward supplementary Jewish education, with the rate of enrollment decreasing from 60% in the 7th grade to 22% in the 11th grade. "There is a steady move away from the Jewish community as *b'nei mitzvah* enter the demanding world inhabited by other American teenagers" (p. 71). The study showed that teenagers increase the time they devote to homework, school-based extracurricular activities, and paid employment, but that Jewish activities are seemingly peripheral and marginal. The teenage respondents did express the sentiment that being Jewish was important, and nearly two-thirds of the adolescents thought it was important to raise their own children as Jews. Finally, most teens felt that their parents strongly influenced the decision to continue formal post-bar/bat mitzvah Jewish education. "Just over half of the parents either required or strongly encouraged post-bar/bat mitzvah Jewish education, and this parental mandate or support was the strongest predictor of actual enrollment" (p. 72).

In another study by Kosmin and Keysar (2000) entitled *Four Up – The High School Year, 1995–1999*, approximately 1,300 teenagers were interviewed twice during 4 years. The first phase of the research involved interviews of 13–14 year olds, and the second phase involved interviewing the same teenagers when they were 17–18 years old. The study revealed that there is overwhelming consistency between the responses of the teenagers at both ages. A large percentage of the 13-year-old students (42%) enjoyed their Jewish education most of the time, whereas 37% of the 17-year-olds felt the same way (p. 24). The study made a clear statement regarding the influence of parents. "Parental engagement in Jewish life shows a clear correlation with the pattern of teenage involvement. Jewishly engaged parents tend to produce Jewishly engaged teenagers" (p. 47). The study also highlighted the response to the question, "How important is it for you to marry somebody Jewish?", with the highest proportions of affirmative responses (75%) coming from those who had attended Hebrew high school (p. 45).

Phillips determined that the more years one attended Hebrew School, the stronger one's Jewish belief and practices are (Phillips, 1997). His previous (1993) *Survey on Mixed Marriage* found that "respondents who continued past age 13 in even a 1 day-a-week school married non-Jews less often than those in more intensive schools who terminated their Jewish education at age 13" (Phillips, 1997, p. 16). He further indicates that adolescent involvement in either formal or informal Jewish education, two or more years of Jewish sleep-away camp or involvement in a Jewish youth group or an Israel teen trip can make a difference in friendships and dating patterns. These are the experiences, then, that have a significant impact on rates of intermarriage and adult Jewish identification.

In a study for the Union of Reform Judaism for teenagers from both in-married and interfaith families, Schaap (2008) notes that what distinguishes "high retention schools is that they display a culture encouraging retention based on a widespread agreement from the stakeholders that this is an important goal" (Schaap, 2008). This explicit goal can strongly influence teenagers to continue their post-bar/bat mitzvah Jewish education. Analysis of the findings yields other significant factors that lead to high retention rates:

- The role of friends and peers – Jewish learning is intrinsically social. Friends are the binding forces. The top factor that all stakeholders agree influences retention rates is the desire of teenage students to be with their friends.
- The parents' role – Ranked second in importance is the statement that parents encourage their children to attend the school. Successful congregations are not just focusing on retaining students but are also making strong efforts to retain parents.
- Family programs and retreats – Both the high-school students and their parents indicate a significantly higher participation rate in family programs and retreats.
- The student's desire to be an active participant in the congregation – In the interviews, several experts indicated that students like to feel that they are significant contributors to a community and thus are seen as key members of their community, rather than being seen as a passive group that is "being served." In high-retention congregations, more high-school students are acting as teachers' aides and are singing in the choir.
- The role of the rabbi and other congregational professionals – In high-retention congregations, the students and their parents are significantly more likely to acknowledge the personal encouragement by the rabbi especially, but also by the other professionals such as the educational director and the teachers.
- The teachers and the educational content – The content of the learning does hold significant relevance for students and their parents. They are likely to rank high as factors in deciding to stay in the school the actual learning and the statement that the topics are relevant to their lives. The teachers at high-retention schools play an important role not only by encouraging the students to continue in the school, but also by making the Jewish learning exciting and relevant (Schaap, 2008).

In 2005, the Greater Boston Jewish Community published a study which indicates that intermarried families choose to raise their children as Jews when the families are themselves deeply engaged in Jewish practice (Chertok, Phillips, & Saxe, 2008). Within Reform-affiliated families, intermarried families with Jewish children are generally as observant as endogamous[1] Jewish families, and their children become B'nai Mitzvah at the same rates. The study reveals that although exogamous[2] families tend to join synagogues later than endogamous households, and a smaller percentage of their teenage children continue their formal Jewish education past their bar or bat mitzvah, many participate in synagogue life in similar ways to other Jews.

---

[1] This term is used to describe marrying within one's religion.
[2] This term is used to describe marrying outside one's religion.

Building on this literature, my own research used a qualitative study to explore the lives of adolescents from interfaith homes, listening carefully to discern what influences their decision to continue their Jewish education through the 12th grade. What emerged was a composite that represents the interplay of factors: the family life, peer relationships, the religious school experience, and finally each student's individual motivation and needs. Utilizing the following case study, one can better understand the significant factors involved for the teenager to be socially and educationally active in the congregation and the Jewish community.

Marlena: Leading the Way

The Family

Sixteen-year-old Marlena stands in the doorway and welcomes me into her home. We begin with the background information about her family. Marlena explains that her family has been a member of the temple for their "whole lives." She says this with conviction and emphasis. She is eager to communicate that being part of the temple is a significant piece of her family story and that it is the reason that she is working at the temple now. She further portrays her mother's connection to religion by saying that she is "not really religious." Marlena's mother Sheryl confirms this fact. Sheryl conveys a sense of pride when she states that her daughter, Marlena, has gone one step further and learned to read Hebrew for her bat mitzvah. When Sheryl was growing up, it was not the norm for a young woman to become a bat mitzvah. Marlena has internalized her mom's thinking in the following passage and shares the positive attitude she has developed regarding her Jewish sense of self.

I mean, they always joke around 'cause like my dad is pretty Catholic and like my mom is not crazy like Jewish ... like she wasn't brought up like that. She's not like that now. We don't go to temple all the time. And like I am very into being Jewish. I have an interest in religion and I think it's really interesting and I like to learn about it. I like to *learn* about Jewish traditions, and I like to *practice* them and *do* the different things, and I'll always like to *make* Shabbat dinners and *bake* challah. They're like, I don't get it. I'm just so into it. I like it. I think it's interesting and I like learning about Jewish customs. I like practicing it too, so ... I do more Jewish stuff than my parents do (Interview, February, 2003).

Marlena uses verbs that illustrate the specific actions that she takes to demonstrate her Jewish connection. She says that she likes to "*learn, practice, do, make and bake*" (my italics) Shabbat dinners. She is able to define what she likes about being Jewish in very specific terms. Marlena has translated her Jewish learning experiences into meaningful Jewish activity.

When I ask Marlena to convey her perceptions regarding her parents' interfaith situation, she is quick to relate that her father, Lou, doesn't really care that she and her brothers are being raised Jewish, but her mother does. Marlena's mother, Sheryl, describes how her children became involved with the temple through participation in the children's choir. The children have literally brought the parents to the religious services, and the parents are both proud and happy to watch their children lead the service and even participate in the children's choir. Sheryl is eager to share the fact that her husband continues to be so supportive of his children's participation in the junior choir. Though she doesn't sing in the public school choir, Marlena tells me that the reason she likes the choir so much is because it gives her the opportunity to be with her friends.

Reaching Out

From the outset, Marlena focuses on the many specific ways in which she actively expresses her Jewish self. First, she is president of the youth group. When I asked her why she became involved, she said, "I was interested in working with the youth group, since I enjoyed leadership positions and wanted to get involved in an organization." Her most significant accomplishment is that she was chosen to be the teen representative on the Temple Outreach Committee. The Outreach Committee organizes activities and programs for interfaith families and addresses ways to include the non-Jewish spouse in temple life. In addition, since she is the president of the youth group, Marlena has been appointed the teen representative to the temple board of Trustees. Marlena realizes that she has been given a position that gives her a sense of responsibility and purpose. She expresses the fact that she feels valued as a teen participant of the temple board and likes the fact that she has been given the opportunity to share her perspective as a child growing up in an interfaith family.

Marlena's work with this Outreach Committee, the temple board, and the youth group has been a positive experience. Her voice becomes animated and she smiles with a sparkle in her eyes. She speaks about this part of her life with a great deal of excitement. Marlena's community service has had a big impact on her. Gaines (2003) notes, "Service has the capacity to radically alter the paradigm of teen empowerment. Community service provides much more than individual involvement in the Jewish community and in the larger world. In a very real way, doing community service allows a hands-on, participatory approach to being a positive force in society" (p. 4).

Smith (2003) observes, "American religious congregations represent one of the few remaining major social institutions in which adolescents participate extensively that emphasizes continuity of interaction. . . .This creates the possibility for youth to form significant relational network ties that cross age boundaries" (p. 25). Marlena communicates her dedication to this volunteer project as an extension of her dedication to the temple and as a result of her positive Jewish educational experience.

Sheryl offers her perspective on Marlena's continuing post-bar/bat mitzvah by saying that, "It's never been a discussion, quite honestly. It's just been assumed" (Interview, February, 2003). I question Sheryl by asking her, "Do you think it would be different if the school wasn't such a positive experience?" She answered by saying, "Possibly. I couldn't say because it has always been a positive experience for them. I'm sure if it was a negative experience; if it was a different type of environment, the situation would be different" (Interview, February, 2003).

My Teacher – My Leader

Marlena is very definite that one of the reasons she has continued her Jewish education is the result of the positive relationships she has developed with certain people in the temple. She builds a very strong case to support the fact that many teachers in the religious school and particularly the student rabbi have played a significant role in her life.

Marlena uses language that describes her emotional connections to people. The context of her narrative is one of relationships and feelings. She speaks about "getting close and having a special bond" and "becoming pretty close" with the new youth advisor/ rabbi. She seems to be proud that she has formed a relationship that feels comfortable and close, while most teens would never go to speak with a rabbi. There is a tone in her voice that expresses the happiness she feels that she can "talk to my rabbi." Research conducted by the National Study of Youth and Religion discovered that 72% of teens find their religious congregation a place to talk about problems (Denton, Pearce, & Smith, 2008).

Marlena describes the numerous and meaningful existential discussions she has had in her confirmation classes. She explains that her Jewish education has provided other important opportunities to discuss big ideas. "I think it has really defined my morals and how I might see the world and how I see other people. That's a lot of what we discuss now that we're like older and we're in class" (Interview, February, 2003). The fact that Marlena mentions the issue of morality as a product of her continued Jewish education is congruent with the research conducted by Kosmin and Keysar (2004). They report that for their sample, the second most important element of being Jewish is "leading an ethical and moral life" (p. 19).

One Direction – Two Religions

Marlena gives thoughtful response to her perspective of religious choice. She sees herself as only Jewish and not a mélange of two religions. Marlena's parents have actually aligned themselves with the smallest percentage of interfaith parents who have selected Judaism to be the only religion in their family. They fall into the smaller cohort of 39% of intermarried couples who are raising their children Jewish as compared to the 53% who are "not being raised Jewish" (Fishman, 2004, p. 7). As her father Lou states, "It worked for us – it may not work for others."

Lou attests to the fact that holiday celebrations are important family gatherings and states that "We are really a close family. I don't think my sisters and brother who are married to Christians, make any bigger deal out of the holidays than I do. It's just really a time to get together" (Interview, 2003). It is interesting to note that Cohen and Eisen (2000) describe the holiday Jewish experience in a similar fashion,

"Holidays celebrated throughout the year, with observance heavily focused on the family at home, therefore constitute the master script of Jewish involvement... Family is thus not only the site and vehicle for holiday observance, but its most important meaning and motivation" (pp. 186–187). For both Lou and Sheryl, holiday celebrations whether Jewish or Christian, provide the closeness and valuable sharing that is important to them.

The Good School

Perhaps the most illuminating aspect of Marlena's story is the way in which both she and her parents pay tribute to the excellent religious school at the temple. There are numerous times when they emphasize the way that the synagogue and the school have positively influenced the children and the parents in the community.

In one conversation, Marlena described some of the highlights of her learning experiences. I was not surprised to hear her speak of the field-trips and the guest speakers who have come to the school. I heard the theme of "engagement" and the issue of active learning and making meaningful connections. Expanding the walls of the classroom to the community and places of historical interest provides students with authentic learning.

Many components of the religious school program have contributed to Marlena's decision to continue her Jewish education to the 12th grade. She has built positive connections with some of the teachers, a caring relationship with the student rabbi, and found value in many of the learning activities. I am impressed that she is able to articulate the inter-relatedness of the entire experience and remembers so many of the details of the specific curriculum.

Marlena has explored many different ways to be part of her synagogue community. She has found a place that she feels valued and accepted and is treated as an adult. She willingly assumes different leadership roles and is given a great deal of support by the teachers, the rabbi, and members of the temple board. She enjoys the fact that she has chosen a path that is not the norm among her peers, and that she can practice what she has learned. Marlena has found many opportunities to be an active member of the Jewish community and she feels both comfortable and committed to linking Jewish learning with Jewish living. She is able to look into the future and see continued ways of connecting to the Jewish community both in college and later into adulthood.

Implications

What can Jewish educators and community professionals glean from Marlena's story and the stories of other students interviewed for this research. How we can possibly use this data to enhance our work with interfaith families, the school community, and finally our students? Though Marlena's story is certainly not the majority case for children of interfaith families, it is all the more important to learn from her experience and to better understand the factors that contribute to the successful Jewish engagement of teenagers.

How Families Respond Makes a Difference

Marlena's story points to the fact that parents who are intermarried have a crucial role in supporting their children's educational choices. When Jewish education is a priority for the Jewish parent, and when parents acknowledge that Jewish learning has benefits for teenagers as well as for younger children, it makes a difference in the attitudes of teens from interfaith families. The question for Jewish educators is why some parents understand the value of Jewish high-school education and other parents do not. How can we utilize the influence of parents who support continued learning to help shift the perception of the other parents who don't? The Jewish community, together with the rabbis, cantors, teachers, and principals, must provide a unified message that post-bar/bat mitzvah Jewish education is in fact critical for the teenage population. The first step is to clearly articulate the position that formative Jewish learning is valuable and essential to adolescent development. When parents feel positive about Jewish learning, they are able to communicate their expectations.

If the community and/or congregation can establish an expectation that Jewish education extends through the high-school years and that Jewish learning is a life-long endeavor, parents will shift their thinking. In my experience, when parents view post-bar/bat mitzvah Jewish education as an important component of their teenagers' lives, the teens are committed to learning. One educator comments:

> Some parents care an awful lot, and they do what they should do, which is to put their foot down and say, look, you don't drop out of junior high school just because you're thirteen. Why do you think that you should stop going now just because you had a bar mitzvah? The whole point is Jewish education and not having a bar mitzvah. Parents who understand that tend to put their feet down and once you do that, the child has to go. And of course those who went to confirmation themselves or had a good Hebrew high school experience tend to assume that their children will continue. (Interview, 2003)

This statement reinforces the fact that teenagers are responsive to their parents' feelings and values. This is further supported by the research of Jewish teenagers (Fishman, 2007; Kosmin & Keysar, 2004) and by the larger National Study of Youth and Religion (Smith & Denton, 2005)

> What we learned by interviewing hundreds of different kinds of teenagers all around the country is that the vast majority of American teenagers are *exceedingly conventional* in their religious identity and practices. Very few are restless, alienated, or rebellious; rather, the majority of U.S. teenagers seem basically content to follow the faith of their families with little questioning. When it comes to religion, they are quite happy to go along and get along. (Smith & Denton, p. 120)

Parents need to be part of the educational process from the beginning. When congregational religious schools are committed to building strong programs that cultivate community and personal relationships, parents will begin to see the value of the experience and support Jewish education throughout the teen years. Parents need to feel empowered to encourage their teenagers to continue their Jewish education. It is important for synagogues and religious schools to include outreach to parents, both the Jewish and non-Jewish parents. Dr. Ismar Schorsch, the former Chancellor of the Conservative Movement's Jewish Theological Seminary, wrote a similar message in a Torah commentary over 10 years ago in 1994: "We should not miss an opportunity to give the non-Jewish spouse of our son or daughter a chance to savor Jewish experience. We should start from strength by taking them into our family and exposing them often to the emotional warmth, ethical standards, intellectual power and artistic beauty of Judaism" (Retrieved May, 2005 from http://learn.jtsa.edu/topics/parashah/576f3/pinhas.shtml).

Leadership – Fostering Caring Relationships

I contend that synagogue schools are in fact part of the solution in keeping teenagers of interfaith families engaged and connected to Jewish life. We look to the congregation to emphasize the value of continued Jewish education. Aron (2000) stresses the role of the synagogue in reaching out to families.

> For the last decade, leaders of the American Jewish community have been wringing their hands over the 'continuity crisis,' whose most obvious symptom is the rising rate of intermarriage, but whose ancillary symptoms include lower rates of affiliation and observance.... Synagogues have tended to be seen as part of the problem rather than as part of the solution. ...Synagogues have the potential for reaching people on a continuous basis throughout their lives and in the context of their families. (p. 7)

Does the professional leadership in the congregation realize the extent to which it can affect a change of vision regarding Jewish education? All the research about educational change points to the fact that the process of change begins with a clearly articulated vision on the part of the school leadership (Evans, 1996).

Professionals play a significant role in conveying this message. Principals, teachers, rabbis, and youth group leaders do have the power to build meaningful relationships that can influence the decision to continue Jewish education. These relationships are highly valued by teenagers, and they cherish the sense of connectedness they feel by being part of the synagogue community. For teens from interfaith families, this sense of belonging to the Jewish community is perhaps even more critical. If we consider the concept of a *kehillah kedoshah* (holy community) as a paradigm for this vision, we can build a foundation for our students to be part of a cohesive and supportive community. Synagogue professionals must understand the critical leadership role they play in encouraging all teenagers, and specifically those from interfaith families, to continue Jewish learning. They are not necessarily trained to work specifically with adolescents and may not understand the developmental need to build strong personal relationships, with both peers and adults. This is an aspect of professional development that requires careful consideration. The professional leadership in the congregation must develop skills and strategies also to reach out to the parent community for support and to connect with teenagers as well.

The Jewish community is beginning to realize that it is important to build strong leadership capacity for Jewish educators. The Leadership Institute for Congregational School Educators sponsored by New York School of Education at Hebrew Union College and the Davidson School at the Jewish Theological Seminary, funded by the UJA Federation of New York, is a result of the growing understanding that a new perception is needed to help educators view themselves as important change agents in the community and to be "charismatic adults" for teenagers. This two-and-half-year professional learning initiative involves 40 principals from both the Reform and Conservative movements, and is designed to build leadership capacity, pedagogical skills, and enhance Judaic knowledge. One of the major goals of the program is to empower educators to create successful schools where shared leadership and collaboration are the building blocks of dynamic learning communities (Wald & Castleberry, 2000).

Re-imagining Jewish Education

Participation in volunteer Jewish leadership experiences during the high-school years is a significant influence to support learning for teenagers from interfaith families. Whether it is the *madrikhim* (teen assistants) program working with elementary age children, the *Gesher le Kesher* program working with 8th graders, being active in a youth group, or creating significant *tikkun olam* (repairing the world) projects, the teenagers in this study expressed the fact that these experiences influenced their decision to continue their Jewish education. In another study of Jewish teenagers, Leffert and Herring (1998) found that volunteer experiences were also powerful predictors of adolescents' involvement in Jewish activities. They found that adolescents who volunteer report significantly higher levels of involvement in Jewish-sponsored activities and value Jewish education and Jewish knowledge. They report further "that if young people can be involved in volunteer or service activities, there is increased likelihood that they will feel that Jewish learning is an important part of their lives and identities as they reach later adolescence and make the transition into early adulthood" (p. 55).

We learn something very important from the students' accounts of the impact of these types of experiences. Our schools must create opportunities for all teenagers to choose among many volunteer options. These would require careful design and structuring and must include time for personal reflection and meaning-making. It is important for teenagers to express their individuality by having choices and finding volunteer situations that are meaningful (Arnett & Jensen, 2002).

The second implication for the field of Jewish education involves building religious school communities that develop strong connections to authentic Jewish living in an open and accepting environment. Marlena and others in this study identify certain aspects of Jewish learning that they found engaging or that provided meaningful connections to their lives, and which made them feel comfortable and supported. They are able to define and characterize these learning experiences in specific detail.

What does engaging Jewish education look like, and how do we strive to provide this kind of experience for our students? I suggest that Jewish learning needs to be personally meaningful. Personal meaning-making is learning that connects an individual to Judaism and Judaism to the individual. Each learner has the opportunity to make Jewish learning a Jewish living experience (Aron, 2000). Creating memorable learning experiences frames knowledge acquisition in vivid experiences, meaningful relationships and connects the individual to emotions, senses, and intellect in ways that create a lasting impression.

Formal religious organizations, while being in a position to assist adolescents in the identity search process, often abdicate such a role (Markstrom-Adams 1992). Religious schools must provide opportunities for a dialogue between parents and teenagers to further exploration of Jewish identity and commitment. It is crucial that parents are brought into the conversation, to help teenagers define the role that Judaism plays in their lives. Parent/child reflections and shared narratives can strengthen the connections between our students and the Jewish community. In speaking about all faith communities, Christian Smith and M.L. Denton (2005) succinctly states, "...parents should be viewed as indispensable partners in the religious formation of youth" (p. 267).

Yearning and Learning

Some students from interfaith families demonstrate a desire to further their Jewish learning which is fostered by the many positive experiences they have had through the years. One educator reflects, "The kids were talking about the confirmation ceremony, and I asked them how many were here in religious school because they were forced to come. No one raised their hands and they all started telling me that they really like coming to learn. You have some kids who are going to go no matter what" (Interview, 2003). We Jewish educators must acknowledge that many of our students have a true desire to learn. Educators, who have high expectations that reflect a teacher's deep belief in a student's capacity to learn, are able to be highly effective.

All religious schools need to have high standards and expectations which convey the message that Jewish learning is important. In addition to having high expectations, Jewish educators must continue to explore important adolescent concerns and frame them within a Jewish context. It is essential to design Jewish high-school programs that address existential questions and contemporary dilemmas that connect to the world outside the school. Resources and texts must reflect adolescent concerns and provide the Jewish perspective. An example is the curriculum presented to the 68th Biennial conference for the Union for Reform Judaism entitled *Sacred Choices: Adolescent Relationships and Sexual Ethics*. Yoffe (2005) describes his perspective on adolescent concerns and the lack of support from the Jewish community.

> The simple truth is this: Our kids are frustrated by the combined failure of their parents and their synagogues to offer them practical help here. More often than not, hookups leave them

depressed, confused, and guilty. But very few of them see the synagogue as a place to go for support, or their Judaism as a source of comfort and direction. And they wonder why. Since we have told them again and again that Judaism is an all-embracing way of life, they expect that their tradition will have something to say about matters of such importance. (Retrieved November, 2005 from www.urj.org)

In addition to grappling with these critical adolescent issues, students want to expand their Jewish knowledge to help them understand the broad existential questions in life that assist in building a strong sense of self. During the last several decades, "religious individualism" has dominated the landscape of American religion. The notion that "an individual should arrive at his or her own religious beliefs independent of any churches or synagogues" (Roof, 2003, p. 139) has an impact on the way in which we must involve Jewish teens in the educational process. This makes our challenge as Jewish educators a significant one; we must offer educational experiences that provide varied opportunities to cultivate deep and meaningful connections to the Jewish community and the synagogue.

Concluding Thoughts

What can we learn that will make a difference in the way we might plan for students from interfaith families? We see that the family plays a central role in the decision to continue post-bar/bat mitzvah Jewish education. When the Jewish parent communicates a positive response to their children's active involvement in the Jewish community it does have a significant impact on the teenager. It is evident that the role of the Jewish parent is crucial in defining expectations and shaping the home environment. In this qualitative study, it doesn't seem to matter if the Jewish parent is the mother or the father, but it is significant for the non-Jewish parent to be either very supportive of Jewish engagement or not involved at all. Sibling and grandparent relationships also play an important role and have considerable impact on the teenagers' decision.

The religious school experience, both during the elementary years and during the beginning years of high school, has a great deal of influence in the decision to continue on to 11th and 12th grades. Many of the programs, trips, retreats, and curricula are appreciated and perceived as meaningful contributions to their strong Jewish connections and the decision to continue. Marlena, like others in the study, finds many of her teachers to be positive role models. The teenagers express their satisfaction with the fact that they are able to build trusting friendships with teachers, rabbis, youth group advisors, and other adults in the community, and that these individual relationships are very significant. Social relationships with peers are critical for these teenagers, and they enjoy the "special" nature of these religious school friendships. Being involved in youth group or the synagogue's *madrikhim* program extends social ties to the congregation and offers the teenager a position of value and honor in the community.

Teenagers from interfaith families are inspired to continue their Jewish education because they are interested in learning and growing spiritually. Their quest for knowledge simply for its own sake – *Torah Lishmah* – is an integral aspect of the decision to continue. The need to understand the spiritual and existential questions of life, which is part of a normative process during adolescents, is another motivating factor. Finally, these teenagers have revealed that their decision to continue Jewish education into the 11th and 12th grades is influenced by their individual experiences in making meaningful connections to their religious school friends, their teachers, rabbis, and youth group advisors and to the curriculum that links Jewish values and Jewish living.

Like resilient youth, who develop a positive attachment to school and therefore defy their cultural environments (Bernard, 2003; Brooks & Goldstein, 2001), these teenagers, unlike many of their peers, have had successful religious school experiences which foster their desire to continue their Jewish education and act in a counter-cultural manner. They attribute their meaningful Jewish learning experience to the powerful influence of caring teachers, rabbis, and youth advisors who are able "to engage the whole child, not just the cognitive but the social, emotional, physical, and spiritual parts. They also understand that student motivation is driven by the need for love and belonging, respect, autonomy/power, mastery, challenge, fun, and meaning, and that successful learning experiences are designed to meet as many of these needs as possible" (Bernard, 2003, p. 121). Creating the opportunity to connect Jewish learning to Jewish living is the foundation of the role of service to the community. The resilient youth literature points to the fact that schools and classrooms that have been successful are often described in terms of "a family, a home, a community – even a sanctuary" (Bernard, 2003, p. 125). This is the very sentiment shared by the Jewish teenagers in this study as well.

Suggestions for Future Research

Sociologist Egon Mayer clearly states, "Those who ignore the potential for Jewish continuity amongst the descendants of the intermarried, given the magnitude of their numbers, are also condemning hope in the American Jewish future" (Mayer, 1994, p. 78). Moreover it is critical for Jewish educators to focus their attention on how to better engage teenagers both from interfaith families and those with two Jewish parents.

The Reform Movement in America has embraced the concept of outreach to interfaith families and has developed many programs and educational materials to support the endeavor. Both the Conservative and Orthodox branches of American Jewry have been less willing to do so. Though the number of interfaith families who raise their children exclusively as Jews is low, many children from a dual-religion household are in fact being exposed to Judaism.

While seeking to shed light on the factors that motivate teenagers from interfaith families to continue their Jewish education, I have discovered that there are many possibilities for further research in the field. More specifically, questions that emerge from this study include further investigation of the following:

- The role of the teacher, rabbi, and youth group leader is an integral factor in the decision to continue post-bar/bat mitzvah Jewish education. What kind of professional training is necessary to guide these professionals to be effective "charismatic adults"? How would this professional development provide innovative models to advance meaningful personal connections to Jewish teenagers from interfaith families?
- There is a potential area of research which involves the teenage quest for spiritual connections. A study of Generation Y (Greenberg, 2004) found that while "the Baby Boom was characterized as a 'generation of seekers,' their offspring, Generation Y, is a 'generation of individuals' " (p. 5). Young people believe it is possible to be "religious" or "spiritual" without belonging to a church, synagogue, or mosque. I suggest that students from interfaith families have a particular pull toward a spiritual quest; I believe that it would be worthwhile to investigate the belief systems of students who do not continue their Jewish education. How do teenagers from interfaith families understand the role of Jewish community in their quest to answer the existential questions of life?

Children from interfaith families are a growing percentage of the students in our religious schools. It is critical that we take their experience into consideration when we design learning for Jewish teenagers. Like the young people in the resilient youth studies, teenagers from interfaith families are bucking the trend and choosing a different set of counter-cultural decisions. We know that most Jewish teens drop out of religious school and that it may seem counter-cultural to continue beyond bar/bat mitzvah; this is even more so the case for students who come from interfaith families. The ultimate success of continued Jewish learning for teenagers from interfaith families is directly related to the success that the individual student feels in finding deep and meaningful connections to both the people in the congregation and to the learning environment.

References

Arnett, J. J., & Jensen., L. A. (2002). A congregation of one: Individualized religious beliefs among emerging adults. *Journal of Adolescent Research, 17*(5), 451–467.
Aron, I. (2000). *Becoming a congregation of learners*. Woodstock, VT: Jewish Lights Publishing.
Bayme, S., Greenwood, D., & Block, J. A. (1998). Intermarriage: Three views. In N. Linzer, D. Schnall, & J. A. Chanes (Eds.), *Portrait of American Jewish community* (pp. 139–164). Westport, CT: Praeger Publishers.
Bernard, B. (2003). Turnaround teachers and schools. In B. Williams (Ed.), *Closing the achievement gap: A vision for changing beliefs and practices* (pp. 115–137). Alexandria, VA: ASCD.
Brooks, R., & Goldstein, S. (2001). *Raising resilient children*. New York: Contemporary Books.
Chertok, F., Phillips, B., & Saxe, L. (2008). *It's not just who stands under the chuppah: Intermarriage and engagement*. Brandeis University. http://bir.brandeis.edu/bitstream/handle/10192/23017/Intermarriage

Cohen, S. (1974). The Impact of Jewish education on religious identification and practice. *Jewish Social Studies, 36*, 316–326.

Cohen, S., & Eisen, A. M. (2000). *The Jew within: Self, family and community in America*. Indiana: Indiana University Press.

Denton, M. L., Pearce, L. D., & Smith, C. (2008). Religioun and Spirituality on the path through adolescence. Research Report Number 8, National Study of Youth and Religion, University of North Carolina at Chapel Hill.

Evans, R. (1996). *The human side of school change*. San Francisco: Jossey-Bass.

Fishman, S. B. (2004). *Double or nothing*. Lebanon, NH: Brandeis University Press.

Fishman, S. B. (2007a). Generating Jewish connections: Conversations with Jewish teenagers, their parents, and Jewish educators and thinkers. In J. Wertheimer (Ed.), *Family Matters: Jewish education in an age of choice* (pp. 181–210). Waltham, MA: Brandeis University Press.

Fishman, S. B. (2007b). *The way into the varieties of Jewishness*. Woodstock, VT: Jewish Lights Publishing.

Fishman, S. B., & Goldstein, A. (1993). *When they are grown they will not depart: Jewish education and the Jewish behavior of American adults* (CMJS Research Report 8). Waltham, MA: Cohen Center for Modern Jewish Studies, Brandeis University.

Gaines, M. (2003). Jewish service as teen empowerment. *Contact, 5*(4), 3–4.

Greenberg, A. (2004). *OMG! How generation Y Is redefining faith in the iPod era*, www.greenbergresearch.com/publications/reports/rebootreport.pdf.

Kadushin, C., Kelner, S., & Saxe, L. (2000). *Being a Jewish teenager in America: Trying to make it*. Cohen Center for Modern Jewish Studies, Brandeis University. www.brandeis.edu/ije

Katzew, J. (2008). Torah at the Center. Union for Reform Judaism.

Kosmin, B. A. & Keysar, A. (2000). *Four up: The high school years, 1995–1999*. New York: Jewish Theological Seminary.

Kosmin, B. A., & Keysar, A. (2004). *Eight up: The college years*. New York: The Jewish Theological Seminary.

Leffert, N., & Herring, H. (1998). *Shema: Listening to Jewish youth*. Search Institute. www.search-institute.org/organizations/Shema.

London, P., & Frank, M. A. (1987). Jewish identity and Jewish schooling. *Journal of Jewish Communal Services, 64*, 4–13.

Markstrom-Adams, C. (1992). A consideration of intervening factors in adolescent identity formation. In G. R. Adams, T. P. Gullotta, & R. Montemayor (Eds.), *Adolescent identity formation* (pp. 173–192). Newbury Park, CA: Sage Publications, Inc.

Mayer, E. (1983). *Children of intermarriage: A study in patterns of identification and family life*. New York: The American Jewish Committee.

Mayer, E. (1994, April). Will the grandchildren of intermarriage be Jews? The chances are greater than you think. *Moment Magazine, 19*(2): 50–53, 78.

Phillips, B. A. (1997). *Re-examining intermarriage: Trends, textures and strategies*. Boston and Los Angeles: American Jewish Committee and Wilstein Institute of Jewish Studies.

Phillips, B. A. (2000). Intermarriage and Jewish education: Is there a connection? *Journal of Jewish Education, 66*(1), 54–66.

Phillips, B., & Chertok, F. (2004). Jewish identity among the adult children of intermarriage: Event horizon or navigable horizon. In *Annual Conference of the Association for Jewish Studies*. Chicago: Cohen Centre for Modern Jewish Studies.

Roof, W. C. (2003). Toward integration of religion and spirituality. In M. Dillon (Ed.), *Handbook or the Sociology of Religion* (pp. 137–148). Cambridge, UK: Cambridge University Press.

Schaap, E. (2008). The Retention of Students Following *B'nei Mitzvah* in Reform Congregational Schools. Retrieved 4/09http://urj.org/_kd/go.cfm?destination=ShowItem&Item_ID=25213

Smith, C. (2003). Theorizing religious effects among American adolescents. *Journal for the Scientific Study of Religion, 42*(1), 17–30.

Smith, C., & Denton, M. L. (2005). *Soul searching: The religious and spiritual lives of American teenagers*. New York: Oxford University Press.

Wald, P. J., & Castleberry, M. J. (2000). *Educators as learners: Creating a professional learning community in your school.* Alexandria, VA: ASCD.

Wertheimer, J., Liebman, C. S., & Cohen, S. M. (1996). How to save American Jews. *Commentary, 101*(1), 47–51.

Yoffe, E. (2005) Biennial Address. Retrieved Nov., 2005 from http://urj.org.

Learning Organisations: Learning to Learn – The Learning Organisation in Theory and Practice

Susan L. Shevitz

The Development of the Concept of "Learning Organizations"

The field of organizational development incorporates many different views of the exact nature of the problems and, hence, the solutions facing American organizations, whether profit or non-profit, religious or secular, small or large.[1] These views entail different foci and different units of analysis, the individual, the group, or the system, and argue for different innovative remedies ranging from system-wide "re-engineering of the corporation" (to use the phrase popularized by Champy and Hammer's highly influential book [1994]) to Argyris and Schon's focus on changing group perception and behavior (1978), or Schein's examination of the role of the leader in creating a culture (1992).

Some theorists and practitioners, discouraged by seemingly intractable problems in all sorts of organizations, began turning to ideas about how people learn in order to find ways to promote lasting improvement. In 1990 Peter Senge, then head of what is today SoL, Society for Learning Organizations at the Massachusetts Institute of Technology, synthesized a range of complex ideas and approaches in the best-selling book he wrote with several co-authors, *The Fifth Discipline: The Art and Practice of the Learning Organization*. The concept wove together personal, organizational, and societal visions of what successful organizations would look like. According to Senge (1990, p. 1) learning organizations are places

> where people continually expand their capacity to create the results they truly desire, where new and expansive patterns of thinking are nurtured, where collective assumption is set free, and where people are continually learning how to learn together.

This view suggests that in most settings people's creativity and capacities are largely untapped and that in an increasingly complex world, where people are

---

S.L. Shevitz (✉)
Brandeis University, Waltham, MA, USA
e-mail: Shevitz@brandeis.edu

[1] See Beckhard, R. What Is Organization Development? In *Organization Development*, ed. Joan Gallos, 3–12, Sage Publications and Burke, W. Where Did OD Come From? in the same volume, 13–37, for a short history of this field.

interdependent in powerful, new ways, people need to create the knowledge and capacities to deal with conditions. Relying on precedent and on outdated assumptions would not help organizations advance the innovative approaches that are needed in a globalized and interdependent world. Senge's approach to learning organizations is a call to both a vision and a methodology:

> We are taking a stand for a vision, for creating a type of organization we would truly like to work within and which can thrive in a world of increasing interdependency and change. (Kofman & Senge, 1993, p. 32)

Learning organizations embody characteristics that Senge claims are generally in short supply in most organizations: (1) they create a culture based on love, wonder, humility, and compassion (he used the Buberian distinction between I–It and I–Thou relationships where the former are objectified, instrumental relationships and the latter are characterized by mutuality, directness, openness, and presence); (2) they develop ways to sustain generative conversations and concerted action; and (3) they see work as part of "the flow of life as a system." (Kofman & Senge, 1993, p. 32) While this might seem to be a "soft" approach to organizational effectiveness, it was based on years of work with corporations of all sizes. Senge and his team developed five "disciplines" that they claim need to be learned and used if significant organizational improvement is to take place. They are the basis of organizational learning:

- Systems thinking: Looking at the widest possible understanding of a system to consider ways things influence each other over long periods of time and at great distance; move from breaking things down into their smaller, manageable parts to see the systems and patterns; this entails seeing the world as consisting of a whole made up of wholes;[2]
- Personal mastery: Continually clarifying and deepening personal vision, developing attitudes and skills that help people see reality more objectively;
- Mental models: Exploring and questioning the assumptions and generalizations one brings to situations (i.e., mental models) and how they influence thought and action and developing new, more appropriate mental models;
- Building a shared vision: Surfacing shared "pictures of the future" that elicit people's deep commitment rather than grudging acceptance or compliance;
- Team learning: Attending to the ways the team members interact that impede learning and creating ways to incorporate the disciplines as it does its work.

These disciplines help individuals and groups within the organization – and through them the organization – to develop the flexibility, adaptability, and productivity to excel by tapping the capacity and commitment of people at all levels of an organization to develop new understandings and forge new approaches. Senge's critics charge that he seriously underestimates the political realities of organizational life so that although organizations might use his ideas, very few "come close to

---

[2] Aronson, D. *Intro to Systems Thinking* provides an accessible exploration of the concept; Aronson host *The Thinking Page* (http://www.thinking.net).

the combination of characteristics that he identifies with learning organizations." (www.infed.org/thinkers/senge/htm). Gavin, writing in 1993, moved away from Senge's interest in personal development as it relates to organizational effectiveness and instead provides a more concrete definition that links learning to performance – i.e., making use of what is learned. He argues that a learning organization "is skilled at creating, acquiring, and transferring knowledge, and at modifying its behavior to reflect new knowledge and insights" (1993 p. 1). Looking at business models, Gavin extrapolates several building blocks associated with organizations that learn:

- Systematic problem solving that uses data and also inquires about underlying assumptions;
- Experimentation that looks for and tests new knowledge in an environment that has incentives for risk taking, creativity, and assessment (of the new ideas and approaches);
- Managers who are trained to support these activities and to be result oriented;
- Learning from past successes and failures;
- Learning from other organizations and sectors (Gavin, 1993, pp. 81–91).

As organizational theorists relied on educational insights into learning, educators began to adapt the model to schools. Michael Fullan and his colleagues at the Ontario Institute for Studies in Education in Canada (as well as others working in the United States and the United Kingdom), provided the theoretical underpinnings for changing educational settings in ways that are consistent with Senge's approach. He wrote a series of books rich in theoretical and empirical data about ongoing attempts to improve schools and school systems and resisted oversimplification by dealing with the different levels within schools and school systems that need to change in order for improvements to take hold (See Fullan, 1991, 1993, 1999, 2005, 2007, 2008). Among the points that Fullan emphasized is that "theories of change and theories of education need each other" (1999, pp. 20–22) and that learning has to take place both within the setting and with the external groups that are also involved in the change. This means that, no matter where it occurs, enabling and supporting new ways of learning that lead to new ways of acting is critically important. Senge's group, eager to help real organizations become learning organizations that effectively deal with their challenges, also published field books including *Schools That Learn*. This provides the conceptual framework as well as specific tools to help the school itself to develop a learning orientation so that learning takes place in the classroom, school, and community and among all the stakeholders (Senge et al., 2000). Fullan produced a similarly practical volume, *Leading in a Culture of Change* (2004) designed to help educational leaders root desired changes in their systems.

Those who assume that learning is the hallmark of educational settings might be perplexed by these forays by educational organizations into the field of organizational development with its emphasis on helping organizations learn. Education is, after all, about learning. The American public, however, had been barraged by evidence that individual students and educational organizations were not learning what they needed to in order to succeed. Standardized tests, high-school graduation rates, problems of literacy and numeracy, and other data indicated that learning was not happening for many students in the American school system.[3] In addition to those who called for strengthening students' basic skills, many critics of American schooling argued that the *type* of learning students need is more sophisticated than recall and use of received information. While this critique was hardly new and had been powerfully made by John Dewey decades earlier, it took a contemporary twist: new technologies that create easy access to unimaginably huge amounts of information and the challenges of globalization require learners to make sense of new situations. Their job is to know how to harness and use information – in essence, to create new knowledge and approaches. Schools, on their part, need to create new instructional models to meet these new demands (Senge et al., 2000, "Orientation"). In order for students to learn in new ways, the different levels of the school system need to become involved: teachers need to know how to learn in this way and then to promote this kind of learning in their classrooms; in order for teachers to do that, schools need to be organized and administered in ways that would support this kind of teacher learning; this, in turn, requires systems that value the new learning, as well. Change, the argument went, would come only when all these levels were addressed and the stakeholders' orientations to learning and to each other would change. *Schools That Learn* gave tools to help people interested in education move forward. Hundreds of other books and trainers promoted orientations to school reform (sometimes called restructuring); many drawing on the insights developed in the Learning Organization approach.

Attempts to Develop Learning Organizations in the World of Jewish Education

The critique of education was not limited to the public sector. In the Jewish world, as well, there was ongoing dissatisfaction with the status quo. As the Atlanta Jewish Times announced on a 1999 cover page, "Reinventing Hebrew School. Most of Us Went to It. Many of Us Hated It. We Need It." Serious studies of Jewish congregational schools looked at different aspects of the failure, or to use Isa Aron's phrase, "the malaise of Jewish education." (1989) Federation heads, foundation directors, educators and academics all expressing the sentiment, much like that about public schools, that something "had to be done" to improve the situation.[4] Fears about

---

[3] The 1983 government report, *A Nation at Risk,* was a clarion call that charged that the population of the United States was too poorly educated to compete in the global economy. This ushered in a period of intense efforts to reform American education on all levels: national efforts (the best example is the No Child Left Behind reform bill) complemented state, local, and school-based efforts.

[4] For other examples see David Schoem's 1989 ethnography, *Ethnic Survival in America,* that vividly portrays deep problems with afternoon schools; Alvin Schiff's controversial 1998 study, *Jewish Supplementary Schooling: An Educational System in Need of Change.* New York: Bureau of Jewish Education.

the intermarriage rate and the future well-being of the Jewish community in North America coalesced as the "continuity crisis" as a 52% intermarriage rate reported by the 1990 Jewish population study (Rosov & Isaacs, 2008, p. 522). Were Jewish education more effective, the popular argument went, then there would be less intermarriage. This reasoning carried both explicit accusation and implicit hope: Jewish education was not effective; it needed to – and could – improve. And since roughly 85% of Jewish children who received a Jewish education were in congregational schools, these schools were considered the first line of defense.

Even before the learning organization wave, there were attempts to look at Jewish education systemically. By the mid-1980s several elements coincided to provide more energy and funds toward efforts to improve Jewish education. Forward thinking executives in Jewish federations, first in Cleveland and Boston, realized that the historic precedent of federations not directly funding congregations – by then being considered the "gateways" to Jewish life – was no longer reasonable and they began to develop and support programs intended to improve Jewish education. In 1993 Boston asserted its mission for its Commission on Jewish Continuity and Education:[5]

Creates connections between people and to the Jewish tradition

Engages teenagers with Jewish values and provides them with life-changing experiences

Helps assure the continued vitality of Jewish life in Boston

Builds a community of Jewish learners of all ages

Empowers synagogues to be a central resource in family life

Allows parents to transmit a love of Jewish learning to their children

Develops professional educators and volunteer leaders

Places day school education within the reach of every family.

Other federations followed and began to fund, and sometimes to themselves run, new modes of Jewish education.

Federations' growing support was augmented by the increased involvement of Jewish family foundations interested in Jewish education.[6] Foundations and philanthropic partnerships began to fund Jewish education, as well. Some philanthropic partnerships worked with particular types of Jewish educational settings (for example day schools or camps) while others invested in a wide range of different Jewish

---

[5]One of the earliest, Boston's Combined Jewish Philanthropies, experimented with a five-pronged model (Shevitz, 1992) and followed with a long-term commitment to Jewish education (see http://www.cjp.org/page.aspx?id=68824).

[6]Examples are the Mandel Foundation, with a long history of supporting Jewish education, the Covenant Foundation that was devoted to "supporting initiatives and ideas and the practitioners who have developed and harnessed them to change the face of Jewish education across the span of a generation" (http://www.covenantfn.org/splash/), the Whizin Foundation which, with its interest in Jewish family life, jumpstarted the field of Jewish family education, and Avi Chai Foundation whose commitment to Jewish education is clear from its mission (http://www.avichai.org/bin/en.jsp?enPage=BlankPage&enDisplay=view&enDispWhat=zone&enZone=AboutUs&enInfolet=Mission.jsp) Others have since become involved.

educational personnel (e.g., heads of day schools, congregational school principals, Hebrew teachers, etc.). In addition to providing funding, the federations and foundations provided another tool with the potential to encourage organizational learning: accountability. They required evaluation of the programs they funded. Before this, systematic program assessment was infrequently done. These mandated evaluations represented a turning point because systematically gathered information could enter the system. Often the evaluations were proprietary but sometimes what was learned was presented in academic or professional forums so that the general knowledge could be shared.

The example of Jewish Family Education (JFE) allows us to trace the shift from narrow programmatic change (the problems would be "fixed" by adding new programs to what was being done) to the wider lens of organizational learning. When JFE emerged in the late 1980s, its pioneers hoped that JFE would "transform" Jewish education and be an effective antidote to the child-focus which emerged as the implicit goal of the school was to prepare students for Bar and Bat Mitzvah ceremonies. By involving parents in their children's Jewish education, educators expected that parents would become good role models for their children, engage more deeply in Jewish life, and that the religious schools would become more relevant and exciting to the children (Wolfson, 1998; Bank, 1998). Some communities realized that to succeed, a community would need to do more than develop new programs; teachers would have to retool if they were to deal successfully with parents and children (both together and separately), prayer services would have to change if they were to become welcoming environments for families with small children, the school would need to modify its curriculum, and so on (Shevitz & Kaye, 1991). At the University of Judaism's (now American Hebrew University) Whizin Center's annual Summer Institute – the primary incubator of Jewish family education – participants were exhorted and instructed to "think systemically," rather than programmatically. Thinking about family education as a program to be added to the ongoing religious school rather than understanding it as a profound shift to thinking about the family as the unit to be educated limited its effectiveness in some settings. This is *not* to suggest that family education was a failure; much good continues to happen as a result of it. Some settings were able to make the perceptual shift and became learning organizations that changed the very way they thought about and delivered Jewish education. But many places were not ready to change their mental models and look systemically at the situation. For that, different learning was required.

From the learning organization perspective, the planners in family education needed to recognize the level at which different stakeholders (in addition to the teachers and children) had to become engaged and what they would need to learn in order to think and act in new ways. In order for the family to be seen as the educative unit, teachers, administrators, parents, other members – really all people who would be directly or indirectly involved – would have to undergo a perceptual shift in order to develop new skills and understandings. To give a small example, if families were aggressively courted to attend Shabbat services, those leading services had to be ready to engage the families with all the wiggling, whispering, and movement that young children bring. Congregants who were the "regulars" at the services had to be willing to open themselves to a different dynamic in the service.[7] This is an example of what Fullan means when he writes about the need for both internal and external partners to learn in order for an innovation to succeed (Fullan, 1999, pp. 31–62). It requires new thinking and new ways of acting on the part of many players who are directly involved (such as teachers, children, parents) and external groups (such as congregants, clergy, custodians).

Some evaluations of early efforts in JFE began to shape the field. Boston, in particular, invested in developing a cadre of Jewish family educators and providing support for their work. Evaluation was an important part of the effort so that lessons learned from early efforts could shape subsequent work (Shevitz, 1998; Sales, Koren, & Shevitz, 2000). Other innovations tried to more explicitly use the learning-organization approach while also applying some of the lessons emerging from JFE. One of the early projects provides the clearest example, both because it was early and, more significantly, it incorporated research and consistently produced analytical and descriptive books and papers from which others could learn (Aron, 2000; 2002; Aron, Lee, & Rossel, 1995).

Concerned about the uninspiring schools found in many congregations, in 1993 the Hebrew Union College Rhea Hirsch School of Jewish Education organized a conference to explore questions related to congregational education (the papers were published in a 1995 book [Aron, Lee, and Rossel]). Several of the presentations looked at the context beyond the individual school. Woocher (1995) brought sociological, ideological, and historical forces to bear on the construction of a new framework for Jewish education; Reimer (1995) looked specifically at the interactions between a congregation and its school when educational change was attempted and argued that education had to become the "favored child" if it were to succeed; and Shevitz (1995) considered the non-linear and non-rational aspect of change and suggested ways to look at the wider system as part of a change process.

The Experiment in Congregational Education (ECE) resulted from this effort and from the experience and theoretical assumptions of several academics at Hebrew Union College whose work involved them in congregational life. The ECE recruited congregations that were willing to engage in an intense two-plus-year process through which each one would look inward at its values and aspirations and outward at the new conditions and opportunities in the community. This deliberation, which also involved text study, would yield a new vision for what Jewish education could become. It was hoped that with the clarity of a shared vision, the team would then align the congregations' plans and programs with the new vision – often creating new approaches and programs.

Influenced by the work of Senge and Fullan, the ECE also believed that the congregants and professionals involved in each setting had to themselves become learning communities in which they would become more comfortable with each other as well as with the use of Jewish texts and values. Participants would be pressed to recognize their own "limiting assumptions" about congregational

---

[7] As experimentation continued, pragmatic solutions to the challenge of organizational learning developed. Some congregations decided to hold "Tot Shabbat" services separately or to designate specific services as Tot Shabbat events.

education and be willing to explore new ideas about Jewish education and congregational change in the quest to transform congregational education. As its critics are quick to point out, the ECE relies heavily on group process. It teaches that this type of reflection and learning is never done; it needs to be embedded in all they do. Aron providing the framework for the ECE, explains why she chose the term "self-renewing" for the project:

> I have chosen the term "self-renewing" to emphasize the reflexive and cyclical nature of this activity, the fact that much of the learning is internal, and that the learning is incomplete without concomitant action. (Aron, 2002, p. 8)

These words echo the writing of Senge and Gavin. They assume that the kind of learning required for transformative change in education is deep and far reaching. Asking people to reconsider the purposes of Jewish education and, consequently, the ways Jewish education is organized and provided, requires that they relinquish or modify their assumptions about how things are – and how they ought to be. In addition, people need to think systemically, engage people who have diverse views, and be empowered to share in decision making and leadership.

A major challenge to this approach occurs when the team that incubates the new ideas has to move them into the larger context, in this case from the planning group that is committed to the new approaches to the rest of the school or congregation that is not. The strategy most often used in schools is to provide some form of "professional development" for teachers and information to others affected by the change. As Sarason argued decades ago (1971 and 1996), these approaches just about guarantee that the intended changes will not occur. As frequently noted, teachers and other stakeholders generally can outlast the many changes thrust upon them without really changing anything significant in how they do their work. Adaptive change and innovation, however, require that people rethink their basic assumptions. For example, a teacher could use new materials designed to replace rote Bible learning with inquiry methods but still teach the way he or she always taught, or a congregation might move to an educational model incorporating informal programs but be unable to provide excellent informal Jewish education. Sarason's insight was that this tendency is not a function of teacher inadequacy or resistance but rather a profound misunderstanding of the culture of schools and how things change (Sarason, 1971/1996).

Learning organization theory advances Sarason's argument. It insists that learning is no longer a "transmission of knowledge model" in which knowledge is organized into a set curriculum which is presented by the expert to the student. Instead the learner encounters the world and, sometimes, a teacher in order to produce knowledge, an approach Barth calls "experiential learning" (Barth, 1998, pp. 96–97). Applied to Jewish education, this suggests that the people closest to the educational process in the congregation, for example – whether teachers, parents, youth educators, leaders, or clergy – have to experience and incorporate the new ways of thinking and acting. It requires reassessing and revising old assumptions and beliefs. These ideas are at the heart of the approach of the ECE and other projects like it. When successful it develops the capacity for the ongoing reflective action needed to succeed over the long haul. This kind of purposefulness is an ongoing process. As the rabbi of a congregation that has been involved with the ECE for many years comments,

> What was unique about our congregation's experience is that we're still doing it. I talked to lots of colleagues who said, "oh yeah, ECE, that was a wonderful thing, yeah yeah yeah, it was a great year." What, are you kidding? We're actually now only beginning to tackle the really deep systemic things and the reality is that it's part of the culture of the temple that we do this.[8]

Learning Organizations and Staff Development

Over time the ECE realized that congregations needed more support and knowledge to help stakeholders throughout the congregational system (such as clergy, parents, preschool teachers, youth educators, teachers, etc.) learn how to teach and learn in ways that would more closely align with their re-imagined aspirations. Toward this end, it ran a pilot project[9] in one region with teams from congregations that had already undergone the ECE process. Small teams of educators, clergy, and lay leaders went through a set of learning experiences in order for them to understand and then develop the type of teaching and learning that their innovations would require. Two factors were important to the project: (1) the teams would have enough time and support to grapple with the new approaches to teaching and learning and to integrate them into their understanding of Jewish education and (2) that this would be done as a team so that the new assumptions would be shared and would be more likely to permeate the system.

This approach to the staff learning is different than the workshop model that Sarason had critiqued. It posits that teachers have to learn differently themselves in order for them to teach and guide their students differently. The same logic applies to principals and other school leaders (Der Bogert, 1999). The school, as an organization, must expect and support the new ways of learning by all its constituents. This is what is often meant by the term "learning communities." As Barth writes,

> We want nothing less than a cadre of new school leaders... who are lifelong learners themselves, modeling the most important purpose of a school; learners who value and trust learning from experience for themselves and who know how to rigorously craft and structure experience so that it yields important personal learning for students, teachers and parents. We want to see the school principal take the big risks necessary to ring the bell atop the schoolhouse of the twenty-first century, so that it may become both a community of learners and a community of leaders. (Barth, 1998, p. 99)

Many recent approaches to staff development are based on these ideas. In general education, the National Staff Development Council [NSDC] asserts that the most

---

[8] Personal email correspondence between Isa Aron and the rabbi (sent to author on 2/1/09).

[9] In this region the ECE process was called RE-IMAGINE and the pilot project was RE-IMAGINING Professional Learning. The pilot, which was showing promising results, was not continued due to funders' changing priorities (I was co-principal of the evaluation of this project. These comments are based on empirical data, discussion with ECE leaders, and representatives of the funder).

significant determinant of whether students learn well is the quality of the teaching and that "teaching quality is improved through *continuous professional learning* which is done as a group in a community" (Hord, 2008, p. 10). Teachers previously have operated as "sole proprietors" who work in isolation. Not only do they not learn from each other, but the school – as an organization – has no way to develop a philosophy and approach that is widely shared by its stakeholders. In organizational terms this means that what is learned stays private and does not help the school develop and improve (Hord, 2008, p. 11). The point of continuous teacher learning in a group is for teachers to engage in purposeful, collegial learning in order to improve teaching effectiveness so that students learn successfully (Hord: 13). Like Garvin's approach to Senge's learning organization, discussed earlier, the NSDC links the purpose of the group learning to the specific goals that are at the heart of the school's mission. Some programs that foster this kind of professional learning at the school level have developed in the Jewish education context.[10] They all face difficult structural challenges: conducting frequent meetings requires finding the time and funds to support the endeavor. They also face difficult conceptual challenges: learning new ways of learning and incorporating them on an ongoing basis requires guidance, practice, and enthusiasm. The model incorporates to varying extents the five disciplines identified by Senge as essential if an organization is to learn: systems thinking, personal mastery, mental models, shared vision, and team approaches. It is commonplace for projects intended to transform Jewish education to require the formation of some sort of team although the make-up and roles of the team vary widely among the different initiatives (see for example Synagogue 2,000 [now 3,000], some PEJE [Partnership for Excellence in Jewish Education] grants for day school, JECEI [Jewish Early Childhood Initiative], the Legacy Heritage Innovation grants, among others).

There are critiques of models that try to engage people in the kind of learning that Senge and others advocate. Too much time is spent on the process of team building, exploring mental models, and developing a shared vision; it could more effectively be used to develop the new approaches. Sometimes mastering the disciplines becomes an end in itself rather than leading to effective action. In addition, the members of the team, having bonded, might feel possessive about the new approaches and find it hard to involve others. It is sometimes hard to move from vision and design to wide-scale implementation while maintaining fidelity to the vision.

Using Information to Foster Organizational Learning

In order to learn, valid information about the system is needed. At least three units of analysis are relevant to Jewish education: the wider system in which Jewish

---

[10] Examples include the Mandel Teacher Educator Initiative, study groups at individual day and congregational schools, peer-supervision methods being developed at some schools, teacher teams at the Jewish Early Childhood Education Initiative, and projects sponsored by central agencies of Jewish education – in Philadelphia, Boston and New York, to name a few.

education operates, the communal system comprised of the different educative settings and organizations in Jewish education, and the individual organization or setting. There are powerful obstacles for getting and using this information. At the communal level, there is no real system but rather many autonomous and semi-autonomous organizations that relate to each other when they need and want to. This reality is seen at the organizational level as well; schools and congregations are "loosely coupled systems," to use Weick's terminology, where the various parts of the system operate in semi-autonomous arenas and do not necessarily or regularly share information or coordinate actions (1976). There is little slack at any level within this "system"; this makes gathering and using data difficult. It is correctly perceived as an extra responsibility, especially when the present demands to run the school, staff the camp, and so on, are so pressing. In some settings, the professionals may not be comfortable with research-based information or know how to interpret and use it. In addition, many congregations and schools have notoriously poor records and lack historical and empirical data. Even simple descriptive statistics are often hard to access or are non-existent. All these conditions make it difficult for Jewish education organizations to learn and need to be addressed in order for organizational learning to take place.

Information and Knowledge from Evaluation and Accountability Efforts

The availability of philanthropic dollars over the last 15 or 20 years has created pressure for information that would help funders consider the impact of their philanthropy. As federation and foundation funding became available for innovation, the beneficiary agencies, whether schools and other settings, became accountable for the expenditures. Funders wanted to know whether new programs were meeting their goals and if the intended impacts were being achieved. Rosov and Isaacs trace the impact of the 1990 population study on the increased demand by funders for program evaluation (2008, p. 522). Simultaneously, a cadre of sophisticated Jewish educators and social scientists in agencies and universities throughout North America and Israel have been available to conduct studies and help groups interpret and use the findings.

While this emphasis on program accountability is a positive development, if looked at from a learning organization perspective there are clear limitations. Program and impact evaluation[11] do not necessarily reveal much about the level of organizational learning that goes on. We might infer that some organizational learning is present when a program shows positive outcomes, though that might not

---

[11] By program evaluation I mean the systematic gathering of valid data that determine the extent to which a program is meeting its stated goals and suggest ways to improve the program. By impact evaluation, I mean following the participants in a program to see whether the longer-term intended impacts are occurring (for example, does going to Jewish summer camp lead to a positive Jewish identity as measured by specific traits?) in later life.

be the case. There can be positive outcomes (increased ability of students to chant prayers, for example) without reaching the long-term impacts that are sought (incorporating some form of Jewish praying in their lives going forward). But program and impact evaluation do not generally look at the organization's capacity to learn in the way that Senge and others understand organizational learning.

Sometimes the results of evaluations and other related research with policy implications have become available and generalizable findings are shared at conferences and through papers. There are several sources of information and I mention only some of them. JESNA's (Jewish Education Service of North America) Berman Center has evaluated many innovative programs (see http://www.jesna.org/program-centers/berman-center/our-projects). JESNA's Lippman Kanfer Institute provides current thinking about emerging issues in Jewish education (see http://www.jesna.org/program-centers/lippman-kanfer-institute/our-projects). The Cohen Center for Modern Jewish Studies at Brandeis University has conducted a great many studies related to Jewish identity as well as evaluations of international, national, and local innovations that have useful information for many Jewish educational settings and are available through its web-site (See http://www.brandeis.edu/cmjs/). The Berman Jewish Policy Archive at New York University's Wagner School and the Jim Joseph Foundation have more recently begun to make information from studies available on their websites. Some of the studies are commissioned by specific organizations and are not available, but many are and the Center has also issued many reports, books, and articles that discuss the findings and new trends (see http://dcoll.brandeis.edu/handle/10192/22946/browse?type=title&sort_by=2&order=DESC&rpp=100).

Some academic and general publishers have published books that provide essential information that is very helpful in the Jewish educational context. For example, see the Hebrew University's Melton Center for Jewish Education (See http://melton.huji.ac.il/eng/ktav.php) and the Mandel Leadership Institute (http://mandel.mli.org.il/MandelCMS/English/VirtualLibrary/Publications/). In addition, some of the web-sites of North American agencies such as PEJE (Partnership for Excellence in Jewish Education) and the URJ (Union of Reform Judaism) include research on education and reports of relevant educational topics. The Avi Chai foundation continues to release studies about aspects of Jewish education of interest to the field (see http://www.avi-chai.org/bin/end88e.html?enPage=BlankPage&enDisplay=view&enDispWhat=Zone&enZone=Publications). Most recently these include Wertheimer's 2005 "Linking the Silos: How to Accelerate the Momentum in Jewish Education Today" and his 2008 "A Census of Jewish Supplementary Schools in the United States, 2006–2007" and 2009 "Schools that Work: What We Can Learn from Good Jewish Supplementary Schools" have stimulated discussion within the field. While these resources and others not mentioned provide valuable information, unless they are used in ways that challenge and deepen the thinking of those who are involved in the educational settings, they really do not contribute to the development of learning communities. This is why many of the recent attempts at educational improvement in the Jewish community have built in specific times and, sometimes methodologies, for analysis and reflection.

One congregational school developed another model that fosters both research and reflection within a learning community. This congregation engaged an independent evaluator who regularly provided feedback and helped the educational team analyze and improve its work (Kur, 2009, p. 3). While focused at first on evaluating specific new programs that the congregation was piloting, the evaluator helps the staff question their assumptions, probe their thinking, and develop new approaches in a supportive way that enhances learning (Kur, 2009; Aron & Moskowitz, 2009). As the director of lifelong learning at the congregation, Kur writes,

> One of the best things an evaluator has done for us... is to bring an independent, objective mind to the table when we are planning a new project, program or curriculum – a person who can identify potential gaps in our thinking and push us to define with specificity what we want to accomplish. (2009, p. 3)

The educational team, on both staff and lay levels, is dedicated to ongoing reflection and adaptation as they create a powerful educational paradigm.[12]

Issues to Be Considered

Can We Learn More About What Is **Really** *Happening?*

It is not surprising that ideas that influence American society, in general, and education, in particular, shape what occurs in the Jewish community. In this case, the learning-organization approach seems intuitively appropriate for Jewish educational settings. The importance of questions in Jewish tradition is compatible with the reflective and probing approach advocated by the learning-organization theory.

Once a phrase that meant something quite specific slips into popular usage it can be indiscriminately used and misused. It would be helpful to know more about what is taking place on the communal and organizational levels, especially where they self-identify as learning organizations. To what extent do they embody the meaning of the term? Educational researchers tend to be more interested in identity formation, educational philosophy, the transmission of knowledge, and other elements close to the teaching and learning process than they are to the decision-making and organizational processes that support or impede successful learning. Using the learning-organization perspective, especially the five disciplines, as a way to explore how Jewish educational organizations operate and change (or do not) would be a valuable contribution to both the literature and the practice of Jewish educational leadership. With few cases that inform the reader in a grounded, illustrative way of the ways Jewish educational organizations "learn to learn" there is a need to understand both the big-picture view (macro level) and the view of the specific details as they play out at, the micro level. Both views are sorely needed.

---

[12] See Aron and Moskowitz (2009) for a fuller portrait of this congregation.

Can Educational Organizations Sustain the Effort to Become Learning Organizations?

We know from the general literature and from the experiences within the Jewish educational sector that becoming a learning organization takes effort. Sustaining it requires commitment over long periods of time. It is not a technique that, once achieved, ends. It requires a change of mind-set by asking people as individuals and groups to continually explore their assumptions ("mental models"), develop shared understandings and goals, learn new ways of thinking and acting, and to embrace a sense of "becoming."

Jewish educational settings are resource-poor environments. There is rarely, if ever, enough time, expertise, money, or energy to do all that is needed, let alone all that is possible. Congregations and schools get caught up in day-to-day operations and respond to the immediate issues that arise. It is difficult for them to be proactive. We need to explore which Jewish educational settings sustain the effort to become learning organizations and how they do it.

We know from the experience of different experimenting Jewish communities that becoming a learning community is often stimulated through external funding for new projects (for example, the ECE, Synagogue 2000/3000, Mandel Teacher Educator Initiative among others) stimulated the efforts in some day and supplementary schools to try to become learning communities, a point also noted in Wertheimer's (2009a,b) studies. They provide the structure, expertise, and personnel to help organizations learn the new approach without neglecting their ongoing work. In a series of field and resource books, Senge and his team (1994, 2000) provide practical tools to help people master and use the disciplines and in his *Dance of Change* he addresses the limitations of insufficient time and support by providing some practical tools. Many of these ideas, such as integrating initiatives, using unstructured time, and making use of coaches and mentors, can be adapted to Jewish educational settings (1999, pp. 67–102).

Can the Learning Organization Be Successfully Scaled Up?

Large, multi-unit organizations interested in becoming learning organizations are counseled to start on a small scale and then to move the innovation out to other units until there is a critical mass using the approach. Once this tipping point is reached, the organization more generally thinks and acts in consonance with the new approach. Moving from the small unit to the larger organization – in their words, addressing the challenge of diffusion – is a difficult step (Senge et al., 1999, pp. 418–486).

As we have seen, this strategy has been used in some of the Jewish community's change initiatives. Small leadership teams are formed to learn, deliberate, and plan together. Successful teams initiate changes in their settings and stimulate other groups to share their approaches. Because the leadership team experience is intense, and its participants bond around the shared experiences, it is frequently hard to engage the larger organization in a meaningful way. Sometimes the planning group takes on a life of its own; in a sense it becomes a counter organization interested in its own separate identity more than in helping to strengthen the larger organization through its efforts.[13] Strategies for moving the approach into the organization must be developed early if change is to become widespread. The use of coaches, CoPs, cultural levers, and data can all help (Senge et al., 1999, pp. 417–456).

Will Information Be Used?

The lifeblood of learning organizations is information and assumptions that can be openly tested and explored. Jewish educational organizations most often operate with a paucity of information and rely on assumptions that are not necessarily articulated, let alone tested. For example, there is very limited, if any, reliable information about student learning or the relationship between how teachers do their work and what students experience and retain. Decisions about curriculum, pedagogy, and much else are made on the bases of assumptions that are often not explicit and, therefore, not discussable. For example, it is widely asserted that teaching liturgical Hebrew deepens students' prayer experience or organizing groups by grades is the best way to support learning. Each of these positions is supported by assumptions about the nature of learning, the relationship of knowledge to experience, and much more. In addition, there is scant empirical information that looks at the issues, whether benefits of organizing students according to interests and/or aptitudes (rather than chronologically) or the outcomes of different approaches to liturgy. From the perspective of learning organization theory, information that relates to these questions needs to be used in an environment of inquiry and learning – and this would generate productive new ideas. To what extent will Jewish educational settings be prepared and able to develop new sources of information and learn to use them in timely and appropriate ways?

Does Becoming a Learning Organization Make a Difference?

A specific change theory is embedded in the learning organization approach: by becoming a learning organization the school (or camp, etc.) will become better at what it does. This will translate into better environments for teaching and learning so that the students will be more positively affected by their religious education. Put another way, although there are many benefits for Jewish educational organizations to become learning organizations – staff may become more involved, planners may be more intentional about school programs, and so on – ultimately we want to know whether becoming learning organizations supports students' learning and strengthens the positive impact of religious education. Research that looks at the organization's internal learning processes and capacities in relationship to outcomes and impacts is needed.

---

[13] The data are drawn from the evaluations of the ECE and Synagogue 2,000 conducted by the Cohen Center for Modern Jewish Studies.

Conclusion

The beginning of A.A. Milne's beloved children's classic, *Winnie the Pooh,* begins with the scene of little Christopher Robin, holding the bear by one arm:

> Here is Edward Bear, coming downstairs now, bump, bump, bump on the back of his head, behind Christopher Robin. It is, as far as he knows, the only way of coming downstairs, but sometimes he feels there really is another way, if only he could stop bumping for a moment and think of it. (A.A. Milne (1926), p. 1)

There is a sense that many of today's Jewish educational organizations want to do better but they too, always busy, can't quite stop in order to figure out how. Accustomed to their own realities, each organization continues to act on many of the same assumptions that have framed its actions in previous decades, even when they do not want to.

The learning organization approach asserts that there are other ways to understand and act upon current conditions but it takes a concerted effort to develop the capacity to recognize and act on them. This entails cognitive and emotional growth through an ongoing process of learning and using the five disciplines – and more. It requires that the group has skill, tenacity, and courage. It also requires time and flexibility. The claim that this approach makes, as applied to Jewish education, is that in order to create settings that will be meaningful in today's world, Jewish educational organizations need to change in significant ways. Without blueprints or formulae, they need to learn how to learn and, in doing so, they will become communities capable of generating and sustaining powerful Jewish educational conceptions that address contemporary conditions and timeless aspirations.

References

Argyris, C., & Schon., D. (1978). *Organizational learning: A theory of action perspective.* Reading, MA: Addison-Wesley.
Aron, I. (1989). The *malaise of Jewish education. Tikkun Magazine, 4*(3).
Aron, I. (2000). *Becoming a congregation of learners.* Woodstock, VT: Jewish Lights Publishing.
Aron, I. (2002). *The Self-renewing congregation.* Woodstock, VT: Jewish Lights Publishing.
Aron, I., Lee, S., & Rossel, S. (1995). *A Congregation of learners.* New York: Union of American Hebrew Congregations.
Aron, I., & Moskowitz, N. S. (2009). Beit Hazon, a visionary synagogue. In J. Wertheimer (Ed.), *Learning and community: Jewish supplementary schools in the twenty-first century.* Hanover, NH: University Press of New England.
Aronson, D. Intro to ST. http://www.thinking.net/Systems_Thinking/Intro_to-ST/intro_to_st.hml.
Atlanta Jewish Times (1999, August 27). (http://www.atljewishtimes.com/archives/1999/082799cs.htm).
Bank, A. (1998). The view from Mulholland Drive. In A. Bank & R. Wolfson (Eds.), *First fruit: A Whizin anthology of Jewish family education.* Los Angeles: The Whizin Institute for Jewish Family Life.
Barth, R. (1998). From puddle dock to the twenty-first century. In V. der Bogert (Ed.), *Making learning communities work: The critical role of leader as learner.* San Francisco: Jossey-Bass.
Champy, J., & Hammer, M. (1993). *Reengineering the corporation.* New York: HarperCollins.

Der Bogert, V. (1999). *Making learning communities work: The critical role of leader as learner.* San Francisco: Jossey-Bass.
Fullan, M. (1991). *The new meaning of educational change.* New York: Teachers College Press.
Fullan, M. (1993). *Change forces.* Bristol, PA: The Falmer Press.
Fullan, M. (1999). *Change forces: The sequel.* Philadelphia: Falmer Press.
Fullan, M. (2005). *Leadership and sustainability.* Thousand Oaks, CA: Corwin Press.
Fullan, M. (2007). *The new meaning of educational change* (4th ed.). New York: Teachers College Press.
Fullan, M. (2008). *The six secrets of change.* San Francisco: Wiley.
Gavin, D. (1993). Building a learning organization. *Harvard Business Review, 71*(4), 78–96, July–August.
Hord, S. (2008, Summer). Evolution of the professional learning community. *National Staff Development Council, 23*(3).
Kofman, F., & Senge, P. (1993) Communities of commitment: The heart of the learning organization. In S. Chawla & J. Renesch (Eds.), *Learning organizations: Developing cultures for tomorrow's workplace.* Portland, OR: Productivity Press.
Kur, A. (2009) *Cheshbon Hanefesh* for Our Schools. *Torah at the Center.* Department of Lifelong Learning, Union of Reform Judaism, 12(1) (Winter).
Milne, A. A. (1926). *Winnie the Pooh.* London: Methuen & Company.
Reimer, J. (1995). When school and synagogue are joined. In I Aron, S. Lee, & S. Rossel (Eds.), *A congregation of learners.* New York: Hebrew Union College.
Rosov, W., & Isaacs, L. (2008). Program evaluation in Jewish education. In R. L. Goodman, P. A. Flexner, & L. D. Bloomerg (Eds.), *What we now know about Jewish education: Perspectives on research through practice.* Los Angeles: Torah Aura Productions.
Sales, A., Koren, A., & Shevitz, S. (2000). *Sh'arim: Building gateways to Jewish life and community.* Boston: Commission on Jewish Continuity, Bureau of Jewish Education and Cohen Center at Brandeis University.
Sarason, S. (1996). *Revisiting the culture of school and the problem of change.* New York: Teachers College Press.
Schein, E. (1992). *Organizational culture and leadership* (2nd ed.). San Francisco: Jossey-Bass.
Schoem, D. (1989). *Ethnic survival in America: An ethnography of a Jewish afternoon school.* Atlanta, GA: Scholars Press.
Senge, P. (1990). *The fifth discipline: The art and practice of the learning organization.* New York: Doubleday.
Senge, P., et al. (1999). *The dance of change: The challenge of sustaining momentum in learning organizations.* New York: Currency/Doubleday.
Senge, P., et al. (2000). *Schools that learn.* New York: Currency/Doubleday.
Shevitz, S. (1992). *What we have learned: The projects of CJP's supplemental school task force, 1987–1992 (Research Report 2).* Bureau of Jewish Education of Greater Boston.
Shevitz, S. (1995). An organizational approach to changing Jewish education: What the literature reveals. In I. Aron, S. Lee, & S. Rossel (Eds.), *A congregation of learners.* New York: Union of American Hebrew Congregations.
Shevitz, S. (1998). Evaluating communal initiatives: Facts can be friendly. In A. Bank & R. Wolfson (Eds.), *First fruit: A Whizin anthology of Jewish family education.* Los Angeles: The Whizin Institute for Jewish Family Life.
Shevitz, S., & Kaye, J. (1991). Writing for *sesame street,* directing traffic, or saving souls: Jewish family educators describe their practice. *Journal of Jewish Communal Service, 67*(4).
Weick, K. (1976). Educational organizations as loosely coupled systems. *Administrative Science Quarterly, 21.*
Wertheimer, J. (2005). *Linking the silos: How to accelerate the momentum in Jewish education today.* New York: The AVI CHAI Foundation.
Wertheimer, J. (Ed.). (2008). *A census of Jewish supplementary schools in the United States.* New York: The Avi Chai Foundation.

Wertheimer, J. (Ed.). (2009a). *Learning and community: Jewish supplementary schools in the twenty-first century*. Hanover, NH: University Press of New England.

Wertheimer, J. (Ed.). (2009b). *Schools that work: What we can learn from good Jewish supplementary schools*. New York: The Avi Chai Foundation.

Wolfson, R. (1998). Growing a field of dreams. In A. Bank & R. Wolfson (Eds.), *First fruit: A Whizin anthology of Jewish family education*. Los Angeles: The Whizin Institute for Jewish Family Life.

Woocher, J. (1995). Toward a 'Unified field theory' of Jewish continuity. In I. Aron, S. Lee, & S. Rossel (Eds.), *A congregation of learners*. New York: Union of American Hebrew Congregations.

Limmud: A Unique Model of Transformative Jewish Learning

Raymond Simonson

Introduction

A key challenge for everyone involved in Jewish education is creating engaging frameworks that are most effective at assisting participants in the lifelong process of acquiring Jewish knowledge, skills, values and ideas whilst enabling them to explore and develop their personal connections to Jewish culture, history, ritual, tradition and spirituality. In the British Jewish community, we hope that such experiences lead to the next generation becoming proud, enthusiastic, committed and knowledgeable members of the Jewish people, who are active and creative in the Jewish dimension of their lives. In short, a key goal is to develop educational frameworks that target what is central to the aims of contemporary Jewish education – the development of positive, authentic Jewish identity and identification. Because of this belief shared by many in Jewish educational circles, there has been a noticeable drive in recent decades in the British-Jewish community to significantly increase the quality, variety and accessibility of educational frameworks and opportunities. This has also led to the search for and growth of additional and alternative methodologies, settings and programmes as anxious community leaders attempt to stem the tide of young adults drifting away from the community (Miller, 1991, p. viii).

With this in mind, this chapter will examine what has become regarded as one of the most vibrant, dynamic and successful examples of alternative educational projects in the Jewish world: Limmud. This chapter will explore the key factors that explain how this unique model has become a powerful vehicle for working towards the above-stated general aims of Jewish education, and why it has been referred to in British Jewry as: "the jewel in our community's crown, as well as a focus of emulation throughout the Jewish world" (*The Jewish Chronicle*, 03/01/2003).

R. Simonson (✉)
Limmud, London, UK
e-mail: raymond@limmud.org

What Is Limmud?

Limmud was initially established in 1980 as a small conference for Jewish educators. This first Limmud event, inspired by the four founders' experience of CAJE in North America, saw approximately 80 British Jewish educators gather from across the denominational, cultural and organisational spectrum to learn with and from each other in a retreat-style setting. The success of this first event led to the call for an annual conference, which began to regularly grow in size, scope, reach and impact on the wider Jewish community.

Three decades on, Limmud is now a world-leader in cross-communal, multi-generational, volunteer-led Jewish learning experiences. It has become British Jewry's premier adult education initiative, with over 7,000 people involved in at least one Limmud activity each year. Its flagship event, the week-long Limmud Conference, is now a landmark in the Jewish calendar, annually attended by over 2,000 participants from across the globe. Alongside this, Limmud attracts ever-increasing number to LimmudFest, its summer outdoor learning and culture residential retreat during the month of Elul; 15 Regional Limmud teams organise Day Limmud conferences in their local communities across the length and breadth of the UK, with over 3,000 people participating in any of six different Day Limmuds each year; over 2,000 people receive a weekly "Taste of Limmud" cross-denominational *parsha* (weekly Torah portion) commentary each week written by a different Jewish educator – all Limmud presenters – from around the world; and over 750 Limmud volunteers engage in learning, training and development sessions, meetings and seminars around the UK throughout the year.

Most strikingly perhaps, is the rapid and unprecedented growth of Limmud across the world. As the new century began, a handful of grassroots activists from Jewish communities in Northern Israel, the Netherlands and Australia who had all experienced Limmud Conference as participants, began planning the first Limmud events outside of the UK. With the guidance and support of experienced British Limmud volunteers and one part-time professional, nascent teams were formed in these communities and their inaugural events were held with much success. Within a few years as increasing numbers of overseas participants of Limmud's events in the UK began to enquire about developing the model in their own communities, Limmud responded by forming Limmud International to oversee this unanticipated growth. By 2008 Limmud International, under the chairmanship of Andrew Gilbert – one of Limmud's most experienced and respected volunteer leaders (and former Chair of the organisation during a key period of growth in the 1990s) – was supporting over 40 Limmud communities around the world providing mentoring, training, development and guidance to the local volunteer leadership. From Budapest to Buenos Aries, Cape Town to Colorado, Los Angeles to Lithuania, Modi'in to Moscow, Sweden to Serbia and from Turkey to Toronto, more and more diverse Jewish communities have been adopting Limmud's approach to Jewish learning with passion and vigour. In 2008 alone, 15 new communities outside of the UK joined the growing Limmud International family.

Limmud: A Unique Model of Transformative Jewish Learning

This chapter will attempt to understand why so many individuals and communities have chosen to embrace Limmud's unique model of Jewish education; what values underpin this model; and what has led it to being described as: "one of the strangest and fastest-growing phenomena of the Jewish world, one that may be transforming how large numbers of Jews gather and study... it may be a new sociological phenomenon" (Haviv Rettig-Gur, *Jerusalem Post*, 31/12/2007).

Guiding Values and Core Principles

On the surface, Limmud is similar to other existing models of Jewish education, such as tried and tested modes of informal education widely in use throughout the arenas of youth movements, summer camps and retreats; and the paradigms of lifelong learning that drive the success of many synagogues' and JCCs' programmes. However, a closer examination of some of Limmud's underlying values and driving principles reveals a counter-cultural and often counter-intuitive model.

Valuing Diversity

One of the defining features of Limmud which was not only radical when it was founded, but which has caused it to be attacked and criticised by a minority of the establishment in every decade since, is that it is a truly cross-communal organisation. One of Limmud's core values declared on its mission statement is: "We value diversity in all we do. We believe in the richness of our diverse community and create cross-communal and cross-generational experiences" (see www.limmud.org/home/about/mission/). As such its activities are open to any type of Jew from all areas of the community – regardless of affiliation (or lack of it), socio-economic background, age, gender, sexuality, level of knowledge, belief or any of the other typical dividing lines found within the Jewish community – and attracts to its events a greater mix of different types of Jew from the widest range of backgrounds than can be found at almost any other Jewish learning event.

Despite claims of some of its critics to the contrary, Limmud does not consider itself to be ideologically pluralist, and nor does it desire to be. Rather than saying that it values every stream, denomination or political leaning equally and that each are valid and contain equally important truths, Limmud simply says that it has no wish to engage in that debate at all. Instead it places a higher premium on the concept of *Am Yisrael* and *Klal Yisrael* – of Jewish peoplehood. In fact explicitly stated in its mission statement is: "Limmud does not participate in legitimising or de-legitimising any religious or political position found in the worldwide Jewish community... Limmud has no part to say in the debates between/across denominations. Limmud will programme its events in such a way as to avoid religious or political conflict" (ibid.). Instead of focusing on that which divides Jews, Limmud seems to share Professor Michael Rosenak's belief that there "is a manifest desire on the part of most educated Jews for community of association and for some agenda that those associated will have in common" (Rosenak in Fox, Scheffler, & Marom, 2003, p. 191).

Limmud's commitment to diversity and cross-communalism is one of the reasons for its increasing popularity, but is also the cause of some of its greatest challenges. It strives hard to ensure its educational programmes represent a balance between different Jewish ideologies and religious and political viewpoints, thus reflecting the diversity of its participants. However, this results in accusations from various opposing sectors of the community that Limmud leans too far to the other extreme, whether this be, for example, left or right, Zionist or anti-Zionist, Orthodox or non-Orthodox and so on. The most notable example of this is that even after nearly three decades Limmud has failed to be accepted by much of the leadership of the mainstream Orthodox movement of the UK (The United Synagogue – the US), with only a handful of the over 50 US rabbis participating and teaching at Limmud's events. Indeed, a number of highly respected Orthodox rabbis and teachers from outside of the UK have commented in the past that the London Beth Din (rabbinical law court of the United Synagogue) explicitly requested that they do not accept Limmud's invitation to participate in their events. Responding to such claims made in the *Jerusalem Post* in December 2007, Rabbi Dr Nathan Lopes Cardozo (teacher, writer and Dean of the David Cardozo Academy in Jerusalem) explained why he has politely rejected such requests and participated at a number of Limmud Conferences: "My response to the Beth Din of London stated my concern that when I eventually stand in front of the Heavenly Court, the Lord will ask me why I did not participate when there was an opportunity to influence thousands of people and provide them with a glimpse into an open-minded and authentic kind of Orthodox Judaism. What would I answer?" (*Jerusalem Post*, 29/12/2007).

Limmud's leadership endeavour to avoid becoming embroiled in debates over what constitutes the "right way" with regards to any Jewish subject, and do not permit such discussions as sessions during Limmud events. Limmud only allows debates or arguments on different Jewish viewpoints or ideologies to take place where they are judged to be *l'shem shamayim* (for the sake of heaven), believing that these debates "can make a positive contribution to furthering our education and understanding" (see www.limmud.org/home/about/mission/). Whilst many applaud this approach as it means Limmud can provide a rare "space in which diverse sections of the Jewish world can meet and moreover meet without antagonism" others are less positive, suggesting that this simply "reveals a deep desire on the part of British Jewry to wish away difficult, problematic and intractable conflicts" (Harris in Rabinowitz, 1998, pp. 39–54).

This neutral position is a delicate and often difficult one to maintain as it leaves Limmud open to the type of criticism personified by veteran columnist and former Chairman of the Governing Board of the World Jewish Congress, Isi Leibler. In one of his public criticisms of Limmud, prompted in part by the participation of former Head of the Jewish Agency and Speaker of the Knesset Avrum Burg at the 2007 Limmud Conference, Leibler accused Limmud of "regularly inviting speakers who represent the antithesis of Jewish values". Leibler rejected Limmud's explanation of the underlying principles and values that guide these decisions, with the derisory: "It is surely grotesque for Limmud to justify such participation on the grounds that 'for the sake of learning' we try to get a wide range of presenters." (Originally published in *Jerusalem Post*, 29/01/2008. Available at http://www.israpundit.com/2008/?p=113.)

Limmud's leadership maintain that they do not intentionally seek controversy and only invite presenters on merit of what they might add to the intellectual debate within the context of enabling the participants to grapple with issues of interest to a broad Jewish audience. However, these tensions between different sections of the Jewish community and the public brickbats thrown at Limmud seem an unavoidable side-effect of pursuing an agenda of diversity and cross-communalism in a community that is better known for its conservatism. These are challenges that Limmud's volunteers are not always best-equipped to face, and they may need to develop a greater level of sophistication over coming years.

Volunteerism and Empowerment

Limmud is a great example of a truly grassroots, volunteer-owned, volunteer-led organisation. From the very beginning it was built by friends who shared a common passion for Jewish learning and engagement in its broadest sense. Limmud was something they were involved with of their own volition, motivated in part by the genuine camaraderie that existed and flourished between team members. None of the professionally staffed organisations around the British-Jewish community have initiated any of Limmud's activities or events – although over the years, some have carried out the important task of providing support to the growing organisation.

Voluntary organisations are not exceptional in and of themselves. In fact, it is estimated that in the UK alone there are around 12 million adults (approx 25% of the adult population) involved in volunteer work (Smith in Deer Richardson and Wolfe, 2001, p. 142). Without the army of volunteers who put in hundreds of thousands of hours of unpaid work every year, most Jewish communal organisations would simply cease to exist in any relevant sense. Where Limmud is different from many of these organisations though is in the nature of the volunteer relationship with the organisation. As articulated by Jacqueline Nicholls, Jewish educator, artist and longstanding Limmud volunteer: "Limmud is not about providing a service for others…but is rather about providing an educational Jewish experience for our community and ourselves. The volunteers 'own' the events with their ideas and their energy" (Nicholls in Boyd, 2003, p. 199).

The key concepts here are empowerment and ownership. Limmud volunteers do not give of their time simply because they feel that Limmud is providing a worthy and important service to other people. Whilst that is a noble and legitimate sentiment that drives a significant amount of the essential volunteerism in the Jewish community, it is by no means the driving force behind volunteering within Limmud.

Instead, Limmud is an organisation "of the people, by the people, for the people", enabling the Limmud community to create the Jewish educational experiences that they themselves want. The agenda is not set and delivered top-down, but is created, developed and delivered bottom-up by those who wish to respond positively to the critique they have of the community, or even to the criticism they have of how Limmud currently does certain things. These volunteers also continue to be (along with thousands of other people) the participants of the events and experiences that they create. Therefore, the volunteers have a fundamental interest in ensuring the educational projects are relevant, creative, dynamic and of an extremely high quality – projects that they themselves would benefit from as participants.

Limmud was an incredibly counter-cultural concept within the very formal mainstream British-Jewish community against which it emerged in the early 1980s. In this context it was antithetical to have a successful organisation, completely independent, where all decisions were taken by the same people who would both implement and be participants in the very events that they themselves were planning and executing. Even more so to have an organisation that rather than discouraging external criticism, has always used such opportunities both to improve what it does and to grow the volunteer base, by encouraging those with the critique to take responsibility for driving the change or fixing the problem. By responding to those with a criticism of Limmud with an invitation to become actively involved in improving it, the organisers have always felt that they could help facilitate the actualisation of ever more people's ideas and visions (Nicholls in Boyd, 2003, p. 198). This is not necessarily the way for the senior leadership of any typical British-Jewish communal organisation to act, especially in the early 1980s.

After three decades, Limmud remains true to its original informal, grass roots volunteer ethos. Organised through a system of teams, volunteers take responsibility for every single aspect of running the organisation and its educational projects and events. Everything from organisational strategy and policy-making, to public relations, budgeting and fundraising is in the hands of the volunteers who are empowered to own, shape and lead the organisation. This includes the recruitment and management of the two or three full-time professional support staff that Limmud now employs.

Whilst the overall structure is more systematic now than it was in the early 1980s in response to the size and reach of its ever-growing activities, much about the informality of the voluntary leadership culture remains the same. Social ti and the culture of friendship still play a significant role across the organisatic Teams consist of people from different backgrounds who genuinely want to wo together, and who believe they are engaged in something of real value and impo They meet regularly and frequently, mostly in each other's homes, both as a wh team and in their smaller sub-teams. They develop meaningful relationships th matter beyond the task they are engaged in. They share Shabbat meals, *chagg* (Jewish holidays) and family celebrations together. Crucially, they engage with ea other as equals, regardless of age, Jewish background or socio-economic statu Whilst it may not be always obvious from the outside, this social capital play a significant part both in Limmud's strength and in the continued motivation an dedication to Limmud demonstrated over the long term by a considerable amount of volunteers. As Professor Mark K Smith appositely notes in an article on social capital: "Interaction enables people to build communities, to commit themselves to each other, and to knit the social fabric. A sense of belonging and the concrete experience of social networks (and the relationships of trust and tolerance that can be involved) can, it is argued, bring great benefits to people" (Smith, 2007, www.infed.org/biblio/social_capital.htm).

What these volunteers have in common is that they all have the desire and ability to "give of themselves because they perceive Limmud as something they can contribute to and impact upon" (Nicholls in Boyd, 2003, p. 198). This is something that Limmud actively encourages. Indeed, within its mission statement and proudly displayed in its printed materials and on its website there are various relevant proclamations including "we encourage all participants to take an active part in all that we do"; "we are all responsible for the communities that we create; everyone has an important contribution to make"; and "we inspire people to be ambitious about their contribution" (see www.limmud.org/home/about/mission/).

One of the practical ramifications of a genuine belief that everyone truly has "an important contribution to make" is that Limmud operates largely as a meritocracy. The vast majority of Limmud volunteers contribute to building the Limmud community through their time, energy and passion, rather than with large financial donations. They invest vast amounts of "sweat equity" to build their Limmud community through sheer determination and hard work. And those who are in the most senior positions – the Chairs of the major events and teams, as well as the Limmud Executive (the board of directors and charity trustees) – are there by virtue of what they have contributed over a number of years, and what they continue to give. They are those who have given the most of themselves and who have demonstrated they are able to continue to give at an exceptionally high level of quality and impact.

Limmud's meritocratic and empowering approach to volunteer leadership is particularly appealing to younger generations who see that in this "adult" organisation, neither their age nor their bank balance is barrier to the level they can get involved or to the roles they can take on. And of course, the benefits of the aforementioned social capital are equally appealing as they are able to widen their communal networks and build new and genuine social ties at the time when they have left the relative comfort of university and youth/student movement life. Indeed, a by-product of the social nature of volunteering within Limmud is the increasing number of long-term relationships and partnerships that have grown out of the volunteer community over the years. Anecdotally at least, this seems to be another motivating factor for many new volunteers, especially those in their early mid-20s.

Educational Philosophy and Approach to Learning

At the heart of everything that Limmud does is a commitment to high-quality, inspiring Jewish learning. In many ways it is difficult to define Limmud through a particular educational philosophy in the way that one can with more traditional educational organisations. Indeed, a participant of any Limmud event is likely to be presented with a wider range of different (and even competing) educational approaches, beliefs, methodologies and styles than they have ever encountered under one roof. However, as with most things Limmud, on closer inspection one can determine underlying core principles and values that determine the learning milieu.

In the centre of Limmud's mission statement is "Limmud's Promise", which is: "Wherever you find yourself, Limmud will take you one step further on your Jewish journey". Like much else about Limmud, this seemingly simple statement represents a fairly radical concept when set against the context of the Jewish education field. The vast majority of Jewish educational organisations and projects have specific outputs and outcomes that they are aiming to achieve. These traditional educational structures focus their energies on taking their students along a set path in order to end up in a set place – from point A to point Z, via points B, C, D, and so on. Limmud, however, sees its task as providing the framework and some tools to enable people to move along their own paths, not necessarily to point B or C, but simply to some position beyond point A. Limmud, in fact, neither concerns itself with what the individual's starting point is nor prescribes a precise endpoint, instead putting its energies and resources into providing multiple paths that are engaging and compelling enough to convince each individual that they should – and can – explore any of them, with the explicit goal of moving. Thus it could be argued that a fundamental guiding principle of Limmud's educational approach is that it ought to be transformational (in the long term at least if not immediately).

In their chapter on adult education in a temporary residential learning community for Jack Mezirow's book *Learning as Transformation*, Dr Judith Beth Cohen and Deborah Piper focus on four critical components of such a learning community if it is to facilitate transformative educational experiences: "the setting, the breakdown of roles among those attending. . ., the element of time, and the structural paradoxes of the curriculum" (Beth Cohen & Piper in Mezirow, 2000, p. 208). We can look at the example of Limmud Conference through these four lenses to gain a better understanding of how it has become such an impactful educational enterprise.

Setting: Setting has always had an important role to play for Limmud. From the earliest days of the Limmud Conference in the serene settings of Carmel College – at the time, a Jewish boarding school in the Oxfordshire countryside – to the current home at the University of Warwick in the Midlands, Limmud's organisers acknowledged the importance of taking people out of their day-to-day settings and creating a temporary physical community. Almost all participants leave their hometowns and travel to arrive at this new location, thus beginning the sense of "one step further on your Jewish journey" with a literal, physical journey.

As with the most celebrated summer camps across the Jewish world, Limmud puts much effort into creating a feeling that one is removed from one's day-to-day world both geographically and perceptually. From the moment one arrives at the gates of the university, one is greeted by huge banners proclaiming that this is Limmud Conference. Before one has even stepped into a classroom, a multitude of signs, posters and banners, all carrying the familiar Limmud logo, colours and unique font will have been passed at every turn. The only people that Limmud participants are likely to encounter for the duration of the event are other Limmud participants, all identifiable from the familiar logoed badges bearing their names, and the programme handbooks and logoed drinks flasks in their hands. The buildings and rooms are transformed with much care and attention by an army of volunteers, so that a vestibule becomes a completely redecorated "Café Limmud" with kosher snacks and drinks and Israeli music playing through the speakers; a seminar building is turned into a fully equipped "Young Limmud" youth camp base; and student union nightclub turns into the "Limmud Shuk" filled with sights and sounds of dozens of Jewish organisations and sellers of Judaica. All rooms are renamed and re-signed accordingly, and large maps of this new Limmud world adorn the walls of corridors and sprout plant-like from poles around the grounds.

Many observers have commented on the attention to detail that goes into this physical transformation that takes place. Limmud's aim here is to create a temporary space where the participant is fully surrounded by multiple stimuli to enhance their Jewish journey. The intended effect is to create a positive Jewish environment that can affect the senses and ultimately the identities of the participants. As noted by Jonathan Boyd, specialist in contemporary British Jewry: "Limmud transforms the social, cultural and educational context into something that is unrecognisable from the rest of the year, and in doing so, enables the context to speak to and influence the individual in a whole host of ways" (Boyd, 2006, p. 33).

In their study of North American summer camps, Leonard Saxe and Amy Sales refer to this creation of a temporary world separated from home, school and work life as a "Brigadoon-like place" where "time and space are compressed" and "everyone seems to live in the here and now" (Sales & Saxe, 2004, pp. 47–48). One of the effects of this is the ability to create a positive atmosphere conducive to learning and potential change, where participants naturally feel more open to new ideas, more comfortable in experimenting and safe to question and be challenged. For Limmud this is not left to chance and is an explicit objective of the organisers. Nicholls has written that part of the organisation's educational aims are to create "a warm and welcoming atmosphere", acknowledging that providing high-quality educators and dynamic, challenging sessions alone will not achieve the goals unless there is also a "warm atmosphere where people feel they want to be and learn" (Nicholls in Boyd, 2003, p. 198). Therefore, the volunteer teams responsible for "Participant Care", "Families & Crèche" and "Space & Decor" play as crucial a role in Limmud's attempts to achieve their overall educational goals as the educational "Programming Team". There is an appreciation of Smith's assertion that in order to create effective, transformational educational programmes, we "need to attend to physical surroundings" and construct environments that "foster conversation, democracy and learning" (Smith in Deer Richardson and Wolfe, 2001, p. 146).

In recent years the voluntary leadership of events such as Limmud Conference and LimmudFest have displayed a growing sophistication in their use of site to increase the overall educational impact on the participants. They have expanded each event over an ever greater number of different spaces and structures, spread out across whichever site they inhabit. In doing so, participants are encouraged to move physically around the site and explore the many paths and corridors that lead to the sessions, lectures, performances, crèches, exhibitions, meals and so on. Some destinations are easy to reach whilst others prove slightly more challenging or are further away from the central areas. Cohen and Piper highlight how this physical sense of journey, choice and exploration can act as a powerful, if implicit "metaphor for the educational journey" that the organisers want the participants to embark on. In their experiences this type of setup can arouse an "infectious sense of curiosity" in the participant, who naturally brings this sense into the classroom, thus creating a "sense of quest and discovery" conducive to transformative educational experiences (Beth Cohen & Piper in Mezirow, 2000, pp. 208–9).

Breakdown of roles: One of the unique features of all Limmud events is the breakdown in roles of those in attendance. Crucial to this is a simple but very powerful statement, laid out as one of Limmud's core values in the mission statement that declares: "Everyone can be a teacher and everyone should be a student". If we break this down, we see that there are three key elements of this which sum up much of Limmud's overall ethos. First, an overarching belief that *all* Jews ought to be involved in learning. A second aspect which may not be immediately obvious is that at Limmud events the teachers should equally be students. Thirdly and perhaps most radically, is the claim that *everyone* is capable, in some way, of being a teacher too. This is in part due to that fact that Limmud "wants people to keep moving and to keep learning; and teaching is a key part of that learning" (Nicholls in Boyd, 2003, p. 199); but also a genuine egalitarian belief that we all have something to learn from each other. This means that in the programme, alongside world famous Jewish educators and thinkers and leaders of their respective fields, sit the dentist with an enthusiasm for and great knowledge of Jewish genealogy and the full-time mother who is passionate and articulate about the poetry of Yehuda Amichai. Both of these may get their one chance in the year to teach their passion to others whilst at a Limmud event. Even more inspiring for them is when they realise that one of the "students" in their class of 20 is the Knesset Member or Yale Professor or Nobel Prize winner who earlier that day they listened to along with another 350 participants.

Putting these three aspects together leads to a highly egalitarian and democratic approach to education which runs through Limmud's DNA. Nicholls explains that at all Limmud events "there is no separation between the presenters and the students. All are participants" (Nicholls in Boyd, 2003, pp. 198–199). The hierarchies and differentiations usually found in educational establishments between teacher and student – and perhaps including auxiliary administrative staff, volunteers and "senior" lay leadership – are non-existent in a Limmud setting. Everyone stays in the same choice of (fairly sparse) accommodation, eats the same food in the same dining rooms with no "top table", dresses relatively casual, and has the same style of name badge, with their first name printed large above their surname. No titles or recognition of status on display – no "Rabbi…" or "Professor…" on badges or indeed in the programme books[1]. The presenters are not paid an honorarium

---

[1] Other than in the mini-biography of each presenter that is included in the handbook in order to ensure participants have all relevant information they may need to help them make informed choices (see below).

(they all voluntarily contribute their time and the majority of them also pay their participant fees to attend) and do not have access to a VIP area or faculty lounge. They eat and drink and socialise and study and debate and discuss alongside all other participants.

This role diffusion creates a particular egalitarian culture in which the potential intimidating distance between teacher and student is minimised as the playing field is levelled (Cohen & Piper in Mezirow, 2000, p. 210). One of the effects of this atmosphere is that genuine and impactful conversations and relationships flourish between who we would traditionally label as students and teachers. These often grow out of sessions as the presenter continues to discuss key points of interest raised with one or more of the students after the session in the informal setting of the bar or over a meal. They also often begin before the learner has even appreciated that their partner in dialogical exchange is one of the invited "teachers". To educationalists from Freire to Smith and Chazan, these continued stimulating conversations and social encounters play a powerful role in developing identities, shaping beliefs and framing our understanding of ourselves and the world[2]. The belief is that through genuine dialogue both educators and students can develop their capabilities to become critical thinkers and shapers of their own worlds as they learn with and from each other.

Some critics of Limmud point to the limitations of an educational experience that does not give the learner much chance either to immerse oneself into any one specific subject at great depth or to methodically develop an understanding through a more traditional learning cycle of *classroom study → reflect → draw new conclusions → bring new conclusions back to the classroom → build on conclusions with classroom study*, and so on. Indeed, it has been noted that "one does not sink roots into a topic at Limmud. Rather, for an hour, one dips gently into it and pulls out" (Haviv Rettig-Gur, *Jerusalem Post*, 31/12/2007). Whilst there is some truth in this, it misses the crucial point discussed above that the learning takes place well beyond the boundaries of any one single session/lesson. Indeed, some argue that the sessions simply act as a catalyst to the main learning, which takes place in the less formal, more natural settings throughout – and after – the event (Boyd, 2006, pp. 30–31). However, not even the keenest Limmud advocate would argue that simply attending a few sessions on one topic at a Limmud event is an equal substitute for a fuller course of study through one of the more traditional routes. Those seeking deep meaningful enlightenment on any one subject are likely to be disappointed if that is their primary goal for participating at any of Limmud's events.

The element of time: Time plays an important role in the transformational nature of the educational process at Limmud's residential events. First, participants have the freedom to build their own timetable. Unlike evening adult education classes or university, there is no set time where each student must attend set lessons. The detailed programme books list all sessions available at any one time, but as much as participants can choose which topics and teachers interest them, they are also free to choose which session slots they will attend and which they will miss altogether.

---

[2] For more, see in particular Jeffs and Smith (1999).

Sessions are programmed throughout the day and do not even follow the traditional norm of stopping for lengthy meal breaks. As with almost everything else with Limmud, the participants choose how they wish to make use of their time – and this is an unusually empowering aspect of the experience.

For the majority of the participants during a residential Limmud event, time is used differently from their day-to-day existence – much like the setting differs as outlined above. The vast majority of participants either work or study full or part time. Outside of the Limmud setting they have a whole host of responsibilities that commands their time, from work to domestic chores to the daily commute. For many, Limmud provides the rare luxury of a break from daily responsibilities and concerns, a suspension of real time, enabling the individual to focus almost uninterrupted on their learning and development, a key factor in maximising the long-term impact of the experience (Beth Cohen & Piper in Mezirow, 2000, p. 212). Kosher meals are provided precluding the need to shop, cook or clean; accommodation is within walking distance of session rooms to avoid the need to spend time commuting each day; inclusive childcare facilities are provided on site so that for large parts of the day someone else is looking after the children; and so on. The various volunteer teams referred to above that are as integral to the success as the programming team, put significant amounts effort and resources into maximising the opportunities for participants to concentrate on their learning experience as uninterrupted as possible.

Structural paradox of the learning programme: A structural paradox exists within Limmud's educational events insomuch as whilst an extremely detailed daily schedule of sessions has been put together by a team of volunteers each participant is completely free to build her own unique programme of study. There is no tutor or course director dictating what topics one needs to take, and no notion of a required set of credits to complete the course. Whilst there are many experienced people – Limmud volunteers, respected educators – willing to give their opinion and recommendations, it is entirely up to the individual to make her own choice. Cohen and Piper acknowledge that "moving away from a teacher-directed format to becoming the active subject who creates her own curriculum is a powerful transition to make" and that this transition plays a significant part in the transformational nature of such an educational endeavour (Beth Cohen & Piper in Mezirow, 2000, p. 216).

There is a belief in a strong element of self-directed learning at place within Limmud. Whilst not in its purest form (given that although there is a wide choice for the learner, it is not infinite, but instead "limited" to some 950 or so sessions and 300–350 different presenters), this is the self-direction that was championed by one of the most influential figures in the field of adult education, Malcolm Knowles. Knowles argues that where individuals take the initiative in their learning, they learn more, and learn better, than passive learners who are taught what others decide they should learn. He claims that as adults make crucial decisions on a regular basis, we should also be trusted to make decisions about our own learning. He explains that proactive, self-directed learners who make their own choices "enter into learning more purposefully and with greater motivation. They also tend to retain and make use of what they learn better and longer than do the reactive learners" (Knowles, 1975, pp. 14–15).

The key concept for Limmud participants here is choice; every individual is empowered and encouraged to choose between multiple topics, diverse presenters and different learning styles. During the week-long Limmud Conference, there are on average between 15 and 25 different sessions taking place at the same time, as many topics, under any one of 10–15 different subject tracks, and utilising as broad a range of methodologies as possible. Each session is described in the handbook that every participant receives, with details of the track, topic, title, learning methodology, level (and if necessary, required prior knowledge) and presenter. In this way the participants are empowered to make an informed choice. Rather than being guided along a conveyer belt of a one-size-fits-all set curriculum, each individual learner creates his or her own study programme to fit his interests or meet her needs; to explore new topics never previously encountered, or find comfort in familiar and favourite subject matter. Each person may arrive with completely different personal aims for their learning, but each may leave feeling their goals have been achieved.

In his seminal work "Liquid Modernity", Polish-Jewish sociologist Zygmunt Bauman examines how modernity's emphasis on the individual has had significant impact on notions of society, largely due to the primacy of concepts of freedom, choice and self-determination of the individual. He writes that "it is up to the individual to find out what she or he is capable of doing, to stretch that capacity to the utmost, and to pick the ends to which that capacity can be applied best – that is, to the greatest achievable satisfaction" (Bauman, 2000, p. 62). Limmud plays into this modern trend by offering multiple options and different entry points. Any Limmud event offers something very similar to Bauman's description of a "buffet table set with mouth-watering dishes" (Bauman, 2000, p. 63) for the individual to choose from based on what they feel may give them the greatest satisfaction.

Amongst the effects of this approach are a fairly radical (certainly within the mainstream British Jewish community) democratisation of Jewish education and empowerment of the learner. Whilst it is true, of course, that Limmud's organisers have made certain choices in advance in order to shape the programme and ensure that particular presenters are part of it, one of their fundamental aims is to ensure that the "buffet table" contains as wide a range of Jewish dishes as possible, and that all dishes are as "mouth-watering" as can be. In order to achieve this variety, the presenters and sessions are determined in part by a 20–30 strong team of programming volunteers who invite some 50–60% of the presenters and encourage them to offer sessions on suggested topics of interest; but also in part by anything from 100 to 200 other individuals who, as described above, are participants who have one or two sessions they wish to present.

This democratisation of the educational programme has seen Limmud described as a "whole new Wikified Jewish world", in reference to the immensely popular online dictionary Wikipedia (Haviv Rettig-Gur, *Jerusalem Post*, 02/02/2008). This uniquely modern phenomenon which has become arguably the world's most popular encyclopaedia is written and edited by its readers, with a set of checks and balances in place to help ensure accuracy. Its popularity has been attributed to a belief "that the combined, continually-edited knowledge of the multitude is more accurate and useful than that of individual experts" (ibid.). Similarly, whilst the overall programme of a Limmud Conference may be shaped, modified and balanced by the programming team, it is essentially built by 300–400 people, who have all contributed at least something to the feast.

It is clear to conclude from this so-called "wikified" approach that the organisers genuinely do not wish to dictate exactly what or how the individual should be learning. This is unlike the majority of Jewish education initiatives where the organisers determine everything from content to learning style to ideological message, and all students go through the same programme, or a variation of it. Instead, every Limmud participant can freely choose his path of learning without any teachers, *madrichim* (guides), or tutors setting the curriculum to be followed. As such, the learning process at Limmud is empowering as it "reinforces the individual's intellectual autonomy" (Haviv Rettig-Gur, *Jerusalem Post*, 31/12/2007) – a highly attractive feature, especially to the younger generation of Jewish adults who are immersed in the age of the internet with its seemingly limitless ability to enable the user to build one's experiences of the world around oneself.

The most effective learning within Limmud takes place through continual and genuine dialogue between presenters and participants, and between participants and other participants. In order for this to happen, the educational activities and environment are – influenced by the thinking of Carl Rogers – consciously constructed to be participant-centred, with the organisers and presenters/teachers "prizing the learner, his feelings, opinions, person" (Rogers, 1969, p. 109). That is not to say that each individual session at a Limmud Conference is purely participant-centred as they are based around the materials or concepts that each presenter has prepared to teach before knowing who her students will be. Rather, Limmud places the individual person in the centre of the overall educational endeavour and acts out a belief in John Dewey's assertions that the learning will be greatly enhanced if it is an interactive, engaging process for the learner (Dewey, 1938, pp. 18–19). This conviction influences almost all key decisions that are made in the planning stages of any major Limmud event, as the Limmud leadership believes that it is central to achieving a genuinely transformational educational experience. Underlying this approach is a profound trust in and respect for the ability of the individual and her commitment to her own learning.

It should be noted that for some there are clear downsides to this "wikified" approach to building the programme, and in particular with adhering to an educational philosophy based on the belief that "everyone can be a teacher and everyone should be a student". Whilst for Limmud's organisers this remains a noble statement of intent, to others it represents a significant weakness in the Limmud's attempts to be taken seriously as an educational organisation. The egalitarian approach that sees all presenters afforded the same status also means it can be difficult to judge in advance which sessions will be of the highest quality. As explained, many of the presenters will have submitted sessions and written their own short biography without being known by the organising team. An enthusiastic amateur may happen to be an inspiring teacher or fascinating speaker, but there is no guarantee that knowledge and enthusiasm for a subject alone will translate into a worthwhile session. The Amichai-adoring mother, or the dentist who loves Jewish genealogy referred to above, may have all the passion but none of the skills needed to present an interesting session. This can be incredibly frustrating for the more serious learner who has sat in angst with the programme handbook trying to choose which session to go to in that hour and which of the others he will have to miss.

Conclusion and Recommendation for Future Research

Perhaps the essence of what makes Limmud such a powerful, successful, transformational endeavour in the field of Jewish education was best captured by the world's oldest Jewish newspaper, *The Jewish Chronicle*, when its Judaism Editor and chief writer wrote in 2009: "Limmud has caught the imagination of Jews worldwide because it offers a broader, more open experience of Jewish community, rather than one bound by hierarchy and convention or riven by religious compartmentalisation. A place of 'yes, we can' rather than 'no, you can't'... It's easy to think that this is the Jewish community as many think it should be: democratic, egalitarian, inclusive, willing to encourage experiment and exposure to different ideas and views" (Simon Rocker, JC, 08/01/2009).

Limmud is not seeking to provide the be-all and end-all Jewish educational experience that leaves all participants with a fully rounded sense of Jewish identity or a complete understanding of how to live a meaningful Jewish life. Instead, following the Freirean tradition it acknowledges its participants as "beings in the process of becoming – as unfinished, uncompleted beings in and with a likewise unfinished reality" (Freire, 1972, pp. 56–57) and wishes to play a role in helping them take one step further on their journey. Limmud's leadership understand that their events and activities act for some as Jewish educational "spas" for those who need a break from their daily routine in order to immerse themselves in a reinvigorating pool of Jewish learning and community; and as a catalyst for others to embark on further Jewish learning.

Dewey taught that the skills, knowledge and values that one learns from any particular situation are not ends in themselves, but if successful become "an instrument of understanding for dealing effectively with situations which follow" (Dewey, 1938, p. 44). Those involved with running Limmud believe that what people take away from their experience at any Limmud event will become such instruments of understanding as they continue to take further steps on their Jewish journeys. Whilst there is no set endpoint for its participants, we can clearly ascribe to Limmud one of Professor Barry Chazan's definitions of effective Jewish education, in that it has a "conscious intent or desire to affect the Jewish character of people – the way they think, feel, and behave" (Chazan, 1991, p. 306). Feedback regularly gathered by Limmud suggests that this is true of a majority of participants, who, through Limmud, encounter a unique community built on principles of egalitarianism, cross-communalism and respect; guided by such values as empowerment, diversity, freedom of choice and mutual responsibility; and with a commitment to "expanding Jewish horizons". If that is true, then how much more so for the community of volunteers who explore these and other concepts all year round, and who put them into action as they create the events, projects and the community that they themselves want to be part of. In almost every community around the world where there is an active Limmud group, it is these volunteers – particularly of the younger generations – who, inspired by their involvement are now amongst the key protagonists driving the rejuvenation of Jewish life, learning and community development, and who are at the forefront of initiatives that are engaging ever-growing numbers of young adults.

Limmud is perhaps a surprisingly under-researched phenomenon. There is little empirical evidence to back up the claims of its leadership, even if there is strong anecdotal support. Of the many potential research projects that might be proposed, I recommend priority be given to the following:

1. *The transformational impact on the individual* – What part has Limmud played in strengthening the Jewish identities and lives of regular participants of its events over a 5, 10 and 15 year period? To what extent does involvement in Limmud lead to involvement in the wider Jewish community?
2. *Limmud's contribution to the British-Jewish community* – How has the UK Jewish landscape changed in the past three decades and what contribution has Limmud made to this? Limmud's leadership – and many observers – believe that Limmud has created fertile ground that has enabled other cross-communal or pluralist organisations, and innovative, creative events and projects to flourish. Without Limmud, would there now be, for example, Jewish Book Week, JCoSS, JCC for London, Jewdas, Wandering Jews – all who have experienced Limmudnikim amongst their leadership and who have followed in Limmud's wake – and others? What have any of these organisations learned from Limmud's experiences, successes and challenges; and gained from its existence and popularity?
3. *Limmud's impact on the Jewish world* – The rapid growth of Limmud around the world is astonishing, and numerically, by any criteria, Limmud International could be said to be a huge success. But what does success mean in qualitative terms? To what extent are the outputs and outcomes impacting on the quality or development of Jewish life in any of the communities where Limmud now has a presence?

References

Bauman, Z. (2000). *Liquid modernity*. Oxford: Blackwell Publishing Ltd.
Boyd, J. (2006). *In search of underlying principles: The case of Limmud*. Unpublished.
Chazan, B. (1991). What is informal Jewish education? *Journal of Jewish Communal Service*, 67(4), Summer 1991.
Dewey, J. (1938). *Experience and education*. New York: Macmillan Publishing Co., Inc.
Fox, S., Scheffler, I., & Marom, D. (Eds.). (2003). *Visions of Jewish education*. Cambridge: Cambridge University Press.
Freire, P., translated by Bergman Ramos, M. (1972). *Pedagogy of the oppressed*. Harmondsworth, Middlesex: Penguin Books Ltd.

Harris, K. (1998). Exploring Jewish space: A critique of Limmud. In R. Rabinowitz (Ed.), *New voices in Jewish thought*. London: Limmud Publications.

Jeffs, T., & Smith, M. (1996). *Informal education – Conversation, democracy and learning*. Derby: Education Now Publishing Co-operative Limited.

Knowles, M. S. (1975). *Self-directed learning. A guide for learners and teachers*. Prentice Hall/Cambridge: Englewood Cliffs.

Mezirow, J. (2000). *Learning as transformation: Critical perspectives on a theory in progress*. San Francisco: Jossey-Bass.

Miller, S. (Ed.). (1991). *Securing our future: An inquiry into Jewish education in the United Kingdom*. London: Jewish Educational Development Trust.

Nicholls, J. (2003). Case study 2: Limmud. In J. Boyd (Ed.), *The sovereign and the situated self: Jewish identity and community in the 21st century*. London: Profile Books Limited.

Rogers, C. (1969). *Freedom to learn*. Columbus, OH: Charles E Merrill Publishing Company.

Sales, A., & Saxe, L. (2004). *How goodly are thy tents: Summer camps as Jewish socializing experiences*. Lebanon, NH: Brandeis University Press.

Smith, M. K. (2001). Place, space and informal education. In L. Deer Richardson & M. Wolfe (Eds.), *Principles and practice of informal education*. London: RoutledgeFalmer.

Smith, M. K. (2007) "Social Capital", in The Encyclopaedia of Informal Education, www.infed.org/biblio/social_capital.htm

Mentoring: Ideological Encounters – Mentoring Teachers in Jewish Education

Michal Muszkat-Barkan

Introduction

A major goal of mentoring teachers[1] is to enhance teachers' professional growth, by increasing their reflective abilities (Glickman, 1990; Zeichner & Liston, 1985; Pajak, 2002).[2] Culture- or religion-based curricula, such as Jewish studies, are embedded within an ideological context. Thus, the ideological context in Jewish studies is an aspect of every lesson and decision taken in the classroom. Teaching Jewish sources is inherently related to the ideological orientation of the participants in the process (Cohen, 1996; Shkedi & Nisan, 2006), including students and their communities, as well as teachers and mentors (Muszkat-Barkan & Shkedi, 2009). Thus, the goals of teacher-mentoring in Jewish education should include enhancing awareness of the ideological-cultural components of personal attitudes toward Jewish resources. This may enable teachers and teachers' mentors to elucidate their own considerations in choosing subject matter for teaching and "translating" it for current learners.

Despite its centrality, the influence of the ideologies of teachers and of teachers' mentors on teachers' professional development has received little critical attention to date. In addition, the effects of the mentors' ideologies on the mentoring process have been rarely recognized or discussed. The aim of this chapter is to define what is unique in the mentoring of teachers in Jewish education as related to the ideologies of participants. This is important because it can help mentors to be more reflective about their practice: to understand what they do and why they do it, and to understand how various components of their beliefs affect their practice of mentoring.

M. Muszkat-Barkan (✉)
Hebrew Union College and Melton Center for Jewish Education, The Hebrew University of Jerusalem, Jerusalem, Israel
e-mail: mbmichal@netvision.co.il

[1] In this article I use the term mentoring as a general term for many kinds of in-service teacher training. See a broader discussion of the terms "mentoring," "clinical supervision," and "coaching" below.

[2] I refer especially to the developmental and reflective models of clinical supervision, see for example Pajak (2002).

This may help mentors identify how their practice is related to their Jewish cultural ideologies. Eventually this may help define needs for mentors' in-service and pre-service training.

Using a qualitative research methodology, I indicate how the personal ideological orientations of both teachers and mentors affect mentoring processes in Jewish education. Based on the case described below and the literature reviewed I discuss how these orientations can be addressed in order to enhance teachers' professional growth.

Background

The Context and Goals of Teachers' Professional Development

There are various ways in which the ends and means of in-service teacher professional development are described. Most commonly the ends of professional development include increasing teachers' professional capabilities; promoting effective teaching practices; encouraging personal and professional growth; and changing school culture (Harris in Firth & Pajak 1998, pp. 12–13). Models for professional development are based on different assumptions regarding teachers' learning, the aims of teachers' development, and the settings in which these processes take place (Feiman-Nemser & Rosaen, 1997; Silberstein, 1998). Teachers' professional development occurs in the context of staff development or in the processes of socialization of new teachers, as part of school improvement or standardization efforts, or in the course of curriculum development (Adey & Hewitt, 2004; Harris, 1998).

A key component of every professional development process is understanding teachers' professional knowledge: What is it that teachers need to know that will improve their professionalism? What kind of knowledge is it and how it is developed? The answers to these questions affect both the aims and the means of professional development processes (Cochran-Smith & Lytle, 1999; Cochran-Smith, 2001; Pajak, 1993). According to approaches that see professional knowledge as an autonomous body of information, mentors should be experts whose role is to introduce and transfer knowledge to teachers, while teachers are those who are expected to acquire and implement the knowledge, what Cochran-Smith & Lytle (1999) call "knowledge *for* practice." From another perspective, the professional knowledge of teachers grows with their ability to reflect on their experience and to create generalizations regarding their goals and patterns of teaching; this is what Cochran-Smith & Lytle (1999) call "knowledge *in* practice" thereby emphasizing reflection in action as a main component of professional development (Schon, 1988; Shkedi, 1996). This concept promotes a more dialogic professional relationship between teachers and their mentors. According to a third concept, "knowledge *of* practice," teachers are experts and their knowledge is created by collaborative learning and critical discussion of their practice (Cochran-Smith & Lytle, 1999; Giroux, 1988). Examining various programs of professional development in Jewish education can reveal assumptions regarding "professional knowledge" in this field. I would like to promote the question of what is that knowledge and how it can be developed by those who are in charge of this task.

The Teachers' Professional Developer: Changes in Terminology and Goals

Teachers' professional developers are often school principals or experienced teachers who serve as role models within their schools or who are called in by outside authorities to guide novice teachers and to promote professional development within schools. The outside authorities might be administrators in teacher training programs, municipal education authorities, or curriculum publishers. Teachers' professional developers are known by one of the following terms: supervisors, mentors, cognitive coaches, trainers, or facilitators. Distinctions between these terms are often related to different understandings of the tasks involved, the status of the participants, and the nature of their relationships.

Table 1 Common descriptions of teachers' mentors, coaches, and supervisors roles[3]

	Mentoring	Coaching	Supervising
The mentee	Beginning teachers	Not restricted	Not restricted
The professional approach	A holistic approach concentrated on helping the novice teachers to "survive" and become competent teachers	A practical approach: the coach trains the teacher and practises with him/her relevant professional skills	An evaluative approach, sometimes based on hierarchy of roles
Characteristics of the trainer	An experienced, appreciated teacher within the school or the teacher training institute	A professional trainer, sometimes trained as a coach	A superintendent or a school principal with an official role

The term "mentor" is invariably used for experienced teachers who work with novice teachers (Godsoe, Ament, & Heilpern, 2007). Yet, the definition of "novice" is flexible, and mentoring programs can be directed at heterogenous groups of teachers in schools, regardless of their professional experience (Portner, 2005, p. 9; Goldsbery in Pajak & Firth 1998, pp. 428–462). Mentors and coaches are described as having different roles: "the work of the mentor is more concerned with the holistic needs of the beginning teacher, including social-emotional needs and personal concerns, while coaches are more concerned with technical proficiency" (Portner, 2005, p. 113). "A critical difference between the role of mentor and the role of supervisor is that a mentor can not be an evaluator" (Portner, 2005, p. 7). However, many times these roles are mixed.

"Supervision for instruction" is rooted in hierarchical relationships (Goldhammer, 1969) but has been transformed in recent years into professional development. This change is reflected in the emergence of the term "clinical supervision." Clinical supervision is a process of teacher professional development

---

[3]Based on integration from various sources, for example (Oliva & Pawlas 1984, p. 5; Costa & Garmston [Hebrew edition] pp. 2–4; Zachary, 2000, pp. 2–6; Rubinshtain 1999 pp. 19–21).

that focuses on a cycle of observing the teacher's work, analyzing it, forward planning, re-observing, etc. (Glickman, 1990; Goldhammer, 1969; Oliva & Pawlas, 1984). Teachers' mentors and cognitive coaches are supposed to observe teachers' practices and discuss them with them (Feiman-Nemser & Rosaen, 1997; Costa and Garmstone, 1999).

Even though different bodies of literature are concerned with teachers' coaching, mentoring, and supervision, the term "mentor" is invariably used as a general name for the professional developer role (Zachary, 2006). Over the years, the objectives of the mentoring relationship have evolved from the mentees learning to an approach rooted in adult learning. "This learner-centered shift . . . requires that a mentor facilitate the learning relationship rather than transfer knowledge to the learner" (Zachary, 2006, p. xv).

In this chapter I use the term "mentoring" to denote professionals who are responsible for teacher learning and professional growth. These mentors are experienced teachers who are appointed to work with teachers in order to increase their capacities and educational achievements in the area of Jewish studies teaching. I prefer the term "mentoring" because of its personal connotation (Davis, 2001, p. 3). Even though teacher–mentor relationships may not be voluntary, they are always personal.

Teachers' Mentoring: Goals and Means

Since mentoring processes entail a meeting between two parties, a teacher and a mentor, hierarchy and the roles of the participants have gained considerable attention. Glickman (1990) presented a "developmental model" of clinical supervision that includes four approaches that differ in the degree of responsibility and the control of the teacher and mentor (or what Glickman calls the "teacher-supervisor") over the mentoring process. This model is applicable to the various possible settings of teacher–mentor relationships and to the evaluation of teachers' needs and the mentors' capabilities. The four approaches to "clinical supervision" according to Glickman (1990) are:

Directive-control behavior: The supervisors are dominant; they set the agenda of the conferences, direct the teachers, and define the parameters of success.

Directive-informational behavior: The supervisors act as the teachers' teachers; they introduce alternatives to the teachers and provide them with useful knowledge.

Collaborative behavior: The supervisory conference is a dialogue that includes the supervisors' and teachers' different roles and experience. The supervisors encourage the teachers to share responsibilities for and control of the process.

Nondirective behaviour: This model focuses on the teachers, their professional world, capabilities, and choices. The teachers lead the conference and set the agenda, and they are responsible for suggesting interpretations, designing solutions, and implementing them. The supervisors' role is to encourage the teachers in these processes.

Although a collaborative and nondirective approach is presented as one of several optional approaches, in a broader developmental context it also represents a shift from a traditional-authoritarian model of mentoring to more democratic models that are based on partnership. This move is somewhat similar to concepts of adult learning, representing a shift from product-oriented to process-oriented mentoring (Zachary, 2000, pp. 3–4).

Many researchers emphasize reflectivity as the main aim of professional conversations among professional developers and teachers (Blasé, 2003; Costa & Garmston, 1999; Zeichner & Liston, 1985; Silberstein, 1998). Pajack (2000) argues that teaching and learning can be understood only in the students' and schools' social, historical, political, and cultural contexts. Mentors, coaches, and supervisors are urged to empower teachers through helping them to deepen their interpretive skills, and increase their awareness of cultural influences on the learners, on curricula, and on the teaching environment (Bowers & Flinders, 1991; Costa & Garmston, 1999). Teachers are encouraged to revisit their own beliefs and become critical and reflective about their assumptions and their taken-for-granted practical choices. This approach assumes that teachers have the ability to improve not only their own teaching but also the entire curriculum and the surrounding educational culture (Cochran-Smith & Lytle, 1999; Glickman, 1990; Zachary, 2006). This emphasis on partnering between mentor and teacher, aimed in turn at generating more reflective abilities, points to a conception of professional knowledge that is a unique amalgam of personal, contextual, and intellectual components.

How should this understanding affect teacher mentoring in a cultural or religion-based curriculum, such as Jewish studies?

Teachers' Ideologies Are Embedded in Any Educational Process

The pedagogical content knowledge of teachers is described as a combination of content knowledge and pedagogical knowledge that develops in relation to the theory learned and experience gained by every teacher. Pedagogical content knowledge is influenced by personal values and beliefs (Schon, 1983; Van-Manen, 1991), including the teacher's perceptions of what is desirable (Nisan, 2009; Shkedi & Horeczyk, 1995). In other words, teachers' pedagogical content knowledge is influenced by their personal ideologies.

Ideologies are intimately related to actions (Althuser, 2006; Lamm, 2002). Thus, teachers' stances regarding education, culture, and society, as they experience it, must be influenced by their beliefs. Teachers' ideals, values, and perceptions regarding the desirable lead their practice (Hansen, 1995). Every curriculum is based on an ideological orientation toward the subject matter and the culture, as well as toward other aspects of the teaching and learning process (Apple, 1990; Schremer, 1999). Interpretation of culturally based texts is affected by the teacher's personal orientation toward the text (Holtz, 2003).

Decisions that are made by teachers in the process of implementing curricula reflect their personal perspectives: they have to "translate" subject matter to "subject matter for teaching" and these processes are linked to personal beliefs regarding the nature of the subject matter and its relevance to the students' lives (Shkedi & Nisan, 2006; Alpert, 2002).

Teachers' Ideologies

Lamm (2002) distinguishes between three main educational ideologies: *socialization*, *acculturation*, and *individuation*. These ideologies differ in their views of what education is, who the ideal graduate is, and in their description of the role of teachers and teaching. "Socialization" strives to train the students for their roles as functional adults in society, and the role of the teacher is to be their trainer for that purpose. According to an ideology of "acculturation," the ideal graduates are scholar-adults who feel comfortable with their culture. Teaching is aimed at instilling knowledge and an appreciation of heritage, and the teachers are the students' role models. The ideology of "individuation" focuses on supporting the unique growth of each student into an autonomous adult. The main teaching task therefore is to release the students from *a-priori* commitments to the authority of the subject matter and to help them find their own "voice" (Lamm, 2002).

Researchers have characterized teachers' educational ideologies as a complex and often contradictory system of loyalties: loyalty to the students, to the content, and, at the same time, to the teacher's own personal ideals (Muszkat-Barkan & Shkedi, 2009; Shkedi & Horeczyk, 1995).

Ideologies in Jewish Education

Jewish education inherently interprets Jewish identity, values, and commitments (Goren D., 1994; Ben-Peretz, 2005), and expresses the explicit and/or implicit ideologies of participants (Ben-Basat, 1997). Educational ideologies include the educators' perspectives on the role of the subject matter (Lamm, 1988, 2002). In Jewish studies, ideologies are manifested in the educators' approaches to teaching Jewish sources, as well as in their prioritizing of contents as "subject matter for teaching" (Holtz, 2003; Shkedi & Nisan, 2006). Teachers are the main players at this scene (Goren D., 1994; Luz, 1994), sometimes without being aware of their important role or even without being invited to bring their personal and professional input.

I have previously classified (Muszkat-Barkan, 2005) Jewish-cultural ideologies according to their degree of identification or criticism toward Jewish culture. These approaches represent a continuum, rather than separated entities:

Identification: The students ought to acquire the core body of authentic Jewish constructs, identify with them, and be committed to them (e.g., Rosenak, 1995; 2003; Ahad Ha'am, 1913; Twersky, 2003).

Critique: Learning Jewish culture should occur without a priori commitment to its authority or expectations regarding its relevance to the learners' life. This approach calls for critical reading, and awareness of the modern perspective of the learners (e.g., Zakovitch, 1995; 2003; Brinker, 2003).

Critique-identification combination: This is a combination between identifying with one's culture and a critical perspective vis-à-vis any cultural paradigm (e.g., Luz, 1994; Simon, 1986; Schweid, 2000).

Teachers' Mentoring and Ideologies in Jewish Education

Teachers' mentoring is a unique personal encounter within the professional educational system. How, then, can one understand the role of the mentor and the effect of ideologies on the underlying assumptions of both mentors and teachers? Such ideologies may remain implicit during mentoring meetings (Cochran-Smith, 2001; Grundy & Hatton, 1995). For example, in a report on mentors' knowledge after working with teachers in Jewish day schools, there is no reference to the Jewish context of the teachers' task (Godsoe et al., 2007). The only reference to this context is to the importance of introducing novice teachers to the school philosophy. Is it because novice teachers are occupied with more basic questions? Or is it because mentors and teachers are educated to leave behind any personal ideology as if it is not relevant to their professional discussion?

Research regarding the role of teachers' and mentors' ideologies in teachers' mentoring is limited. Particularly, there is a limited account of the unique challenges faced by mentors and teachers in Jewish education. In the following case study, I discuss the ways in which teachers and teachers' mentors deal with their personal ideologies in teachers' mentoring. Based on the case presented I then describe what I understand as the unique challenges and directions for mentoring teachers in Jewish education.

Methods

The data presented herein were generated in the course of a broader study on the role of ideologies in teachers' mentoring.[4] This study was conducted according to the principles of constructivist-qualitative research (Stake, 2000). The general questions of the study were the following: What roles do the different ideologies of mentors and teachers play in the mentoring of Jewish studies teachers? What are these ideologies, how they are manifested in the mentoring process, and how do they affect it? The sub-questions were ultimately defined only after the final analysis of the data and the construction of a "grounded theory" (Strauss & Corbin, 1990). The research aim was to describe and understand the subjects of the research through their own language and interpretations of their unique experiences (Lincoln & Guba, 1985; Tzabar-Ben Yehoshua, 1997).

---

[4] Previously (Muszkat-Barkan, 2005), I used the term supervision to translate the Hebrew terms "hanchaya" or "hadracha." In this chapter I use the term mentoring for the reasons explained below.

The research focused on 14 participants; teachers and mentors, within the framework of four case studies. Each case included one mentor and the teachers that he or she mentored. Three of the four mentors served as official supervisors in Israeli public high schools that prepare students for the matriculation exams, in Jewish Studies. Two of the mentors were mentors in Bible Studies, one a mentor in Jewish Philosophy, and one a mentor in TALI[5] elementary schools. All of the mentors were known as experienced and successful teachers. The 10 participant teachers were all mentees of one of the four mentors.

In this chapter I present one of the four cases broadly and use what I have learned from the other cases to generate findings and discussion.

Case Study: Mentor Rachel

Rachel is in her 50 s. She has been working in the TALI system for 25 years as a general and Judaic teacher and this is her fifth year as a TALI mentor. Rachel describes herself as an "open orthodox-observant Jew." Rachel sees her main role as a mentor in enabling teachers to create connections to Jewish content so that they will be able to teach the Judaic resources in ways that are close to their world. At the same time she feels responsible that content chosen by the teachers will be "authentic" to the Jewish world. Rachel tells about her work with a particular teacher in one TALI elementary school:

> The teacher had prepared the "Bulletin Board for the Month of Cheshvan" following our meeting, and I felt that as much as we tried to bring Judaism to the teacher it was not picked up, so I told the teacher: "Let's make the board look more Jewish."
> ...Then suddenly we were painting big clouds that had written on them, *"mashiv haruach u'morid hagashem"* ["who causes the wind to blow and the rain to fall"]. Now, when someone looks at the board, this is the sentence that jumps off the wall after the word "Cheshvan." So we cut out the display [together], I really took her by the hand.

Rachel believes that the teacher is the one who needs to choose the materials for teaching. Yet, she is critical and feels that these materials are not "Jewish enough." Rachel is fluctuating between encouraging the teacher's autonomy in creating the bulletin board and "taking her hand by hand" in order to create a "more Jewish" bulletin board.

Who is responsible for curricular decisions: the teacher or the mentor? What kind of professional dialogue can be expected when the mentor feels responsible for the professional growth of the teacher and at the same time for the Jewish agenda of the school?

Rachel feels that she is responsible for bringing Jewish content knowledge to the teachers. Her goal is to enhance the Jewish content in the schools. As she puts it,

---

[5]TALI is a nationwide network of over 120 Israeli public schools that are committed to providing pluralistic Jewish education. http://www.tali.org.il/

> For several years now I have been talking about it – where to bring in prayer, because in school they don't have prayers, they don't learn about prayers. In the fifth grade they have a little introduction to the *Siddur* [prayer book], and that's all. So this year I suggested that we bring in a 2-day prayer curriculum for all grades.

For Rachel, the prayers and the language of the *Siddur* are central components of Jewish culture and experience. Thus, she argues with the school's avoidance of prayer and with the short introduction to the *Siddur*.

Rachel tends to see her primary mentoring aim as encouraging teachers to teach content that is central to the Jewish world, according to her beliefs. But what happens when the teachers have different perceptions of the core of Jewish culture? We can see such a conflict in the following report from Sharon, a veteran Judaic studies teacher, who works with Rachel:

> Sharon: So the mentor,... She really wanted us to incorporate prayers in the school in first and second grades. I was toning her down on certain things, I told her it won't fly here. ... It was very important to her that the children learn about *Zom Gdaliah, Taa'nit Esther* [Jewish fast-days]. She would fax stuff to me [...but I think that] it doesn't do anything for the children. I can make a connection between *Zom Gdaliah* and [the assassination of Prime Minister], Rabin, but I don't want to do it just as she wanted ...so it was very difficult, really very difficult for her.

While the mentor sees learning about the festivals, and experiencing and learning the prayers as her professional contribution, the teacher sees it in a very different way. The teacher interprets such input as foreign to the school and as dictating a Jewish message that is not oriented to the school's population. Rachel had tried to introduce some ideas regarding how to promote prayers in the school but got negative reactions from the teachers.

> Rachel: The teacher's reaction to my ideas was "Not now. " So I felt hurt, and here I have to differentiate my personal feelings from what is going on: I felt that Judaism is being hurt, I am being hurt. [...] because I am... my aim at school is to lead it [Judaism] forward and not backward.

The mentoring orientation of Rachel reflects her identification with Jewish culture and a desire to acculturate the teachers within the Jewish world, directing the process within the boundaries of what she perceives as legitimate to Judaism. Her personal Judaic approach affects her professional framework, her perception of what is the "language" of Judaism (Rosenak, 2003), and thus the sense of what needs to be introduced to the students is directly related to her own perception of Judaism. The ideology of the mentor is reflected here in the construction of the subject matter of Jewish studies through a decision about what is at the core of Judaic studies and what is not.

While Rachel directs the teachers to focus on what she sees as the core Jewish constructs, she also seeks to engage them in the process of personal knowledge development. She wants them to find their own identification with central components of Jewish culture. Rachel avoids confrontations over ideological differences, and strives to create alternatives that will enable the teachers to find Jewish components with which they can identify, without having to expose and directly discuss their own beliefs. The consequence of this approach is that sometimes the teachers accept Rachel's suggestions and interpretations on Jewish curricula resources, and incorporate them into their teaching. On other occasions, when the mentor's suggestions do not fit their orientations they might ignore those suggestions. As one of the teachers says,

> "I listen to her ideas. If I like them, I take them and if not – in the class I am on my own..."

Yet, this is not the only pattern of ideological interaction between the mentor Rachel and the teachers she works with. A different behavior is described by Rachel regarding her work with veteran teacher Dina, when Dina became a teacher of a TALI class within the school.

Rachel tells that at the beginning Dina was angry about becoming a TALI teacher, because she saw the TALI principles as religious and felt that they contradicted her own beliefs:

> Rachel: I had to show Dina that Judaism is more than black and white. I looked for materials and interpretations that would allow her to find her own voice. I wanted her to see the plurality of Judaism.

Dina trusted Rachel. She accepted her professionalism and did not hesitate to ask her provocative questions but at the same time accepted her guidance. Both of them felt that their professional connection was a fruitful one.

Rachel sees herself as the teacher of the teachers she works with. She believes that her role is to enrich their Jewish content knowledge so that they will feel competent and be motivated to teach more Jewish content in their classrooms. She wants the teachers to be more knowledgeable and she is certain that the Jewish tradition is so wide as to enable every teacher to find within it her/his own orientations and those of their students.

There is a difference between the two professional encounters involving the same mentor, but with two different teachers. Both teachers were secular and had different ideological approaches toward Judaism from that of the mentor. In the first encounter there was no explicit dialogue regarding the reasons for the teacher's resistance to the Jewish pedagogical choices of the mentor and regarding the differences between their perceptions of Judaism. In the second encounter the differences provided the starting point for the mentoring relationship. Here, both the teacher and the mentor described an experience of mutual listening and openness. The teacher was active in expressing herself and the mentor made an effort to bring Judaic content that suited the teacher's world. Neither Dina nor Rachel could have anticipated the educational outcomes of their meetings. They both noticed that the outcome of the process was different from what they had planned in advance and that it evolved through the course of their dialogue. In contrast, the encounter with Sharon was frustrating for both the teacher and the mentor, since both of them avoided discussions regarding the ideological differences between them. As such, the professional discussion was about what should be taught while ignoring the question of why and what for, as if attitudes and beliefs were irrelevant. At the end, the mentor felt that the school was taking a step backwards in teaching Judaic studies and the teacher felt that the mentor did not understand the school's orientation.

A Framework for Discussing Mentors' Ideologies: A Proposal

This representative case study and others as well show that either an explicit or an implicit ideological discourse between teachers and mentors can have a profound impact on the mentoring process. Mentors' ideologies affected the selection of subject matter for teaching, in its preparation and interpretation, as well as the way in which the mentors dealt with teachers' own ideologies.

In order to analyze the effect of mentoring ideologies on the mentoring process, I describe the characteristics of mentors' ideologies and propose a framework for the discussion of the inter-relationship between the components of mentors' ideologies. I suggest that the individual mentoring ideology (defined below as a "mentoring orientation in Jewish studies") can be characterized according to two main components: a Jewish-cultural component, and an educational component. The individual combination of the Jewish cultural and the educational components determine the mentoring orientation in Jewish studies and the ways by which mentors' orientations are expressed in the mentoring process.

1. *Jewish-cultural component*: This component includes the mentor's attitude toward Jewish content and Jewish texts, how they are understood, and how they should be studied (Holtz, 2003, pp. 73–102). In an earlier work, I classified Jewish-cultural ideologies according to their degree of identification or criticism toward Jewish culture (Muszkat-Barkan, 2005). These approaches represent a continuum rather than separate entities. They include *Identification, Critique, and a Critique-identification combination* (as described above). For example, in the case presented here, the mentor expressed "identification" toward the Jewish content. She wanted the teachers and students to acquire the core body of what she perceived as authentic Jewish constructs.
2. *Educational component*: Above, I used Lamm's (2002) classification of educational ideology: *acculturation, socialization,* and *individuation* to describe the educational attitudes of the mentors. There is a close interaction between and alignment of educational ideologies and teachers' professional development and mentoring approaches.

    To analyze mentoring approaches I use Glickman's classification of supervisory behaviors (1990). This classification includes varying degrees of responsibility and control as exercised by both the mentor and the teacher in relation to the mentoring process. In *directive-control* and *directive-informational* behaviors the mentor leads the professional encounter with teachers. The mentors set the agenda and provide the teachers with "useful knowledge." Both behaviors reflect a professional development perception of "knowledge *for* practice" (Cochran-Smith & Lytle, 1999) that sees professional knowledge as an autonomous body of information. In this approach, the mentor is an expert whose role is to introduce and transfer the knowledge to the teachers, while the teachers are those who are expected to acquire and implement the knowledge. The *collaborative* mentoring approach is conceived as a dialogue, despite the mentors' and teachers' differing roles. This behavior leads to generation of "knowledge *in* practice" (Cochran-Smith & Lytle, 1999) where the professional knowledge of teachers grows with their ability to reflect on their experience.

The mentor's role in a *nondirective* approach is to encourage teachers to set the agenda for the mentoring process, suggest interpretations, design solutions, and implement them. This may lead to creating "knowledge *of* practice" (Cochran-Smith & Lytle, 1999) where teachers' knowledge is generated by collaborative learning and critical discussion of their practice. Interestingly, in my research I did not observe "nondirective" supervisory behavior among the mentors studied. While the reasons for this finding are yet to be explored, this may be related to the central role of ideologies in mentoring Jewish studies teachers that makes it hard for the mentors to stay neutral and act in a nondirective fashion.

Based on this framework, I propose the following three mentoring orientations in Jewish studies that use three Jewish concepts to describe various relationships between mentor and mentee: (i) a collaborative-provoking mentoring orientation, termed "*Hevruta*" (ii) a directive mentoring orientation, named "*Rav-U-Moreh*," and (iii) a control-functional mentoring orientation (a mentoring focused on achieving implementation), named "*Posek*." Usually a single mentoring orientation is used by each mentor but sometimes mentors use different orientations in relation to different teachers and curricula.

In the case presented here, the mentor saw the aim of Jewish education in terms of acculturation. She wanted the teachers to be able to bring the core of the Jewish culture to their students in order to "upgrade" the Jewish culture of the school. She believed that content knowledge is crucial to the Jewish background of the teachers. Thus, the acculturation educational ideology was related to a directive-informational behavior: the mentor looked for ways to enrich the teachers' Jewish content knowledge so that they would bring it to their students. When the mentor was open to ideological discussion her approach became more collaborative and the meeting took an exploratory course. The combination of these components defines the *Rav-U-Moreh* mentoring orientation (as shown in Table 2).

Jewish Studies Mentoring Orientations

"*Hevruta*" Collaboration Learning

This orientation combines a critical attitude toward the Jewish sources without a-priori commitment to their authority (Zakovitch, 2004, Brinker, 2003) with an educational ideology that sees the role of the teacher as responsible for increasing the autonomy of the individual student ("*individuation*" (Lamm, 2002)). According to this orientation, the subject matter is a tool for enhancing the learner's capacity, and not an end in itself. The role of the teacher is to help the student to find his or her own voice free of any authority. This ideology encourages a critical educational dialogue toward common sacred assumptions regarding Jewish content (see, e.g., Lamm, 2002, pp. 316–318).

Table 2 Mentoring orientations in Jewish studies and their components

Jewish-cultural component[a]	Educational components		Mentoring orientation in Jewish education
	Educational Ideologies[b]	Supervisory Behaviors[c, d]	
Identification	Acculturation	Directive-informative	*Rav-U-Moreh*[e]
Critique	Individuation	Collaborative	*Hevruta*
Critique or identification	Socialization	Directive-control	*Posek*

[a]Muszkat-Barkan (2005)
[b]Lamm (2002)
[c]Glickman (1990)
[d]As stated above, the "non-directive" behavior was not observed in the current study. For possible explanations, see p. 890 above.
[e]The mentoring orientation of *Rav-U-Moreh* is characterized by the combination of directive-informative behavior and an educational ideology of *acculturation*. It may be combined with the *identification* Jewish cultural ideology or with the *critique-identification* ideology, both Jewish cultural ideologies that the mentor might feel he/she needs to instill in the teachers and their students.

According to this orientation, teachers' professional development is rooted in "knowledge *in* practice" (Cochran Smith & Lytle, 1999). In the context of mentoring in Jewish education this implies that Jewish content is developed within the particular context of a Jewish cultural orientation, and within a school community that includes students and parents, as well as teachers. This orientation is characterized by collaboration between mentor and teacher that is aimed at knowledge development (Zachary, 2000). The mentor sees herself as a "Hevruta," a partner for the process of joint learning. The term "*Hevruta*" traditionally means two people who study Jewish text together.[6] Here I use this term to describe the collaboration and partnership between the mentor and the teacher in the reflective exploration of the teacher's practice. During this process the mentor not only guides the teacher but also reveals her own pedagogical content knowledge.

Reconstructing the subject matter for teaching often requires the mentor to ask provocative questions during mentoring meetings regarding the teacher's assumptions and beliefs, in order to enhance awareness of tacit perceptions. The mentor perceives the stimulation of such discussions as a part of her role as mentor.

The role of the mentor according to this orientation is to guide deconstruction and reconstruction processes, so that teachers become more critical of their own beliefs and practices as well as regarding myths that are embedded in the curriculum. The mentor should be aware of her own assumptions, and be ready to expose them.

---

[6]See a description of "*Hevruta*" in teachers' professional training settings in Eli Holtzer (2002) and in the chapter of that name above. I use this term as a description of collegiality partnership between a mentor and a teacher in the reflective exploration of the teachers' practice.

"*Rav-U-Moreh*": The Directive Mentoring Orientation

This mentoring orientation is based on the Jewish cultural approach of *identification* and commitment to the authority of Jewish culture and tradition (Rosenak, 1995; 2004; Ahad Ha'am, 1913; Twersky, 2003). This mentoring orientation sometimes includes a combination of critical orientation with identification (*Critique-identification*), inculcating a desire to identify with one's culture while encouraging a critical perspective vis-à-vis any cultural paradigm.

The educational ideology related to the *Rav-U-Moreh* orientation is acculturation, but can be also socialization (Lamm, 2002). The mentors see their primary responsibility as increasing the teachers' "knowledge," capabilities, and motivation to bring Jewish content to the classroom. The main assumption according to this orientation is that obstacles to identifying with Jewish culture are related to the lack of knowledge or personal connection of students and teachers to Jewish culture. Thus, it is hoped that the professional engagement of teachers with Jewish culture will model a similar engagement for their students. The role of mentors is to expose teachers to the richness of Jewish culture so that they will be convinced that it can be valuable to their students.

This professional development orientation can be defined as "knowledge *for* practice" (Cochran-Smith & Lytle, 1999). The role of the mentor is to present to the teacher a body of "pre-made" knowledge freighted with the mentor's interpretations, and to direct the teacher toward what is perceived as the best way of introducing this knowledge to students.

In these terms, mentors see themselves primarily as the teachers of teachers. The Jewish term of *Rav-U-Moreh* emphasizes the responsibility of the mentors for increasing the knowledge of their students as well as the hierarchy between them. The "*Rav-U-Moreh*" is supposed to "keep the Torah"[7] and pass it on to his students. Mentors holding this orientation may feel that they have to protect the Jewish content from being misunderstood. They feel responsible for ensuring that the teachers represent Jewish content to their students in proper ways. Therefore, in mentoring meetings they actively direct the teachers to select materials for teaching, and interpret them, encouraging *identification*.

Mentors that hold this orientation may attribute ideological differences between them and the teachers to the teachers' lack of understanding of the true meaning of the Jewish cultural sources. They try to avoid confrontation with the teachers, but when resistance becomes explicit they will try to explain and to "teach" the teachers, seeking to encourage greater empathy with the Jewish sources. One of the important goals of mentoring according to this orientation is to lead teachers to find ways of interpretation with which they can identify and feel comfortable. Open discussions with teachers may occur when the mentor is sure that the teachers' resistance doesn't come from devaluing Jewish sources.

---

[7] Lamentations/Eichah Rabbah, Petichtah 2, ed. Buber 1b: "Who are the guardians of the city? They are the teachers of the written Torah and the oral Torah/tradition that contemplate, review, and preserve the Torah day and night." See also Aberbach (1982).

Directing teachers to find their own personal meaning in the Jewish sources can be perceived as a declared goal of professional development or as a means to increase the teachers' motivations. Personal discussions might be perceived as an integral part of the mentoring meetings or as a (welcomed) deviation from the agenda.[8] Perhaps not surprisingly, in this research, mentors who hold the "*Rav-U-Moreh*" orientation were orthodox Jews who work with secular teachers, and expressed identification with Jewish sources.

"*Posek*" Functional Mentoring Orientation

This mentoring orientation is outcome driven. The mentor sees her role as directing the teachers to improve the performance of their students, regardless of the students' or the teachers' personal approaches toward Judaism or education. The term "*Posek*" is related to the traditional role of rabbis in determining the normative behaviors of Jewish individuals and communities.[9] This orientation is predicated on the educational ideology of socialization (Lamm, 2002). According to this concept, the teachers' goal is to train students to become active members of society. In terms of Jewish education this can be translated into instilling habits (*Hergel*, in the words of Twersky, 2003, pp. 82–83) that assure the continuity of the community. Professional development is perceived as "knowledge *for* practice" (Cochran-Smith & Lytle, 1999), i.e., providing the teachers with what is required in order to achieve the goals of society. The mentor (as a "*Posek*") has the authority and the relevant knowledge for this task. The mentor directs and controls the selection and interpretation of Jewish contents in a way that is expected to fit the desirable students' outcomes (Glickman, 1990).

The socialization approach in this mentoring orientation is expressed as a commitment toward an external authority, such as students' achievements in standardized testing such as matriculation exams. The mentor might expect that the teachers' Jewish orientation will be identical with the Jewish orientation of the official curriculum of the state system. Mentors might see ideological differences as an obstacle, especially for orthodox teachers who teach in the secular public system. According to this perception those teachers must put aside their personal beliefs but at the same time mentors may doubt if it is possible. This is reflected in mentors' comments arguing that orthodox teachers working in the secular system can not identify with the contents and messages of the system's curriculum; they cannot leave behind their personal orientations and therefore are unable to teach it in the way that is required by the system. Accordingly, the mentors hardly ever discuss

---

[8] In previous research (Muszkat-Barkan, 2005) I divided the orientation of *Rav-U-Moreh* into different titles because of two distinct emphasis among mentors in relation to the personal component in the professional development processes. Looking at the data again, I see many commonalities in the various components of their mentoring orientation in Jewish education and merge them into one title.

[9] A relevant discussion on the influence of the personal ideologies of the rabbi on his way of making normative decisions, "Psikot," is discussed in A. Rosenak (2009). See especially pp. 2–3, 138–139.

their own Jewish orientation. They feel that as mentors they need to represent the school system's attitudes and socialize the teachers to do so too. In this way, the mentors dictate the "right" attitudes needed for teaching and expect that the teachers will "do their duty" accordingly.

Mentors with this mentoring orientation can thus be defined as *"Posekim"* because they direct the teachers to observe external standards of the educational system (that can be described as *Halacha* [a legal/normative requirement]), rather than be affected by individual approaches.

Conclusions and Further Directions

The Presence of Ideology in Professional Mentoring Discussions

The study reported here shows that the personal ideologies of teachers and mentors are an influential presence within the processes of teacher mentoring in Jewish studies. By integrating conceptions of Jewish-cultural and educational approaches, it has been possible to define three mentoring orientations in Jewish studies. The mentoring orientations of *"Hevruta," "Rav-U-Moreh,"* and *"Posek"* reflect presumptions regarding teachers' knowledge, teachers' professional growth, and the mentors' role in Jewish education.

The Association between the Jewish-cultural and the Educational Components

A general correlation could be observed between the Jewish-cultural and educational components: the Jewish-cultural approach of critique was associated with the educational approach of individuation, and with a tendency toward a more collaborative mentoring approach. The Jewish term *"Hevruta"* denotes the perception of professional development as a collaborative inquiry of partners.

The Jewish-cultural approach of identification was associated with the educational approach of acculturation, and was reflected in a tendency toward a more directive mentoring approach. This association can be explained by a traditional perception of the teacher as a role model who represents and translates the Jewish resources for students. In the mentoring context, the term *"Rav-U-Moreh"* represents a traditional educational ideology that sees the aim of education as acculturating the students to the dominant culture. It assumes that the role of the teacher as well as of the mentor is as a mediator and sometimes protector of that culture.[10] In a Jewish educational context this leads to hierarchical relationships.

The functional mentoring orientation – *"Posek"* – relates to a normative – behavioristic attitude. Both can be correlated with the approaches of critique or identification as much as those are the expected standards for Jewish education in

---

[10] Idealization of teachers as knowledgeable and well respected was a rabbinic trope, and it didn't always reflect the reality of the relationships between a teacher and the community. See Gafni (1999).

a specific setting. Thus, if the critical approach toward the Jewish sources is an external requirement it will not reflect an educational ideology of individuation, and won't lead to a more democratic mentoring. The primary commitment of the *Posek* is that teachers will meet the system's standards and be socialized with them.

Mentors' Commitments and Teachers' Ideologies

While the teachers in my study expressed their primary commitment to their students, the mentors expressed the ideologies of the systems they represent. This is reflected in the commitment of the mentors to the formal curriculum which they invariably defend (Muszkat-Barkan & Shkedi, 2009).

The mentors studied were aware of the influence of the teachers' ideologies on their pedagogical content knowledge and practice, and sometimes saw these ideologies as a potential obstacle for teaching Jewish studies. However, at the same time, the mentors did not acknowledge the influence of their own ideologies on their mentoring orientation and practice. For the most part, the mentors avoided direct discussions of their own and of the teachers' personal approaches regarding the Jewish content, possibly because they perceived such a discussion as a threat to the mentoring process.

Different mentoring orientations can be used by the same mentor, as exemplified in the case study presented above. Rachel moved from a more directive to a more collaborative approach, a move from the *Rav-U-Moreh* approach, to a partnering or *Hevruta* orientation. The readiness of both the mentor and the teacher to discuss openly the ideological tensions led to the change expressed in the mentoring process.

My data showed that the professional knowledge of both teachers and mentors developed during the mentoring meetings. The mentoring process provides opportunities for teachers and mentors to reexamine their own perceptions, especially when they are willing to deal with their ideological orientations.

In light of the observed reluctance of both teachers and mentors to discuss their own ideological orientations during the mentoring meetings, increasing their awareness to the effects of such discussions may be of critical importance. Such open discussions of the ideological contradictions can create an ideological "map" (Geertz, 1990) for the participants and enable them to deal with different opinions and reconsider their own views, during "deep talk" with teachers, colleagues, and among themselves (Himley & Carini, 1991). The findings of this study therefore support the call for mentors to become more aware of teachers' personal attitudes (Bowers & Flinders, 1991). The teachers in the current study echoed these calls, arguing that their mentors did not pay enough attention to, nor respected, their ideological orientations.

Will Ideological Discussion Lead to Ideological Indoctrination?

Some authors have argued that when Jewish cultural ideologies are allowed into an educational system they can be used as a tool for indoctrination or "thought control" (Apple, 1990; Schremer, 1999; Lamm, 1988). While such concern is understandable, my study shows that in Jewish education, both Judaic-cultural and educational ideologies inevitably act as motivating forces for both mentors and teachers, as others have suggested in different contexts (Hansen, 1995; Nisan, 2009; Palmer, 1998). My study suggests that an open and reflective ideological intercourse can actually protect against such ideological indoctrination. It can create opportunities for both teachers and mentors to reexamine their own ideologies, in a professional-personal setting, and can therefore serve as an opportunity for professional development.

Recommendations for Further Research

1. *Mentors' professional knowledge*: Further research on the mentors' professional knowledge is needed. Such research may elucidate ways to help mentors become more reflective about their practice and about teachers' needs. Defining mentors' knowledge may help mentors develop awareness and flexibility regarding their own role perception.
2. *When should we invite ideological discussions into the mentoring process?* Further research is required to define when discussions between teachers and mentors regarding their respective cultural and educational ideologies can promote teachers' professional development. Elucidating the various levels of reflection that could be achieved in such discussions may help mentors and teachers define the influence of these on the professional growth of teachers.
3. *Teacher training*: The professionals' ability to discuss Judaic approaches may influence mentoring meetings as well as the teachers' practice. Exploring such practices might affect the training of Jewish Studies teachers. Future research may explore in what ways ideological sensitivity can influence teachers' in-service training.

References

Aberbach, M. (1982). *Jewish education in the time of the Mishna and the Talmud [Hebrew]*, (pp. 94–109). Jerusalem: Reuben Mass Ltd.

Adey, P. & Hewitt, G. (2004). *The professional development of teachers: Practice and theory.* Dordrecht: Kluwer Academic.

Alpert, B. (2002). Concepts and ideas in the study of curricula as key texts. In A. Hoffman & Y. Shenall (Eds.), *Values and goals in Israeli curricula [Hebrew]*. Kfar Saba and Kadima: Beit Berl College, Rekhes Publishing House.

Althuser, L. (2006). *On the ideology [Hebrew]*, (translated from French by A. Azulai). Tel-Aviv: Resling Publishers.

Apple, M. (1990). *Ideology and curriculum* (2nd ed.). London: Routledge.

Ben-Bassat, N. (1997). Additional directions in Jewish identity education in Israel. *Studies in education: The Israeli Journal for Research in Education [Hebrew]*, New Series, 2(1), 168–184.

Ben-Peretz, M. (2005). The Jewish heritage and the aims of education in Israel. In M. Bar-Lev (Ed.), *Jewish Heritage in a changing world [Hebrew]* (Vol. 10, pp. 57–72). Jerusalem: Hebrew University, School of Education, Teachers Training Department.

Blasé, J. R. (2003). *Handbook of instructional leadership: How successful principals promote teaching and learning*. Thousand Oaks, CA: Corwin Press.

Bowers, C. A., & Flinders, D. J. (1991). *Culturally responsive teaching and supervision: A handbook for staff development*. New York: Teachers College Press.

Brinker, M. (2003). Jewish studies in Israel from a liberal-secular perspective. In S. Fox, I. Scheffler, & D. Marom (Eds.), *Visions of Jewish education* (pp. 95–122). Cambridge: Cambridge University Press.

Cochran-Smith, M. (2001, Jan/Feb). Learning to teach against the (new) grain. *Journal of Teacher Education, 52*(1), 3–4.

Cochran-Smith, M., & Lytle, S. L. (1999). Relationship of Knowledge and Practice: Teacher Learning in Communities. *Review of Research in Education, 24*, 249–305.

Cohen, J. (1996). *Jewish thought for the sake of education: Can Jewish tradition be 'Translated'? Molding and rehabilitation, papers in memory of Prof. Akiva Ernst Simon and Carl Frankenstein [Hebrew]* (pp. 164–182). Jerusalem: The Hebrew University Magnes Press and The School of Education of the Hebrew University of Jerusalem.

Costa, L., & Garmstone, J. (1999). *Cognitive coaching*. Published in Hebrew by The Branco Weiss Institute for Development Thinking, Jerusalem.

Davis, O. L., Jr. (2001, Fall). A View of authentic mentorship. *Journal of Curriculum and Supervision, 16*, 1–4.

Feiman-Nemser, S., & Rosaen, C. (Eds.). (1997). *Guiding teacher learning insider studies of classroom work with prospective & practicing teachers*. Washington, DC: American Association of Colleges for Teacher Education.

Gafni, Y. (1999). Education of the young in the time of the Talmud – tradition and reality. In R. Feldhi & E. Etkes (Eds.), *Education and history: Cultural and political contexts [Hebrew]*. Jerusalem: Zalman Shazar Center.

Geertz, C. (1990). *The interpretation of cultures [Hebrew]*. Jerusalem: Keter Publications.

Giroux, H. (1988). *Teachers as intellectuals*. New York: Bergin and Garvey.

Glickman, C. D. (1990). *Supervision of instruction* (2nd ed.). Boston: Allyn and Bacon.

Godsoe, B., Ament, A., & Heilpern, M. (2007). *Experience speaks, the impact of mentoring in the classroom and beyond*. New York: Avi Chai Foundation.

Goldhammer, R. (1969). *Clinical supervision: Special methods for the supervision of teachers*. New York: Rinehart & Winston.

Goldsbery, L. (1998). Teachers involvement in supervision. In G. R. Firth & E. Pajak (Eds.), *Handbook of research on school supervision* (pp. 428–462). New York: Macmillan.

Goren, D. (Ed.). (1994). *People and world: Jewish culture in a changing world, recommendations of the committee for examining Jewish studies in Israeli general state schools*. Jerusalem: Ministry of Education, Culture and Sports.

Grundy, S., & Hatton, E. J. (1995). Teacher educators' ideological discourses. *Journal of Education for Teaching, 21*(1), 7–24.

Haam., A. (1913). *The national morality. Ahad Haam's writings [Hebrew]*. Tel-Aviv and Jerusalem: Dvir and Ivrit Publications.

Hansen, D. T. (1995). *The call to teach*. New York: Teachers College Press.

Harris, B. M. (1998). Paradigms and parameters of supervision in education. In G. R. Firth & E. Pajak (Eds.), *Handbook of research on school supervision* (pp. 1–34). New York: Macmillan.

Himley, M., & Carini, P. (1991). The Study of works: A phenomenological approach to understanding children as thinkers and learners. In M. Himely (Ed.), *Shared territory* (pp. 17–56). New York: Oxford University Press.

Holtz, W. B. (2003). *Textual knowledge: Teaching the Bible in theory and practice*. New York: Jewish Theological Seminary.

Holtzer, E. (2002). Conceptions of the study of Jewish texts in teachers professional development. *Religious Education, 97*(4), 377–403.

Lamm, Z. (1988). The ideological bases of Jewish studies in Israeli education. *The Joint Education [Hebrew]., 130*, 57–76.

Lamm, Z. (2002). *In the turbulence of ideologies: The foundations of education in the twentieth century [Hebrew]*. Jerusalem: Magnes Press.

Lincoln, Y. S., & Guba, E. G. (1985). How do teachers manage to teach? Perspectives on problems in practice. *Harvard Educational Review, 55*(2), 178–194.

Luz, E. (1994). A secular alternative: Teaching Jewish studies in the state school system. In M. Eyali (Ed.), *Tura 3: A collection of articles on Jewish thought and philosophy* (pp. 15–27). Tel-Aviv: The United Kibbutz – Sifriat Poalim Publishing group.

Muszkat-Barkan, M. (2005). Ideological Encounters: Case Studies of Teacher Supervision in Jewish Studies. Ph.D. Diss., Hebrew University of Jerusalem.

Muszkat-Barkan, M., & Shkedi, A. (2009). Ideological commitment in the supervision of Jewish studies teachers: Representing community. In A. Pomson & H. Deitcher (Eds.), *Jewish day schools Jewish communities* (pp. 270–288). Oxford: The Littman Library of Jewish Civilisation.

Nisan, M. (2009). *Educational identity as a major factor in the development of educational leadership*. Jerusalem: Mandel Leadership Institute.

Oliva, P. F., & Pawlas, G. E. (1984). *Supervision for today's schools*. New York: Longman Inc.

Pajak, E. (1993). *Approaches to clinical supervision*. Norwood, MA: Christopher-Gordon Publishers, Inc.

Pajak, E. (2002). Clinical supervision and psychological functions: A new direction for theory and practice. *Journal of Curriculum and Supervision, 17*(3), 189–205.

Palmer, P. (1998). *The Courage to Teach Exploring the Inner Landscape of a Teacher's Life*. San Francisco: Jossey-Bass.

Portner, H. (2005). *Teacher mentoring and induction: The state of the art and beyond*. Thousand Oaks, CA: Corwin Press.

Rosenak, M. (1995). *Roads to the palace: Jewish texts and teaching*. London: Berghahn Books.

Rosenak, M. (2003). On second thought the Hebrew University Magness Press.

Rosenak, M. (2003). *On second thought, tradition and modernity in Jewish contemporary education [Hebrew]*. Jerusalem: Magnes Press and Lifshitz Academic College.

Rosenak, A. (2009). *Halakhah as an agent of change: Critical studies in philosophy of Halakha [Hebrew]*. Jerusalem: Magnes.

Rubenstein, I. (1999). *The mentor as a professional: Teachers' perspective in a training role*. Jerusalem: The Ministry of Education, Culture and Sports, Pedagogic Administration, Training Office.

Schon, D. A. (1983). *The reflective practitioner: How professionals think in action*. New York: Basic Books.

Schon, D. A. (1988). Coaching reflective teaching. In P. P. Grimmett & G. L. Ericson (Eds.), *Reflection in teacher education*. New York: Teachers College Press.

Schremer, O. E. (1999). *Education in Israel: Between radicalism and tolerance [Hebrew]*. Jerusalem: Magnes Press.

Schweid, E. (2000). *Humanistic Jewish education in Israel: Content and methods [Hebrew]*. Tel-Aviv: The United Kibbutz – Sifriat Poalim Publishing Group.

Shkedi, A. (1996). Teacher education: What we can learn from experienced teachers. *British Journal of In-Service Education, 22*(1), 81–99.

Shkedi, A., & Horeczyk, G. (1995). The role of teacher ideology in the teaching of culturally valued texts. *Teaching and Teacher Education, 11*(2), 107–117.

Shkedi, A., & Nisan, M. (2006). Teachers' cultural ideology: Patterns of curriculum and teaching culturally valued texts. *Teachers College Record, 108*(4), 687–725.

Silberstein, M. (1998). *Teaching as a reflective practice: Guidelines for alternative training programs [Hebrew]*. Tel-Aviv: Mofet Institute.

Simon, U. (1986). *The teaching of Akiva Ernst Simon. Chapters in my life: Building-up in the time of destruction [Hebrew]* (pp. 181–232). Tel-Aviv and Jerusalem: Sifriat Poalim and Leo Baeck Institute.

Stake, R. E. (2000). Case Studies. In N. K. Denzin & Y. S. Lincoln (Eds.), *Handbook of qualitative research* (pp. 435–454). Thousand Oaks, CA: Sage.

Strauss, A. & Corbin, J. (1990). Grounded Theory Methodology. In N. K. Denzin & Y. S. Lincoln (Eds.), *Handbook of qualitative research* (pp. 273–285). Thousand Oaks, CA: Sage.

Twersky, I. (2003). What must a Jew study – And why? In S. Fox, I. Schefler, & D. Marom (Eds.), *Visions of Jewish education*. Cambridge Press, Hebrew edition.

Tzabar Ben-Yehoshua, N. (1997). *Qualitative research in teaching and learning [Hebrew]*. Ben-Shemen: Modan.

Van-Manen, M. (1991). *The tact of teaching: The meaning of pedagogical thoughtfulness*. Albany, NY: SUNY Press.

Zachary, L. (2006, Summer). *Creating a mentoring culture*. San Francisco: Coalition for the Advancement of Jewish Education.

Zachary L. J. (2000). *The mentor's guide: Facilitating effective learning relationships*. San Francisco: Wiley

Zakovitch, Y. (2003). Teaching the book of Joshua in our times. In M. Frankel & H. Deitcher (eds.), *Understanding the Bible in our times: Implications for education* (pp. 11–20). Studies in Jewish Education (Vol. IX) Magness Press.

Zakovitz, Y. (1995). Distance requires closeness. In S. Gelander (Ed.), *Topics in education 4, Bible and education [Hebrew]* (pp. 7–16). Kiryat Tivon: Oranim Publications.

Zeichner, K. M., & Liston, D. (1985). Varieties of discourse in supervisory conferences. *Teaching & Teacher Education, 1*(2), 155–174.

Parents and Jewish Educational Settings

Jeffrey S. Kress

Introduction: The Challenges of Ecological Complexity

To summarize the intersection of parents and Jewish educational settings[1] is to attempt to encapsulate in static prose a dynamic and interactive system. More accurately, it is an attempt to summarize several dynamic systems and the interactions among them. Such a description, focusing on components of the various systems and their points of intersection, would be able to encompass parts of the picture, but these parts would inevitably add up to less than the "whole." Moreover, excellent reviews and original research on aspects of this topic have recently been published and are cited frequently throughout this chapter (in particular: Goodman, Flexner, & Bloomberg, 2008; Pomson & Schnoor, 2008; Wertheimer, 2007); it is not my intention to reiterate in detail their contents. Rather, my goal is to provide a structure for understanding multiple elements of this complex system.

Psychologist Urie Bronfenbrenner (1979, p. 14) described such complex systems as *ecologies* of development or education.[2] Ecological developmental systems consist of several components, each of which has the potential to impact on one's behaviors, attitudes, and learning:

1. the roles and relationships in which one is a direct participant, referred to as *microsystems*, which bring experiences, rules, and expectations that shape development (for parents, for example, a place of employment; for students, a school);

J.S. Kress (✉)
Jewish Theological Seminary, New York, NY, USA
e-mail: jekress@jtsa.edu

[1] It is understood that parents are also agents of Jewish education. The focus of this chapter, however, is on the parents as they relate to educational institutions.

[2] Bronfenbrenner generally used the term "development" as opposed to "education" to refer to the process of growth on many levels—cognitive, affective, social, identity, and group membership, etc. Since the goals of Jewish education encompass a similar range of outcomes, Bronfenbrenner's analysis applies to the current situation even though it is grounded in an "education" context.

2. connections among microsystems (referred to as *mesosystems*, such as, from the standpoint of a parent, the interaction between a child and his or her teachers, each of whom has direct "microsystemic" connections with the parents);
3. contexts in which an individual does not directly participate but which nonetheless impact on the individual's experience, referred to as *exosystems* (a teacher's organization or union is an exosystem from both the parents' and child's perspective; neither is a member, unless the parent is also employed by the school, but the organization creates policy that impacts upon the experience of both).
4. social and/or cultural norms, expectations, assumptions, beliefs, or shared understandings, referred to as *macrosystems*; for example, the idea that Jewish children should have a bar or bat mitzvah that involves certain ritual and celebratory components; or a communal vision that Jewish education is central to the survival of the Jewish people in the face of anti-Semitism and/or intermarriage.

While Bronfenbrenner's original formulation did not include a temporal dimension, later articulations described a fifth component, the *chronosystem*, or the understanding that the individual as well as the entire set of ecological relationships has a history, a course of development preceding the current point in time. It is not just the array of roles and relationships existing at any given moment that holds developmental potential; the evolution of these elements over time is also relevant. As such, for example, an understanding of the chronosystem would predict that the way in which a parent interacts with a child (a microsystem) at a given point would be influenced by, among many other things, the history of such interactions leading up to that point.

Of course, each of the five ecological components functions in relation to all of the others. As a brief example, a parent's interaction with the teachers at a school (from the parents' point of view, a microsystemic interaction) will be shaped by, to provide just a partial list, his or her relationship with the child (microsystem), the child's relationship with the teachers (mesosystem), policies set by the school leadership (exosystem) regarding parent interaction, the perceived norms (by parents and teachers alike) regarding accepted modes of interaction with teachers (macrosystem), the parent's own history of interaction with teachers in his or her past educational experience (chronosystem), and the prior interactions between the parent and the teacher in question (also chronosystem).

Further complicating the matter, an individual's developmental ecology cannot be separated from those of others; similar to Ezekiel's circles within circles, ecologies are seen as "nested" among one another. While a parent's ecological system may include a direct microsystemic relationship with a teacher, that teacher has his or her *own* set of ecological relationships. Also, the composition of a system varies depending on the reference point. A parent and a child have a direct microsystemic relationship (from the perspective of the parent and child) which, from the point of view of the teacher, may be primarily an exosystem in which she does not participate but which impacts on her role. An important implication of the nesting of ecologies is reciprocal interaction among those ecologies. If one could imagine a diagram of ecological systems, the arrows among those systems would have arrows on both ends. As parents influence the development of their children, for example, children, in turn, help shape the actions, attitudes, and knowledge of their parents. As parents bring their developmental history (chronosystem) into an interaction with a teacher, that teacher is, in turn, influenced by her own developmental history.

I begin by identifying the complexity of the situation not as an excuse or explanation for falling short of capturing the enormous richness of the story, as will inevitably be the case. Rather, my intention is to set up a framework for understanding this intricate system of relationships. Further, such complexity is the rule in developmental/educational settings and, therefore, it is into this web that both educators and researchers alike peer as they try to make sense, either as a matter of applied practice or as an analytic interpretation, of any given piece of information emerging from an interaction or observation at any particular point in time. A parent speaking with a teacher in a school hallway, or with a researcher in the context of an interview, shines light on parts of the system, but because the system is ever-evolving and extends beyond any single participant, the picture that emerges is more like a snapshot taken with strobe-lighting than a documentary video. Elements of the system are likely to be unknown and potentially unknowable by that parent, let alone the educator or researcher with whom she or he interacts.

Implications of this complexity are discussed later in this chapter. For now, this introduction should serve to set the proper perspective for the reader for understanding the material that follows. In the next section, I will highlight some of the ecological elements involved in the intersection of parents and Jewish education. The theory and research described bring together many of these "strobe-light" photos. They are, by necessity, described as discrete elements, or elements with relatively simple points of intersection with one another. The reader should imagine these elements as interrelated, with changes in one area holding the potential to change the system as a whole along with all of the component parts.

Parents and Jewish Education: Ecological Elements

Today's Parents

As parents are the node around which this analysis centers, it is worth highlighting themes emerging from recent findings with regard to Jewish parents and families.[3] Data from the 2000–2001 National Jewish Population Survey in the United States show that, in that country, Jewish parents of school-age children are overwhelmingly likely to have themselves received some form of Jewish education, and that this education is overwhelmingly likely to have taken place in a supplemental school (Cohen, 2004; Phillips, 2008). Along with high levels of Jewish education, intermarriage is also common among the parents of children receiving Jewish education

---

[3] This is not meant as a demographic overview, but rather a discussion of data most relevant to the intersection of parents and Jewish education.

today. Phillips (2008) reports that slightly less than half of Jewish children under the age of 18 come from families with two Jewish parents. "In other words, what once was the 'typical' Jewish family consisting of two Jewish parents living together with their children is now the exception rather that the rule" (Phillips, 2008, p. 66). The increase in intermarriage is associated with an overall decline in numbers of children receiving a Jewish education (Phillips, 2008; Wertheimer, 2008).

The intersection of trends in work status (a parental microsystem) and gender roles (a macrosystemic "norm") also has implications for the interaction of parents and Jewish schools. The Jewish population is increasingly likely to have both parents participating in the workforce (Wertheimer, 2008). It is generally mothers who take the role of "managers" of the family (Prell, 2007), regardless of whether or not they are employed full-time in paying jobs. "In the realm of mother as manager her attention to children's education is paramount, it is one of her key portfolios" (Prell, 2007, p. 9). Mothers, again regardless of employment status, tend to be the ones that adapt their schedules to accommodate a child's needs and logistical constraints. As such, "[w]omen assume responsibilities for children and family that make them key to an understanding of how the family's Jewishness is shaped and how children are educated" (Prell, 2007, p. 9). While mothers with full-time employment value their dual role, they nonetheless experience role-conflict (Prell, 2007). Parental employment status and gender roles interact, with the result that "mothers, particularly non-working mothers, are more likely to be the face of the family in the school" (Prell, 2007, p. 14).

Not surprisingly, between work and childcare, parents feel that they have very little personal time (Prell, 2007). The challenge of making time for Jewish education within the demands of extracurricular activities, work, and children's social lives, particularly for those in middle school when the logistics of navigating the "*bar/bat mitzvah* circuit" has the potential to create stressful situations for parents and families (Fishman, 2007; Kress, 2007).

Parents' conceptualizations and beliefs about parenting are important determinants of parenting behavior (Sigel, 1985). Prell (2007) found that parents talk about Jewish parenting in terms of specific family and communal rituals and practices, even if the family actually observes few of these. Because these items involve the management of family time, these often fall under the mother's purview. Parents not raised within Judaism, in contrast to Jews by birth, will often use terms related to spirituality and a relationship with God with regard to both parenting and expectations of Jewish schooling.

Finally, parent involvement in adult Jewish education can also be seen as an important exosystemic factor. Research has pointed to the flowering of adult education initiatives and the broad impact these may have. In particular, the discourse of adult learning has shifted from content learning to meaning-making, or Jewish education framed within a process of developmental growth (e.g., Grant, Schuster, Woocher, & Cohen, 2004). This highlights the dynamism of this system—at the same time that a youth is learning in school, a parent's Jewish experience is evolving through experiences out of, as well as associated with, the school (as discussed below).

Setting the Child's Ecological Stage: Parents as Decision Makers

School is a central microsystem in the experience of a child, who may spend more waking hours there than in any other setting. In making decisions about their children's education, parents are setting the parameters for this important element in the ecology of childhood. The most consistent finding with regard to parents and Jewish educational decision making is that parents have, in general, become much more active in choosing educational settings for their children than they have been in past generations. "Whereas Jewish parents at mid-century enrolled their children in the closest synagogue school, today's families are more apt to insist on just the right fit between *each* child and the type of schooling they choose to deliver that education" (Wertheimer, 2008, p. 14, emphasis in the original). Wertheimer (2008, p. 14) sees this as "consumer orientation" toward education and a "greater insistence on quality."

Individualization of educational choices to meet the needs of individual children results in a range of educational decisions even within the same family, with different children potentially receiving different forms of Jewish (and secular) education. Again, it is mothers in particular that tend to assume the lead role in assuring that the unique educational needs of their children are met, though educational decisions are often made more jointly (Prell, 2007). Ecological complexity suggests that while "parents" are an ecological unit, each parent also has his or her own ecological system, with some overlapping and some unique elements. For example, as we have seen above, mothers tend to have a stronger microsystemic connection with schools than do fathers (for whom the school may be more of an exosystem, experienced through their spouse). This has implications for parental decision making. Because of their more frequent exposure to the school, a "mother's perceptions of the school will clearly influence how the family may respond to children's educational needs" (Prell, 2007, p. 14).

The primary dimension of decision making discussed in the literature has to do with the choice between day school and supplemental school education.[4] The range of reasons provided by parents illustrates the numerous ecological factors that can influence a parent's decisions. These include cost, lack of the parents' own Jewish knowledge, and concern that a child may become more observant than a parent would prefer (Kress, 2007; Pomson, 2007; Prell, 2007). Logistical concerns can be a factor in educational decision making; distances to and from various educational settings and the availability (or unavailability) of transportation options can help determine the viability of various options (Fishman, 2007; Kress, 2007). The quality of the local public schools is also pertinent, with excellent public schools complicating a decision to pursue a private school education. Parents also consider the particular learning needs of each individual child and the perceived ability of the local schools (secular or day) to provide for such needs.

---

[4] Actually, the decision is often framed in the literature as whether to send a child to a day school or not. Supplemental school is often seen as a "default" position (Kress, 2007).

Macrosystemic beliefs and perceived norms are also relevant. Some parents see it as un-American to reject a public school education; they feel conflict "between an ideology of diversity and a loyalty to the American public school system, and a commitment to 'Jewish continuity,' their stated responsibility to transmit Jewish culture" (Fishman, 2007, p. 191). Further, some parents believe that a day school education does not prepare a child for the "real world," and want their child to encounter more diversity than they believe exists in day schools. Cohen and Kelner (2007) posit that an overall declining concern about ghettoization may help explain the growth in day school attendance among non-Orthodox Jews. These authors find little statistical relationship between income and the decision to send a child to day school. Rather, such decisions were found to be predicted by a variety of indicators of Jewish engagement.

Day or supplemental school is only one of the educational choices facing Jewish parents. Even among those for whom day school education is essentially a given (because of macrosystemic norms related to day school education, primarily among Orthodox Jews), there is a process of choice regarding which day school would be best for a child, at least in geographic areas in which a variety of choices can be found (Prell, 2007). Among parents of children in supplemental school, this second level of decision (regarding which religious school to send a child) is generally predetermined by a prior decision (made based on a variety of issues) regarding which congregation to join. That is, parents see themselves as choosing a congregation (because of the "feel," the rabbi, geography, the denomination, etc.) and not specifically a school (Kress, 2007). As independent, "community" (non-congregational) supplemental schools become more common; such decisions may become more complex and should be explored further.

Some components of school choice can be seen as relatively straightforward, involving a rational comparison of the relative benefits and shortcomings of the available educational options. However, chronosystemic factors such as a parent's personal/educational history also play an important role in these decisions. Pomson (2007) sees school choice within the evolving narrative of parents' lives. Choosing a day school "emerges, then, from a particular mix of relationships, experiences, and events, but it should not be seen as a terminal moment in which an adult with a fully formed Jewish identity makes a decision about the Jewish life of another...choosing a school for one's children both clarifies and changes the meaning one attributes to past experiences from one's own life" (Pomson, 2007, p. 120).

With regard to decision making related to Jewish education for teens, Fishman (2007) describes several factors considered by parents and their teenage children alike. These include social/peer factors, educational quality, the potential for Jewish education to serve as "a possible resume or portfolio builder, or as a resource for networking for future career advancement" (Fishman, 2007, p. 191), competition for time from other activities, and prior experiences, particularly bad experiences, teens have had with Jewish education. It is important to note that teens in Fishman's study reported that their parents' expectations and desires figured strongly in their decision to remain in Jewish education past their bar/bat mitzvah. Even when parental influence was particularly powerful, in terms of the decision to initially remain in Jewish education post-bar or bat mitzvah, Fishman (2007) found a surprising number of teens that embraced the decision even when they felt that they were initially "forced" to do so. This is consistent with research findings showing that teens, rather than rushing to reject their parents' ideals as typically portrayed, are strongly influenced by their parents' value systems (Smith & Denton, 2005).

Parent Involvement in Schools

Once a decision regarding an educational venue is made (and it is acknowledged that this is not a one-time event; decisions may be reconsidered and re-made), there are a variety of ways in which parents can be involved in schooling. In this light, the school serves as a microsystem for the parents as well as the children, and parents have the potential to provide a mesosystemic bridge for a child between school and home environments. Inherent in the discussion of parental involvement is the assumption that actions that parents take can enhance the learning experience of their children (Epstein & Sanders, 2003). Attending and participating in school events, helping children with homework and assignments, and even asking a child about his or her school day are all forms of parental involvement.

Drawing on the ideas of Boleman and Deal, Pomson and Schnoor (2008) provide a framework of four modalities of parent involvement in Jewish day schools.

1. The *Structural Frame* describes parents as volunteers, stepping up to fill needed roles that the school would have difficulty staffing with paid personnel. The authors provide a variety of examples ranging from serving as chaperone for school events to helping in the office. Parents recognize the pragmatic need for their help (usually initiated by school personnel who seek volunteers) and see it as a chance to become more engaged with the school and with their child's education in general.
2. The *Human Resource Frame*, similar to the Structural, involves parents volunteering for the enhancement of the school. However, involvement in this category is generally parent-initiated (rather than educator- or administrator-initiated) and involves provision of a service that, in benefiting the child of the volunteering parent, benefits the school community more broadly as well. Parents coaching sports teams or running other extracurricular activities in which their children (and, of course, others as well) participate are an example of participation in this category.
3. The *Political Frame* describes the involvement of parents in the governance and policymaking of the school. This can happen formally (e.g., through a position on a board) or informally (e.g., through expressing their opinions to school leaders). Participation of this type brings the potential for contentious interactions and may call upon a parent to voice publicly opinions about Judaism and/or education that were previously a matter of private belief.
4. The *Symbolic Frame* involves parent participation in (or attendance at) communal events and celebrations. Occasions such as model *seders*, while often viewed

skeptically by educators, can be emotionally meaningful moments for parents for whom they serve as public recognition of their children's milestones.

Kress (2007) found only limited involvement of parents in supplemental schools, mainly involving occasional attendance at school events (e.g., model *seders*) and contact with school personnel regarding logistical or educational concerns. However, some parents volunteer in, or are employed by, the supplemental schools, and some schools use parents in a variety of important roles. Parents of supplemental school children also serve on school committees. Prell (2007) points out that findings such as this exist in stark contrast to the more active and involved role that these same parents may take in their child's secular school. One exception to this general lack of involvement may be the functioning of parents as educators in supplemental schools. Because of personnel needs, parents are often called upon to teach in such schools (e.g., Aron, 1997; Kaplowitz & Feiman-Nemser, 1997). Also, parents are involved in governance of such schools through participation in education and synagogue committees, though there is a large degree of variation in the degree of activity and involvement of such committees among synagogues.

The Impact of Children's Jewish Educational Settings on Parents

In all ecological systems, those that take action or exert influence are themselves influenced through the relationship. The discussion up to this point has focused on parents as the more active partner in the parent–school relationship, being the ones to make educational decisions and to become involved in the school. Emerging research points to the impact of a child's Jewish educational experience on parents. To begin with, parents are also learners themselves in a variety of ways. They learn from their children, who bring home information, customs, or practices (including songs, or newly learned Hebrew words) which may be unfamiliar to parents. More subtly, participation in a religious–educational community may lead parents to re-examine their current modes of Jewish engagement in light of newly encountered macrosystemic norms or perceived expectations. Further, schools may address educational efforts to parents directly, through "adult education" initiatives, possibly linked to that which their children are learning.

Research findings point to the strong association of a child's participation in Jewish education and the participation of a parent in an adult learning program. "Half of the respondents [to the 2000–2001 NJPS] with children currently enrolled in Jewish education reported participating in some kind of adult education during the previous year as compared with only 13% of respondents whose children were not currently enrolled" (Phillips, 2008, p. 65). In addition to learning in parallel, parents are also involved as learners alongside their children. Jewish family education, as described by Kay and Rotstein (2008) addresses not only children but also parents as adult learners (of Jewish content and also issues related to parenting), the interaction of parents and children, and the development of the family as a unit.

Of course, the association between a child's and a parent's learning cannot be assumed to be a result of a child's school experience. However, theorists speculate about how the involvement of a child in a Jewish educational setting can facilitate a parent's pursuit of adult Jewish education for themselves. As their children enter Jewish schools, parents, already involved in considering issues of Jewish identity for themselves and their families, may become aware of the limitations in their own Jewish knowledge and/or be motivated to enhance the child's school experience through their own learning efforts (Katz & Parker, 2008). Katz and Parker (2008) see the emergence of parents as recipients of Jewish education as related to a number of Jewish and general social trends. As attendance at day schools and Jewish summer camps increase, parents may find that their children's Jewish knowledge soon eclipses their own. Further, there is a growing unwillingness on the part of parents to cede responsibility for instilling Jewish identity to the schools. Finally, there is a general trend, in and out of Jewish education, toward ongoing education for adults.

These trends coincide with a growing appreciation on the part of educators that "[t]he role model parents can provide their children as engaged learners is invaluable in demonstrating the seriousness of Jewish education. Moreover, the well-educated parent, it has been argued, might serve as a powerful advocate for higher educational standards" (Wertheimer, 2008, p. 16). Katz and Parker (2008) discuss the developmental context of young adulthood (while acknowledging the increasing age-span at which adults are having children) and point to literature showing the priority young adults put on contributing to both family and career, and their particular interest in "practical learning" (p. 155). They also cite some evidence that younger adults, in contrast to older adults, are more apt to change their behavior in response to Jewish learning. Parents, pursuing learning and other forms of Jewish involvement, may hope to inspire their children's Jewish education through their own example (Fishman, 2007).

Parents of students in day schools (Pomson, 2007) and supplemental schools (Kress, 2007) have also described the impact of their children's schools on their Jewish experience. While neither study of these two studies was designed to quantify the extent of such impact (that is, to ascertain how many parents were impacted and how strongly), they did provide converging results about the form that impact may take. A child's participation in both types of schools has the potential to result in a parent's pursuit of adult learning, including learning from one's child as well as seeking structured learning opportunities to address deficits that might have come to light through seeing a child's gains. Beyond knowledge, a child's school experience can enhance the range of family Jewish ritual practice as well as what Pomson (2007) refers to as *enculturation* or "increasing integration of Jewish culture into [the parents'] lives" (p. 135). Finally, day schools and supplemental schools can both create social connections with other Jewish parents. Kress (2007) also points out the potential for supplemental schooling to lead to friction in a family as children may resist attending and parents may resent additional demands on their schedule. Though this issue is not discussed in the parallel Pomson (2007) study, day schools certainly hold the potential to bring up similar concerns within a family.

There is also evidence that Jewish education may play a role in *maintaining* changes in the Jewish experience of a family in addition to initiating such changes. As an ecological approach would suggest, reduction in environmental support for a change, through withdrawal from an educational setting, for example, would attenuate changes associated with that setting. In this vein, Fishman (2007), found that:

> When teenagers stopped attending Jewish schools after bar/bat mitzvahs, they reported that their family Jewish observances and activities, such as Shabbat service attendance, gradually declined without the reinforcing effect of Judaic discussion in classes and invitations for holiday celebrations with classmates' families. In contrast, when they continued attending Jewish schools after bar/bat mitzvah, family activities tended to remain constant. (p. 189)

Acknowledging History: Parental Chronosystems

It is significant that parents not only *are* learners, but *were* learners. Many Jewish parents had some form of Jewish education in their youth; parents who are not Jewish or did not grow up as Jews may have had religious education within their own faith traditions. Regardless of their religious schooling, all parents were students in some type of educational setting in the past. These experiences can exert strong influences on the expectations, attitudes, and affects that parents bring with them in experiencing their children's education. Further, parents' past experiences with Judaism, Jewish communal organizations and professionals can color their current attitudes toward Jewish education and Jewish educational settings.

To begin with, there is evidence that the decision a parent makes regarding a child's Jewish education is predicted by the decisions their own parents made for them (that is, the type of Jewish education they received). Overall, there is an intergenerational cycle of Jewish commitment and Jewish education with parents more engaged with Jewish ritual and communal life disproportionately choosing day schools (Cohen & Kelner, 2007). Furthermore, a parent's past experiences may operate on a more emotional or attitudinal level. A parent's "personal–historical context" (Pomson, 2007, p. 117) is an important component in understanding his or her choice of, and experience of, a child's education. A particularly powerful interaction of current experience and personal history occurs while "visiting a school and finding something parents themselves missed in their own childhoods ad perhaps all of their lives up to now" (Pomson, 2007, p. 119).

Cohen and Kelner (2007) hypothesize that "Jewish involvement yields higher aspirations for children's Jewish development, which leads to belief in (or hope for) the efficacy of day schools, which in turn promoted day school utilization" (pp. 82–83). Research from general education suggests that the impact of a parent's educational history on his or her expectations for a child may be mediated by their negative self-feelings with respect to that education (Kaplan, Liu, & Kaplan, 2001). As such, the affective experience of the parent's education may be an important factor in decision making.

Parents' decisions about their children's Jewish education are steps along a parents' Jewish journey as well as that of a child's, and the interaction of parents and

Jewish educational settings must be understood within this broader context. Fishman (2007, p. 191) found that:

> Many parents felt ambivalent about who they were as Jews, and they were interested in talking about the ways in which decisions about their children's education became a stage on which their own mixed feelings were acted out.

Further, the broader communal context frames the relationship of parents and Jewish education. In particular, the ways in which parents relate to other Jewish organizations, particularly synagogues, can have an impact on their experiences and expectations of Jewish education (Fishman, 2007; Kress, 2007). For example, a warm feeling or experience of caring from a rabbi or, conversely, a feeling of disenfranchisement from the synagogue, can color a parent's view of a supplemental school.

A parent's own educational history can also influence the way he or she understands or interprets a child's school experience. Early experiences create schema, or frameworks of understanding that integrate knowledge, beliefs, emotion, and attitudes, related to Jewish education that, in turn, serve as filters for the processing of new information related to Jewish education (Kress, 2007). Kress (2007) found that parents' negative experiences with supplemental school education can cast a pessimistic view of their child's education in such settings even when the child's experience has been, by the description of the parent, more positive. Of course, a child's complaints are likely to reinforce such a schema, which can lead to what Prell (2007) describes as parents coming to the conclusion that there is an "inevitable dilemma—how to make children enjoy and learn in a meaningful way" (Prell, 2007, p. 25).

The issue of the maintenance of negative parental schema regarding supplemental school education provides an interesting example of the interaction among various ecological issues, including a parent's history, a child's current experience, the involvement (or lack thereof) of the parent in the school and the interaction (or lack thereof) between parents and children around the school experience. Explaining the persistence of negative supplemental school schema even in the face of admitted evidence countering these negative assumptions, Kress (2007) writes,

> While schema can change based on disconfirming data, it is noteworthy that parents generally had very little direct experience with the religious school, especially as children grow older...Until the actual event of the bar/bat mitzvah, when a child gets to demonstrate his or her gains, parents may experience this focus on synagogue ritual as a decrease in emphasis on home ritual, thereby further adding to the difficulties (already imposed by developmental issues, increasingly busy schedules, etc.) of interacting with their children around religious school activities. (p. 153)

Coupled with findings, discussed earlier, that in general parents have generally limited involvement in their child's supplemental school education, Kress (2007) continues:

> Negative preconceptions and limited involvement constitute a negative feedback loop. Parents with negative schema are unlikely to be motivated to become involved in the school. This lack of involvement both decreases chances for parents to encounter data that may exist to disconfirm their schema, and may also reinforce children's own misgivings about religious schooling.

Future Directions

While emerging research is painting a more complete picture of the dynamic interaction between parents and schools, and, of course, more research is called for in those areas, there are some topics which have been generally overlooked in the literature. For example, while research has been conducted about choices among educational options, we know less about the nature of decisions to maintain or change these initial decisions. What factors lead a parent to change a child's initially chosen educational venue?

Further, little is known about parents and informal Jewish educational settings. How do the dimensions above (parent as decision maker, the reciprocal impact and involvement of parent and educational setting, the parent's educational history) play out with regard to the experience of, and decisions regarding, youth in summer camps, youth groups, and the like? This issue becomes more salient with the emergence of research supporting the efficacy of informal Jewish education (e.g., Cohen, 2007). Looking specifically at camping as a case in point, several questions can be raised: Based on what factors do parents choose to send their children to a Jewish summer camp? How do they choose between the ever-growing array of "specialty camps" (e.g., sports camps, computer camps and even, as I recently learned about, circus camp, at which campers learn juggling and other skills) and those with a more Jewish educational focus? How do "Jewish style" camps, or camps in which a vast majority of campers are Jewish but have no Jewish ritual or educational elements, fit into the equation? In what way do parents' own camping experiences influence their choices? Anecdotally, we hear of more parents concerned with the cost of paying for both day school and summer camps. As the efficacy of camps in promoting Jewish outcomes becomes better documented, how do parents decide where to allocate their funds? What rituals do campers bring home with them, and to what degree are these maintained in the home and community?

Likewise, little international data are available related to the topic of parents and Jewish schools. An ecological perspective, however, would suggest that the functioning of any system would be sensitive to local trends; the number of potential inputs into a system creates the potential for idiosyncratic outcomes. In fact, this can be seen as a direction for all research, in North America and beyond: to explore local ecologies and to compare and contrast these, with the goal of understanding the key variables that drive the system (e.g., geography, size of local Jewish population, educational options, etc.).

The impact of increased adult Jewish education on the relationship of parents and schooling is a topic of further research as well. As parents participate in (independent) adult education, or learn (formally or informally) through a child's experience in a school, or participate in parent education programs, they may bring with them not only increased "literacy" (i.e., familiarity with Jewish subject matter) but also may develop motivation for involvement in their children's education and, perhaps, even a new conceptualization of Jewish education as a life-long process of meaning-making. What are these changes in attitude and conceptualization and how are they manifested in the intersection of parents and schools?

The attitudes of educators toward parents and parental involvement are also in need of further exploration. Educators often speak of parent involvement with ambivalence, lamenting lack of parent concern for their children's education while resisting parents' attempts to exercise too much influence over what goes on in the classroom. Gruber and Trickett (1987) describe the dynamics of parent involvement as quite complicated, involving structural elements of schools that impede the full participation of parents as full partners to educators in public schools. Grossman (1999) talks about the potential for educators (in general education) to assume that the values of the families in which they themselves were raised—in which education and parent involvement in education may have been prized—are also the values held by the families of their students. Disappointment can result when parents make decisions which educators see as inconsistent with these values. Just as parents seem to hold schema, or preconceived attitudes and opinions, about religious schooling, it seems likely that educators may hold preconceptions about parents as well. This can be seen in the articulated assumptions on the part of religious school educators that parents are "Only in it for the *bar/bat mitzvah*" and of the implied judgment of educational and communal professionals that the parents sending a child to a supplemental school are in some way uninterested in the Jewish development of that child. An ecological framework would suggest that opinions such as these might color an educator's interaction with parents, possibly leading to further alienation on the part of a parent.

The impact of the increase in so-called "non-traditional" family constellations, particularly same-sex couples, on schools is also a matter for inquiry. The broadening of the macrosytemic norms regarding same-sex unions has the potential to impact on the language and images used by educators and also calls into question how schools are addressing—both with students and in their own policies—the various *halachic* opinions related to the issue.

Finally, this chapter is being written during a time of severe economic turmoil in the United States and beyond. This economic downturn has had and will continue to have an impact on parents and schools. It is likely that shifts in the ecological system will result. Might financial challenges to school necessitate more or different parent involvement in lieu of paid professionals? How will economics impact decision making?

Conclusion: Harnessing Complexity

Trends point toward parents increasingly seeking educational venues, Jewish and/or otherwise, that best meet the needs of each individual child. While often discussed as a static choice point, parental decision making takes place within a dynamic of evolving components including the nature of the family and its individual members (particularly the changing perception of the needs of the child in question); the school, its leadership and personnel, and the instructional methods and curricular focus of any given grade; and the nature of the interaction among child, parents, and school. As such, while we can look at parents and Jewish education at a given point in time, the relationship is one of constant motion.

How can such an ever-changing relationship be managed? Certainly, it would not be enough to market different educational options, let parents decide, and assume that a steady course would be set into motion. What would be needed is the involvement of the parents in a process, or an ongoing dialogue. However, there is reason to believe that such conversations are not the norm. Kress (2007, p. 168), commenting on interviews with parents about expectations for supplemental school education, notes that "it appeared that many had not been posed with this question before nor had they previously articulated their ideas about these issues." Even in settings with high levels of parental involvement, it cannot be assumed that parents and educators have engaged in sustained discussion about parental goals and expectations.

Opportunities to articulate educational goals and expectations for their children, and possibly also for themselves (Aron, 2000), cannot only capture the thoughts of the moment, but in creating an expectation of, and space for, reflection on the topic can call upon parents to consider, and possibly question, their assumptions and to realize alternate possibilities for their children's (and their own) Jewish growth. Educational transitions provide particularly apt entry-points for such conversations between educators and parents and

> can provide an opportunity for an educational leader and/or rabbi to engage parents in a serious discussion of their goals and hopes for their children, what they want their children to gain from the experience, what they expect from the school, how they can help in the process of achieving these goals, etc. This conversation can be repeated at various intervals, and can even take place with students (particularly at the older grades). (Kress, 2007, p. 169)

The articulation of parental expectations would thus become part of the educational process itself. Not only would this lead to more direct communication of needs and concerns, but could also serve to provide an opportunity for reflection on the part of educators, parents, and children alike. Such an approach acknowledges the interactive nature of the relationship between parents and Jewish educational settings and uses this understanding as a springboard for growth.

References

Aron, I. (1997). Avocational teaching: The genesis and diffusion of an idea. *Religious Education*, 92, 430–439.

Aron, I. (2000). *Becoming a congregation of learners*. Woodstock, VT: Jewish Lights.

Bronfenbrenner, U. (1979). *The ecology of human development: Experiments by nature and design*. Cambridge, MA: Harvard University Press.

Cohen, S. M. (2004). *Jewish educational background: Trends and variations among today's Jewish adults*. New York: United Jewish Communities.

Cohen, S. M. (2007). The differential impact of Jewish education on adult Jewish identity. In J. Wertheimer (Ed.), *Family matters: Jewish education in an age of choice* (pp. 34–56). Lebanon, NH: University Press of New England.

Cohen, S. M., & Kelner, S. (2007). Why Jewish parents choose day schools. In J. Wertheimer (Ed.), *Family matters: Jewish education in an age of choice* (pp. 80–100). Lebanon, NH: University Press of New England.

Epstein, J. L., & Sanders, M. G. (2003). Family, school, and community partnerships. In M. H. Bornstein (Ed.), *Handbook of parenting* (Vol. 5, 2nd ed., pp. 407–438). Mahwah, NJ: Lawrence Erlbaum Associates.

Fishman, S. B. (2007). Generating Jewish connections: Conversations with Jewish teenagers, their parents, and Jewish educators and thinkers. In J. Wertheimer (Ed.), *Family matters: Jewish education in an age of choice* (pp. 181–210). Lebanon, NH: University Press of New England.

Goodman, R. L., Flexner, P. A., & Bloomberg, L. D. (Eds.). (1998). *What we now know about Jewish education: Perspectives on research for practice* (pp. 151–159). Los Angeles: Torah Aura Productions.

Grant, L., Schuster, D. S., Woocher, M., & Cohen, S. M. (2004). *A journey of heart and mind: Transformative Jewish learning in adulthood*. New York: JTS Press.

Grossman, S. (1999). Examining the origins of our beliefs about parents. *Childhood Education, 76*, 24–27.

Gruber, J., & Trickett, E. J. (1987). Can we empower others? The paradox of empowerment in the governing of an alternative public school. *American Journal of Community Psychology, 15*, 353–371.

Kaplan, D. S., Liu, X., & Kaplan, H. B. (2001). Influence of parents' self-feelings and expectations on children's academic performance. *Journal of Educational Research, 94*(6), 360–370, July–August 2001.

Kaplowitz, S. A., & Feiman-Nemser, S. (1997). Parents as religious school teachers a survey of participants in the avocational teacher project at Congregation Kehillat Israel. *Religious Education, 92*, 500–515.

Katz, B. D., & Parker, M. (2008). The Jewish education of parents. In R. L. Goodman, P. A. Flexner, & L. D. Bloomberg (Eds.), *What we now know about Jewish education: Perspectives on research for practice* (pp. 151–159). Los Angeles: Torah Aura Productions.

Kay, J., & Rotstein, E. (2008). Jewish Family Education. In R. L. Goodman, P. A. Flexner, & L. D. Bloomberg (Eds.), *What we now know about Jewish education: Perspectives on research for practice* (pp. 143–150). Los Angeles: Torah Aura Productions.

Kress, J. S. (2007). Expectations, perceptions, and preconceptions: How Jewish parents talk about "supplementary" Jewish education. In J. Wertheimer (Ed.), *Family Matters: Jewish education in an age of choice* (pp. 143–180). Lebanon, NH: University Press of New England.

Phillips, B. (2008). The demography of Jewish learners. In R. L. Goodman, P. A. Flexner, & L. D. Bloomberg (Eds.), *What we now know about Jewish education: Perspectives on research for practice* (pp. 59–74). Los Angeles: Torah Aura Productions.

Pomson, A. (2007). Schools for parents: What parents want and what they get from their children's Jewish day schools. In J. Wertheimer (Ed.), *Family matters: Jewish education in an age of choice* (pp. 101–142). Lebanon, NH: University Press of New England.

Pomson, A., & Schnoor, R. F. (2008). *Back to school: Jewish day school in the lives of adult Jews*. Detroit: Wayne State University Press.

Prell, R. -E. (2007). Family formation, educational choice, and American Jewish identity. In J. Wertheimer (Ed.), *Family Matters: Jewish education in an age of choice* (pp. 3–33). Lebanon, NH: University Press of New England.

Sigel, I. E. (1985). A conceptual analysis of beliefs. In I. E. Sigel (Ed.), *Parental belief systems: The psychological consequences for children* (pp. 345–371). Hillside, NJ: Lawrence Erlbaum.

Smith, C., & Denton, M. L. (2005). *Soul searching: The religious and spiritual lives of American teenagers*. Oxford: Oxford University Press.

Wertheimer, J. (Ed.). (2007). *Family Matters: Jewish education in an age of choice* (pp. 3–33). Lebanon, NH: University Press of New England.

Wertheimer, J. (2008). The current moment in Jewish education: An historian's view. In R. L. Goodman, P. A. Flexner, & L. D. Bloomberg (Eds.), *What we now know about Jewish education: Perspectives on research for practice* (pp. 13–20). Los Angeles: Torah Aura Productions.

Practitioner Enquiry and Its Role in Jewish Education

Alex Sinclair

What Is Practitioner Enquiry?

In the world of education, it sometimes seems as if there are two separate endeavors going on. The world of research and theory asks its questions, comes up with its findings, its theories, and its hypotheses, writes papers, and holds conferences. Meanwhile, the world of practice goes about its business: planning, teaching, debriefing, facilitating, grading, meeting, assessing, talking. Sometimes these worlds brush against each other; usually they do not. Sometimes, researchers and practitioners have the greatest of respect for each other and view each other as collaborators and colleagues; often they do not. Educational practitioners may view education professors and researchers as "out of touch with reality" and "stuck in the ivory tower"; and education researchers may view practitioners as doing work which, while objectively important, they are grateful that they personally no longer have to do.

While both practitioners and researchers are rightfully wary of panaceas, in this chapter I argue that practitioner enquiry is a critical endeavor that not only unites the worlds of research and practice, but also has the chance to improve both research and practice simultaneously.

There is nothing so practical as a good theory: the aphorism, originally Kurt Lewin's, was often used by Seymour Fox in his teaching, and can be found in an adapted version "there is nothing as practical as a great idea" in his writing (Fox, 1997, p. 1). What Fox meant by his use of the aphorism, I would suggest (which is not necessarily the same thing that Lewin originally meant), is that the world of theory and research, when refracted and utilized appropriately, is an extremely powerful tool that can have a real impact on practical questions and concerns. Conversely, the best educational research is work that directly responds to, challenges, highlights, or investigates real questions of practice. Practitioner enquiry adds a third layer to this discussion, namely, that the practitioner and the researcher can be the same person.

A. Sinclair (✉)
Jewish Theological Seminary, Jerusalem, Israel
e-mail: dralexsinclair@gmail.com

History of Practitioner Enquiry

Practitioner enquiry has a long history. When Piaget made hypotheses based on his observations of his children's development, that was practitioner enquiry (Matthews, 1980). When Dewey's students reflected on their pupils' work in the laboratory school, that was practitioner enquiry (Tanner, 1997). Indeed, Dewey was one of the first to advocate research by teachers on their own practice. In 1929, he wrote,

> It seems to me that the contributions that might come from classroom teachers are a comparatively neglected field... For these teachers are the ones in direct contact with pupils and hence the ones through whom the results of scientific findings finally reach students. They are the channels through which the consequences of educational theory come into the lives of those at school... As far as schools are concerned, it is certain that the problems which require scientific treatment arise in actual relationships with students. (cited in Hubbard & Power, 1999, p. 4)

Several recent surveys of practitioner enquiry indicate that practitioner enquiry as a discipline has existed, in one form or another, since the mid-twentieth century. Zeichner and Noffke (2001) identify five traditions of practitioner enquiry: first, the action research tradition, beginning with the work of Kurt Lewin, and brought into the educational world by Stephen Corey, Dean of Teachers College at Columbia University, in order to improve teachers' instruction; second, the teacher-as-researcher movement in the United Kingdom, led by Lawrence Stenhouse (1975), John Elliott, and others; a North American teacher research movement, basically independent of the British one; the tradition of self-study research, in which teachers explore their own practice; and the tradition of participatory research, which has mostly taken place in Latin America, Africa, and Asia.

Cochran-Smith and Lytle (2004) employ a slightly different tack in surveying the field, and rather than a historical overview, they offer six terms that are part of the "conceptual umbrella" of practitioner enquiry (they prefer "practitioner inquiry" to "practitioner research," on the grounds that it is more resonant with the community of practitioners. I follow their preference; there is no significance in the spelling of the word here "enquiry" rather than "inquiry"). The six terms they discuss are action research, teacher research, self-study, narrative/autobiographical inquiry, the scholarship of teaching, and finally, using teaching as a site for research. They call the term practitioner enquiry itself "protean" because of this blurriness in its meaning (609).

Despite this protean nature, Cochran-Smith and Lytle are able to identify seven common elements in all these variant traditions of practitioner enquiry: practitioners also function as researchers; practitioners' knowledge is a valuable and important resource for thinking about teaching; practitioners' professional contexts are the sites for inquiry and their professional practice is the focus; there are blurred boundaries between practice and enquiry; questions of validity or, in their preferred term, trustworthiness, are raised by critics (on this, more below); the enquiry has a systematic rather than ad hoc nature, especially in its focus on what students are learning; and finally, the importance of the inquiring community of professional peers in making public the knowledge gained by practitioner enquiry.

Despite these longstanding and variant traditions, most researchers agree that it is not until quite recently that practitioner enquiry has really become widespread. Cochran-Smith and Lytle suggest that although various forms of teacher research were discussed throughout the twentieth century, it was during the 1980s that teacher research gained new standing because of its potential to lessen the divide between theory and practice (Cochran-Smith & Lytle, 2004, p. 603). Indeed, the same two researchers, as late as 1990, were still writing that "few teachers participate in codifying what we know about teaching, identifying research agendas, and creating new knowledge" (Cochran-Smith & Lytle, 1990, p. 2).

The Version of Practitioner Enquiry Discussed in This Chapter

It was in the 1990s that the field of Jewish education began to be influenced by practitioner enquiry, and many of its manifestations in Jewish education follow what Zeichner and Noffke call the self-study tradition, or what Cochran-Smith and Lytle call "Using teaching as a site for research." Most of the rest of this chapter therefore focuses on this particular tradition of practitioner enquiry and its manifestation in Jewish education.

This type of practitioner enquiry began to flourish in the 1990s, when several researchers began publishing studies of their own teaching, using a wide variety of data (including classroom videos, transcripts of the chalkboard, student work, and teacher journals). These studies truly bridged the worlds of theory and practice: from the researcher's perspective, they added new knowledge and understanding about a wide variety of educational questions, and from a teacher's perspective, they were exemplars of reflective practitioners thinking about their professional questions. What was most innovative about this research was that the researchers were all genuinely educational practitioners as well, splitting their time between the academy and the field.

One of the most articulate of these practitioner enquirers was Magdalene Lampert, whose book *Teaching Problems and the Problems of Teaching* (2001) is a paradigmatic example of this kind of research. In the book, Lampert studies a single teacher: herself.

> Using [a problems-based approach to Mathematics], I teach them [my students] that they all can learn and that they can do it in school. But I do not attempt to prove that teaching with problems "works." I explain what kind of work is involved in doing it in an ordinary classroom in relations with students and subject matter. (p. 1)

One initial observation about practitioner enquiry, highlighted nicely here, is that it is one of the most helpful ways in which we can deepen our knowledge of pedagogical content knowledge (Shulman, 1986) in a particular subject. It is no accident that many of these early practitioner researchers were students of or otherwise connected to Lee Shulman. Lampert echoes Shulman's critique of the polarization between subject matter and pedagogy when she writes,

> Conventional academic categories would have me limit a scholarly investigation of this work either to an analysis of the curriculum or to a study of the instructional methods... Decomposing the practice of teaching into curriculum, instruction, students, and content leaves troublesome gaps, rendering the most fundamental aspects of the work invisible. (p. 28)

Lampert's book is replete with examples of her attempts to recompose the study of her own teaching. Her work, like all work in this subfield of practitioner enquiry, is at its heart an exploration of pedagogical content knowledge. As such, some of her work is somewhat inaccessible to the non-mathematician. This is perhaps to be expected and even desired, if the term pedagogical content knowledge is to be taken seriously. After all, it is subject-*specific* pedagogy, and if I don't understand the subject, I shouldn't expect to understand its pedagogy.

This example helps distinguish this kind of practitioner enquiry from action research, one of its other traditions. Action research is usually focused on shared problems within a wide community of practice. This kind of self-study practitioner enquiry is a little different. As Hubbard and Power note (1999, 2003), while it may lead to large-scale educational change, its initial and primary focus is always on a particular and personal context: how do my students' questions change after participating in certain activities? What happens when my students choose their own reading material? How do my colleagues change their practice after participating in in-service workshops? And so on. Lampert's approach clearly falls under this rubric. However, *practitioner enquiry is most significant when its results move beyond particular educational contexts and speak to wider questions faced by educators in general*; in that sense it is similar to many other types of qualitative research. Chazan discusses this tension between the particular and the general in his study of his own high-school algebra classroom.

> And I do not expect that my experience generates a set of findings that can be readily applied by others. That said, this sort of stance toward teaching does not imply that one cannot draw conclusions from experience... I have found fault with commonplace views of mathematics for their chilling effect on discussion in the mathematics classroom... I hope to have contributed to a growing literature in which problems of teaching practice are viewed from the perspective of the teacher and seen as intellectually challenging and important, without implying that such problems have "solutions". (Chazan, 2000, p. 149; see also Heaton, 2000)

A good example of the felicitous move from particular to general is Ball and Wilson's (1996) research on how moral issues are addressed in the teaching of mathematics and history. Their own individual, necessarily particular experiences as teachers, speak also to wider questions of morality in the hidden curriculum in general. In this chapter Ball and Wilson make precisely that move: they begin with specific analysis of their own teaching, and then quickly use those insights to make some remarkable arguments about teaching and education in general; (incidentally, for a long list of early works of this type of practitioner enquiry, see the in-text citation that Ball and Wilson offer at the beginning of this article). So Wilson begins by thinking about her own teaching from a somewhat narrow, pedagogical perspective:

> I felt like I was being sucked into a black hole of student understanding, a veritable whirlpool of misconceptions... I found out even more about things we needed to examine, to question. At the same time, I felt like I was getting pulled further and further off the central topic: Why Lansing was the capital of Michigan, and what a capital was. (p. 161)

However, she soon moves on to much bigger questions:

> How do you deal with children's preconceptions about others – for example, Matthew's assumptions about the homeless? (p. 163)

In Ball's section of the article, on teaching fractions, this move is made even more clearly. She begins with several pages of typical practitioner self-investigation, with careful analysis of students' language, attention to the minutiae of specific classroom interactions, and reflection on what her students are actually thinking, much of which has the tone and scope of this excerpt:

> I considered the two girls' apparent understanding of the content. I wondered about what Mei was saying. What did she mean when she said, "I'm not saying the numbers are the same. I'm just saying the part you shade in is the same." Did she think 4/4 and 5/5 both represented one whole? And what was Cassandra focusing on? Numerals? The number of pieces in each rectangle? (p. 167).

Ball then moves onto profound questions of morality in education: what is her responsibility to her students' legitimate arguments, even when they are different from mathematical convention? How does she balance her moral commitments to her students with those to the teacher they will encounter next year? What difference does it make to her responses to her students that they are girls? Or come from a variety of ethnic minorities? Ball and Wilson conclude that one cannot separate the moral from the intellectual in teaching: they are "fused." Whether or not one agrees with their analysis, their argument, or their conclusion, one must be struck by the way in which they build a profound philosophical discussion around their reflections on their own practice, and how their practitioner enquiry becomes not just a springboard to a complex philosophical debate, but actual, valid, legitimate arguments within that debate.

From these examples, we can begin to see why practitioner enquiry is so important. It is a unique way of looking at education which bridges between theory and practice, taking both equally seriously.

Practitioner Enquiry and New Media

The development of this form of practitioner enquiry may be understood in a particular historical context, too: the emergence of new, multimedia technologies. Before the 1980s, the only teachers who could see themselves recorded on videotape were Hollywood actors pretending to be teachers. When camcorders and other new technology became more accessible and affordable, new vistas for practitioner enquiry suddenly opened up; indeed, it is probably no exaggeration to say that this kind of practitioner enquiry would have been impossible without those technological developments. While other earlier traditions of practitioner enquiry (such as the British school, led by Stenhouse (1975), Elliott, and others) did not depend on these technologies, this kind of practitioner enquiry, with its focus on self-study and analysis of one's own documented teaching, is highly technology dependent.

An important early work that recognized and explored this new technological frontier was *Teaching, Multimedia, and Mathematics: Investigations of Real Practice*, which Lampert co-authored with Ball (1998). In this book, Lampert and Ball set out an agenda for teacher education that is rooted in reflective investigation of multimedia samples of actual teaching practice. This isn't strictly speaking "pure" practitioner-enquirer investigation, because their agenda is directed at how their materials can be used by learning teachers, but the practitioner-enquirer mode of thinking is present throughout the book (I return to the place of practitioner enquiry in teacher preparation later).

Lampert and Ball were the pioneers of the use of new technologies in practitioner enquiry. Nevertheless, that technology had its limits.

> At this point, we found ourselves bumping up against the ever-changing boundary between what we could imagine and what was real in the world of new technologies. The dream of hypermedia developers in the 1980s was that large and diverse collections of information... could be stored electronically, accessed instantaneously, cataloged and cross-referenced in multiple ways for multiple users, and – most important of all – linked... Most fundamentally, we learned that what we were able to imagine far outstripped the multimedia hardware and software available at the time to consumers in the educational marketplace. (pp. 55–57)

Today, those limits have been radically reduced. The kind of technological arrangements that required expensive equipment, often operated by specially trained technical personnel, when Lampert and Ball began, are now available to any teacher at much more affordable costs and are for the most part layperson-operable. As an educator, in virtually any physical space or context, I can do all those things that Lampert and Ball dreamt of, at nominal cost. While practitioner enquiry can certainly be conducted without using new technologies, it is much richer when done using videotape, scanned documents, online survey assessments and evaluations, saved smartboard files, and the like. Contemporary technology offers the practitioner enquirer a wealth of potential data sources that were simply unavailable in the past, and it is thus likely that this mode of research will further develop in the coming years.

Practitioner Enquiry in Educational Training

Practitioner Enquiry as Teacher Professional Development

It is a mistake to see practitioner enquiry as just another kind of research, where the word "practitioner" is merely a substitution for "ethnographic," or "statistical," or any number of other qualifiers. We must also take note of the "practitioner" side of the phrase. That is, as well as whatever emerges from the research itself, practitioner enquiry is a form of reflective practice itself that is to be encouraged and advocated. Its fruits are in research *and* in practice. The habits of practitioner enquiry are closely related to those of the "reflective practitioner" (Schön, 1983, 1987), and those of the kind of reflective teachers who we would like to see inhabit the profession. We should note that there is a subtle but important difference between practitioner enquiry and Schön's notion of the reflective practitioner. The latter refers primarily to what Schön calls "reflection in action." Schön's distinction between these two areas is illuminating:

> We may reflect *on* action, thinking back on what we have done in order to discover how our knowing-in-action may have contributed to an unexpected outcome. We may do so after the fact, in tranquility... our reflection has no direct connection to present action. Alternatively, we may reflect in the midst of action without interrupting it. In an *action-present* – a period of time, variable with the context, during which we can still make a difference to the situation at hand – our thinking serves to reshape what we are doing while we are doing it. I shall say, in cases like this, that we reflect-*in*-action. (Schön, 1987, p. 26, his italics)

The practitioner enquirer is therefore engaged in a somewhat different activity from Schön's reflective practitioner, and it's important to note this, because Schön's work has (rightly) been so influential that the ubiquity of his coined phrase might impinge on or blur the importance of practitioner enquiry. Practitioner enquiry is in essence reflection *on* action. The practitioner-researcher, while not denying the importance of Schön's reflection-*in*-action, nevertheless believes that really significant results can be achieved from looking *back* at the educational act, using as much documentation as appropriate or necessary.

Zeichner and Liston (1996) discuss several critiques of Schön's work from the perspective of reflective teaching. These critiques include Schön's ignoring of the importance of social or dialogical work in teacher reflection (indeed, it is noteworthy that many practitioner-researchers collaborate in pairs), and his lack of attention to contextual or milieu-based details that influence teaching. Zeichner and Liston, basing themselves on the work of Griffiths and Tann, two teacher-educators from the UK, suggest that Schön's work be seen as two or three levels within a five-level chart of teacher reflection (Table 1 below):

This helpful table positions practitioner enquiry at levels 4 and 5 and, to my mind, indicates that while Schön's notion of the reflective practitioner has become a fashionable and ubiquitous term, it is really a stepping stone, a mile marker on the first few steps on the way to practitioner enquiry. In research terms, the results of levels 4 and 5 are more likely to be robust and permanent, given the written and

Table 1 Five levels of teacher reflection

1. Rapid reflection	Immediate and automatic reflection-in-action
2. Repair	Thoughtful reflection-in-action
3. Review	Less formal reflection-on-action at a particular point in time
4. Research	More systematic reflection-on-action over a period of time
5. Retheorizing and research	Long-term reflection-on-action informed by public academic theories

Zeichner and Liston (1996, p. 47)

documentary nature of both data and analysis; thus while levels 1, 2, and 3 in the table are important in the realm of practice, levels 4 and 5 (the levels of practitioner enquiry) are perhaps more significant for the world of research.

Practitioner Enquiry in Teacher Preparation

While most practitioner enquiry is written by teachers with several years of experience behind them, it is also increasingly seen as an important resource for teacher preparation and induction. In the widely acclaimed and documented teacher-preparation program at Michigan State University, study of one's own teaching is one of the areas focused upon and a course entitled *Reflection and Inquiry in Teaching Practice* consists of 6 credits out of a total of 48 (Carroll, Featherstone, Featherstone, Feiman-Nemser, & Roosevelt, 2007, pp. 22–23). One of the professional standards for their teaching interns is "work on developing their practice by raising questions and investigating problems and issues that arise in their teaching and seminars (59). One of the themes of the teacher-preparation program at MSU is "inquiry":

> Finally, we learned about the complexities and importance of making inquiry a central thread in the teacher preparation program... Because teachers need the habits and skills of inquiry in order to get good at what they do, and stay good at it as they travel along a changing river, inquiry is a cross-cutting theme in the Team One program... Introducing a program-long curriculum of inquiry... showed [prospective teachers] how they might become makers, not just consumers, of knowledge in teaching.

While the preservice teachers in this program were not fully fledged teacher-researchers, it is clear that they were being trained to be able to inhabit that role in the future, and it is also clear that the habits of investigation into one's own teaching (as well as that of others) were seen by the program leaders as core intellectual and professional habits that aided the interns in their journey to becoming teachers (see also Ball & Cohen, 1999).

Another important benefit of researchers engaging in practitioner research is a level of credibility that is attained in the eyes of practitioners. As Seymour Fox warned (1972, 1997), educational change is unlikely to happen unless teachers are both able and willing to enact it. And (as we noted earlier) one of the greatest complaints of practitioners is that educational scholars live in the "ivory tower" and are unconnected to practice. Scholars who are engaged in practitioner research have more chance of attaining credibility among the community of practitioners and thus influencing practice with their ideas and research.

Critiques of Practitioner Enquiry

Recent surveys of practitioner enquiry in general education have noted several critiques that have been made of it. It is beyond the scope of this chapter to delve into these critiques in depth. Cochran-Smith and Lytle suggest five main complaints made against practitioner enquiry: first, a skepticism that educators thinking about their own practice can actually produce "knowledge" as it is epistemologically understood in the research world; second, a methodological claim that teachers are untrained and unprepared to do proper research (see also Huberman, 1996); third, a critique related to the first two, but specifically rooted in the science-based approach of the Federal Government's educational agenda, in which initiatives like No Child Left Behind rely strongly on more traditional empirical data; fourth, a political critique, suggesting that practitioner enquiry is often motivated by politics rather than pure research; and fifth, a critique that suggests that practitioner enquiry is either highly personal, and therefore not generalizable, or is a valuable professional development tool, but not research.

Zeichner and Noffke (2001) offer a similar but not identical list of critiques. They also focus on teachers' lack of training in research methods, and on the positivist critique that practitioner enquiry cannot be generalized from small environments into larger claims. In addition, they raise the concern that practitioner enquiry takes away from teachers time that could and should be spent teaching, and finally, an interesting suggestion that practitioner enquiry may lead to "stagnation" among teachers who believe that certain ideas have, through that enquiry, been "proven," and that they therefore may cease questioning them (pp. 298–299).

None of these varied critiques is entirely without basis. Nevertheless, as Schwab (1964) has taught us, the syntactic structures of a discipline are never neutral choices, and what appear to be disputes over "knowledge" in the discipline of educational research are in fact disputes over the selection of appropriate syntactic structures. It probably behooves us to view the dispute over the legitimacy of practitioner enquiry in this light.

Practitioner Enquiry in Jewish Education

Practitioner Enquiry in K-12 Jewish Educational Settings

In Jewish education, practitioner enquiry is still in its infancy, but a small number of practitioner researchers have already created a modest corpus of interesting studies. In the following section, I discuss a few such studies.

A recent study by Susie Tanchel (2006), focusing on her own practice as a Bible teacher in a community high school, has its research roots directly in the work of Lampert and others already noted. Tanchel taught Bible in a community Jewish high school. Her approach to Bible sees Biblical scholarship in general, and source criticism in particular, as an essential interpretive approach to which to expose Jewish high-school students. Yet the teaching of source criticism is a highly complex educational dilemma, fraught with difficult questions about its effect on Jewish identity, its developmental appropriateness, its "Jewishness," and so on. In the field of Bible education, many writers have struggled with these questions; see, for example, the treatments by Greenberg (1959, 1990/1995), Dorph (1993, 2002), Holtz (2003), and Sinclair (2004). However, practitioner enquiry offers extra and perhaps more authentic ways to shed light on these questions.

So, for example, Tanchel's practitioner enquiry can do what neither Greenberg, Dorph, or Holtz are able to do in their thinking about the identical research questions: it can investigate the thoughts and voices of her own students, who have actually learned about the documentary hypothesis with her. Her research contains many illuminating windows into the reactions, both cognitive and spiritual, of her high-school students. When she writes that:

> They struggle mightily with how to integrate this material into their religious experience and wonder about the far-reaching implication of doing so. These include concerns about the continued sacredness of the text. (Tanchel, 2008)

We, the readers of the research, know that this is not a cognitive psychologist wondering what might happen, nor a Biblical scholar ruminating on possible implications. It is a real teacher, documenting and analyzing actual reactions received from her students, which took place in the framework of her own classroom teaching. Tanchel juxtaposes her students' reactions with a discussion of the pluralist vision of the school, and offers curricular warrants for the teaching of the documentary hypothesis for a variety of different typologies of student: typologies that are, again, drawn from her own direct classroom experience.

Thus when Tanchel concludes that teaching the documentary hypothesis "offers students openings to continue crafting their own theologies, establishing their own relationship to Jewish sacred texts, and envisioning their own Jewish lives," the reader is aware that her conclusion is rooted in her observations and analyses of her own teaching of actual teenagers in a real-life setting. Tanchel's research position as practitioner enquirer may therefore add more to our knowledge of the problem than research methods that are rooted in philosophy, external interviews, or the discipline itself. As we saw with Ball and Wilson in mathematics and history, practitioner enquiry is able to move from discussion of a particular context onto more general and wider conclusions about the teaching of a subject in general: indeed, about teaching in general.

While Tanchel's probably represents the fullest piece of practitioner enquiry to date in the teaching of Bible in Jewish educational contexts, there have been a few other forays into this area: Epstein (2004), who reflects on her own classroom use of "tableau" as a creative midrashic method; Cousens, Morrison, and Fendrick (2008), who, like Tanchel, discuss the use of the contextual orientation to teaching Bible (Brettler, 2005; Holtz, 2003), but with adults rather than high-school students, and my own experiment (Sinclair, 2005) with practitioner research on Bible, which taught me that when one person is doing the teaching, philosophical reflection on that same teaching, and the written analysis of the former in the light of the latter, powerful and significant insights can be gained.

Just as we noted earlier, with regard to the contribution of practitioner enquiry to the preservice preparation of teachers and their in-service professional development in general education, so too in Jewish education, the potential contribution of practitioner research for improving practice is great. There is no more effective way to improve practice than encouraging practitioners to be more reflective and research-minded about their own work. "A teacher-researcher is not a split personality, but a *more complete teacher*" (Hubbard & Power, 1999, p. 3, their italics). In an ideal world, every educator would also be a researcher on his/her own educational practice. In cutting edge in-service curricular projects, like the Melton-AVI CHAI Standards and Benchmarks project, or the Mandel Teacher Education Institute, teachers are encouraged to research each other's classrooms and to investigate their own teaching using video and student work artifacts. And when we think about Jewish educational research agendas, the more that research is directly rooted in the real and tangible issues and questions of educational life, the more it is likely to be compelling, meaningful, and useful.

Practitioner Enquiry in Jewish Tertiary Settings

Elie Holzer's (2006) and Orit Kent's (2006) work on the Beit Midrash component of a teacher-preparation program is an example of practitioner enquiry in a tertiary setting (see also Feiman-Nemser, 2006). Holzer and Kent are both faculty members in a teacher-preparation program, educators whose daily business is to help their students become more skilled Jewish teachers. Holzer and Kent's studies of their work use the same method as Ball and Wilson (1996) did: they begin from the particular and move to the general; from data and interpretation of their own particular program and the students in it, toward more grandiose goals about the field of teacher education in general.

In one statement made by Kent, we can see this move from the particular to the general happening in three clearly discernible steps. "For the last three summers," writes Kent, "I have been collecting data from a modern *beit midrash* [a traditional Jewish study hall, now often used to refer to many forms of non-academic communal Jewish learning] that I co-design and co-teach... my study of *hevruta* [the format of traditional Jewish learning, in which students study text in pairs while engaged in conversation and debate about the text] learning in the *DeLeT beit midrash* is intended to help develop a conceptualization of this often used but seldom studied form of learning." We can break down this statement into three steps as follows:

1. "For the last three summers I have been collecting data from a modern *beit midrash* that I co-design and co-teach..." *[step 1: practitioner researcher credentials]*
2. "My study of *hevruta* learning in the *DeLeT beit midrash*" *[step 2: particular, narrow-focused study of particular practitioner context]*
3. "Is intended to help develop a conceptualization of this often used but seldom studied form of learning" *[step 3: suggestion that the practitioner enquiry may have larger and broader applications].*

These three steps represent in skeleton form the research rationale of this particular version of practitioner enquiry.

Two further comments are worth making here. First, Kent's research method is so entrenched in this particular-to-general mode of practitioner enquiry that she argues that from a close reading of just *one* hevruta session between two of her students, she is able to draw out conceptual conclusions that are applicable to a wider field. Second, while Kent's interpretation is informed by a variety of theoretical frameworks, such as research on teaching and learning, cooperative learning, classroom discourse, and norms of social interaction, it is also clear that her own wisdom of practice as the co-designer and co-teacher of this program informs and enriches her interpretation of her data at least as much as these external theoretical frameworks. An outside researcher, examining the same data with the same external theoretical frameworks, would not have been able to write the rich research paper that Kent, as practitioner-researcher, was able to.

Another practitioner-researcher in a Jewish tertiary setting is the emeritus professor of theology at the Jewish Theological Seminary, Neil Gillman. Gillman, although he does not use the formal language of practitioner enquiry that we have so far explored in this chapter, is, I would suggest, a practitioner enquirer nevertheless. Gillman's writing, as well as focusing on "pure" subject matter, also focuses on his reflection on his own work as a teacher of Jewish theology. His collection of essays, *Doing Jewish Theology*, contains two articles that explicitly deal with his teaching and many more in which the subject occurs implicitly. In these essays, Gillman (2008a, b) refers in an organic fashion to his research questions as a teacher, to statements his students have made and written, to documentations of and reflections on his own pedagogical content knowledge (again, he doesn't use that term himself), and to the ways in which his classroom activity has changed over the years: all elements that fit squarely into the discipline of practitioner enquiry.

Gillman's stance as a practitioner enquirer has been an inspiration for some of my recent work, as seen below.

Suggestions for Practitioner Enquiry in Jewish Educational Contexts

We have seen that the teaching of Bible is one area of Jewish education that has seen some early practitioner enquiry work. This chapter ends with a series of suggestions for practitioner enquiry in various other areas of Jewish education.

Formal educational contexts in the general educational world have been the ones that have been most researched by practitioner-enquirers, and the day-school context in the Jewish world is fertile ground for such work. The formal educational setting contains many structural elements that facilitate practitioner enquiry, such as the easy availability of electric outlets, possibilities for substitutes or colleagues to assist with data collection, the increasingly widespread adoption of technology and software such as PowerPoint presentations, smart boards, and online forums, that can be saved and documented, and the large quantity of written student work available for study. It behooves us to train preservice teachers in the skills of practitioner enquiry and to create as many opportunities as possible for in-service teachers to practise these skills. Schools of education should be encouraged to include practitioner enquiry classes in their requirements, just as MSU does.

However, practitioner enquiry need not only happen in formal, full-time educational contexts. Summer camps, Israel trips, congregational schools, and alternative Shabbat services are all contexts which are well suited to serious and systematic practitioner enquiry. While these contexts may have greater logistical barriers than practitioner enquiry in the day school, creative solutions can almost always be found for practitioner enquirers in these and other contexts.

One example of an educational context that could be greatly illuminated by more work by practitioner-researchers is the organized trip to Israel, or what is often known as the "Israel Experience." We have a reasonably significant corpus of research that investigates different aspects of the sociology and culture of the educational and social experience of participants in various forms of Israel trip. These include ethnographic studies of teenagers' trips (Goldberg, Heilman, & Kirshenblatt-Gimblett, 2002; Heilman, 1999); participant-observer reports of adult education and professional development trips (for example, Pomson & Grant, 2004); conceptual or philosophical discussions about the very nature of the Israel trip (for example, Kelner, 2002); and various evaluations of trips' efficacy along a range of measurable criteria (Saxe & Chazan, 2008). (Most recently, see Kelner's (2010) extensive study of Birthright trips). What we don't have is practitioner enquiry, and I would argue that our thinking about the Israel experience would be immeasurably improved by such additions to the research corpus. In this and other informal contexts, there are many practical, financial, and logistical barriers that are greater than in formal contexts, but it is clear that this is the direction that we should be moving in.

A Vignette: Practitioner Enquiry on the Israel Experience

I end this chapter with a brief summary and analysis of a practitioner enquiry paper (Sinclair, Backenroth, & Bell-Kligler, 2010) in the context of the Israel experience, in order to illustrate the kinds of thinking that practitioner enquiry can contribute to Jewish education. The practitioner-enquirers – Backenroth, Bell-Kligler, and Sinclair (the author of this chapter) – are all practitioners as well as researchers of Jewish education. The subject of our research was a seminar in Israel for students doing an MA in Jewish Education at the Davidson School of Education of the Jewish Theological Seminary. This seminar has run annually since 2004, and the three of us, to varying extents, have been its creators, leaders, and evaluators since its inception.

The seminar is entitled "Visions and Voices of Israel" and attempts to bring these young educators-in-training into innovative professional conversations about Israel education and engagement. We are interested in having them explore what it might mean to engage with Israel with all its complexities; how to create commitment to Israel because, despite, and along with, its realities (Gringras, 2006; Sinclair, 2003, 2006, 2009).

As practitioners, one thing that we noticed in our students' responses to the seminar over the years is that many of them find it troubling and painful to move from what might be called a "romanticized-idealized" relationship with Israel to one that is more complex and nuanced. Some students ended the seminar with these feelings of pain and even anger unresolved. To further complicate the picture, we began to see an emerging phenomenon of students coming back to us 2 or 3 years after their time on the seminar, and saying that only after that extended period of reflection have they begun to truly see its profound educational benefits. Our own sense of unease was deepened by considering the educational career and approach of one of our senior colleagues, Neil Gillman. As we noted above, he can also be seen as an example of a practitioner researcher in a tertiary setting. Like us, Gillman seeks to move students from romantic understanding to more complex ones. His theology classes confront and challenge students with the implications of Bible scholarship for traditional understanding of revelation. In a recent exploration of Gillman's philosophical and pedagogical positions, it is suggested that Gillman is "disturbing" to some students; Gillman nevertheless "believes that the potential discomfort associated with confronting such an understanding of marginality – not only for the philosophically minded, but rather for all of his students – is a necessary step in the professional preparation of rabbinical students" (Tauber, 2007). To what extent are Gillman's struggles the same struggles with which we as Israel educators must also grapple? As practitioner-enquirers, we decided to explore these difficulties ourselves.

The Process of Practitioner Enquiry

What, then, as practitioner-enquirers, did we do? What is the process of practitioner enquiry? To begin with, we spent a lot of time reading, analyzing, thinking about, and talking about our students' responses to the program. Each year our students filled in extensive evaluations, using online data collection software; through these evaluations, we were able to probe the thinking of our students in the immediate aftermath of the seminar. We also collected and analyzed many emails that we had received from students days, weeks, and months after their time in Israel. Since the seminar required no formal written work on the part of the students, these evaluation responses and emails became our primary window into what our students were thinking, feeling, and asking. We did not, as Ball and Lampert did, watch our students on videotape, transcribing and analyzing their words, but, through this internet technology, we were able to collate a large quantity of authentic student voices.

As we analyzed our students' voices, we also went back and analyzed our own planning and thinking. We went back over emails we had sent each other, planning documents we had written, and handouts from activities that we had run. We tried to reconstruct and reconsider our intended outcomes, and compared these with our students' voices.

We then sought to contextualize our findings within theoretical and conceptual frameworks offered by educational, sociological, and psychological researchers. Not content with just stating that this was what we had seen, we attempted to place our observations within wider frameworks. We moved (as Ball did, above) from the particular to the general.

This chapter is not the place for an extended discussion of the interpretations we made, or the conclusions we drew. Briefly, we began to understand that it is not easy for students to move – or, more accurately, be moved – from their previous romanticized-idealized relationship with Israel into a more complex, multidimensional, "reality"-based relationship. Foundational beliefs are subverted; deep-held convictions are questioned; identity based on comfort must instead be based on disequilibrium. We were aided by the approach of Kegan (1982), who claims that transitions from one stage of identity to another involve leaving a consolidated self behind before any new self can take its place; until a new balance is achieved, the individual feels a loss of control and is in a state of disequilibrium. As we reflected on our own practice, we saw that it may well have been this sense of disequilibrium that our students found most upsetting. Our research therefore led us to some tentative conclusions about how to interpret this phenomenon present in some of our students' immediate frustration and subsequent belated understanding: namely, that we should accept these transitions as necessary and perhaps even desirable parts of the educational process that we hoped they would go through. Our research also led us ask to further questions about our own practice: is it okay to leave students in disequilibrium? How might we provide better scaffolding to help them move beyond that disequilibrium into a more nuanced but consolidated position? How do we respond personally to students who express anger and frustration? As we have seen several times so far in this chapter, practitioner enquiry enables us to move from particular contexts to larger educational questions.

The advantages of practitioner enquiry in this research setting are clear. On a most basic level, the feedback loop between practice, evaluation, and re-imagined practice based on evaluation, is much shorter when practitioner enquiry is the mode of research used for evaluation. Outside researchers would have to spend a considerable amount of time learning about the program, its goals, language, and details; talking with us, the practitioners, to help develop the research questions; and then interpreting and formulating the data into a form in which it could be usefully channeled back to us. Instead, we, as practitioner researchers, were able to do all three of these steps much more quickly, and most often, not in linear, but in a more helpful circular fashion. As we do the research, we become more skilled practitioners; as our practitioner skills and knowledge base develop, our research questions and analytical tools become sharper and more focused; as knowledge from our research is created, it is transferred to the field in "real time."

Looking Forward: Encouraging Practitioner Enquiry in Jewish Education

Practitioner enquiry, therefore, holds significant promise as a mode of research for the field of Jewish education. What steps can we make in the field of Jewish education in order to encourage and seed further research of this type? I would suggest that there are two major areas in which we need to make progress: appropriately, given the nomenclature of this mode of research, those areas are, on the one hand, persuading enquirers (researchers) to do more as practitioners, and on the other, persuading practitioners to do more as enquirers.

First, there are many researchers in the academic world of Jewish education who used to be practitioners. A glance through the list of authors of this handbook will quickly indicate that the vast majority of writers have also been practitioners too. Some of these experiences may have been in the dim and distant past, as teachers or camp counselors and division heads, but for some of the researchers in our field, their experiences as practitioners are closer and perhaps even current. How many researchers of Jewish education teach adult-education classes in their local communities? How many writers in this handbook teach a session every now and then at the local summer camp, day school, or synagogue school? My guess is (certainly among the younger members of the field) that the number is quite considerable. And, of course, if we consider the teaching of graduate-level classes in Jewish education, nearly all the writers in this handbook are, like Neil Gillman, practitioners too. The field of Jewish educational research would be greatly enriched if we were able to provide incentives for researchers to increase the amount of time they spend being practitioners and to use that time as grist for their research mill. This means that academic institutions must rethink structural questions like what counts as course load for educational researchers, and what kinds of achievements should be considered in making decisions about tenure. These two structural issues in particular are significant barriers for practitioner enquiry, and those interested in seeing more practitioner enquiry in Jewish educational research would do well to seek to lower those barriers (I would also suggest that practitioner enquirers have significant pedagogical advantages in the teaching of graduate-level classes, given their proximity to the field and therefore their increased sensitivity to the actual challenges their students will face; nevertheless, this issue is beyond the scope of the current chapter).

Second, there are many practitioners in the field who, with the right incentives, assistance, and structural facilitation, could make valuable contributions to educational research. There are dozens of thoughtful, reflective, research-minded day-school teachers who could offer significant papers on the myriad issues of day-school education: barriers in achieving differentiated instruction; approaches toward pluralism in text study; the tension between the goals of Hebrew language acquisition and philosophical classroom discourse; and so on. There are dozens of congregational school principals who could offer significant papers on questions like the influence of the milieu on the learner; formal versus informal educational methodologies in the congregational school context; possibilities for professional development in environments with many part-time staff members; and so on. There are dozens of camp directors, division heads, and camp heads of education, who could offer significant papers on questions like the most successful enculturating frameworks within camp; the place of children with special needs in the camp environment; the contribution of outdoor education to Jewish educational philosophy; and so on. In these questions, and countless others like them, the field of Jewish educational research is simply missing the voices of these potential practitioner enquirers, and the field is impoverished as a result.

Several recent initiatives have sought to tap into these potential contributions to practitioner enquiry. The Mandel Center for Studies in Jewish Education at Brandeis University has developed a project on Bridging Scholarship and Pedagogy in Jewish Studies. This project spawned two conferences, the first in 2005, and the second in 2008, on the teaching of Bible and the teaching of Rabbinic literature respectively. The purposes of this project are immediately recognizable as supportive of the work of practitioner enquiry:

(1) Teachers of Jewish studies at all levels and settings share common questions and may productively engage in collaborative inquiries, even if they arrive at different answers.
(2) Jewish education ought not to be isolated from the academic pursuit of Jewish studies scholarship.
(3) Meaningful research into the practice of pedagogy in Jewish studies can and should be conducted by teachers at all levels and settings, both within and outside of academia. The subfields of Jewish studies will benefit from the development of a "scholarship of teaching," much as has occurred in the fields of mathematics, history, and elsewhere (http://www.brandeis.edu/mandel/projects/bridginginitiative.html, retrieved July 13th, 2009).

A conference on Israel education, held at the Melton Centre for Jewish Education of the Hebrew University in 2009, also contained several papers in the area of practitioner enquiry.

What else could Jewish educational systems do in order to facilitate such contributions by practitioners? It is my belief that an award must be established to enable educators in varied contexts to apply for funding that would enable them to conduct practitioner enquiry research projects. Practitioners would apply to this award with a research project proposal, and each year, a certain number of awards would be granted to successful applicants. The awards would provide funding to the applicant's educational institution with the proviso that the funds be used to grant the applicant a reduction in course load or administrative responsibilities significant enough to enable the person to spend the year doing some serious practitioner research.

It has been said that a structural weakness in Jewish education is that it consists of many "silos" that are not sufficiently linked together (Wertheimer, 2005). In the context of Jewish education as a whole, certainly as presented in this handbook, the two biggest silos that are not yet linked are the worlds of educational theory and educational practice. It is high time that we linked those two silos together.

If the field of Jewish education could make the necessary structural changes in order to facilitate practitioner enquiry from both of these sides – enabling researchers to get out in the field more and apply their research skills to their own practical endeavors, and granting practitioners the time to do serious enquiry on their own practice – then, as a field, Jewish education would be immeasurably enriched.

References

Ball, D. L., & Cohen, D. K. (1999). Developing practice, developing practitioners. In G. Sykes & L. Darling Hammond (Eds.), *Teaching as the learning profession* (pp. 3–32). San Francisco: Jossey-Bass.

Ball, D. L., & Wilson, S. M. (1996). Integrity in teaching: Recognizing the fusion of the moral and intellectual. *American Educational Research Journal, 33*(1), 155–192.

Brettler, M. Z. (2005). *How to read the Bible*. Philadelphia: Jewish Publication Society.

Carroll, D., Featherstone, H., Featherstone, J., Feiman-Nemser, S., & Roosevelt, D. (2007). *Transforming teacher education: Reflections from the field*. Cambridge, MA: Harvard Education Press.

Chazan, D. (2000). *Beyond formulas in mathematics and teaching: Dynamics of the high school algebra classroom*. New York: Teachers College Press.

Cochran-Smith, M., & Lytle, S. L. (1990). Research on teaching and teacher research: The issues that divide. *Educational Researcher, 19*(2), 2–11.

Cochran-Smith, M., & Lytle, S. L. (2004). Practitioner inquiry, knowledge, and university culture. In J. J. Loughran, M. L. Hamilton, V. K. LaBoskey, & T. Russell (Eds.), *International handbook of self-study of teaching and teacher education practices* (pp. 601–649). The Netherlands: Springer.

Cousens, B., Morrison, J. S., & Fendrick, S. P. (2008). Using the contextual orientation to facilitate the study of Bible with generation X. *Journal of Jewish Education, 74*(1), 6–28.

Dorph, G. Z. (1993). *Conceptions and preconceptions: A study of prospective Jewish educators' beliefs about torah*. New York: Jewish Theological Seminary of America.

Dorph, G. Z. (2002). What do teachers need to know to teach Torah? In B. I. Cohen & A. Ofek (Eds.), *Essays in education and Judaism in honor of Joseph S Lukinsky*. New York: Jewish Theological Seminary of America.

Epstein, S. D. (2004). Reimagining literacy practices: Creating living midrash from ancient texts through Tableau. *Journal of Jewish Education, 70*(1–2), 60–73.

Feiman-Nemser, S. (2006). Beit midrash for teachers: An experiment in teacher preparation. *Journal of Jewish Education, 72*(3), 161–181.

Fox, S. (1972). A practical image of "the practical." *Curriculum Theory Network, 10*, 45–57.

Fox, S. (1997). *Vision at the heart*. Jerusalem: Mandel Institute.

Gillman, N. (2008a). On the religious education of American rabbis. In *Doing Jewish theology: God, torah and Israel in modern Judaism*. Woodstock, VT: Jewish Lights.

Gillman, N. (2008b). Teaching the akedah. In *Doing Jewish theology: God, torah and Israel in modern Judaism*. Woodstock, VT: Jewish Lights.

Goldberg, H., Heilman, S., & Kirshenblatt-Gimblett, B. (2002). *The Israel experience: Studies in youth travel and Jewish identity*. Jerusalem: Melton Centre for Jewish Education.

Greenberg, M. (1959). On teaching the Bible in religious schools. *Jewish Education, 29*(3), 45–53.

Greenberg, M. (1990/1995). To whom and for what should a Bible commentator be responsible? In M. Greenberg (Ed.), *Studies in the Bible and Jewish Thought* (pp. 235–243). Philadelphia: Jewish Publication Society.

Gringras, R. (2006). *Wrestling and Hugging: Alternative Paradigms for the Diaspora-Israel Relationship*, from http://www.makomisrael.net/NR/rdonlyres/05584E5A-ED59-45BF-8485-E5F5481B6496/57984/MAKOMWrestlingandHugging.pdf

Heaton, R. M. (2000). *Teaching mathematics to the new standards: Relearning the dance*. New York: Teachers College Press.

Heilman, S. (1999). From T-shirts to peak experiences: Teens, the Israel trip and Jewish identity. In Y. Rich & M. Rosenak (Eds.), *Abiding challenges: Research perspectives on Jewish education* (pp. 231–250). Tel Aviv: Freund Publishing House Ltd.

Holtz, B. W. (2003). *Textual knowledge: Teaching the Bible in theory and in practice*. New York: Jewish Theological Seminary of America.

Holzer, E. (2006). What connects "good" teaching, text study and Hevruta learning? A conceptual argument. *Journal of Jewish Education, 72*(3), 183–204.

Hubbard, R. S., & Power, B. M. (1999). *Living the questions: A guide for teacher researchers.* York, ME: Stenhouse.

Hubbard, R. S., & Power, B. M. (2003). *The art of classroom inquiry: A handbook for teacher-researchers.* Portsmouth, NH: Heinemann.

Huberman, M. (1996). Moving mainstream: Taking a closer look at teacher research. *Language Arts, 73*, 124–140.

Kegan, R. (1982). *The evolving self: Problem and process in human development.* Cambridge, MA: Harvard University Press.

Kelner, S. (2002). *Almost pilgrims: Authenticity, identity and the extra-ordinary on a Jewish tour of Israel.* New York: City University of New York.

Kelner, S. (2010). *Tours that bind: Diaspora, Pilgrimage, and Israeli Birthright Tourism.* New York: NYU Press.

Kent, O. (2006). Interactive text study: A case of Hevruta learning. *Journal of Jewish Education, 72*(3), 205–232.

Lampert, M. (2001). *Teaching problems and the problems of teaching.* New Haven and London: Yale University Press.

Lampert, M., & Ball, D. L. (1998). *Teaching, multimedia and mathematics: Investigations of real practice.* New York: Teachers College Press.

Matthews, G. B. (1980). *Philosophy and the young child.* Cambridge, MA: Harvard University Press.

Pomson, A., & Grant, L. D. (2004). Getting personal with professional development: The case of short-term trips to Israel for Diaspora teachers. In J. Bashi, M. B. Peretz, & A. Bouganim (Eds.), *Education and professional training.* Jerusalem: Jewish Agency.

Saxe, L., & Chazan, B. (2008). *Ten days of birthright Israel: A journey in young adult identity.* Boston: Brandeis University Press.

Schwab, J. J. (1964). Problems, topics, issues. In S. Elam (Ed.), *Education and the structure of knowledge* (pp. 4–47). Chicago: Rand McNally.

Schön, D. A. (1983). *The reflective practitioner: How professionals think in action.* New York: Basic Books.

Schön, D. A. (1987). *Educating the reflective practitioner.* San Francisco and London: Jossey-Bass Publishers.

Shulman, L. S. (1986). Those who understand: Knowledge growth in teaching. *Educational Researcher, 15*(2), 4–14.

Sinclair, A. (2003). Beyond black and white: Teaching Israel in light of the matzav. *Conservative Judaism, 55*(3), 69–80.

Sinclair, A. (2004). A Dialogical approach to critical Bible study: The use of Schwabian deliberation to integrate the work of Bible scholars with educational philosophy. *Religious Education, 99*(2), 107–124.

Sinclair, A. (2005). An exercise in the theory of practice: The Hermeneutics of Bibliodrama in the Sinclair classroom. *Journal of Jewish Education, 70*(3), 61–73.

Sinclair, A. (2006). A conservative Jewish educational approach to Post-Zionism. *Conservative Judaism, 59*(1), 29–38.

Sinclair, A. (2009). A new heuristic device for the analysis of Israel education: Observations from a Jewish summer camp. *Journal of Jewish Education, 75*, 1.

Sinclair, A., Backenroth, B., & Bell-Kligler, R. (2010). Breaking myths, building identity: Practitioner-researcher reflections on running an Israel seminar for Jewish education graduate students. *International Journal of Jewish Education Research, 1*, 49–74.

Stenhouse, L. (1975). *An introduction to curriculum research and development.* London: Heinemann Educational Books.

Tanchel, S. (2006). *Honoring Voices: Listening to the Texts and the Teacher, the Scholars and the Students.* Boston: Brandeis University.

Tanchel, S. (2008). "A Judaism that does not hide": Teaching the documentary hypothesis in a pluralistic Jewish high school. *Journal of Jewish Education, 74*(1), 29–52.

Tanner, L. N. (1997). *Dewey's laboratory school: Lessons for today*. New York: Teachers College Press.

Tauber, S. (2007). Between reason and emotion: Intellectual and existential tensions in contemporary rabbinic education; a portrait of Neil Gillman. *Journal of Jewish Education, 73*(3), 227–259.

Wertheimer, J. (2005). *Linking the silos: How to accelerate the momentum in Jewish education today*. New York: AVI CHAI.

Zeichner, K. M., & Liston, D. P. (1996). *Reflective teaching: An introduction*. Mahwah, NJ: Lawrence Erlbaum Associates.

Zeichner, K. M., & Noffke, S. E. (2001). Practitioner research. In V. Richardson (Ed.), *Handbook of research on teaching* (4th ed., pp. 298–330). Washington DC: American Educational Research Association.

Preparing Teachers for Jewish Schools: Enduring Issues in Changing Contexts

Sharon Feiman-Nemser

Skepticism about teachers and teacher education runs deep in American society and both have been easy targets of criticism by sympathetic and unsympathetic observers. The familiar quip says it all: "Those who can, do; those who can't, teach; those who can't teach, teach teachers." Such sentiments are deeply rooted in beliefs about gender, social class, and intellectual activity. They also reflect the history of teaching and teacher education in the United States, a story of professional aspirations colliding with social forces and political realities.

Since the establishment of normal schools in the mid-nineteenth century, the question of how best to recruit and prepare teachers has been hotly debated. Some leaders like Cyrus Pierce, president of the first normal school, concentrated on "making better teachers," but their ideals were quickly overwhelmed by the insatiable demand for teachers to staff the rapidly growing public school system. Still, the debate continued among advocates of technical, liberal, and professional education as normal schools became teachers' colleges in the opening decades of the twentieth century and some of the most prestigious universities created departments and schools of education (Borrowman, 1956).

A projected teacher shortage and persistent concerns about the achievement gap heightened concerns about teacher quality and qualifications at the start of the twenty-first century. Despite general agreement that teaching matters and growing empirical support for this claim, there is still no consensus about how to get good teachers. Some advocate strong programs of professional preparation (National Commission on Teaching & America's Future, 2006), while others argue for alternate routes that bypass most requirements in favor of academic background and on-the-job learning (Finn & Madigan, 2001). Despite changing times and conditions, questions about recruiting and preparing teachers persist.

Where does Jewish teaching and teacher education fit into this narrative? One might expect that the high value Judaism places on learning and intellectual achievement would result in a high regard for Jewish teachers and an appreciation for the knowledge, skills, and dispositions they need to do the important work of Jewish

S. Feiman-Nemser (✉)
Brandeis University, Boston, MA, USA
e-mail: snemser@brandeis.edu

education. This is far from the case. As Leo Honor, an important figure in the movement to modernize Jewish education and professionalize Jewish teaching in the twentieth century, writes,

> One of the anomalies of Jewish life has been the contrast between the intensity with which Jews...have concentrated upon the task of instructing the young to live in accordance with the precepts of Torah and their comparative lack of concern with the qualifications of the personnel entrusted with the responsibility of performing the duties which this task entails. (Gannes, 1965, p. 177)

The shortage of qualified personnel is a recurring theme in the history of Jewish education in America, linked to the improvement of Jewish schooling and the future of Jewish life in this country. For the early-twentieth-century reformers, replacing the old fashioned *melamed* with American-born, American-trained teachers was a key element in modernizing Jewish schools and safeguarding the future of Judaism in the new world.

Concerns about the quality and quantity of Jewish educators persist today as career opportunities for women expand, young people anticipate having multiple careers, and issues of status and remuneration persist.

This chapter examines two "experiments" in Jewish teacher preparation, one historical and one contemporary.[1] The first occurred in the Hebrew teachers colleges, established in large Jewish communities before, during, and after World War I to provide qualified teachers for "modern," communal Talmud Torahs. The second is currently taking place in a handful of programs designed to prepare teachers mainly for community and non-Orthodox day schools which have sprung up since the 1980s. In both cases, the emergence of a new kind of Jewish school which depended on a new kind of Jewish teacher led to the creation of new programs of Jewish teacher preparation.

Two vantage points frame this inquiry. First, I want to understand these Jewish teacher-education initiatives as educational responses to a set of conditions, needs, and aspirations within the American Jewish community and among its educational leaders. So I ask, what circumstances led to the founding of these new programs for Jewish teachers? What were/are the programs like? What ideas about the role of the teacher and the purposes of Jewish education guide(d) the selection of content and the design of learning opportunities?

Second, I am interested in how these experiments in Jewish teacher education relate to prevailing ideas and practice regarding the education of teachers. Thus I consider the teacher training programs offered by the Hebrew teachers colleges in relation to developments in American teacher education in the early twentieth century. I also consider how contemporary efforts to prepare day-school teachers relate to current ideas and debates about the preparation of teachers in the twenty-first century. My goal is to bring together lines of historical and contemporary inquiry in Jewish education with general scholarship about teaching and teacher education

---

[1] Special thanks to Gail Dorph, Jon Levisohn, and Alex Pomson for their thoughtful feedback and to Jonathan Krasner for directing me to historical sources.

to identify and illuminate some enduring issues in the preparation of teachers for Jewish schools.

The chapter has two main sections. In the first, I briefly examine the rise of the Hebrew teachers colleges, then focus on the teacher training program at the Teachers Institute (TI) of the Jewish Theological Seminary. I chose TI as my example because of its national and local status and its eventual relationship with Teachers College, Columbia University, a pioneer in professional teacher education, leadership development, and educational research. The second section focuses on the recent development of a handful of programs designed to prepare teachers mainly for non-Orthodox day schools. Here my example is DeLeT (Day School Leadership in Teaching), a program I created at Brandeis University in 2001. In both sections, I consider how each of the focal programs relates to prevailing ideas about teacher education. A brief conclusion offers some comparative observations and suggests an agenda for future research.

From *Melamdim* to Professional Teachers

Between 1881 and 1914, unprecedented numbers of Jewish immigrants came to the United States from Eastern Europe and settled mainly in large cities. These immigrants faced enormous challenges in building a life and making a living. They embraced free public education as the key to becoming American and securing a better social and economic future. Without a communal system of Jewish education, they had difficulty providing an adequate Jewish education for their children to supplement their secular studies.

The immigrants tried to transplant the educational institutions they had developed in Europe, including the *heder*, a one-man private Hebrew school for young boys, the *yeshiva*, and the *Talmud Torah*, a charity school for children of the poor. Some, inspired by cultural Zionism and the revival of the Hebrew language, created schools modeled after the *heder metukan*, or improved heder, where they pioneered the natural method of teaching Hebrew, *ivrit b'ivrit*, as a living language (Dushkin, 1918; Pilch, 1969; Rauch, 2006). These eventually inspired the modern Talmud Torahs which reached their high point in the 1920s.

Jewish educational leaders surveying the state of Jewish education at the time found "medieval" and "modern" forms of Jewish schooling, often existing side by side (Dushkin, 1918; Hurwich, 1958; Kaplan & Cronson, 1949). They directed most of their critique at the infamous *hadarim* where untrained teachers used rote methods to produce a mechanical reading of Hebrew. Most Jewish children received no Jewish education at all, and those who did learned little and often developed negative attitudes toward Judaism. Something had to be done.

Visionary leaders thought the problem should be tackled at the communal level. They believed that the future of Jewish life in America depended, in part, on the preparation of American-educated Jewish teachers who would embody the old-world tradition of textual knowledge and love of learning and the new-world commitment to modern methods of scholarship and pedagogy. Their vision found expression in the Hebrew teachers colleges, established in major Jewish cities to train Jewish teachers and advance Jewish learning.

The Hebrew Teachers College

Two related developments enabled the formation and growth of the Hebrew teachers colleges—the creation of "modern," communal Talmud Torahs and the takeover of their curriculum by members of the Hebraist movement in America. In response to the problematic state of Jewish education, Jewish communal organizations established local boards or bureaus of Jewish education, beginning with New York in 1910. These agencies created community-wide schools based on the Talmud Torah model.[2] According to Mintz, the incipient Talmud Torah movement represented a kind of "popular front" for young men and women committed to the Hebraist ideology. They turned the supplementary Talmud Torahs into "Hebrew" schools by advancing an intensive Jewish education based around *Eretz Yisrael*, the Hebrew language and a cultural Jewish nationalist interpretation of the Bible, Jewish history, and the Jewish holidays (Ackerman, 1993; Mintz, 1993).[3]

Most of the Hebrew teachers colleges were established after World War I as larger Jewish communities began to address the needs and problems of Jewish education in an organized way.[4] Besides their stated purpose of training teachers, they offered advanced Jewish study to Talmud Torah graduates, eventually setting standards for the lower schools and becoming the capstone of local systems of Jewish education.

As their name implies, they had a strong *Hebraist* ethos fostered by the study of Hebrew language and literature and by the use of Hebrew as the medium of instruction. Each institution reflected the personality of its leaders and local community, yet for all the differences between them, the Hebrew teachers colleges had a remarkably uniform "language-centered and heritage-centered" curriculum (Janowsky, 1967, p. 331).

The Hebrew teachers colleges never fully met their goal of supplying all or even most of the Hebrew teachers needed by the market. Still they produced a considerable number of graduates[5] and established a new model of Jewish teacher

---

[2] Benderly saw the Talmud Torah as the most promising model because it was a communal institution like the public school and because it had already been reshaped into an afternoon school so as not to conflict with public schooling.

[3] School systems inspired by this model were created in New York, Boston, Baltimore, Detroit, Minneapolis, Indianapolis, Pittsburgh, and Chicago.

[4] The institutions established during this general time frame include Gratz College, Philadelphia (1898); Teachers Institute of the Jewish Theological Seminary, New York (1910); Baltimore Hebrew College (1919); Herzliyah Teachers Institute, New York (1921); Hebrew Teachers College of Boston (1921); Chicago College of Jewish Studies (1924); and Cleveland College of Jewish Studies (1926).

[5] Margolis (1964) states that 2,191 teachers graduated from the six Jewish teacher training institutions which he studied (Gratz, Cleveland College of Jewish Studies, Boston Hebrew College, Herzliyah, Teachers Institutes at JTS and Yeshiva University) from the times of their opening

preparation which raised the standard of Jewish schooling in their area. Surveys of the early courses of study reveal some common patterns (Dinin, 1967; Margolis, 1964; Ackerman, 1989), for example, the subordination of pedagogy to subject matter and the lack of differentiation between education for teachers and education for scholarship.

While such generalizations provide an overview, they convey little of the enacted curriculum and culture of these institutions. For that, I turn to the program at the Teachers Institute of the Jewish Theological Seminary. Established in 1909 to supply trained teachers for the Jewish schools of New York City, the Institute served as the prototype for Hebrew teachers colleges around the country and influenced Jewish education far beyond the confines of New York.

Teachers Institute of the Jewish Theological Seminary[6]

Solomon Schechter, President of the Jewish Theological Seminary, recognized the urgent need in America for trained teachers. In 1910, he appointed Mordecai Kaplan, a 28-year-old graduate of the Seminary, as principal of the Teachers Institute of the Jewish Theological Seminary. Thus began a most exciting experiment in Jewish teacher education.

Under Kaplan's leadership, the Institute became a partner with the newly established Bureau of Jewish Education, a center of Hebraist culture, and a platform for Kaplan's teaching of "reconstructionist" Judaism (Kaufman, 1997). Shortly after the Institute was established, the Jewish community of New York (the *Kehillah*) created the first Bureau of Jewish Education and appointed Dr. Samson Benderly as its director.[7] Kaplan's collaborations with the Bureau and with Benderly, the father of modern Jewish education in America, placed the Teachers Institute at the forefront of these reforms.

Benderly needed teachers for his modern Talmud Torahs and the Teachers Institute needed students to train. The requirement that schools under the Bureau's supervision could not hire untrained teachers enabled the Institute to become a full-time school offering 18–20 h of coursework during the weekday mornings, rather than relying exclusively on part-time or evening classes. The Institute reorganized into two divisions, an academic course for those who wanted to continue their Jewish studies, and a professional course for aspiring Hebrew teachers. This change

---

through 1950. Hurwich (1958) gives a figure of 1,885 graduates among the eight institutions he studied—the same six as Margolis plus Baltimore and the Hebrew Training School for Girls in New York—from their beginnings through 1949. He concludes that this output met 20–25% of the need.

[6]This portrait draws heavily on David Kaufman's (1997) detailed and illuminating account of the development and early history of the Teachers Institute at the Jewish Theological Seminar.

[7]Benderly emigrated to the United States from Palestine in order to complete his medical studies. He settled in Baltimore where he pioneered the use of *ivrit b'ivrit* in an experimental Hebrew school. Benderly eventually left medicine to devote himself to Jewish education.

coincided with a move in 1916 to new quarters close to the immigrant neighborhoods where most of the TI students lived. During the 15 years that the Institute spent at the Hebrew Technical Institute on the Lower East Side, the faculty and students created a self-conscious, educative community and TI became "the leading vocational school for Jewish teachers in America" (Kaufman, p. 587).

The collaboration of Kaplan and Benderly not only influenced the recruitment of TI students, it also affected the choice of faculty, the shape of the curriculum, and the character of the institution. The faculty included a group of European-educated Jewish scholars and Hebrew writers, and a group of Americans, including some Seminary rabbis trained by Kaplan, specialists in the arts, and two "Benderly boys."[8] This composition reflected Kaplan's idea about living simultaneously in two civilizations—American and Jewish. Among the Eastern European, yeshiva-educated faculty were religious teachers who could convey the culture of Eastern Europe to young American Jews and *maskilim* (enlightened ones) who embodied the Hebrew nationalism and cultural Zionism that inspired Benderly and his followers. The latter group profoundly influenced the culture of the Teachers Institute, making it a center for Hebraist culture in America (Ackerman, 1993; Kaufman, 1997).

Hebrew, Bible, Jewish history and religion were the core subjects and this became the model at other Hebrew teachers colleges (Dinin, 1967). Hebrew, the main language of instruction, was the primary subject and the "heart" of the culture at TI. The Hebraists were more interested in contemporary literature than "sacred texts" and taught Torah as a literary and historical source and the classical basis of modern Hebrew literature. They "suffused the classroom with their passionate Hebraism" and promoted the use of Hebrew outside the classroom as well (Mintz, 1993, p. 92).

The arts also played an important role. A course in "Jewish Music and Methods of Teaching Jewish Songs," was introduced in 1924, followed by courses in graphic arts, drama, and dance. Besides these formal opportunities for arts education, folk dancing, group singing, and student dramatic productions were regular features of life at the Institute, contributing to a strong sense of community.

Still, the central element of the TI experience was Kaplan's course in "Religion," as Kaufman (1997) explains, "If Hebrew and the arts were the heart and soul of the curriculum, then Kaplan's course in Biblical interpretation and Jewish thought was its mind" (p. 602). Kaplan taught from the opening of TI until his retirement and he used the course to work out his ideas about Judaism as an evolving religious civilization. Offered in 1- or 2-h-a-week lessons over 3 and eventually 4 years, the course covered (a) Biblical interpretation; (b) ceremonies and liturgy; and (c) ethics.

---

[8] Benderly searched out male college students who might be recruited for careers in Jewish education. He arranged for them to teach in the Bureau's experimental schools and to study with Kaplan and other TI faculty. Many received doctorates from Teachers College, Columbia, where they studied with Dewey, Kilpatrick, and other well-known progressive educators of the time. Known as the Benderly boys, these men disseminated Benderly's ideas by serving as leaders in Hebrew teachers colleges and heads of bureaus of Jewish education around the country.

The essence of the course was Kaplan's approach to Biblical interpretation, as he explained, "I teach my subject from the evolutionary point of view and I regard it as necessary to help students to adjust themselves to the problems of modern life" (Kaufman, p. 602).

While Kaplan's course left some students confused, it opened the eyes of others. Reactions ranged from "breaking up my orthodox views" and "losing my sense of a personal God and the desire to pray" to gaining "more real faith" and "new ways to think about God, Torah and the Jewish people" (Kaufman, pp. 604–605). Looking back on his studies with Kaplan at the Teachers Institute, philosopher Israel Scheffler (1995) writes that the experience "plunged him into a turmoil of belief" (p. 134). For many students, Kaplan's course and the whole experience at the TI was "a journey of personal transformation" (Kaufman, p. 606).

Details about education courses are harder to come by. The Institute offered the first courses in pedagogy in 1916 when Leo Honor was hired to teach history and pedagogy. These included courses in the history of Jewish education in the United States, the curriculum of the Jewish school, and methods of teaching Bible, ceremonies, liturgy, and Jewish music (Margolis, 1964, p. 84). Plans for giving students opportunities to observe and practise teaching were also developed, but not implemented until later (Gannes, 1965, pp. 190, 204). Overall, pedagogical training remained a secondary consideration.

This changed to some extent when the Institute moved uptown in 1930 to its own spacious, new building adjacent to the Seminary. Kaplan negotiated a joint program with nearby Teacher College, Columbia University, which enabled students to earn a Bachelor of Science degree from Columbia and a Bachelor of Jewish Pedagogy degree from the Teachers Institute in 5 years. The first 2 years were devoted to Jewish studies at the Institute. The last 3 years were divided between Jewish studies, general education, professional studies, and supervised teaching.[9] The Institute's attempt to open an experimental and practice school at Temple Ansche Chesed in 1939 was unsuccessful as Margolis (1964) explains: "Financially, pedagogically and administratively, the school was not ready for experimentation. Its limited staff and limited number of classes made it of little help in practice teaching" (pp. 117–118).

With each strengthening of the program, the Institute increased admission requirements. At first, admission was limited to young people at least 16 years old with an elementary knowledge of Hebrew. Once Hebrew high school graduates were available, the Institute required 3 years of attendance at a secular high school, 2 years of Jewish study beyond elementary school, and sufficient knowledge of spoken Hebrew to participate in courses taught in Hebrew. When the Institute was reorganized into three departments—Preparatory, Academic, and Teacher Training—admission to the latter required graduation from an academic high-school course or completion of the courses in the Preparatory Department. These requirements remained unchanged until 1925 when a new kind of requirement

---

[9]In 1924 the New York legislature gave the Seminary the right to confer the degrees of Bachelor, Master, and Doctor of Jewish Pedagogy.

was added. Successful applicants had to possess, in the opinion of the faculty, "the personal qualifications essential to success as teachers" (Margolis, 1964, p. 91).

What were those qualifications? Benderly maintained that the successful Jewish teacher needed the same qualifications as the public-school teacher, with particular stress on an inspiring personality, a thorough knowledge of Judaism, and understanding of the American Jewish child, religious enthusiasm, and faith in the future of American Jewry (Gannes, p. 187). Having moved next door to Teachers College,[10] one of the premier schools of education, the Teachers Institute had contact with leading exponents of a professional education for teachers. What were their views and how did they fit in with the program for teachers at TI?

Teacher Education in the Early Twentieth Century

The Hebrew teachers colleges were established during a period of enormous expansion in every sector of teacher education and much debate about teacher education.[11] The main issues concerned the place of general education, its relation to professional preparation, and the balance of a liberal and a technical emphasis in the professional sequence (Borrowman, 1956). Although teacher education was largely viewed as a technical undertaking, there were countervailing ideas about how the normal school ideal of superb craftsmanship could be integrated with the liberal arts ideal of the literate teacher. Teachers College was a leading exponent of that position.

Between 1895 and 1930, normal schools converted to teachers colleges, spurred by sky-rocketing demands for teachers and by pressure from their own students for affordable, accessible higher education. Teacher education entered the university through a second route as elite institutions, including Columbia University, created chairs of pedagogy which quickly became departments and eventually colleges or schools of education. On university and normal school campuses, academic faculty who considered general education and subject matter knowledge sufficient preparation for teaching distanced themselves from educationists who advocated specialized training for teachers. A deep rift developed between these two groups which never really healed.[12] Ironically, this was also the time when medical education moved to the university, but no one questioned whether medical training should be both scientific and practical.

Some important thinkers called for the coordination of general/liberal education and professional education on the grounds that teachers need to understand the aims of education and the child as learner as well as the content to be taught. If teachers were to rely on their own intelligence rather than follow the directives of others, they needed a broad social vision of education and an understanding of the social

---

[10] Teachers College, founded in 1897 as the New York College for the Training of Teachers, affiliated with Columbia University as a professional school of education. According to Borrowman (1956), TC became the "ideal" university-level professional school, embracing the traditions of both liberal and technical education (p. 119).

[11] For different versions of this history, see Borrowman, 1956; Clifford & Guthrie, 1988; Labaree, 2004; Lageman, 2000.

[12] A similar divide often separates Jewish educators and Jewish studies scholars.

and psychological factors affecting learning. This position was articulated in a study by the Carnegie Foundation (Learned et al., 1920) on the professional preparation of teachers and in an essay by Dewey (1904) on the relation of theory and practice in education.

The Carnegie study argued that in order to meet the demands of modern society, teachers needed a professional education that promoted intelligence and insight. William Bagley, a co-author of the study and a faculty member at Teachers College, favored a unified program which avoided the distinction between "academic" and "professional." He objected to special methods separated from content, calling instead for college-level subject-matter courses in which approved methods of teaching were modeled and discussed. Bagley and his colleagues decried the common practice of adding a few education courses to a general college course.

Dewey's 1904 essay dealt with a central issue in professional education—the relationship of theory and practice. Dewey agreed that teacher preparation required a certain amount of practical work and he outlined two approaches with different purposes:

> On the one hand, we may carry on practical work with the object of giving teachers-in-training...control of the techniques of class instruction and management, skill and proficiency in the work of teaching. With this aim in view, practice work is of the nature of apprenticeship. On the other hand, we may use practice work as an instrument in making real and vital theoretical instruction—knowledge of subject matter and principles of education. This is the laboratory point of view. (p. 318)

Dewey favored the laboratory view. He outlined a sequence of field experiences designed to help prospective teachers gain an understanding of principles of learning, the organization of subject matter, and classroom management before they undertook independent practice. The quality of both laboratory and apprenticeship experiences depended on the quality of the schools that served as observation and practice sites.

For many deans and professors of education at the time, the teaching hospital attached to university medical schools was a model for laboratory schools where educational theories could be tested and applied research conducted, while student teachers learned to adopt an experimental stance toward their teaching. Teachers College opened four demonstration and practice schools serving different student populations and educational purposes, but they rarely lived up to Dewey's vision[13] In fact, the ideal of serious professional education for teachers was more often a dream than a reality. Still, it was in the air as Kaplan and his colleagues taught aspiring teachers at the Teachers Institute.

TI and Prevailing Ideas about Teacher Education

The course of study for teachers at the Teachers Institute in its early decades aimed to produce graduates, mainly female, with a unique Jewish literacy, a love of Jewish culture and learning, and confidence about the future of Judaism in America. More

---

[13] For a discussion of the fate of practice schools, see Clifford & Guthrie (1988), pp. 109–116.

academic than professional, the curriculum made little distinction between "education for elementary and secondary teachers and training for scholarship" (Janowsky, 1967, p. 337). What graduates learned about teaching children is harder to discern.

The academic orientation of the TI curriculum is evident in the space devoted to Jewish studies compared with education. The emphasis on Judaics reflects the collegiate status of the Institute and the fact that students often took education courses at secular colleges where they studied. It also reveals the skepticism of scholars toward the study of pedagogy.

Jewish literacy at TI privileged Hebrew over knowledge of classical texts and treated halacha and mitzvoth as customs and ceremonies (Mintz, 1993, p. 91). The formal curriculum and the institutional culture produced graduates who were models of Jewish living. Did it also teach them how to turn their adult knowledge of Judaism into teachable content and learning activities for young students and how to address children's questions about God, miracles, or the historicity of the Bible?

From their education in the Jewish arts and their participation in the rich cultural life of TI, graduates likely formed images of how the arts could enrich and enliven the curriculum and how holiday celebrations could foster positive attachments to Judaism. Did they also have opportunities to consider the purposes of Jewish education in America and develop a progressive vision of what that education should look like? For example, would they agree with Dushkin (1918), a Benderly disciple, that "instead of teaching Hebrew or Bible or prayers or Talmud, the Jewish schools should teach Jewish children, and, for these purposes, the selections from the religious-national treasure house of the Jewish people should be such as will best prepare these children for their life as American Jews?" (p. 317). How did they understand the religious and/or cultural needs of their future students, sons and daughters of immigrants who might not share their passion for Hebrew?

Samuel Dinin, an instructor in history and education at TI, identified several "unsolved problems" with the program. He thought the Institute needed a model school like the Horace Mann School at Teachers College to serve as a laboratory for and existence proof of the program's vision of progressive Jewish schooling. Dinin also thought the program paid too much attention to the Jewish past and not enough to the Jewish present. "There is too much emphasis on subjects and texts...and no discussion of economic or vocational problems facing Jewish young people today, nor of Jewish community life and organization in this or other countries" (1967, p. 80).

Preparing Professional Day-School Teachers

Well before the start of the twenty-first century, Jews individually and collectively secured their place in the social, economic, political, and cultural life of this country. Still, the challenge of how to be Jewish in America endures. While signs of Jewish creativity and renewal abound, there is hard evidence of declining numbers, weakening ties, and widespread Jewish illiteracy. Some observers see a small, engaged Jewish minority and a large majority of unengaged and indifferent Jews. Others suggest that between the highly involved and the uninvolved is a big, diverse middle whose Jewish identity and connections fluctuate in relation to life stage and circumstances.

If being Jewish in the twenty-first century has become a matter of individual choice, what can be done to encourage this choice? In a move back to the future, communal leaders have turned again to Jewish education as the key to Jewish continuity. In the last 30 years, the forms and venues of Jewish learning have expanded to include every stage of the life cycle from early childhood to senior citizenship. Jewish education has come to mean much more than Jewish schooling and Jewish schools have taken on expanded functions traditionally met by home and community. The proliferation of options for Jewish learning is partly a response to the contemporary preoccupation with individual choice and personal meaning, but it leaves open the question, Jewish education for what. While scholars and educators examine alternative visions of Jewish education, the fundamental issue, why be Jewish, begs for a contemporary answer.

The Expansion of Jewish Day Schools

In this context, one of the most unexpected developments has been the growth of non-Orthodox Jewish day schools and the diversification of the day-school student population. This represents a change of heart and a change of place in the larger society. The early-twentieth-century leaders in Jewish education believed that Jewish schools should not interfere with "America's cherished plan of a system of common schools for all the children of all the people" (Dushkin, 1918, p. 138). Alexander Dushkin, one of Benderly's followers, wrote this at a time when the newly arrived Jewish immigrants were facing the challenges and uncertainties of life in America. Fifty years later, after a long and distinguished career in Jewish education, he changed his mind:

> ...There has grown up a third generation of American Jewry whose parents are American born and who...feel themselves at peace as citizens of the American democracy... In the years ahead, it will be increasingly obligatory for Jewish educators to promote the establishment of day schools as the intensive core of the American Jewish school system...to include 25% of our children. (1967, pp. 44–48)

Interestingly, Dushkin's recommended percentage fits the current numbers, though perhaps not the demographics he had in mind. According to the National Jewish Population Study (2000), Jewish children today receive more full-time Jewish schooling than their parents' generation, with 29% attending a day school or yeshiva, as compared to 12% of Jewish adults who attended Jewish day school or yeshiva. While most day school students come from Orthodox homes, increasing numbers of non-Orthodox families have chosen a day-school education for their children.

Day-school enrollments took off in the 1940s as different Orthodox groups advocated intensive Jewish education to insure the survival of traditional Jewish life in America. Some wanted to segregate their children from secular learning and outside influences, while others sought to combine strong Jewish and secular education.[14] After World War II, the Conservative movement set up day schools to perpetuate its brand of Judaism, founding the Solomon Schechter Day School Association in 1964. After many years of opposition to the idea, in 1985 the Reform movement passed a resolution supporting day schools.

Schick (2009) reports 800 day schools, up from 676 in 1998 and 759 five years ago. Of these, 200 (25%) are non-Orthodox, which includes 98 community schools, 17 Reform schools, and 50 Solomon Schechter schools. Most of the growth in the non-Orthodox sector occurred in community day schools which reported a 40% increase in the last decade, mainly at the high-school level.

Outside the Orthodox community, day schools educate a relatively small segment of Jewish children compared to congregational schools. Still, some communal leaders and Jewish educators believe that non-Orthodox Jewish families need day schools even more because they are more integrated into American society and more at risk of assimilation. Others see day schools as an effective way to foster strong Jewish identities and sustain a vital Jewish community.

The growth of non-Orthodox day schools led some to wonder where teachers would come from, particularly teachers who could help realize the vision of community day schools. The prospect of full-time teaching positions, concerns about a shortage of qualified teachers,[15] and a belief that a new kind of teacher was needed made it possible once again for visionary funders and educational leaders to contemplate full-time Jewish teacher-education programs.

New Programs to Prepare Day-School Teachers

Since the start of the twenty-first century, a handful of programs were launched with generous support from Jewish foundations and funders, including the PARDES Educators Program sponsored by the Pardes Institute of Jewish Studies in Israel, Melamdim sponsored by the Shalom Hartman Institute in Israel, and the DeLeT (Day School Leadership Through Teaching) Program sponsored by Hebrew Union College-Jewish Institute of Religion in Los Angeles and Brandeis University.[16] These well-subsidized programs vary in length, substantive focus, institutional sponsorship, and terminal degrees, but they share a commitment to enhancing the

---

[14] In 1935, there were 16 day schools in the US enrolling 4,600 students. By 1965, there were over 300 elementary and secondary schools with over 55,000 students. Torah U'Mesorah was established in 1944 and set out to create day schools in every community. The National Council of Beth Jacob Schools was founded in 1947, to promote schools for girls, modeled after those in Poland (Pilch, 1969, pp. 140–144).

[15] Ben-Avie and Kress (2006) found that 46% of all day-school teachers are over the age of 50 and will likely retire within 10 years and 24% of Judaic and general studies teachers are recent hires. Whether the latter finding is a reflection of teacher turnover or school growth, it suggests the need for strong preparation and induction to increase teacher retention.

[16] Three other programs created around the same time were short-lived—the Jewish Teacher Corps, Ha-Sha'ar, and a new masters program in Religious Education at the University of Pennsylvania.

quality of teaching and learning in Jewish day schools by preparing passionate and knowledgeable day-school teachers at the elementary, middle, and/or high-school levels.

The lack of research about these initiatives limits what we can learn from them in systematic ways. For example, we cannot tell if different candidates are attracted to different programs, what vision of day-school teaching animates them, what learning opportunities are provided in courses and field work, how long graduates of different programs stay in teaching, and what kind of teachers they become. Because I know the DeLeT program from the inside and because it has been the focus of some research at the Mandel Center for Studies in Jewish Education, I present it as an example of one contemporary program designed to prepare beginning day-school teachers.[17]

The DeLeT Program

The DeLeT (Day School Leadership Through Teaching) program was started in 2001 because Laura Lauder, a visionary venture philanthropist, wanted to help address the shortage of qualified teachers for liberal elementary day schools, particularly teachers who could teach both general and Jewish subjects in an integrated way.[18] Impressed with Teach for America (TFA), a service-oriented program that recruits talented graduates from elite colleges and universities for 2 years of teaching in hard-to-staff public schools, Lauder wanted to create a prestigious, selective, intensive fellowship to recruit and train day-school teachers.

Lauder organized a group of funders who supported DeLeT during its first 5 years when it functioned as a national fellowship program.[19] She invited Michael Zeldin, professor of Jewish education at the Hebrew Union College-Jewish Institute of Religion and me, newly arrived at Brandeis University, to design and launch the program at our respective institutions. During the planning phase, a national design team articulated beliefs about teaching and learning and the mission of liberal Jewish day schools in order to lay a strong conceptual foundation for the program. When DeLeT became part of the educational offerings at HUC-JIR and Brandeis, these ideas provided a common framework for faculty, mentor teachers, and students in both sites.[20]

---

[17]DeLeT is part of three research projects at the Mandel Center: a longitudinal survey of alumni from HUC and Brandeis; a comparative study of beginning teachers in Jewish, Catholic, and urban teacher-education programs, and a study of DeLeT's Beit Midrash for Teachers. For more information, see www.brandeis.edu/mandel.

[18]DeLeT, the Hebrew word for "door," is designed to open a door to a career in day-school education. Jonathan Woocher created the name which stands for "day school leadership through teaching."

[19]DeLeT now benefits from generous funding from the Jim Joseph Foundation which enabled the program to continue.

[20]At Brandeis, DeLeT became the Jewish day school concentration in the Master of Arts (MAT) in Teaching Program. At HUC, DeLeT became one of several certificate programs.

DeLeT is a full-time, 14-month, post-BA teacher preparation program that combines Jewish and education studies with an intensive internship. Fellows spend two summers on campus taking courses and participating in cocurricular activities. During the intervening school year, they spend 4 days a week in a local day school, learning to teach with the support and guidance of experienced (mentor) teachers and clinical instructors. During their internship year, fellows return to campus 1 day a week to continue their formal studies.

The program links a vision of liberal day-school education with a vision of the kind of teacher the program aims to prepare. According to the DeLeT MAT Handbook at Brandeis (2008), the central task of Jewish day schools is to enable students "to form integrated identities as they study and experience their dual heritage and responsibilities as Americans and as Jews" (p. 4). To advance this vision, DeLeT aims to prepare elementary day-school teachers who "(a) take students and their ideas seriously; (b) create democratic classrooms infused with Jewish values and experiences; (c) make meaningful connections between general and Jewish studies; (d) welcome parents as partners in children's education; (e) value Jewish text study as a core Jewish activity; (f) learn well from experience" (Feiman-Nemser & Zeldin, 2007, p. 6).

Several elements stand out in this formulation. The list gives primacy to pupils and their capacity to think. It signals the Jewish day-school teacher's responsibility to model and teach both Jewish and democratic values and to help students learn to be citizens in two communities. It implies that such learning may be enhanced by curricular integration. It highlights the value of learning from texts and from experience for both students and teachers (Hammerness, 2007)

At Brandeis, five strands or components make up the DeLeT curriculum: classroom teaching, subject-matter pedagogy, learners and learning, Jewish literacy and identity, and field studies which include a practicum in teaching reading, an internship, and classroom research. A seminar on teaching, tightly coordinated with the internship, runs through the program and provides a context for learning about planning, classroom instruction, assessment, classroom organization, management, and culture. Subject-specific methods courses address the learning and teaching of core subjects in the elementary curriculum, both general (mainly reading and math) and Jewish (Torah, prayer, holidays). A seminar on becoming a Jewish educator enables DeLeT students to clarify their personal stance on basic theological and ideological issues and consider the implications for day-school teaching.

The first summer emphasizes teachers as students of Jewish texts. As the year unfolds, the focus shifts to teachers as students of children, learning, subject matter, and teaching. The overall goal of the program is to prepare reflective teachers with a strong beginning practice and an identity as Jewish educators, whether they teach Jewish studies, general studies, or both. Those who come with a strong Judaic studies background often end up teaching Jewish studies, but all are prepared to integrate Jewish themes into their teaching, situate classroom experiences in a Jewish frame of reference, and serve as Jewish role models. According to the latest alumni survey, administered in 2009, 40% of the DeLeT graduates teach general studies, 40% teach Jewish studies, and 20% teach both.

DeLeT also works to build a professional learning community that models the intellectual and ethical dispositions teachers should foster in their own classrooms. One vehicle for doing this at Brandeis is the Beit Midrash for Teachers where students in their first summer are paired with students in their second summer to study classical Jewish texts about teaching and learning. As *hevruta* partners learn to listen to each other and the texts and to frame and refine their interpretations, they begin to form habits of mind and heart that shape their approach to text study and the study of teaching and learning (Feiman-Nemser, 2006). Thus the Beit Midrash helps foster a community of critical colleagues who support each other's learning during the intense year of DeLeT and beyond.

A signature feature of the DeLeT program which distinguishes it from other Jewish teacher preparation programs past and present, and from programs like Teach for America, is the year-long, mentored internship.[21] The opportunity to observe and assist experienced teachers as they work with students across the school year, to be part of a day-school community and to interact with parents and administrators is strong preparation for teaching. Besides their mentor teacher, each fellow has a clinical instructor who helps them connect what they are learning at the university with what they are doing and learning in their internship classrooms.

Contemporary Discourse in Teacher Education

DeLeT and other contemporary programs for preparing day-school teachers emerged during a period of intense debate about the quality and control of teaching and teacher education. Basically there are two strategies for getting good teachers. The first, associated with the deregulation agenda, relies on recruitment and selection. The second, associated with the professionalization agenda, relies on providing people with opportunities to develop the capacities required for effective teaching. The two agendas reflect different assumptions about teaching and learning to teach.

Deregulators take a minimalist approach. They advocate reducing or removing requirements ("barriers") so that more and different people will be attracted to teaching. Since the mid-1980s, the proliferation of alternative routes to teaching has dramatically changed the landscape of teacher education and the number of teachers prepared through such routes has grown exponentially. Alternative certification programs have also succeeded in attracting a different pool of candidates, more diverse with regard to race, age, and gender and, in some highly selective programs, academic qualifications.

The second strategy associated with professionalization rests on a view of teaching as a clinical practice that depends on the purposeful use of specialized knowledge, skill, and judgment in the service of student learning (National Commission on Teaching and America's Future, 1996). According to proponents, developing professional teachers depends on high-quality initial preparation and

---

[21] DeLeT is an example of an "eased-entry" program compared with "fast-track" programs like TFA which place teachers in classrooms as teachers of record after a brief summer of training.

continuous professional development. Exemplary preparation programs feature extensive, carefully supervised fieldwork integrated with courses that cohere around a shared vision of good teaching.

Advocates of professional teaching and teacher education are critical of the narrow definition of a "highly qualified teacher" enshrined in *No Child Left Behind*, the federal legislation enacted by the Bush administration in 2002. According to NCLB, verbal ability and subject-matter knowledge are the relevant indicators of teacher quality. Accordingly, articulate liberal arts graduates with academic majors in their subject area should be able to figure how to teach while doing it.

Clearly teachers cannot teach what they do not know, but teachers must also know how to transform their knowledge into teachable subject matter with a structure and logic that students will understand. They need multiple ways of representing core concepts and explaining big ideas. They also need to know what students may find confusing or difficult and how to approach those topics in intellectually honest and age-appropriate ways (Ball & McDiarmid, 1990; Wilson, Shulman & Richert, 1987). An academic major does not provide this kind of subject-matter knowledge for teaching.

One obstacle to promoting a professional view of teaching is the belief held by many that teaching is relatively straightforward work, not "an extraordinarily difficult job that looks easy" (Labaree, 2004, p. 298). Because everyone has been to school, everyone thinks she/he knows what teaching involves. Teaching also seems straightforward because we all engage in a kind of teaching, "showing, telling, and helping others," as part of our daily lives. This contributes to the notion that teaching is a "natural" skill, not something learned through rigorous professional preparation (Ball & Forzani, 2009).

But classroom teaching is different from the everyday showing, telling, and helping that we do as parents, spouses, and friends. Inside the classroom, teachers perform a wide range of activities—explaining, listening, questioning, managing, demonstrating, assessing, inspiring—all aimed at promoting the learning of 25 or more diverse students. Outside the classroom, teachers design instructional plans, assess student work, interact with colleagues, parents, and administrators. Based on a deep understanding of classroom teaching, some leading teacher educators are now recommending that the curriculum of teacher education be (re)centered on core tasks and activities that beginning teachers must understand and enact (Ball & Forzani, 2009; Grossman & McDonald, 2008).[22]

The simple dichotomy between "alternative" and "traditional" teacher-education programs is breaking down as researchers discover more differences within than between categories. Moreover, since the effect of any program is a combination of selection and learning opportunities, the solution to the problem of teacher quality may depend on balancing strong recruitment with rigorous opportunities to learn about teaching through connected coursework linked to supervised field experience (Grossman & Loeb, 2008, pp. 184–185).

---

[22] The recentering on practice is a counter measure to what some see as an over-emphasis on teacher planning, reflection, knowledge, and beliefs.

DeLeT in the Context of Contemporary Teacher Education

Where does DeLeT fit in contemporary discourse on teacher education? Clearly the program reflects the professionalization agenda in its goals, structure, and curriculum. The model of an integrating teacher is appropriate for the elementary grades where most teachers are generalists, but the day school's dual curriculum poses challenges. In terms of recruitment, DeLeT offers some of the same incentives as other highly selective alternate route programs, but program leaders face trade-offs in their effort to recruit strong candidates.

DeLeT incorporates many features associated with programs that have a positive impact on teachers' preparedness and performance (Darling-Hammond, 2000). These include (a) a clear vision of teaching and learning that gives the program coherence; (b) well-defined standards of practice and performance used in program design and student assessment; (c) a core curriculum based on knowledge of child development, learning, and subject-matter pedagogy, and taught in the context of practice; (d) strong partnerships with schools; (d) extended clinical experience integrated with coursework; and (e) extensive use of pedagogies that relate theory and practice (e.g., child study, performance assessment, classroom research).

Overall, DeLeT has succeeded in recruiting academically able, Jewishly committed candidates with diverse backgrounds and experience. Many DeLeT fellows attended top-ranked universities where they majored in a variety of subjects, including Jewish studies (57%).[23] Nearly three-quarters enrolled in DeLeT within 2 years of college graduation; the rest came to day-school teaching as a second or third career; 39% place themselves outside conventional denominational labels. The rest are equally divided between Conservative (22%) and Reform (22%), with 12% identifying as modern Orthodox. In terms of their own Jewish education, 35% attended a Jewish elementary day school and 20% attended a Jewish day high school. The rest participated in other forms of Jewish education (supplementary school, camping, Hebrew high school); 71% spent time in Israel touring, visiting, studying; 9% grew up there (Tamir, Feiman-Nemser, Silvera-Sasson, & Cytryn, 2010).

Incentives like a year-long internship, full tuition scholarship, a modest living stipend, the chance to earn a state teaching license, and an advanced degree support a selective-admission process and help broaden the pool of candidates. Program leaders puzzle over accepting people who are exploring a possible career in day-school teaching or sticking with people who seem to have such a commitment. Unlike some service-oriented programs where people teach for 2 years and then move on to other careers, DeLeT aims to build a cadre of teacher-leaders for Jewish day schools. So retention is as important as recruitment.[24]

---

[23] The ranking of colleges and universities is based on SAT scores, using data and guidelines from the College Board (http:/www.collegeboard,com)

[24] Besides the 14-month program of initial preparation, DeLeT offers support during the first 2 years of teaching and continuing professional development opportunities for alumni. This reflects the program's vision of a professional learning continuum (Feiman-Nemser, 2001).

A second trade-off facing program leaders has to do with candidates' Jewish studies background. Some outsiders question whether DeLeT should ever accept someone with a strong Jewish identity but a limited Judaic studies background, but that misses a central aspect of the program. DeLeT prepares elementary day-school generalists who see themselves as Jewish educators, whatever their teaching assignment. This represents a sea change in how people think about day-school teacher preparation. In the past, day schools outsourced the training of elementary generalists to general schools of education. DeLeT prepares teachers who identify with the Jewish mission and contribute to the Jewish life of the school. Whether they teach general studies, Jewish studies, or both depends on their background and interests, and the needs of the field.

Conclusion

Separated by almost a century, the program for teachers at the Teachers Institute of the Jewish Theological Seminary and the DeLeT program at Brandeis University, and the Hebrew Union College-Jewish Institute of Religion were launched at times of transition, experimentation, and uncertainty in the American Jewish community (Sarna, 1995; Woocher, Rubin-Ross, & Woocher, 2009). Both programs were created to prepare Jewish teachers for a kind of Jewish school that would not have existed in each other's era. Just as a 5-day-a-week supplementary Talmud Torah is hard to imagine today, so a non-Orthodox day school, especially a pluralistic one, was unthinkable in the opening decades of the twentieth century. The invention of these new institutions under different historic circumstances to help perpetuate Judaism in modern America reflects an enduring faith in the power of Jewish education.

The teacher training program at TI and the DeLeT program offer different answers to this question: What do Jewish teachers need to know, care about, and be able to do, and how can they be helped to learn that? In this concluding section, I use these differences to highlight some enduring issues about the curriculum and pedagogy of Jewish teacher education. I close with a call for research on the preparation of day-school teachers. In the current climate of accountability, school leaders, educational researchers, and policy makers want to know what kind of teacher education produces teachers who stay in teaching and make a difference in students' lives and learning. Jewish funders, day-school leaders, and teacher-education providers also need answers to this question.

A report commissioned by the National Academy of Education[25] outlines three broad areas of knowledge, skill, and commitment that teachers need to be effective: (a) knowledge of subject matter and curriculum goals in relation to the purposes of schooling; (b) knowledge of learners and their development in social contexts; and

---

[25] A synthesis of several decades of research and practical experimentation, this framework reflects the current state of research and professional consensus about what teacher education needs to accomplish.

(c) knowledge of teaching (e.g., instruction, assessment, management) (Darling-Hammond & Bransford, 2005, p. 10). The TI and DeLeT programs emphasize different kinds of knowledge across these domains.

While the Teachers Institute emphasized Judaic subject-matter knowledge, the DeLeT program emphasizes pedagogical knowledge. It is not surprising that a collegiate program preparing teachers for an intensive Jewish afternoon school would focus on Judaic content, including Hebrew language skills, while a graduate level, professional preparation program for elementary teachers in all-day Jewish schools would emphasize general and subject-specific pedagogical knowledge. We should not, however, let this difference reinforce the familiar and persistent separation between content and pedagogy and between the student and the curriculum.

Teachers need a solid grasp of their subject matter and an understanding of their pedagogical aspects (Shulman, 1986). Such knowledge helps teachers make important content accessible to a range of learners.[26] Moreover, since teachers teach particular content to particular students in particular contexts, they also need to know how to get to know their students as individuals and learners, create, and maintain a productive learning environment, monitor student engagement and understanding, and promote moral and civic development.[27] These responsibilities require principled and practical knowledge best learned in the context of practice.

A persistent challenge for teacher education is creating well-designed field experiences that serve the purposes of both laboratory and apprenticeship. Securing appropriate schools of observation and practice was an "unsolved problem" for the Hebrew teachers colleges. On the other hand, DeLeT makes extensive use of pedagogies that help future teachers link theory and practice and develop a beginning repertoire of curricular, instructional, and assessment strategies, including a year-long internship. Strong field experiences have clear goals, frequent opportunities for practice with feedback, modeling by more expert teachers who make their thinking visible, multiple opportunities to relate coursework to field experiences, and structured opportunities for analysis and reflection (Darling-Hammond & Bransford, 2005, p. 410). Such arrangements depend on long-term partnerships between day schools and teacher-education programs based on mutual self-interest and a negotiated vision of good teaching and learning.

The importance of knowing one's students has its parallel in teachers' self-knowledge. Teaching and learning to teach are deeply personal work, engaging teachers' emotions as well as their intellect and shaping their personal and professional identities. We saw how Kaplan provoked TI students to confront and transform their own religious beliefs and practices. Similar transformations occur in the DeLeT program as teacher candidates explore their Jewish identities in a

---

[26] Preparing subject matter teachers is especially daunting at the elementary level where teachers are responsible for multiple subjects. This is a continuing challenge for the DeLeT program.

[27] The DeLeT standards place these teaching responsibilities in a Jewish framework. Standard 2 calls for teachers to know their students as individuals, learners, members of families, spiritual beings. Standard 3 calls for teachers to create classroom learning communities infused with Jewish values and experiences.

pluralistic environment and consider what it means for Jewish educators to be "textpeople" (Heschel, 1966). If we want day-school teachers to support their students' religious, cultural, and spiritual development, we need to attend to these aspects in teachers.

Research in teacher education emerged in the last half century as an identifiable field of inquiry. Amid contemporary debates about how to get good teachers, there are increasing calls for research that identifies the critical elements of teacher education that produce teachers who have a positive influence on students. The existence of different pathways to Jewish day-school teaching creates a unique opportunity to gather data about (a) who attends different programs; (b) what kind of preparation they receive; (c) what sort of work environment they enter; (d) what they are like as teachers. With comparable data about individual teachers, their preparation, and their schools, we can examine how these factors interact to promote (or inhibit) a sense of preparedness and success. Understanding which combinations yield the most committed and effective teachers can help strengthen the design of programs to prepare day-school teachers.

Research in Jewish education is still a young enterprise with few structural supports for serious and sustained inquiry. This makes it hard to mount a program of research in Jewish teacher education. At the same time, support for such an investigation would signal a new regard for the preparation of day-school teachers and the work of day-school teaching. It would also produce usable knowledge to inform policy and practice.

References

Ackerman, W. (1989). Strangers to the tradition: Idea and constraint in American Jewish education. In H. Himmelfarb & S. DellaPegola (Eds.), *Jewish education worldwide: Cross-cultural perspectives* (pp. 71–116). Lanham, MD: University Press of America.

Ackerman, W. (1993). A world apart: Hebrew Teachers colleges and Hebrew speaking camps. In A. Mintz (Ed.), *Hebrew in America: Perspectives and prospects* (pp. 105–128).

Ball, D. & Forzani, F. (2009). The work of teaching and the challenge for teacher education. *Journal of Teacher Education, 60*(5), 497–511.

Ball, D., & McDiarmid, W. (1990). The subject matter preparation of teachers. In W. Houston (Ed.), *Handbook of research on teacher education* (pp. 437–449). New York: MacMillan.

Ben-Avie, M., & Kress, J. (2006). *The educators in Jewish schools study*. New York: JESNA.

Borrowman, M. (1956). *The liberal and technical in teacher education: A historical survey of American thought*. Westport, CN: Greenwood Press.

Clifford, G. J., & Guthrie, J. (1988). *Ed school: A brief for professional education*. Chicago: University of Chicago Press.

Darling-Hammond, L. (Ed.). (2000). *Studies of excellence in teacher education* (3 Vols.). Washington, DC: American Association of Colleges for Teacher Education.

Darling-Hammond, L., & Bransford, J. (2005). *Preparing teachers for a changing world: What teachers should learn and Be Able to Do*. San Francisco: Jossey Bass.

Dewey, J. (1904). The relation of theory to practice in education. In C. Murray (Ed.), *The relation of theory to practice in the education of teachers. Third yearbook of the national society for the scientific study of education* (pp. 9–30). Chicago: University of Chicago Press.

Dinin, S. (1967). "The curricula of the Hebrew teachers colleges. In O. Janowsky (Ed.), *The education of American Jewish teachers* (pp. 61–81). Boston: Beacon Press.

Dushkin, A. (1918). *Jewish education in New York city*. New York: Bureau of Jewish Education.

Dushkin, A. (1967). Fifty years of American Jewish education: Retrospect and prospects. *Jewish Education, 37*(1/2), 44–57.

Feiman-Nemser, S. (2001). From preparation to practice: Designing a continuum to strengthen and sustain teaching. *Teachers College Record, 103*(6), 1013–1055.

Feiman-Nemser, S. (2006). Beit midrash for teachers: An experiment in professional education. *Journal of Jewish Education, 72*(3), 161–181.

Feiman-Nemser, S., & Zeldin, M. (July, 2007). *Final Report: The DeLeT Program at Brandeis University and Hebrew Union College-Jewish Institute of Religion, 2002–2007*. A report submitted to the National Advisory Committee.

Finn, C., & Madigan, K. (2001). Removing the barriers for teacher candidates. *Educational Leadership, 58*(8), 29–31.

Gannes, A. (Ed.). (1965). *Selected writings of Leo Honor*. New York: The Reconstructionist Press.

Grossman, P., & Loeb, S. (2008). *Alternative routes to teaching: Mapping the new landscape of teacher education*. Cambridge, MA: Harvard Education Press.

Grossman, P., & McDonald, M. (2008). Back to the future: Directions for research in teaching and teacher education. *American Educational Research Journal, 45*(1), 184–205.

Hammerness, K. (2007). *Examining coherence in context-specific teacher preparation programs: Looking for alignment across program goals, teachers' goals for students, and opportunities to learn*. Waltham, MA: Brandeis University, Mandel Center for Studies in Jewish Education.

Heschel, A. J. (1966). Jewish education. In *The insecurity of freedom*. Philadelphia: Jewish Publication Society.

Hurwich, L. (1958). Jewish education in Boston (1843–1855). *Jewish Education, 26* (Spring).

Janowsky, O. (1967). The education of American Jewish teachers: Pattern and prospect. In O. Janowsky (Ed.), *The education of American Jewish teachers* (pp. 317–346). Boston: Beacon Press.

Kaplan, M., & Cronson, B. (1949). First community survey of Jewish education in New York City-1909. *Jewish Education, 20*(3).

Kaufman, D. (1997). Jewish education as a civilization: A history of the Teachers institute. In J. Wertheimer (Ed.), *Tradition renewed: A history of the Jewish theological seminary* (Vol. I, pp. 567–629). New York: The Jewish Theological Seminar.

Labaree, D. (2004). *The trouble with Ed Schools*. New Haven, CT: Yale University Press.

Lageman, E. (2000). *An elusive science: The troubling history of educational research*. Chicago: University of Chicago Press.

Learned, W., & Bagley, W., et al. (1920). *The Professional Preparation of Teachers for American Public Schools*. Bulletin No.14, The Carnegie Foundation for the Advancement of Teaching. New York: The Foundation.

Margolis, I. (1964). *Jewish teacher training schools in the United States*. New York: National Council for Torah Education of Mizrachi-Hapoel Hamizrachi.

National Jewish Population Study. (2000) *National Jewish population survey*. New York: United Jewish Communities.

DeLeT MAT Handbook at Brandeis *MAT-JDS DeLeT handbook* (2008). Mandel Center for Studies in Jewish Education. Waltham, MA: Brandeis University.

Mintz, A. (1993). *Hebrew in America: Perspectives and prospects*. Detroit, MI: Wayne State University Press.

National Commission on Teaching and America's Future (1996). *What matters most: Teaching for America's future*. New York: Author.

Pilch, J. (Ed.). (1969). *A history of Jewish education in America*. New York: National Curriculum Research Institute of the American Association of Jewish Education.

Rauch, E. (2006). *The education of American Jewry: The past is a prologue*. New York: Liberty Publishing House.

Sarna, J. (1995). *The great awakening: The transformation that shaped twentieth century American Judaism and its implications for today*. New York: Council for Initiatives in Jewish Education.

Scheffler, I. (1995). *Teachers of my youth: An American Jewish experience*. Boston: Kluwer Academic Publishers.
Schick, M. (2009). *A census of Jewish day schools in the United States*. New York: Avi Chai Foundation.
Shulman, L. (1986). Those who understand: Knowledge growth in teaching. *Educational Researcher, 15*(2), 4–14.
Tamir, E., Feiman-Nemser, S., Silvera-Sasson, R., & Cytryn, J. (2010). *DeLeT Alumni: A comprehensive report on the journey of beginning day school teachers*. Waltham, MA: Mandel Center for Studies in Jewish Education, Brandeis University.
Wilson, S., Shulman, L., & Richert, A. (1987). "150 different ways of knowing: Representations of knowledge in teaching. In J. Calderhead (Ed.), *Exploring teachers' thinking* (pp. 104–124). London: Cassell.
Woocher, J., Rubin-Ross, R., & Woocher, M. (2009). *Redesigning Jewish education for the 21st century*, A Lippman Kaufer Institute Working Paper. New York: JESNA.

Professional Development of Teachers in Jewish Education

Gail Zaiman Dorph

Introduction[1]

In the last decades, a consensus has emerged concerning both the importance and the critical features of high-quality professional development for teachers.[2] Grounded in the idea that students' educational experience depends on the caliber of teachers' instructional skills, this chapter explores the following questions:

- What makes it challenging to create effective professional development for teachers in both general and Jewish education?
- What are the critical principles of effective professional development?
- What happens when these principles are implemented in Jewish educational settings—what do these principles look like in action, what seems to work, and what obstacles arise?

To provide images of the kind of professional learning experiences that can profoundly improve the capacity of our teachers, the chapter concludes with examples of principle-based professional development in Jewish educational settings. These examples also suggest that more effort and research are needed to figure out how to make these kinds of experiences even more effective and more common.

G.Z. Dorph (✉)
MTEI - Mandel Teacher Educators Institute, Jerusalem, Israel
e-mail: gaildorph@gmail.com

[1] The author wishes to thank Sheldon Dorph, Barry Holtz, Vicky Kelman, Sharon Feiman-Nemser, and Susan Stodolsky for reading earlier drafts of this chapter. In addition, special thanks to Kathy Simon for her careful and thoughtful suggestions, which greatly improved the clarity of this chapter.

[2] In particular, see three recent reports of large-scale studies: Barber and Mourshed (2007); Darling-Hammond et al. (2009); Porter et al. (2000).

Challenges to Creating Effective Professional Development for Teachers

Four challenges face Jewish and general education as we aim to create effective professional development for teachers. The first two relate to teachers and teaching; the second two relate to professional development and professional developers.

Teachers Often Lack Solid Preparation in Their Subject Matters for Teaching

While many of the challenges of professional development arise both in general and Jewish education, the issue of teacher preparation appears in a unique form in Jewish educational contexts. In a study of Jewish education in three diverse American Jewish communities, researchers found that only 19% of teachers, across Jewish school settings—this includes day, pre and congregational schools—have professional preparation in both Jewish Studies and Education (Gamoran, Goldring, Robinson, Tammivaara, & Goodman, 1998). The situation does not seem to have changed dramatically over the course of the last decade. When we look only at Jewish studies knowledge, the lack of subject-matter knowledge is the most extreme in congregational and early childhood settings and least extreme in day school high schools, where generally teachers have subject-matter knowledge. Additionally, teachers affiliated with the Orthodox movement have more Jewish studies background (Gamoran et al., 1998). In a more recent study of day and congregational schoolteachers (Ben-Avie & Kress, 2008), a somewhat different set of questions were asked to learn about professional-level teacher education in supplementary and day school settings. On the Jewish studies dimension, findings indicate that in day schools 53% of teachers had received some Jewish studies courses in college; 22% were Jewish studies majors; 8% were rabbis. Among congregational schoolteachers, 4% were rabbis; 19% were Jewish studies majors; 60% had taken Jewish studies courses in college. While the majority of teachers had degrees beyond a BA, 44% of day school teachers, and 68% of congregational schoolteachers did not have teaching certificates.

This lack of subject-matter expertise poses real challenges for the curriculum of professional development in education in general and in Jewish education in particular. In general education, the claim is often made that teachers are unprepared to teach their subjects (Ma, 1999; Stodolsky, 1988); however, there is probably no one teaching a math class who has not studied math at least through high school. Yet, it is common for teachers of Hebrew in many Jewish schools to have weak knowledge of Hebrew[3] (Gamoran et al., 1998) and for teachers of Bible to have no experience studying the Bible either as children or as adults.

---

[3] When ascertaining the knowledge base of teachers in Jewish schools, researchers ask participants to rate their fluency in reading Hebrew, translating Hebrew, and speaking Hebrew.

So, unlike other contexts, where one might rely on teachers' content knowledge (sometimes solid; sometimes not) and work on developing pedagogical content knowledge (Shulman, 1986), professional development in Jewish schools needs centrally to attend to content knowledge. What would it take for teachers to "get up to speed" in Hebrew or Bible as they teach those subjects? In order for professional development to be effective in the sphere of Jewish education, it needs to grapple with the fact that teachers may be both novice instructors and also novice students of the subjects they are teaching.

Teachers Often Have a Mimetic View of Teaching and Learning

The dominant instructional mode in both Jewish and general education over the past generation fits what Jackson (1986) refers to as the "mimetic tradition." In this tradition, instruction has been widely designed as though people learn through transmission—by listening carefully and then remembering or practicing what they have heard. Considerable research, however, has shown that learning involves not imitation and replication, but change and transformation (Bransford, Brown, & Cocking, 1999; Jackson, 1986; Kegan, 1982). Often referred to as transformative or constructivist, this paradigm suggests that learning is not additive, but requires internal change. Further, this research demonstrates that learning—of skills and facts along with big ideas—is more effective when it is experiential and interactive. This vision of teaching and learning emphasizes conceptual understanding and the social construction of knowledge. Following Dewey (1938), it claims that learning generally does not take place in isolation, but most often occurs in social situations where teachers and students (and students among themselves) discover and make meaning through their interactions with the subject and with each other. Since most teachers have learned within the "mimetic" paradigm, their years of experience as students are unlikely to support them in teaching in the constructivist/transformative paradigm that we currently understand as most effective. This suggests that effective professional development, rather than just adding to teachers' repertoire of skills, will also help teachers transform deeply engrained understandings about the nature of teaching and learning.

Most Professional Development Is Aligned with the Mimetic Model of Teaching and Learning

Unfortunately, most professional development experiences reflect the mimetic or "delivery" tradition. Think of the models we most often see—the one-shot workshop that focuses on generic teaching skills, the "make and take" workshop that focuses, for example, on teaching a Jewish holiday, in the one-size-fits-all community learning day. Typically, all of these are more aligned with the mimetic model of learning. They tend to focus on generic pedagogical skills, rather than on specific pedagogical approaches that align to the uniqueness of the various subject matters. Typically, these experiences do not build images of transformative teaching and learning and do not help teachers reconsider their modes of teaching, so the possibility of their having lasting value on improving practice is limited.

There is a double challenge, then, in supporting teachers to adopt a transformative model of teaching: Teachers have had an "apprenticeship" of learning throughout their youth that suggests to them that learning is about transmission. Further, teachers' experiences of professional development reinforce this point of view. It makes sense that the modes of professional development be aligned with the modes of teaching that we are trying to promote; therefore, we need professional development to be not just informative, but transformative. Both the curriculum and pedagogy of professional development for teachers need to be redesigned in order to meet this double challenge.

Most Professional Developers Have Not Been Prepared to Create Learning Experiences That Reflect This New Model of Teaching and Learning

The first three challenges suggest the fourth challenge: how to support the "new" professional developer (Ball & Cohen, 1999; Stein, Smith, & Silver, 1999). They too "suffer" from the same maladies, i.e., they were educated in a mimetic fashion and they have experienced mimetically inspired professional development. Our current understanding about teaching and learning demands that professional developers create and implement transformative professional development for teachers. The challenge we (in Jewish and general education) face is formidable. We need to simultaneously change the nature of learning experiences for children, for teachers, and for professional developers.

Professional Development: Curriculum and Principles

In the last decades, a consensus has emerged about the critical principles of effective professional development for teachers that takes into account this transformative vision of teaching and learning (Darling-Hammond, Wei, Andree, Richardson, & Orphanos, 2009; Knapp, 2003; Little, 1993; Porter, Garet, Desimone, Yoon, & Birman, 2000; Sparks & Hirsch, 1990). These principles suggest designing learning opportunities that change teachers' *thinking* about teaching and learning and also affect their teaching *practices*. Not surprisingly, these principles are aligned with a more general constructivist vision of teaching and learning.

Curriculum of Effective Professional Development

In the teaching and learning model proposed here, there are three elements that are always present: teacher, student, and subject matter. Additionally, there is a fourth factor referred to as the "environment" that includes such things as a classroom, a family, a synagogue, or professional development setting. Figure 1 depicts what we

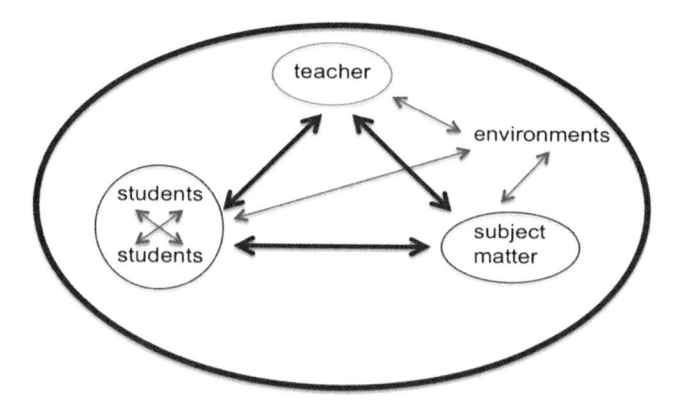

Fig. 1 Student instructional learning triangle

might think of as the default situation, where a teacher teaches students in a classroom. The arrows in between the vertices depict the interactive nature of teaching and learning. Let us consider this triangle.[4]

This interactive triangle (Cohen, Raudenbusch, & Ball, 2003; Hawkins, 1967; McDonald, 1992; Sizer, 1984/1992) is an attempt to describe enacted teaching. It indicates that opportunities for student learning reside in interactions of students with each other, with their teachers and with the subject(s) they are studying.

> Nearly all formal learning in schools involves the interactions of three actors: the student, the teacher, and the subject of their mutual attention. The character of this triangle is subject to change, varying from pupil to pupil, teacher to teacher, subject to subject, day to day, even minute to minute. (Sizer, 1984, pp. 151–2)

Figure 2 includes the same three elements: teacher, learner, and subject matter and the same conception of the dynamics of the relationships. But, in Fig. 2, the professional developer is in the teacher's role. The professional developer's students are the teachers who participate in professional development sessions, and the "subject matter" is "teaching and learning" itself, that is, the entire student instructional triangle. It is worth noting the parallel processes between student and teacher learning.

In studying this triangle, we see that opportunities for teachers' professional learning reside in the interaction among professionals, the subject matter of professional development, and the professional developers. These opportunities for learning can take place outside of the practice of teaching, in workshops, courses, and in study groups designing curriculum or examining student work; or within practice itself, through mentoring and peer coaching (Ball & Cohen, 1999; Feiman-Nemser, 1998 and 2001; Knapp, 2003).

Most importantly, the triangle illuminates the "content" of the subject matter of professional development. The curriculum of professional development for teachers is not adult study of the subject matter (no matter how rich that may be). It is, rather, learning Humash, Siddur, Talmud, and other topics *for the purposes of* teaching

---

[4]This graphic appears in Cohen et al. (2003) with an additional circle around it to depict the environment.

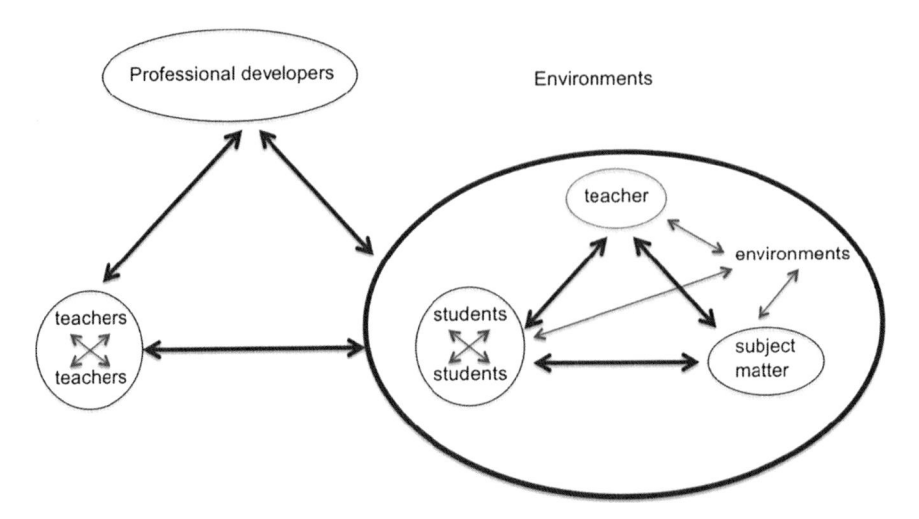

Fig. 2 Teacher instructional learning triangle (Deborah Ball introduced this graphic into the design and curriculum work of MTEI in 1996)

them to specific learners in specific contexts—what Shulman (1986) called pedagogic content knowledge. As Dewey (1902/1964) said, teachers must be able "to psychologize" the subject matter (p. 352). This means that a teacher must be able to "view the subject matter through the eyes of the learner, as well as interpret[ing] the learner's comments, questions, and activities through the lenses of the subject matter" (McDiarmid, Ball, & Anderson, 1989, p. 194). Integrating the study of subject matter with issues of teaching and learning provides a path toward addressing the first challenge raised in this chapter—that teachers in Jewish education may be novices at the subject matter and novice teachers (see Appendix for the extension of this approach to thinking about the curriculum for the professional developer). Focusing on pedagogical content knowledge supports teachers in gaining expertise in both subject matter and teaching at once.

Principles of Effective Professional Development (PD)

Educational researchers[5] argue that to affect teachers' thinking and practice, professional development programs should:

1. Take place within teachers' regular work day or work week
2. Continue over time with sessions building on each other

---

[5]There are different versions of this list (Bolam & McMahon, 2004; Knapp, 2003; Little, 1993; Stein et al., 1999). On most lists, "align with new standards" is a key feature. As Jewish education does not have a standards movement to which these PD interventions could align, I have omitted this feature.

3. Model active learning
4. Foster a collegial, collaborative environment
5. Focus on building teachers' pedagogical content knowledge
6. Include learning in and from practice

The first two principles speak to the structural characteristics of these initiatives; the next two involve the norms, social contexts, and processes of learning; and the last two relate to elements of the content of the curriculum itself. As I unpack these key features, I will situate them in the contexts of Jewish education in order to help illustrate implications for professional development in these settings.

Take Place Within Teachers' Regular Work Day or Work Week

It is clear that increasing the number of hours that teachers learn together will not in and of itself improve the quality of learning for their students, but without such time set aside for learning, no change can be expected. Teachers' work in Jewish educational settings needs to be redefined. We can no longer assume that the teaching role includes only preparing and teaching one's class, coming in 15 minutes before, leaving directly afterward, and attending an occasional teachers' meeting. Making time for teacher learning requires thinking creatively about how to build this into teachers' ongoing work. How might the work of teachers be designed so that they have time to think, talk, and learn together? Depending on the setting, it might mean paying teachers for an extra evening or Sunday afternoon a month; it might mean figuring out a system of release time, which may involve paying a substitute or organizing times for teachers to work together during electives; it may involve changing the nature of teachers' meetings and taking care of logistical issues through written communication.

Continue Over Time with Sessions Building on Each Other

Recent research has shown that it takes (at least) between 30 and 50 hours or more for professional learning experiences to begin to effect changes in teachers' thinking and practice; it likely takes even more to support enough change in practice to effect student outcomes (Darling-Hammond et al., 2009; Knapp, 2003; Wayne, Kwang, Pei, Cronen, & Garet, 2008). In Jewish education, a study done in five communities (Holtz, Gamoran, Dorph, Goldring, & Robinson, 2000), reported that 37% of programs met for only one session, and another 49% met for between two and five sessions. Just 12% of programs met for six or more sessions: even those programs included only 18 or fewer hours of learning time. Thus, none of the programs were sustained enough to have a reliable impact on teachers' thinking or practice.[6]

---

[6] A recent JESNA (Jewish Educational Services of North America) study (2008) suggests that professional development opportunities attended by teachers in day school and after-school programs,

Model Active Learning

If teachers are to create "transformational" learning environments where students learn to challenge each other, question ideas, and build new knowledge, it makes sense that professional development for teachers model these features (Lieberman, 1996). Active learning is often mistakenly conflated with interactive techniques, like using manipulatives in mathematics or learning centers when studying Israel. Creating active learning environments is not the opposite of learning from frontal teaching. Aiming for understanding and using one's knowledge is the hallmark of this kind of learning.

What might it look like to apply the principles of active learning to professional development settings? This paradigm suggests that we think about teachers as learners who would benefit from learning opportunities that encourage curiosity, inquiry, analysis, and reflection. Professional development that models active learning supports teachers by creating opportunities for them to work with their colleagues on real problems, to share their own work, and give and receive feedback and build new professional knowledge.

Locate Professional Learning in a Collegial, Collaborative Environment

In an intensive study of the norms of ten Jewish schools in one community, Stodolsky and her colleagues (2006) found that teachers report a congenial atmosphere in which they were generally helpful to one another and could count on one another. Yet there was little indication that this congeniality translated into meaningful professional discourse among teachers. Only a few schools (3 of 10) reported regular collaboration among teachers on instructional matters, such as coordinating curriculum.

Despite congenial relationships, the work of teaching is overwhelmingly solitary (Lortie, 1975). Teacher-writers Troen and Boles (2003) reflect on the way the isolated nature of teaching practice affects teachers' learning:

> ...isolation means that each teacher must learn things by trial and error...Teachers have few opportunities and little encouragement to work together and learn from one another...and collaboration and teamwork are not the cultural norm. (pp. 69–70)

Teacher isolation prevents teachers learning from one another and building professional learning communities. Professional school cultures that support teacher learning (Little, 1987), on the contrary, feature sustained interaction among teachers about teaching and learning.

However, just creating opportunities for teachers to talk together will not create such communities, for the social norms of conversation do not necessarily lead

---

still are mostly in programs of 1 day. Only 13% of teachers in complementary (after school) schools and 16% of teachers in day schools have participated in programs of 4–6 sessions.

to meaningful learning. It might be fair to say that most adults do not know how to engage in constructive yet critical conversations with their peers, to function as "critical colleagues" (Achinstein & Meyer, 1997; Lord, 1994). In their conversations with each other, teachers tend to practice the conventions of politeness that are common in the wider culture. In most circumstances, teachers refrain from asking probing questions about a colleague's practice, even when they have the opportunity to talk about professional issues because they do not want to "rock the boat," to appear critical, or to create tension with their colleagues (Grossman, Wineburg, & Woolworth, 2001). As Lord suggests, teachers must be willing "to serve as commentators and critics of their own and other teachers' practices" (p. 185). This challenge suggests a question. How can we create professional development opportunities in which the unfamiliar norms of critical colleagueship are valued, and explicit experience, practice and support for engaging in these kinds of behaviors are provided?

Focus on Pedagogic Content Knowledge

In research on programs of professional development in five American Jewish communities, only 13% focused on Jewish content per se, and another 18% focused on methods for teaching a particular Jewish content. The remaining programs (69%) centered on issues of pedagogy, leadership, or other topics without articulating a concrete connection to Jewish subject matter (Holtz et al., 2000). Given most teachers' lack of Jewish subject-matter knowledge, creating professional development opportunities that deal both with Jewish subject matter and also with issues of teaching and learning those subjects is of critical importance.

The goals, challenges, pedagogic strategies of subject matters are different one from another (Stodolsky, 1988). Teaching Hebrew is different from teaching Bible, Values, Rabbinics, or Jewish Customs and Practices. Articulating this point, Shulman described pedagogic content knowledge as follows:

> [Pedagogical content knowledge consists of knowing]...for the most regularly taught topics in one's subject area, the most useful forms of representation of those ideas, the most powerful analogies, illustrations, examples, explanations, and demonstrations—in a word, the ways of representing and formulating the subject that make it comprehensible to others....[also,] an understanding of what makes the learning of specific topics easy or difficult; the conceptions and preconceptions that students of different ages and backgrounds bring with them to the learning of those most frequently taught topics. (Shulman, 1986, p. 9)

If Shulman is right, we need to think about how to provide forums to help teachers in the varied settings of Jewish education develop appropriate pedagogic content knowledge.

Jewish education calls for yet another kind of knowledge related to content. It is the knowledge related to the theological and ideological issues inherent in the subjects we teach as well as the demands of each particular setting. For example, we know that students are troubled with such issues as: Who wrote the Bible? Does God answer prayer? How can one believe in God after the Holocaust? How can I support Israel when I do not support its policies toward the Palestinian people? Professional development for teachers would certainly need to include opportunities to encounter multiple authentic Jewish approaches to these ideas, and opportunities for them to develop ways to articulate their own beliefs. What would professional development look like that would give teachers the inner and external resources they need to deal with thorny issues related to foundational beliefs and ideas raised in the questions above?

Learn in and from Practice

Teachers often claim that they learn the most about teaching from experience, but teaching experience alone does not create good teachers. Experience is a great teacher when one has the opportunities, practices, and support to learn from experience. Teacher educators have designed a variety of approaches to help teachers learn in and from practice (Ball & Cohen, 1999). Strategies for supporting teacher learning include investigating records of practice—like student work, videos of classrooms, curriculum (Ball & Cohen, 1999; Grossman, 2005; Lampert & Ball, 1998)—and creating opportunities to "rehearse and develop discrete components of complex practice in settings of reduced complexity... approximations of practice" (Grossman & McDonald, 2008). Examples of the latter include planning lessons or units, role-playing explanations or responding to questions, simulating various lesson openings. All of these practices have the potential to provide the support necessary for teachers to learn from their experience of teaching.

How Do These Characteristics Take Shape in the Context of Real Professional Development in Jewish Educational Settings?

Given the varied contexts and realities of Jewish schools, can these principles become hallmarks of professional development in these settings? To explore this question, I offer a set of case studies, drawn from the work of the graduates of the Mandel Foundation's Mandel Teacher Educators' Institute (MTEI). Founded in 1995, MTEI prepares senior Jewish educators to design and implement professional development for teachers that embodies the principles and practices outlined in this chapter, while addressing the challenges of Jewish education (Appendix). MTEI has four main goals:

1. To promote a vision of Jewish education that:
    - Takes subject matter seriously
    - Emphasizes text study
    - Values children's thinking
    - Fosters children's collaborative learning
    - Sees teachers' learning as central to teaching

2. To support participants in creating a collaborative culture for teacher learning in their schools.
3. To help participants develop deeper and useable Jewish content knowledge.
4. To help participants develop a repertoire of professional development principles and practices that engage teachers in the study and improvement of their teaching.

Multiple evaluations of the MTEI program and its graduates over the last decade have shown that the graduates of the program have enacted professional development initiatives that are consonant with the principles discussed above (Dorph, Stodolsky, & Wohl, 2002; Stodolsky, 2009; Stodolsky et al., 2006; Stodolsky, Dorph, & Rosov, 2008; Stodolsky, Dorph, Feiman-Nemser, & Hecht, 2004).

The programs described below are examples of three such programs not designed by academics or educational researchers; rather, they are initiatives constructed by practicing educators in the field. They can be thought of as "existence proofs"—that is, they present solid evidence that the model of professional development described, though challenging, can be learned and enacted in Jewish educational settings. I have selected these three cases as examples because each takes place in a different setting, has different goals, and uses different professional development strategies. Yet they all feature rigorous, cumulative, collaborative learning opportunities that engage teachers in challenging their ideas and each other while thinking carefully about issues of teaching and learning. Although these examples emanate from American settings, international studies of education support these very same principles and practices—and I am confident that with attention to context could be applied in other Jewish communities across the globe (Barber & Mourshed, 2007; Bolam & McMahon, 2004; Darling-Hammond et al., 2009; Day & Sachs, 2004).

Case 1: Day High School—Creating Professional Learning in a Collegial, Collaborative Environment

Tamar[7] and Aaron, faculty members in a large Orthodox day high school, designed this initiative. Tamar was the head of the language department; Aaron was a teacher in the rabbinics department. Together, they instituted an optional teacher study group, open to all faculty members. Given the typical divide between teachers of Jewish and general studies in Jewish day schools and the disciplinary divide among departments in most high schools, this was a bold move in and of itself. Between 16 and 22 teachers, out of a possible 36, participated regularly. They met once a month during a 42-minute lunch-break for an entire school year. None of the teachers were compensated for their time, although Aaron and Tamar did receive very modest remuneration for playing a coordinating role.

---

[7] All the names used in this chapter are pseudonyms.

Tamar and Aaron had two goals:

1. To get teachers talking about their practice in a way that opened up a sense of curiosity about teaching strategies and teaching decisions.
2. To create a professional learning environment for teachers.

There were two aspects to their program: (1) a study group in which teachers studied videos of classes in order to practice observing and discussing teaching and learning in a safe context, and (2) classroom observations in which group members would visit each other's classes and then discuss teaching and learning in their "real lives."

The group began by examining a video of a teacher who did not teach in their high school, before moving on to study videos of Tamar and Aaron and one other faculty volunteer. In order to make these videos both practical and engaging, Tamar and Aaron edited a 42-minute class length video into 15-minute clips, carefully selecting some moments they thought represented their best teaching and some representing "problematic" moments. During each of the sessions, the group discussed what they had noticed, working as partners (hevruta-style)[8] to talk about particular topics raised in the discussion of the video-clip.

Although it had been rare at this school for veteran teachers to observe each other unless someone was having trouble and needed advice, teachers in the group made time to visit each other's classrooms, and reported that the opportunity was "intellectually stimulating" and "fun" and that the spirit of these conversations was open and trusting.

Teachers wanted to continue discussing issues that emerged in their study group, and so they self-organized four additional study sessions. One such issue involved the question of when and if it is appropriate for teachers to share personal stories or information in class. Another session involved teachers exploring the role of reinforcement in learning and the nature of reinforcement that is appropriate during the high school years.

Aaron and Tamar measured their success by (1) the large proportion of teachers who attended all the sessions (2) the fact that teachers made the time to observe each other (3) the comments teachers made, and (4) the additional sessions that teachers set up for themselves. In their evaluations, teachers reported loving the intellectual inquiry in which they were engaged. Although Tamar and Aaron did not have data to show how much teachers actually changed their teaching practice, they did witness changes in the dimension of colleagueship and in how the teachers talked about their teaching.

---

[8]Hevruta study is a traditional method of Jewish learning, which involves two people studying a text together helping each other ascertain its meaning.

Case 2: Congregational School—Building a Collaborative Environment for Part-Time Teachers to Focus on Student Learning

The principal of a congregational school for over a decade, Lucy had always offered professional development to her teachers (there are nine teachers on Lucy's faculty; the average length of employment in her school is 11.5 years). These sessions were usually facilitated by outside experts and were "stand alones," not tied to each other in any substantive way. Although not paid for the time, teachers were contractually obligated to annually attend about 18 hours of professional development. The 18 hours often included the orientation at the beginning of the year, a community professional learning day, and several discrete sessions during the year.

After participating in a year-long professional development program led by an MTEI graduate, Lucy began to facilitate her faculty's professional development and work with her teachers in a more sustained fashion. Her goals were similar to those of Aaron and Tamar; she wanted to support teachers talking about their practice in ways that opened up a sense of curiosity about teaching and learning and to create a professional learning environment for teachers. There was one big difference—Lucy's starting point. Lucy was concerned that when she spoke with her teachers after observing them teach, they did not seem to focus on what children were learning. This focus was of critical importance to her. In order to work on all these goals, she decided to study videos from the MTEI videobank[9] with her teachers.

After 2 years, Lucy decided she wanted to move teachers' attention to student learning in the "real life" of their congregational school, and she introduced a methodology called Japanese "Lesson Study" (Lewis & Tsuchida, 1998). This strategy involves several deliberate steps: Teachers design a single lesson collaboratively; one member of the group teaches the lesson, while others, including the co-planners, observe it; the lesson is filmed and is analyzed by the group which has watched it; and then the lesson is revised and re-taught by others. Lucy modified the process in order to "make it work" in her setting and time frame.

The first time she tried it, Lucy and her faculty planned a session on Psalms that was part of the curriculum of the sixth grade. They used printed curriculum materials as their jumping-off point. The lesson they created added an opening exercise that framed the lesson and other exercises to help their students find the content more meaningful. These activities included having students look at greeting cards as ways of expressing gratitude and other emotions, reading Psalms, and finally writing their

---

[9] The MTEI videobank (2000): Reading the classroom as text: a videobank and resource guide for investigations of teaching and learning, is a project of the Mandel Foundation. It includes tapes and transcripts of lessons in congregational schools, textual, and student curriculum materials relevant to each lesson, examples of student work, and suggested activities that professional developers can use in conjunction with these records of practice.

own Psalms. Lucy and the teachers were delighted with the student engagement in the lesson and felt that the opening exercise did help the students "get into" the notion of expressing gratitude via the written word.

The following year, Lucy and her faculty once again engaged in lesson study. This time, they planned a session about Hanukkah. Lucy added an additional dimension to the design: She taught the lesson twice—once to each of two different fifth grade classes. The lesson included students studying in groups, presenting their learning to the class, and collaborating on the development of skits. Teachers also created a "pop quiz" to assess students' learning. Between the first and the second teaching of the lesson, the teachers assessed the students' learning and redesigned aspects of the lesson. Between classes, teachers suggested that Lucy work more actively with the students' small groups, listening as they worked and asking probing questions to encourage their thoughts. The second class did better on the pop quiz than the first class.

Lucy felt that the seminars succeeded in establishing a collective collegial forum for teachers to share their ideas and learn from each other. In particular, Lucy felt that teachers were becoming more reflective and were focusing on teaching in ways that would enhance student learning. In an interview study done after the first 2 years of the program, teachers' comments support Lucy's assessment. The following comments give some sense of their experience and their learning midway through the experience just described:

> [I am] trying to have a big idea when I am teaching... critically looking at myself.... Okay these were my goals, did I get there? If I didn't get there, where did we go? How can I start this again next week? (Lisa)

> When we have a chance to meet professionally like this, this is a whole different story. It is so wonderful to be able share ideas and share thoughts and share methods with colleagues in this way that wasn't really afforded to us before, when it was like meeting style or you know, somebody else coming here (Rivka).

> I think it put teachers on the same wave length...Where are we as a group of teachers? My kids are going on to other teachers. We are all teaching the same kids. If we have different ideas, having a team philosophy. We do it differently, but have the same goals (Mimi). (Stodolsky et al., 2008)

Case 3: Central Agency Sponsored Initiative—Increasing Pedagogical Content Knowledge

This central agency sponsored program was a year-long professional learning experience, including a trip to Israel, focused on teaching about Israel. In contradistinction to the two other programs, this one was highly subsidized. Participants paid only $750 for the 10 day Israel trip that was core to their learning experience. In addition, among the 30 educators who participated, there were both novices and veterans. The participants delivered services to children and youth from fifth grade through high school in both formal and informal settings. The group met monthly during the academic year.

Two central agency consultants, Susie and Sarah, directed this initiative, which had two distinct goals: (1) increasing participating educators' knowledge and connection to Israel, and (2) engaging these educators in a collaborative and interactive learning experience that they could use as a model for creating active learning for their students. Susie and Sarah designed an intervention using the principles of problem-based learning (PBL), which is a strategy that challenges students to find and use appropriate resources and work cooperatively in groups to better understand and seek solutions to real-world problems.

Sarah and Susie wanted to connect participants to Israel via interests and passions that they trusted would be shared by their participants and which could connect them to Israel's land and people. They chose to focus on environmental issues in Israel and asked group members to choose among six different aspects of Israel and the environment. Participants formed teams to investigate issues, such as water, sustainable communities, air, animals, plants, and land.

Susie and Sarah framed problems on which team members did research over the course of the months prior to the 10-day Israel trip. For the group studying sustainable communities, Susie and Sarah framed their problem as follows:

> Israel has not developed a strong carbon free energy strategy. As Israel's energy demand grows, Israel continues to invest in natural gas, a carbon-based energy source that is imported from Africa, rather than develop solar energy that is local and more sustainable....
>
> What does Israel need to do to develop more carbon-free/solar alternative energy for use inside Israel? What barriers exist and how can Israel get past them? What Jewish sources can inform our thinking about sustainable environments and the importance of using alternative energy? (Written communication from Susie and Sarah)

In Israel, the group visited Kibbutz Lotan, a sustainable community in action, where members are dedicated to making their kibbutz totally self-sufficient in terms of energy. They saw solar panels and ovens, and multiple creative ways in which this kibbutz reuses and recycles products and materials that others would relegate to garbage or waste. Participants had a chance to ask experts and regular kibbutz members about their thinking about alternative energy sources and to probe the obstacles to spreading these strategies more widely. Participants crawled in and out of igloo-like solar huts, shaped bricks from mud and straw and baked them in the sun, and baked brownies in the solar ovens. They developed an experiential understanding of what it means to be energy independent—off the national grid.

When the participants returned from Israel, members of all the groups organized a fair for each other (and invited guests) to share what they had learned about the problem they had been studying and created problem-based learning experiences for their students. One example of team members' engagement with their own students serves as an illustration of this work. Students did a project on improving the school environment by using found materials in the waste bins of the synagogue and creating lightshades and artistic sculptures. Students shared their learning, displaying pictures of different stages of the PBL learning process along with a variety of artifacts that illustrated their work, e.g., the identified problem, the worksheets that they created indicating what information they needed to gather to learn more about the issues, evidence of group work and evaluation.

Given the relatively short time line and the ambitious goals of the project, Sarah and Susie were able to see that educators were indeed working with their students on PBL learning experiences. They wished that funding for the program had been longer than 12 or 13 months so that they could monitor and assist participants in the program develop PBL learning experiences related to Israel and other curriculum-based projects, but worried that inviting participants to join an 18-month initiative would have put them off.

Analysis of Cases

When we examine these three cases, we see the enactment of the principles of effective professional development (see Table 1). Each case was embedded in a different context, each was at least a year in length and involved multiple sessions that were linked and each involved serious, collaborative work on the part of participants. Facilitators carefully chose goals for teachers' learning and provided learning opportunities, which encouraged teachers to engage in inquiry into the practices of teaching and learning. The facilitators created active learning environments through developing records of practice (videos in the case of Aaron and Tamar; problem-based learning challenges in the case of the Susie and Sarah consultants) and also "approximations of practice" (co-planning, evaluating, and re-planning a lesson in the case of Lucy; the learning fair in the case of Sarah and Susie).

These cases give us a sense of what is possible, even within the significant constraints of the real world of Jewish education. Yet each of these cases seems a bit precarious, for each relied upon energetic leadership and groups of teachers that were willing to go beyond the call of duty and beyond their paid hours to work together on improving their teaching craft. The third also relied on a generous grant to support educators' trips to Israel. For these kinds of programs to be sustainable over the long term, they would need to be built into the system more fully. This kind of ongoing learning would need to become part of a teacher's job description, part of the regular school day and school year, and part of the educational budget. In the meantime, the cases are inspiring stories of what is possible when teachers find ways to learn together, investigating their practice, in a context of curiosity and trust.

Table 1 A comparison of the three PD cases

Principles of effective PD	Day high school	Congregational school	Central agency
Cumulative and ongoing	X	X	X
Job embedded	–	X	–
Active learning	X	X	X
Collegial, collaborative environment	X	X	X
Pedagogical content knowledge	–	X	X
Learn in and from practice	X	X	X

Conclusion

From the perspective of scholarship and developing a more extensive knowledge base, this chapter suggests a variety of avenues for future research related to teachers' knowledge and practice. While we know that it is possible to produce professional developers who can design and implement quality programs infused with the principles of effective PD, we do not know much about the impact of these initiatives on participating teachers' ideas about teaching and learning and their classroom practice.

In terms of pedagogic practices, we need to study what and how teachers modify their teaching practices based on their PD learning experiences and whether any of the changes "make them" more effective pedagogues. Do any of the PD practices change the nature of communication in the classroom; help teachers become more powerful designers of active learning experiences; encourage the development of powerful pedagogic content knowledge?

With regard to student outcomes, the gold standard for assessing effective PD in general education is the connection between professional development for the teacher and students' achievement. Although there is insufficient research[10] on this relationship in general education, there is even less in Jewish education.[11] Moreover, in Jewish education outcomes for student learning are underspecified even when goals are stated. In order to track the impact of PD on student learning, we would have to take the arena of learning in Jewish subject areas more seriously and be willing to invest in substantive work on developing clear and worthwhile outcomes for Jewish learning in the variety of settings in which it takes place.[12] Assessments of student learning that can produce data about changes in students' knowledge and understanding will also need to be developed.

Other avenues of inquiry relate to professional developers and their education and practice. We can ask questions about professional developers that are similar to those asked about teachers and students. Starting with the notion of outcomes, if the gold standard of evaluating the effectiveness of teacher professional development is change in student outcomes, does it not make sense that the gold standard for professional developers is "teacher outcomes?" Does the PD offered using the new paradigm suggested in this chapter help teachers develop more effective teaching practices? We have little research in general or Jewish education that provides a window on this question (Stodolsky et al., 2008; Wayne et al., 2008). Based on research in general education (Ball & Cohen, 1999; Knapp, 2003), this chapter has

---

[10] Darling-Hammond et al., 2009; Porter et al., 2000; Wayne et al., 2008.

[11] The Jewish Educational Services of North America (JESNA) evaluation (2006) of the Nurturing Excellence in Synagogue Schools (NESS) project used student attitude toward education and continuing beyond Bar Mitzvah as measures of outcomes. Although they are both very important, neither is the kind of subject-matter outcome being measured by current educational research.

[12] See the Benchmarks and Standards Project for an example of such work in the area of Bible teaching and learning in day schools, a project of the Melton Research Center of the Jewish Theological Seminary.

suggested that there is an isometric relationship between the education of students, teachers, and professional developers. Because there are few programs designed to develop professional developers, there is little to no research that examines this premise in an empirical way. As we try to make more robust PD an ongoing feature of teacher work, we could benefit from more research that investigates these questions.

Policy Implications

Because we are addressing a practical problem here, that is, the improvement of teachers' practice in the service of improved student learning, there are other implications as well. If we believe that students' learning is connected to teachers' learning, and we want to improve students' learning, we know what to do:

- Make ongoing learning part of what it means to be a teacher
- Set aside time, money, and human resources at each school and central agency to design and facilitate professional development that follows the principles outlined in this chapter
- Develop programs for the "trainers of trainers"

What can be done to help make this a reality? Because of the complexity of the issues, action needs to come from all the stakeholders who care about the supporting the work of teachers and improving the learning experiences of students. For academicians and professional developers, the implications are obvious:

Professional Developers: provide principle-based PD; develop rich cases of principle-based professional development to augment those offered in this chapter; develop records of practice that could be used in the learning opportunities for teachers and professional developers.

Academicians and Educational Researchers: prepare personnel to lead PD efforts; evaluate PD programs[13] and their impact; investigate the impact of PD on teachers' ideas and practices; study the impact of PD on teachers' practice and student achievement.

Other stakeholders also need to step up to the plate in order to create the necessary climate and infrastructure supports for the implementation of professional development as a leverage strategy to improve the field of Jewish education. For example:

Parents: let the principal know that you value both professional development for teachers and those who are skilled in providing it; use parent education committees to help finance and structure in the time for this work.

Teachers: demand that ongoing professional learning opportunities be built into your contracts.

---

[13] Sales, Samuel, and Koren (2007) and JESNA updates include listings of PD offerings, but one cannot ascertain which, if any, are grounded in the principles of effective PD.

School Leaders: support ongoing professional development for your teachers by building in time and opportunities for PD; create formal positions (part-time or full-time depending on size and complexity of your institution) for professional developers; support the ongoing professionalization of those who will plan and lead these initiatives in your institutions.

Central Agency Personnel: develop personnel and programs that offer PD and/or consult and support school based personnel in planning and facilitating principle-based PD.

Foundation Supporters and Personnel: encourage the development of and support for grants (and the development of grants) for PD that embody these principles.

This call to many stakeholders draws attention to an issue that goes beyond the educational challenges that this chapter addressed. It is clear from the cases presented in this chapter that even very experienced, knowledgeable teachers value substantive, collaborative professional learning opportunities. It is also clear that leaders can be prepared and supported to head up such ambitious initiatives. What remains unclear is the extent of Jewish communal commitment. How committed are we to student learning and, by extension, to teacher learning?

Appendix[14]

In the same way that teachers need to think about the student as learner, the professional developer must think about the teacher as learner. The subject matter of the curriculum for professional developers is the learner instructional triangle as well as the teacher instructional triangle. It includes engaging with fellow professional

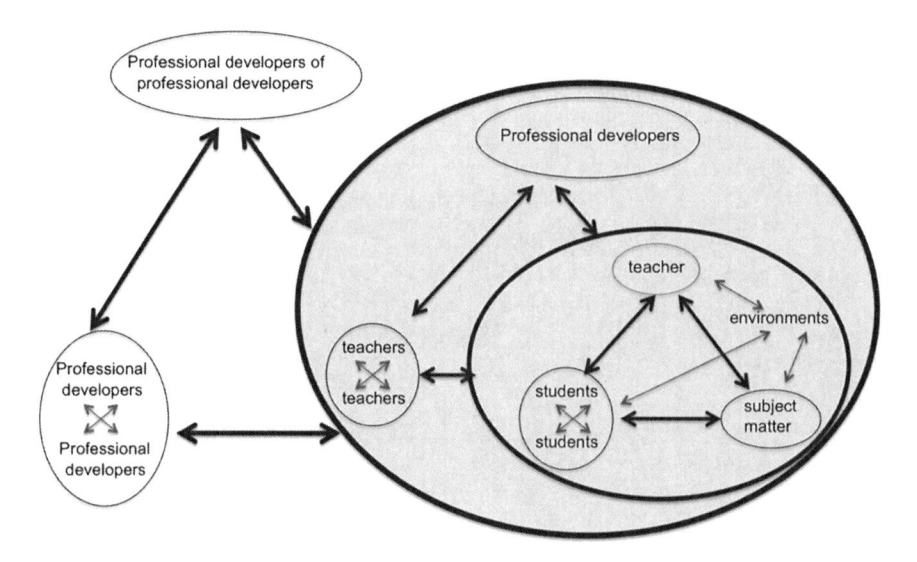

Fig. 3 Professional developer learning triangle

---

[14]Deborah Ball introduced this graphic into the design and curriculum work of MTEI in 1996.

developers and together "getting smarter" about how to help teachers learn to teach their students to become active learners of "X." This process also assumes a teacher, the professional developer of professional developers.

References

Achinstein, B., & Meyer, T. (1997). *The uneasy marriage between friendship and critique: Dilemmas of fostering critical friendship in a novice teacher learning community*. Paper presented at the Annual Meeting of the American Educational Research Association, Chicago, IL.

Ball, D. L., & Cohen, D. K. (1999). Developing practice, developing practitioners: Toward a practice-based theory of professional education. In L. Darling-Hammond & G. Sykes (Eds.), *Teaching as the learning profession: Handbook of policy and practice*. San Francisco: Jossey-Bass Publishers.

Barber, M., & Mourshed, M. (2007). *How the world's best-performing school systems come out on top*. New York: McKinsey & Company.

Ben-Avie, M., & Kress, J. S. (2008). A North American study of educators in Jewish day and congregational schools: Technical report of the educators in Jewish schools study. www.JewishEducationalChange.org.

Bolam, R., & McMahon, A. (2004). Literature, definitions and models: Towards a conceptual map. In C. Day & J. Sachs (Eds.), *International handbook on the continuing professional development of teachers*. UK: Open University Press.

Bransford, J. D., Brown, A. L., Cocking, R. R. (Eds.). (1999). *How people learn*. Washington, D.C: National Academy Press.

Cohen, D. K., Raudenbusch, S. W., & Ball., D. L. (2003). Resources, instruction and research. *Educational Evaluation and Policy Analysis, 25*, 119–142.

Darling-Hammond, L., Wei, R. C., Andree, A., Richardson, N., & Orphanos., S. (2009). Professional learning in the learning profession: A status report on teacher development in the United States and abroad. Report by National Staff Development Council.

Day, C., & Sachs, J. (2004). Professionalism, performativity, and empowerment: Discourses in the politics, policies and purposes of continuing professional development. In C. Day & J. Sachs (Eds.), *International handbook on the continuing professional development of teachers*. UK: Open University Press.

Dewey, J. (1902/1964). The child and the curriculum. In R. D. Archambault (Ed.), *John Dewey on education: Selected writings*. Chicago: University of Chicago Press.

Dewey, J. (1938). *Experience and education*. New York: Collier Books, Macmillan Publishing Co.

Dorph, G. Z., Stodolsky, S. S., & Wohl, R. (2002). Growing as teacher educators: Learning new professional development practices. *Journal of Jewish Education, 68*, 58–72.

Feiman-Nemser, S. (1998). Linking mentoring and teacher learning. *Velon Tijdscrift voor Lerarenopleiders*, June/July 1998.

Feiman-Nemser, S. (2001). Helping novices learn to teach: Lessons from an exemplary support teacher. *Journal of Teacher Education, 52*, 17–30.

Gamoran, A., Goldring, E. B., Robinson, B., Tammivaara, J., & Goodman., R. (1998). *The teachers report: A portrait of teachers in Jewish schools*. New York: Council for Initiatives in Jewish Education.

Grossman, P. (2005). Research on pedagogical approaches. In M. Cochran-Smith & K. M. Zeichner (Eds.), *Studying teacher education*. Mahwah, NJ: Lawrence Erlbaum.

Grossman, P., & McDonald, M. (2008). Back to the future: Directions for research in teaching and teacher education. *American Educational Research Journal, 45*, 184–205.

Grossman, P., Wineburg, S., & Woolworth, S. (2001). Toward a theory of teacher community. *Teachers College Record, 103*, 942–1012.

Hawkins, D. (1967). I, thou, and it. In *The informed vision: Essays in learning and human nature*. New York: Agathon Press.

Holtz, B. W., Gamoran, A., Dorph, G. Z., Goldring, E., & Robinson, B. (2000). Changing the core: Communal policies and present realities in the professional development of teachers for Jewish schools. *Journal of Jewish Communal Service, 76*, 173–185.

Jackson, P. W. (1986). *The practice of teaching*. New York: Teachers College Press.

Jewish Education Service of North America. (2006). *Nurturing excellence in synagogue schools*. New York: Author.

Jewish Education Service of North America. (2008). *Educators in Jewish schools study*. New York: Author.

Kegan, R. (1982). *The evolving self: Problem and process in human development*. Cambridge, MA: Harvard University Press.

Knapp, M. S. (2003). Professional development as a policy pathway. *Review of Research in Education, 27*, 109–157.

Lampert, M., & Ball, D. L. (1998). *Teaching, multimedia, and mathematics: Investigations of real practice*. New York: Teachers College Press.

Lewis, C. C., & Tsuchida, I. (1998). A lesson is like a swiftly flowing river: How research lessons improve Japanese education. *American Educator, 22*(12–18), 50–52.

Lieberman, A. (1996). Practices that support teacher development: Transforming conceptions of professional learning. In M. W. McLaughlin & I. Oberman (Eds.), *Teacher learning: New policies, new practices*. New York: Columbia University, Teachers College Press.

Little, J. W. (1987). Teachers as colleagues. In V. Richardson-Koehler (Ed.), *Educators' handbook: A research perspective*. New York: Longman.

Little, J. W. (1993). Teachers' professional development in a climate of educational reform. *Educational Evaluation and Policy Analysis, 15*, 129–151.

Lord, B. (1994). Teachers' professional development: Critical colleagueship and the role of professional community. In N. Cobb (Ed.), *The future of education: Perspectives on national standards in America*. New York: College Entrance Examination Board.

Lortie, D. (1975). *Schoolteacher*. Chicago: University of Chicago Press.

Ma, L. (1999). *Knowing and teaching elementary mathematics: Teachers' understanding of fundamental mathematics in China and the United States*. Mahwah, NJ and London, England: Lawrence Erlbaum Associates.

McDiarmid, W., Ball, D. L., & Anderson, C. W. (1989). Why staying one chapter ahead doesn't really work: Subject-specific pedagogy. In M. Reynolds (Ed.), *Knowledge base for beginning teachers*. Elmsford, New York: Pergamon Press.

McDonald, J. P. (1992). *Teaching: Making sense of an uncertain craft*. New York: Teachers College Press.

Porter, A. C., Garet, M., Desimone, L., Yoon, K. S., & Birman, B. F. (2000). *Does professional development change teaching practice? Results from a three-year study*. Report from the U.S. Department of Education, Office of the Under Secretary, Planning and Evaluation Service, Elementary and Secondary Education Division.

Sales, A., Samuel, N., & Koren, A. (2007). *Mapping professional development for Jewish educators*. Waltham, MA: Brandeis University's Fisher-Bernstein Institute for Jewish Philanthropy and Leadership.

Shulman, L. S. (1986). Those who understand: Knowledge growth in teaching. *Educational Researcher, 15*, 4–14.

Sizer, T. (1984/1992). *Horace's compromise*. New York: Houghton Mifflin.

Sparks, D., & Hirsch, S. (1990). *A national plan for improving professional development*. Oxford, OH: National Staff Development Council.

Stein, M. K., Smith, M. S., & Silver, E. A. (1999). The development of professional developers: Learning to assist teachers in new settings in new ways. *Harvard Educational Review, 69*, 237–270.

Stodolsky, S. S. (1988). *The subject matters: Classroom activity in math and social studies.* Chicago: University of Chicago Press.

Stodolsky, S. S. (2009). *A decade of learning: An evaluation of the Mandel Teacher Educator Institute.* Report to the Mandel Foundation, Cleveland, OH.

Stodolsky, S. S., Dorph, G. Z., & Feiman-Nemser., S. (2006). Professional culture and professional development in Jewish schools: Teachers' perceptions and experiences. *Journal of Jewish Education, 72*, 91–108.

Stodolsky, S., Dorph, G. Z., Feiman-Nemser, S., & Hecht., S. (2004). *Boston MTEI: Leading the way to a new vision for teachers and schools.* Report to Boston Jewish Community and sponsoring foundations and agencies.

Stodolsky, S. S., Dorph, G. Z., & Rosov, W. (2008). Teacher professional development in congregational settings. *Religious Education, 100*, 240–261.

Troen, V., & Boles, K. (2003). *Who's teaching your children? Why the teacher crisis is worse than you think and what can be done about it.* New Haven, CT: Yale University Press.

Wayne, A. J., Kwang, S. Y., Pei, Z., Cronen, S., & Garet., M. S. (2008). Experimenting with teacher professional development: Motives and methods. *Educational Researcher, 37*, 469–479.

Professional Development: *Vini, Vidi, Vici*? Short-Term Jewish Educators Trips to Israel as Professional-Development Programs

Shelley Kedar

Introduction: Foundations and Definitions

In 47 BCE, Julius Caesar claimed an overwhelming Roman victory in the battle of Zela and sent the famous, simple yet powerful, message back to the Senate in Rome: "Veni, Vidi, Vici" (Latin: *I came, I saw, I conquered*). Using this quote as the heading of a chapter about Jewish educators' trips to Israel is a calculated risk, as the relationship between Israel and the Jewish people is often described in confrontational language, ranging from Rabbi Joesph Soloveitchik's (1971) "six knocks" on the doors of world Jewry to an "alternative" paradigm for Israel engagement termed "hugging and wrestling" (Gringras, 2005). Assuming that "Veni" and "vidi" are possible however difficult to attain: that is to say, whereas we do know that an educational trip to Israel has a profound impact on young adult participants (e.g., Kelner, 2004; Kirshenblatt-Gimblett, 2002; Saxe, Sasson, & Hecht, 2006) "vici" is as yet unclear—how can it have a personal as well as professional effect on Jewish educators?

I will hereafter relate to the term "professional development" as the work-related learning opportunities for practicing teachers, aimed at nurturing knowledge, skills, and commitments required for professional practice (Feiman-Nemser, 2006). Based on literature, I assume that any educational system requires a professional-development plan for the teachers who work in its domain, and even more so in Jewish education as teachers are characterized by weakness of backgrounds and general lack of preparation for the field (Zaiman-Dorph & Holtz, 2000).

A long-standing debate exists between two competing concepts defining the purpose of a professional-development program: on the one hand, is the focus on providing educators with tools and methods, and on the other hand, engaging them in an ongoing learning process, one that fosters an investigative stance toward the teaching and learning of a particular content (Stodolsky, Zaiman Dorph, & Feinman- Nemser, 2006). This relationship was described by Corchan-Smith and Lytle (1999) as a metaphoric pendulum swinging between "teaching better" and

S. Kedar (✉)
Bet Hatfutsot, Museum of the Diaspora, Tel Aviv, Israel
e-mail: shelleykedar@gmail.com

"knowing more." The authors (ibid.) offer three conceptions of teachers' learning stemming from this "swinging" relationship between the two:

(1) On the one hand is "Knowledge *for* practice:" the more teachers know the better they teach, therefore knowledge is to be directly applied in the classroom.
(2) On the other hand is "Knowledge *of* practice:" teachers have personal knowledge and are partners and leaders in the knowledge construction process, thus knowledge acquisition is a broad social-political process.
(3) Swinging between the two is "Knowledge *in* practice:" teachers knowledge is grounded in the teaching act itself and reflecting upon it. This third type of relationship echoes theories by Dewey (1938) and Schon (1987).

Zaiman-Dorph and Holtz (2000) offer a slightly different look at "good professional development." They define it as a program connected to *knowledge of the content* that is being taught; has a clear and focused *audience* in mind; has a *coherent plan* that is sustained over time; and gives teachers opportunities *to reflect, analyze, and work* on their practice. Stodolsky et al. (2006) add another dimension to the above definition and propose that "new style" professional development enables teachers *first hand experience* as well as *collaborative learning*, which they, in turn, may enact in their classrooms.

Tachlit: The Purpose of Jewish Professional Development

> R' Tarfon and the elders were gathered in the upper chamber of Nit'zah's house in Lod. This question was asked in their presence: Is talmud (i.e. learning) greater or is ma'aseh (i.e. action) greater? R' Tarfon replied and said, 'Ma'aseh is greater.' R' Akiva replied and said, 'Talmud is greater.' Everyone replied and said, 'Talmud is greater, because talmud leads to ma'aseh ...' (Kiddushin 40b)

From this Talmudic discussion, we learn about the inseparability of learning from action in the Jewish world of study. Following the discussion of the relationship between the two in the former section, I wish to propose a purpose for *Jewish* professional development that demands inseparability of learning from action: *Tachlit*. Nowadays, *Tachlit* or *Tachlis* is a colloquial way of saying "in practical terms" as the origin of the word in Hebrew derives from the root "tool" or "instrument."[1] I propose that, the *Tachlit* of a Jewish professional-development program includes "tools" or "instruments" such as: knowledge, ability, and skills to perform the educators' task, emphasizing the means to achieve the aims of the educational work (Nisan, 1997). As the word *Tachlit* also interprets as "meaning,"[2] another inseparable component includes a focus on the teacher as a person standing at the heart of the educational work—in the sense that "you cannot teach anything well until you make meaning of it for yourself" (Grant, 2008). This idea is often associated with

---

[1] The word in Hebrew stems from the root which is literally a tool.

[2] The word will is the translation of "meaning" in a phrase like "the meaning of life."

Parker Palmer (1998) who argued that the human heart is the source of good teaching, and therefore, good teaching is not just about "tools" but rather comes from the identity and integrity of the teacher. Therefore, the other side of the *Tachlit*, purpose of Jewish professional development, is the identity of the teacher, seen as an adult traveling the life-long identity journey (Schuster, 2003).

Hence, I propose that the purpose of a meaningful Jewish professional-development program is the synergy between two often competing concepts: *means*—the tools or instruments needed to perform the act of teaching, and *meaning*—developing and crystallizing the educational identity (Nisan, 1997) of the Jewish educator, an identity constituted through the commitment to an educational endeavor, guided by knowledge-based conceptions of education and of the good and the worthy.

Israel Experience as Jewish Professional Development

As a phenomenon, educational trips to Israel (that will hereafter be referred to as "Israel experiences") are an example of the longest running, well-documented, and researched example of educational religious tourism—focusing mainly on young adult participants (To name a few: Chazan & Koraznsky, 1997; Cohen, 2000; Cohen, 2006b; Saxe, Sasson, & Hecht, 2006). Indeed, research indicates that it is one of the most powerful educational tools available for affecting identity and continuity among young Jews (Chazan, 1999). However, only a small body of research has accumulated on teachers' Israel experiences and an even smaller number of studies have specifically researched Israel experiences as professional-development programs (e.g., Reisman, 1993; Grant, Kelman, & Regev, 2001; Pomson & Grant, 2004).

A recent survey of Israel engagement in North American community day schools found that 77% of the respondents, who were mostly heads of school and heads of Jewish studies, participated in a professional-development program related to Israel, and 60% of them in a program that included a trip to Israel (Kopelowitz, 2005). The same survey mentioned that almost 92% of educators expressed interest in participating in professional-development programs in Israel (Kopelowitz, 2005). This interest has already translated into policies, for example, NACIE (North American Coalition for Israel Engagement, a project initiated by the Jewish Agency for Israel—now called Makom) has defined among its objectives for day and congregational schools: "(to) send (more) educators to Israel" (Katz, 2004). While a successful Israel program may very well reinforce Jewish identity, a question is raised whether the length time spent on the Israel trip program allows effective professional development (Stodolsky, Zaiman Dorph, & Feinman-Nemser, 2006). As an Israel experience program is in no way a long-term undertaking[3], it may

---

[3]This span of time relates to the time spent *in* Israel. Although some programs are an integral part of long-term professional-development processes, including pre- and post-programming in the country of origin, I wish to focus on the program in Israel and its potential to be a holistic unit.

even cause an adverse affect: "We came, we saw, we can't remember a thing!"[4] (Kirshenblatt-Gimblett, 2002, p. 3). Considering this framework of Israel experience programs, can they be more than elaborate one-time seminars?

Since Israel experience stands at the crossroads of three fields: religion, tourism, and education that have been melded into one concept in the post-modern age, namely educational religious tourism (Cohen, 2006), re-focusing on each field, separately, may enhance our understanding on how to create an Israel experience that is a Jewish professional development program.

Education—The "Eyes" of the Program

Israel education in Jewish communities around the world, presents an ongoing challenge for Jewish educators (Grant, 2008). It seems only natural, that the subject matter of a program in Israel will be *Israel education*, through a multifaceted approach (Chamo, Sabar Ben Yohushua, & Shimoni, 2009). This may assist in enhancing the teachers' ability to perform Israel education ("means") as well as strengthen their personal connection and understanding of Israel ("meaning"). Furthermore, the "new paradigm" formulated in recent literature (e.g., Zaiman-Dorph & Holtz, 2000) that outlines the "central tasks" for the practice of professional development, may be adapted and serve as the guiding "eyes" of the program in Israel:

1. *Intellect*: deepening and extending teachers' Israel knowledge.
2. *Instrument*: extending and refining teachers' repertoires so that they can perform relevant, connecting Israel education for students.
3. *Inspiration*: strengthening the attitudes and skills of teachers toward study and improving their own teaching of Israel.
4. *Influence*: increasing leadership development so that teachers can influence (as leaders) the life of the school with specific regard to Israel.
5. *Identity*: nurturing the teacher's personal connection and commitment to Israel.

Considering *all* the five "eyes" in creating the educational content of the Israel experience program paves the way toward fulfilling the purpose of professional development.

Tourism: From Trip to Experience

Much energy is directed at getting more people to *visit* Israel on organized *trips*. Intuitively, the framing of the program as an "Israel trip" impedes its ability to become a professional-development program. Use of the term *experience*, rather than "trip" or "visit" is not merely semantic, but signifies the belief that the participating educators are not travelers on a one off tourist vacation, and thus entails

---

[4] Printed on a T-shirt.

the possibility that the program becomes an important educational event (Chazan & Koraznsky, 1997).

Dewey (1938) offered a theory of education based on experience, grounded on two abstract principles: (i) continuity—all experiences are carried forward and influence future experiences and (ii) interaction—present experiences arise out of the relationship between the situation and the individual's stored past. Building on Dewey, I suggest the Israel experience program be structured as a continuous process, beginning prior to the arrival in Israel and ending after the return from Israel. Moreover, this process must build on the participating educators *existing* values, knowledge, and skills, as many times Israel education, similarly to Jewish education, is conversed from a deficit point of view (Chamo, 2008).

Religion: Community as Structure and Content

Assuming that reality is a web of communal relationships and that we understand reality when we are "in community" with it (Palmer, 1998) helps facilitate the understanding that teacher learning is improved when it takes place within a professional-learning community (Feiman-Nemser, 2006). This community is what Palmer (1998) calls "Community of Truth:" a rich and complex network of relationships in which we speak and listen, make claims on others, and make ourselves accountable. It is also a safe environment for adults to explore the meaning of their religious faith (Schuster & Grant, 2005), what Berger and Luckman (1966) defines as "plausibility structure" allowing individuals to engage in conversation with significant others in matters of religion. Put together, these two concepts can be Jewishly articulated in the term "*Sacred Community*" of Jewish educators.

Whereas in somewhat technical terms, any Israel experience entails building a supportive community as a core structure (Klein-Katz, 1998), creating a sacred community is not just "means," but also "meaning"—an end of its own. It is created and maintained by spiritual rituals like: texts study, prayer, and the gathered life of the community itself' (i.e., actually functioning in a community) that should be incorporated, possibly daily, into the program (Palmer, 1983).

To sum up, I suggest that an Israel experience program be constructed through the "eyes" of Israel education professional development, be considered and thus formulated as an *educational experience* and inspire as well as be implemented through the formation of a *sacred community* of Jewish educators.

Encounter Between Person and Place: Introducing Four Conceptual-Practical Models

Many Israel experience programs are built around the idea that it is the tangible contact with Israel as a physical place (landscape, archeological remains, settlements, and people) that produces a feeling of attachment to Jewish identity (Kirshenblatt-Gimblett, 2002). The actual act of walking the land, for example, nature hiking, is considered a way of strengthening *ahavat ha'aretz* (one's love for the land) through the development of *yediat ha'aretz* (an experiential knowledge of the land) (Katriel, 1995).

The importance of the relationship between the person and the place visited lacks research (Poria, Reichel, & Biran, 2006). However, it is proposed that this relationship is what defines the meaning of the visiting experience, through a continuum that has, at the one end, the person's socio-psychological motives for visiting a place and, at the other end, cultural-educational ones. A recent study on the significance of tourists' experiences of a heritage site, conducted by an Israeli research team at the Anne Frank House in Amsterdam (Poria, Reichel, & Biran, 2006), identified three categories or approaches to the person–place relationship: (1) willingness to feel connected to the history presented; (2) willingness to learn; and (3) motivations not linked with the historic attributes of the place whereby an element of social "obligation" is apparent: visiting because you feel you "should."

When Jews visit Israel, their approaches spread across a continuum of recreational, educational, cultural, and religious motives (Klein-Katz, 1998) corresponding with Poria's et al. (2006) categories. Moreover, as mentioned before, the relationship between the Jewish visitor and the place (Israel) is also very much influenced by the visitor's personal factors, such as the individual's Jewish biography, past experiences, and education (Cohen, 2003; Horowitz, 2003), and these in turn have a profound impact on the encounter with Israel. The different relationships between the person, the Jew, and the place, Israel, were articulated in an unpublished theory on Israel experience created and experimented by MELITZ: an independent non-profit informal Jewish–Zionist education agency established in 1973, centered in Jerusalem. MELITZ introduced to its staff an educational conception called "Site as Text,"[5] stemming from the idea that the Jewish visit to Israel is an educational process, during which Jewish identity and their belonging to the Jewish people is explored. According to this perception, Israel was defined as an educational resource, encountered by four model persons, each representing a different relationship between person and place:

1. *The Observer* who is visiting the site as an estranged outsider. He has the advantage of being able to be critical, supposedly "objective," without emotional involvement or commitment. However, his disadvantage is in the lack of value-based meaning of the visit.
2. *The Landlord* visits the site from a position of ownership and belonging. In this case the visit is an ideological standpoint, a political declaration of control. This is the other side of the observer approach: the site is related to emotionally and thus referring to it in critical and analytical terms is virtually impossible.

---

[5]The heading of the conception as well as its articulation were only used internally, in staff training—however they have had a substantial influence on many informal educators who have "carried" this conception with them to other Jewish educational venues.

3. *The Pilgrim* arrives at the site with respect, sacredness, and glorification. Expecting a transformative, highly emotional, "once in a lifetime" experience.
4. *The Person Looking for Meaning*: a title borrowed from Victor Frankl's 1946 book, this person visits the site as if he is visiting himself. During the visit a dialogue is created and the site turns from a neutral location to an arena for meaning making.

These encounters are constructed along four assumptions:

(1) The sites chosen in Israel are relevant to Jewish life and to core questions occupying Jews today.
(2) Each site has a historical and cultural depth, and gives rise to different layers of meaning.
(3) The encounter with the site engages the person, enabling him or her to find him/herself and relate to his or her circles of belonging.
(4) Site encounters are performed though active experience, whereby the person is required to engage in dialogue and interact with the site.

I will hereafter discuss each model, suggesting ways in which each one could implement the purpose and practice of Jewish professional development. These following is not based on analysis of existing programs, but are rather offered as theoretical outlines, based on examples from my own professional experience.

The Power of Sights: Observer-Oriented Professional Development

וַיַּעַמְדוּ מֵרָחֹק (שמות כ':י"ד) They stayed at a distance (Exodus, 20:14)

... after a missile hit a hillside in Haifa ..."They[6] seemed detached from it, in a way" ... The Sidkins did not send Sam to Israel for a dose of Zionist indoctrination, but because they subscribe to a widespread view in the Jewish community that, as part of a small and rapidly assimilating ethnic minority in the UK, Jewishness can be reinforced by sending your children to the one place where Jews are everywhere ..."I'm not heavily into politics. I watch the news but I don't have very strong views. You'd have to talk to my husband, but he isn't here at the moment." (Grant, 2006). However critical one can be of this position, viewing Israel from a distance even while touring it is indeed prevalent among Israel trips and Jewish visitors (Cohen, 2003). And so, in order to make these a professional-development program, they should be educationally constructed and implemented through the five "eyes" as follows:

---

[6]The youth group touring Israel.

1. *Intellect*: the experience needs to encourage "considering anew the opportunities, pitfalls, and responsibilities of meeting Israel as a foundational space and place of the Jewish experience" (Copeland, 2008, p. 8). The program should therefore confront educators with contemporary, mind-provoking acquaintance with Israel allowing discourse without alienation, which builds on their past knowledge. For example, meeting people and organizations representing the creativity and complexity of Jewish life in Israeli context such as—secular rabbis; Jewish environmentalists; Rabbis for Human Rights.
2. *Instrument*: The Talmudic method of *shakla ve' taria*, negotiating truths and ideas, engaging in debate-based learning is a unique tool that can be demonstrated on site in Israel as well as implemented in the classroom back home. It may involve: programming daily *chevrutah* (collaborative, small groups) study on core texts articulating conflict and connection of the Jewish people in the land of Israel, like the Carmel Mountain representing the dilemma between prophets and kings in Biblical times and its articulation in modern day Israel, that is, religion and state.
3. *Inspiration*: "Knowing what we do not know" is crucial in educators' development and is very important for relevant Israel education (Copeland, 2008; Gringras, 2005) therefore the program should provoke educators' apparent knowledge of Israel with contemporary Israeli realities. For example, visiting an urban Kibbutz, an emerging concept—where the ideals of communal socialist life are implemented through education and not agriculture.
4. *Influence*: Educators should be the sources of their own learning (Knowles, 1980) and thus the program should encourage and cater for educators to initiate and facilitate on-site discussion with their peers, so they may be inspired to do so at their own educational settings. This can be implemented despite the educators presumed lack of familiarity with a specific site, through preparing *divrei torah* short-text studies relating to the site and Jewish historical context, for example, a text from the book of Exodus in the desert, a text from Prophets in the Valley of Elah.
5. *Identity*: notwithstanding the biblical quote heading this section is: "they stayed at a distance," Israel as the physical *place* can become part of the observing educator's identity by placing a programmatic emphasis on the afore-mentioned nature walks and hikes as a way of strengthening *ahavat ha'aretz* (one's love for the land) through the development of *yediat ha'aretz* (an experiential knowledge of the land) (Katriel, 1995).

Israel as a Jewish Homeland: Landlord-Oriented Professional Development

לְךָ אֶתְּנֶנָּה (בראשית, י"ג:י"ז; בראשית כ"ח :י"ג ; בראשית ל"ה:י"ב ; שמות ל"ג, א')

"I am giving it to you" (Genesis 13:17; Genesis 28:13; Genesis 35:12; Exodus 33:1)

The foundation of the State of Israel, in 1948 re-established "in *Eretz-Israel* the Jewish State, which would open the gates of the homeland wide to every Jew" (from the *Declaration of Independence*). For some, the idea of Israel as the promised homeland for the Jews was not abandoned (Chazan & Koraznsky, 1997) and it resonates through the new millennium: in a recent paper Copeland (2008) reinforces Israel as being both the holy land and the *homeland* of the visiting Jew.

Considering the visiting "Landlords" yields two different Jewish audiences: one comprises Israeli born educators who have chosen to live outside Israel and bring with them a complex relationship with the state of Israel as Israeli emigrants are often viewed as violators of the Zionist ideology, or even a threat to the survival of the Jewish state (Sabar, 2002). Indeed, when visiting Israel, Israeli born educators express feelings of ownership: "this is mine" (Sabar, 2002) and these feelings have been known to affect their experience (Pomson & Grant, 2004). Another audience comprises Jews *expecting* to encounter their Jewish homeland: Cohen (2006) describes a clear connection between religious self-definition across Jewish denominations, that is, Reform, Conservative, and Orthodox, and the level of viewing Israel as a homeland—appearing at a higher level among orthodox and conservative Jews. The program should therefore include:

1. *Intellect*: extend educators' knowledge of the historical roots of the Jewish people in the land of Israel with a contemporary perspective, and in this respect the tension between "vision" and "reality." For example, programming visits to biblically mentioned sites that have revived and evolved Jewishly in modern day Israel like Gezer, mentioned in the Bible as the site of battles headed by Joshua and David against the Canaanite kings, today the site of a Progressive Jewish Kibbutz struggling for the recognition of its female Reform rabbi by the State of Israel.
2. *Instrument*: Holm et al. (2003) claim that a group's religion is inseparably linked to a particular environment or homeland via ceremonies. Therefore, creatively engaging teachers' with renewed Jewish ceremonies in Israel should be an instrumental focus. For example, exploring the Kibbutz approach to "Land" festivals in the *Shitim* Institute for Jewish holidays, attending a *Tikkun Leil Shavuot* led by a "secular" Jewish institution such as Alma—home for Hebrew culture in Tel Aviv.
3. *Inspiration*: I suggest that educators from a Landlord point of view connect and learn how to express their relationship with Israel as love based; this intuitive emotion held by the two possible educator populations should not be ignored. However, as in a personal relationship, idealized love can never survive the actual responsibilities of a living relationship (Copeland, 2008). The program should therefore enable educators to strengthen their attachment to the land itself and its symbolic homeland meaning while farming this attachment in a realistic framework. For example, visiting the Shalom Center in Tel Aviv, the former site of the first Hebrew high school, Herzliyah—while examining the vision of Ahad Ha'Am for Israel as a cultural–spiritual center versus the reality pressed by Herzl of a vibrant, normal state like all states.[7]
4. *Influence*: Palmer (1983) established that the act of knowing is an act of love. This approach is particularly relevant for empowering educators to evoke love for Israel and strengthen Jewish peoplehood. Considering you cannot educate

---

[7] This experience may be even more powerful when attention is drawn to the face that the building itself stands on the crossroads between the Ahad Ha'Am and Herzl streets.

someone to love a land and that love is not contagious (Oz, 1983), I suggest that a focus should be placed on experimenting with how to transfer this love into the classroom, as an art (Fromm, 1956). This may happen through allowing room for personal choice during the program, and creating a flexible itinerary based on the participants own emphases.

5. *Identity*: dissonance may occur through the identity discussion undertaken by the educators who feels a sense of ownership of Israel, especially when experiences contradict their expectations. For example, I personally found a group of educators quite shocked to discover that Israeli Arabs living in Tel Aviv-Jaffa consider themselves Palestinians, although they are officially citizens of the State of Israel. This echoed through the program evoking emotions from anger and disappointment to despair. As one participant told me, "It's true I chose to live outside Israel and I haven't been here for a long time. But I cannot remember Arabs saying such things! It took me by complete surprise and shock! I don't know what to do next!" Indeed, reality is a paradox of apparent opposites, and educators must learn to embrace those opposites as one (Palmer, 1998). Although not prevented, I suggest these paradoxes can be "embraced" during reflection and processing sessions, imbedded in the program itinerary.

The Pilgrimage: Pilgrim-Oriented Professional Development

שָׁלֹשׁ רְגָלִים, תָּחֹג לִי בַּשָּׁנָה (שמות כ"ג:י"ד)

Three times a year you are to celebrate a festival to me (Exodus 23:14)

Generally speaking, religion has long been a motive for embarking on journeys and non-economic travel and moreover, spiritually motivated travel has become popular in recent decades alongside the growth of tourism in the modern era (Cohen, 2003). Current day "pilgrimages" are usually journeys to a place that a person considers embodies a valued ideal (Poria et al., 2006): in this sense, pilgrimage is extended beyond religious travel to include travel to places which include nationalistic values and ideals, disaster sites (like Ground Zero), war memorials, and cemeteries for example Mount Herzl National Cemetery, places related to literary writers (like the Agnon House in Jerusalem), music stars, genealogy, and places one visits because of a personal sense of "obligation" to the area or its narrative (e.g., Massada).

The pilgrimage to Israel may be framed as a peak experience that may only happen once in a persons' life, a journey from the "periphery" (the Jewish Diaspora) to the "center" (Cohen, 2006). The pilgrims' decision to come to Israel is based on it being the place to strengthen spiritual or religious identity (Cohen, 2003; Grant, 2000) and as such, the program is structured along a duality of geography and spirituality (Cohen, Ifergan, & Cohen, 2002). An example of constructed pilgrimage that is seemingly different yet similar is the educational program in Poland for Israeli youth (Feldman, 2005), constructed around well-defined "sacred" places, sites sanctified by Jewish suffering and death, leaving modern Poland irrelevant.

Similarly, "pilgrims" see the experience in Israel primarily as an opportunity to learn about Judaism, not necessarily about the country itself or its residents and therefore have less interest in socializing and encountering Israelis and Israeli culture (Cohen, 2003) and may even be disinterested in understanding today's Israel. "Pilgrim"-educators may visit sites with the interest to have what is they perceive as an "authentic experience" of their romantic, idyllic image of the land of Israel: a Biblical Land, a desert with camels and patriarchs. Therefore, the professional-development Israel experience from a pilgrim perspective may look like this:

1. *Intellect*: Pilgrimage depends on liturgy, ritual, and the "protocols" specific to a site (Kirshenblatt-Gimblett, 2002), therefore I suggest engaging educators, prior to their arrival, in creating resource booklets to accompany the experience, used on a daily, hourly, basis on sites as a *midrash*—an interpretive complementary text—to the "core" text which is the site itself. For example, booklets prepared for Jerusalem's Old City could include: the story of the Binding of Isaac (the Biblical location of Temple Mount); the texts describing the building of the Temples; an Israeli poem about the Western Wall;[8] and perhaps a time line and a map of the Old City including the Quarters, the gates, etc. There should be various booklets depending on the group's themes for the visit.
2. *Instrument*: As in fact, much that the pilgrims have come to see sites that cannot be seen and must be visualized and imagined (Kirshenblatt-Gimblett, 2002) this situation is similar to a classroom outside Israel, for example, the Western Wall, this is just a small part of the remaining wall of the Temple Mount and imagining the Temple that once stood there is necessary. Therefore, educators should experiment with methods that bridge this gap between reality and history, like: booklets, actual guiding, models, simulations, recreations, reenactments, and other such theatrical techniques (Kirshenblatt-Gimblett, 2002) so they may take them back with them to their classrooms.
3. *Inspiration:* The skills and attitudes to be nurtured in a pilgrim-oriented experience should stem from andragogy, a concept associated with Malcolm Knowles (1980). In the context of Israel education, this means creating opportunities for *self-directed learning* for educators during the Israel experience program, allowing educators an initial exploration and understanding of a site, before providing them with "final answers." Again, in the case of the Western Wall, perhaps beginning with a quiet, individual experience of the site, and only later farming it in text and discussion.
4. *Influence:* Following the former, pilgrim educators can effect the Israel education at their schools by treating their students as "people" (Brooks & Brooks, 1999) empowering them to ask their own questions, reach their own answers, and take responsibility for their own leaning. This means educators invite their

---

[8] For example, the 1967 poem "The Paratroopers Cry" by Haim Hefer describing Israeli paratroopers liberating the Western Wall during the Six-Day War.

students to become "pilgrims away from the pilgrim site" by creating opportunities for them to explore and emotionally connect, building on their perhaps existing knowledge or their ability to find information.
5. *Identity*: The Biblical pilgrimage was planned long before it occurred, sometimes even a few years, in collaboration by a group based on family or community. The professional-development Israel experience program should incite and facilitate this process: sharing or even transferring the responsibility for the learning by explicitly engaging educators in the planning process from the creation of the program. This means that the organizer takes a "step back," not an easy task, and trusts the program design with the educators who may or may not have been to Israel. Involvement in the specific details of the journey would stem from and enhance the educators' personal commitment to the experience as a pilgrimage.

The Odyssey: Meaning-Oriented Professional Development

לֶךְ-לְךָ מֵאַרְצְךָ וּמִמּוֹלַדְתְּךָ וּמִבֵּית אָבִיךָ, אֶל-הָאָרֶץ, אֲשֶׁר אַרְאֶךָּ. (בראשית י"ב:א')

Leave your country, your people and your father's household and go to the land I will show you (Genesis 12:1).

The conception of Odyssey, a journey of transformation and return to the original place of departure, contrasts dramatically with the journeys expressed in the narratives of the Jewish people (Haberman, 2006). This approach emphasizes the place as a tool (albeit a meaningful one) inciting personal identity exploration and the transformation. Above is the famous quote describing God's commandment to Avram, expected to embark on a journey to an unknown land—the land of Israel—never to return to his geographical homeland again. However, it is this type of journey transforms Avram's identity. Although probably hoping to return to their geographical homeland, the "Odysseyan" educators are embarking on a journey of self-change (Cohen, 2006), a conscious activity whereby they hope to be transformed in a meaningful way. This is an "inward voyage" (Noy, 2003) from the familiar to the unknown.

Identity exploration and meaning making is very much dependent on the perception of the journey as an authentic experience (Chambers, 2008) and therefore, "Odyssian" educators do not consider themselves tourists, visitors, or strangers to Israel (although locals may consider them as such); they wish to integrate with Israeli culture, and hope to avoid staged "tourist" attractions (ibid.).

The "meaning – full" Israel experience professional-development program may look like this:

1. *Intellect*: The program's content is arranged thematically, exploring circles of identity and key components of Jewish identification such as: collective memory, religious practice, Hebrew language, Jewish values, Jewish texts, and Israel (Chamo, 2008). Insomuch that learning may occur "off the beaten track," the

itinerary choices stem from the meaning of the site as opposed to any other consideration. For example, when wishing to explore the meaning of sacredness, *Kedushah*, the program focuses on Haifa as a holy city for unique sects (Bahai, Ahmediyyah, Carmelite order, etc.), although Haifa is not frequently visited as part of tourist programs in Israel and would usually not be included in short-term experiences for logistical reasons.

2. *Instrument*: The main instrument used during the program should be *Mifgashim*—intentional, constructed, lengthy encounters (Cohen, 2000) with Israeli peers who share the search for Jewish meaning. Educators should be taught to structure and facilitate *Mifgashim* by personally participating in them. The educational framework of these encounters should be explicitly articulated and their meaning explored through discussion groups, from a reciprocal approach, on relatively "neutral" ground (ibid.). For example, a residential week away from where the Israelis reside, meeting Jewish educators, comparing and sharing best practices in terms of Jewish studies meeting as equals, ready both to teach and to learn (ibid.).

3. *Inspiration*: engaging educators in *beit midrash* before, during, and after the program means that educators will engage daily, in a traditional learning structure adapted to the purposes of professional development explicit in the selection of texts and the language of instruction (Feiman-Nemser, 2006). It will serve as an "odyssey" within an "odyssey" and become the connecting line between the home country, the journey and the return. An overall thematic concept, such as Jewish peoplehood: the knowledgeable identification and connection to the Jewish people (Chamo, Sabar Ben Yohushua, & Shimoni, 2009) can be studied and debated prior to leaving, can serve as the connecting theme while during Israel experience, and carry through the return as a spectrum for reflection on the personal meaning of belonging to the Jewish collective.

4. *Influence*: *beit midrash* described above will allow for the creation of a platform for networking and collaboration between educational peers from Israel and abroad, starting before and continuing beyond the Israel experience. This means a broadening of the before mentioned "sacred community" concept to include educators from both sides, practicing what Parker Palmer (1993) would define as "hospitality:" receiving each other with openness and care and placing the search for meaning at the heart of the communal practice.

5. *Identity*: Nisan (1997) claims that educators should commit themselves to a comprehensive conception of aims and values with respect to their educational work. I suggest the value placed at the heart of the Israel experience be a journey to Jewish peoplehood, thus it becomes not merely a personal Odyssey but rather a visionary commitment to the Jewish people and the land of Israel. Therefore, the program should encourage and allow participants' personal involvement as partners in the process; room to express their values and abilities; and a process imbuing them with a sense of responsibility for the future (Nisan, 1997).

Not Exactly a Fifth Model: The *Madrich*—Leading Educator

מַדְרִיכְךָ בְּדֶרֶךְ תֵּלֵךְ (ישעיה, מ"ח:י"ז)

Leads you along the paths you should follow (Isaiah 48:17)

The four models described above lack an important connecting link: that of the mediator between the person and the place—namely, the educator leading the experience. These educators often provide the "lenses" for the experience by taking an active role in planning and executing the program. Cohen et al. (2002) describe their dual role: on the one hand, they are pathfinders, providing access to an unknown territory. And, on the other hand, they are mentors, providing geographical and spiritual guidance. The authors (ibid.) also suggest a third type, "the model:" positioned in symmetry with the participants, as they share the search for identity and connection. In this latter sense the extents of their knowledge is not as important in so much as their ability to facilitate learning, create a space within the group for questioning and generate meaning.

I find the process facilitated by "the model" (ibid.) educator on an Israel experience is what Borowitz (1992) described as *Tzimtzum*: using Jewish mystical terminology, he promotes a notion of contemporary Jewish leadership based upon the understanding that learners increasingly demand to be treated as persons (similar to the andragogical approach described before). Borowitz offers a three-stage process carried out by this leading educator: (1) "Contraction"—withholding presence and power so that the followers may have a space to "be," helping them create their *own* knowledge, an ability to facilitate a process as first among equals; (2) "Breaking"—an inevitable consequence brought about by disappointment and frustration from what seems to be irrelevant or immature conversation within the group, completed by forgiveness, modeled by the leader and enabled through the creation of a sacred community of educators; (3) "Amendment"—a third and final stage that builds on its predecessors, empowering the group to work out of their own initiative and assume full responsibility for their own learning. This third stage is the stage Borowitz calls "person making."

This educational-leadership process is relevant and applicable in all four conceptual models. The leading educator's task on an Israel experience professional-development program is therefore to initiate a professional and personal process, created through the interaction between person and place, by limiting themselves and inviting group responsibility—thus being *models* of this process (Meyer, 2003).

Next Steps: A Framework for Programming and Further Research

While each of the four conceptual models can serve as a basis for an Israel experience professional-development program, they are somewhat compromised if applied as exclusive models. Research has already established that there are many different and even conflicting personal assumptions with regard to an Israel experience (Marom, 2003): since at any moment, adult educators can be shifting from a vacation mode of curiosity-seeker to that of a religious pilgrim, internalizing instrumental knowledge or be seeking meaning for their existence (Klein-Katz, 1998). Therefore, to end this chapter I would like to suggest one integrative dynamic framework:

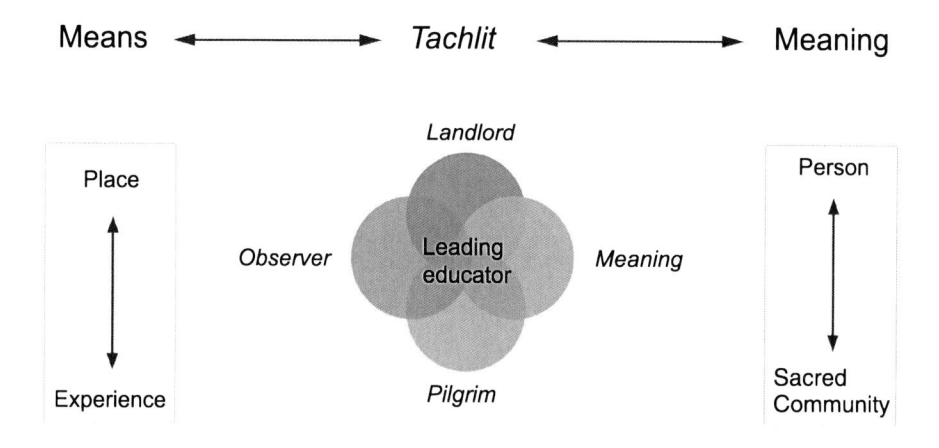

Means ⟵⟶ *Tachlit* ⟵⟶ **Meaning**

```
                     Landlord
     Place                                       Person
              Observer    Leading    Meaning
                          educator
                      Pilgrim                    Sacred
     Experience                                  Community
```

This suggested framework has a dynamic structure, moving from side to side and from top to bottom, thus creating a matrix:

- On top is the *Tachlit*—the dual purpose of means and meaning—as the overall, organizing frame. The *Tachlit* provides the primary *horizontal synergy* between "means" (on the left) and "meaning" (on the right). Both "means" and "meaning" sides simultaneously nourish and are being nurtured by each other.
- The relationship between "Place" and "Person," which was discussed in length through the four conceptual models, are placed on either side on the *Tachlit*: "Place" under "means" and "Person" under "meaning." The core foundations of an educational tourist religious program, namely "Experience" and "Sacred Community," which were discussed earlier in this chapter, are presented on either "Means" or "Meaning" sides, respectively,
- The positioning of Place and Experience on the Means side and Person and Sacred Community on the Meaning side of the framework create a *vertical dynamism*—movement from top to bottom and vice versa. Thus, on the Means side (left) is the conceptual dialectic between Place and Experience, and on the Meaning side (right) the conceptual dialectic between Person and Sacred Community.

Therefore, the horizontal synergy of *Tachlit* and the two sided vertical dynamism create a complex system of interactions, where the four conceptual models become perceptible, presented as separate yet overlapping fields, with the conceptual "leading educator" shared by all four:

(1) Landlord is predominantly positioned in the interaction between Place and Person
(2) Pilgrim is predominantly positioned in the interaction between Experience and Sacred Community
(3) Observer is predominantly positioned in the interaction between Place and Experience
(4) Meaning is predominantly positioned in the interaction between Person and Sacred Community

Because of its complexity, this framework provides a versatile and multi-dimensional field for programming, thus when one wishes to plan an Israel experience professional-development program, one can find a variety of ways to cater for the different and sometimes conflicting goals—without loosing sight of the purpose *Tachlit* and the core elements (Place, Person, Experience, Sacred Community).

Being theoretical, this framework is yet to be put to the test. As mentioned at the beginning of this chapter, the entire field of Israel experience as professional development is lacking and more solid, empirical research on the implementation and effects of these programs is greatly needed. First and foremost, I recommend further research focuses on using the integrative-dynamic framework as an *evaluative* tool of current Israel experience programs in general, and for professional-development programs in particular. The framework should assist in creating a shared language and criteria for critical conversation about these programs, which is currently quite absent.

Moreover, further research should look into:

- The people: what are the characteristics and origins of each of the four conceptual perceptions toward the Israel experience professional-development program: Who are the observers? Pilgrims? Landlords? Odyssians? How or can an understanding of these four separate yet overlapping personas contribute toward an understanding of contemporary Jewry's relationship with Israel?
- The place: what are the essential sites and experiences suitable for creating each conceptual program?
- The experience: how is this framework effective in helping educators acquire the attitudes, skills, and knowledge they need for Israel education at their own classrooms?
- Sacred community: what would be effective methods for preparation, reflection, and processing and follow up to the program?
- Leading educator: who is the leading educator and how can they be trained and evaluated?

These five questions open a window into each element, helping in creating a broader understanding of this framework—as a basis for the initial question posed above.

Vici?

This chapter began with a question: how can the short-term experience in Israel serve as a professional-development program? This question entailed exploring a seldom-researched topic, while relying on a large volume of adjacent international research and conceptualization and years of personal–professional experience in the field of Israel experience professional-development program. The integrative framework presented at the end of the chapter provides a substantial basis for programming. Without compromising articulation of an explicit, unifying overall purpose, yet allowing much flexibility and adaptability to the various profiles of the educators, organizational needs, and goals. Notwithstanding, this framework needs to be put to the test: application in the field and research must be the next steps in order to validate it.

Indeed, the heading of this chapter is: "Veni, vidi, vici." However, the first two parts of this statement, "I came" and "I saw" were not at all addressed, and this is not an indication of their insignificance. On the contrary, bluntly put: there are not enough educators who have been offered the opportunity or perhaps wish to partake in Israel experience professional-development programs. Therefore, there is also a clear need to research *how* to get educators to Israel. This needs to be a comprehensive effort covering issues like community and school policies, budget allocations, as well as the educators' perceptions and motivations.

In conclusion, what has been achieved here? I draw from a famous Talmudic discussion, describing an argument between rabbis, whereas toward the end of the argument Rabbi Eliezer calls out: *"If the law is as I say then let it be proved by Heaven"* and indeed a voice from heaven came and asserted that Rabbi Eliezer was right. However, Rabbi Yehoshua stood up and said (quoting Deuteronomy 30:12) *"It is not in Heaven"* and a later sage explained further (quoting Exodus 23:2): *"it is for the people to decide"* (*Babylonian Talmud, Bava Metzia: 59*). I will take Rabbi Yehoshua's stance and say that an Israel experience professional-development program is not "in the heaven"—it is not an unreachable goal, a distant idea or a theoretical concept. And as such, *Vici* can be achieved.

Acknowledgments I would like to thank Professor Lisa D. Grant for her friendship, mentoring, and empowerment that accompany my work and enabled the writing and completion of this chapter.

Bibliography

Berger, P. L., & Luckmann, T. (1966). *The social construction of reality: A treatise in the sociology of knowledge*. Garden City, NY: Anchor Books.

Borowitz, E. (1992). Tzimtzum: A mystic model for contemporary leadership. In S. L. Kelman (Ed.), *What we know about Jewish education*. Los Angeles: Torah Aura Productions.

Brooks, J. G., & Brooks, M. G. (1999). *In search of understanding: The case for constructivist classrooms*. Alexandria, VA: ASCD – Association for Supervision and Curriculum Development.

Chambers, E. (2008). *From authenticity to significance: Tourism on the frontier of culture and place*, Futures.

Chamo, N. (2008). Parents' Consciousness and Educational Expectations Regarding Jewish-Secular Identity. Dissertation, Tel Aviv University. (In Hebrew).

Chamo, N., Sabar Ben Yohushua, N., & Shimoni, G. (2009). *Jewish peoplehood*. Tel Aviv: Beth Hatefutsoth. (In Hebrew).

Chazan, B. (1999). Teaching Israel in the 21st century. In R. E. Tornberg (Ed), *The Jewish educational leader's handbook*. Denver, CO: A.R.E. Publications.

Chazan, B., & Koraznsky, A. (1997). *Does the teenage Israel experience make a difference?* New York: Israel Experience Inc.

Cohen, E. H. (2000). MIFGASHIM: A meeting of minds and hearts. *Journal of Jewish Education, 66*(11), 23–37.

Cohen, E. H. (2003). Tourism and religion: A case study – visiting students in Israeli universities. *Journal of Travel Research, 42*, 36–47.

Cohen, E. H. (2006b). Research in religious education: Content and methods for the postmodern and global era. *Religious Education, 101*(2), 147–152.

Cohen, E. H., & Cohen, E. (2000). *The Israel experience program: A policy analysis*. Jerusalem: The Jerusalem Institute for Israel Studies. (In Hebrew).

Cohen, E. H., Ifergan, M., & Cohen, E. (2002). A new paradigm in guiding the madrich as a role model. *Annals of Tourism Research, 29*(4), 919–932.

Cohen, S. M. (2006a). *A tale of two Jewries: The "Inconvenient truth" for American Jews*. New York: Steinhardt Foundation for Jewish Life; Jewish Life Network.

Copeland, S. (2008). How shall we speak about this land – making sense of the work of israel travel education. Paper written for Makom, Israel Engagement Network. www.makomisrael.net

Corchan-Smith, M., & Lytle, S. L. (1999). Relationships of knowledge and practice: Teacher learning in communities. *Review of Research in Education, 24*, 249–305.

Dewey, J. (1938). *Experience and education*. New York: Simon and Schuster.

Feiman-Nemser, S. (2006). Beit midrash for teachers: An experiment in teacher preparation. *Journal of Jewish Education, 72*(33), 161–181.

Feldman, J. (2005). In search of the beautiful land of Israel: Youth voyages to Poland. In: E. H. Cohen & H. Noy (Eds.), *Israeli backpackers and their society: From tourism to rite of passage*. New York: State University of New York Press: Israeli Studies Series.

Fromm, E. (1956). *The art of loving*. New York: Bantham.

Grant, L. (2006). *What British Jews Think of Israel*. The Independent UK, Tuesday, 18 July. Available online: http://www.independent.co.uk/news/uk/this-britain/what-british-jews-think-of-israel-408400.html

Grant, L. D. (2000) Paradoxical Pilgrimage: American Jewish Adults on a Congregational Israel Trip. Ph.D. Dissertation, Jewish Theological Seminary.

Grant, L. D., & Pomson, A. D. M. (2003). From In Service Training to Professional Development: Alternatives Paradigms in Israel for Diaspora Educators. Report commissioned by the Research and Evaluation Unit of the Jewish Agency for Israel, Jerusalem.

Grant, L. D., Kelman, N., & Regev, H. (2001). Travelling towards the self while visiting the other: Israeli TALI School educators on a U.S. study tour. *Journal of Jewish Communal Service, 77*(3/4).

Grant, L. D. (2008). A Vision for Israel Education. Paper presented at the Network for Research in Jewish education conference, 2 June 2008.

Gringras, R. (2005). Wrestling and Hugging: Alternative paradigms for the Diaspora-Israel relationship. Paper written for Makom, Israel Engagement Network. www.makomisrael.net

Haberman, B. D. (2006). Journeying on the Zion cycle: An odyssey of a different sort. In A. B. N. Nachanson & M. Natan (Eds.), *MASA time for a journey*. Jerusalem: The Jewish Agency for Israel and the MASA Company.

Holm, T., Pearson, J. D., & Chavis, B. (2003). *Peoplehood: A model for the extension of sovereignty in American Indian Studies*. Wicazo SA Review.

Horowitz, B. (2003). Connections and Journeys: Assessing Critical Opportunities for Enhancing Jewish Identity. A report to the Commission on Jewish Identity and Renewal UJA-Federation of New York.

Katriel, T. (1995). Touring the land: Trips and hiking as secular pilgrimages in Israeli culture. *Jewish Folklore and Ethnology Review, 17,* 6–13.

Katz, S. (2004). *NACIE: A Partnership to Deepen Community-Wide Engagement with Israel in North American Jewish Life.* Agenda Jewish Education, 18. Published by JESNA, the Jewish Education Service of North America.

Kelner, S. (2004). Somebody Else's Business: The Deliberate Attempt to Influence Individual Belonging through Israel Experience Programs. Paper Presented at Conference on Dynamic Belonging: Shifting Jewish Identities and Collective Involvements in Comparative Perspective, Institute for Advanced Studies, Hebrew University of Jerusalem, Jerusalem, Israel. June 20, 2004

Kirshenblatt-Gimblett, B. (2002). Learning from ethnography: Reflections on the nature and efficacy of youth tours to Israel. In H. Goldberg, S. Heilman, & B. Kirshenblatt-Gimblett (Eds.), *The Israel experience: Studies in youth travel and Jewish identity.* Jerusalem: Studio Kavgraph, Andrea and Charles Bronfman Philanthropies.

Klein-Katz, S. (1998). *Jewish adults as learners in family education: The family Israel experience.* Jerusalem: Melitz – The Centers for Jewish-Zionist Education.

Knowles, M. S. (1980). *The modern practice of adult education. Andragogy versus pedagogy.* Englewood Cliffs, NJ: Prentice Hall/Cambridge.

Kopelowitz, E. (2005). Towards What Ideal Do We Strive? A Portrait of Social and Symbolic Engagement with Israel in Jewish Community Day Schools. Survey commissioned by RAVSAK and The Jewish Agency for Israel.

Koren, A., & Sales, A. L. (2005). Israel in Professional Development for Informal Jewish Education: Current Programs and Future Needs. North American Alliance for Jewish Youth, Maurice and Marilyn Cohen Center for Modern Jewish Studies, Brandeis University.

Margolis, D. (2004). *Towards a Vision of Educational Re-Engagement with Israel.* Agenda: Jewish Education, 18. Published by JESNA, the Jewish Education Service of North America.

Marom, D. (2003). Before the gates of the school: an experiment in developing educational vision from practice. In: S. Fox, I. Scheffler, & D. Marom (Eds.), *Visions of Jewish education.* USA: Cambridge University Press.

Meyer, M. A. (2003). Reflections on the educated Jew from the perspective of reform Judaism. In S. Fox, I. Scheffler, & D. Marom (Eds.), *Visions of Jewish education.* USA: Cambridge University Press.

Mittelberg, D. (1994). *The Israel visit and Jewish identification.* New York: American Jewish Committee, Berman Jewish Policy Archive.

Nisan, M. (1997). *Educational identity as a primary factor in the development of educational leadership.* Jerusalem: Monographs from the Mandel Institute.

Noy, C. (2003). This trip really changed me: Backpackers' narratives of self-change. *Annals of Tourism Research, 31*(1), 78–102.

Oz, A. (1983). *In the Land of Israel.* Jerusalem: Keter (in Hebrew).

Palmer, P. J. (1983, 1993). *To know as we are known. Education as a spiritual journey.* San Francisco: Harper San Francisco.

Palmer, P. J. (1998). *The courage to teach. Exploring the inner landscape of a teacher's life.* San Francisco: Jossey-Bass.

Pomson, A. D. M., & Grant, L. D. (2004). Getting personal with professional development: The case of short-term trips to Israel for diaspora teachers. In J. Bashi, M. B. Peretz, & A. Bouganim (Eds.), *Education and professional training.* Jerusalem: The Jewish Agency for Israel.

Poria, Y., Reichel, A., & Biran, A. (2006). Heritage site management: Motivations and expectations. *Annals of Tourism Research, 33*(1), 162–178.

Reisman, B. (1993). *Adult education trips to Israel: A transforming experience.* Merlitz, Melton Centre, Hebrew University, JCC Association, Israel.

Sabar, N. (2002). Kibbutz L.A.: A Paradoxical social network. *Journal of Contemporary Ethnography, 31,* 68–94.

Saxe, L., Sasson, T., & Hecht, S. (2006). *Taglit-birthright Israel: Impact on Jewish identity, peoplehood, and connection to Israel*. Waltham, MA: The Maurice and Marilyn Cohen Center for Modern Jewish Studies.

Schon, D. (1987). *Educating the reflective practitioner*. San Francisco: Jossey-Bass.

Schuster, D.T. (2003). *Jewish lives, Jewish learning: Adult Jewish learning in theory and practice*. New York: UAHC Press.

Solovetchik, J. (1971). *Lonely man of faith*. Jerusalem: Mossad haRav Kook. (In Hebrew).

Stodolsky, S. S., Zaiman Dorph, G., & Feinman-Nemser, S. (2006). Professional culture and professional development in Jewish schools: Teachers' perceptions and experiences. *Journal of Jewish Education, 72*(2), 91–108.

Tickton-Schuster, D., & Grant, L. D. (2005). Adult Jewish learning: What do we know? What do we need to know? *Journal of Jewish Education, 71*, 179–200.

Zaiman-Dorph, G., & Holtz, B. W. (2000). Professional development for teachers: Why doesn't the model change? *Journal of Jewish Education, 66*(1/2), 67–76.

Rabbis as Educators: Their Professional Training and Identity Formation

Lisa D. Grant and Michal Muszkat-Barkan

Introduction

By definition, a rabbi is a teacher. Yet, few rabbis actually pursue extensive formal studies in education as part of, or in concert with their rabbinical schooling. Though this remains the case for the majority of rabbis trained in Reform and Conservative seminaries both in the United States and Israel, many rabbis today choose to serve in educational roles instead of or in addition to their pulpit responsibilities. Orthodox rabbis have long served in senior educational positions in Orthodox day schools, although there does not seem to be any consistent standard for their educational training. In the liberal movements, there appears to be a growing trend to combine formal educational training with rabbinical studies. These dual-degree graduates find positions in day schools, community settings, and congregations as classroom teachers, directors of Jewish studies, principals, heads of school, school rabbis, and sometimes a combination of several roles. In Israel the situation is somewhat different since there are still relatively few Reform and Conservative congregations that can afford to pay for a full-time rabbi. Thus, many graduates of Reform and Conservative Rabbinical programs in Israel look to Jewish education as a means of realizing their rabbinic calling. They serve as educators in several settings including public schools, pre-schools, the army, and in congregations. Indeed, in both the United States and Israel, the field is still so new, it appears that new job titles and responsibilities are crafted at times based on the skill set and interests of particular individuals and the needs and vision of the institution in which they serve.

How do these rabbi-educators define their roles? What distinguishes them from educators who serve in similar kinds of positions? Are there skills, capabilities, and perspectives that rabbi-educators possess which are different from individuals with advanced training in Jewish studies and senior positions in Jewish education? How do rabbi-educators describe their professional identity? Do they see themselves as rabbis who serve in educational settings, as educators who happen also to be rabbis, or is their identity as a rabbi-educator somehow unique and integrated? While there

L.D. Grant (✉)
Hebrew Union College, New York, NY, USA
e-mail: lgrant54@gmail.com

is an abundance of literature on teacher development and a much smaller base about the professional preparation of rabbis, there is virtually no research that has explored the question of what this combined role entails. This study offers a first step in developing the field of inquiry about the identities and roles of rabbi-educators. Our focus is on how rabbi-educators themselves describe and define their professional identity and roles. We examine their self-reports through two principle lenses—Mordechai Nisan's work (2009) on the self-construction of educational identity, and a theoretical framework for clergy education developed by a team of researchers from the Carnegie Foundation for the Advancement of Teaching who undertook a comprehensive study of the pedagogical practices of faculty who train rabbis, ministers, and priests in North American seminaries and schools of theology (2006). As we learn more about the qualities and contributions of rabbi-educators to Jewish educational settings, we can better reflect on what specialized training is required to support and develop individuals who choose this path?

Our interest in these questions emerges out of our experiences as two professors of Jewish education who teach education courses to rabbinical students in the United States and Israel. We are interested in the findings both from a theoretical and practical perspective. In other words, we want to explore what factors shape professional identity, so that teachers like us who are involved in the process of preparing rabbi-educators can better understand their specific academic and professional needs. We are also interested in exploring cross-cultural similarities and differences in professional-development needs in the US and Israel.

The research is based on a qualitative study of a small pool of American and Israeli rabbi-educators who are currently serving in congregations or as a rabbi in a Jewish day school.

The following questions shape our preliminary investigation:

1. What factors do rabbi-educators perceive as central in reflecting their professional identity?
2. What do rabbi-educators perceive as their central goals?
3. What skills, knowledge, and orientations to Jewish learning and Jewish living do rabbi-educators perceive that they bring to their work in educational settings?
4. What aspects of their training as rabbis and educators do they see as most valuable to their dual role?

Throughout the analysis, we also explore what are the common denominators and what distinguishes the perspectives of their roles for American and Israeli rabbi-educators.

Research Methodology

During the 2006–2007 academic year, we sent out a brief survey to individuals working as rabbi-educators in Reform, Conservative, or community day schools, and Reform and Conservative congregations both in the United States and in Israel.

Respondents were given the option of giving their name and voluntarily agreeing to participate in a follow-up telephone interview. The Americans were invited to participate based on their job function. The Israelis were drawn from a group who participated in Jewish education professional-development seminars during the 2006–2007 academic year. It was important to us that participants in this study all saw themselves as rabbi-educators. We also chose individuals who we thought would still have fairly clear memories of what aspects of their professional preparation most helped them in their rabbi-educator role. Some were still students in the final stages of their training; others had been in the field for 6 years or less.

In addition to descriptive questions such as education background, current job title, and key responsibilities, we asked respondents to comment on the challenges and rewards of their position, and how their rabbinical training and education training (if any) shapes their performance. We also asked them about their current professional-development needs.

We received responses from 18 American rabbi-educators and 16 Israelis rabbis and rabbinical students working in a variety of Jewish educational settings. From this pool of 34 respondents, we conducted in-depth follow-up telephone interviews during the spring of 2007 with ten American and nine Israel rabbi-educators. Each interview took between 30 and 60 minutes. It is clear that we have neither the numbers of respondents nor the depth of data to draw a comprehensive portrait of the individuals who choose this career path, their perceptions of their role, and its requirements. Rather, we see this research as a means of opening the field of investigation into these questions of what distinguishes a rabbi-educator in terms of professional identity and practice?

Table 1 presents a general breakdown of the respondents by school where they studied and whether they have formal training in education. All the rabbis who study at Hebrew Union College take courses in Jewish education as part of their rabbinic training. Almost all of the Americans who also completed a masters in Jewish education did so concurrent with their rabbinical studies. The six Israelis who indicated

Table 1 Summary of research participants

	United States	Israel
Reform ordination[a]—dual-degree rabbinics and education	8	5
Reform ordination—no education degree	2	6
Conservative ordination[b]—dual-degree rabbinics and education	6	2
Conservative ordination no education degree	1	3
Other ordination[c]	1	

[a]Four of the HUC graduates studied at the Los Angeles campus and the Rhea Hirsch School of Jewish education; four studied at HUC's New York campus and the New York School of Jewish education; two were ordained at HUC New York and did not have a degree in education.
[b]The Americans studied at the Jewish Theological Seminary in New York and the Israeli rabbi-educators studied at Machon Schechter, the sister institution to JTS in Israel.
[c]This individual received private ordination and has masters degrees in Jewish studies, elementary education, and special education.

Table 2 Jewish educational setting

	United States
Day school rabbi	9
Congregational rabbi with substantial education responsibilities	2
Congregational educator	7

Table 3 Jewish educational setting

	Israel[a]
Rabbi in public schools	15
Community rabbi	6
Adult educator	6
Army educator	3
Pre-school rabbi	3

[a]These numbers represent 16 individuals who have multiple part-time jobs as rabbi-educators in various settings.

they have a formal degree in education, studied general education at an academic institution outside of their seminary training.

Table 2 provides the breakdown of American respondents by type of position they were in at the time of contact for this study. Half work in day schools where they have a range of titles such as "Rabbi-in-Residence," "School Rabbi," and "Director of Judaic Programming." Two respondents are congregational rabbis with substantial responsibilities in education. For example, one of the study participants described one of her central roles in the congregation as "the rabbi of the religious school community." The other seven serve as directors of Jewish education in congregations. Here too, titles vary greatly including "Director of Lifelong Learning," "Director of Religious Education," and "Director of Youth and Family Education."

Israeli rabbi-educators have somewhat different roles than their American counterparts as shown in Table 3. They are also much more likely to work in multiple part-time positions in different settings. For example, we see that 15 people work in public schools. Although the setting is a so-called "secular" school, their role is somewhat similar to a school rabbi in an American-Jewish day school. They may be responsible for creating ceremonies, teaching teachers, and developing a *beit midrash* for students and/or parents. Several rabbi-educators also serve as educational consultants in the Israeli army to help build and strengthen soldiers' Jewish identity. Rabbi-educators who work in Reform and Conservative congregations may or may not be the pulpit rabbi. As there are no formal congregational schools in Israel, their education work tends to be more informal, creating study groups for *b'nai mitzvah* students, parents, and adults. These rabbi-educators also might be involved with the congregation's pre-school, and the public schools in the area. Position held does not seem to correlate in any way to denomination of the rabbi-educator.

Theoretical Framing

One of the challenges of undertaking this research is the absence of a literature in which to ground our analysis. As we have noted, there is almost nothing that has been written about this combined role of rabbi-educator.[1] Our search revealed three papers that address some aspect of this field of study. The first two are written by school rabbis and focus on explaining this role (Koren, 1993 and Gottfried, 2000). The third article is written by a professor of Jewish education who is also a rabbi and concerns the preparation of rabbis as teachers (Schein, 1988).

Koren describes the role of rabbis in religious (Orthodox) Israeli schools as an extra-curricular function. His research shows that the position is not clearly defined. The rabbis' main responsibilities appear to involve serving as a resource for Jewish knowledge and working with the faculty, students, and parents in informal settings. The rabbi is expected to help solve educational and personal challenges as they relate to tensions between secular and sacred studies and the surrounding Israeli society.

Gottfried makes similar observations about the school rabbi's role in Solomon Schechter schools in America. Her paper is more of a personal reflection on an individual's role in a Conservative Jewish day school. Here, the author describes her primary function as serving as a religious role model to faculty, students, and parents (Gottfried, 2000, p. 47). She understands her role to be multi-faceted, helping to create a religious environment for the entire school community, serving as a resource for religious knowledge and guidance through formal teaching, counseling, consulting, and informal encounters.

Koren identifies several key roles and skills that school rabbis need in their practice. He notes that rabbi-educators need to serve as facilitators of group process and as teachers to faculty and students. They must organize informal educational experiences and ceremonies for parents and students. And, they also must have the sensitivity and ability to advise and support parents in the school community.

Schein's paper focuses on the task of preparing rabbis to be teachers, what he describes as the "art of translation" (p. 15). He provides an educational framework for how rabbinical students can develop better skills to make Jewish sources relevant and accessible to American-Jews with a wide range of backgrounds, motivations, and needs.

These papers just begin to open the discussion about what characterizes the professional identity of rabbi-educators. They suggest that rabbi-educators see themselves as active teachers and spiritual guides in the school community. Their teaching often takes place in informal settings and through counseling and pastoral work rather than as part of the formal curriculum. The findings suggest that certain pedagogies are central to this role, among them facilitating, guiding, and the ability to "translate" Jewish sources to contemporary contexts.

---

[1] For this study, we focused on the literature most directly pertaining to rabbi-educator training. Literature from related fields such as guidance counseling, life coaching, and pastoral care may yield some fruitful comparisons as the research develops.

While helpful, these three papers alone do not provide a strong enough theoretical base upon which to build a more comprehensive analysis of what characterizes the identity and role of a rabbi-educator. Since the literature about rabbi-educators is so thin, we decided to examine how the literature on professional identity formation of educators and the training of rabbis can shed light on our questions and findings. Two sources were particularly helpful in framing our analysis. First is Mordechai Nisan's monograph entitled "'Educational Identity' as a Major Factor in Educational Leadership" (2009). Our second source comes from a comprehensive study of clergy education in America (Foster, Dahill, Goleman, & Tolentino, 2005).

Nisan's philosophy of educational-leadership development provides an initial lens through which we can explore how rabbi-educators describe their professional identity. According to Nisan, professional self-identity is constructed based on several different factors. Frequently, a significant part of adult identity is defined by one's professional life. Adults seek meaning and self-actualization through their work. While educational leaders define themselves first and foremost as educators, they distinguish themselves as educational *leaders* by going through a process of deliberation in deciding which factors are more significant in defining the qualities and priorities of their leadership.

Nisan identifies key characteristics of educational-leadership identity as including an educational vision, goals, beliefs about education that derive from personal experience, and an understanding of the reality in which educators work. Once individuals become aware of their own vision and goals they need to become more reflective about the reasons for choosing them. Educational leaders who have the opportunity to discuss their goals, enhance their abilities to choose and implement educational strategies to actualize their vision. Ideally, part of any process of professional education should include work to help individuals form their professional vision and provide a laboratory for them to strengthen the bridge between goals and means.

We turned to Foster et al. (2005) as a framework for understanding the key factors that characterize clergy education. We wanted to see which of these factors were most salient from the perspective of the rabbi-educators in our study. We also were curious to see if the rabbi-educators identified any other aspects of their training that fell outside of the Foster et al. framework.

According to this extensive study of the training of rabbis, priests, and ministers, there are four core pedagogies that characterize the nature of clergy education and shape their professional practice. These include pedagogies of (1) interpretation; (2) formation; (3) contextualization; and (4) performance.

Pedagogies of interpretation focus on developing critical thinking and reflection skills in reading and analyzing texts. The emphasis is not only on understanding the text in its own context but also on helping learners to see that the text has something relevant and significant to say about the contemporary human condition.

Pedagogies of formation are designed to cultivate interdependence between the learners' spiritual and professional development. They seek to cultivate a sense of authenticity and integrity by aligning religious identity with religious leadership and practice. The authors describe this approach as one that is best reflected in elevating the presence of God and holiness in all aspects of life.

Pedagogies of contextualization are closely related to pedagogies of interpretation, but here the emphasis is reversed. These pedagogies focus on strengthening religious tradition as something relevant and meaningful to contemporary life. They stress the ideas that knowledge is constructed and that context shapes educational goals, processes, and experiences. They also emphasize the importance of helping learners become self-reflective about their own biases and assumptions through their encounters with the "other."

Pedagogies of performance are rooted in the assumption that the role of clergy is extremely public and therefore imbued with high expectations from the audiences who they are intended to serve. As the authors note: "Performance is a way of thinking and being revealed in the act of doing, carrying out, or putting into effect" (p. 158). These pedagogies focus on developing the ability to interpret and perform "scripts" that can engage and motivate the audience to further action as individuals or collectively.

The research through which these pedagogies are derived is based solely on clergy education. We recognize that rabbi-educators go through the same process of professional training as their rabbinic colleagues. Many, but not all, also receive additional professional preparation as educators. We were interested in understanding whether and how these four pedagogies that are so central to clergy development are manifest in the professional identity construction and role definition of those working as rabbi-educators as well.

Summary of Findings

As noted, our findings are based on two sets of data: (1) 34 written survey responses from 18 American and 16 Israeli rabbi-educators; and (2) follow-up telephone interviews with 19 of this original 34. Only four of the total pool are men. The appendix provides a profile of the interviewees, their name, country, year and school of ordination, and current position(s).

Components of Professional Identity

The rabbi-educators in our study tend to define their identity in one of three ways. Some see themselves predominantly as rabbis serving in an educational role or setting. A handful sees themselves predominantly as educators who happen to be rabbis. Many describe their role as fused with both aspects being essential to their professional identity. Role or setting did not seem to have a direct impact on self-ascription for those who described their identity as fused. For instance, Patty who has more pulpit responsibilities than many of our other respondents, seemed to give her educator role more priority. She said, "I've been an educator forever. It has always been part of my identity. In fact, this was a huge draw for me in rabbinical school. I see everything I do as education." Similarly, Eyal, another congregational rabbi who also works in a school said, "As a congregational rabbi, I do a lot of education. Even when I accompany a family going through a process of mourning, it's education." Likewise, Anat who also serves as both a pulpit and school rabbi, said, "I see myself as an educator in a broad sense. When I teach in a bar mitzvah class as well as when I conduct a committee meeting ... For me, education is always related to faith. An educational action is a faith action."

Most of the respondents who serve as congregational educators see their roles as fused. For instance, Julia who is director of Lifelong Learning at a congregation, said, "I see the roles as really integrated. I wanted to be a rabbi and also wanted to be able to look at my rabbinate through the lenses, the way educators are trained to think. They've always been integrated." Shoshana, a newly appointed congregational educator, made a similar observation: "I am not sure I could do my job if I was not a rabbi and an educator. My training in both fields has already been of specific use in the short time I have been here ...Who I am as a person is an educator ... but, I also can't imagine being an educator without being a rabbi."

Others of our respondents also saw their roles as fused, but more in an ideal sense than in terms of their day-to-day reality. Leah, a congregational school principal, said, "I'd like more integration in my job. I didn't go to rabbinical school so I would learn how to order chicken. I wish I had fewer administrative responsibilities and more time to work with adults and parents." Neil, who has a similar position, said, "I've been saying I have two jobs. I'm the educator and I'm the rabbi. I'd like to connect them more. The people you see often cross both worlds. How do you build on that relationship to help the families and further the congregation's mission? I'm thinking a lot about that."

In contrast to those who described a fused role are a few who noted one or the other aspect as more predominant. Melissa and Leah, both congregational educators, seemed to think that any skilled educator should be able to do most of what they do, including leading services and writing divrei Torah. As Melissa noted: "The only time I feel like a rabbi is when I do life cycle events for friends and family." Similarly, Ilana, who doesn't see herself serving as a congregational rabbi, said, "Education is going to be the heart of my rabbinical practice."

On the other hand, Alice who has worked in a day school for 7 years, described herself more as a rabbi than an educator. She said she chose to work in a school mainly because she wanted to balance her time between work and family. She remarked, "My sense of mission as a rabbi always had to do with children and families. That could have been played out in the pulpit as well."

Perceptions of Preparation

Respondents also reflected on how the various aspects of their professional preparation contribute to their professional identity. Many of the American rabbi-educators we interviewed said they felt they were a better rabbi because of the education training they received. They describe their educational training as providing them with the practical tools and organizational expertise for working in the field, skills they did not acquire through their rabbinical school curriculum. For example, Julia, a graduate of the Rhea Hirsch School of Education at HUC in Los Angeles, remarked, "What I learned during that education year helped me bring all the rabbi stuff together. In the education program, you get a perspective on the field and Jewish world that you don't get in rabbinical school." Leslie, another Rhea Hirsch graduate now working in a day school, said, "If I was just the rabbi, I feel I wouldn't know the inner workings. I can see a bigger picture. I get a more holistic perspective of the school." Another JTS graduate working in a day school who responded to the initial questionnaire wrote: "I'm very thankful that I took the time to complete an education degree before rabbinical school. The rabbinical program was so academic in nature. It doesn't teach you how to connect with people. It helps you figure it out through internships."

Many respondents also highlighted particular education courses that they felt were essential to their professional success. Courses in organizational dynamics, leadership, supervision, and reflective practice were those most frequently mentioned. Whereas most of their American colleagues pursued a formal degree in Jewish education while in rabbinical school, the Israelis who train at HUC in Jerusalem take only two courses in education during their tenure, and those who train at Schechter take almost none[2]. Most of the Israeli respondents indicated they would prefer to get more formal training in education during rabbinic school. The Israeli rabbi-educators (trained at HUC) mentioned as helpful the course that exposed them to visions and practice in Jewish education and leadership. Some also mentioned the importance of deliberating with colleagues about their educational goals and their opportunity to visit and practice teaching in an Israeli high school. As Amit noted, "It was important that we had a safe space in rabbinical school to discuss Jewish education without the pressure of day to day practice."

Machon Shechter graduates mentioned almost no formal training in education during rabbinical school but a general spiritual and leadership preparation that helped them as rabbis. Thus, Hila said, "Each rabbi is first of all an educator but, I didn't get any educational tools in my training at Machon Shechter." Indeed, most of the Israeli respondents felt that they would have benefited from more practical tools during their rabbinic-educational training.

At the same time that many rabbi-educators said that their education training made them better rabbis. American and Israelis alike expressed the sentiment that they can do more as educators because of their rabbinic training. Several noted the fact that the title rabbi commands more respect. For instance, Melanie, a congregational school educator said, "The title gives me *kavod* [respect]. People tend to respond differently. I wish it were different .... Lots of people pushed me to the rabbinate, but no one ever said 'have you ever thought about education instead of or in addition to the rabbinate'?" Many also observed that rabbis bring more of a

---

[2]Recently, rabbinical students at Machon Schechter have begun taking classes in education. At the time when the interviewees in our study were in school, this was not the case.

spiritual perspective and orientation to education than do many of their education colleagues. For example, Julia described supervision of her staff as a spiritual practice. Several respondents spoke about how as rabbis, they can see and respond to the "whole person" in ways they feel many educators are not as prepared to do. This is reflected in Alice's observation: "I'm more interested in the children's personal development right now than their intellectual development." Shoshanna, elaborated even further: "People want to come to you for mentoring, spiritual needs, help with celebration and coping with sorrow. People don't tend to look at their educator in that light ... When a parent comes to me with a child with special needs, the fact that I can approach that relationship as a rabbi and not only be thinking about the child's educational needs, really makes a difference."

Just as many respondents named specific education courses that they saw as essential to their role, so too did they itemize what they felt was most valuable about their rabbinical school training. Virtually every American rabbi-educator listed pastoral care and counseling, and text skills. Neil, a congregational educator described how he links these two skills together: "My pastoral care skills are really important in listening to parents and students as they describe the challenges they have. I do a lot of listening, and where appropriate, I do a lot of linking of Jewish tradition to the responses I hear, trying to demonstrate some of the wisdom of our tradition and how it can help people today." Israeli respondents mentioned a strong Jewish studies background as the main contribution of their rabbinate training. For some of them it was what they needed and for others it was not enough. Eran, a school rabbi said, "In rabbinical school I got a lot of Jewish knowledge, but the title of rabbi does not transform you into an educator."

Vision and Goals of Rabbi-Educators

As mentioned above, Nisan (2009) identifies vision, goals, and beliefs that derive from personal–professional experience as key components of professional identity. At times, the visions that rabbi-educators articulate are specific to the particular context or setting in which they work, such as with *b'nai mitzvah* students or school faculty. At other times, their vision relates more to their general view of the human life journey and its relation to the Jewish world. We identified three core themes that the rabbi-educators in our pool touched upon as they articulated their visions: (1) a desire to connect the Jewish world to everyday life experience; (2) to guide spiritual growth; and (3) among the Israelis, to promote a pluralistic agenda in Israeli society.

Align the Jewish World with Everyday Life

Most of our respondents see their role in helping people create meaningful connections to Jewish life as a central aspect of their rabbinate that they can uniquely contribute to their educational settings. This aspiration was expressed by rabbi-educators working in a wide range of settings. Esther, an American day school rabbi said, "This job is a chance to educate young families and children and staff as to what it means to think and learn Jewishly." Sarah, who works in Israeli public schools and the Israeli army, said, "My job is to link Jewish content with Jewish living and belief." Likewise, Shoshanna, a congregational educator said she sees her job as creating "opportunities for living Jewish culture, and transmitting the necessary skills to be able to do so." And Eyal, who works in a congregation and several different schools in Israel, said, "I would like to help students, teachers, and adults to see everything through the prism of the tradition, Jewish culture, religion and faith."

This theme relates to what Schein (1988) calls "the art of translation" or what Foster et al. (2005) name as "pedagogy of contextualization." Yet, our respondents did not narrow their role to translating only text (Schein, 1988), but saw their mission more broadly in terms of translating the Jewish culture. They stress the role they play in reshaping Jewish knowledge in order to make it relevant to the educational contexts in which they work. They describe themselves as Jewish role models who work to bring the best of the Jewish culture to their learners in order to create stronger commitments to and engagement in Jewish life.

It is not altogether surprising that the rabbi-educators in our study emphasized this pedagogy as a professional goal, since they are enmeshed in the multiple contexts of students, teachers, families, school culture, and ideologies on a daily basis. It may also be that the rabbi-educators' responses in this regard are not all that different from what we might hear from congregational rabbis whose work is also focused on helping people find and make meaning through Jewish texts and tradition.[3]

Spiritual Guidance

Many of both the American and Israeli respondents in our research describe their role as spiritual guides and role models in educational settings, as something that distinguishes them from educators who do not have rabbinic training. They note their training in counseling and pastoral care, as well as their ability to work with people more holistically as key features that set them apart. Some spoke directly about their role as spiritual guides. For instance, Hava, who teaches in a TALI school and the IDF, said, "I try to bring out the spiritual aspects of Judaism, to be a *moreh derech*." One of the American day school rabbi-educators responding to the written questionnaire wrote, "I want to increase the sense of spirituality and *esprit de corps* among the staff so everyone feels more invested in the Jewish mission of the school." Mark, another day school rabbi-educator extended this to a broader audience when he described how he was asked to write his own job description: "I wrote that I would be the spiritual guide for the Solomon Schechter school family – students, faculty, parents, staff, and the wider community."

Other respondents focused more on their potential as rabbi-educators to influence and shape lives. For example, Anat, a congregational rabbi in Israel who also works in schools, remarked, "I love to see people who believe in our ability

---

[3] See Muszkat-Barkan M. "To Mend Myself, To Mend the World: The Choice to Study for the Reform Rabbinate in Israel" (in press).

to change who they are. When I see the changes occur within the group (congregants, students); when I see people apply what we learned to their own lives I feel successful."

Julia, whose responsibilities include supervising faculty noted how she saw her job as supporting both their professional and personal development: "Ultimately, I'm hoping they will grow, primarily in their professional practice, but also as Jews."

This theme fits within a pedagogy of "interpretation" (Foster et al., 2005) which is manifested as an internal guide that leads to pedagogic choices such as discussing values, searching for meaning, and creating affective educational/spiritual experiences that sometimes compete with or supersede cognitive emphasis or gaining knowledge. In comparison to Koren (1993) and Gottfried (2000) they do not emphasize their rabbi-educator role as a source for Jewish knowledge as much as it serves as a source for guidance about Jewish life and personal change.

Pluralism

One of the most significant distinguishing features of the Israeli respondents in our study is their emphasis on pluralism as an important value in their professional identity. Most articulated a pluralistic vision, specifically noting values such as creativity within the Jewish world, relevance as a vehicle for identification with Jewish culture, and the legitimacy of different perspectives as a part of Jewish learning and Jewish living. [4]. They also see the dichotomy between the orthodox and secular perspective in Israeli society as a gap that constrains the engagement of many Israelis with the Jewish world.[5]

This tendency grows out of the cultural and ideological environment in which these rabbi-educators chose to study and the movement in which they choose to serve. Both the Conservative and Reform institutions in Israel mention pluralism as one of the main characteristics of their mission and agenda. Expressions like "the multifaceted Jewish culture," "pluralistic Jewish education," and more, attest to the centrality of a pluralistic standpoint in these movements.[6] Thus, we can understand the context for our Israeli respondents' pluralistic agenda. They use the pedagogy of contextualization in order to emphasize the many ways that can be used in understanding, interpreting, and living Jewish culture in contemporary Israeli life.

---

[4] Both the TALI system and HUC-educational programs in Israel have the term "Pluralism" in their missions and title programs.

[5] This is one of the main "calling" motivations for studying at rabbinic school for Israelis. See Muszkat-Barkan M. "To Mend Myself, To Mend the World: The Choice to Study for the Reform Rabbinate in Israel" (in press).

[6] For example, see: http://www.masorti.org/: "The Masorti movement is a *pluralistic*, religious movement in Israel, affiliated with Conservative Judaism;" http://rac.org/advocacy/irac/ "IRAC was founded in 1987 with the goals of advancing *pluralism* in Israeli society and of protecting and defending the human rights of all Israeli citizens;" http://www.tali.org.il/english/index.asp "TALI is a nation wide network of over 120 Israeli state schools that are committed to providing a *pluralistic* Jewish education for Israeli's non observant majority."

The Israeli rabbi-educators wish to promote a positive Jewish-values agenda in contrast to the often polarized perceptions most Israelis hold toward Jewish tradition: Eran, a school rabbi said he is struggling to "actualize Jewish experience for teachers and students based on values of humanism, pluralism and equality." Amit described how she hopes "to create a fit between the pluralistic Reform Jewish culture and Israeli experience ... I want to help people internalize a pluralistic perspective which would allow them to become creative within the Jewish world."

Ilana articulated the feeling that as a liberal rabbi she has to model a pluralistic perspective: "With my Reform agenda I come to the process of teaching and learning with more responsibility to make room for the entire range of voices. My voice is only one of them."

The absence of this agenda among our American respondents can be explained by the pluralistic reality of American and especially Jewish-American society. Pluralism is already a core value in American society that shapes how Americans understand their choices in life, including whether and how they engage in religious practice. This creates a different set of challenges for American rabbi-educators. For Israelis, the emphasis appears to be more on changing society through effecting change in particular educational settings. The personal challenges are understood as a part of the national challenges. The Americans lack this sense of collective agenda; rather they seem to see their work more in terms of motivating and supporting individuals within their communities in building a relationship to Judaism and Jewish life.

Pedagogies Shaping Identity

Our initial research suggests that two of the four pedagogies identified by the Carnegie Foundation study on clergy education predominate as key factors in shaping the self-perception of rabbi-educators' professional identity. These are what Foster et al. (2005) label pedagogies of formation and contextualization. Participants in our study focused on these two aspects of their work to a much greater extent than they did on the other two pedagogies—interpretation and performance. These latter two pedagogies appear somewhat more focused on skill development, while both formation and contextualization appear to be concerned with integration. In the former case, pedagogies of formation focus on integrating personal and professional elements of self, while pedagogies of contextualization concentrate on learning how to make religious texts, traditions, and beliefs relevant and meaningful in contemporary life.

Pedagogies of Formation

The Carnegie Foundation researchers describe pedagogies of formation as "the dispositions, habits, knowledge, and skills that cohere in professional identity and practice, commitments and integrity" (Foster et al., 2005, p. 100). These pedagogies aim to integrate the processes of spiritual and professional development, bringing together personal belief with professional practice. Three inter-related strategies contribute to formation: (1) awakening students to the presence of God; (2) imbuing their work and life with holiness; and (3) practicing religious leadership (pp. 103–104).

While they did not use this exact language, many of the rabbi-educators in our study stressed the importance of integrating religious knowledge with character development. They spoke about their roles as spiritual leaders and their ability to serve as spiritual role models in ways above and beyond what they believed many educators without rabbinic training could do. As we have already noted, a great number used the term "spiritual guide" to describe their work with students, teachers, and parents.[7] For example, this perception is clearly reflected in the written comments of one of the American day school rabbi-educators.

> Being a rabbi I believe I am *kli kodesh*, a spiritual exemplar, and everything I do I do with that hat on. Even though I play an administrative role at the school, I am always a rabbi. Every time I speak, whether publicly or with people privately I think about what I am saying, whether the content or the tone. If I upset someone it isn't me the individual who is upsetting them it is me the rabbi upsetting them and the impact can be devastating.

Remarks made by Hava, an educational counselor in the IDF, and Eran who works with students and teachers in Israeli public schools, also reflected on the integration of their role as teacher and spiritual role model:

> I work with army officers and like to use educational opportunities to raise human questions such as my place in the wilderness, loneliness, and the meaning of life. As a rabbi, I give myself permission to delve into the spiritual aspects of life. It's not the learning but the spirituality. I started with halacha but have moved to a deeper engagement with spirituality. (Hava)
> A rabbi-educator doesn't just talk about Judaism like an anthropologist or scholar. It's something internal. I try not to talk about Judaism but to live Judaism with the students and their parents. There's a difference between teaching about Judaism and teaching how to be a Jew. (Eran)

While we might read these remarks as imbued with a sense of the holiness of their mission, few actually used this explicit language. Indeed only a handful of our interviewees spoke either directly or indirectly about God. In one instance, Leah, a congregational school rabbi-educator reflected on her role as a religious leader. She said, "Being a rabbi gives the position more gravity. It says that religious school is important and that rabbis aren't 'beyond' the most holy of tasks of helping to educate our children and their families."

In another case, Alice, a day school rabbi-educator, described her work helping teachers prepare for a second grade tefilah ceremony: "I talk with teachers about their questions about God. We write tefilot together. Not that there aren't teachers who can't do that, but many can't." Likewise, when speaking about prayer, Hila,

---

[7] Interestingly the term "spiritual guide" was not found in interviews with teachers or teachers' mentors. Teachers who are not rabbis seem to distance themselves from the use of the term spirituality. See, for example, the Chapter "Ideological Encounters…" by Muszkat-Barkan (2011).

who works in a TALI school in Israel, said, "A rabbi has a special energy. I believe this energy reaches the kids and they can experience tefilah with their soul and not only with their minds." Echoing within these statements is the question of whether the actual educational work of rabbis is different from that of educators who are not rabbis. Further research needs to be undertaken in order to answer this more fully. It does appear that the rabbi-educators feel comfortable and confident to tackle questions of spirituality and belief while many educators who are not rabbis seem to be less confident in doing so.

Pedagogies of Contextualization

In the broadest sense, pedagogies of contextualization refer to "the task of making explicit the socially situated nature of all knowledge and practice" (Foster et al., 2005, p. 132). This pedagogy focuses on learning how to present religious tradition as something relevant and meaningful to contemporary life.

Our respondents frequently noted the importance of helping people negotiate with and make meaning from Judaism. Indeed, some described their role as a mediator between Jewish texts and tradition and people's lives. Neil, a congregational educator, put it like this:

> I do a lot of listening to parents and students as they describe the challenges they have. Where appropriate, I do a lot of linking of Jewish tradition to the responses I hear, trying to demonstrate some of the wisdom of our tradition and how it can help people today.

Similarly, Sarah, who works in several Israeli educational settings, said, "I want to connect content to living and also belief. I believe that Jewish tradition has important things to teach us in actual contexts." In like fashion, Amit, a congregational rabbi who also works in schools, said, "It's important for me to connect what people know and do but don't see as something Jewish to Jewish life and to create a bridge between Jewish identity and global identity. That's my Zionism."

Esther, who works in an American Reform day school reflected on her role in trying to find the appropriate level of observance in her particular context of a Reform Jewish day school:

> Being a Rav Beit Sefer in a Reform day school is not so clear. Families aren't really sure what they are looking for and what it means to lead a Jewish life. While there may be debate and alternatives explored about how to learn tefilah in an Orthodox or Conservative school, they aren't debating whether kids should learn tefilah at all.

Pedagogies of Interpretation and Performance

The survey and interview data yielded fewer references to tasks and skills needed that relate to pedagogies of interpretation and performance than those related to pedagogies of formation and contextualization. In delineating pedagogies of interpretation, the Carnegie Foundation researchers stress the importance of developing critical thinking and critical reflection skills in reading and analyzing texts. While virtually all of the participants in our study highlighted the importance of the text study skills they developed through their rabbinic training, almost no one described how they put these skills into practice. Thus, we have no evidence to show whether or how these skills of interpretation are brought to bear in their day-to-day work. We wonder how the rigorous preparation rabbis receive in textual analysis might contribute to their roles as rabbi-educators in ways different from educators without rabbinic training. However, at this stage, we can only pose the question for further investigation.

Several of our respondents explicitly noted the benefit of the critical thinking and reflection skills they developed through their formal training. However, these skills were more typically associated with their education courses than they were with their rabbinic training. They also focused more on the applied benefits of critical reflection in action rather than the intellectual process of textual analysis. For example, Melanie, a congregational educator, said, "The cornerstone of my educational training was all about how to be a reflective practitioner. In the rabbinic program there was a weak attempt to build in reflection but it was more haphazard." Julia described how her education work helped her organize and synthesize her rabbinical school program: "What I learned in my education program really helped me bring all of the rabbinical school stuff together. It really made a difference tying a lot of loose pieces together." Ilana remembered: "In our education course we learned to ask the 'why' questions that are so important in planning every educational activity."

Pedagogies of performance involve those aspects of training that prepare clergy to be effective public leaders. Indeed, there are performative qualities in virtually everything clergy do, including classroom teaching, preaching, liturgical leadership, counseling, and even running meetings. The Carnegie Foundation research team focuses on how seminary educators cultivate professional proficiency through pedagogies that emphasize these performative aspects of the work.

The rabbi-educators in our study touched upon some of these aspects of performance, mostly frequently mentioning teaching and counseling as core skills needed to perform effectively in their roles. They also described some of the challenges they perceive in adequately performing in their roles. Some of those without formal education training acknowledged an absence of good teaching skills. For instance, two of the Israeli respondents said they would have liked to learn more practical tools for teaching during their professional training. Sarah said, "I wish we learned more about how to develop a personal teaching style." Several of the American rabbi-educators also noted some missing pieces in terms of their educational practice. Knowledge about learners with special needs, classroom management, and administrative skills such as budgeting and grant writing were among the most frequently mentioned gaps they perceived in their training. An Israeli rabbi-educator also mentioned the lack of background regarding dealing with families and family education.

Missing from the Framework

The Carnegie Foundation study does not focus on educational training per se as a core aspect of clergy education. Our research suggests that some of the qualities reflected in each of the four pedagogies may be enhanced and enriched through course work in education, perhaps most explicitly with regard to pedagogies of contextualization and performance which are the most directly related to teaching and helping people to make meaning out of religious tradition. In addition, our interview data revealed two areas of professional practice that are not addressed in the framework identified by Foster et al. These have to do with organizational management and curriculum development. Our respondents who had formal training in education referenced these skills which were outside of their rabbinical school curriculum as essential to their vision, self-understanding, and daily practice. Many also noted that they would like further training in these areas to enhance their education practice.

Discussion

What can we conclude from these findings? From the rabbi-educators' comments and the way they described their practice, we learned about their "lived ideology" (Billig, Cordal, Edwards, Gane, & Middleton, 1988) which is a central component of their professional identity as leaders (Nisan, 2009). While they share a great deal in common with educators who do not have rabbinic training, they clearly perceive themselves as having skills and dispositions distinctly formed as a product of their combined rabbinic and education preparation. Our study reveals that the professional identity of these rabbi-educators is shaped around three distinct goals. These include (1) their educational mission to align the Jewish world with personal life; (2) their desire to serve as a spiritual mentor or guide for their various constituents; and (3) for the Israelis, a broader mission of promoting a pluralistic agenda in Israeli society. Whether or not these goals are shared by educators who are not rabbis remains an open question worthy of further study. For this group, perhaps it is not the individual goals that distinguish these rabbi-educators but their interrelationship. Indeed, it may be that the first goal is something that they share with other educators; the second goal is something they share with other rabbis; and the third goal is something that they share with others working to create a more pluralistic society in Israel. But, our findings suggest that it is not just the educational setting for their work that defines their role. This is most evident by those respondents who referred to a synergy between the two roles when they said in effect "I'm a better rabbi because of my education training, and I'm a better educator because I'm a rabbi." They emphasized the importance of the educational-training components during rabbinical school as shaping their professional identity and their abilities to perform their dual role as rabbi-educators. And at the same time they emphasized how their rabbinical training helped them to develop deep content knowledge and a sense of holistic responsibility for the various constituencies they serve.

Further Directions

We began this preliminary exploration of the evolving role of rabbi-educators with the awareness that the research might raise as many questions as it answers. It seems crucial to continue to work to better understand how seminaries that train rabbi-educators can address the professional development needs of the many students who are now choosing this dual path, both in Israel and North America. As we conclude this phase of our inquiry, we pose several additional questions to frame the next level of study.

1. Perhaps most significantly, this study does not resolve the question of whether rabbi-educator is a profession distinct from rabbi or educator. The participants in our study clearly see themselves as a different group. This is most noticeable in how they define their purposes around issues of spirituality, belief, and religious practice. This question needs further investigation with a larger pool of participants. It will also be interesting to explore how the goals and self-perceptions of rabbi-educators are shaped by their roles. In other words, how does professional identity change over time? What impact does the specific job requirements have on shaping this identity?
2. As noted, in contrast to the Carnegie Foundation study, our research findings did not reveal significant emphasis on the performative aspects of the rabbi-educator role. It very well may be that we did not ask the right questions of our respondents. A future study might want to focus more specifically on this area of professional practice to determine what specific skills and capabilities are developed through educational training that enhance the job performance of rabbi-educators?
3. We also wonder how do the colleagues and people served by rabbi-educators in their work environments perceive their contributions? Are they perceived as differently in their beliefs and practices from educators who are not rabbis as they think they are? How do rabbi-educators differ in the performance of their roles from rabbis who are not educators and educators who are not rabbis? How do these perceptions compare to the self-perceptions of the rabbi-educators themselves?

Thus far, our findings suggest that rabbis who serve as educators recognize that the dual components of educational and rabbinical preparation are essential to the success of their work. To varying degrees, they perceive a synergy between the educational and rabbinic perspectives of their professional identity. This combination is reflected in the professional goals shared among our American and Israeli rabbi-educators, with the notable exception of the Israeli emphasis on the promotion of a pluralistic agenda. Further study that explores the questions we outline above will help us better understand the contributions of this dual role and how those who serve in this position develop over time.

Appendix Profile of Interviewees

Name[a]	Country	Year of ordination	School	Current position
Sara	Israel	2007	HUC Jerusalem	Social justice coordinator—public school; Teacher in IDF Training Program; Jewish studies curriculum writer; Beit midrash facilitator—public school
Hava	Israel	2005	Machon Schechter	TALI[b] (public) school rabbi; Educational counselor for Jewish identity in IDF
Hila	Israel	2006	Machon Schechter	TALI (public) school rabbi
Alice	US	1999	HUC—NY	Director of Judaic programming—day school
Amit	Israel	2005	HUC Jerusalem	Congregational rabbi—works with pre-school and other educational activities in the congregation and community
Anat	Israel	2005	HUC Jerusalem	Congregational rabbi—works with public schools in the area and other educational activities in the congregation and community
Eran	Israel	2004	HUC Jerusalem	Rav Beit Sefer—public schools; Facilitator of teacher batei midrash
Esther	US	2000	Other	School rabbi and Jewish studies curriculum coordinator—day school
Eyal	Israel	2003	Machon Schechter	Congregational rabbi—works as a rabbi of a TALI school and other educational activities in the congregation and community
Ilana	Israel	2008	HUC Jerusalem	Bat Mitzva program in public schools; Facilitator of teacher and adults batei midrash, Jewish studies curriculum writer
Julia	US	2003	HUC—LA	Director of lifelong learning—congregation
Leah	US	2005	JTS	Education director—congregation
Leslie	US	2000	HUC—LA	School rabbi and principal of Jewish studies—day school
Mark	US	2007	JTS	Rav Beit Sefer—day school
Melanie	US	2002	HUC—LA	Director of religious school, youth, and camping—congregation
Miriam	Israel	2004	HUC Jerusalem	Public school and congregational pre-school rabbi
Neil	US	2005	HUC—NY	Director of Jewish Learning—congregation
Patty	US	2004	JTS	Associate rabbi, spiritual leader of the religious school—congregation
Shoshana	US	2006	HUC—NY	Director youth and family education—congregation

[a] All names are pseudonyms.
[b] TALI schools are part of the public school system in Israel. They are secular schools that have decided to enrich their curriculum and school community with Jewish studies and experiences.

References

Billig, M., Cordal, S., Edwards, D., Gane, M., & Middleton, D. (1988). *Ideological dilemmas: A social psychology of everyday thinking*. London: Sage.

Foster, C. R., Dahill, L., Golemon, L., & Tolentino, B. W. (2005). *Educating clergy: Teaching practices and pastoral imagination*. San Francisco: Jossey-Bass.

Gottfried, L. (2000, summer). A new role for rabbis in Solomon Schechter schools. *Conservative Judaism, 52*(4), 47–52.

Judaism the Masorti movement in Israel: http://www.masorti.org/

Koren, G. (1993) Preparation and training of School rabbis. The Annual Lifshiz College Yearbook (Hebrew).

Muszkat-Barkan, M. (2011). 'Ideological encounters: *Mentoring teachers in Jewish Education*. In H. Miller, L. Grant & A. Pomson (Eds.), *International handbook of Jewish education*. Dordrecht: Springer.

Muszkat-Barkan, M. To mend myself, to mend the world: The choice to study for the reform Rabbinate in Israel (in press).

Nisan, M. (2009). *'Educational identity' as a major factor in the development of educational leadership*. Jerusalem: Mandel Leadership Institute.

Schein, J. (1988, summer). Rabbi as teacher: The process of formulating educational goals for Jewish leadership. *Jewish Education, 56*(2), 15–17.

TALI Education Fund (a Hebrew acronym for Enriched Jewish Studies) http://www.tali.org.il/english/index.asp

The Reform movement in Israel http://rac.org/advocacy/irac/

Special Education: "And You Shall Do That Which Is Right and Good ..." Jewish Special Education in North America: From Exclusion to Inclusion

Rona Milch Novick and Jeffrey Glanz

Introduction

> And you shall do that which is right and good ...
>
> (*Devarim*, 6:18)

Jewish education, like its secular counterpart, has increasingly sought to address the needs of students with learning, behavior, emotional, social, and physical challenges. From the earliest secular programs that largely segregated students with homogeneous disabilities such as the Perkins School for the Blind and Gallaudet School for the Deaf (Winzer, 1993), and those that were designed to offer "asylum" for children seen as too disabled and uneducable (Paul, French, & Cranston-Gingras, 2001), special education has expanded exponentially. Initial efforts led to massive specialization and differentiation (Sailor & Roger, 2005). Confronted with less than positive outcomes in specialized programs, and ethical mandates to revise exclusionary policies, American reforms moved to decrease the number of students in segregated special education placements. This not uniquely American process is echoed in the 1994 UNESCO Salamanca statement urging the international community to "endorse the approach of inclusive schooling" (p. x). Across the globe, developed countries such as Ireland (Shevlin, Kenny, & Loxley, 2008) and Italy (Begeny & Martens, 2007) and those recently obtaining independence like Ukraine (Raver & Kolchenko, 2007) or emerging into industrialization like China (Ellsworth & Zhang, 2007) have moved toward inclusion. Israel passed its Special Education Law in 1988 giving priority to integration of special needs students into regular classrooms (Schanin & Reiter, 2007). Jewish special education, most often a private endeavor, has moved slowly toward inclusive practice, confronting unique challenges and ethical imperatives.

R.M. Novick (✉)
Yeshiva University, New York, NY, USA
e-mail: Rnovick1@yu.edu

Historical Factors: Early Models and Their Influences

Teach them diligently to your children

(*Devarim*, 6:7)

Winzer's (1993) noteworthy history documents the horrendous treatment of the "deformed," "feebleminded," "insane," "socially maladjusted," "stupid," "incapables," "unteachable," and "handicapped" prior to the eighteenth century. In the nineteenth century, exclusion was commonplace, although the beginnings of "charity" toward, if not education of, the disabled emerged. She cites the pioneering work of Diderot for the blind, Ferrus for the mentally retarded, and Tuke for the deaf, among prominent others, whose work formed the basis for caring and educating "handicapped" students. In America, the spirit of the Revolution fueled the view that all individuals could and should contribute to the emerging democratic society. This supported the move toward increased schooling for individuals with special needs. Unlike prior paternalistic models, early special education in the United States was geared toward vocational training, preparing all to become "productive" citizens rather than a drain on the new country (Osgood, 2008).

The history of Jewish special education appears to have been more influenced by secular culture and history than by Jewish understandings of disability and difference. In her introduction to the 2006 Partnership for Excellence in Jewish Education (PEJE) series on *Noteworthy Practices in Jewish Day School Education*, Miller-Jacobs highlights multiple Jewish perspectives that shape attitudes regarding diverse students. The precept that all individuals, disabled or not, are made in G-d's image is underscored by the blessing one says when seeing an individual who is disabled. Thanking G-d for creating diversity (*Baruch ata Hashem ... mishaneh et habriyot*, Blessed are you our G-d who diversifies living creatures; *Mishneh Torah*, Hilchot B'rachot) reminds us that every child, no matter how different, is a creation of G-d. Also relevant is the principle that Jews are responsible for each other (*kol Yisrael arevim zeh lazeh*; Babylonian Talmud). Being responsible for the well-being of fellow Jews includes assuring their access to Jewish communal institutions. Miller-Jacobs quotes Kushner's editorial comment in *Etz Hayim* on *Mishpatim* arguing, "the decency of a society is measured by how it cares for its least powerful members" (PEJE, 2006, p. 4).

Astor (1985) contrasts the Jewish view of disability with other cultures whose notions embody a sense of creation "failures" (i.e., Sumerian myth regarding inept gods molding disabled individuals from clay). The Old Testament offers the examples of Isaac who was blind for much of his life, Jacob who dealt with lameness, and Moses, the great teacher/leader of the Jewish nation, who was speech-impaired. When Moses argues that his disability renders him unfit he is reminded: "who gives man speech ... who makes him dumb, deaf, seeing or blind? Is it not I, the Lord? Now go, and I will be with you as you speak and instruct you what to say" (*Shemot* 4:11–12). Disability is not to be viewed as an immutable limitation.

Kaminetsky (1977) underscores the "responsibility to integrate the handicapped with the Jewish education effort" (p. 105) and its connection to Torah law. There is a requirement to educate all Jews, including those who have the potential to reach adult legal status. Fulfilling the precept "... so that he may live by your side as your brother" (*Vayikra*, 25:36) requires including those who will not reach adult legal status, but for whom education can promote their integration in society.

Talmudic sources provide further support. Schloss (2008) cites the discussion in the Babylonian tractate of *Sanhedrin* quoting Rav Yehuda who says in the name of Rav

> whoever withholds the teaching of the law from the mouth of a student, i.e. whoever neglects to teach Torah to a student, is as if he robs [the student] of his ancestral heritage. For it is stated: The Torah that Moses commanded us is the heritage of the congregation of Jacob. This means: It is a heritage to all of Israel since the six days of creation. (Babylonian Talmud, Tractate *Sanhedrin*, 91b)

Schloss further cites Rabbi Shmuel Halevi Edels in the *Maharsha* stating that each and every child, regardless of academic prowess, is entitled to a Jewish education.

Despite these perspectives on inclusion, Jewish education paid little attention to special needs until recently. The Jewish Education Service of North America publication *So That All May Study Torah: Communal Provision of Jewish Education for Students With Special Needs* commented, "in the rhetoric of inclusion and outreach which typifies the continuity deliberations (i.e. how to best maintain the Jewish population) and which extends to so many other subpopulations (the intermarried, the non-traditional family, the elderly, teens, college students, etc.) the sub-populations of physically, emotionally and mentally challenged individuals and their families are rarely mentioned or considered and, therefore, plans are rarely made for meeting their needs" (Isaacs & Levine, 1995, p. 6).

Special Education in the Modern Age

> We are all brought forth for one purpose, every scion that comes to birth in Israel is to be Israel's son or Israel's daughter; for this one purpose you are to bring up your child, for this ultimate purpose it was given to you. You commit treason, treason against what is most holy, if you neglect this.
>
> (Samson Raphael Hirsch, 1962, p. 407)

Until the late 1950s, the US federal government largely left the business of education to the states. The cold war need for scientists engaged the federal government in pumping funds into elementary- and secondary-level science education. Federal involvement initially expanded to special needs issues by providing support to colleges training teachers of the mentally retarded and in 1963, broadened to support preparation of a variety of special education teachers. In 1967, PL89-313 allowed federal funds to be delivered to state schools for the "handicapped."

Through the 1960s and 1970s, advocates pushed for increased funding for students with disabilities, enforceable entitlements, and perhaps most importantly a single entity to coordinate national efforts for special needs children. In 1975, Congress passed Public Law 94–142 (Education of All Handicapped Children Act). More recent legal mandates (Individuals with Disabilities Education Act (IDEA) 1997, 2004) require states to develop and implement policies that assure a free appropriate public education (FAPE) for all children (Wiebe Berry, 2006). PL 94–142 and later reauthorization of IDEA also guaranteed parents due process regarding their children's educational needs. Despite federal mandates, advocates have consistently been required to appeal to state law makers and mount litigation to ensure that children receive the services they require and to which they are entitled (Martin, Martin, & Terman, 1996).

Statutes and litigation decisions have created legal precedents for students to receive publicly mandated and funded services regardless of where they are schooled. This has allowed Jewish schools to petition districts to supply limited special educational services including speech, occupational therapy, learning support, counseling, and other services. Ideally, these services would be offered by culturally sensitive district-funded practitioners at convenient and appropriate times in Jewish schools. In reality, districts frequently require that Jewish special needs students come to their sites during school hours.

Segregated special education classes in Jewish schools are reportedly "close to a century old" (Schloss, 2001, p. 2). Considering possible reasons for limited inclusion of diverse students in Jewish education, Kaminetsky (1977) discusses the prestige of accomplished learning and the association of scholarship with piety. He suggests that "slow learners" attending some Jewish programs found the material challenging and withdrew, or parents, concerned that children would be subject to ridicule, kept them from Jewish programs. Kaminetsky alludes to a survey of Jewish educators that revealed an overwhelming majority in favor of Jewish education for special needs populations; however, less than half felt that such children should be educated with the general population. The Coordinating Committee on Religious Education for the Handicapped, founded in the mid-1960s, offered advocacy, information, and training to increase the access of the disabled to Jewish education (Schloss, 2008). A recent PEJE review (2006) confirms that parents had to fight to have their special needs children attend Jewish schools until recently.

Largely in response to parents' efforts, there has been a substantial increase in the number of Jewish schools including special needs students (PEJE, 2006). Schloss (2008) echoes the critical role of parent advocacy, especially when combined with professional efforts. The AVI CHAI foundation census of US Jewish day schools in the 2003–2004 school year reviewed enrollment in denominationally affiliated schools, and an additional 100 schools located through government and Jewish community records (Schick, 2005). Of the 759 schools included, 43 were special education schools, serving a total of 1,780 students. The report noted 331 additional special education students in non-special education schools, although it is unclear how inclusive such settings were. Schick states:

> It is difficult to track special education students in Jewish schools, the majority of whom are now in institutions with a special education mission. Other such students are in separate programs that have been established in regular day schools. In line with an expanding societal and governmental commitment to special education, there has been significant growth in this sector. Almost certainly, the census undercounts the number of special education students enrolled in day schools under Jewish sponsorship. (p. 8)

The expansion of Jewish education to include special needs students has occurred across communities and continents. Glaubman and Lifshitz (2001), describing changes in Israeli education, explain that until recently, both the *Haredi Talmud-Torah* and *Beit Yaakov* systems were virtually closed to special needs pupils. Changing attitudes to the disabled within ultra-orthodox culture, and Rabbinic attention and support to families with special needs children has prompted significant changes, including a Ministry of Education supervisor assigned to work with the *Haredi* population, and a special education track in the *Beit Yaakov* teachers' college.

Special Education and the Move to Inclusion: Trends in Public and Jewish Schools

> If a teacher has taught a subject and the pupils failed to understand it, he must not be angry with them nor get excited, but should review the lesson with them many times until they finally grasp it.
>
> (Maimonides, *Mishneh Torah*, 4:4–5.)

Inclusion is more than a service delivery model, it is a belief system (Stainback & Stainback, 2000) and a process of facilitating an educational environment that provides access to high-quality education for all (Lambert et al., 2003). In inclusive settings, removal of children with special needs occurs only when the nature or severity of the disability is such that education in the general classroom cannot be achieved even with supplementary support (Individuals with Disabilities Education Act, 33, U.S.C., 1400, 1997; Kochhar, West, & Taymans, 2000; Viachou, 2004; Young, 2000).

Movement toward inclusion has been slow and resistance formidable (see, e.g., Fuchs & Fuchs, 1994). Despite clear increases in the identification of students with disabilities since 1970, the percentage placed in inclusive classrooms remains "minimal" (p. 22). Momentum for inclusion is growing, however (see, e.g., Shepherd & Brody Hasazi, 2007). Support from local, state, national, and international professional organizations has fueled interest and advocacy. Court cases have challenged schools that segregate students with disabilities. Lay groups, parent advocates, and educators have begun to "push" for inclusion on a human rights basis (see, e.g., International League of Societies for Persons with Mental Handicap, 1994, June).

In the United States, the number of students with special needs, approximately 15% of the total public school population, is over 5 million. For Jewish day schools this would translate into approximately 38,000 students who may need special services. Assuming socio-cultural factors reduce incidence in the Jewish community, it is still likely that students with special needs sit in every Jewish classroom in America. Addressing the needs of these students, who, for the most part, are learning disabled but may also have visual/auditory/physical/emotional disabilities, has become a major issue for both research and practice.

In 2006, PEJE collated information on special education programs as a resource for schools and parents. Not meant as an exhaustive survey, 22 programs were described, drawn from interviews with school professionals that attended a 2005 conference of the Consortium of Special Educators in Jewish Central Agencies and additional schools known through work with PEJE. Nine served elementary through high school, with the remaining programs geared to particular grades. Only one was disability-specific (emotional/behavioral disturbance), others served students with diverse difficulties. Although 12 programs identified themselves as providing inclusion, review of program descriptions revealed only 2 employing full inclusion. For others, inclusion was one model of service delivery, along with self-contained programs, pull-out and push-in support, and the use of shadows or aides.

Reviewing comments of the program directors, three critical issues emerge: (i) successful inclusion requires time and effort, with significant attention to teacher buy-in and training. (ii) directors almost unanimously cited the critical role of top-level administration. (iii) finally, financial support was a major issue, often necessitating significant advocacy, sophistication regarding funding, and scholarship programs. Not all programs provided cost information, but those that did ranged from a few thousand dollars to $18,000 above regular day-school tuition. Such programs may be inclusive in the children they educate, but will remain exclusive to wealthy families, unless alternate financial supports are developed.

Currently, Jewish schools deal with the placement of children with disabilities in a variety of ways. Some schools do not address the issue. Many adopt a mainstreaming approach in which a child leaves general education classes to receive special services such as resource room, speech therapy, etc. In some schools, these students are initially segregated from the mainstream, and later placed in general education classrooms for specific subjects. Many students are excluded entirely for academic subjects, and placed for social reasons into general classes for art, music, or physical education.

Despite limited inclusive options for Jewish students, many agencies that support Jewish education are embracing the need for increased inclusion. The Jewish Education Service of North America (2009) includes in the mission of its Consortium of Special Educators in Central Agencies for Jewish Education "dissemination of information on program models and development, specialized curriculum and technology, *inclusion*, professional development and support, advocacy and legislation, and community relations and awareness" (emphasis added). RAVSAK: The Jewish Community Day School Network (2009), on its website, identifies itself as "the international center for the advancement and support of pluralistic Jewish day school education. We promote academic excellence, *maximal inclusion*, Jewish diversity and religious purposefulness ..." (emphasis added). It is unclear whether the referred to inclusion is intended across students with disabilities, or from varied Jewish backgrounds. PARDES, the coordinating agency for

Reform schools lists among its goals the "development of the full potential of the personal-intellectual, emotional, social, spiritual and creative-blending of the best of our Jewish and American heritage" (PARDES, 2009).

When the spirit of inclusion takes root in Jewish agencies and communities, greater inclusive practices in Jewish special education become possible. As the program director of the Amit Community School in Atlanta, GA wrote, "When those outside of the Jewish community look at our success and ask how we have accomplished so much, it is an easy answer. We are fortunate to live in a community that understands the key principles of creating an environment in which families can truly feel part of Klal Yisrael. Our community values diversity, believes in a sense of belonging, and strives to offer community support" (Zimmerman, 2008, p. 2).

Ethical Issues

> Just as you are required to teach your own children, so are you responsible to educate all children.
> (Rabbi Judah the Pious)

Inclusive practice requires moral commitment. Zweiter's (2006) incisive critique challenges Jewish educators to critically examine their own practices on many levels. Zweiter questions grouping students homogeneously stating, "... it is far from clear that bright children learn less when they are with a mixed group of students than when they are with other bright children" (p. 15). Most of our classrooms are homogeneously grouped because, according to Oakes (1985), traditional conceptions of learning remain with us even though they no longer make sense. Zweiter cautions against such educational "inertia" which can stifle creative solutions and change.

Advocacy for inclusion is also grounded in a broader critique of classroom life (Jackson, Boostrom, & Hansen, 1993). Kohn (1999) describes our schools and classrooms as joyless. Levine (2004) charges, "instructional practices and curricular choices fail to provide educational opportunities for diverse learners" (p. 8) and asks, why children have to "wait until adulthood to experience success?" (p. 10). According to Shapiro (2006) "school is a place that conveys, and endlessly reinforces the idea that people are necessarily and inevitably to be ranked in ability and worth, and that those who are deemed of most worth are recognized and celebrated ..." (p. 40). For a discussion of the strong ethical argument for inclusion, the reader is referred to Glanz (2008).

Why Inclusion and What Stands in the Way

> A student should not be embarrassed if a fellow student has understood something after the first or second time and he has not grasped it even after several attempts.
> (*Shulkhan Arukh, Yoreh De'ah*, 246:11)

Along with moral and Jewish arguments, research findings should inspire Jewish educators to move toward inclusion. In a review of the literature, Salend and Garrick (1999) found "increases in academic achievement, increased peer acceptance and richer friendship networks, higher self-esteem, avoidance of stigma attached to pull-out programs, and possible lifetime benefits" (as cited in Wiebe Berry, 2006, p. 490). Vaughn, Elbaum, Schumm, and Hughes (1998) have cited positive social outcomes for students with and without disabilities (also, see Hunt & Goetz, 1997; Staub & Peck, 1994–1995). Studies indicate that inclusive classrooms do not contribute to academic decline of non-disabled students (Peltier, 1997; Power-deFur & Orelove, 2003; Sharpe & York, 1994). Research also indicates that acceptance of inclusive practices is based on the amount of administrative support, resources, and training teachers receive (Ainscow, Howes, Farrell, & Frankham, 2003; Bishop & Jones, 2002). Effective inclusion also "depends on classroom climate factors as well as effective instructional strategies" (Erwin & Guintini, 2000; Myklebust, 2006; Wiebe Berry, 2006, p. 520).

To better understand the delayed move to inclusionary practices in Jewish schools, issues that support or compromise inclusion are discussed below.

Attitudes/Efficacy

Developing confidence about teaching "special learners" is important for both general and special education teachers, especially in considering more inclusive models (Jung, 2007). A survey of regular and special education teachers indicated a lack of confidence in their instructional skills and in the support staff provided to address special students' needs (Center & Ward, 1987).

Teachers' beliefs about struggling students may translate into different expectations and instruction for those students, as well as negatively impact their sense of responsibility for teaching them (Scharlach, 2008). In her qualitative case study, Scharlach found teachers with high efficacy had high expectations for students, and the opposite was also true. Four out of the five teachers studied felt that it was the responsibility of someone other than the classroom teacher to address difficulties of struggling readers.

Jung (2007), reviewing the impact of training on attitudes and efficacy of 68 education students, suggests, "training might need to be extended to help raise the confidence level of pre-service teachers" (p. 110) with guided field experiences more effective in creating positive attitudes than a course in inclusion. Jung further questions how teachers who graduate with inclusionary practices and attitudes will be supported once in the "real world?"

Critical for Jewish schools are the attitudes of their teachers. An exploration of Israeli ultra-orthodox Jewish teachers' attitudes (Glaubman & Lifshitz, 2001) revealed interactions between gender and level of disability with male teachers more positive toward inclusion of mildly disabled and female teachers more positive toward inclusion of severely disabled, students. The ultra-orthodox teachers defined disability differently than other professionals, grouping mild visual and auditory impairments with blindness and deafness, and learning disabilities with mild retardation. These definitions impacted willingness to include such students. Further research across denominations would be important in assessing and developing Jewish teacher attitudes that support inclusion.

Teacher Training, Supervision, and Administrative Support

Research on successful inclusion implementation indicates that administrative support is crucial (Newmann, Rutter, & Smith, 1989; Rieck, 2000). Many teachers are not properly trained to teach differentially, and are not committed to an inclusive philosophy (Sapon-Shevin, 2007). Teacher training and professional development post-graduation are required (Bowe, 2005). McLaughlin and Warren (1994), studying special education administrators, found "many of the increased costs . . . are seen as one-time start-up costs and not necessarily costs that will continue . . . as a core of staff within school buildings gain confidence and experience" (p. 16).

Supports essential for successful inclusion are summarized in Table 1, many of which represent challenges for Jewish schools. There are fewer teacher-training programs and not all Jewish schools employ trained teachers, with informal education programs and supplementary schools least likely to have such personnel. Professional development funds are limited, and resources difficult to access. Jewish teachers participating in publicly funded training may find the content minimally relevant to Jewish subjects.

Table 1 Summary of factors identified as critical for successful inclusion

Common planning	Inclusive practice requires shared planning time for participants (Fuchs, Fuchs, & Bahr, 1999)
Teacher training	Initial training is inadequate unless continually supported (Meijer, 2001)
Resources	Support personnel, technologies, and all necessary resources must be provided (Boyd, 1992; Hord, 1991)
Continuous assessment	School leaders must take the time and effort to assess staff and student progress (Boyd, 1992; Hord, 1991)
Consultation	Coaching, consulting, and continued development further the objectives established by administrators and participants (Boyd, 1992; Hord, 1991)

Cost

In 1999, US public schools spent, on average, $6,556 annually to educate a student without disabilities, and $12,639 to educate a student in special education, with significant variability based on the disability (Chambers, Parish, & Harr, 2002). Some critics view inclusion as cost cutting, aimed at decreasing specialized teachers and centralizing services (McLaughlin & Warren, 1994), yet most inclusion programs involve considerable special education personnel and support costs. Advocates for special education, and for enhanced services for all students, suggest that funds spent to educate at-risk students will save money in the decreased costs of psycho-social and educational support in the future. Hummel-Rossi and Ashdown (2002) caution that links between educational funds and specific student outcomes have been difficult to establish, and the methodologies somewhat controversial. The authors further argue against exclusive focus on student achievement, when satisfaction, self-esteem, or good citizenship, though difficult to measure, may be just as important. Cost-benefit analyses typically compare taxpayer costs of education with predicted taxpayer costs of educational failure. There is an assumed increase in public revenue when education produces members of society who will, themselves, pay taxes. The costs of failure for Jewish education are significant. Research on Jewish continuity (American Jewish Committee, 1997) and at-risk adolescents (Pelcovitz, 2004) underscores the centrality of Jewish education for Jewish individual and community development.

Other Factors

Feiler and Gibson (1999) highlight four concerns that warrant attention. First, precise definitions and a consensus about practice are necessary. Second, research on long-term social and academic benefits or dangers of inclusion is necessary (Armstrong, 2004). Third, having an inclusive classroom does not mean exclusion does not occur (Wiebe Berry, 2006). If teachers' espoused beliefs or theories do not match their actions (Osterman & Kottkamp, 2004), inclusion will not work, as demonstrated when one author observed a collaboratively taught class. At the lesson's end, one teacher announced, "Okay, time for language arts. Those in special-ed move to the back of the room." A final caution is that inclusion best practices may exist in individual classrooms, but not be reinforced by the larger school culture (also see, Lindsay, 2003; Wedell, 2005).

There is no question that problems remain in proper inclusion implementation. As Wolfe and Hall (2003) suggest, however, "let's end the debate about *whether* to include students with severe disabilities in the general education classroom. Let's focus on *how* and *when* and *where*" (p. 56; italics in original).

Models of Service for Special Needs Students

Pull-Out Programs/Resource Room Settings

Early conceptualizations of reading difficulties resulting from specific learning disabilities led to the creation of "resource rooms" where disabled students could receive specialized reading instruction (Bentum & Aaron, 2003). Unfortunately, their efficacy has not been extensively researched. A meta-analysis of 11 studies comparing mainstream to special education (including resource room) found no advantage to separating poor readers (Wang & Baker, 1985). Bentum and Aaron, caution that resource room placement actually results in decreased achievement in some cases. In their longitudinal study, students showed no significant reading improvement and a decline in spelling and IQ, which was positively correlated with the length of time in resource room, suggesting that they provide impoverished learning environments.

Wiener and Tardiff (2004) studied 117 Canadian children in grades 4–8, comparing pairs of support paradigms; in-class vs. resource room, or self-contained class vs. inclusion. Evaluating social and emotional functioning in both pairs, students in the more inclusive environment fared better. Rea, McLaughlan, and Walter-Thomas (2002) compared US eighth graders in inclusive vs. pull-out programs and found significant academic advances for students in inclusive settings. The only published study of resource rooms in US Jewish schools, completed over a decade ago, found that parents, administrators, students, and teachers voiced some general positive comments and some concerns (Luchow, 1992). Given the relatively weak and/or negative findings summarized above, pull-out models are less than compelling, particularly in the face of ethical imperatives for inclusive practice.

Collaborative Team Teaching

Collaborative team teaching occurs when multiple teachers teach together in the same classroom in order to promote the learning and emotional development of students. Commonly, the team has one general education- and one special education-certified teacher. Teachers benefit from collaboration, and from assistance with planning, implementing, and evaluating lessons (Fishbaugh, 1997). Students benefit from lower teacher–student ratios and improved quality of lessons.

Team teachers share responsibility for developing, delivering, and monitoring instruction and progress of students. Arrangements vary, from teachers assuming responsibility for particular curriculum areas, to both teaching the same material to smaller groups. Alternatively, the classroom teacher may teach the lesson to the class with the supplementary teacher adapting and developing material for those students who require support (Ripley, 1997).

Research indicates that effective collaborative team teaching requires that teachers be given time to learn how to team-teach, be able to plan cooperatively, and buy-in to the team-teaching process. When teachers set weekly co-planning time as a priority, they are able to make adjustments, evaluate students, and address strategies that best service the needs of their students (Walther-Thomas, Bryant, & Land, 1996). Volonino and Zigmond (2007) conclude that co-teaching, a common occurrence in full inclusion placements, "is complicated by the theory-practice divide... and is not often implemented as proposed." In an investigation of team teaching in a Jewish school, Fishman (2002) found that without adequate training and support, this model can do more harm than good.

Consultant Teaching/Push-In Programs

Consultant teaching may be similar to team teaching, or it may provide the general education teacher with the opportunity to consult with a special education colleague. Whereas team teaching focuses on supporting all students in a classroom, the push-in or consultant model generally focuses on supporting individual students within the classroom. When collaborative/consultant teachers co-plan and regularly discuss particular students, the likelihood of student achievement rises dramatically, and improvement in student behavior is also evidenced (Krueger, 1994 as cited in Gerber, 1995).

Consultant teacher models may evolve from more traditional pull-out programs, recognizing that the support of a special education consultant can benefit greater numbers of students when available in mainstream classrooms. Scheindlin (2009), describing such a move at the Sinai Akiba Academy explains, "the specialist goes into classrooms knowing who her primary target population is, but she is there to support other students as well."

Paraprofessionals

Many special education programs employ paraprofessional staff. In their review, Giangreco and Doyle (2007) lament that teacher assistant utilization appears driven more by politics, local practice, and advocacy, than by careful, compelling research. Since most aides have little or no training (Riggs & Mueller, 2001), orientation or supervision (French, 2001), and struggle with unclear role delineation (Riggs & Mueller, 2001) it is not surprising that research has yet to support aides as integral to improved student outcomes.

When first deployed over three decades ago, such aides served largely management/housekeeping roles; supervising playgrounds and hallways, preparing materials and taking attendance (Giangreco & Doyle, 2007). Increasingly, aides are serving students' instructional needs, coinciding with greater numbers of special needs students in general education and with budget constraints limiting additional teachers in the classroom. Unfortunately, there is little research to inform educators' decision-making regarding the responsibilities of aides.

Jewish schools often operate beyond the realm of certification requirements creating challenges around paraprofessional use. If classroom teachers of record are not credentialed, how might they support the professional development of an aide? Additionally, Jewish schools need aides who can support students across general and Jewish studies. In the general population, the majority of aides are women who live in the communities where they work (Riggs & Mueller, 2001), a finding both relevant and disconcerting for Jewish schools, especially in small, tight-knit communities. The insular nature of many communities suggests that classroom aides in Jewish schools are likely to be neighbors, synagogue members, or friends of some or all students. Families may feel uncomfortable with students' limitations becoming "public knowledge" and delicate issues of confidentiality and dual roles require careful consideration.

Community Consortia

Economic realities and the desire to develop the best services possible even for low-incidence difficulties have led the public sector to develop consortia. The New York Board of Cooperative Educational Services (BOCES) was founded in 1948 and allowed school districts to combine purchase power and share the costs of services and programs. "School districts ... choose to purchase a BOCES service rather than providing it on their own when they believe that the cost and quality warrant it" (Board of Cooperative Educational Services, 2009).

Jewish communities have begun to recognize that they can do more together than apart. Examples of such collaborations are offered below.

Etta Israel Center—Rather than construct one school, or create supports in a single environment, the Etta Israel Center developed a cadre of professionals to support inclusion of Jewish students throughout the Los Angeles area.

> Of the 10,000 students enrolled in Jewish Day Schools throughout Los Angeles County, 20% have learning differences or developmental disabilities that affect their ability to learn ... Because each child with special needs is different, the Etta Israel Center provides Jewish families with a range of educational services. (Etta Israel Center, 2008)

Gateways: Access to Jewish Education (2009)—This Greater-Boston organization enables students to access Jewish education in the setting their parents choose by working on-site with students and teachers. The goal is for students to succeed academically, socially, and spiritually and become participants in the Jewish community.

CAHAL—Communities Acting to Heighten Awareness and Learning—This regional Long Island/Queens partnership serves students in 11 yeshivas. CAHAL reasoned that while virtually all local schools had learning disabled children, most did not have "enough students on the same grade level to open a class, nor the funding to provide related support services or professional guidance"(CAHAL, 2005). CAHAL operates with joint decision-making, involving principals and lay leaders from each school, and aims to decrease isolation and move students toward full integration.

Selected Research Issues

As special education research begins to explore increasingly complex issues, research on North American Jewish special education remains in its infancy. Jewish educators therefore borrow from their non-Jewish counterparts, extrapolating from studies of considerably different students in clearly different settings. We offer a brief review of four areas with implications for Jewish education; curriculum-based measures, language learning, family involvement, and technology.

There has been considerable research of curriculum-based measurement (CBM) as a means for both identifying students with special needs and developing and monitoring interventions to advance their learning. CBM, contrary to its name, does not relate to the curriculum, but the "generic representations" (Alonzo, Ketterlin-Geller, & Tindal, 2007) or underlying skills that allow success. Widely used in reading and math, CBM's have been documented as effective, and can help educators better understand students' learning needs, and the impact of their teaching (Alonzo et al., 2007).

Increasing awareness of the clear differences in Hebrew language learning has spurred development of curriculum-based measurement tools for Hebrew (Goldberg, Weinberger, Goodman, & Ross, 2010; Institute for University-School Partnership, 2009). Significant effort would be required to develop CBM's for other Jewish subjects. Without CBM's, or other standardized assessment tools, Jewish schools will continue to rely on widely variable, subjective measures (teacher developed tests) to identify students who require support.

The impact of learning disabilities on reading, writing, and spoken language has been studied extensively (Hallahan, Lloyd, Kauffman, Weiss, & Martinez, 2005). There has also been considerable attention to the increased likelihood for English language learners to require special education (Harry, 2007). Mastery of Hebrew facilitates entry into the world of Jewish learning and living. Since Hebrew is the language of prayer in many Jewish schools, students who struggle with Hebrew may feel spiritually disconnected (Goldberg, 2005). There are Jewish emigrant students for whom Hebrew represents not a second, but a third, or fourth language. Research exploring Hebrew language challenges, the role of accommodation in curriculum, and remediation tools and strategies is critical in supporting inclusion of all Jewish students.

Another focus of research is the involvement of families with schools. That family engagement in children's learning supports better academic outcomes is well documented (Epstein, 1987; Henderson & Mapp, 2002). It is what families do *at home* with their children that has the greatest impact on learning (Schargel & Smink, 2001). To benefit their students, including those with special needs, Jewish schools must consider what support and education families need to be role models, teachers, and educational catalysts for their children.

An intriguing finding has been the role that advocacy for special needs students plays in supporting the adjustment and well-being of their parents (Leyser, 1994). Parents of children in Jewish settings could benefit from parent-advocacy training programs similar to those in the public sector, especially since laws and entitlements for students in non-public schools can be challenging to understand and enforce.

Education technology researchers have explored how computer simulations might improve problem solving and whether word processors might improve writing (Woodward & Ferretti, 2007). Assistive technologies that allow students greater access to instructional materials have also been studied, with new devices developed regularly. Technology relevant to Jewish students includes computerized text learning packages that concretize difficult, abstract Judaic concepts, as well as support and/or remediate lagging literacy skills. Schloss (2001) cites the challenges of a rapid proliferation of Judaic software and the limited number of Jewish educators with the knowledge and skill to best utilize these advances. Significant research is necessary to determine both the best use of these new technologies, and the training required for teachers to employ them to include diverse learners.

Future Directions

Our review of Jewish special education has been at once exhilarating and disappointing. Despite the dearth of research, our work has provided two distinct satisfactions. First, Jewish educators realize the communal, educational, and moral imperative to create learning environments of high quality for all students. Inclusionary practices, in particular, are gaining serious attention (e.g., Glanz, 2008). Second, the lack of research provides an array of exciting, relevant, and rewarding opportunities for serious scholarly investigation. Some avenues of inquiry with Jewish special needs students include the following:

- Teaching spirituality
- The impact of inclusion on general education students
- Differentiated instruction in a variety of Jewish subjects across grade levels
- Teaching Jewish texts
- Supplemental/complementary and informal education
- Impact of longer school days
- Teacher preparation and professional development to support inclusion
- Effective measures of student progress
- Family involvement

Conclusions

While writing this chapter, the first author discovered a video on inclusion for her graduate Jewish special education class. In *"If you believe in me, I'll believe in me"* (Youtube, 2009), the parent of a Down's syndrome child explains, "It was very important to us that she be a member of the community, the same way our older children were." The principal of the family's private school remarks, "we already had five children from the family in our school, and I remember … saying to the teachers there is no way we can say no to that baby." In a tearful voice the mother continues, "I received a card from the principal that said when our daughter becomes kindergarten age, we're going to be ready for her" and St. Anne's, a participating school in the Washington, DC consortium providing for special needs students in Catholic schools, was ready. The principal concludes, "I think it's a matter of just realizing that once you say I'm going to do it, God's graces are with you, and people start jumping on with you." It is the authors' hope that Jewish schools will resist the temptation to remain as they are, serving some, but unable to address the needs of all. For our communities and our children to grow, we need every parent of every Jewish child to be greeted by schools that open their doors and say "we are ready."

References

Ainscow, M., Howes, A., Farrell, P., & Frankham, J. (2003). Making sense of the development of inclusive practice. *European Journal of Special Needs Education, 18*(2), 227–242.

Alonzo, J., Ketterlin-Geller, L. R., & Tindal, G. (2007). Curriculum-based measurement in reading and math: Providing rigorous outcomes to support learning. In L. Florian (Ed.), *The Sage handbook of special education* (pp. 475–485). Thousand Oaks, CA: Sage.

American Jewish Committee (1997). *Jewish continuity: Policy statement and action plan*. Retrieved March 30, 2009 from http://www.ajc.org/site/apps/nl/content2.asp?c=ijITI2PHKoG&b=841105&ct=1048717

Armstrong, F. (2004). *Action research for inclusive education: Changing places, changing practices, changing minds*. London: RoutledgeFalmer.

Astor, C. (1985). *Who makes people different: Jewish perspectives on the disabled*. New York: United Synagogue of America.

Begeny, J. C., & Martens, B. K. (2007). Inclusionary education in Italy: A literature review and call for more empirical research. *Remedial and Special Education, 28*, 80–94.

Bentum, K. E., & Aaron, P. G. (2003). Does reading instruction in learning disability resource rooms really work? A longitudinal study. *Reading Psychology, 24*, 361–383.

Bishop, A., & Jones, P. (2002). Promoting inclusive practice in primary initial teacher training: Influencing hearts as well as minds. *Support for Learning, 17*(2), 58–63.

Board of Cooperative Educational Services of New York (2009). Retrieved March 28, 2009 from http://www.boces.org/wps/portal/BOCESofNYSe

Bowe, F. (2005). *Making inclusion work*. Upper Saddle River, NJ: Pearson.

Boyd, V. (1992). *Creating a text for change*. Austin, TX: Southwest Educational Development Laboratory.

CAHAL. (2005). Retrieved March 28, 2009 from www.cahal.org

Center, Y., & Ward, J. (1987). Teachers' attitudes towards the integration of disabled pupils in regular schools. *Exceptional Child, 31*, 41–56.

Chambers, J. G., Parish, T. B., & Harr, J. J. (2002). *What are we spending on special education services in the United States, 1999–2000?* Palo Alto, CA: American Institutes for Research, Retrieved March 1, 2009 from http://csef.air.org.

Ellsworth, N. J., & Zhang, C. (2007). Progress and challenges in China's special education development: Observations, reflections and recommendations. *Remedial and Special Education, 28*, 58–64.

Epstein, J. L. (1987). Parent involvement: State education agencies should lead the way. *Community Education Journal, 14*(4), 4–10.

Erwin, E. J., & Guintini, M. (2000). Inclusion and classroom membership in early childhood. *International Journal of Disability, Development and Education, 47*, 237–257.

Etta Israel Center. (2008). Retrieved March 28, 2009 from http://www.etta.org/educational.html

Feiler, A., & Gibson, H. (1999). Threats to the inclusive movement. *British Journal of Special Education, 26*, 147–152.

Fishbaugh, M. S. E. (1997). *Models of collaboration*. Boston: Allyn and Bacon.

Fishman, A. (2002). *Team teaching in the Jewish day school: A case study*. Unpublished Master of Education Dissertation, Toronto: York University.

French, N. K. (2001). Supervising paraprofessionals: A survey of teacher practices. *Journal of Special Education, 35*, 41–53.

Fuchs, D., & Fuchs, L. S. (1994). Inclusive schools movement and the radicalization of special education reform. *Exceptional Children, 60*(4), 294–309.

Fuchs, D., Fuchs, L. S., & Bahr, M. W. (1999). Mainstream assistance teams: A scientific basis for the art of consultation. *Exceptional Children, 57*, 128–139.

Gateways. (2009). Retrieved March 28, 2009 from http://www.jgateways.org/about

Gerber, P. J. (1995). The efficacy of the collaborative teaching model for serving academically-able special education students: Review of literature. Retrieved March 10, 2009 from http://www.soe.vcu.edu/merc/briefs/BRIEF29.HTM

Giangreco, M. F., & Doyle, M. B. (2007). Teacher assistants in inclusive schools. In L. Florian (Ed.), *The Sage handbook of special education*. London: Sage Publications.

Glanz, J. (2008). *The ethics of exclusion: Pedagogical, curricular, leadership, and moral imperatives for inclusive practice in Jewish schools* [Monograph]. The Azrieli Papers: Yeshiva University.

Glaubman, R., & Lifshitz, H. (2001). Ultra-orthodox Jewish teachers' self-efficacy and willingness for inclusion of pupils with special needs. *European Journal of Special Needs Eductionn, 16*, 207–223.

Goldberg, S. J. (2005). Hebrew reading difficulties and social exclusion: A path to aggressive behavior. *Jewish Educational Leadership, 4*(1), Retrieved March 28, 2009 from http://www.lookstein.org/online_journal.php?id=74

Goldberg, S. J., Weinberger, E. R., Goodman, N. E., & Ross, S. (2010). Development of an early Hebrew oral reading fluency measure. *Journal of Jewish Education, 76*, 198–214.

Hallahan, D. P., Lloyd, J. W., Kauffman, J. M., Weiss, M. P., & Martinez, E. A. (2005). *Learning disabilities: Foundations, characteristics, and effective teaching*. Boston: Allyn and Bacon.

Harry, B. (2007). The disproportionate placement of ethnic minorities in special education. In L. Florian (Ed.), *The Sage handbook of special education* (pp. 475–485). Thousand Oaks, CA: Sage.

Henderson, A., & Mapp, K. (2002). *A new wave of evidence: The impact of school, family, and community connections on student achievement*. Austin, TX: Southwest Educational Development Laboratory, Retrieved March 30, 2009 from www.sedl.org/connections/resources/evidence.pdf

Hirsch, S. R. (1962). *Horeb*. London: Soncino Press.

Hord, S. (1991). *Leadership: An imperative for successful change*. Austin, TX: Southwest Educational Development Laboratory.

Hummel-Rossi, B., & Ashdown, J. (2002). The state of cost-benefit and cost-effectiveness analyses in education. *Review of Educational Research, 72*, 1–30.

Hunt, P., & Goetz, L. (1997). Research in severe disabilities. *Journal of Special Education, 31*, 3–29.

Individuals with disabilities Education Act, 33, U.S.C., 1400 (1997).

Individuals with disabilities Education Act, 20, U.S.C., 1400 (2004).

Institute for University-School Partnership (2009). Retrieved March 26, 2009 from http://www.yu.edu/azrieli/schoolpartnership/index.aspx?id=28234

International League of Societies for Persons with Mental Handicap. (1994, June). The Inclusion Charter. UNESCO World Conference on Special Educational Needs: Access and Quality. Salamanca, Spain.

Isaacs, L. W., & Levine, C. N. (1995). *So that all may study Torah: Communal provision of Jewish education for students with special needs*. New York: Jewish Education Service of North America.

Jackson, P. W., Boostrom, R. E., & Hansen, D. T. (1993). *The moral life of schools*. San Francisco: Jossey-Bass.

Jewish Education Service of North America. (2009). Retrieved March 30, 2009, from http://www.jesna.org/our-work/special-needs

Jung, W. S. (2007). Preservice teacher training for successful inclusion. *Education, 128*, 106–113.

Kaminetsky, E. (1977). *Studies in Torah Judaism: Sins of omission – The neglected children. A special education mandate for the Jewish community*. New York: Yeshiva University Press.

Kochhar, C. A., West, L. L., & Taymans, J. M. (2000). *Successful inclusion: Practical strategies for a shared responsibility*. Upper Saddle River, NJ: Merrill.

Kohn., A. (1999). *The schools our children deserve*. Boston, MA: Houghton Mifflin.
Lambert, L., Walker, D., Zimmerman, D. P., Cooper, J. E., Lambert, M. D., Gardner, M. E., et al. (2003). *The constructivist leader* (2nd ed.). New York: Teachers College Press.
Levine, M. (2004). Helping those in need: Celebrating diverse minds. *Educational Leadership, 61*, 8–12.
Leyser, Y. (1994). Stress and adaptation in Orthodox Jewish families with a disabled child. *American Journal of Orthopsychiatry, 64*(3), 376–385.
Lindsay, G. (2003). Inclusive education: A critical perspective. *British Journal of Special Education, 30*(1), 3–12.
Luchow, J. P. (1992). Three-year study of resource rooms in yeshivot and day schools. *The Jewish Special Educator, 1*(1), 20–22.
Martin, E. W., Martin, R., & Terman, D. L. (1996). The legislative and litigation history of special education. *Special Education for Students with Disabilities, 6*(1), 25–39.
McLaughlin, M. J., & Warren, S. (1994). *Resource implications of inclusion: Impressions of special education administrators at selected sites*. Center for Special Education Finance, Policy paper 1, US Department of Education, Office of Special Programs.
Meijer, C. J. W. (2001). Inclusive education and effective classroom practices. Report of the European Agency for Development of Special Needs Education. Retrieved March 10, 2009 from http://www.european-agency.org/site/info/publications/agency/ereports/docs/05docs/ie_effectivecp.doc
Myklebust, J. O. (2006). Class placement and competence attainment among students with special educational needs. *British Journal of Special Education, 33*(2), 76–81.
Newmann, F. M., Rutter, R. A., & Smith, M. S. (1989). Organizational factors that affect school sense of efficacy, community, and expectations. *Sociology of Education, 62*, 221–238.
Oakes, J. (1985). *Keeping track: How schools structure inequality*. New Haven, CT: Yale University Press.
Osgood, R. L. (2008). *The history of special education: A struggle for equality in American public schools*. Westport, CN: Greenwood.
Osterman, K. E., & Kottkamp, R. B. (2004). *Reflective practice for educators: Improving schooling through professional development* (2nd ed.). Thousand Oaks, CA: Corwin.
PEJE. (2006). *Noteworthy practices in Jewish day school education*. Boston, MA: Partnership for Excellence in Jewish Education.
Pardes Day Schools. (2009). Retrieved from http://www.pardesdayschools.org/about.php, March 30, 2009.
Paul, J., French, P., & Cranston-Gingras, A. (2001). Ethics and special education. *Focus on Exceptional Children, 34*(1), 1–16.
Pelcovitz, D. (2004). *The at-risk adolescent in the Orthodox Jewish community: Implications and interventions for educators* [Monograph]. The Azrieli papers. New York: Yeshiva University.
Peltier, G. L. (1997). The effects of inclusion on nondisabled students: A review of the research. *Contemporary Education, 68*, 234–240.
Power-deFur, A., & Orelove, D. (Eds.) (2003). *Inclusive education: Practical implementation of the least restrictive environment*. Gaithersburg, MD: Aspen Publishers.
RAVSAK, The Jewish Community Day School Network. (2009). Retrieved from http://www.ravsak.org/about-ravsak/who-we-are
Raver, S. A., & Kolchenko, K. (2007). Inclusion of school-age children with disabilities in Ukraine. *Childhood Education, 83*, 370–373.
Rea, P. J., McLaughlan, V. L., & Walter-Thomas, C. (2002). Outcomes for students with learning disabilities in inclusive and pullout programmes. *Exceptional Children, 68*, 203–223.
Rieck, W. A. (2000). Inclusion: Administrative headache or opportunity. *NASSP Bulletin, 84*, 56–62.
Riggs, C. G., & Mueller, P. H. (2001). Employment and utilization of para-educators in inclusive settings. *Journal of Special Education, 35*, 54–62.

Ripley, S. (1997). Collaboration between general and special education teachers. ERIC Digest. ERIC Clearinghouse on Teaching and Teacher Education Washington DC. Retrieved March 11, 2009 from http://www.ericdigests.org/1998-1/general.htm

Sailor, W., & Roger, B. (2005). Rethinking inclusion: Schoolwide options. *Phi Delta Kappan, 86*(7), 503–510.

Salend, S. J., & Garrick, L. M. (1999). The impact of inclusion on students with and without disabilities and their educators. *Remedial and Special Education, 20,* 114–126.

Sapon-Shevin, M. (2007). *Widening the circle: The power of inclusive classrooms.* Boston: Beacon Press.

Schanin, M., & Reiter, S. (2007). From integration to inclusion. *Childhood Education, 83,* 347–350.

Schargel, F. P., & Smink, J. (2001). *Strategies to help solve our school dropout problem.* Larchmont, NY: Eye on Education.

Scharlach, T. D. (2008). These kids just aren't motivated to read: The influence of preservice teachers' beliefs on their expectations, instruction and evaluation of readers. *Literacy Research and Instruction, 47*(3), 158–172.

Scheindlin, L. (2009). Meeting the needs of diverse learners at Sinai Akiba Academy. Retrieved March 23, 2009 from http://www.ssdsa.org/content/pdf/Rabbi%20Larry%20Scheindlin%20Sinai%20Akiba.doc

Schick, M. (2005). *A census of Jewish day schools in the United States, 2003–2004.* New York: Avichai Foundation.

Schloss, M. (2001). Yesterday, today and tomorrow: Special education. *Consortium of Special Educators in Central Agencies for Jewish Education, 12,* 2–3.

Schloss, M. (2008). *Mental retardation: Halakhah and Education.* Unpublished doctoral dissertation, Azrieli Graduate School of Jewish Education and Administration, Yeshiva University.

Shapiro, H. S. (2006). *Losing heart: The moral and spiritual miseducation of America's children.* Mahwah, NJ: Lawrence Erlbaum.

Sharpe, M. N., & York, J. L. (1994). Effects of inclusion on the academic performance of classmates without disabilities. *Remedial and Special Education, 15,* 34–44.

Shepherd, K., & Brody Hasazi, S. (2007). Leadership for social justice and inclusion. In L. Florian (Ed.), *The Sage handbook of special education* (pp. 475–485). Thousand Oaks, CA: Sage.

Shevlin, M., Kenny, M., & Loxley, A. (2008). A time of transition: Exploring special educational provision in the Republic of Ireland. *Journal of Research in Special Education Needs, 8,* 141–150.

Stainback, S., & Stainback, W. (Eds.). (2000). *Inclusion: A guide for educators.* Baltimore: Paul H. Brookes.

Staub, D., & Peck, C. A. (1994/1995). What are the outcomes for nondisabled students. *Educational Leadership, 52,* 36–40.

Vaughn, S., Elbaum, B. E., Schumm, J. S., & Hughes, M. T. (1998). Social outcomes for students with and without learning disabilities in inclusive classrooms. *Journal of Learning Disabilities, 31,* 428–436.

Viachou, A. (2004). Education and inclusive policy-making: Implications for research and practice. *International Journal of Inclusive Education, 8*(1), 3–21.

Volonino, V., & Zigmond, N. (2007). Promoting research-based practices through inclusion? *Theory into Practice, 46*(4), 291–300.

Walther-Thomas, C. S., Bryant, M., & Land, S. (1996). Planning for effective co-teaching: The key to successful inclusion. *Remedial and Special Education, 17*(4), 255–264.

Wang, M. C., & Baker, E. T. (1985). Mainstreaming programs: Design features and effects. *Journal of Special Education, 19*(4), 503–521.

Wedell, K. (2005). Dilemmas in the quest for inclusion. *British Journal of Special Education, 32*(1), 3–11.

Wiebe Berry, R. A. (2006). Inclusion, power, and community: Teachers and students interpret the language of community in an inclusion classroom. *American Educational Research Journal, 43*(3), 489–529.

Wiener, J., & Tardiff, C. Y. (2004). Social and emotional functioning of children with learning disabilities. Does special education placement make a difference? *Learning Disabilities Research and Practice, 19*, 20–32.

Winzer, M. A. (1993). *The history of special education: From isolation to integration*. Washington, DC: Gallaudet University Press.

Wolfe, P. S., & Hall, T. E. (2003). Making inclusion a reality for students with severe disabilities. *Teaching Exceptional Children, 14*, 56–61.

Woodward, J., & Ferretti, R. (2007). New machines and new agendas: The changing nature of special education technology research. In L. Florian (Ed.), *The Sage handbook of special education*. London: Sage Publications.

Young, I. M. (2000). *Inclusion and democracy*. Oxford: Oxford University Press.

Youtube. (2009) Retrieved March 26, 2009 from http://www.youtube.com/watch?v=HP8pRlADNcY

Zimmerman, L. (2008). Consortium news. *Consortium of Special Educators in Central Agencies for Jewish Education, 19*, 3.

Zweiter, S. (2006). From the inside looking in: Some musings on day school education. In Z. Grumet (Ed.), *Jewish education in transition: Proceedings of the first international conference on Jewish education* (pp. 11–27). Teaneck, NJ: Ben Yehuda Press.

Teacher Education: Ensuring a Cadre of Well-Qualified Educational Personnel for Jewish Schools

Leora Isaacs, Kate O'Brien, and Shira Rosenblatt

Introduction

There is strong consensus among researchers of teaching and learning that while a variety of dynamics influence the successful education of children, the effectiveness of teachers is the single most important educational determinant (Education Commission of the States [ECS], 2003). Since the mid-1980s, a growing number of education reformers, policymakers, and researchers have argued that many shortcomings in the US elementary and secondary education system are the result of inadequate working conditions, resources, and support provided to teachers. Many of these reformers contend that professionalization of teachers will result in higher commitment, which will positively affect teachers' performance and ultimately lead to improvements in student learning (ECS, 2003). Whether or not the field accepts this proposition, a broad review of extant research about public, private, and Jewish education reveals that a deep understanding of the motivations, personal and professional needs, and career trajectories of teachers enhances our ability to identify levers for change in the critical areas of recruiting, retaining, and developing well-qualified teachers to meet the current and emergent needs of the Jewish community. At the same time, teachers exist within the context of a complex environment that influences their teaching, learning, motivations, and decisions. Historical developments and trends, in addition to an array of elements of the Jewish and broader zeitgeist, cannot be ignored. Efforts to ensure that the field of Jewish education has a cadre of well-qualified educational personnel for Jewish schools therefore must be part of a systemic vision of Jewish education. What the field learns about the factors that affect recruiting, retaining, and developing teachers, and the policies derived from that learning, must be understood with an eye toward improving learning and outcomes for students.

L. Isaacs (✉)
The Jewish Education Service of North America (JESNA), New York, NY, USA
e-mail: lisaacs@jesna.org

An Evolution in North American Jewish Education

Jewish texts emphasize the pivotal role of the teacher in cultivating knowledgeable, passionate, and dedicated Jewishly identified individuals.[1] Frequently, Jewish education in America has followed trends in secular society; families choose different venues for their (and their children's) education and institutions often modify their programs to respond to these demographic and cultural changes. For example, in response to increasing secularization, Germanization, and the influence of Protestant Christian Sunday schools in mid-nineteenth century America, enrollment shifted from religious day schools to Sunday schools. In the early twentieth century, Jewish schools relied heavily on teachers from eastern Europe and, later, from Israel (Dushkin, 1980). Among the Jewish day and complementary[2] school teachers who responded to the *Educators in Jewish Schools Study* (EJSS) *Educator Survey*, more than 85% were raised in the United States (EJSS, 2008). In the mid-twentieth century, the blossoming of congregational religious schools accompanied the expansion and suburbanization of synagogues (Zeldin, 1983). Another aspect of the evolution of Jewish schooling was a change in the students who patronized these schools (Dushkin, 1980) from immigrant families and children to native-born American children. Similarly, a decline in anti-Semitism and restrictions that previously consigned Jews to "their own kind" in educational, professional, and social settings allowed them to circulate more widely, resulting in greater assimilation into North American secular society. No longer was the home the locus of Jewish learning and observance for many Jews affiliated with "liberal" denominations. Increasingly, these families relied on their synagogues for their children's pre-*b'nai mitzvah* education. In 1990, the Commission on Jewish Education in North America, among others, called the dilemma of increased assimilation and a less Jewishly identified and Jewishly interested population a "crisis," declaring: "The responsibility for developing Jewish identity and instilling a commitment to Judaism for this population now rests primarily with education" (Commission on Jewish Education in North America, 1990).

Currently, the education of Jewish children in some type of "Jewish schooling" is the norm in North America. According to the 2000–01 National Jewish Population Survey (NJPS), more than 70% of all Jewish children receive some form of Jewish

---

[1] Well-known among the multitude of sources is this Talmudic dictum: "Rabbi Yehudah the Prince sent Rabbi Chiya and Rabbi Yossi and Rabbi Ami to tour the towns of Eretz Israel to establish there teachers and sages. They came to one place and found there neither teachers, nor sages. Thus, they spoke unto them: 'Bring us the guardians of the city.' They went and brought the policemen of the city. The rabbis asked: 'Are these the guardians of the city? Nay, these are the destroyers of the city.' They asked: 'Who then are the guardians of the city?' The rabbis answered: 'The teachers and sages'." (*Yerushalmi, Chagiga, Ch. 1, 7*).

[2] "Complementary schools" refers to congregational, supplemental, religious, Hebrew schools, and other *part-time* Jewish education for students in grades K–12 of any denomination and those who are unaffiliated. The data collected and reviewed for this chapter deal most frequently and specifically with "congregational schools." As such, this appellation is used for the sake of consistency.

education (NJPS, 2002) in approximately 800 Jewish day schools and 2,000 congregational schools run by congregations and other Jewish communal organizations in North America (EJSS, 2008). Not only do Jewish children today receive more full-time Jewish schooling compared to their parents' generation (29% versus 12%), but also fewer children today receive no Jewish education (NJPS, 2002). Alongside these developments is the marked growth of intensive all-day Jewish schooling (approximately 200,000 students in grades K–12 in schools representing different streams of Judaism and diverse ideological bents). Similarly, we have witnessed advances in congregational Jewish education. The field also has seen significant growth and expansion in Jewish early childhood education and in supplementary Jewish education for high school students (Wertheimer, 2007). The continuing trend toward "reinventing" and "revitalizing" synagogues has had an impact on Jewish educational opportunities at all levels[3] and has broadened the reach of Jewish education to families and adults. Many communities are developing an effective culture of experiential Jewish education (e.g., camps, service learning, youth movements, and Israel programs) to support and extend the learning that occurs in school settings. Following decades of decline, serious adult learning, including the growth of Jewish studies in universities, is on the upswing.

Throughout the research, two factors continually surfaced as catalysts for substantive change in Jewish education content, pedagogy, and resources that significantly improve educational environments. First is a widespread lack of satisfaction among key stakeholders within Jewish academic institutions, central agencies for Jewish education, emergent educational organizations, and individual schools (Sales & Koren, 2007). Second is the increased involvement of foundations and philanthropists who support Jewish education with their intellectual and financial resources and who serve as engines for positive change. As the Jewish community has begun to heed the call to enhance and improve Jewish education in the last few decades, these developments—and the emergence of serious evaluation and empirical research in the field—are transforming the "crisis" into an opportunity.

Still, challenges abound. Professional and lay leaders, consumers, and researchers point to multiple concerns: the continuing "pediatric" focus of Jewish education, a significant drop-out rate post-*b'nai mitzvah*, structural issues in formal Jewish schooling, and external contextual factors. The rampant change that characterized the twentieth and early twenty-first centuries has forced Jewish education to adapt to revolutionary technologies, changing definitions of community, and new norms of communication (Woocher, 2006). Especially among young adult Jews, identities are fluid, cultures are intermingled, and religious/Jewish studies are simply one choice among many attractive pursuits. The Jewish community's expectations are also in flux, driven by a culture that provides unfettered access to resources

---

[3] National programs, such as Synagogue 2000 and its successor Synagogue 3000, STAR (Synagogues: Transformation and Renewal), The Experiment in Congregational Education (ECE), and local initiatives (e.g., Hartford's La'Atid: Synagogues for the twenty-first century), are a few notable examples of programs designed to re-imagine and re-invigorate synagogue life.

and a world of "mass customization" that grants consumers the ability to get what they want, when and where they want it. Jewish institutions (e.g., federations) and entrenched causes (e.g., Israel) are often met with ambivalence. They cannot expect the community loyalty they once enjoyed and must continually prove their worth in response to funders' increasing expectations for accountability. These rapid developments give new urgency to issues relevant to Jewish teachers: who they are; how they are trained, recruited, and retained; and the potential for systemic and ongoing professional development to ensure there is a cadre of high-quality Jewish teachers to provide excellent learning for students.

Teacher Shortage

Although no systematic empirical data exist about the number of teachers or teaching positions in Jewish schools in North America, some researchers estimate that there are 66,000 teaching positions (28,000 in congregational schools; 22,000 in Jewish day schools; and 16,000 in Jewish early childhood programs) (Goodman, Schaap, & Ackerman, 2002). The American Jewish community chronically declares a critical shortage of Jewish educational personnel. Data from recent research echo the perception that there is currently a shortage of "fully qualified" or "high-quality" teachers in Jewish day and congregational schools in North America, which will have a negative impact on Jewish students and their learning. Anecdotal and empirical evidence shows that Jewish day and congregational school administrators find it difficult to fill open positions with *fully qualified* teachers (e.g., EJSS, 2008). Research indicates that if current trends continue (e.g., an aging teacher population, younger teachers' uncertainty about staying in the field, and certain inhospitable workplace conditions), the Jewish community will continue to face a critical teacher shortage. This shortage is a matter of both the quality and quantity (absolute number) of teachers. A 2005 report emphasized, as have others, "It is not just about ensuring an adequate number of teachers ... but having teachers in the profession who are as accomplished as possible" (ECS, 2005).

The field of Jewish education is starting to recognize the need to constantly monitor and adapt teacher training and support to respond to changes in Jewish education and learners. Without accurate and up-to-date data about Jewish teachers and their professional lives and working conditions, the field cannot effectively conceive successful recruitment and retention policies. Worse, it may misdiagnose the problem and waste precious resources on approaches that are fruitless or even detrimental to Jewish education and to students. Isa Aron notes, "teachers alone cannot make the difference.... Good research is needed to understand the nature and dimensions of the shortage, assess the realities, and develop research-informed solutions" (Aron, 1992). To ensure a cadre of well-qualified educational personnel for Jewish schools, the field must understand who the teachers are, how they are trained, the mechanisms by which they are recruited, the factors that influence retention, and how to keep them inspired and fulfilled.

A Profile of Jewish Teachers

In an effort to address the paucity of empirical data about teachers in Jewish schools, the Jewish Education Service of North America (JESNA) undertook an important first step toward creating a research-based portrait of teachers in Jewish day and congregational schools in North America. The *Educators in Jewish Schools Study* (EJSS, 2008) is a large-scale national study that collected descriptive information about Jewish teachers, administrators, and specialty personnel in Jewish day and congregational schools.[4] The findings not only painted a vivid snapshot of the teachers in the field today, but also provided data to inform key stakeholders about the factors that motivate Jewish day and congregational school teachers to enter and to remain in their schools and in the field of Jewish education. Without this information, decision-makers lack a sufficiently complete context in which to consider Jewish education policy and plan educational change.

Who Are the Teachers?

Demographic data about Jewish teachers presented in the EJSS report corroborate other research in regional Jewish communities (Frank, Margolis, & Weisner, 1992; Gamoran, Goldring, Robinson, Goodman, & Tammivaara, 1998; Goodman & Schaap, 2007) and in general education. Across Jewish school classrooms in the United States, teachers are predominantly female (75–80%), white (94%), and married (more than 70%). Of EJSS respondents, 43% were 50 years or older (EJSS, 2008). This rapid "graying" of Jewish teachers mirrors the national demographic trend in education[5] and points to the need to replenish the number of teachers in the field in significant ways over the next two decades.[6]

Recent research presents an overall profile of teachers in Jewish schools who are highly motivated, have considerable experience in the fields of general and/or Jewish education, and who have participated in formal and/or informal Jewish education. They tend to be highly "degreed," particularly in general studies, but lack teaching certification. Studies also show that there is great variation in the Jewish educational backgrounds of these teachers. While approximately 90% of both day and congregational school teachers who responded to the EJSS *Educator Survey* reported that they participated in formal and experiential Jewish education as youth

---

[4]These data include key demographics, details about current positions, teachers' motivations, professional development, factors influencing retention, and more.

[5]"The proportion of K–12 teachers who are 50 years of age and older has risen from 24% in 1996 to 42% in 2005" (National Center for Education Information, Washington, DC. *Profile of Teachers in the U.S., 2005*). "Over the past two decades, the median age of primary and secondary [public] school teachers [in the US] increased from 36 to 43 [years old]" (AmeriStat, August, 2002).

[6]"A historic turnover is taking place in the teaching profession. While student enrollments are rising rapidly, more than a million veteran teachers are nearing retirement. ... Overall, we will need more than two million new teachers in the next decade" (National Education Association (NEA), 2003).

and/or adult learners (EJSS, 2008), further research is needed about the settings, duration, and content of those experiences. A study of Jewish teachers in Atlanta, Baltimore, and Milwaukee found that one-third of those Jewish teachers ended their own Jewish education after *bar/bat mitzvah* (Gamoran, Goldring, Robinson, Goodman, & Tammivaara, 1998). In congregational school settings, where teachers tend to be part-time, many do not have formal Jewish education backgrounds (EJSS, 2008).

In a study of teachers in six communities (Kelner, Rabkin, Saxe, & Sheingold, 2004), researchers discovered that while all of the teachers teaching Judaic content in their local day schools were Jewish, 32% of general studies teachers and 11% of educational administrators (20% of day school staff overall) were not Jewish. Similarly, increasing numbers of teachers who are not Jewish are being employed in Jewish early childhood education settings to meet the growing needs of the field.[7] These realities may have significant implications for the ability of Jewish schools to transmit Jewish values, content, culture, and identity to their students.

Why Do They Teach?

Studies in both Jewish and general education frequently demonstrate that teachers choose their profession and their jobs out of a sense of mission and passion for connecting with students and playing an influential role in their lives. However, findings among EJSS respondents demonstrated that more than half of Jewish day and congregational school teachers did not plan their careers in Jewish education (EJSS, 2008). Rather, they were motivated by their own Jewish educational experiences (e.g., Jewish camp, schooling, or experiential education) or were "tapped" by people they trust (usually a Jewish communal or educational professional) who encouraged them to enter the field (EJSS, 2008). These findings suggest that mobilizing influential individuals and/or mentors in a more purposeful way could be beneficial in attracting and recruiting promising Jewish teachers. When asked about their motivations to work in their particular schools (and by extrapolation in the Jewish educational field), EJSS respondents most frequently said they want to make a real impact on students, work individually with students, and get to know students well. Other intrinsic motivators varied according to the teaching venue: 76% of day school teachers are motivated to teach in their settings out of a desire to work with students who are self-motivated to learn. Contributing to the Jewish community is a prime motivator for 88% of congregational school teachers (EJSS, 2008).

---

[7] According to 2006 figures from the Coalition for the Advancement of Jewish Education (CAJE), "30% [of teachers] in the JCC [Jewish Community Center] preschools, 10–25% in Reform schools, and 12–20% in Conservative schools [are not Jewish]. The percentage is highest in the western United States, where almost 40% of preschool teachers are not Jewish." ("Growing Number of Non-Jews Teach the Aleph-Bet at Preschool." Sue Fishkoff (2006). Retrieved from http://www.InterfaithFamily.com on April 7, 2009.)

Where Do They Work?

Gamoran and his colleagues discovered that while there appears to be "considerable stability in the field of Jewish teaching," teachers in the communities they studied were likely to move from position to position during their careers (Gamoran, Goldring, Robinson, Goodman, & Tammivaara, 1998). The majority of teachers who responded to the EJSS *Educator Survey* had teaching experience in Jewish education settings other than their current positions (EJSS, 2008).[8] A sizeable percentage of EJSS respondents in Jewish day and congregational schools were "new" to their schools, working in their current positions for two or fewer years. On the other end of the spectrum, 22% of congregational school teachers and 34% of day schools teachers worked in their current schools for more than 10 years. Not only do a sizeable percentage of teachers in Jewish schools work in multiple schools during their careers, but many also hold multiple teaching posts simultaneously. EJSS found this is more likely among congregational school teachers than among their day school colleagues. While Jewish day school teachers work substantially more hours overall at their schools than congregational school teachers, as one might expect, the majority of teachers in the EJSS study (2008) and in the community study by Gamoran et al., (1998) professed they had a "career" in Jewish education.

Pre-service Training

Isa Aron defined a professional Jewish teacher as one "who has a degree or credential in Jewish education, and who thinks of teaching as his or her career" (Aron, 2004). Relatively few Jewish teachers who responded to the EJSS study had pre-service academic preparation in Judaic studies or education; a minority had formal training in Judaic studies for the content area in which they taught. Data collected by Kelner et al. (2004) indicate a similar lack of formal preparation among administrators and teachers. Commonly, informal Jewish teachers lack pre-service training entirely (Commission on Jewish Education in North America, 1990). EJSS demonstrated that the large majority of teachers in the study were highly educated in secular studies, but nearly half of responding day school teachers and two-thirds of congregational school teachers did not hold valid teaching credentials. A growing body of research shows that investment in "teacher knowledge" is among the most productive ways to increase student learning; creating rigorous standards for teachers is one way to accomplish this. In the world of general education, formal pre-service training (usually in a college or university setting and including in-class student teaching) is a prerequisite for sitting for intensive, state-mandated teacher certification exams, which are in turn required for employment in public and many

---

[8]A study of Jewish teachers in Greater Boston reflects this national trend: 70% of those Jewish teachers had been in their current jobs for four or fewer years; 53% had been teaching in some Jewish setting for five or fewer years, and 50% or more had been in their current jobs for three or fewer years (Frank, Margolis, & Weisner, 1992).

independent schools. Unlike public school, the field of Jewish education currently lacks national or state-mandated requirements or a standard measure against which it can evaluate the basic competence of teachers in Jewish schools (Teacher Support Network, 2007).[9]

One lingering question is whether it is possible, in light of the perceived crisis in Jewish education personnel, to raise standards and still have enough teachers. Sharon Feiman-Nemser (1992) reframes the issue with two questions: "What do teachers need to know in order to teach?" and "How do teachers learn the practice of teaching?" She offers four basic propositions in response to these questions. First, teachers are learners who should be challenged to reevaluate their assumptions about teaching and subject matter. Second, Jewish teachers require a "conceptual understanding of Judaica and lots of chances to observe/experience exemplary teaching" in addition to academic courses. Third, on-the-job experience should be enhanced by reflective practice, support from administrators and colleagues, and regular ongoing learning. Fourth, research about Jewish education and Jewish teachers should inform their practice. In 2007, Feiman-Nemser revisited the essential question, "What do teachers need to learn?" and added that novice teachers need to know "How to think ... know ... feel ... and act like a teacher." This process demands intellectual inquiry about education and pedagogy; knowledge of subject matter and key educational/learning processes; interpersonal, spiritual, and/or psychological work; and "a repertoire of skills, routines, strategies, and the capacity to think on your feet in the context of changing circumstances" (Feiman-Nemser, 2007). Because education neither starts nor stops with the teacher, and because many uncontrollable environmental and contextual factors affect teachers, the goal of preservice training (and ongoing professional development) is improving the quality of *teaching*, not only the quality of the *teacher* (Kennedy, 2006).

Recruitment

Recruiting well-qualified Jewish teachers is situated within the broader context of recruiting and retaining a professional workforce for the Jewish communal sector. Kelner's review of existing research on the subject (Kelner, Rabkin, Saxe, & Sheingold, 2004) analyzed professional recruitment in private, non-profit, and Jewish sectors. The researchers revealed that leaders of diverse Jewish communal institutions struggle to recruit and retain all levels of professionals. They posited an array of factors that may impact the recruitment of Jewish professionals (including

---

[9] A teaching credential is the license conferred by a state to teachers who have completed certain state-mandated requirements for teaching certification and have passed state-mandated teaching examinations. The National Board of License for Teachers and Principals in Jewish Schools in North America (NBL) attempts to establish standards and criteria for the certification of professional teachers in the Jewish community (day schools, congregational schools, early childhood programs, and family education). Although this certification process is designed to recognize qualified teachers and encourage teachers to acquire professional training, it is not mandated within Jewish schools. As of this writing, the future operations of the NBL are uncertain.

teachers), such as organizations' perception that the labor pool lacks "dual-skills of Jewish and professional competencies" and the increasing desirability of graduate training. They acknowledged that gender bias, especially persistent barriers for women in leadership, is widespread and detrimental to recruitment and retention. Further, they asserted that organizations fail to create sustainable and inspiring workplaces and systems, thereby curtailing career advancement and limiting professional mobility. Because most of the solutions proffered in this area do not focus on underlying structural and cultural challenges, the researchers advocate for systemic thinking and detailed assessment of the needs of different stakeholders. They encourage the Jewish community to declare its intent to accurately diagnose issues and prescribe contextually appropriate solutions.

Alongside these factors is the reality that many well-qualified candidates do not choose jobs in Jewish education. According to some leaders in the field, formal Jewish education is not perceived as a career track that offers rewards for "advancement, good work, merit, inventiveness, and all the things that in another profession would move you up the ladder" (JESNA, 2004). Supporting this view, Gamoran et al. (1998) found that while becoming a Jewish teacher is relatively easy (i.e., the barriers are low, especially for part-time teaching positions), the scarcity of full-time positions with substantial salary and benefits makes recruitment to the field more difficult. Some suggest that addressing the issue of recruitment is inextricably linked to raising the visibility and status of Jewish teachers in our communities. Others advise raising salaries and increasing benefits. Still others, such as Ben-Avie and Kress (2007), take an ecological-developmental approach that emphasizes the importance of the interconnected nature, function, and relationships of people and systems within a school culture.

Financial incentives often top the list of proposed solutions to the challenge of recruiting highly qualified teachers. The rationale is that if the salaries (and thereby the status) of teachers are increased sufficiently, more professionals will be attracted to the field. Other voices in Jewish and general education approach financial incentives cautiously, since few rigorous studies of teacher salaries and their impact on recruitment and retention exist and extant data do not provide clear direction. For example, a study of the Massachusetts signing bonus concluded, "Increasingly, research suggests that the challenge of attracting and retaining new teachers depends on making sure the schools are places where teachers can achieve the intrinsic rewards that a career in teaching offers. Short of that, no financial inducements will suffice" (Liu, Moore, & Peske, 2004).

Schools can prepare more effectively for the complex process of teacher recruitment (Stronge & Hindman, 2003). Researchers recommend obtaining accurate assessments of the current status of the teaching profession and the labor market for teachers (ECS, 2005) to develop strategies that will incline qualified candidates toward the field of education. The challenge of attracting and recruiting the most qualified candidates who are most likely to succeed is complicated by the fact that administrators of day and congregational schools express very different criteria for hiring teachers in their respective settings. Isa Aron (2004) advocates a systemic approach that identifies and categorizes different types of teachers within a "differentiated staffing pyramid." Different constellations of skills are required within each level of the pyramid (e.g., classroom teachers, administrators, trainers/mentors, Judaic studies specialists, and a senior educator/principal). Therefore, recruitment efforts should target appropriately qualified candidates for distinctly different functions.

Reimer and Finkel have offered several strategies for successful teacher recruitment (JESNA, 2004). These include facilitating adults' mid-career transitions into Jewish education. They suggested that potential recruits, who often are inspired by new Jewish learning and leadership positions, need a "bridge person" to encourage and facilitate the transition from their previous work. In the case of congregational schools, recruiters should consider a range of sources for professional and avocational teachers, including local college-age and graduate students; unemployed, "underemployed," or retired adults; congregants; full-time and part-time Jewish day school and public school teachers; and Israelis. Other strategies to attract promising candidates include continuous promotion of the field; placing recruiters where young Jews congregate; scoping out good candidates and enticing them into the field (e.g., camp counselors and *shlichim*: Israelis who come to work as camp counselors or teachers in the US); and hiring strong pre-service teachers whose steep learning curves could be addressed through professional development. They also emphasized that Jewish education leaders and schools should take advantage of technology for training teachers locally to meet the needs of local Jewish schools. Other researchers (e.g., Goodman, Schaap, & Ackerman, 2002) point to the value of formal programs that help college students explore a career in Jewish education, such as JESNA's Lainer Interns for Jewish Education[10] and the CAJE Schusterman College Program.[11]

Recruitment, of course, is only one aspect of ensuring a cadre of well-qualified educational personnel for Jewish schools. Once these teachers are in Jewish day or congregational school classrooms, the field must understand how to keep them and encourage them to pursue their careers in the field.

Retention

Multiple national studies in general education broadcast statistics about the "staggering" teacher turnover and attrition rate in US schools, which many (including the National Commission on Teaching and America's Future) have determined is much higher than in other professions requiring comparable education and skills (Sparks, 2002). While some degree of teacher turnover is inevitable and even healthy for teachers and schools, consistently low retention of teachers (let alone "high-quality"

---

[10]See http://www.jesna.org/our-work/israel-lainer-interns/about-the-program for more information.

[11]The Schusterman College Program was a week-long experience as part of the larger CAJE conference, including pre-conference and Shabbat. As of spring, 2009, CAJE ceased operation; information about the future of the Schusterman College Program is unavailable at this time.

teachers) carries tremendous financial, human resource, and educational costs that may have a negative impact on educational outcomes. A 2000 study by the US Department of Education indicated that 40–50% of teachers leave within their first 7 years of teaching and two-thirds of those leave within their first 4 years (McCreight, 2000). Generally, this attrition declines markedly after 4–5 years in the classroom, then increases again after 25–30 years in the profession, when teachers are nearing retirement (ECS, 2005). A review of recent research in Jewish education (Kelner, Rabkin, Saxe, & Sheingold, 2004) revealed that teacher turnover in the first 3 years in Jewish day schools is approximately 12%. The rate more than doubles (27%) for congregational school teachers, many of whom work part-time in their primary school setting.

Darling-Hammond's research in general education (2003) revealed that the top four factors that influenced attrition and teacher retention were salary, working conditions, adequate teacher pre-service preparation, and mentoring support (especially early in a teacher's career). EJSS (2008) showed that in addition to these, the most important retention-related factors common to responding Jewish day and congregational school teachers were work/home balance, how the school responds to students who are not thriving, and recognition and/or validation from school administrators. Salary also was rated among the most prevalent factors (particularly for day school teachers) and was most important to those for whom it is the main source of household income. Overall, however, it was not ranked substantially higher than other important factors. In addition to salary, benefits are a key component of teachers' compensation packages. Among the Jewish day and congregational school teachers responding to the EJSS *Educator Survey*, between 66 and 70% of teachers who work more than 31 hours a week received health insurance, retirement benefits, and paid time off for professional development. Between 33 and 50% said they received life insurance, dental insurance, and/or partial/full tuition for their children.[12] Among teachers in general education settings, there is strong evidence that compensation plays a key, yet complex role in recruitment and retention. For example, while increasing compensation tends to increase rates of teacher retention, the impact of salary as a factor varies by gender, level of experience, and job satisfaction (ECS, 2005). One should keep in mind that for most teachers, "compensation" extends far beyond salary to include intrinsic and intangible compensation.

Several factors distinguish a teacher who is "likely to leave" from one who is "likely to stay." Common sense and research both demonstrate that the more satisfied a teacher is with her/his career and workplace conditions, the more likely s/he is to remain (Center for Comprehensive School Reform and Improvement, 2007). More than 80% of teachers who participated in the EJSS study expressed overall job satisfaction and 70% believed they had a good career "compared with people

---

[12] See Shoshanna Sofaer and Lynne Page Snyder (2004). *Addressing Uninsurance Among Jewish Educators: Background Analysis and Options.* Unpublished paper. Executive summary available at http://www.ou.org/index.php/ylc/article/2411. See also the press release issued by RAVSAK: The Jewish Community Day School Network. Retrieved on January 7, 2008, from http://www.ou.org/pdf/ylc/1831_001.pdf.

of their same age and gender." More than 75% reported that given everything they know now, they would choose their job again (EJSS, 2008). A study of Jewish teachers in the Greater Boston area similarly revealed that 70% were satisfied or very satisfied with their jobs (Frank, Margolis, & Weisner, 1992). These Boston teachers said their sense of job satisfaction could increase with support and help in teaching (especially from the principal), increased salary, the ability to reach more students in class, students who were more interested in Judaism, and greater respect from students.

Characteristics common to teachers who are "likely to stay" include, but are not limited to: passion, commitment, curiosity, determination, resilience, flexibility, commitment to intellectual stimulation, and deep care about their students and work (Williams, 2003). Teachers' need to feel capable and effective is a critical determinant in their decision to remain in a position (or in the field). Teachers with long tenures commonly cite several reasons for staying in teaching: love (for students, intellectual work, and subject matter), a feeling of hope/possibility, a drive toward democratic practice and social justice, and a perceived ability to shape the future. Teachers "likely to stay" believe that their jobs fill a strong personal need for creativity, provide meaningful relationships, and show them that they are making a difference in students' lives. Other environmental factors that influence teachers' decisions to stay in a school include a balance of connectedness and autonomy with colleagues and administration, the ability to be decision-makers, and/or opportunities to contribute substantively to school policy and change (Sparks, 2002).

Similarly, teachers who say they are "likely to leave" their schools and/or the field of Jewish education share commonalities, especially regarding work environment. The study of Jewish teachers in the Greater Boston area revealed that teachers "likely to leave" experience job dissatisfaction related to troublesome students, inadequate pay for their time and energy, and the need to discipline students. They characterized a "bad day" in teaching as one in which they were tired or in a bad mood, they felt they didn't teach anything, the students were bored, and/or the class was out of control (Frank, Margolis, & Weisner, 1992). Many studies of retention and attrition in public schools have found that teachers who are "likely to leave" were not adequately trained for their work as teachers, lacked resources, had high populations of low-achieving students, and/or had students with disruptive behavioral issues. In addition, these teachers often felt unsupported by administration, did not perceive a career ladder open to them, did not have access to ongoing learning or coaching, and/or perceived that they could not sustain their households on a teacher's salary (Guarino & Santibanez, 2006).

Based on this and other evidence, schools are likely to retain their high-quality teachers if they prepare and nurture them effectively, get to know their teachers well and understand "the difference that makes the difference" for them, improve the working environment, provide compelling intrinsic and extrinsic incentives, and ensure strong school leadership (National Education Association, 2003). Some schools are taking immediate steps to reform their recruitment processes to improve their chances of identifying and hiring well-qualified teachers who will succeed in teaching and improve student learning.[13] When schools seek teachers whose preparation, personalities, and values mesh with those of the school, they increase the potential for long-term relationships with those teachers. In addition, there is evidence that schools benefit from understanding and responding to what teachers are seeking from a teaching position, such as a school that makes good teaching possible; order and stability; opportunities to work with colleagues and develop their skills; a reasonable workload; and accessible, respectful, supportive leadership (Johnson & Birkeland, 2003). Reimer and Finkel advocate "the big three" approaches to Jewish teacher retention: ongoing excellent professional development (especially mentoring), intellectually exciting experiences, and networking (JESNA, 2004). They also stress the importance of creative lay and professional institutional leadership, and collaboration among schools, Jewish communal organizations, students, and parents.

Professional Development

Professional development is a key to promoting the induction, intellectual and professional growth, and tenure of teachers (Feiman-Nemser, 2003). It also is the critical link between improving the quality of teaching and improving student learning in Jewish schools. Many studies across Jewish and general education show that teachers value, seek, and/or are engaged in ongoing professional development. Nearly all of the teachers profiled in EJSS said they had participated in some professional development in the previous 12 months, including workshops, university courses, and distance learning (EJSS, 2008). Across the studies explored for this chapter, professional development emerged as *the* essential tool to increase teacher satisfaction, contribute to the retention of new teachers, enhance the work and investment of veteran teachers, and improve teaching and student learning.[14] This research also found that addressing the professional development needs of teachers, particularly in their first one to five years in the field, can improve both the rate of teacher retention and the quality of the teaching profession.

A review of available research makes clear that the educational processes and products that become normative in general education settings (e.g., public schools) often have an impact on operations in other school settings (e.g., Jewish day and

---

[13]See Barbara Sargent (2003). "Finding Good Teachers – And Keeping Them" *Educational Leadership*. (ASCD). (60)8. Sargent highlights a NJ district's success using a rigorous selection process and providing new teachers with structured and nurturing (professional and emotional) support, and shows the degree to which working conditions are a significant factor in retention.

[14]See, for example, New Jersey State Department of Education (2001). *Standards for Required Professional Development for Teachers: A New Vision.* "The New Jersey Professional Teaching Standards Board believes that teachers must be dedicated to a continuous plan of professional development that begins with their pre-service activities, that continues with their induction into the profession, and that extends through the life of their professional career in education through on-going and sustained professional development endeavors."

congregational schools). In the context of professional development, it is reasonable to believe that the growth and success of well-developed teacher professional development programs in general education settings will influence the creation and implementation of effective professional development programs in Jewish educational settings. Still, the US school system has much to learn from its international colleagues. For example, a recent study (Wei, Andree, & Darling-Hammond, 2009) found that in contrast to US schools, professional development in other countries is embedded in a teacher's regular job responsibilities. The authors cite a number of compelling statistics from a 2004 report of the Organisation for Economic Cooperation and Development (OECD). For example, "more than 85% of schools in Belgium, Denmark, Finland, Hungary, Ireland, Norway, Sweden, and Switzerland provide time for professional development in their teachers' workday or week." In many European and Asian countries, about "half of a teacher's working time" is devoted to collaborative planning, observing classrooms, preparing lessons and assessments, and working directly with families and students outside the classroom. Another striking difference in policy is that in the majority of school systems in Asia, Australia, and Europe, formal professional development and induction programs for new teachers are mandatory.

These and similar data indicate that rather than isolating professional development as an "event," it should be part of the school's overall plan and "rooted in a systems approach that focuses on identifying and managing a wide range of factors that impact student outcomes" (Weissman, 2007). In some cases, educational systems or school structures make it difficult for teachers to take advantage of learning opportunities. Researchers have found that fewer than half of the general education teachers received "release time" for professional development and nearly 25% were not given any support time or credit for professional development (Sparks & Hirsch, 1999). Similarly, EJSS study respondents revealed that even in cases in which their school administrators perceive a strong need for (or require) professional development, most teachers pay their own expenses for professional development activities, whether or not they received paid time to attend (EJSS, 2008).

Professional development for Jewish teachers also is complicated by the reality that Jewish schools tend to be more "resource poor" than public schools. Additionally, the nature of Jewish education involves different social-emotional and spiritual priorities than general education. Since the goals and standards for Jewish education remain in large part undefined, and since there is little extant research about professional development in Jewish schools, aligning professional development theory and practice is not yet possible. Weissman emphasizes the importance of training teachers to function as "action researchers" to fill this gap (Weissman, 2007).

A significant disconnect exists between teacher professional development as it is currently provided and where it must be situated if schools are to achieve their desired outcomes. Both researchers and practitioners indicate that there is not yet enough staff development and what exists is not up to par. Teachers seeking professional development are most likely to find "one shot" workshops (many of which assume homogeneous needs among teachers) or courses lacking well-planned agendas. As a result, teachers are taking part in a hodgepodge of unrelated courses. Just as teachers prepare engaging, intellectually challenging lessons for their students, so professional development should help teachers actively synthesize concrete aspects of teaching (behaviors, attitudes, skills, and knowledge), their desire to find meaning in their work, and critical self-reflective practice (Darling-Hammond & Richardson, 2009).

Effective professional development for teachers integrates goals and contents in a way that is results-driven and embedded in a teacher's job (Sparks, 2002). It provides meaningful cognitive, social, and emotional engagement with ideas, fellow teachers, and a variety of materials (Intrator & Kunzman, 2006). Professional development likely to be successful also is sustained (i.e., rigorous, cumulative, and long-term) and relationship-focused (i.e., it prepares teachers to succeed in all aspects of their work). Finally, effective professional development uses evaluation and research data and applies techniques and perspectives of critical inquiry. Although the field of professional development is just gathering steam in the realm of Jewish education, several noteworthy programs already exist.[15] On a broad level, many central agencies and bureaus of Jewish education provide in-service training and resources for Jewish schools and for Jewish teachers, especially for avocational teachers in congregational schools.

One frequently studied and widely advocated avenue of professional development is "mentoring." More than a "buddy system," mentoring brings together a novice teacher and a senior educator in a collaborative relationship defined by specific expectations, roles, and responsibilities. Darling-Hammond's research has shown that teachers who experience strong teacher preparation combined with ongoing professional development are more "likely to stay" and that well-designed mentoring programs "raise retention rates for new teachers by improving their attitudes, feelings of efficacy, and instructional skills" (Darling-Hammond, 2003). The growing popularity of formal mentoring programs has generated a corresponding need to identify and develop good mentors. Many schools intuitively target their veteran teachers for these mentoring roles. Studies indicate that serving as a mentor provides a new lease on life for many veteran teachers; many say mentoring and/or coaching other teachers creates an incentive for them to remain in teaching as they learn from and share with their colleagues (Darling-Hammond, 2003). Increasingly, these mentors receive some type of training to enable them to fulfill their roles effectively. According to recent research, several countries (including Israel, Switzerland, France, Norway, and England) require formal training for mentor teachers (Wei, Andree, & Darling-Hammond, 2003).

Another increasingly popular form of professional development is the community of practice (CoP). CoPs allow teachers who have a shared practice to work

---

[15]Examples of intensive professional development programs for formal and informal Jewish educators that JESNA has formally evaluated over time include: Nurturing Excellence in Synagogue Schools (NESS), Mandel Teacher Teachers Institute (MTEI), Leadership Institute for Principals, Machon L'Morim: B'reshit, TeKiaH, and Shofar.

together to improve that practice by creating and sharing knowledge and insight through a diverse range of social interactions, research projects, and presentations. New technologies are expanding the possibilities for professional development through formal distance learning, independent study, ad hoc online relationships in groups and networks, and learning with wikis and blogs (Ferriter, 2009). In addition, Jewish educators have access to expanded resources through online centers, such as JESNA's Sosland Online Resource Center, e-chinuch, Mofet Institute's Teacher Education Resource Center, and the Lookstein Institute for Jewish Education.[16]

Our knowledge about professional development points to the essential need to conceive, develop, and sustain a well-planned continuum of learning opportunities for Jewish teachers at all stages of their careers, with particular emphasis on the formative years. It also encourages teacher-administrator collaboration to establish connections between knowledge and practice to improve teacher performance and student outcomes. Collegial relationships with peers, senior teachers, and administrators who are supportive and able to offer constructive criticism will be indispensible to this project. At its most grand, what the field now knows about professional development for teachers—and the potentially enormous impact well-qualified teachers and high-quality teaching can have on student learning—demands a transformation in our commonplaces about teaching and learning (Feiman-Nemser, 2007).

Approaching Solutions and Policy in Jewish Education

The link between excellence in teaching and excellence in student outcomes demands a systemic approach to Jewish education that attends to multiple tasks at once. This is a "field in motion;" it cannot wait for a complete set of standards before beginning to focus on teaching excellence. The challenge is meeting current needs and anticipating the emergent needs of an evolving community of learners and forms of Jewish education. Policy-makers must understand the dynamics of this active system and plan strategically to prepare and sustain teachers and educational leaders in new and creative ways. While the field can expect short- and intermediate-term gains, significant progress toward true excellence will take time.

While the field of Jewish education as a body has a limited ability to influence change directly on the level of individual schools and learners, levers for change that directly impact excellence in teaching are more immediately within our reach. These include: investment in Jewish teachers, teacher preparation and professional development, school cultures that foster respect and learning, research and evaluation, and resources supporting excellence.

---

[16]JESNA's Sosland Online Resource Center (http://www.jesna.org/sosland/home), e-chinuch (http://www.chinuch.org), Mofet Institute's Teacher Education Resource Center (http://mofetjtec.macam.ac.il/Pages/default.aspx), and the Lookstein Institute for Jewish Education (http://www.lookstein.org).

Investment in Jewish teachers includes, but is not limited to, financial support to improve salaries. Other important areas for immediate and long-term investments include: pre-professional training, supervision and mentoring, adequate preparation time, peer-to-peer collaboration, ongoing professional development, and developing a school culture of learning that attracts and retains excellent teachers. While Jewish day and congregational school teachers have unique concerns, both require holistic policies that reflect commitment to improving teacher quality and student outcomes today and planning for these teachers' futures. These widespread investments may increase the likelihood that qualified candidates will enter the field, that recruiters will be able to attract the best and brightest, and that teachers will stay in the field of Jewish education.

High-level teacher preparation is essential to nurturing a generation of highly qualified Jewish teachers who will raise the caliber of teaching and learning in Jewish schools. Because most extant teacher training programs produce teachers and administrators for Jewish day schools and higher education settings, there is a need to enhance and/or create robust pre-professional programs to prepare a greater number of high-quality congregational school, early childhood, and informal Jewish educators. The field of Jewish education must engage in a discussion about what this pre-professional training ought to look like, what kind of investment is required, and how the field will measure its progress toward its desired outcomes. The field also must diversify avenues through which potentially excellent teachers can enter the field, secure attractive compensation packages, and develop multiple career ladders for their advancement. While induction, mentoring, and professional development are essential components of the learning mosaic, they ultimately must promote retention in a climate where up to one-third of teachers leave the profession or their schools in their first few years.

Professional development for all teachers must be relevant, ongoing, rigorous, sustained, and technologically adaptable. Extant studies report that while most Jewish teachers possess high levels of general education, they tend to be deficient in one or more key knowledge areas: Jewish content, pedagogic skills, and/or pedagogic content knowledge. Research demonstrates it can take upward of 5–10 years before a teacher masters the art and science of teaching (e.g., Huberman, 1989). This reality makes clear that lifelong educational and Jewish learning is paramount for current and potential teachers who might not otherwise find success in the field (Feiman-Nemser, 2003). According to Sparks and Hirsch (1999), ideally 10% of a school's budget and 25% of a teacher's time should be devoted to teacher learning. Despite this and other research on excellence in professional development, too many schools still rely on isolated events without a well-conceived plan for long-term professional growth. Alternatives to ad hoc events include mentoring, which leverages master teachers and creates individualized learning programs for teachers and mentors. With training and support, veteran/more-skilled teachers can become master teachers, mentors, and team leaders. Research shows the positive and meaningful impact of these relationships on teaching and learning. Other activities that foster learning include, but are not limited to: distance learning, CoPs, and other real and virtual tools that link resources. Professional development also must anticipate that the changing relationship between teaching and technology in Jewish and general education might well demand a different kind of teacher and a different type of teacher training that puts teachers on the cutting edge of advances in technology, pedagogy, and learning. The Jewish educational world must catch up with technological advances that can unite local and national resources and integrate them into teacher induction, mentoring, and professional development.

A school culture, or "professional learning community," that fosters respect and learning encourages and sustains teachers and students. According to Ben-Avie and Kress (2007), a professional learning community refers to "the effectiveness and efficiency with which teachers collaborate on teams, as well as create a culture in which they learn together and from one another." Ben-Avie and Kress demonstrate that a professional learning community can encourage and support knowledge-sharing among faculty, between faculty and students/families within and beyond the institution's walls, and among institutions. Creating a professional learning community means valuing educational experimentation, autonomy in teacher decision-making, clear policies and structures, and measurable performance outcomes. In keeping with this idea, the field cannot discount a student's home as an essential locus of teaching and learning. Fostering a school culture of respect and learning must include family education to create lasting improvement in student outcomes.

Research and evaluation require a systematic program of collecting, analyzing, and reporting qualitative and quantitative data that will help the field make wise decisions about developing benchmarks, assessing student and teacher performance, and investing in the key leverage points highlighted in this chapter.[17] A learning community is dedicated to wrestling with complex results and translating them into digestible and meaningful training for teachers. Teachers must have the tools and training to become "action researchers" to help conduct the evaluation and research that will lead to necessary resources to ensure success. To maximize the impact of meaningful research and evaluation, the field must advocate for and set aside resources for codifying these innovative ideas, developing curricula, and creating lending libraries for teachers to share resources.

Resources supporting excellence are indispensible if the field is serious about focusing on key leverage points through which it can begin to make change. Reimer and Finkel (JESNA, 2004) note that success is contingent upon the commitment and vision of institutions, substantial construction and efficient use of infrastructure/funding, successful and adaptable lab communities and pilot projects, creative use of resources, and plowing the fruits of investment back into the field. Feiman-Nemser (2007) adds to these a concerted effort to educate lay/professional leaders about the critical relationship between high-quality teaching and high-quality professional development, support for multiple pathways into Jewish teaching, and

---

[17] This may be accomplished by focusing on specific areas of content (e.g., the Jewish Theological Seminary's Tanakh Project), stages in program development, different venues within Jewish education, and program scale (local and/or national).

alignment of career-long teacher development with what the field knows about good teaching and optimal learning.

Next Steps

The Jewish community will not awaken tomorrow to find thousands of well-qualified Jewish teachers waiting to be scooped up like manna from heaven. Therefore, it must begin today to increase the proficiency of the current cadre of teachers in our schools in educational theory and methods, subject matter, pedagogy, and the "art and science" of becoming excellent classroom teachers. This chapter points the way toward ensuring a cadre of well-qualified educational personnel for Jewish schools by recruiting, retaining, and developing excellent teachers to meet the current and emergent needs of the Jewish community. In order to take some of the next steps, the field needs additional research. Possible rubrics and examples of questions to be explored include, but are not limited to:

1. *What does the field need to know about recruitment, retention, and development?*

   a. In what venues, and at what times, are potential Jewish teachers most open to the influence of individuals who may lead them to a career in Jewish education?
   b. Which types of Jewish educational experiences are most likely to tap into teachers' intrinsic motivations to channel their skills and passions into Jewish education?
   c. What steps can the field take to increase the likelihood that teachers feel they have satisfying careers in specific settings?
   d. What is the impact of teacher recognition on Jewish teachers? What types of recognition, if any, are most effective for which teachers?
   e. What are the differential effects of financial incentives for different cohorts of teachers (novice versus veteran teachers, etc.)?

2. *What does the field need to know about teachers, how students learn, and what it takes to help students learn certain things?*

   a. What do beginning Jewish teachers need to know, learn, and do in order to be successful in their early placements?
   b. What are the key things students should learn over time in different settings? What do teachers need to know, feel, or do to facilitate/encourage the students to meet the articulated outcomes?
   c. What is the relationship between specific teacher knowledge and behaviors and student outcomes? How can the field best assess this? Which gaps in knowledge or behavior are most "learnable" through pre-service training or professional development?

d. What are the requisite skills and knowledge that teachers need to develop non-cognitive outcomes in students in Jewish schools? What are the best ways to prepare and support teachers to develop and use these skills?
3. *What does the field need to know about what works—and how it can be refined/applied in Jewish contexts?*
   a. How relevant/comparable are findings from recent general literature about teacher induction, development, developmental stages, etc. to various Jewish educational settings?
   b. How might these practices be adapted to the reality of a diverse Jewish schooling environment?
4. *What are the indicators for success?*
   a. What are the criteria for "Jewish teacher excellence" in different settings?
   b. How would we measure these criteria?
   c. How might we use the learnings from external assessments as tools for self-reflective practice among educators in Jewish school settings?
   d. How would the field measure excellent performance?
   e. How could the field connect student outcomes with teachers' activities/performance?
   f. What are our indicators of success for teachers? For students? In different settings?

The research explored in this chapter brings the field of Jewish education closer to understanding the Jewish teachers in the field today and provides data that will inform key stakeholders about the factors that influence teachers to enter and to remain in (or to leave) the field of Jewish education in Jewish day and congregational schools. While providing an empirical basis for advocacy and strategic planning for change to improve quality teaching and improve student outcomes, it also raises fresh questions to stimulate critical discussions about responsible policy and decision-making. The resulting local, national, and institutional conversations will educate the field of Jewish education and related stakeholders toward a cultural shift of respect and advocacy on behalf of Jewish teachers in their communities to benefit learners, teachers, Jewish schools, and all Jewish communities in North America.

References

Aron, I. (1992). What we know about…Jewish teachers. In S. Kelman (Ed.), *What we know about Jewish education: A handbook of today's research for tomorrow's Jewish education.* Los Angeles: Torah Aura Productions.

Aron, I. (2004). *Realism as the key to excellence in congregational education. Agenda: Jewish Education* (Vol. 17). New York: JESNA.

Ben-Avie, M., & Kress, J. (2007). *A North American Study of Teachers in Jewish Day and Congregational Schools.* Full text available online at http://www.jewisheducationalchange.org

Center for Comprehensive School Reform and Improvement. (2007). *Improving Teacher Retention with Supportive Workplace Conditions*. Full text available online at http://www.centerforcsri.org
Commission on Jewish Education in North America. (1990). *A time to act*. New York: University Press of America.
Darling-Hammond, L. (2003). Keeping good teachers: Why it matters, what leaders can do. *Educational Leadership*, (ASCD), *60*(8), 6–13.
Darling-Hammond, L., & Richardson, N. (2009). Teacher learning: What matters? *Educational Leadership*, (ASCD), *66*(5), 46–53.
Dushkin, A. M. (1980). *Jewish education: Selected writings*. Jerusalem: Magnes Press (Hebrew University).
Education Commission of the States (ECS). (2003). Eight Questions on Teacher Preparation: What Does the Research Say? *Teaching Quality Research Reports*. Full text available online at http://www.ecs.org/html/educationissues/TeachingQuality/tpreport/home/summary.pdf
Education Commission of the States (ECS). (2005). Eight Questions on Teacher Recruitment and Retention: What Does the Research Say? *Teaching Quality Research Reports*. Full text available online at http://www.ecs.org/html/educationissues/TeachingQuality/TRReport
Feiman-Nemser, S. (1992). What We Know About Learning to Teach. In S. Kelman (Ed.), *What we know about Jewish education: A handbook of today's research for tomorrow's Jewish education*. Los Angles: Torah Aura Productions.
Feiman-Nemser, S. (2003). What new teachers need to learn. *Educational Leadership*, (ASCD), *60*(8), 25–29.
Feiman-Nemser, S. (2007). Learning to teach. In P. Flexner, R. L. Goodman, & L. D. Bloomberg (Eds.), *What we now know about Jewish education: Perspectives on research and practice*. Los Angeles: Torah Aura Publications.
Ferriter, B. (2009). Learning with blogs and wikis. *Educational Leadership*, (ASCD), *66*(5), 34–38.
Fishkoff, S. (2006). Growing Number of Non-Jews Teach the Aleph-Bet at Preschool. Retrieved on April 7, 2009, from http://www.Interfaithfamily.com
Frank, N., Margolis, D., & Weisner, A. (1992). *Research report III: The Jewish school teacher*. Boston: Bureau of Jewish Education of Greater Boston.
Gamoran, A., Goldring, E. B., Robinson, B., Goodman, R. L., & Tammivaara, J. (1998). *The teacher's report: A portrait of teachers in Jewish schools*. Council for Initiatives in Jewish Education. Jerusalem: The Mandel Foundation.
Goodman, R. L., Schaap, E., & Ackerman, A. (2002). *What are the numbers of Jewish teachers and students in formal Jewish educational settings?* New York: CAJE.
Goodman, R. L., & Schaap, E. (2007). Jewish Education Personnel. In P. Flexner, R. L. Goodman, & L. D. Bloomberg (Eds.), *What we now know about Jewish education: Perspectives on research and practice*. Los Angeles: Torah Aura Publications.
Guarino, C. M., & Santibanez, L. (2006). Teacher recruitment and retention: A review of the recent empirical literature. *Review of Educational Research*, *76*(2), 173–208.
Huberman, M. (1989). The professional lifecycle of teachers. *Teachers College Record*, *91*(1), 31–57.
Intrator, S. M., & Kunzman, R. (2006). Starting with the soul. *Educational Leadership*, (ASCD), *63*(6), 38–43.
JESNA. (2004). *Agenda: Jewish Education: Educator Recruitment and Retention*, *1*(17), 1–18.
JESNA. (2008). *Educators in Jewish Schools Study (EJSS)*.
Johnson, S. M., & Birkeland, S. E. (2003). The schools that teachers choose. *Educational Leadership*, (ASCD), *60*(8), 20–24.
Kelner, S., Rabkin, M., Saxe, L., & Sheingold, C. (2004). *Recruiting and retaining a professional work force for the Jewish community: A review of existing research*. New York: Brandeis University.
Kennedy, M. M. (2006). From teacher quality to quality teaching. *Educational Leadership*, (ASCD), *63*(6), 14–19.

Liu, E., Moore, S., & Peske, H. G. (2004). New teachers and the Massachusetts signing bonus: The limits of inducements. *Educational Evaluation and Policy Analysis, 26*(3), 217–236.

McCreight, C. (2000) *Teacher attrition, shortage, and strategies for teacher retention.* Texas: Texas A&M University. (ERIC Document Reproduction Service no. ED444986).

National Education Association. (2003). *Meeting the challenges of recruitment and retention: A guidebook to promising strategies to recruit and retain qualified and diverse teachers.* Washington, DC: National Education Association.

National Jewish Population Study 2000–2001. (2002). New York: United Jewish Communities (UJC).

New Jersey State Department of Education. (2001). *Standards for Required Professional Development for Teachers: A New Vision.* Retrieved on December 19, 2007, from http://www.nj.gov/education/profdev/standards.htm

Sales, A. L., & Koren, A. (2007). *Re-imagining congregational education: Lessons from the RE-IMAGINE project.* Waltham, MA: Brandeis University.

Sparks, D. (2002). *High-performing Cultures Increase Teacher Retention.* Oxford, OH: National Staff Development Council. Full text available online at http://www.nsdc.org/library/publications/results/res12-02spar

Sparks, D., & Hirsch, S. (1999). *A national plan for improving professional development.* Oxford, OH: National Staff Development Council.

Stronge, J. H., & Hindman, J. L. (2003). Hiring the best teachers. *Educational Leadership,* (ASCD), *60*(8), 48–52.

Teacher Support Network. Retrieved on November 4, 2007, from http://www.teacherssupportnetwork.com

Wei, R. C., Andree, A., & Darling-Hammond, L. (2009). How nations invest in teachers. *Educational Leadership,* (ASCD), *66*(5), 28–33.

Wertheimer, J. (2007). *Recent trends in supplementary Jewish education.* New York: Avi Chai Foundation.

Weissman, C. (2007). Professional development requires a discipline for seeing wholes. In P. Flexner, R. L. Goodman, & L. D. Bloomberg (Eds.), *What we now know about Jewish education: Perspectives on research and practice.* Los Angeles: Torah Aura Publications.

Williams, J. S. (2003). Why great teachers stay. *Educational Leadership,* (ASCD), *60*(8), 71–74.

Woocher, J. (2006). *Redesigning Jewish education for the 21st century.* New York: Jewish Education Service of North America (JESNA).

Zeldin, M. (1983). Jewish schools and American society: Patterns of action and reaction. *Religious Education, 2*(2), 182–192.

Ultra-Orthodox/Haredi Education

Yoel Finkelman

Haredi Judaism in Context

Modernity brought enormous freedoms and opportunities to Western Jewry. For the most part, modern Jews happily integrated themselves into the cultures of the countries in which they lived. And, for the most part, Jews saw these developments as positive, cherishing their newfound freedoms. In the process, the nature of Jewish religious identities changed dramatically. Some Jews abandoned their Jewish commitments, and others modified them into new Jewish movements, ideologies, and identities that matched their intellectual proclivities and social aspirations.

Beginning in Hungary in the middle of the nineteenth century, and then spreading to Eastern Europe and later throughout the globe, a small minority of Jews focused less on the opportunities and more on the spiritual and religious dangers that they associated with increased freedoms. They became worried, with more than a little justification, that modernity would lead to neglect or alteration of what they took to be the immutable word of God. Torah, they claimed, was self-sufficient, and becoming "like the gentiles" would do incurable harm to Jews who adopted such a strategy. Instead, Jews should isolate themselves from others and maintain allegiance purely to the traditions of the past. These Jews became known as Haredim, or Ultra-Orthodox.

Haredi Judaism presents itself as self-contained and as the simple continuation of what Judaism had always been and always should be. *Hadash asur min haTorah* (novelty is prohibited by the Torah) became a kind of rallying cry, a slogan penned by a founding leader of Haredi Judaism, Rabbi Moshe Sofer (1762–1839): continue to study Torah, to keep *mitzvot*, to dress as one's predecessors dressed, and to maintain allegiance exclusively to Torah—just as, it is claimed, Jews have always done—rather than to the new-fangled modernistic values that have tempted some away from God's truth (for a basic introduction to Haredi Judaism, see Friedman & Heilman, 1991).

Y. Finkelman (✉)
Bar Ilan University, Tel Aviv, Israel
e-mail: yoel.finkelman@gmail.com

Historians have questioned this Haredi self-understanding of a seamless continuation of the tradition from the past. Instead, historians argue that much of Haredi Judaism's reactions to modernity have, ironically, made it quite modern (Silber, 1992). Still, Haredi Judaism has continued, in different times and places and in slightly different forms, to define itself through sharp contrast with the cultures that surround it. It is, broadly speaking, rejectionist, isolationist, and counter-cultural. Haredi Jews attempt to create an enclave culture, one in which Jews can surround themselves in Orthodox Jewish culture and values, and where they can be protected from the dangerous and destructive values of the outside world (Sivan, 1995).

Obviously, the attempt to create and maintain an enclave culture under the relatively open conditions of modernity requires a network of social and educational institutions to construct and reinforce collective values (Rosenak, 1993). Schools—along with families, synagogues, mutual aid organizations, and the like—do much of the work in Haredi attempts to construct individual and collective identities. Indeed, one of the dramatic changes that Haredi society has undergone over the centuries is the increased emphasis on formal education for all members of society. If, in the Jewish past, higher formal education was a privilege of a minority of men, in Haredi society every member of society, both male and female, acquires higher formal education in order to provide children and young adults with the knowledge and acculturation that they need to be protected from the lures of non-Haredi culture.

This chapter attempts to familiarize the reader with basic issues in Haredi formal education, focusing on educational institutions for members of the Haredi community. I cannot deal with several central issues here, as important as they may be: informal education, parenting (Finkelman, 2007 and Finkelman, 2009), teacher training, special education (Glaubman & Lifshitz, 2001), and institutions designed for outreach to non-Haredim (Caplan, 2001; Danzger, 1989; Safer, 2003). Furthermore, I will limit the discussion by focusing on the two largest and most influential Haredi communities, those of Israel and North America, and pay scant attention to smaller Haredi communities in Europe and South America. In addition, I will mention Sephardic Haredim (those deriving from Jewish communities originating in Muslim countries) only in passing (Ravitzky, 2006 and Caplan, 2003, pp. 264–269).

I will begin with a description of the centrality of Torah education within a Haredi context and then move to an explanation of some key dividing lines that separate different subgroups of Haredim from one another. Then, I will trace the educational experiences of Haredi males and females through their separate educational institutions from childhood through adulthood, examining the institutions of study, the function of those institutions, the religious education that they provide, and the access that they give students to general education and vocational training.

The Centrality of Torah Study in Haredi Education

Haredi Jewish education differs from that of other segments of the Jewish community, and it is impossible to understand the Haredi community and its educational system without reference to that difference. To put it simply, Torah education is more central in the cultural economy of Haredi communities than it is in that of other Jewish communities.

To begin with, the Haredi birthrate is higher than that of the general population. Children, therefore, are ubiquitous in the community, and institutions for their education take up a particularly central place. But the birthrate is only one aspect of the centrality of education in Haredi communities. While the discourse of Jewish education in non-Haredi communities (pardon the generalization) often focuses on education as a means of intellectual and spiritual enrichment, as a way of encouraging Jewish continuity, and as a method of enabling participation in Jewish practice, for the Haredi community, education, at least for men, is valued as an end in and of itself and is taken to be a lifelong endeavor.

For Mitnagdic streams (more on this group below) in Haredi theology, Torah study is the be-all-and-end-all of Jewish experience, the very purpose of creation. But even in non-Mitnagdic communities, male Torah study is absolutely central, and Torah education does not end with a degree, job qualification, or certificate of completion. Even if a student receives rabbinic ordination, this is not a sign to stop formal education. Furthermore, decades-long immersion in Haredi educational institutions also reinforces the community's isolationism by surrounding young people and adults for as long as possible in institutions in which Haredi values and culture hold sway. And, by not providing extensive general education or vocational training for men, these institutions limit their social and economic independence, thereby making individuals dependent on the communal infrastructure.

Hence, Haredi men in Israel are expected to continue their studies into their 30s and 40s, and even in North America men commonly study full time at least until their mid-20s, either without or in addition to some vocational training. Some men continue full-time study for their entire lives. In Israel and parts of North America this has resulted in a historically unprecedented expansion of what the sociologist Menachem Friedman has called the "society of learners": a Haredi community in which full-time Torah study is the primary vocation of adult men (Friedman, 1991, pp. 80–87). North American Haredi men are more likely than their counterparts in Israel to take part in the workforce, but even in that context, full-time Torah study well into adulthood is a norm to strive for. If, for pre-modern traditional Jewish society, Torah study at an adult level was the inheritance of a small minority of the male intellectual, spiritual, and often economic elite, in today's Haredi community it is a mass phenomenon (much as adult formal education has become a norm throughout the developed West).

As a result, there are quantitatively more institutions of Torah study in Haredi neighborhoods than in other Jewish neighborhoods,[1] and Torah scholarship is a central linchpin in defining leadership, social status, and rank within the communal hierarchy. Indeed, one of the central planks in Haredi ideology is that of *da'at Torah*, a doctrine according to which great rabbis and Torah scholars have exclusive

---

[1] Furthermore, because Haredi society is divided into numerous groups and subgroups, each subgroup often maintains separate educational institutions for its own population (Friedman, 1991, p. 155, but see p. 159; Schiffer, 1998, pp. 12–15).

authority over virtually all aspects of individual and communal life (Brown, 2005; Kaplan, 1992). In short, Torah education is more central within Haredi communities than in other Jewish communities.

Some Basic Dividing Lines

Despite an oft-heard stereotype, Haredi Judaism is not monolithic. It is divided by a crisscrossing network of separations between groups and subgroups. It is not possible in this context to trace the nuances of every distinction between different subgroups. But three must occupy us. First, the distinction between Hasidim and Mitnagdim; second, the distinction between Israel and North America; and third, the distinction between men and women.

Hasidim and Mitnagdim

The Hasidic movement developed in the eighteenth century, founded by Yisrael Ba'al Shem Tov (1698–1760) and his students, and it quickly became influential throughout Eastern Europe. In its early years, before the Haredi community had taken firm shape, the movement tended to downplay Torah scholarship as a marker of religious success. Instead, it emphasized certain kinds of mystical experiences for the elite, and an emotional attachment to God as well as service through daily activities of life for the masses (Lamm, 1999). The rabbinic elite, the Mitnagdim, opposed the Hasidic movement, because they continued to see Torah study as the central pillar of religious success and were upset both by Hasidic devaluation of scholarship and by hints of antinomianism in theology and practice. While the Hasidic rabbis and their institutions appealed to the masses, even to ignorant laborers, the Mitnagdim established yeshivas, elite institutions for long-term Torah study, in order to raise the next generation of (exclusively male) *talmidei hakhamim* (Torah scholars) (Nadler, 1999).

Educationally, Hasidim invested less in traditional Torah scholarship than did their Mitnagdic peers. Yet, Hasidism adopted a fear and rejection of secular education and science, which translated into bitter opposition to the Haskalah, the modern Jewish Enlightenment movement that called for educational reform and increased openness to general culture (the animosity was mutual). Instead, the Hasidic movement tried to preserve a simple-faith attitude among followers. The cerebral Mitnagdic movement was, for the most part, more open to general education, but Mitnagdim worked to keep their followers segregated in yeshivas for many years.

Gradually, from the late nineteenth century and particularly in the years after the Holocaust, the two communities grew closer together, discovering that what they have in common, particularly the fear of non-Haredi society and culture, is more important than what they have disagreed about in the past. Hasidim, over the years, have come to put more emphasis on the study of Torah, and have even developed networks of yeshivas (Stampfer, 1998, and Breuer, 2003, pp. 55–57). At the same time, Mitnagdic Haredi Judaism has expanded from a small elite minority into a mass culture, a "society of learners" (Friedman, 1991), thereby finding more room for laypeople (or, put differently, converting the plurality of the community's men into members of the elite).

North America and Israel

On the whole, the North American Haredi community is a great deal more acculturated than its counterpart in Israel. American Haredim, particularly among the Mitnagdim, are more likely than their Israeli counterparts to have a high school, college, and even graduate school education. Many work in non-Haredi workplaces; they may follow sports or popular music; and they are more likely to read "secular" books (Caplan, 2006). Israeli Haredim, while also integrated to a certain degree into contemporary Israeli culture (Caplan & Sivan, 2003), tend toward greater isolationism. They acquire very little general education, and remain more confined to their own enclave communities.

The nature of Israel as a Jewish State pushes Israeli Haredim in more isolationist directions. The general culture and government in North America are gentile, while those in Israel are Jewish, and constructed by secular Jews at that. Hence, American Haredim can more easily view the surrounding culture as neutral, while contemporary Israeli Haredim will view the surrounding culture as heretical Judiasm, making it more threatening. Furthermore, the relationship with the Israeli government and its funding, in conjunction with the thorny issue of military service, constructs a more isolated Israeli Haredi experience. In Israel, yeshiva students earn a postponement and often exemption from otherwise mandatory military service, and Haredi culture views military service as the high-road to abandonment of a Haredi life (though small numbers of Haredim do join the army—see Hakak, 2003; Stadler, 2009). This pushes young adult Haredim into yeshiva, and limits their options to leave.

Limited government funding of Haredi education in North America, compared with the larger Israeli government funding of Haredi education, helps construct the educational differences between the two Haredi communities. With the passing of Israel's mandatory education law in 1949 and the national education law of 1953, the State established the *Hinukh 'Atzmai* (Independent Education) stream, in which Haredi schools receive State funds, but remain largely independent in terms of curriculum and educational programming (Schiffer, 1998; Sebba & Schiffer, 1998, 28–33).[2] Hence, Haredi schools had reliable and consistent official funding, which allowed them to grow rapidly (Friedman, 1991, 56).[3] Furthermore, the

---

[2] Some groups, particularly the more radically isolationist *Edah Haredit*, do not accept government funding for their schools, but they are a small minority even on the Israeli Haredi scene.

[3] As of 2007, Haredi education in Israel included 27.0% of the student body in elementary schools and 20.5% of high school age students, meaning approximately 161,000 elementary school students and 57,000 high school age students. See the information

government also provides stipends for advanced study in yeshivas, in addition to child allowances and other social-welfare payments. Hence, while the Haredi sector remains one of the most impoverished segments of Israeli society, Haredi society can still afford to encourage all males to study Torah full time well into adulthood because of access to funding provided by other segments of society (Berman, 2000; Gottlieb, 2007; Schiffer, 1998).

In contrast, the US government provides very little support for private schools, which almost all Haredi children attend, and Haredi society does not gain government funding beyond the welfare state's provisions for the poor.[4] Some Haredi elementary and high schools in North America are organized under the loose umbrella of the Torah U'Mesorah organization, which provides a small measure of centralization and oversight, but the organization provides little or no funding (Kramer, 1984). Hence, the burden of tuition payment falls on the shoulders of parents, which pressures them to enter the workplace and earn a living.[5] Further, there is no threat of military service in North America. Hence, leaving yeshiva for the workplace and acquiring the general education that allows for such a thing are more accepted among North American Haredim than among Israeli ones.

Even with these generalizations about the more open American community and the more isolationist Israeli one, it can be more helpful to think about all Haredi communities as existing on a continuum between more isolationist and less isolationist. Some communities, in both North America and Israel, speak Yiddish primarily, dress in ways that are less influenced by contemporary fashion, are less open to general education, and more thoroughly oppose any emergence, even temporary, from the boundaries of the enclave (Schneller, 1980). Other communities speak the vernacular, dress in ways that are more influenced by contemporary fashion, are more open to general education, and are more willing to allow or encourage temporary leaving of the enclave, at least for a good reason. While Israeli Haredim tend, on the whole, toward greater isolationism, this is not a hard and fast rule, with both Israeli and American Haredim appearing at every and any spot on the continuum between isolation and acculturation, ranging from Jerusalem's *Edah Haredit* at the most isolationist, to yeshivas like Baltimore's Ner Yisrael on the less isolationist side.

Men and Women

Certainly, the single most important distinction for understanding Haredi life in general, and education in particular, involves gender. According to the Haredi cultural

---

from Israel's Central Bureau of Statistics, available at http://www.cbs.gov.il/reader/shnaton/templ_shnaton.html?num_tab=st08_12&CYear=2008 and http://www.cbs.gov.il/reader/shnaton/templ_shnaton.html?num_tab=st08_10&CYear=2008.

[4]Marvin Schick (2005) puts the number of students in Haredi schools in the United States at just over 100,000.

[5]Certain Canadian Provinces do provide government funding for parochial schools.

ideal, there are essentialist differences between men and women, which are reflected in radically different social and communal roles (El-Or, 1994). Ideally, men should become pious Torah scholars. In contrast, a woman should be characterized by her *tzniut*, modesty in both dress and demeanor, and her normative cultural role centers on domesticity and child rearing. Men should participate in, and control, the community's religious public sphere of worship, politics, and decision making; women should find fulfillment in the privacy of their roles as mothers and wives (though they are often expected to leave their homes to work in order to support their husbands' study). Further, Haredim allow little mingling of the sexes and disallow public representation of sexuality, in conscious opposition to the eroticization of much of contemporary general popular culture. Much of the responsibility for public modesty lies with women, who are expected to dress in clothing that covers the body and does not invite the "male gaze." Under these circumstances, communal worship and almost all public events are gender separate.

As we shall see below, different social and religious roles for males and females require different kinds of education and different kinds of schools. Haredi schools are segregated by gender from the youngest ages, and the separate male and female educational institutions provide dramatically different experiences and curricula, which launch members of the different genders "into entirely different orbits" from their earliest childhood (Bilu, 2003, p. 173).

In particular, Torah study ranks at the top of the Haredi axiological hierarchy, and women are exempt from much of that study. Indeed, they are prohibited from studying the Talmud, the most important text of Haredi study. Hence, while men are encouraged and expected to study Torah and Talmud full time from a young age until early adulthood, and part time for their entire lives, women are expected to end their formal education in their early 20s at the latest, and their schooling provides a truncated religious curriculum (El-Or, 1994; Shaffir, 2004). Furthermore, despite the emphasis on female domesticity, women often work outside the home in order to help support their families and their husbands' full-time Torah study. Hence, young women are encouraged to gain the vocational training and/or college education they will need to do so effectively, even in sub-communities where such training is frowned upon for Haredi men (Caplan, 2003; Friedman, 1995).

The Educational Pathways of a Haredi Jew

Haredi education, like all education, does more than just impart information. It is central in the work of cultural transmission, in socializing young people into the ways and norms of a particular community. Haredi Jews, both male and female, learn a great deal more in their schools than Bible, Jewish law, Talmud, or Jewish history. They learn also a complete worldview: what makes for valuable and important information; what one can do with valuable information; and how to use that in ways that the Haredi community considers worthwhile (Krakowski, 2008a). Schools teach Haredim how to behave in acceptable ways, how to navigate the community and the outside world, and what roles they should play as either Haredi males or females. Formal and informal educational institutions help construct their pupils' identities.

In the coming sections, I will trace the separate educational experiences of males and females as they enter the school system until they emerge decades later. I will focus particularly on the structures of the various school systems, their roles in constructing identity, and the kinds of general education that they make available.

Male Education

The Yeshiva

The cornerstone of Haredi male education is the yeshiva (Breuer, 2003; Helmreich, 1982; Stampfer, 2005).[6] It is worth dwelling on this institution for adults even before discussing elementary and secondary education, largely because the yeshiva's uniqueness exemplifies the value of men's Torah education from a Haredi perspective. The ideal Haredi male is the *talmid hakham*, the pious scholar, whose lack of physical prowess derives from a dedication to and expertise in the "sea of the Talmud" and in Jewish law, which in turn engenders a soft-spoken personal piety. While Haredim can be attracted to other more aggressive images of masculinity, such as athletic or military (Stadler, 2009), the yeshiva remains the institution that does the most to inculcate the mastery of the Talmud and the personal piety that is seen as the hegemonic male norm (on Haredi masculinity, see Aran, 2003).

Generally, the yeshiva day is divided into three units, or *sedarim*, one each in the morning (approximately 8:30 a.m.–12:30 p.m.), afternoon (approximately 3:00 p.m.–6:00 p.m.), and evening (approximately 8:00 p.m.–the end of the student's energies, but sometimes as late as midnight or beyond). For the most part, the students focus on Talmud for at least most of each of these three periods, though they might schedule some time for the study of Jewish law, Bible, *mussar* (religious ethics and self-development), or other disciplines of Torah study. In Hasidic institutions, students may dedicate significant time to studying the ideological and theological works of the particular Hasidic community. Advanced students, particularly those who are preparing for rabbinic certification, might dedicate a great deal of time and energy to systematic study of Jewish law, but students could not ignore Talmud entirely in their daily schedules.

---

[6]In the academic year 2006/2007 there were 44,395 young men registered in yeshivas in Israel, and 67,313 in kollels, according to Israel's Central Bureau of Statistics (see http://www.cbs.gov.il/reader/shnaton/templ_shnaton.html?num_tab=st08_10&CYear=2008).
Numbers for North America are much more difficult to come by, though yeshiva students certainly number in the tens of thousands. For now out-of-date numbers, see Helmreich (1982, pp. 48–49).

Most of this study occurs not in the classroom, but in the *beit midrash*, the study hall. A *beit midrash* is typically a large, book-lined room in which tens if not hundreds of teens and adults study in pairs, or *havrutot* (sing. *havruta*). Each *havruta* prepares a passage in the Talmud with its traditional commentaries, often spending hours if not days on a single page of the Talmud. The less-advanced students attend a class, or *shiur*, each day, often occupying about one hour of each *seder*, in which a teacher will review, expand on, and deepen the material they were to have covered on their own. As students become more advanced, *shiur* attendance will diminish, and they will be freer to simply study on their own (On yeshivot as educational institutions, though without particular reference to Haredi Judaism, see Halbertal and Hartman-Halbertal, 1998).

Generally, after a few years in yeshiva a student will be considered of marriageable age. Upon finding a suitable spouse, the young man will begin his studies in *kollel*, a yeshiva for married men. While largely identical to yeshivas in terms of pedagogic style and curriculum, a *kollel* student receives a stipend to help support his family, and he is more likely to study for rabbinical ordination in order to enable him to work as a teacher or religious functionary in the future.

Success as a yeshiva student helps the student climb the ladder of the Haredi social and cultural hierarchy and reach the status of the *talmid hakham*. An *illuy* (young and diligently studious genius) earns the respect of his peers and community, is more likely to find a prestigious teaching job in a yeshiva, and makes for a more desirable spouse and son-in-law, thus giving the young man better opportunities to marry into a respected and/or well-to-do family.

In North America, many advanced yeshivot allow if not encourage their students, after a year or two, to gain some kind of general education and/or vocational training. Students may attend undergraduate or graduate degree programs, more often than not in a field of study such as accounting that can translate directly into a job and income and which does not require in-depth study of the humanities or social sciences, fields that are deemed problematic from an ideological or theological perspective. Many yeshivas maintain arrangements with local universities or institutions of higher learning in which students attend night school and receive at least some college credit for their yeshiva studies.

For Haredi communities where college attendance remains completely taboo—a phenomenon that dominates the Haredi scene in Israel—the community may supply alternative vocational programs to provide training in computer programming, web design, or similar professions that would allow a young Haredi man to make a living without too much exposure to general education. Such programs exist in the United States (Heilman, 2006, Chapter 5) and are developing in Israel as well (Hakak, 2004; Lupo, 2003).

The Path to Yeshiva

While the research has not systematically examined early-childhood education for Haredi males (but see Heilman, 1992, Chapter 12), by way of generalization it is fair to say that kindergartens for Haredi boys are similar in structure to those of the general population, only they are same sex and impart knowledge related to Biblical stories, religious holidays, Jewish law and custom, and Haredi worldview. Actual text study can begin for boys as early as 3 years of age, often before the children can themselves read (Bilu, 2003). Further, Yoram Bilu has pointed to various rituals associated with male early childhood education—the child's first day in school and his first haircut, for example—which help to socialize Haredi Jewry's youngest boys into proper images of Haredi masculinity, particularly regarding the central role that text study is to play in their lives (Bilu, 2000; Bilu, 2003).

Elementary schools teach young Haredi students basic material in Bible, Jewish law, and other areas of religious study. In early years, the curriculum focuses more on Bible and ritual practice, but beginning generally in the fourth of fifth grades, male students begin to study Mishnah and later Talmud as well. Gradually, over the course of the coming years, Talmud will take up more and more of the schedule to the point that by the end of *yeshiva ketanah*/high school, it dominates the curriculum.

In the more isolationist groups, elementary age children attend a *heder* or *talmud Torah* type of school, dedicated almost exclusively to sacred studies, sometimes teaching only the most basic arithmetic and vernacular literacy. Among the less isolationist groups, elementary schools are modeled after a conventional elementary school, only with a dual curriculum. More often than not, a separate teacher, often a male *rebbe*, teaches sacred studies, usually in the morning, on the theory that students will concentrate better on the more important religious studies early in the day. In the afternoon, students will learn general studies, perhaps with a female or even non-observant teacher (Krakowski, 2008b). The curriculum downplays general education, often including only what is absolutely necessary to meet government requirements and/or provide students with enough background to function in the workaday world (Shaffir, 2004). The general education "is conceptually isolated and restricted in content, [and its] purpose is limited to the acquisition of basic skills necessary to function in daily life," rather than being seen as inherently valuable (Krakowski, 2008a, p. 18, though in some cases, general education can also be drafted into support of the group's religious worldview, Schweber, 2008).

For communities with less focus on general education, students advance from elementary *heder* to a *yeshiva ketanah*. This institution, often including a dormitory, introduces pre-teens and teens into the learning environment of a *beit midrash*, with less focus on formal classes, grades, and homework, and more focus on the study of Talmud in a *hevruta* format during *seder* in the *beit midrash*. In schools with more focus on general education, Haredi junior-high and high schools look much like a regular school in terms of structure and framework, with students attending departmentalized classes in various topics, again with sacred studies often in the morning and general education in the afternoon. Even here, however, as students advance they are likely to spend more time studying Talmud, and more of their time preparing for their Talmud lectures in a *beit midrash*. Whether they attend *yeshiva ketanah* or Haredi high schools, by the time young Haredi men reach their late teens, they enter the most highly valued educational institution, the yeshiva.

Female Education

One opinion in the Talmud (BT, Sotah, 21b) prohibits the teaching of Torah to females, which is part of the reason that, over the centuries, Jewish women generally received little or no formal education (Zolty, 1993). Today, however, the Haredi community most certainly does provide formal Torah education to its female members. However, if Haredi male education focuses on achieving intellectual independence in Talmud, and if the boy's educational path is designed to lead him to the yeshiva and its *beit midrash*, such is decidedly not the case for the education of Haredi females.

Formal religious education for Haredi women traces its roots to the growth of the Beth Jacob school system, originally founded by an anonymous young Cracow seamstress, Sara Schneirer, shortly after World War I. As East European Jewish society became less observant, and as the community could be less counted on to acculturate girls and women into observance, formal schooling became necessary for Orthodox females, despite the breach with tradition. While not all of East European Haredi Judaism backed Beth Jacob, and not all Haredi schools for girls associate with the movement (Granot, 2007–2008), Beth Jacob was the institution which popularized formal schooling for Orthodox girls, spreading from Schneirer's own one-woman school to a movement of some 35,000 European students at the outbreak of World War II (Weissman, 1995; Zolty, 1993). Gradually, the movement spread to Israel and the United States (Bechhofer, 2004; Weissman, 1993). While there is no official Beth Jacob organization with any kind of office or membership, a great many of today's schools associate themselves with the informal movement, and are associated with that movement by constituents and outsiders.

Beth Jacob and other Haredi girls' schools do not educate students to become *talmidot hakhamim*, female parallels of the male pious scholar. Instead, these schools are designed to provide girls and women with the basic religious literacy necessary to function and thrive in Haredi society, inculcate in them an attachment to certain kinds of spiritual experiences, and acculturate young women into the roles that they are assigned in the Haredi hierarchy. In a paradox that Tamar El-Or refers to as "educated and ignorant," Haredi women learn about the religious practices they are expected to do and about their roles in the family and community, but remain ignorant about the theory and larger textual tradition that construct their roles. Haredi women should take interest in formal study primarily to the extent that it enables them to fulfill their domestic tasks and earn a living to support their families and their husbands' Torah study (El-Or, 1994). From the youngest ages, Haredi girls are trained in domesticity and in Haredi notions of modesty (Yafeh, 2007; Yafeh, 2009; Zalcberg, 2009), and are prevented from achieving expertise in the fields of traditional Torah scholarship that would inevitably cast them into public roles that are deemed inappropriate (but, see El-Or, 2009, on female Haredi leadership).

In the absence of an image of female scholarship, and with Talmud study entirely unacceptable, Haredi female educational institutions, from kindergarten and onward, are structured much more like conventional schools than like the yeshivas and *batei midrash*. In this "school-like model," students attend compartmentalized classes on particular topics, do homework, take tests, receive formal report cards, and graduate on to higher classes. This pattern continues from elementary school, through high school, and on to post-high school seminaries. These school-like institutions are less likely than a *beit midrash* to encourage intellectual independence and expertise in primary sources, since the learning is mediated more thoroughly by the teacher. Furthermore, the curriculum focuses more on Bible, practical law, religious ideology, and the development of a pious personality, rather than the Talmud that dominates the boys' and men's curricula (though there remains significant variation and dispute among Haredi schools from different subgroups regarding how much Torah women should study and why, Granot, 2007–2008).

Upon completion of high school, many young Haredi women attend seminary, a post-high school program, sometimes with a full-time program of Torah study and character building, and sometimes with a teacher-training or vocational element as well. In any case, Haredi young women are expected, whether during or after seminary, to learn a trade or vocation so that they can provide financial support for their eventual husbands and families, ideally without undue exposure to the dangers of the outside culture (El-Or, 1994; Friedman, 1995; Shaffir, 2004). Indeed, according to official Haredi doctrine, particularly in Israel, the woman earns an equal share of her husband's credit for his Torah study if she provides for him and the family on a material and emotional level (Caplan, 2003).

Hence, teaching in religious schools, whether in the Haredi or the non-Haredi sector, is often considered an ideal job for a young Haredi woman, especially in Israel, and much Haredi vocational training for women focuses on preparing them to be teachers. Not only does this leave the young woman within a religious context during work hours, but the academic schedule allows a mother to be home with her (ideally large) family during mother and children's shared school vacations. In Israel and the more isolationist communities in North America, where college education is prohibited or frowned upon even for women, alternatives might include secretarial work, web design, bookkeeping, a small business run out of the home (cosmeticians, wig sales), or other jobs that do not require higher education (though degree-granting programs have recently opened for Haredi women in Israel in fields such as social work and other helping professions). In America, where college and even graduate school is acceptable or even desirable for some Haredi women, other options such as accounting or helping professions like speech pathology or occupational therapy are viewed by some as good educational options, particularly if workplaces allow for the flexible hours that are helpful for mothers.

Current Challenges

In the aftermath of World War II, few could have imagined the dramatic growth of the Haredi sector that took place over the second half of the twentieth century. At the time, Haredi Jewry (like much of Orthodoxy) was weak and defensive, perceived by many to be grasping at its last breaths before an inevitable demise in the face of the forces of modernization and history. Today, few would speak in such terms, with

Orthodoxy in general and Haredi Jewry in particular, thriving in the context of an outside culture perceived to be threatening (Caplan, 2008; Friedman, 2006). But challenges in general, and educational challenges in particular, remain.

Every educational system struggles to transmit information, knowledge, literacy, mastery of subject matter, and values, as well as those character traits that are part of the overt and hidden curriculum of a school. In this sense, Haredi education is no exception. Furthermore, these pedagogic matters are tied up with the perennial educational problems of discipline and classroom order. However, while the particular texts and values differ between Haredi and non-Haredi contexts, Haredi and non-Haredi schools share these classroom-centered pedagogic and disciplinary problems. Two other challenges to Haredi education are currently receiving the most public attention, both in internal Haredi discourse and outside of it: finances and drop-out.

The Haredi community, particularly in Israel, suffers from crippling poverty. The "society of learners"—in which a particularly high percentage of adult males study full time and in which men are barred or discouraged from college education or vocational training—leaves Haredi families without adequate sources of income. In addition, large Haredi families add expenses. In Israel, government subsidies moderate at least some of the poverty and help pay for schooling, but the greater rejection of general education and the ways in which men are confined to yeshiva by threat of military service make financial problems more severe (Berman, 2000; Gottlieb, 2007). North American Haredim often have more general education, vocational skills, and earning power, but the high cost of unsubsidized private education takes an enormous toll on families' budgets.

In Israel, Haredi parties have been hard at work lobbying for greater subsidies for families and educational projects. In America, the Haredi lobbyists advocate government spending for parochial schools, whether in the form of subsidizing general education or various vouchers and tax credits (to date, this lobbying has not met with much success, and it often irritates the mainstream American Jewish establishment that advocates strict church–state separation, Heilman, 2002, pp. 323–324). However, another more direct educational solution involves increasing earning power by opening Haredi-run and regulated vocational training institutions for both men and women (Heilman, 2006, Chapter 5; Hakak, 2004; Lupo, 2003). At the margins of Israeli Haredi society, some even advocate limited military service for some Haredi men to give them greater access to the job market (Hakak, 2003). The successes of these endeavors, particularly given the economic challenges currently facing the worldwide economy, can only be measured with hindsight that is not yet available.

The second challenge that currently occupies Haredi educational discourse is the problem of defection, youth who leave a Haredi life. Inevitably, a community that places such emphasis on boundary maintenance and isolation, yet lives as a minority within the larger and attractive culture, is going to find some of its members opting to leave and join the general culture, particularly in the context of a free democracy in which religious belief and practice are essentially voluntary. Indeed, the problem of defection has been one of Orthodoxy's central fears from its inception during the early parts of the nineteenth century. Obviously, successful educational experiences help maintain the allegiance of youth.

The problem of defection has several aspects, the first of which gets more attention from academic researchers and the second of which receives more attention in internal Haredi discourse. The first is what is referred to as *hazarah bashe'elah*, those who abandon their Haredi identities and lifestyles, adopting instead a secular or other non-Haredi identity (Barzilai, 2004). The second, referred to in English as Kids-at Risk and in Hebrew slang as *shabab* (Arabic for "youth"), involves youth who, despite often maintaining some connection to Haredi society, leave their educational institutions and get involved in delinquency, substance abuse, sexual promiscuity, and petty crime. Some eventually return to the straight and narrow of Haredi culture, while others eventually leave Haredi Judaism entirely. In any case, this has led to significant calls in the Haredi community on both sides of the ocean for increased attention to each student and his or her individuality. Further, concern over these issues has led to the creation of schools and educational programs designed to prevent drop-out or to encourage those who have already dropped out (Danziger, undated; Metropolitan Coordinating Council, 2003).

Conclusion: Is Communication Possible?

Recent years have witnessed a renaissance of academic interest in the Haredi community, particularly in Israel (Caplan & Sivan, 2003; Caplan & Stadler, 2009). Yet, scholars have not focused particular attention on Haredi education (but see Krakowski, 2008a, 2008b). In part this is because much educational research stems from a desire to improve practice. However, the Haredi community is at best ambivalent, if not actively hostile, to the academy and its intellectual methods (Caplan, 2003, 253–260). Hence, the Haredi community as a whole and its educational institutions in particular are not likely to produce a body of methodologically grounded reflective educational research. Research on Haredi education comes from outsiders.

Internal Haredi reflection on religious and educational practice takes a very different form from what university-trained academics find useful, and it is more likely to be couched in the language of traditional religion, ideology, and halakhah, rather than the language of the social sciences or philosophy of education. This colors what the academic community knows and does not know about Haredi education. Scholars tend to focus on topics currently on the agenda of the academic community: the history of institutions such as yeshivas or Beth Jacob schools, construction of gender identity, Haredi relations to the Israeli army and to the workplace, and (at least in Israel) how government budgets are spent in the Haredi sector. But the academic community knows little of the kinds of things that might be most useful for Haredi educators: effective and ineffective pedagogic methods, best practices, level of Haredi schoolchildren's knowledge of the curriculum, effective teacher training, etc.

This lack of communication stems from the vastly different worldviews and vocabularies of Haredi educators and their counterparts outside the Haredi community. By identifying Torah study as the very meaning of existence and by spending so much cultural capital on boundary maintenance and isolation, Haredi society deliberately sets itself apart from others, even from well-meaning and serious Jewish educators and scholars. Non-Haredi educators and scholars, even those most sympathetic to Haredi Judaism, often treat the Haredi community as an anthropological or historical case study. Critical distance means approaching Haredi Judaism and its education as an Other that needs to be "translated" in order to be understood. Could the Haredi community gain some self-understanding by appreciating what the scholarly community has learned? Could it gain some educational wisdom by applying social–scientific research tools to its own institutions? Could the non-Haredi Jewish world gain something by a less-distanced appreciation of Haredi dedication to Torah study and to a passionate and encompassing Jewish life? Perhaps, but at the moment I suspect that the cultural gaps between Haredi educators and the academic community are too large for widespread cooperation.

References

Aran, G. (2003). The Haredi body: Chapters of a developing ethnography (Hebrew). In Caplan, K. & Sivan, E. (Eds.) *Israeli Haredim: Involvement without assimilation?*. (Hebrew) (pp. 99–133). Tel Aviv: Van Leer Institute and Hakibbutz Hameuchad Publishing House.

Barzilai, S. (2004). *To storm a hundred gates: A journey into the world of the newly secular.* (Hebrew). Tel Aviv: Yediot Aharonot and Sifrei Hemed.

Bechhofer, S. 2004. Ongoing constitution of identity and educational mission of Bais Yaakov Schools: The structuration of an organizational field as the unfolding of discursive logics, Ph.D. Dissertation, Northwestern University.

Berman, D. (2000). Sect, sacrifice, and subsidy: An economist's view of ultra-orthodox Jews. *The Quarterly Journal of Economics*, *115*, 904–952.

Bilu, Y. (2000). Circumcision, the first haircut, and torah: Ritual and male identity in the ultraorthodox community of Israel. In M. Ghoussoub & E. Sinclair-Webb (Eds.), *Imagined masculinities: Male identity in the modern Middle East* (pp. 33–64). London: Saqi Books.

Bilu, Y. (2003). From milah (circumcision) to milah (word): Male identity and rituals of childhood in the Jewish ultraorthodox community. *Ethos*, *31*(2), 172–203.

Breuer, M. (2003). *Tents of torah: The yeshiva, its structure and history.* (Hebrew). Jerusalem: Zalman Shazar Center.

Brown, B. (2005). The doctrine of da'at torah: Three stages. (Hebrew) *Derekh HaRuah*, *2*, 537–600.

Caplan, K. (2001). Israeli Haredi society and the repentance (*Hazarah Biteshuvah*) movement. *Jewish Studies Quarterly*, *8*(4), 369–399.

Caplan, K. (2003). The internal popular discourse of Israeli Haredi women. *Archives de Sciences Sociales des Religions*, *123*, 77–101.

Caplan, K. (2006). Haredim and western culture: A View from both sides of the ocean. In M. Litvak (Ed.), *Middle Eastern societies and the west: Accommodation or clash of civilizations* (pp. 269–288). Tel Aviv: Moshe Dayan Center for Middle Eastern and African Studies.

Caplan, K. (2008). The ever-dying denomination: American orthodoxy, 1824–1965. In M. L. Raphael (Ed.), *The Columbia history of Jews and Judaism in America* (pp. 167–188). New York: Columbia University Press.

Caplan, K., & Sivan, E. (Eds.). (2003). *Israeli Haredim: Involvement without assimilation?*. (Hebrew). Tel Aviv: Van Leer Institute and Hakibbutz Hameuchad Publishing House.

Caplan, K., & Stadler, N. (Eds.). (2009). *Leadership and authority in Israeli Haredi society*. (Hebrew). Tel Aviv: Van Leer Institute and Hakibbutz Hameuchad Publishing House.

Danzger, H. (1989). *Returning to Judaism: The contemporary revival of orthodox Judaism*. New Haven, CT: Yale University Press.

Danziger, Y. (undated). *The incidence of at-risk youth in the orthodox Jewish community of Brooklyn, New York*. New York: City of New York Department of Youth and Community Development.

El-Or, T. (1994). *Educated and ignorant: Ultraorthodox Jewish women and their world*. Reinner: Boulder, CO.

El-Or, T. (2009). "All Rights Reserved for Anat": Great and small female leaders in the religion and repentance industries (Hebrew). In Caplan, K. & Stadler, N. (Eds.). *Leadership and authority in Israeli Haredi society*. (Hebrew) (pp. 129–163). Tel Aviv: Van Leer Institute and Hakibbutz Hameuchad Publishing House.

Finkelman, Y. (2007). Tradition and innovation in American Haredi parenting literature. In D. Zisenwein (Ed.), *Innovation and change in Jewish education* (pp. 37–61). Tel Aviv: Tel Aviv University.

Finkelman, Y. (2009) Relationships between parents and schools in Haredi popular literature in the United States. In A. Pomson & H. Deitcher (Ed.), *Jewish day schools, Jewish communities: A reconsideration* (pp. 237–254). Oxford and Portland, OR: Littman Library of Jewish Civilization.

Friedman, M. (1991). *The Haredi (ultra-orthodox) society: Sources, trends and processes*. (Hebrew). Jerusalem: The Jerusalem Institute for Israel Studies.

Friedman, M. (1995). The ultra-orthodox woman. (Hebrew). Y. Atzmon (Ed.), *Jewish women in Mediterranean communities* (Hebrew). (pp. 273–290). Jerusalem: Zalman Shazar Center.

Friedman, M. (2006). "For the miracles": The prosperity of the "Torah world" (Yeshivot and Kollels) in Israel. (Hebrew). E. Etkes (Ed.), *Yeshivas and houses of study* (Hebrew). (pp. 431–442). Jerusalem: Zalman Shazar Center and Dinur Center.

Friedman, M., & Heilman., S. (1991) Religious fundamentalism and religious Jews: The case of the Haredim. In M. Marty & R. S. Appleby (Eds.), *Fundamentalisms Observed* (pp. 197–264). Chicago and London: University of Chicago Press.

Glaubman, R., & Lifshitz., H. (2001). Ultra orthodox Jewish teachers' self-efficacy and willingness for inclusion of pupils with special needs. *European Journal of Special Needs Education, 16*(3), 207–223.

Gottlieb, D. (2007). *Poverty and labor market behavior in the ultra-orthodox population in Israel*. Jerusalem: Van Leer Institute (available at http://mpra.ub.uni-muenchen.de/4024/1/MPRA_paper_4024.pdf, viewed April, 2009).(Hebrew).

Granot, T. (2007–2008). Women's status and the education of girls according to the Hasidic Rebbe (*Admor*) Rabbi Yequtiel Yehudah Halberstam of Sanz-Klausenburg. (Hebrew) *Hagut, 8*, 37–86.

Hakak, Y. (2003). *Yeshiva learning and military training: An encounter between two cultural models*. (Hebrew). Jerusalem: Floersheimer Institute for Policy Studies.

Hakak, Y. (2004). *Vocational training for ultra-orthodox men*. (Hebrew). Jerusalem: Floersheimer Institute for Policy Studies.

Hakak, Y. (2005). *Spirituality and worldliness in Lithuanian Yeshivas*. (Hebrew). Jerusalem: Floersheimer Institute for Policy Studies.

Halbertal, M., & Hartman Halbertal, T. (1998). The yeshiva. In A. Oksenberg Rorty (Ed.), *Philosophers on education: New historical perspectives* (pp. 458–469). London: Routledge.

Heilman, S. (1992). *Defenders of the faith: Inside ultra-orthodox Jewry*. Berkeley, Los Angeles, and London: University of California Press.

Heilman, S. (2002). Haredim and the public square: The nature of the social contract. In A. Mittleman, J. D. Sarna, & R. Licht (Eds.), *In Jewish polity and American civil society* (pp. 311–336). Lanham, MA: Rowman and Littlefield.

Heilman, S. (2006). *Sliding to the right: The contest for the future of American Jewish orthodoxy.* Berkeley, Los Angeles, London: University of California Press.

Helmreich, W. (1982). *The world of the Yeshiva: An intimate portrait of orthodox Jewry.* New York: Free Press.

Kaplan, L. (1992) Daas torah: A modern conception of rabbinic authority. In M. Sokol (Ed.), *Rabbinic authority and personal autonomy* (pp. 1–60). Northvale, NJ and London: Jason Aaronson.

Krakowski, M. 2008a. Isolation and integration: Education and worldview formation in ultra-orthodox Jewish Schools, Ph.D. Dissertation, Northwestern University.

Krakowski, M. (2008b). Dynamics of isolation and integration in ultra-orthodox schools: The epistemological implications of using rebbeim as secular studies teachers. *Journal of Jewish Education, 74*(3), 317–342.

Kramer, D. Z. (1984). *The day school and Torah Umesorah: The seeding of traditional Judaism in America.* New York: Yeshiva University Press.

Lamm, N. (1999). *The Religious thought of Hasidism: Text and commentary.* New York: Yeshiva University Press.

Lupo, J. (2003). *A shift in Haredi society: Vocational training and academic studies.* (Hebrew). Jerusalem: Floersheimer Institute for Policy Studies.

Metropolitan coordinating council on Jewish poverty. (2003). *Teenage orthodox Jewish girls at risk: Study and recommendations.* New York.

Nadler, A. (1999). *The faith of the Mithnagdim: Rabbinic responses to Hasidic rapture.* Baltimore, MD: Johns Hopkins University Press.

Ravitzky, A. (Ed.). (2006). *Shas: Cultural and ideological perspectives.* (Hebrew). Tel Aviv: Am Oved.

Rosenak, M. (1993) Jewish fundamentalism in Israeli education. In M. Marty & R. S. Appleby (Eds.), *Fundamentalisms and society* (pp. 374–414). Chicago and London: University of Chicago.

Safer, L. B. 2003. The Construction of identity through text: Sixth and seventh grade girls in an ultra-orthodox Jewish Day School, Ed.D. dissertation, University of Pennsylvania.

Schweber, S. (2008). "'Here there is no why': Holocaust education in a Lubavitch girls' yeshiva. *Jewish Social Studies, 14*(2), 156–185.

Shaffir, W. (2004). Secular studies in a Hassidic enclave: "What do we need it for?" *Jewish Journal of Sociology, 46*, 59–77.

Schiffer, V. (1998). *The Haredi educational system: Allocation, regulation and control.* (Hebrew). Jerusalem: Floersheimer Institute for Policy Studies.

Schick, M. 2005. *A census of Jewish Day Schools in the United States, 2003–2004.* Avi Chai.

Schneller, R. (1980). Continuity and change in ultra-orthodox education. *Jewish Journal of Sociology, 22*(1), 35–45.

Sebba, L., & Schiffer., V. (1998). Tradition and the right to education: The case of the ultra-orthodox community in Israel. In D. Gillian & L. Sebba (Eds.), *Children's rights and traditional values* (pp. 160–193). Dartmouth: Ashgate.

Silber, M. (1992). The emergence of ultra-orthodoxy: The invention of a tradition. In J. Wertheimer (Ed.), The Uses of Tradition: Jewish Continuity in the Modern Era (pp. 23–84). New York and Jerusalem: Jewish Theological Seminary of America.

Sivan, E. The enclave culture. In M. Marty & R. S. Appleby (Eds.), *Fundamentalisms comprehended* (pp. 11–63). Chicago and London: University of Chicago Press.

Stadler, N. (2009). *Yeshiva fundamentalism: Piety, gender, and resistance in the ultra-orthodox Jewish world.* New York and London: New York University Press.

Stampfer, S. (1998). Hasidic Yeshivot in Interwar Poland. *Polin, 11*, 3–24.

Stampfer, S. (2005). *The development of the Lithuanian Yeshiva.* (Hebrew). Jerusalem: Zalman Shazar Center.

Weissman, D. (1993). *The education of religious girls in Jerusalem during the British mandate: The establishment and development of five educational strategies.* (Hebrew), Ph.D. diss., The Hebrew University of Jerusalem.

Weissman, D. (1995). Bais Ya'akov as an innovation in Jewish women's education: A contribution to the study of education and social change. *Studies in Jewish Education, 7,* 278–299.

Yafeh, O. (2007). The time in the body: Cultural constructions of femininity in ultraorthodox kindergartens. *Ethos, 35*(4), 516–553.

Yafeh, O. 2009. Women's pedagogic authority and its limits: Education and psychology, text and practice in ultraorthodox girls kindergartens (Hebrew). In Caplan and Stadler, 2009, 31–56.

Zalcberg, S. (2009). Channels of information about menstruation and sexuality among Hasidic adolescent girls. *Nashim, 17,* 60–88.

Zolty, S. P. (1993). *"And all of your children shall be learned": Women and the study of Torah in Jewish law and history.* Northvale, NJ: Aaronson.

Section Four: Geographical

Introduction

This final section of the International Handbook reveals the extent to which Jewish education emerges at an intersection between the global and the local. The 12 chapters in this section, written by practitioners of Jewish education, Jewish educational researchers, and scholars from cognate fields of Jewish studies, provide an opportunity to explore ultimate questions in the social scientific study of Jewry regarding the influence of factors in the local environment and of transnational Jewish cultural patterns on the norms, modalities, and goals of Jewish education. Such questions, familiar to historians, sociologists, and anthropologists of Jewry, are rarely taken up by researchers and practitioners of Jewish education because of the isolated character of their work, within their subfields, and within the national contexts in which they labor. The Handbook—and particularly this section—makes it possible to ask such questions; indeed, we hope that the following chapters may inspire a new commitment to the cross-cultural study of Jewish education.

While other sections of the Handbook gravitate mostly around the State of Israel and the US, the contributors to this section provide an opportunity to appreciate nuances in communities that lie outside the orbit of these two magnetic poles. What emerges is a sense of the varieties of Jewish education; how the push and pull of localized forces—community demographics, history (and particularly the twin upheavals of the Shoah and communism), the relationships between church and state, and those between Jews and the popular majority—have birthed diverse narratives of Jewish education.

As will be seen, the opportunities and modalities for Jewish education in the Netherlands, Eastern Europe, and parts of Latin America have been both constrained and enlivened by the small number of potential clients in these places, especially when compared with what is possible or not possible in larger Diaspora communities or in the State of Israel. By the same token, the goals of Jewish education look different in communities decimated by the Shoah and/or by communism, compared with those such as Canada and Australia built in large part by Holocaust survivors, or those like the UK and the US that have experienced relatively uninterrupted institutional development over more than 100 years. No less importantly, the place of parochial Jewish education in public life, and of Jews as a religious/ethnic minority, has also produced some of the sharpest differences between the supply of and demand for Jewish education, as seen, for example, in the differences in how Jewish day school education is incorporated and conceived in France, Russia, and the UK.

Yet, for all of the differences brought in to view in this section, these chapters provide evidence, first, of certain phenomena that challenge most if not all Jewish communities whatever their circumstances, and, second, of a general tendency to pursue certain common educational solutions to these challenges. Thus, in all Diaspora Jewish communities, there are doubts about the sustainability of systems for intensive Jewish education because of a declining demographic base outside the ultra-orthodox sector, and because of doubts about the capacity of these systems to graduate future generations of knowledgeable educational leaders. These concerns have led almost everywhere to a concentration of investment in what Wertheimer calls in his chapter, "the most immersive forms of Jewish education": all-day Jewish schools, summer camps, and Israel trips; these being the few educational experiences that are viewed as having a better than even chance of sustaining Jewish identification and cultural creativity. In turn, this narrowing tendency has intensified global concerns about the financial burdens placed on the broader Jewish community by increased dependence on such programs. As the two chapters concerned with Jewish education in Israel show, even in the Jewish state, this same cycle of concerns plays out, only with larger sums of money at stake.

If, at the start of the twenty-first century, all-day Jewish schooling constitutes in many communities the educational medium of choice for providing intensive Jewish education to young people, a number of chapters demonstrate that this state of affairs has come about as a result of sharply different processes in different places. Compare, for example, two chapters that carefully analyze the rise of day school education. David Mendelsson, in his chapter on Jewish education in the UK, makes evident that acceptance of Jewish day schools by British parents since World War II occurred most directly in response to cultural and demographic changes in English society and to changes in government educational policy that democratized state schools. The turn to day schools, such that today more than 50% of Jewish children ages 5–18 attend such schools, was not, what he calls, "internally driven," it was an "unintended side effect" brought about in large part because of parental flight from state schools.

The title of Forgasz and Munz's chapter on Australia, "The Jewel in the Crown of Jewish Education," indicates how different was the view of Jewish day schools in that country. Although these schools have maintained their appeal over the course of more than half a century by making the best use of government assistance for independent schools and by offering a quality private school education, their founding was galvanized and then sustained by waves of Jewish immigrants first from post-war Europe and then more latterly from South Africa who have displayed "a strong desire to replicate the intensity of the Jewish life" they experienced in the places from which they came. These internal drivers explain some of the highest rates of day school enrollment in the world.

It is fascinating to compare these two chapters with the sections of Bouganim's chapter on France that are also concerned with day school education. In all three contexts, the government is deeply implicated in the certification and supervision of Jewish school programs, and provides substantial support for Jewish schools. But the cultural context in France—where there is such a contested relationship between religion and the state—has until recent times strongly deterred the widespread development of parochial Jewish schooling in that country. These conflicted commitments produced one of the most fascinating (but poorly studied) paradoxes of Jewish education over the last 100 years whereby the Paris-based Alliance Israelite Universelle—a quintessentially French organization—supported the largest Jewish school system in the world for more than half a century before it was prepared to support even a single school in France.

The peculiarities of the French context provide a pristine setting for observing how the development of Jewish education is so much colored by local context. In France, where the regular school year is just 140 days long, and is broken up by frequent vacation periods, there is vivid evidence of how Jewish education abhors a vacuum. Informal Jewish education, and especially Jewish Scouting, has filled the available time creating an unusually vital environment that has been ahead of its time both in its commitment to environmentalism and in creating a shared space for the religious and secular. It is hard to find a parallel to this organization anywhere else in the world.

It is geographic *singularities* such as this that make the final section of the Handbook such stimulating material. Repeatedly, readers will find themselves wondering what might be inferred or applied from a particular instance to other, radically different, settings. Take, for example, Lerner-Spectre's chapter on Paideia, the European Institute for Jewish Studies in Sweden. The author details the development of a program that responds to a phenomenon she coins "dis-assimilation," a pattern in which "young adults who, before the fall of communism, were unaware of their Jewish heritage but who, in confronting this disclosure, choose to identify themselves as Jews." She asks the reader to consider that the kind of education offered by Paedeia, one that is distinctly literary and intellectual, can have implications for contemporary Jewish adult education outside of Europe.

Similar questions about applicability are provoked by Bar-Shalom and Ascher-Shai in their chapter on innovations in secular schooling in Israel. The cases they present from schools in Israel derive from the collision of Jewish and non-Jewish immigrants with the religiously polarized Israeli school system. These collisions may be a unique outcome of the attempted absorption of such diverse minorities into the only public Jewish school system in the world, but, as in the best instances of case study, these particular cases provoke more general questions. They invite one to wonder about the potential forms and content of secular Jewish education, and its capacity to engage Diaspora communities that seek to make intensive Jewish education attractive and meaningful to liberal and secular Jews.

In parallel fashion, Gross's chapter on State Religious Education in Israel reconstructs the competing ideologies, political, and educational worldviews that have shaped this substantial system. She leaves the reader in no doubt as to the sociological significance of these schools as both shapers and markers of the developing Jewish state. Though a unique Israeli phenomenon, the dilemmas and debates she interprets concerning educational goals, the relationships between Jewish and general studies, the profile of educational leadership, and the considerations in student selection, echo strongly the more localized balance of forces and beliefs that shape modern Orthodox Jewish education in any number of communities around the world.

Goldstein and Ganiel, in their chapter on Latin America, similarly argue for the application of conceptual models across diverse environments. In fact, in pioneering fashion given how little research there has been on Jewish education in Latin America, they highlight how different Jewish education looks in the largest communities of the region, in Argentina, Brazil, and Mexico. And yet, they advance a set of models—pragmatic change, spiritual renewal, and insularity—that can be observed as common responses to the forces of democratization and globalization across the continent. Further, they argue strongly that these models can help make sense of developments in Jewish education elsewhere.

By contrast, Michael Brown, with an historian's sensitivity to the particular, demonstrates how, in Toronto and Montreal, the vigor and stability of Jewish education derives from special features in the Canadian context: Canada's bi-national structure; public attitudes to religion and state; the Jewish community's relatively recent arrival; and a level of antisemitism higher than in the neighboring US. These factors have produced institutional diversity, high levels of participant enrollment, innovative research and strong central education bureaus. Ironically, while it will be difficult, as Brown implies, to reproduce such outcomes elsewhere (especially south of the Canadian border), he indicates that in recent years these distinctive strengths have been eroded by forces that are more global in nature.

These global forces are detailed by Wertheimer in his chapter on the US. It seems, in fact, that the US is ground zero for many of the corrosive trends which Brown identifies. Wertheimer points to heightened consumerism on the part of families, rising rates of intermarriage, and severe time constraints limiting the availability of children and their families. These trends have led to a decline in the numbers of children receiving a Jewish education and to a shift toward providing immersive educational forms to a shrinking minority of consumers. In turn, these developments have driven a wave of experimentation funded in large part by private foundations. Employing a broad canvas, Wertheimer shows how these trends account for efforts such as Birthright Israel, the remaking of Hillel, the encouragement of day school education, the expansion of Jewish residential camping, and the training of educational leadership.

A mark of the globalization of Jewish educational patterns is best appreciated by comparing these American trends with what has emerged over the last 20 years in the Former Soviet Union. Of course, the social and historical backdrop in Russia and parts of Eastern Europe could not be more different, and as Markus and Farbman show in their chapter, there are some especially challenging problems that derive from the Communist past, most obviously the absence of the synagogue as a support for Jewish community, and also a residual difficulty in collecting reliable data about the community. And yet despite these differences, some of the educational foci for community investment in the FSU today bear an uncanny similarity to those in America. These include a focus on supporting all-day Jewish schools, Birthright programs, leadership training initiatives, and Hillel activities. Reading across chapters, it seems that one explanation for these commonalities is the dependence on common funders and providers, but this is just one of many hypotheses that would benefit from further research.

If and how communities might be created anew is the central thread that connects the chapter on the FSU with chapters about smaller Jewish communities in Europe and about the Netherlands. In Eastern Europe, as Steve Israel indicates, the residential camp—a total Jewish environment for children, young adults, and for families—seems to have been more successful than any other educational intervention. Such camps have served as incubators for resuscitating communities that have lost much of their memory and most of the organs of healthy Jewish life. The dilemma, as Israel writes, is whether there is a reasonable balance between the resources invested and the benefits involved. He asks, if so much has to be rebuilt and for so few people, might there be better uses for what are always limited financial resources?

As van het Hoofd shows, the Jewish community in the Netherlands took a different path after emerging from the decimation of the Shoah. Before the war, or at least until an influx of refugees from Germany in 1938, the Dutch Jewish community, one of the most acculturated and well-integrated Jewish communities in Europe, largely turned its back on the availability of state aid for denominational schools, an opportunity seized by both Catholics and Protestants. After the war, a handful of schools were opened to serve a ravaged community. And yet, more than 50 years later, enrollment levels continue to be minimal, barely different from what they were before 1938. Certainly, they do not stand comparison with the situation in Belgium, a country in which Jews were no less traumatized by the Holocaust, but where today 90% of Jewish children attend day schools. It seems that in the Netherlands the Jewish community's commitment to integration runs very deep no matter what traumas it has endured.

This conclusion confirms a deep current that runs through all of the chapters in this section. While Jewish education is an international enterprise and this section of the Handbook provides strong confirmation that it is, in the final analysis it is a local endeavor. Both its form and content are indelibly shaped by where it is located. To be properly understood, those localities must be encountered in all of their rich detail, as in the chapters to come.

Helena Miller
Lisa D. Grant
Alex Pomson

American-Jewish Education in an Age of Choice and Pluralism

Jack Wertheimer

With its multi-billion dollar budget, thousands of schools and informal-educational settings, and expanding scope, stretching from early childhood to adult education, the sprawling field of Jewish education in the United States defies easy generalization. At times, it has been the object of severe criticism for real or imagined failings; and at other times it has been lauded for great accomplishments, sometimes earned, other times not. Built over a long period of time by dedicated cadres of champions, both professional educators and lay leaders, the field today is the product both of experiments conducted by past generations and of recent initiatives to address emerging needs. The one constant has been the voluntaristic ethos of American society, which encourages the formation of different kinds of associations, even as it favors none. Unlike the situation in some other countries where government funding is made available for particular types of programs, complete separation of church and state in the United States has meant that Jewish-educational programs depend entirely upon the creativity and sustained support of Jews.

Given these circumstances, the field has confronted a set of perennial challenges as follows:

- Adapting to continually shifting demographic and social realities
- Responding to parental and communal expectations
- Rebalancing the mix of vehicles delivering a Jewish education
- Setting goals and devising proper educational content
- Working with limited financial resources
- Recruiting and retaining personnel

These concerns continue to animate discussions in the field during the present era, no less than they did in the past. To highlight what is new, I will compare contemporary concerns to the issues of 50 years ago. In so doing, my purpose is not to lament the loss of a golden age, for in truth, Jewish-educational programs in that period

---

J. Wertheimer (✉)
Jewish Theological Seminary, New York, NY, USA
e-mail: jawertheimer@jtsa.edu

were often shallow or misguided. Rather such a comparison will set into bold relief just how much the field has changed, even as similar challenges have persisted.

New Demographic and Social Realities

The postwar era, like today, was a time of massive transformation, with two primary social dynamics driving change: one was the Jewish baby boom, which for Jews began in the early 1940s and took off after the war; the second was an exodus from the cities to newly built sub-divisions on the suburban frontier. In short order, a vast army of Jewish families, many of whom had little experience with synagogue life and only a minimal Jewish education engaged in the great civic activity of the time: like their fellow Americans, Jews joined a house of worship in record numbers, but unlike others, they did so primarily in order to enroll their children in religious schooling.

As a consequence, the setting for Jewish education shifted irrevocably from communal institutions to congregations, and the latter were inundated with seemingly inexorable waves of families entrusting them to serve as the primary Jewish educators of the baby-boom generation.[1] According to one informed estimate, roughly 600,000 young people were enrolled in formal-educational programs by the early 1960s, with the overwhelming majority in congregational schools (American Association for Jewish Education, 1976, p. 12). This, in turn, created great demand for teaching and other personnel to deliver a Jewish education, the construction of classroom space, new curricula and textbooks, expanded synagogue budgets, input from denominational education offices, and, in some communities, school and teacher certification.

A half-century later, the scene looks quite different in important ways. Despite the fact that the total Jewish population has remained stable (or according to some has even increased), enrollments in formal Jewish education by school-age children have declined significantly, hovering somewhere around 460,000 students by the end of the first decade of the twenty-first century.[2] While some forms of Jewish education continue to expand, the challenge in most communities is to cope with contraction, rather than massive growth, as was the case 50 years ago.

Moreover, as Jews today are settling at an ever greater remove from centers of population, a great many schools are enrolling small student bodies. Nearly 40% of day schools enroll 100 or fewer students; supplementary schools tend to be even smaller, with 60% enrolling fewer than 100 children.[3] In short, today's geographic mobility is bringing a diffusion of student populations in contrast to the shift to

---

[1] The great Jewish suburban migration was studied contemporaneously by Sklare & Greenblum, 1967. For two more recent views, see Prell, 2007, and Wertheimer, 2005b.

[2] The latest census has enumerated some 228,000 students between preschool and grade 12 in day schools (Schick, 2009, p. 5). And a census of supplementary schools estimated an enrollment of some 230,000 students from grades 1 to 12 (Wertheimer, 2008, p. 9).

[3] Day-school figures are based on Schick, 2005, p. 21. Supplementary school figures are from Wertheimer, 2008, p. 14. Forty percent of supplementary schools enroll 50 or fewer students.

suburbia which represented geographic mobility by a large body of Jews moving together to the same areas. The delivery of a good Jewish education to such a far-flung student population poses a new challenge to educators.

How is the field responding to these demographic shifts? To date, little systematic thought has been given to the overall enrollment decline. Rather than tackle the larger issue, smaller stop-gap solutions are in place: in some localities, day schools are merging or dropping their allegiance to a single denominational identity in favor of a communal orientation; some synagogues are also merging their supplementary schools in response to lower enrollments, at times joining with other synagogues of the same denominational orientation, and at times with ones of a different religious movement. Some institutions are also offering inducements to lure parents. Several national and local foundations are underwriting tuition reduction programs to help families stay in the system and induce others to enroll their children.[4] Some effort is now underway by Jewish residential camps to offer scholarship funds in order to draw thus far unengaged families.

We only are beginning to see responses to the heightened population diffusion in the form of more talk about harnessing the Internet for online or video instruction. A program funded by the AVI CHAI Foundation offers the services of Jerusalem-based teachers to nine separate day schools in the United States, with the latter providing a teacher to be present during the video-cast instruction.[5] A very different model has been founded by the Institute for Southern Jewish Life to address small supplementary school programs far from large centers of Jewish life. Here distances are bridged through the use of a common curriculum devised for small schools in southern towns and cities and experiments with traveling "education fellows" who advise local teachers, a model that could be copied in other regions.[6] It remains to be seen whether other such efforts will address the widely scattered population of students through the creation of consortia, circuit-riding educators, regional-education centers, and retreat programs bringing learners together from distant places.

Parental and Communal Expectations

Shifting expectations have accompanied the new social patterns. In line with so much else in American life, Jewish education is increasingly seen as a commodity and families have assumed the role of consumers. This means, in the first instance, that they sift carefully through the options available and demand choices. Where once it was natural for parents to enroll all of their children in the nearest

---

[4]The Samis foundation has played this role in Seattle. For a summary of some early programs, including that of AVI CHAI, see JESNA, 1999. More recently, David Magerman offered such tuition assistance to day schools in Philadelphia (Schwartzman, 2009).

[5]On the remote learning, see http://www.avi-chai.org/bin/en5caf.html?enPage=BlankPage& enDisplay=view&enDispWhat=Zone&enZone=JLPC. For a description of the experience with one school in Charleston, see Lookstein 2009, p. 5.

[6]The educational work of the Institute is outlined at its website, http://www.isjl.org/education/index.html

congregational school of their denominational preference, it has now become far more common for parents to select a different educational vehicle for each of their children. It is not unusual for parents to enroll one child in a supplementary school, another in a day school, and hire a private tutor for a third child, all in the service of finding just the right fit for each child. The same may hold true for the informal-educational experiences parents select, with a residential summer camp experience chosen for some children and Israel experiences or youth movement activities for others.[7]

To add to the complexity, educational choices for children also are increasingly entangled with the needs of parents. When deciding on a day school for their children, parents are likely to consider not only the values and orientation of a particular school to which they want to expose their children, but also whether the school will meet the parents' own needs. Increasingly, day schools and supplementary schools have been pressed to attend to the Jewish educational and communal needs of parents both because they want to enlist parents as partners in the enterprise of educating their children and also because parents are looking to the school for their own continuing Jewish education. Parents also expect to find a worthwhile peer group within the school's parent body (Pomson, 2007, pp. 101–142; Pomson & Schnoor, 2008).

Even as schools must contend with these new parental expectations, they are also held accountable for the outcome of their programs in relation to the Jewish identities of the children they educate. In this sense they have become victims of rising communal expectations. Beginning already in the 1980s, a movement to strengthen Jewish education began to sweep American-Jewish life, which only accelerated in response to heightened worries over long-term "Jewish continuity" generated by the 1990 National Jewish Population Study, with its dramatic evidence of spiraling intermarriage rates. Suddenly, Jewish education, which had long been treated by communal leaders as a stepchild (most obviously by the general skittishness of federations of Jewish philanthropy when it came to investing in formal Jewish education) was pushed front and center, with attendant claims for its efficacy in reversing assimilatory trends. And indeed, much evidence has suggested strong correlations between intensive and diverse Jewish educational experiences for young people and their eventual later adult commitments to Jewish life. But as more money has been channeled to certain types of educational programs, they have also faced higher standards of accountability: What do graduates of a program actually learn and experience? How do educational experiences translate into adult commitment? And most urgently, if more money has been channeled to Jewish education, can we document the impact of that investment?[8]

Expectations of a different sort have risen as a result of the inclusion of intermarried families in programs of Jewish education. With the dramatic upward spike

---

[7] This is central to the thesis of several essays included in Wertheimer, 2007b.

[8] Foundations have been the most likely to pose these questions publicly, but, more generally, funders of all kinds have linked their giving to successful outcomes.

of intermarriage rates, proponents of outreach have demanded of Jewish institutions that they invest in educational programs for intermarried parents that completely integrate children whose parents are intermarried. This demographic shift alone confronts educators with dramatically new circumstances because they cannot expect all children to come from a home that unambiguously transmits a single religious identity and because non-Jewish parents now become participants in the educational process, and they may come with a distinctive understanding of what religious education ought to impart. As one study has put it,

> The contrast in outlook of Jewish-born parents and those not born Jewish [is] often quite dramatic, perhaps best understood as an emphasis upon a Judaism of family and festivals as compared to a Judaism of faith and feelings. (Wertheimer, 2005a, p. 22)

The operative assumption has been that Jewish education and other experiences will engage this population in Jewish life and win over the children. But these great hopes also come with a price in the form of heightened expectations of success, even though no experiment of such a magnitude has ever been tried in the past and there is no way to know whether Jewish education can accomplish what outreach proponents demand (Olitzky & Golin, 2008, pp. 94–96). Put in quantitative terms, a recent study of educational programs under the auspices of the Reform movement found that nearly half the children (49%) have one parent who had not been raised as a Jew—i.e., had either converted from another religion or are not Jewish (Katzew, 2008, p. 1). This novel challenge, moreover, has been addressed thus far with barely any special training provided to educators, no new curricula geared to this specific population and no additional financial resources.

Responding to Great Expectations

All of these shifts have pushed and pulled Jewish educational institutions in new directions. The consumerist orientation of parents coupled with declining numbers of children, for example, has required all kinds of educational programs to compete, perhaps more intensively than ever before. Educators of necessity have become marketers of their products, pitching the benefits of what they offer as compared to other educational products. Advocacy, thus, has risen in importance. To help them, a number of new national umbrella organizations have appeared on the scene since the mid-1990s, mainly established by groups of concerned funders, and all designed to make the case for a particular form of Jewish education and to offer guidance to educators seeking to improve their marketing work. Among the new organizations are one for day schools, the Partnership for Excellence in Jewish Education (PEJE); supplementary schools, the Partnership for Effective Learning and Innovative Education (PELIE); the Foundation for Jewish Camp (FJC); and the Jewish Early Childhood Education Initiative (JECEI). In addition to their advocacy role, these organizations also recruit funders and champions for their particular fields and offer services to programs in their domains.

Still another response to the new consumerism has been a vast expansion in the number of educational providers. To be sure, some of this also stems from the voluntaristic American model, which tends to encourage the spawning of ever more institutions, the heightened emphasis on attending to the diversity within the American-Jewish population and the ever-wider dispersal of Jewish populations to remote areas. As a result, the number of day schools and supplementary schools continues to rise, even though the total number of students receiving a formal Jewish education has continued to decline. New players have arrived on the scene, such as Chabad, which now runs 73 day schools (Schick, 2009), mainly for non-Orthodox Jews, and over 350 supplementary schools (Wertheimer, 2008, p. 4). Independent operators of schools[9] and private tutors have also multiplied.[10] Efforts are underway to build more residential summer camps, encourage the growth of youth programs, and to multiply the number of Israel programs. To be sure, the goal is to expose ever larger numbers of young people to Jewish educational experiences, but at the same time the insistence on options and in some cases on finding programs just right for each child are also fueling this proliferation of educational ventures.

To accommodate more demanding families, these programs are also tailoring their offerings. The most blatant example of this tendency has been evident in the field of supplementary Jewish education. Because so many schools under Conservative auspices, which had once regarded 6 hours per week of instruction as mandatory, cut back on instructional time, the educational office of the United Synagogue for Conservative Judaism ratified a set of six acceptable substitute options of shorter duration, explaining that with the increase in distance between where families live and their synagogues, the high incidence in which both parents work outside the home, and the growing population of single parents, it is unrealistic to expect children to make their way to schools three times a week.[11] Supplementary schools, moreover, are also creating multiple tracks to accommodate the time constraints and interests of children. In some settings, formal education has been replaced by a mix of Shabbat programming offering religious worship and other experiences with family education programs. Other schools permit parents to choose the days that work best for them and their children. Some supplementary high school programs offer a wide range of class electives, and in some cases have eliminated requirements entirely.[12] All of these examples speak to the insistence on choices.

More generally, Jewish-educational programs of all kinds have become far more attuned to the diversity of their student bodies. Educators attend to gender

---

[9]One of the most successful and innovative supplementary school programs, Kesher, is run independently at two sites in the Boston area.

[10]We have no way to estimate how many such independent programs and tutoring services exist. For a report on one such operation, see Sarah, 2004 and Spence, 2008.

[11]I have discussed these issues in Wertheimer, 2007a, p. 13.

[12]Examples of such schools are discussed in Wertheimer, 2009.

differences,[13] racial diversity, the sexual orientation of parents, and many other formerly ignored special interests and needs (Schwartzapfel, 2009; UAHC, 2000). To be sure, much of this is prompted by a new attunement of educational thinking in the wider American society to these types of differences, but they also stem from the insistence of parents that Jewish educational efforts attend to these considerations.

Communal Concerns About the Vitality of Jewish Life

High expectations have also come from another quarter—American-Jewish communal leadership. As concern has mounted over the past decades about the erosion of Jewish life through intermarriage, disengagement from organizations, and declining levels of participation in synagogues, Jewish leaders have fastened on ignorance of Jewish civilization as a key source of disengagement, and conversely have identified intensified Jewish education as the cure for these weaknesses. As already noted, this approach has served as a double-edged sword: on the one hand, it has attracted supporters and champions; on the other hand, it has challenged educational vehicles to justify new investments by demonstrating just how much impact they have had.

Not surprisingly, given these concerns, the forms of Jewish education that offered the greatest hope for increased vitality and a demonstrated track record of success tended to win wide public attention and significant new funding. The most successful on both scores were the most immersive educational programs as follows:

1. Day-school education embraces young people in school programs beginning before 9:00 a.m. in the morning and in some schools concluding with extra-curricular activities that may last as late as 7:00 p.m. Students also spend time together with their peers and educators on occasional Shabbatonim, weekend retreats, and other forms of social gathering during non-school hours. All of this time makes it possible for day schools to expose students both to advanced levels of study and also to powerful socialization experiences. When it became apparent from survey research that day-school graduates tend to be more strongly engaged in Jewish life as adults than graduates of other educational programs (and not coincidentally tend to intermarry at far lower rates than other Jews),[14] Jewish leaders searching for ways to strengthen Jewish life increased their investment in day schools and worked to expand the number of students enrolled, particularly by trying to enlarge the non-Orthodox sectors of day schools. The two decades

---

[13]See, for example, the work of Shira Epstein on evaded issues in Jewish education, http://www.jtsa.edu/William_Davidson_Graduate_School_of_Jewish_Education/Addressing_Evaded_Issues_in_Jewish_Education.xml.

[14]Data from the 1990 National Jewish Populations Study already pointed in this direction. On the general impact of more Jewish education, see Lipset, 1994 who concluded: "The longer and more intensive the Jewish training, the more likely people are to be committed to and practice Judaism" (57). On the specific adult impact of day-school education, see Cohen, 2007, p. 43. Extensive supplementary school education also was found to have positive outcomes.

spanning the end of the twentieth century and the beginning of the twenty-first witnessed some growth in day schools and enrollments in the non-Orthodox sector. In the 1990s alone, according to an estimate by Marvin Schick, enrollment in non-Orthodox day schools grew by some 20% and a number of communal and Conservative high schools opened during those years, too (Schick, 2000, p. ii).

2. More recently, Jewish residential summer camps have attracted new support from funders. Living in camp settings 24 hours a day for anywhere from 3 to 7 weeks, young people can be exposed to intense Jewish living. In some camps, they experience regular prayer daily or at least on the Sabbath for the first time in their lives. They live according to the Jewish calendar, with Sabbath observed as a special day unlike all other days of the week. Those who are in camp on the Ninth of Av are exposed to a fast day that is widely ignored by most American Jews. Some Jewish camp settings also offer only kosher food, some forms of educational programming, the opportunity to learn Hebrew songs; they also involve young people in Jewish dance, art addressed to Jewish themes, and other forms of Jewish cultural expression (Sales & Saxe, 2004). This type of immersion in Jewish living was touted by educational leaders such as Mordecai Kaplan (Winter, 1966, p. 166), a long-time scholar-in-residence at Cejwin and other Jewish camps, as far back as the 1920s and then taken up by all the religious movements in the middle of the century. Camping is now more clearly on the communal agenda again because through its immersive environment it offers unparalleled opportunities to shape young Jews and convey to them how pleasurable and enriching Jewish living can be. The establishment of the Foundation for Jewish Camp in 1998 and its ability to attract new funding for residential camps reflects a renewed interest in this type of informal Jewish education.

3. By contrast, immersive programs of study in Israel reflect a more recent phenomenon. Prior to the Six-Day War, only very small numbers of such programs existed. Since then, there has been an explosion of yeshivas and seminaries, principally attracting Orthodox men and women, in their gap year between high school and college, if not for longer periods. Parallel programs have been established by the Conservative and Reform movements, by a few youth movements, and by enterprising Israeli institutions offering a range of options stressing ecology, service work, study, and intensive language instruction.[15] Israel Experience programs for high school students were popular, especially in federation circles in the 1990s, which dangled trips as a reward for participating in Jewish teen programs and schooling. The most popular form of Israel program today is the 10-day all-expenses-paid Birthright Israel trip, now undertaken by nearly 200,000 American Jews between the ages of 18 and 26. All of these programs are premised on the assumption that taking young Jews away from their normal

---

[15] A long listing of these programs may be found at the MASA website, http://www.masaisrael.com/Masa/English/

environment, exposing them to aspects of Israel, infusing their trip with educational content, and allowing time for social interactions will serve as powerful experiences to strengthen the Jewish identity of participants.[16]

Day schools, residential camps, and Israel programs share two things in common: one is the way in which they each immerse participants in intensive educational settings, minimally for entire school days, or else for weeks at a time, round the clock. They also have been studied extensively for the purpose of gathering evidence as to their long-term impact. Given the concerns that have prompted funders to invest in Jewish education, it is hardly surprising that more research has gone into tracking these forms of Jewish education than any other types of programs. We should not take for granted that 50 years ago, of the three options, only residential camping attracted even the slightest attention.

Lifelong Jewish Learning

If a concern about building strong Jewish identities has prompted a new emphasis on immersive educational experiences, a mix of other factors accounts for the turn to expanding opportunities for learners of all ages. Options have multiplied in response to a number of pressures: the heightened emphasis on choice, parental insistence that programs meet individual needs, disappointment over the inability of formal education programs to reach the full spectrum of learners, and also the hunger of some adults for continuing Jewish education to make up for the weak education they received while growing up. Educational programs are now far more attuned to underserved segments of the Jewish population, such as preschoolers and their parents, teens, college students, and single adults. New initiatives now seek to strengthen Jewish educational vehicles directed at each of these sub-groups as follows:

- Early childhood is now recognized as a critical time for educators to reach young children and their parents; indeed, this age is often seen as a potential portal of entry into Jewish involvement not only for the children, but also for their entire families. Hence, the upgrading of training programs for teachers of this age group and the ferment in the field (Vogelstein, 2008, pp. 365–372). The great challenge confronting efforts to upgrade this form of Jewish education stems from the reality that early childhood work has traditionally come with little status, and Jewish programs have relied heavily on teachers who themselves have little Jewish or pedagogical training; a substantial number are not even Jewish.
- Youth programming is also getting a second look. During the middle decades of the twentieth century, Zionist and denominational youth movements attracted

---

[16] An extensive list of follow up research studies on Birthright participants may be found at the website of the Cohen Center for Modern Jewish Studies at Brandeis University. See http://ir.brandeis.edu/handle/10192/22946/advanced-search. See also Saxe & Chazan, 2008.

an important share of highly committed teens. But by the close of the century, these youth movements had waned, attracting only small fractions of teens and making virtually no dent on Jewish public consciousness. Youth activities are now picking up through local efforts housed either in synagogues, as community-wide efforts[17] or through the non-ideological B'nai B'rith Youth Organization, a recipient of significant new foundation money.[18] These settings for informal Jewish education are seen as important vehicles for bringing young Jews together for social activities with some elements of informal Jewish education.

- Given the disproportionately high percentage of Jews who attend college, a range of groups have organized efforts to offer educational programming on campuses. Though not formally an arm of Jewish communities, many Jewish studies programs in fact serve to educate college students about aspects of Jewish life. The explosion of such programs is unprecedented and represents still another dramatic shift in the delivery of Jewish educational content since the middle decades of the twentieth century. Many hundreds of courses are now offered on Jewish languages—Hebrew, Yiddish, even Ladino—Jewish texts and their interpretations, and Jewish culture and its history that were unavailable except in the most limited form 50 years ago, but now are commonplace at hundreds of colleges and universities, including those under state or Christian auspices.[19] Additionally, interested students can now take classes and engage in informal education at campus Hillel buildings,[20] Chabad Houses,[21] and other sites on or near their campuses.

- With young adults more likely to delay marriage and family formation until well into their thirties, a vast population of Jewish singles with some discretionary time and a desire to socialize with other Jews is being served by a network of organizations and innovative initiatives, many including elements of educational programming. Conventional organizations such as federations, Jewish community relations groups such as the American Jewish Committee and the ADL, welfare groups such as the American Jewish Joint Distribution Committee, and Israel centered groups such as AIPAC, all run programs for Jews of this age group and aggressively court them to participate in more advanced training programs where they are groomed to assume leadership roles. In addition, a panoply of initiatives has been launched by and for young adults by their peers, including

---

[17] On the various informal teen programs supported by the Combined Jewish Philanthropies in Boston, see http://bbyo.org/news/releases/bbyo_and_panim/

[18] "Philanthropists Pledge $3.5 Million to BBYO ..." http://bbyo.org/news/releases/bbyo_and_panim/

[19] A directory of endowed chairs in Jewish fields enumerates 250 such positions; they are augmented by considerably more non-endowed positions plus courses offered on aspects of Judaica by specialists in ancillary fields. For the directory, see http://www.ajsnet.org/chairs.php

[20] Hillel claims there are Jewish life offices on 500 US campuses. See http://www.hillel.org/about/default

[21] Chabad claims it fields over 150 on-site campus centers. http://www.chabad.org/centers/campus_cdo/jewish/Campus-Directory.htm

independent minyanim (worship communities), ecologically oriented groups, service programs, cultural gatherings, and groups either advocating on behalf of Israel or critical of its policies. These are augmented, in turn, by a broad array of affinity groups that attend to the needs of sub-populations, such as young adults of Russian or Israeli origin, seekers of Orthodox outreach programs, gays, and lesbians wishing to socialize with each other, outdoor enthusiasts, or others with a shared interest. All of these efforts include Jewish-educational programming either about contemporary Jewish culture or text learning (Wertheimer, forthcoming).

- As for middle aged and older adult populations, new national educational programs have proliferated, offering set curricula over a period of 2 years or other educational opportunities. The Florence Melton Adult Mini-School based at the Hebrew University and offered in communities around the United States[22] and the Meah curriculum devised at the Boston Hebrew College[23] have reached thousands of Jewish adults over the past decade. In addition, the Wexner Heritage Foundation has offered serious 2-year learning programs for future lay leaders at sites across the country. They are augmented by synagogues, Jewish Community Centers, Orthodox outreach programs, and many other providers actively offering Jewish-educational programming in person and online.[24]

All of these efforts are consistent with a slogan that has taken hold in the American-Jewish community in recent years, namely that Jews should think about Jewish education as a matter of "lifelong Jewish learning." Few of the programs I have mentioned are unique to the present age, but the sheer mass of options and the message of urging Jews to continue their Jewish education over their life course are reflections of the current mood. Despite the opportunities and the message, however, only a minority of American Jews can be described as lifelong Jewish learners, and most programs attract only a relatively small share of the potential market of Jews.

Curricula

Once students are enrolled, what should be the focus of the curriculum? This is a perennial challenge facing all educational institutions, and even more so Jewish ones, which must choose from a vast body of learning and many possible options. Curriculum providers can offer some guidance, but the key players are shifting. Whereas once the education departments of the religious movements played a central role in developing curricula, their influence has diminished of late. The Reform

---

[22]Information about the Melton courses can be found at http://www.fmams.org.il/1a_aboutus/9_leadership.htm

[23]The Meah program was launched at two Boston-area sites in 1994. It now claims over 2,500 alumni around the country. http://www.hebrewcollege.edu/meah

[24]For an analysis of the impact of these programs, see Grant and Schuster 2003 and Grant, Schuster, Woocher, & Cohen, 2004. See also Grant and Schuster in this handbook.

movement has invested more in developing new curriculum than any of its counterparts, producing the Chai curriculum for supplementary schools and a Hebrew complement called Mitkadem. A significant portion of schools under Reform auspices have adopted parts of this curriculum, as have some schools under other denominational auspices. Much of the slack in curriculum has been picked up either by individual schools that tailor curricula to the strengths of their teaching staff and by commercial educational publishers, such as Behrman House Books and Torah Aura Productions. Day-school curricula which tend to be more labor intensive because they cover more extensive material have been produced under grants for large foundations.[25]

Still, questions of focus and emphasis cannot be resolved entirely by curriculum providers. Individual schools tend to shape their own approaches to the vexing question of how to allocate limited time and what goals should be set for student learning. Schools of all sorts struggle with how much time to devote to Hebrew-language instruction, and which registers of Hebrew to stress—Biblical, liturgical, rabbinic, or modern Israeli Hebrew—let alone the question of spoken versus written Hebrew. They must also resolve how much time to allocate to teaching skills versus conceptual issues versus textual study versus action-oriented activities. Clearly, these are not air-tight categories, but they continue to vex educators in all kinds of settings, all the more so when students are available only for the most limited amount of time in supplementary programs and settings of informal education.[26]

Among the more challenging issues in curricular development today is the matter of Israel education. In the two decades after the Six-Day War, Jewish schools of all kinds invested considerable effort in teaching about contemporary Israel and enjoyed the benefit of an outpouring of textbooks and other resources;[27] today, by contrast, Israel education is widely understood as an unresolved set of dilemmas. Veteran teachers lament how much the ground has shifted from the heroic era when every Jewish child knew of Golda Meir, Moshe Dayan, and Yitzhak Rabin; today by contrast, Israeli leaders are largely unfamiliar to students. Even more important, media coverage has presented at best a portrait of Israel in shades of gray, and educators are now flummoxed as to what to teach about Israel and from which perspective: Should students be exposed to an idealized portrait of the Jewish homeland or to a society that struggles with intractable issues, sometimes in an uplifting fashion, sometimes less so? Should Israel be viewed primarily through the prism of

---

[25] The AVI CHAI foundation, for example, has invested large sums in the Neta Hebrew curriculum for day schools and in a benchmarks project for Bible study in day schools. On the former, see http://www.avi-chai.org/bin/en5caf.html?enPage=BlankPage&enDisplay=view&enDispWhat=Zone&enZone=JLPC#48; on the latter, see http://www.jtsa.edu/William_Davidson_Graduate_School_of_Jewish_Education/Melton_Research_Center_for_Jewish_Education/Melton_Standards_and_Benchmarks.xml

[26] Some of these issues are explored in the section on Curriculum in Goodman, Flexner, and Bloomberg, 2008, pp. 269–362.

[27] For research on the state of Israel education, see Pollak, 1984–1985, Ackerman, 1996; Chazan, 2000; Krasner, 2003.

its conflicts with neighboring Arabs or through the prism of culture and religion? Should Israel education focus, as it had in the past, on the many ways Israel is similar to the United States or should it emphasize the radically different circumstances in which Israeli and American Jews live? Much new thinking is going into addressing these and other questions, but for the moment, Israel education is viewed as a problem to be solved, rather than as an automatically positive feature of Jewish educational institutions.[28]

Even more broadly, there is great confusion about the purpose of Jewish-educational programs—or at least much debate about the proper emphasis. Some educators aspire for their students to attain high levels of Jewish literacy through exposure to the classic texts of Judaism and the broad sweep of Jewish civilization.[29] Others regard socialization as the primary task of educational institutions, by connecting students with other Jews and enculturating them so that they feel anchored in a living Jewish community.[30] And still others go further and stress the importance of using Jewish educational experiences as a means of developing the affective side: let children feel good about being Jewish and enjoy participation in a set of Jewish activities; that will linger long after skills and information have been forgotten. These different approaches have enormous consequences for the way educational institutions allocate their limited time with students. Though the issues are not entirely new, the intensity of clashing views and the divergence of opinion today may be greater than in the past.

Resources of Personnel and Funding

At precisely the time when Jewish educational options proliferated and communal attention was riveted on education as a critical building block for strengthening Jewish life in the United States, it began to dawn on some educational leaders that shortages in qualified personnel might torpedo ambitious efforts to rebuild Jewish educational options. To be sure, the work of educators never carried high prestige in Jewish life: the *melamed* is remembered in Jewish literature as somewhat of a schlemiel who spends his time in the classroom because he could not find better work.

For much of the twentieth century, the field of Jewish education recruited immigrants to staff its schools, initially drawing on first generation Jews from Europe and

---

[28]For some recent discussions of these issues, see *Jewish Educational Leadership* September 2008, http://virtualmelton.huji.ac.il/course/view.php?id=8 for a collection of papers devoted to this topic, and also Alick Isaacs' chapter in this handbook.

[29]This is the model adopted by most Jewish day schools in the Orthodox world with Haredi and Hasidic day schools more likely to emphasize textual proficiency above other considerations, while modern Orthodox and other day schools add some content on aspects of Jewish civilization—thought, literature, the arts, music, and history.

[30]Isa Aron has argued for enculturation as the primary goal, which requires a living community to engage in anchoring young people (Aron, nd).

then later from Israel. Women who served primarily as homemakers picked up the slack, particularly in supplementary education where their services were required for only a few hours per week. Shifts in social patterns have made it far harder in recent decades to recruit teachers.[31] As ever larger numbers of Jewish women have entered the labor force as full-time employees, but this source of teachers has dried up considerably. Moreover, as Jewish immigration has slowed to a crawl and those who have immigrated generally come with advanced degrees in other fields, still another pool of teaching personnel has evaporated. By the closing decade of the twentieth century, serious attention has been lavished on the entire question of teacher recruitment and retention, leading to several important studies designed to learn more about who are current teachers, where and how they are recruited and what are their perceptions of their work and their levels of job satisfaction.[32]

A slew of new programs have arisen over the past two decades to address the shortages of personnel and shape educational leaders. To begin with, new training programs have been established at several universities, and existing ones at the major religious seminaries have received new infusions of scholarship support in order to help them recruit students to teacher training programs. Other programs select teachers who show promise as future school heads; and still others work with camp heads, classroom teachers, and youth group leaders, among others.[33] All of these are in line with a major preoccupation in Jewish communal life that has no earlier parallel: deliberate and highly organized leadership training. Where once it was taken for granted that leaders would emerge as a matter of course, now dozens of programs recruit, train, and nurture future leaders in a deliberately self-conscious fashion.[34]

Limited Financial Resources

Finally, we come to the most pervasive and intractable of all challenges facing the field: the mismatch between needs and financial resources. Jewish-educational programs in the United States always have relied upon a mixture of communal support, philanthropic contributions, and tuition fees paid by families. As in the past, the funds available have not sufficed to cover budgets—the costs of infrastructure, curriculum development, new technologies, the training and on-going learning of educators, and, most important, salaries and benefits for educational personnel. What has changed in recent decades is the prominent role assumed by foundations as the decisive force propelling educational change. Several large foundations have spearheaded efforts such as Birthright Israel, the remaking of Hillel, the support and encouragement of day-school education, the expansion of Jewish residential

---

[31] Shevitz, 1988 has argued that teacher recruitment has been a perennial problem.

[32] This new interest is well captured in an excellent overview by Goodman and Schaap, 2008, pp. 199–211. Among the new studies, see especially Ben-Avie & Kress, 2006.

[33] For a good overview of these recent efforts, see Sales, Samuel, and Koren, 2006.

[34] This larger effort is analyzed in Kelner, Rabkin, Saxe, and Sheingold, 2005.

camping, and the training of educational personnel. In short, the current situation differs dramatically from earlier times because of the work of foundations and major philanthropists.

Despite these remarkable investments and creative new thinking by foundations, large financial problems remain, and, if anything, are growing. Spiraling costs of day-school education, which now can exceed over $30,000 per high school student and huge costs associated with summer camping are but two of the many examples of how the high cost of Jewish living has become prohibitive to the point where it is driving some families to abandon the most immersive forms of Jewish education in favor of less costly options.[35] Some foundations have begun to experiment with Hebrew charter schools as a means of bringing government money to bear on language instruction. No one believes that such schools can replace the rich Judaic content of day schools, but such is the desperation for new funding sources that the charter model is seen as an aspect of the mix, which will also include after-school religious instruction. Other philanthropists are playing a role in their own local communities by offering financial support to specific schools, camps, or programs, all with the intention of helping struggling families with the affordability challenges.

None of these issues is unique to the present moment, but some of the solutions are novel—free 10 days trips to Israel, vouchers to families who never enrolled their children in day school before, national loan programs to schools, extensive leadership training for potential school heads, and plans for vast day school endowment projects all reflect new thinking. Moreover, the fact that foundations are spearheading these efforts dramatizes the extent to which the locus of educational innovation has shifted to a new sector of the Jewish community and away from traditional centers of influence—bureaus of Jewish education, the religious movements and federations of Jewish philanthropy. The crisis of financing and the general anxiety over the quality of Jewish education has brought new players onto the scene who are assuming a central role in addressing some of the major challenges.

As we consider the shifting contours of the field of Jewish education in the United States in recent decades, we would do well to acknowledge the overarching new reality confronting the field. It is now evident to most observers that Jewish education is seen not only as facing a set of challenges in its own right, but writ large is also touted as *the* solution. No other sector of the Jewish community is promoted so ubiquitously as the silver bullet for reversing trends eroding Jewish life—not synagogues, not Jewish organizations, not service programs, not cultural enterprises. None of these is regarded as capable of stemming the tide of losses. Jewish education alone is on the lips of leaders as they offer up hope for renewal. This in itself reflects a remarkable turn-around for the former "stepchild" of the Jewish community. It also places a heavy, unprecedented, and perhaps unrealistic burden of responsibility on the ever-changing field of Jewish education.

---

[35] On the high costs of Jewish living, see Bubis, 2008.

References

Ackerman, W. (1996). Israel in American Jewish education. In A. Gal (Ed.), *Envisioning Israel: The changing ideals and images of North American Jews* (pp. 173–190). Detroit, MI: Wayne State University Press.

American association for Jewish education. (1976). *Trends in Jewish school enrollment in the United States, 1974/5*. New York: American Association for Jewish Education.

Aron, I. (nd). The teacher's role in curriculum reform. Retrieved from, https://www.policyarchive.org/bitstream/handle/10207/10160/TeachersRoleInCurriculumReform.pdf?sequence=1

Ben-Avie, M. & Kress, J. (2006). *The educators in Jewish schools study: Preliminary findings from a registry of day and congregational/supplementary schools in North America*. New York: Jewish Educational Services of North America.

Bubis, G. (2008). *The costs of Jewish living: Revisiting Jewish involvements and barriers*. New York: American Jewish Committee.

Chazan, B. (2000). Through a glass darkly: Israel in the mirror of American Jewish education. In A. Gal, & A. Gottschalk (Eds.), *Beyond survival and philanthropy: American Jewry and Israel* (pp. 123–130). Cincinnati, OH: Hebrew Union College Press.

Cohen, S. M. (2007). The differential impact of Jewish education on adult Jewish identity. In J. Wertheimer (Ed.), *Family matters: Jewish education in an age of choice* (pp. 34–56). Hanover, NH: Brandeis University Press.

Goodman, R. L., Flexner, P. , & Bloomberg, L. D. (Eds.) (2008). *What do we now know about Jewish education: Perspectives on research and practice*. Los Angeles, CA: Torah Aura Productions.

Goodman, R. L. & Schaap, E.(2008). In R. L. Goodman, P. Flexner, & L. D. Bloomberg (Eds.), *What do we now know about Jewish education: Perspectives on research and practice* (pp. 199–212). Los Angeles, CA: Torah Aura Productions.

Grant, L. D., & Schuster, D. T. (2003). *The impact of adult Jewish learning in today's Jewish community*. New York: United Jewish Communities.

Grant, L. D., Schuster, D. T., Woocher, M., & Cohen, S. M. (2004). *A journey of heart and mind: Transformative Jewish learning in adulthood*. New York: The Jewish Theological Seminary of America.

JESNA (1999). *Consultation on day school tuition subvention programs*, NY: Jewish educational services of North America. Retrieved from, https://www.policyarchive.org/bitstream/handle/10207/15609/Consultation%20on%20Day%20School%20Tuition%20Subvention%20Programs.pdf?sequence=1.

Katzew, J. (2008). Director's message. *Torah at the Center*, *11*(2), 1–4. Retrieved from, http://urj.org/kd/_temp/9C4C0318-D191-EC76-728931B2B6B2569D/TATC_April2008%20.pdf.Spring 2008.

Kelner, S., Rabkin, M., Saxe, L., & Sheingold, C. (2005) *The Jewish sector's workforce: Report of a six community study. Professional leaders project*. Report No. 2. Cohen Center for Modern Jewish Studies. Brandeis University.

Krasner, J. (2003). Israel in American Jewish text books, 1948–Present. Paper delivered at the 2003 conference of the Midwest Jewish Studies Association.

Lipset, S. M. (1994). *The power of Jewish education*. Los Angeles, CA: Wilstein Institute.

Lookstein centre for Jewish education. (2009). *Look: The newsletter of the lookstein center for Jewish education*, Spring 2009. Retrieved from, http://www.lookstein.org/newsletter/look11.pdf

Olitzky, K., & Golin, P. (2008). Outreach and Jewish Education. In R. L. Goodman, P. Flexner, & L. D. Bloomberg (Eds.), *What do we now know about Jewish education: Perspectives on research and practice* (pp. 87–98). Los Angeles, CA: Torah Aura Productions.

Pollak, G. (1984–1985). Israel in American Jewish schools in the 1980s. *Jewish Education*, *52*(4), 12–14.

Pomson, A. (2007). Schools for parents: what parents want and what they get from their children's Jewish day school. In J. Wertheimer (Ed.), *Family matters: Jewish education in an age of choice* (pp. 34–56). Hanover, NH: Brandeis University Press.

Pomson, A., & Schnoor, R. F. (2008). *Back to school: Jewish day school in the lives of adult Jews.* Detroit, MN: Wayne State University Press.

Prell, R. E. (2007). Community and the discourse of elegy: The postwar suburban debates. In J. Wertheimer (Ed.), *Imagining the American Jewish community* (pp. 67–90). Hanover, NH: Brandeis University Press.

Sales, A., Samuel, N., & Koren, A. (2006). *Mapping professional development for educators.* Retrieved from, http://www.jimjosephfoundation.org/PDF/Final%20Report%20on%20Professional%20Development.pdf

Sales, A., & Saxe, L. (2004). *"How goodly are thy tents?" Summer camps as Jewish socializing experiences.* Hanover NH: Brandeis University Press.

Sarah, R. (2004). B'nai Mitzvah boosters: One-on-one tutors ease the way to coming of age ceremony. *JWeekly.com* March 4, 2004. Retrieved from, http://www.jweekly.com/article/full/25312/b-nai-mitzvah-boosters/

Saxe, L., & Chazan, B. (2008). *Ten days of Birthright: A journey in young adult identity.* Hanover, NH: Brandeis University Press.

Schick, M. (2000). *A census of Jewish day schools in the United States.* New York: AVI CHAI Foundation.

Schick, M. (2005). *A census of Jewish day schools in the United States, 2003–2004.* New York: AVI CHAI Foundation.

Schick, M. (2009). *A census of Jewish day schools In the United States, 2008–2009.* New York: AVI CHAI Foundation.

Schwartzapfel, B. (2009). A teacher's toolkit for tackling tough issues: Jewish educators learn to address bullying, harassment and eating disorders. forward, January 20. Retrieved from, http://www.forward.com/articles/14970/

Schwartzman, B. (2009). Tuition incentive seeks to boost enrollment. *Philadelphia Jewish Exponent,* Nov. 20. Retrieved from, http://www.jewishexponent.com/article/17669/

Shevitz, S. (1988). Communal responses to the teacher shortage in the North American supplementary schools. *Studies in Jewish education 3* (pp. 25–61). Jerusalem: Magnes Press.

Sklare, M., & Greenblum, J. (1967). *Jewish identity on the suburban frontier: A study of group survival in an open society.* New York: Basic Books.

Spence, R. (2008). Tutors tackle Tinsel-Town: Bar Mitzvah tutors give hollywood hopefuls a leg up. *Forward,* Jan. 16. Retrieved from, http://www.forward.com/articles/12476/

Union of American Hebrew congregations. (2000). *Al pi darco/according to their ways: A special needs educational resource manual.* New York: UAHC Press.

Vogelstein, I. (2008). Early childhood and Jewish education–if not now, when?. In R. L. Goodman, P. Flexner, & L. D. Bloomberg (Eds.), *What do we now know about Jewish education: Perspectives on research and practice* (pp. 373–386). Los Angeles, CA: Torah Aura Productions.

Wertheimer, J. (2005a). *Linking the silos: How to accelerate the momentum in Jewish education today.* New York: AVI CHAI Foundation.

Wertheimer, J. (2005b). The postwar suburban synagogue in historical context. In E. Lederhendler, & J. Wertheimer (Eds.), *Text and context: Essays in modern Jewish history and historiography in honor of Ismar Schorsch* (pp. 578–605). New York: JTS Press.

Wertheimer, J. (2007a). *Recent trends in Jewish supplementary education.* New York: AVI CHAI Foundation.

Wertheimer, J. (Ed.) (2007b). *Family matters: Jewish education in an age of choice.* Hanover, NH: Brandeis University Press.

Wertheimer, J. (2008). *A census of Jewish supplementary schools in the United States, 2006–2007.* New York: AVI CHAI Foundation.

Wertheimer, J. (Ed.) (2009). *Learning and community: Jewish supplementary schools in the 21st century*. Hanover, NH: Brandeis University Press.

Wertheimer, J. (forthcoming). Mapping the scene: How young Jewish adults engage in Jewish life today.

Winter, N. H. (1966). *Jewish education in a pluralist society: Samson Benderly and Jewish education in the United States*. New York: New York University Press.

Anglo-Jewish Education: Day Schools, State Funding and Religious Education in State Schools

David Mendelsson

Introduction

This chapter will explore three central issues in Jewish education in England since the end of the Second World War. These issues arose in the wake of social, cultural and demographic changes in post-War England generally, and, to a lesser degree, within the Jewish community. First, the chapter will trace the dramatic shifts in Anglo-Jewish attitudes to Jewish day school education. Next, it will examine how the state's convoluted approach to the funding of denominational education impacted Jewish education, particularly day schools. Finally, it will analyse the provision of Jewish religious education to pupils in non-denominational State schools. Each issue, though rooted in the Anglo-Jewish context, has parallels in other contexts worldwide, and understanding the factors that have shaped Jewish education in England – parental responses to societal transformations, state funding of religious schools, and religious education in State schools – may offer insights applicable elsewhere. The chapter focuses primarily on day school education, and, to a lesser extent, on another 'formal' framework for imparting Jewish learning, namely, supplementary education in Sunday or afternoon classes.[1] These institutions merit examination because they have undergone dramatic reciprocal changes that reflect a shift in Jewish identity and self-perception. This shift took place against the backdrop of a significant recontouring of England's social, cultural and demographic landscape, and the chapter focuses on the impact these *broader* changes have had on Jewish education. To provide a context for this analysis, I begin by outlining the structure of English schooling, both general and Jewish, during this period.

D. Mendelsson (✉)
Hebrew Union College and Rothberg International School, Hebrew University of Jerusalem, Jerusalem, Israel
e-mail: dmendelsson@huc.edu

[1] See Mendelsson, 2002, Chapter 5, for more on supplementary school Jewish education. While informal Jewish frameworks of various sorts have also had some educational impact on Anglo-Jewish youth, this internal pedagogic development, interesting though it is, does not fall within the purview of the present chapter.

Structure of the Educational System

The Education Act, 1944 set out three stages in the education of English and Welsh children. Children between the ages of 5 and 11 were to attend primary schools. Attendance at secondary schools was compulsory until age 15, and optional from 15 to 18. First and second stage schools were funded mainly by the local education authority (LEA). The third stage was further education at colleges and universities.

Unlike the primary schools, non-denominational State secondary schools were selective, and a series of exams taken at age 11 – referred to as the 'Eleven plus' – determined a child's educational and often occupational and class destiny. Grammar school places were available to the approximately 20% who passed the Eleven plus; the other pupils were placed at Secondary Modern and Secondary Technical schools. In 1965, the Labour Government adopted a policy of abolishing the selective non-denominational Grammar schools and replacing them with large Comprehensive schools where the mixing of different populations and expansive, varied, curriculum would, it was hoped, create greater opportunity for all children. From 1965 to 1979, comprehensive education was a matter of considerable political manoeuvring, generating much uncertainty and acrimony (Simon, 1994).

In dramatic contrast to the American scene, the State school system encompasses both non-denominational and denominational schools, the latter run by Anglican, Roman Catholic or Jewish organisations.[2]

In addition to State schools, there are also privately-run schools, referred to as Independent schools, which include both boarding and day schools. Until the late 1960s, Independent schools, most of which had been established by religious foundations, often had tacit quotas for non-Christian pupils. The Jewish schools were similarly divided into State denominational and private fully-independent fee-paying day schools; there was also a Jewish private boarding school – Carmel College – modelled on Eton and Harrow, but providing an Orthodox Jewish education and ethos.

Independent schools often sought to secure 'voluntary aided' status, which enabled them to have the bulk of their costs borne by the state. This status was awarded only to schools meeting stringent criteria with respect to the premises, syllabus, teacher qualifications, and local demand for school places. Voluntary-aided status afforded parents the assurance that the schools in question met the LEA's academic and other standards.

The *Schools Standards and Framework Act*, 1998 re-categorised State schools. 'Community schools' are non-denominational and fully state-funded; Voluntary schools are owned or administered by an education trust, usually religious. There are two principal types of Voluntary schools: 'Voluntary Controlled' and 'Voluntary Aided'. With regard to the former, the LEA controls the school, employs the

---

[2] Since 1993, aided status has been extended to nine Muslim, Greek Orthodox, Hindu and Sikh schools.

staff, and sets the admissions policy. The charitable foundation makes no monetary contribution to maintaining the school. The teaching of Religious Education is predominantly non-confessional and multi-faith, but the school ethos and worship are confessional (Cush, 2003). By contrast, at 'Voluntary Aided' schools the charitable foundation is responsible for the building and its upkeep, with government grants available to defray these sums. It employs the staff and sets the admissions policy, but the LEA pays salaries and other costs. Some schools, formerly called 'Direct Grant' schools, receive funding directly from the state, rather than the LEA. Abolished in 1976 and reintroduced in 1988, they are now known as 'Grant Maintained' schools.

Today, the 33 larger Jewish day schools in Britain, attended by the majority of Jewish day school pupils, are voluntary-aided. In addition, there are numerous small Independent day schools, most of which serve the fervently-Orthodox (*Charedi*) population. Until recently, the latter generally eschewed government funding, fearing loss of autonomy over admissions policy, curriculum and teaching staff. But rising costs have led the fervently Orthodox to seek state funding to help maintain their schools. Since the girls' schools devote more time to general studies, their chances of securing state financial aid are greater than those of the boys' schools. There are no Voluntary Controlled or Direct Grant schools in the Jewish sector.

Parental Receptiveness to Jewish Day School Education

Over the past 35 years, preferences of Jewish parents vis-à-vis their children's education have undergone a sea change. In 1944, of those receiving Jewish education, only 1 in 16 attended a Jewish day school, whereas the corresponding figure for 1987 is 1 in 2. This dramatic increase in Jewish day school attendance was accompanied by a decline in attendance at part-time frameworks such as afternoon Hebrew classes. To accommodate the growth in demand for Jewish nursery and day school places, the number of such institutions rose steadily, from 23 in 1954 to 57 in 1975, 70 in 1989 and 135 in 1999. This growth is particularly salient in light of the decline in the overall number of Jewish children in England, which dropped by 25% from the 1950s to 2002 (Valins, Kosmin, & Goldberg, 2002).

Part of the explanation for the increased attendance at day schools is demographic: the robust growth in the fervently-Orthodox communities. In the 1950s such growth had seemed improbable, but outreach and fecundity have enabled the fervently-Orthodox community to increase from 2.6% of Anglo-Jewry in 1970 to 10% at the end of the millennium (Alderman, 1992; Valins et al., 2002). Future trends can be projected from the statistic that of all synagogue marriages in 2006, almost 26% were fervently Orthodox (Graham & Vulkan, 2007). As the fervently Orthodox community does not, for the most part, send its children to non-*Charedi* Jewish schools, let alone State schools, the *Charedi* schools have experienced enormous expansion since the founding of the Yesodey Hatorah schools in 1942 with just six pupils: by the year 2000, there were over 10,000 pupils in fervently-Orthodox schools in England (Valins et al., 2002).

In the non-*Charedi* sector, however, the shift in parental attitudes has been remarkable. To understand this development, let us first examine the situation prior to the rise of the day schools.

Post-War Parental Attitudes to Schooling

Overall, Jewish day school attendance had been in decline since well before the Second World War (Steinberg, 1989). The general opinion was that the purpose for which the day schools had been established – to protect children from proselytisers, provide them with basic Judaic and general knowledge, and above all, 'Anglicize' them – had been achieved. Now native born and culturally integrated, the majority of Anglo-Jewry took the primary goal of schooling to be academic achievement and upward mobility (Alderman, 1992; Miller, 2001). Motivated to extricate itself from working-class neighbourhoods, the community viewed a good education at a selective Grammar school as the best entryway to business and the professions, and the key to socialisation into the middle class. Jewish children were, indeed, quite successful at winning Grammar school places (Gould, 1984; Krausz, 1969).

Believing that the middle class, to which it aspired, disapproved of denominational schooling, the Jewish community took the stance that ethnic identity in general, and religion in particular, should be confined to the home and synagogue. Since most of the non-Jewish middle-class children who received religious education acquired it at Sunday school, it was this model of part-time classes unconnected to 'real' school that the Jewish community adopted, whether the sponsoring organisation was the London Board of Jewish Religious Education (LBJRE), representing centrist Orthodoxy, or the growing Reform and Liberal movements.

Until the 1970s, most Anglo-Jewish children received their Jewish education in supplementary classes on Sundays or after school. These classes, attended mainly by children aged 8 to 13, sought to instil the ability to read Hebrew and follow the synagogue service, familiarity with festivals, and a basic knowledge of Jewish history, Bible stories and religious rituals. They were better attended on Sunday mornings than during the week. Complaints about the teachers, pedagogy and curriculum abounded (Mendelsson, 2002).

Both the embrace of non-denominational schools, and the willingness to relegate religious education to a few hours of instruction weekly, reflect the fact that British Jews, though culturally integrated into mainstream society, nonetheless felt uncertain as to their status in England. Antisemitism, encouraged by Mosley's Fascists, resurfaced in the 1940s, and was exacerbated by violence in Palestine directed at the British Mandatory authorities. Opinion polls revealed considerable antipathy to Jews. The Jewish community responded apologetically, calling on its members to blend in, on the assumption that that if they became more 'like' non-Jews, the antagonism would disappear (Kushner, 1989).

Jewish Day School Constituencies

As noted, the overall trend prior to the late 1960s was decreased day school attendance. Nevertheless, during the 1950s and early 1960s, Jewish day school education was preferred by three small sectors of Anglo-Jewry. One was the strictly-Orthodox community led by Rabbi Solomon Schonfeld, whose Jewish Secondary Schools Movement was the largest of the Jewish day school providers. This sector upheld Samson Raphael Hirsch's programme of *Torah im Derekh Eretz*, with its commitment to Jewish studies alongside secular knowledge. It saw Jewish schooling as conducive to robust Jewish life with limited social but full professional integration into society at large. Like the rest of Anglo-Jewry, this sector, and the schools it sponsored, endorsed English middle-class values: financial security, upward social mobility, industriousness (Schonfeld, 1943, 1958).

Not surprisingly, the second group that rejected the prevailing preference for State schools was the *Charedi* sector. At first the Yesodey Hatorah schools were alone in the field, but in 1959 the Lubavitch movement started its own schools. Thereafter, various other Hassidic and Lithuanian groups opened schools. The fervently Orthodox had little interest in integrating into either British society or the middle class. Immersed in punctiliously applying Torah law to every aspect of life, they accepted an exiguous existence. The chief parental educational goals were Torah scholarship and strict levels of religious observance.

The third group that sent its children to day schools was drawn from working-class London Jews who preferred to send their children to the schools that had been established by the Anglo-Jewish 'Cousinhood' and later came under the aegis of the LBJRE. Most such parents did so because, though themselves working class, they were leery of their children's social interaction with schoolmates who might not aspire to a Grammar school education. After 1953, when the Zionist movement entered the field of day school education, it too harnessed Anglo-Jewry's reservations about the English working class, and later, ambivalence towards New Commonwealth (West-Indian and Indo-Pakistani) immigrants (Bermant, 1970). As a result, the Zionist Federation schools, several of which were situated in working-class districts, were often oversubscribed.

The Shift to Day School Education

By the mid-1960s, the bulk of Anglo-Jewry was successfully integrated into the British middle class. Yet as the decade came to a close, the demand for Jewish day school education had begun to rise, while attendance at supplementary schools was falling (Table 1 below).[3] Many have sought to account for this transition by invoking

Table 1 National trends in full- and part-time Jewish education for children between 5 and 17

	1962/1963	%	1967/1968	%	1975/1976	%	1986/1987	%	1992	%	1999	%
part-time	21,075	36	24,843	42	17,346	32	11,957	25	9,900	22	8,810	20
full-time	8,854	15	9,015	15	10,908	20	12,085	25	12,700	28	20,700	47

Source: Jewish Educational Development Trust, 1992, p. 7, and Board of Deputies, 2000.

---

[3] As noted, the shrinking percentage of children attending supplementary schools also reflects the growth of the fervently-Orthodox population within British Jewry.

an Anglo-Jewish religious and spiritual revival associated with the Six Day War and the campaign for Soviet Jewry (Bermant, 1990; Braude, 1981). But the importance of these factors has been exaggerated. In fact, it was the 1965 decision of the Labour Government to end selective education by dismantling the Grammar schools that led to withdrawal of Jewish children from the non-denominational state system (Valins et al., 2002). For the affluent, private education was the preferred alternative: the Independent schools continued to be perceived as the best means of ensuring academic achievement. By the early 1980s, Jews comprised 40% of the enrolment at several Independent schools in London and Hertfordshire. For those parents who were unable or unwilling to pay for private education, however, Jewish voluntary-aided schools became a means of circumventing the comprehensive system (Mendelsson, 2009).

Heightening the sense that Independent schools produced academic excellence, and thus contributing to the withdrawal of Jewish children from non-denominational State schools, was the assumption that the growing number of ethnic minority children in State schools had led to a decline in academic standards. Jewish schools were now achieving much improved academic results (Black, 1998). Moreover, they were perceived, albeit naively, as impervious to the turbulence associated with the permissive society. Parents believed that in sending their children to Jewish schools, they were shielding them from the dangers of political radicalism, promiscuity and drugs, which could impede their academic success and derail their future.

Another factor contributing to the newfound acceptance of Jewish day schools was Britain's gradual transformation from a basically monolithic to a multicultural, multi-faith society. New Commonwealth immigrants had arrived in Britain in growing numbers in the 1950s and 1960s, but multiculturalism was adopted as both a general policy and an educational objective only in the late 1970s. Initial expressions of cultural diversity involved acceptance of diversity in dress and cuisine, but soon spread to more substantive exposure to ethnicities, e.g., broadcasts of non-Christian prayer services, ethnic radio programmes such as Radio London's 'You Don't Have to Be Jewish', and events like the distinctively Caribbean Notting Hill Carnival. This openness to 'otherness' encouraged many Jews to be more self-affirming of their Jewish identity, though the embrace of ethnicity remained a matter of debate within Anglo-Jewry.

Attitudes to Jewish day school education reflected this debate: those who confined their Judaism to the private realm tended to oppose day school education, those comfortable with expressing their Jewish identity in public tended to support it. Despite the growing legitimacy of public expression of ethnic identity, most of the community, and certainly, its representative agencies, preferred its traditional profile as a religious denomination rather than a self-avowed ethnic group (Mendelsson, 2002).

Yet the search for community in an increasingly individualistic society impelled some Jews to re-examine their links to Judaism and the Jewish people. Despite the community's formal self-presentation as a religious group, and its discomfort with the 'ethnic minority' rubric, the term now accurately reflected its character. Except among the Orthodox, ritual observance was becoming less uniform, and Jewish identity was increasingly conceived in terms of belonging to a cultural or ethnic group rather than religious belief. A survey of United Synagogue members showed that about 90% 'strongly agreed' with the statements 'an unbreakable bond unites Jews all over the world' and 'it is important that Jews survive as a people' (Kalms, 1991). Rejection of the 'ethnic' label was thus a tactical consideration motivated by apprehension about being associated with minorities perceived as less acculturated. Despite integration into the political, cultural, social and economic realms of British life, Anglo-Jewry continued to harbour fears regarding its acceptance.

To summarise, different segments of the community had different objectives as to their children's education. For the *Charedi* sector, the primary considerations were a curriculum featuring intensive Torah studies, and organisation of the school in conformity with desiderata set by the rabbinical authorities, e.g., gender separation. For those affiliated with centrist Orthodox and Progressive (Liberal and Reform) congregations, and the unaffiliated, the dominant consideration was academic excellence (Valins et al., 2002). In the immediate post-War years, Independent schools were beyond the means of most British Jews, who had working or lower-middle-class incomes, hence State primary schools, and at the secondary level, Grammar schools, were seen as the best choice. Two decades later, changes to the educational system, particularly the phasing out of Grammar, and later, Direct Grant schools, impelled parents to seek alternatives. Due to upward economic mobility, Independent schools were now within the reach of some. But Jewish voluntary-aided schools attracted growing numbers of parents. As with all state-supported schools, the pupils' academic success was monitored and publicised by government agencies, endearing these schools to Jewish parents (Valins et al., 2002). Moreover, the legitimacy conferred on denominational schooling by Britain's embrace of multiculturalism allowed those who sent their children to Jewish day schools to see doing so as entirely compatible with being fully 'English' (Alderman, 1999).

Legislation on Denominational Schools

While the 1944 Education Act was still in committee, senior civil servants had suggested ending state funding for denominational schools. To avoid conflict with the ecclesiastical authorities, it was decided to offer two funding options for denominational schools. 'Controlled status' gave the denomination funding for, and autonomy over, religious instruction, in return for surrendering jurisdiction over the school to the LEA. 'Voluntary aided status' let the denominational authority retain partial autonomy over curriculum and administration in return for funding half the building and maintenance costs of each school. The former option was chosen by the Anglican Church, the latter by the Catholics and Jews. In 1959, the government raised its subsidy of voluntary-aided schools from 50 to 75%, and in 1967 and 1975, raised the building and maintenance grants to 80 and 85%, respectively. In 2001, it was decided to cover 90% of total costs (Parker-Jenkins, Hartas, & Irving, 2005).

Superficial analysis of the government's denominational schools policy might suggest growing sympathy for this type of education. In fact, however, budgetary restrictions and later, political opposition, limited expansion of the state-aided sector. According to the 1944 Education Act, the denominational authorities had to prove that within the locale of a proposed school there was not only parental demand but also an overall need for additional school places. During the 1950s, the post-War baby boom ensured that there was little difficulty in proving the requisite shortfall in school places. Yet whereas the Catholics were committed to denominational schools, the Jews evinced only slight interest in this option (Steinberg, 1989), as explained above. By the time Jewish attitudes changed in the late 1960s, state funding was more difficult to procure because declining birth rates had reduced the overall need for school places. After 1973, the inflationary spiral caused by the Arab oil embargo led to severe cuts in government expenditure on education. To establish additional schools, therefore, the community had no recourse but to fund the building projects on its own, in the hope that subsequently, applications for the coveted 'voluntary aided' status would be granted.[4]

Political considerations also limited the expansion of state-aided denominational schools. Beginning in the late 1970s, multiculturalism was a hot-button issue on the national and local political agendas. In this debate, the Labour party was perceived as more sensitive to the needs of ethnic minorities. In those London councils it controlled, it adopted a policy of affirmative action. But Labour disapproved of separate ethnic and religious schools, contending that such schools tended to foster religious, racial and cultural divisiveness. It preferred multicultural schools where ethnic and religious diversity would be encouraged, e.g., by classes on world religions and the celebration of diverse religious festivals. In keeping with this policy, Labour rejected applications for voluntary-aided status by *Charedi* and Muslim schools, justifying this rejection by citing the schools' failure to meet national and local criteria.

The Conservatives, in power from 1979 to 1997, shared Labour's fears that ethnic minorities were requesting public funds to further separatism. However, they viewed the existing *denominational* voluntary-aided schools – Anglican, Roman Catholic and Jewish – as upholding moral teachings that were broadly in line with Tory thinking. Moreover, they often contrasted perceived failings of the comprehensive schools, about which the Conservative party remained sceptical, to the acknowledged academic achievements of the denominational schools. Committed to parental choice, the Conservatives had to support denominational schooling. When the Muslim Parents' Association in Bradford demanded state-aided status for its schools, the Conservatives were in a quandary. They could not deny to one religious group what they had granted to others.

Meanwhile, in non-denominational State schools, incidents of racism and insensitivity to ethnic minority children were mounting. South Asian parents, for instance, claimed that their languages and cultures were not sufficiently respected in non-denominational schools. Muslim parents demanded schools whose behavioural standards were more in keeping with their religious outlook. Having pledged to

---

[4]Chief Rabbi Jakobovits' Jewish Educational Development Trust raised substantial funds for Jewish day school education for precisely this purpose; see Mendelsson, 2002, Chapter 6.

honour parental choice and diversity, the New Labour party had no choice but to reverse its stance and support denominational schools. Under this new policy, the Islamia School in the London Borough of Brent secured state-aided status, the Al-Furqan School in Birmingham followed suit, and shortly thereafter three additional Muslim schools became state-aided (Parker-Jenkins et al., 2005). They were joined by two Sikh, one Greek Orthodox and one Seventh Day Adventist School. State-aided status had now become available to so-called 'visible' religious minorities and to peripheral denominations.

In this changed climate, the Jewish community was able to secure state-aided status for more schools. Between 1992 and 1999, 12 new Jewish schools were added to the list of state-aided institutions (Valins & Kosmin, 2003).[5] Among these were two schools sponsored by the Progressive movement, which had traditionally evinced hostility to the very idea of Jewish day schools. So entrenched was this hostility that Rabbi Dow Marmur critiqued it during his keynote address at a Reform Synagogues conference in 1972, proposing that the movement adopt a policy of founding its own day schools (Marmur, 1972). Since 2004, several *Charedi* schools have also attained aided status.[6]

Not long after this expansion of the denominational schools (popularly known as 'faith' schools), race-related riots broke out in Bradford, Oldham and Burnley in July 2001; tensions were rekindled following the 9/11 terrorist attacks in the United States. In the wake of these disturbances, faith schools were reproached for allegedly fostering separatism rather than interaction between religious and ethnic groups. From the perspective of the minority leaders, however, day schools constituted the front line in the struggle against assimilation and communal disintegration. The controversy over the right of denominations to state funding for their schools continued to ignite popular passions as fears of isolationism and fundamentalism challenged the cohesion of the multicultural society. A MORI opinion poll found that 27% of interviewees opposed expansion of faith schools; this number increased to 43% when the same question was asked vis-à-vis Muslim, Sikh and Greek Orthodox schools (Times Educational Supplement (TES), 2001b).

Labour continued to support faith schools, introducing a White Paper, *Schools Achieving Success*, that defended proposals for more faith schools not only on the basis of the parental right to choose, but also because faith schools under state supervision were preferable to private institutions not subject to national curriculum, testing and performance standards. Attempting to placate critics, the government proposed integrating children of other faiths or no faith into denominational schools (Jackson, 2004, pp. 41–42; TES, 2001a).

The religious authorities were divided over the proposals. The Archbishop of Canterbury supported the idea that a percentage of places in voluntary-aided schools

---

[5] By contrast, in the preceding decade only two Jewish schools had been awarded this status.
[6] They include the Yesodey Hatorah Senior Girls School and Lubavitch Girls Primary School, both in London, the Beis Yaakov High School in Salford and the Manchester Mesivta School. In girls' schools, the ratio of general to religious studies is higher than in the parallel boys' schools.

be reserved for children of other faiths and no faith; the Roman Catholics, Muslims and Jews opposed it. Chief Rabbi Sacks argued that it was not the inclusivity of the student makeup that would nurture tolerance in faith schools, but rather the content of the syllabus, which he recommended be the subject of a national assessment (TES, 2001c). In response to a *Times Educational Supplement* editorial warning that 'establishing more Muslim schools in areas where the racial cauldron is still bubbling would be potentially disastrous', Ibrahim Hewitt, head teacher at the Al Aqsa primary school in Markfield, Leicestershire, remarked: 'the racial cauldron is bubbling because young people have a shortage of faith in their education, and not the reverse' (TES, 2001d). To the relief of the Catholic, Muslim and Jewish authorities, the plan to integrate children of other faiths or of no faith was dropped.

Governmental support, or more precisely, the Jewish community's acceptance of state funding for its schools, has created a dilemma. Community demographers predict that within the next decade, as the size of the mainstream community declines, Jewish schools may have difficulty filling school places. By law, voluntary-aided schools are obliged to fill surplus places, if necessary, with children of other religions. While some remain confident that the number of parents seeking Jewish day school education will continue to grow, others disagree, and predict that, given the schools' academic success, LEAs will not agree to reduce the intake, but will fill open places with non-Jewish pupils. The situation is not without precedent: Jewish voluntary-aided schools in the small and shrinking provincial communities of Birmingham and Liverpool have for many years enrolled non-Jewish children. At the King David Grammar School in Liverpool, over 50% of the student body has for some time been non-Jewish.

This puts the schools in a difficult position. On the one hand, they are committed to educating a minority-faith constituency in the tenets of its religion, on the other, they are responsible for the academic success and integration of a sizeable non-Jewish minority. The King David school was the subject of a government report. The inspectors were impressed:

> The school is a model of a multi-cultural institution. An environment is provided where pupils from more than two cultures work and live in harmony. The warm relationships are remarkable and pupils from all cultures and backgrounds co-exist happily. The school can be very proud that its pupils show mutual respect for one another and for each other's way of life. (UK Department of Education and Science, 1986)

Nevertheless, the integration of children of other faiths or no faith demands much planning and pedagogic resources. Hence the community preference is to avoid being mandated to 'top up' enrolment with children of other faiths (Commission on Jewish Schools, 2008).

Another challenge has recently (re)emerged for faith schools: the charge that many are not educating their pupils towards an understanding of other faiths and ethnicities. Critics of denominational schooling have called for exchange visits between different schools and the introduction of education for multiculturalism. Aware of this challenge, the Jewish community initiated a study of its schools' attitudes to multicultural education. The three schools found to be most energetic in this sphere were affiliated with the Progressive movement, whereas those found to be indifferent or hostile to such education were centrist Orthodox. The report acknowledged the burden imposed by the dual mandate of teaching the full national curriculum alongside comprehensive and not just token Jewish studies (Short, 2002). The issue of multicultural education will clearly remain a challenge, especially if ethnic/racial tensions intensify.

Religious Education in Non-denominational State Schools

Under the terms of the 1944 Education Act, all schools were required to begin the day with a collective act of worship, and all children were to receive religious instruction on a regular basis. The nature of the religious education was to be determined by a conference of representatives of the Church of England; other religious denominations deemed appropriate by the LEA; the LEA; and the teachers' association. Although the Act did not specify which religion or religions were to be taught, it was understood that the instruction would be generically Christian. Perusal of the various Agreed Syllabuses confirms that they indeed sought to inculcate Christian teachings, and schools were taken to be 'Christian communities preparing children for Christian living in the wider society' (Parsons, 1994). Similarly, the collective worship was broadly Christian in nature.

By the late 1950s and early 1960s, pupils were complaining that the religious education being imparted was dry and irrelevant. In response, religious education specialists suggested re-orienting the aims, methods and content of the classes to make them child-centred and directly relevant to the pupils' lives. Instead of discussing abstract religious concepts or Church and biblical history, a thematic approach informed by developments in the social and behavioural sciences was proposed. In 1966, the West Riding Education Authority presented the first of a new set of Agreed Syllabuses, which in its form and content acknowledged the child's psychological development. A section entitled 'Underlying Principles' mandated that the material must relate to life as experienced, and prompted teachers to address spiritual voids and encourage shared faith encounters. Other LEAs followed suit, and many began incorporating units on world religions and even non-religious philosophies. Yet despite placing the child at the centre of the curriculum, and the putative commitment to openness, the new approach to religious education basically remained Christian in orientation, seeking to foster a Christian outlook.

Two crucial changes in British society during the late 1960s and the 1970s gave rise to a different conception of religious education. The first was the growth of secularism, attested to by declining church attendance and ritual practice (Cook & Stevenson, 1996). The second, discussed above, was the rise of the multi-ethnic multi-faith society. The mainline Christian groups no longer dominated religious life, having been joined by an array of other denominations, especially Islam, Hinduism, Buddhism and Sikhism, and smaller sects such as the Mormons. In areas where the population was highly diverse, the presentation of religion in purely Christian terms clearly conflicted with the assumptions of the 1944 Education Act.

There was increasing demand, both by the minorities themselves and by others, that the religious education syllabus be changed to reflect this diversity, in the hope that this would facilitate greater understanding and tolerance of the non-Christian communities. The task of the teacher, it was now argued, was 'to portray a variety of religious positions and religious beliefs sympathetically, displaying an imaginative grasp of their significance, content and claims while not advocating one religious tradition rather than another' (Parsons, 1994). Religious education fast came to be conceived as an academic discipline much like any other school subject, and the cultivation of Christianity was replaced by a commitment to multiculturalism and religious pluralism (Wright, 1993).

How did Anglo-Jewry respond to the changing nature of religious education in State schools? Under the 1944 Education Act, parents were permitted to withdraw their children from religious education classes to receive instruction in their own denomination. Secondary schools were to provide facilities for this activity if the transfer of the children to a venue outside the school premises was impractical. By the early 1950s, the LBJRE had taken advantage of this clause and established 'withdrawal classes' for over 3,000 children in some 25 schools. By 1975, however, these classes had declined in number dramatically, with only eight centres, attended by some 680 pupils, remaining operative (Ziderman, 1989). The LBJRE attributed this decline to the new religious education syllabus, since its neutral, multi-faith approach challenged the legitimacy of withdrawing children from classes that no longer inculcated Christian beliefs (Biennial Report of LBJRE, 1977). Obviously, though, much of the decline resulted from the fact that many parents were no longer enrolling their children in non-denominational State schools, preferring, as discussed above, either Independent schools or voluntary-aided Jewish day schools.

Some were pleased by the new approach. A number of Jewish teachers at non-denominational State schools spoke out in favour of the change, asserting that the new religious education succeeded in being positive about all faiths and conducive to empathy and tolerance. Two Jewish religious education teachers at a secondary school in multiracial Bedford declared: 'We would be horrified if our Jewish, Muslim, Hindu and Sikh children withdrew from Religious Education. We welcome and enjoy their contribution to the subject. We hope that all of them will gain some insight into each other's beliefs and be strengthened in their own' (Canter and Walker to Jewish Chronicle, 1980). Parents who had formerly been reluctant to single their children out by having them withdraw from religious education classes were more comfortable with the non-dogmatic, values-free approach to religious education. And some members of the Jewish educational establishment viewed the new approach favourably. Clive Lawton, chairperson of the Board of Deputies' Youth and Education Committee and former principal of the Liverpool Jewish high school, predicted that it would engender in some Jewish children a more positive attitude to their Judaism because it was 'validated in a non-Jewish environment'. Moreover, the academic–objective, as opposed to confessional–doctrinal, nature of the syllabus, meant that instead of being 'preached at', these children would be taught their tradition in a 'more palatable way' (Lawton & Sless, 1982).

Other educators felt differently. Some preferred the traditional approach to religious education, arguing that the withdrawal classes had been an opportunity to provide an affirmative, values-orientated Jewish education to children who would otherwise receive no Jewish education at all (Ingram and Manasseh to Jewish Chronicle, 1982). Fred Worms, a lay leader of the community's education effort and a governor of the North London Collegiate School for Girls, an Independent school, expressed satisfaction when the new principal of that school announced a more Christian focus to the religious education lessons. This enabled him to organise parallel classes, similarly committed to inculcating religious principles, for Jewish children (Worms, 1996). Indeed, the LBJRE sought to open new withdrawal-type classes in Independent schools with high Jewish enrolment, suggesting that it was cognisant of the growth in the number of Jewish pupils attending these schools, and aware that many were continuing to teach old-style religious education as a means of imparting Christianity.

The *Education Reform Act, 1988*, stimulated spirited discussion of religious education in State schools. Rabbi Jonathan Sacks, then principal of Jews' College, addressed the subject on BBC Radio's 'Thought for the Day'; his remarks were soon invoked by Chief Rabbi Jakobovits during a debate in the House of Lords. Rabbi Sacks critiqued the world faiths syllabus as superficial, as a 'touch of Christianity, a dash of Judaism, a slice of Islam', arguing that this approach failed to recognise that 'only one faith resonates with personal meaning: the faith of our community [whatever faith it be], our culture, our family, our past' (Sacks, 1988). He preferred a return to the policy whereby each denomination was permitted to teach its own religious doctrines. Sacks recalled his childhood experience at a local school, where the religious education had been Christian: 'The effect of this schooling on our Jewish identity was curious. It made us, of course, acutely aware that we were different. But because those around us were taking their religion seriously, it made us consider Judaism seriously too.' Chief Rabbi Jakobovits concurred with this opinion, and attacked the neutral–pluralistic approach to religious education. He proposed that instead of employing religiously indifferent teachers, religiously committed educators be hired to teach pupils of their own faiths. 'Effective religious instruction can no more be administered by and to persons of a different faith than can a blood transfusion be safely given without first ensuring blood-group compatibility. Indiscriminate mixing of blood can prove dangerous and so can the mixing of faiths in education' (Sacks, 1988).

The Education Reform Act established a national curriculum that set out attainment targets, programmes of study and assessment arrangements for basic subjects. Such specifications for religious education, however, were not included. Rather, syllabuses agreed on by a Standing Advisory Council on Religious Education (SACRE) were to be reviewed by the LEAs (Rose, 1988). The SACREs were to have the same four constituent groups as the Agreed Syllabus conferences set out in the 1944 Education Act, namely, representatives of the Church of England; other religious denominations deemed appropriate by the LEA; the LEA; and the teachers' association. The Act stated that religious education should 'reflect the fact that religious traditions in Great Britain are in the main Christian whilst taking account of the teaching and practices of the other principal religions represented in Great Britain'.

Within a few years, however, even this comparative approach to religious education, and the much weakened primacy accorded to Christian input vis-à-vis curriculum, was deemed insufficiently pluralistic, and subjected to further modification. In 1994, the Department of Education's School Curriculum and Assessment Authority published two model syllabuses that reflected the authority's views on how religious education was to be interpreted under the 1988 Act. The two models were very similar and essentially covered the teachings of the six predominant religions in Great Britain: Christianity, Islam, Buddhism, Hinduism, Judaism and Sikhism. It has been claimed that the syllabuses represent 'a significant step forward in acknowledging the multi-faith nature of British society', and are of considerable pedagogic merit, allowing students to learn from religion in addition to learning about religion (Hobson & Edwards, 1999). But they have also elicited criticism. The study of religions separately, critics have argued, is overly descriptive and unimaginative, and fails to challenge the students as would a comparative approach. It has also been faulted for not inviting students to reflect on their own understanding of spirituality, and for ignoring secular–humanist perspectives. In any event, the syllabuses clearly seek to minimise the number of children withdrawn from religious education classes. At the annual meeting of the SACREs in 2001, it was claimed that the nature of the agreed syllabuses has had the effect of reducing the number of withdrawals to an 'extremely small number' (Qualification and Curriculum Authority, 2001).

In response to these changes in the teaching of religious education in state-maintained schools, the relevant Anglo-Jewish bodies have redirected their efforts. Rather than providing withdrawal facilities for Jewish children, they now focus on ensuring that the study materials on Judaism will adequately convey the spirit and teachings of Judaism.[7] The Board of Deputies of British Jews has assumed responsibility for this effort, providing resources and educational materials. It has encouraged members of the Jewish community to take an active part in their local SACREs, to ensure that Jews are well represented.[8] When contrasted with the activities of the LBJRE in the 1950s and 1960s, such efforts highlight the changed role of communal agencies in the wake of multi-faith education in non-denominational State schools. The community realised it could no longer provide a forum – withdrawal classes – for nurturing Jewish identity in Jewish pupils in the non-denominational State schools, as it had in the past. It would instead need to ensure that instruction about Judaism supplied to the entire student body as part of the general curriculum did justice to the community, its faith and its values.

---

[7] Neil Levitan, Coordinator, Jewish Activities in Mainstream Schools (JAMS) for the United Jewish Israel Appeal (UK), pointed out in a personal communication (February 2009) that in some schools, Jewish agencies also provide informal activities for Jewish pupils in non-classroom settings.

[8] Hannah Ashleigh, Education Projects Manager, Board of Deputies of British Jews, articulated this approach in correspondence (March 2009).

Conclusions

One conclusion to be drawn from this study is that neither the communal agenda, the objectives set by the state authorities, nor the wider social, cultural, political and economic context determined the prevailing mode of Jewish education in post-Second World War England. Rather, it was the parental agenda that determined what form the delivery of most Jewish education would take. From the end of the war until the mid-1960s, neither generous governmental subsidies for day school education, nor the poor quality and general unpopularity of supplementary Jewish education, sufficed to persuade many Anglo-Jewish parents to send their children to day schools. Exceptions to this general rule included the *Charedi* community, the strictly-Orthodox community led by Rabbi Solomon Schonfeld, and some working-class inner-city parents who were unhappy with the educational level of their local State schools. The provision of separate instruction in Judaism within the framework of non-denominational State schools, we also saw, made very little difference with respect to parental educational choices.

What determined parental choice of an educational framework was not, then, the Jewish institutional–communal agenda, which endorsed maximal Jewish education for its own sake, nor the governmental agenda, which sought to create a non-tiered educational system to equalise opportunity for all, but rather, the Jewish *parental* agenda. Initially, parents sought to ensure their children's integration into British society and the middle class, and later, when this was taken for granted, into the professional classes. Also important was ensuring that their children's affiliation with the Jewish community was maintained. When comprehensive education was introduced, they did not accept it, but sought ways to preserve selective high-level secular education, even if that meant embracing denominational education, or paying for Independent schools. The unintended side effect was that, for the many parents who chose Jewish day schools, this entailed giving their children a better quality Jewish education – the very outcome sought by the communal leadership, but previously ignored by parents. The Jewish parental agenda persisted despite changes in the funding and organisation of the broader educational system. Though the state system endeavoured to provide a modicum of religious education, the same parents who were satisfied by minimal Jewish education in the pre-comprehensive era, nonetheless – when they feared their goal of facilitating high academic achievement for their children was in jeopardy – abandoned state education and shifted towards denominational education with a fairly substantial religious studies component. They were not driven by the rabbinical–communal agenda of imparting Jewish education to preserve religious observance and communal continuity, but by their own agenda of maximising quality secular education.

Another conclusion to be drawn from our survey of the main parameters of Jewish schooling in England is that overall, the profile of community–state relations in the field of education has been positive. The Jewish community, like other major denominations, has – to a degree unparalleled in other Diaspora Jewish communities – benefited from considerable state largesse in day school funding. Although funding is contingent upon meeting stringent national and local educational standards, once these standards have been met the schools have flourished, producing impressive academic results as well as imparting meaningful Jewish experiences and an acceptable to high-level Jewish education.

Third, due to the constraints imposed by the acceptance of state aid in the provision of denominational education, Anglo-Jewish education must be attuned to educational imperatives adopted by the state. In the wake of multiculturalism and the embrace of diversity, the past 20 years have seen substantial changes in the delivery of religious education in non-denominational State schools, as well as in the demands made of voluntary-aided denominational schools. The community will continue to straddle the twin mandates of adhering to national and local educational directives, and providing affordable Jewish education. For *Charedi* Jews, the walls between their community and society at large remain particularly high in the realm of education. Nevertheless, due to the community's rapid expansion, the growing strain on its financial resources has in some cases led the ultra-Orthodox to seek state support for their schools. *Charedi* leaders remain ambivalent about state support, as it comes with strings attached that some perceive as undermining communal mores.

At the same time, the Jewish schools will have to be vigilant in ensuring that they continue to fulfil a third and equally or perhaps more important mandate: satisfying the educational aspirations of Anglo-Jewish parents for their children. In the final analysis, we have seen, apart from the strictly- and fervently-Orthodox sectors, the chief concern of Anglo-Jewish parents has generally not been the Jewish education imparted to their children. Most parents have been willing to be flexible as to the quality and quantity of Jewish knowledge acquired by their children, but consistently seek the highest quality secular education accessible to them.[9] Synthesising the foregoing, we can predict that should demographic developments and government funding policies impel widespread opening of places at Jewish day schools to children of other faiths – a scenario that could create parental apprehension, warranted or not, as to the schools' ability to sustain a high academic level – the popularity of day schools may yet wane.

The debates over faith schools and the religious education curriculum in non-denominational schools illustrate that Britain remains uncertain as to the extent to which multiculturalism should be mandated. Some contend that faith schools support disadvantaged populations, solidify their pupils' identity, and encourage a mosaic of British identity. Others view them as divisive and conducive to insularity and bigotry. Common schools, these critics claim, would strengthen inter-group solidarity and the overall social fibre. But both Britain's major political parties, the Conservatives and New Labour, have expressed commitment to parental choice in education. They are committed to educational diversity and recognise a historic debt to faith schools. It thus seems unlikely there will be a challenge to the continued existence of these schools in the immediate future. On the other hand, calls

---

[9] At least one study has found that very recently, some parents have begun to take the quality of their children's Jewish education more seriously, see Miller, 2007.

to reform these schools vis-à-vis the imparting of multicultural values, admission of children of other faiths or no faith, and interaction with other schools, may result in legislation that challenges their present autonomy.

Despite the significant increase in the study of Anglo-Jewish education during the last 30 years, much room remains for further research. Given the enormous expansion of Jewish day school education and the fact that by now, many of the graduates of these schools have reached adulthood, it is to be regretted that so little empirical research has been undertaken to assess the impact of this framework on individuals and the community. Although much philanthropic and communal funding has been channelled to day school education, surprisingly little effort has been made to measure its efficacy vis-à-vis transmission of Jewish knowledge and values. Another area yet to receive in-depth examination is that of day school curricula, syllabuses and textbooks. Study of these tools would allow researchers to uncover and deconstruct the underlying ideological and educational commitments of the various organisations that establish Jewish day schools. A comparative study of the teaching of subjects such as Bible, Talmud, and Israel across different schools would provide much insight into the respective organisations' philosophical and socio-cultural assumptions. A further lacuna in Anglo-Jewish educational research is informal education, which has yet to be adequately studied. It is likely that this is to some extent due to the inherent nature of the youth group environment, in which the experiential dimension is key, and the importance of measuring and documenting educational impact is not emphasised. Some scholarly attention has been paid to the Zionist youth movements, but given the strong impact of this mode of education, as attested to by its graduates' subsequent life choices, far more research remains to be done. In conclusion, Jewish education in England is a fertile area for further research, not only in and of itself, but also due to its historic influence on the former Commonwealth communities.

References

Alderman, G. (1992). *Modern British Jewry*. Oxford: Clarendon.
Alderman, G. (1999). British Jews or Britons of the Jewish persuasion? The religious constraints of civic freedom. In S. Cohen, G. Horenzyk (Eds.), *National variations in Jewish identity* (pp. 125–135). Albany, NY: SUNY.
Bermant, C. (1970). *Troubled Eden*. New York: Basic.
Bermant, C. (1990). *Lord Jakobovits*. London: Weidenfeld and Nicolson.
Black, G. (1998). *A History of the Jews' Free School*. London: Tymsder.
Board of Deputies of British Jews. (2000). *Education statistics 1992–2000*. London: Board of Deputies Research Unit.
Braude, J. (1981). Jewish education in Britain today. In S. Lipman & V. Lipman (Eds.), *Jewish Life in Britain 1962–1977*. New York: H. G. Saur.
Commission on Jewish Schools. (2008). *The future of Jewish schools*. London: Jewish Leadership Council. http://www.thejlc.org/commissiononjewishschoolsreportfinal.pdf.
Cook, C., & Stevenson, J. (1996). *British history from 1945*. London: Longman.
Cush, D. (2003). Should the state fund schools with a religious character?. *Journal of the Professional Council for Religious Education, 25*, 10–15.
Gould, J. (1984). *Jewish commitment: A study in London*. London: Institute of Jewish Affairs.

Graham, D., & Vulkan, D. (2007). *Britain's Jewish community statistics 2006.* London: Board of Deputies of British Jews. http://www.boardofdeputies.org.uk/file/CommunityStatistics2006.pdf

Hobson, P., & Edwards, J. (1999). *Religious education in a pluralist society.* London: Woburn.

Jackson, R. (2004). *Rethinking religious education and plurality.* London: Routledge.

Jewish Chronicle. (1980). Letter to editor by Marcia Canter and Jean Walker, 25 Jan.

Jewish Chronicle. (1982). Letter to editor by Rabbis C. Ingram and C. Manasseh. 12 March.

Jewish Educational Development Trust. (1992). *Securing our future: An inquiry into Jewish education in the United Kingdom.* London: JEDT.

Kalms, S. (1991). *A Time for change: United Synagogue review.* London: Kalms Foundation.

Krausz, E. (1969). The Edgware survey: Occupation and class. *Jewish Journal of Sociology, 11,* 75–95.

Kushner, T. (1989). *The persistence of prejudice: Antisemitism in British society during the Second World War.* Manchester: Manchester University Press.

LBJRE. (1977). Biennial Report of London Board of Jewish Religious Education, London.

Lawton, C., & Sless, S. (1982). Provision of Jewish Education in Non-Jewish Schools. Unpublished report in archives of Chief Rabbi Jakobovits (CR C3 7 1983), housed at Greater London Record Office.

Marmur, D. (1972) A genuine search for new ways. *Living Judaism, 5,* 35–46.

Mass Observation Poll M-O A FR: 2463, M-O A TC: 62/4/B University of Sussex

Mendelsson, D. (2002). Between Integration and Separation: The History of Jewish Education in England 1944–1988. PhD dissertation, Hebrew University of Jerusalem.

Mendelsson, D. (2009). Embracing Jewish day school education in England, 1965–1979. *History of Education, 38,* 543–563.

Miller, H. (2001). Meeting the challenge: The Jewish schooling phenomenon in the UK. *Oxford Review of Education, 27,* 501–513.

Miller, H. (2007). *Accountability through inspection: Monitoring and evaluating Jewish schools.* London: Board of Deputies of British Jews.

Parker-Jenkins, M., Hartas, D., & Irving, B. (2005). *In good faith: Schools, religion and public funding.* Aldershot: Ashgate.

Parsons, G. (1994). *The growth of religious diversity: Britain from 1945* (vol. 2). London: Routledge.

Qualification and Curriculum Authority (QCA). (2001). *Religious education and collective worship: An analysis of 2000 SACRE reports.* London: HMSO. http://www.qcda.gov.uk/resources/publication.aspx?id=7eb2bed7-debc-44b2-b071-f117e48e6735

Rose, W. (1988). A survey of representative groups on SACRE. *Journal of Contemporary Religion, 13,* 383–393.

Sacks, J. (1988). Three Lords' addresses. *L'Eylah: A Journal of Judaism Today, 26,* 3–7.

Schonfeld, S. (1943). *Jewish religious education.* London: National Council for Jewish Religious Education.

Schonfeld, S. (1958). *Message to Jewry.* London: JSSM.

Short, G. (2002). *Responding to diversity: An initial investigation into multicultural education in the United Kingdom.* London: Institute for Jewish Policy Research.

Simon, B. (1994). *The State and educational policy.* London: Lawrence and Wishart.

Steinberg, B. (1989). Anglo-Jewry and the 1944 Education Act. *Jewish Journal of Sociology, 31,* 81–108.

Times Educational Supplement. (2001a). K. Thornton. Lose faith in others and lose funding. 16 November.

Times Educational Supplement. (2001b). B. Passmore & N. Barnard, Voters oppose expansion of faith schools. 30 November.

Times Educational Supplement. (2001c). M. Samuel, Talking point. 30 November.

Times Educational Supplement. (2001d). I. Hewitt. Faith schools do not create ghettos. 7 December.

UK Department of Education and Science. (1986). Report by HM Inspectors on King David High School, Liverpool, 10–14 November.
UK Statutes. (1988). *Education Reform Act 1988*. Ch. 40. London: HMSO.
UK Statutes. (1998). *School Standards and Framework Act 1998*. London: HMSO.
Valins, O., & Kosmin, B. (2003). *The Jewish day school marketplace: The attitudes of Jewish parents in greater London and the South-East towards formal education*. London: Institute of Jewish Policy Research.
Valins, O., Kosmin, B., & Goldberg, J. (2002). *The future of Jewish schooling in the United Kingdom*. London: Institute for Jewish Policy Research.
Worms, F. (1996). *A life in three cities*. London: Halban.
Wright, A. (1993). *Religious education in the secondary school*. London: Fulton.
Ziderman, A. (1989). Jewish education in Great Britain. In H. Himmelfarb & S. DellaPergola (Eds.), *Jewish education worldwide: Cross-cultural perspectives* (pp. 267–300). Lanham: University Press of America.

Australia: The Jewel in the Crown of Jewish Education

Paul Forgasz and Miriam Munz

Setting the Context

Jews were present in Australia from the very beginning of European settlement in 1788, when a fleet of ships arrived bearing a contingent of British convicts, of whom at least eight were Jewish. (Rutland, 1997). The history of the first four decades of Australian Jewish life is, in fact, not the history of a community but one of individual Jewish convicts. It was only with the arrival of the first free Jewish settlers during the late 1820s that we see the beginnings of organised Jewish communal life, regarding which Rutland (1997) observes, "The close ties the early Jewish settlers had with leading Anglo-Jewish families imprinted the English pattern of Jewish practice on Australian Jewry and this influence was to remain strong throughout the nineteenth century" (p. 49). But she also notes that during this period "Australian Jewry continued to be plagued by the problems of low levels of religious observance, poor standards of Jewish education, and the pressures of integration into the general community" (p. 75). In fact, by the 1920s things had deteriorated to a point where, according to Rubinstein (1986), "the near disappearance of the Anglo-Saxon Jewish community by assimilation seemed almost inevitable within a few generations" (pp. 61–62).

However, the arrival on Australian shores of thousands of European refugees and Holocaust survivors after World War II radically transformed the face of Jewish community life in Australia, both demographically and in terms of a prevailing Jewish mind-set and value system. These migrants also played a key role in cementing within the Australian Jewish community a strong and lasting sense of commitment to Israel and Zionism. Not surprisingly, Rubinstein (1986) writes that "by 1950 Australian Jewry was very different from what it had been 15 years before" (p. 70). Indeed, the legacy of this dramatic post-war development is reflected today

P. Forgasz (✉)
Monash University, Melbourne, Australia
e-mail: Paul.Forgasz@monash.edu

M. Munz (✉)
Monash University, Melbourne, Australia
e-mail: Miriam.Munz@monash.edu

in a remarkable array of organisations and facilities which cater to the religious, cultural, welfare and varied leisure needs of Australian Jews. However, for Rubinstein (1986, 1991), the most significant change that came over the Jewish community in Australia was the emergence of a Jewish day school system which he regards as "entirely novel and entirely the product of the post-World War II period" (1986, p. 71). In fact, he goes so far as to suggest that Australia's Jewish day school system is "the 'jewel in the crown' of post war Jewish experience" (1991, p. 211). Moreover, he argues, it is this "which gives Australian Jewry its special international distinction, and which is, possibly more than any other factor, responsible for the evolution of the type of community that has arisen here since 1945" (p. 211). He also views the success of the day school movement as "unique among any ethnic minority in Australia" (p. 240). In view of this, we have chosen to focus our discussion on the Jewish day school movement in Australia.

Historical Evolution of Australian Jewish Day Schools[1]

Australian Jewish day schools operate today within the larger framework of a well-developed private school system which includes independent schools associated with various religious affiliations or particular educational philosophies as well as a separate Catholic parish school system. In fact, private schooling existed from the earliest days of European settlement in Australia, when education was provided by state-supported denominational schools. However, by mid nineteenth century, state-administered non-denominational public schools had been established, as well as a separate denominational school board which administered government funds to church schools and a tiny number of Jewish schools. During the latter half of the nineteenth century, each of the colonial (state) governments expanded their systems of public schooling and between 1872 and 1895 passed the "free, compulsory and secular" Education Acts which made primary (elementary) education a state responsibility and stopped most financial assistance to church schools. Nevertheless, a residual system of private schooling continued, composed mainly of Catholic parish schools and Protestant grammar schools. In the decades that followed the federation of the individual colonies in 1901, Church leaders campaigned for the restoration of state aid and, as Angus (2003) notes, "by the 1950s there was bipartisan political support for the resumption of some form of government support" (p. 113); furthermore, "since the 1970s state funding of private schools has been a fact of Australian life" (p. 112). This had the effect of energising the private sector and encouraged a remarkable growth of private schools, including a diverse and robust Jewish day school system.

The first day schools in Sydney and Melbourne were established during the latter half of the nineteenth century in response to expressions of concern about the

---

[1] The brief historical overview which follows is based on a number of more extensive accounts of the development of Jewish education in Australia. In particular, see Rubinstein (1991); Rutland (1997, 2000); Conyer (1998).

lack of adequate Jewish educational facilities. However, by the end of the century they had closed their doors, plagued as they were by a lack of community support and the withdrawal of government aid. Almost 50 years later, Abraham Rabinovitch founded the North Bondi Jewish Day School in 1942, which was then established as Moriah College in 1953. Rabinovitch remained its president until his death in 1964, exercising autocratic control over a school which operated along narrow Orthodox lines. Consequently it attracted the support of only a very small number of mainly refugee immigrant families. Conyer (1998) observes that because the Board of Deputies, the representative body of Jews in New South Wales, "was not a party to the school, the school was never considered nor regarded as a project of the community for the community" (p. 333). It was not until the 1970s that the Jewish day school movement in Sydney showed any real signs of expansion. In fact, the development of a highly successful day school movement occurred first within the Melbourne Jewish community which witnessed the growth of a number of day schools during the 1950s and beyond. Australian Jewish day school education is thus aptly described by Solomon (1973) as a "post war phenomenon" (p. 169).

Mount Scopus College was Melbourne's first post-war Jewish day school. A birth child of the Victorian Jewish Board of Deputies (VJBD), the representative body of Victorian Jewry, it opened its doors in 1949. What is particularly fascinating about the school as a case study in the development of Jewish day school education is that it was created by the community for the community. Of particular interest are various issues which dominated debates at VJBD meetings and in the community at large regarding the creation of a community-based day school:

- The desirability of segregating Jewish children from the wider society.
- Would the creation of such a school foster anti-Semitism?
- The question of whether religious instruction should be compulsory. Although it was eventually decided that it should be, there was debate about what form of religious instruction would be acceptable to all. Following many discussions and formal debates, the wording agreed upon in the school's 1947 constitution was that "Jewish religious instruction shall be based on traditional lines but shall be taught in a modern way" (cited in Patkin, 1972, p. 126). Although potentially this was open to manifold interpretations, from its inception the school adopted a stance which Rubinstein (1991) describes as "'soft' but observant Orthodoxy" (p. 222).
- Given that the VJBD contained vigorous and vocal Yiddish speakers, there was considerable debate over whether Yiddish should be made compulsory alongside Hebrew and religious instruction. Although the decision was negative, it was agreed that provision would be made for its teaching for those who desired it.

Mount Scopus emerged as one of the great success stories of Jewish education not only in Australia, but throughout the Diaspora. Referring to a report that was presented to the Executive Council of Australian Jewry Annual Conference in 1958, Rutland (1997) outlines the reasons identified by its author as accounting for the school's initial success. First, the establishment of the State of Israel in 1948 led to a strengthening of Jewish identity among Jews throughout the Diaspora. In addition, the stream of Eastern European Holocaust survivors who migrated to Melbourne during the 1950s brought with them a strong desire to replicate the intensity of Jewish life that had characterised pre-war Poland. It was also suggested that a reason for the school's success was

> the fact that by clever but dignified propaganda of Jewish education, it has became gradually fashionable and "the proper thing to do", as were "endeavours to make Jewish teaching more attractive by furnishing brighter classrooms, employing enthusiastic teachers, and introducing modern and appealing curricula". (cited in Rutland, 1997, p. 349)

Beginning with an enrolment of 120 in 1949, school numbers rose dramatically in the following years, reaching a peak of more than 2,600 by the mid-1980s. An important reason for the school's continuing appeal was, and still is, the achievement of consistently high scholastic standards, especially at year 12: a factor which also accounts for strong levels of parental support across most Australian Jewish day schools.

Although Mount Scopus was set up as a school for the community, a succession of ideologically diverse day schools began to spring up in Melbourne in the wake of its establishment, clearly indicating that various sectors of the community did not feel that their needs were being adequately met. During the 1950s, Chabad established Yeshiva and Beth Rivka, a day school for boys and girls respectively, and the Adass Israel School was set up by the predominantly Hungarian ultra-Orthodox community. In 1962 the Mizrachi organisation established Yavneh College as a religious Zionist day school. The 1960s also saw the Bialik kindergarten and supplementary Hebrew language school emerge as a secular Zionist day school but in which teaching about the Jewish religion was included. According to Israel Kipen, one of the school's founders, what set it apart was that "in many other Jewish schools, Jewish culture is considered a part of the Jewish religion while at Bialik the Jewish religion is considered a part of the overall Jewish culture" (Rubinstein, 1991, p. 226). Perhaps alluding to the ideological debates which surrounded the establishment of Mount Scopus, Kipen also claimed that Bialik was not founded "in a haze as was the case when Scopus started" (Rutland, 2000, p. 81). The 1970s saw the Progressive (Reform) Jewish community coming into its own when it established The King David School. As Conyer (1998, p. 332) notes, however, it "was met with strong resistance by the community at large, headed by the Orthodox mainstream leadership". Even the local Jewish press adopted "a policy of virtually boycotting any positive reporting of the school" (p. 332). Finally, during the mid-1970s the Yiddishist/Bundist community established the Sholem Aleichem School as a Yiddish kindergarten and primary school, building on the foundation of two part-time Yiddish schools. Thus, a particularly remarkable aspect of Melbourne's day schools is that they represent the full ideological spectrum of the Jewish world, from ultra-Orthodox to secular Yiddishist. This reflects the ideological divisions which exist within the Melbourne Jewish community itself, a product in large measure of the diversity that characterised Jewish life in interwar Poland.

The success enjoyed by the day school movement in Melbourne was much slower in coming to Sydney. Mention has already been made of the internal problems that plagued Sydney's first post-war Jewish day school. Unlike Mount Scopus College, it failed to attract broad-based communal support. Nor did the establishment during the 1960s of Masada College on Sydney's North Shore and of the Yeshiva primary school do much to boost total enrolments in Sydney's day school system. In considering the evolution of Sydney's day school movement, account must be taken of the demographic makeup of Sydney Jewry. Whereas Jewish life in Melbourne was dramatically transformed by a significant post-war influx of Eastern European Jewish migrants, Sydney's Jewish immigrant community consisted of what Rutland (2000) describes as "the more assimilated and culturally sophisticated remnants of Western and Central Europe" (p. 78). Conyer (1998) thus suggests that Sydney's "history of immigration meant that a primarily Anglo-Australian culture dominated the community. The competition between competing ideologies, a characteristic of Melbourne, was never a primary motivating force for the community. Furthermore, this highly Anglicised community preferred to be less conspicuous and therefore were (*sic*) more hesitant about the creation of a distinctive day school" (p. 332).[2]

However, during the late 1960s, Sydney's day school movement underwent a dramatic transformation. Abraham Rabinowitch, who had maintained an autocratic stranglehold over Moriah College for more than two decades, passed away in 1964. Under the leadership of a new principal the school went from strength to strength, with enrolment numbers growing to a point where Moriah eventually overtook Mount Scopus as the largest Jewish day school in Australia. In fact, the latter has experienced a progressive decline in enrolments since the late 1980s. During the 1970s and 1980s Sydney's Yeshiva primary school was expanded to include both a boys' and a girls' secondary (high) school. In 1981 Mount Sinai College opened as a modern Orthodox primary school in Sydney's south-eastern suburbs. Following the lead of Melbourne's King David School, The Emanuel School was established in 1983 as Sydney's first Progressive Jewish day school. Furthermore, this whole period witnessed a remarkable increase in the overall rate of day school enrolments.

According to Rutland (1997, 2000) there are a number of factors that account for this success. There was a visible strengthening of Jewish identity in the wake of the 1967 and 1973 Arab/Israeli Wars. This was also a period during which the government adopted multiculturalism as official government policy and as Rutland (2000) notes, this "made the idea of separate ethnic and religious schools more acceptable" (p. 83). The increase in Jewish day school enrolments was also part of a developing and continuing trend within the wider community, characterised by a growing loss of confidence in government schools and a corresponding increase in private-school enrolments. At the same time, the expansion of Jewish schools was aided

---

[2]Solomon (1978) argues that from the outset the Melbourne Jewish community was more conscious of its Jewish minority identity. Thus, with the removal of state aid from denominational schools in the late nineteenth century, the Sydney Jewish community closed its day school but the one in Melbourne continued for a further 25 years.

by the provision since the early 1960s of generous levels of government funding to private schools. As had been the case in Melbourne, new waves of Jewish immigration – to some extent from the Soviet Union, but more so from South Africa – also had a considerable impact on the growth of Sydney Jewish day schools, especially Masada College. The South Africans were particularly strong supporters of these schools because, as Rutland (1997) points out, they

> brought with them a strong belief in the day school movement, a belief which is largely a product of their homogenous Lithuanian background...In addition, the very nature of South African society tends to encourage groups to be introverted, while the fear of intermarriage is also a strong motivating factor. (pp. 371–372).

Mention must also be made of developments in the smaller centres of Jewish population. In Perth, Carmel College was established in 1959 but suffered initially from a lack of community support which was driven by issues relating to segregation and the school's educational standards. However, this resistance was overcome because of a concerted effort to employ quality teachers and because people were also influenced by the success of the day school movement in Melbourne. A wave of South African migration to Perth impacted very positively on the growth of Carmel, presently regarded as one of the leading academic schools in Perth. Nevertheless, one particularly contentious issue which hangs over the school is the policy of not accepting children of mothers who have converted to Judaism through the Progressive movement. Beyond Perth, Jewish primary day schools have been established in what might be regarded as the more marginal centres of Australian Jewish life – Adelaide, Brisbane and the Gold Coast.

Today there are 21 Jewish day schools throughout Australia, 12 of them operating from K-12 and serving an estimated total Jewish population of 107,000. About 60% of Jewish children in Australia receive a full-time Jewish education; approximately 70% of the total Jewish preschool age population is enrolled in Jewish preschools.[3] Through a roof body structure, the Australian Council for Jewish Schools, the day schools have developed a well-coordinated and highly effective approach to negotiating the intricate complexities of government funding of private schools. The principals have also formed their own association, the role of which is to provide a forum for cooperation between the schools regarding matters of common concern.

While Australia's Jewish day school movement may well lay claim to being "the 'jewel in the crown' of post war Jewish experience" (p. 211), the success of Jewish education in Australia extends beyond the day school movement.[4] A significant

---

[3] See Rubinstein (1991) and Rutland (2000) for a more detailed analysis of enrolment patterns and statistics, though these are now dated.

[4] Moreover, Rutland (2000) suggests that Jewish day school education has not been an unqualified success story. She refers to two studies regarding the effectiveness of "mainstream Jewish day schools" that were undertaken during the 1980s and "reached fairly negative conclusions" (p. 95). Rutland also argues that apart from the *haredi* schools, the others succeed more in terms of fostering Jewish association, commitment to Israel and knowledge about the Holocaust, but fare less well in the transmission of knowledge about Judaism and Hebrew language. She also claims that

number of children who do not receive a full-time Jewish education participate in a creative mix of both formal and informal programmes of supplementary Jewish education under the auspices of local boards of Jewish education. In Melbourne, the United Jewish Education Board (UJEB) provides after-school and Sunday classes for students at non-Jewish schools. It also provides Jewish religious education classes in 40 Victorian primary state schools for half an hour per week. The equivalent organisation in Sydney is the Board of Jewish Education (BJE).[5] The difference between the two organisations is that both the BJE and the NSW Board of Progressive Jewish Education are funded by the Jewish Communal Appeal (JCA): whereas UJEB operates on a far smaller budget funded by donors whose loyalty is mainly directed to the day schools their own children and grandchildren attend. The BJE has also managed to develop a professional staff, act as a resource centre for the Jewish day schools and supply distance education to rural and regional areas in New South Wales.

Beyond the classroom, informal Jewish education of Australian youth is served by a diverse network of mainly Zionist youth movements which also maintain a presence in a number of the day schools.[6]

Challenges Confronting Jewish Day Schools

In 2009 Jewish education in Australia stands at critical crossroads in view of the many and varied challenges which confront it. In some cases, these challenges mirror those facing other Jewish communities throughout the world. In others, the challenges are particular to religious and ethnic schools in largely secular Australia.

Sustaining Jewish Day School Enrolments

Affordability

Every discussion with significant stakeholders in the Jewish school system concludes that affordability is and will be the greatest challenge to Jewish education in Australia. As Nechama Bendet, chairperson of the Victorian Council of Jewish Schools, points out, school costs increase annually at twice the rate of the consumer price index.[7] Jewish schools must maintain buildings, pay for security and

---

"many students complete 13 years of Jewish schooling feeling disillusioned and negative about their experiences" (p. 96).

[5] In addition to UJEB and BJE classes, the Progressive movement and individual Chabad Centres offer after-school and Sunday classes.

[6] See Rubinstein (1991) and Rutland (1997, 2000) for descriptions of other aspects of Jewish education in Australia. Forgasz and Jones Pellach (2006) discuss the phenomenal success in Australia of the Florence Melton adult Jewish education programme.

[7] Interviewed 10 November 2008

ensure that they are at the cutting edge of educational initiatives, both Jewish and general, since they compete with top academic private schools. In fact, it is the recognised academic excellence, the variety of subjects, the committed teachers and the sophisticated facilities which play a significant role in attracting parental support for Jewish schools. Additionally, Jewish schools have to bear the cost of paying for a dual curriculum and a longer than usual Australian school day.

In 2009, parents pay between 22,000AUD and 25,000AUD (17,000USD – 19,500USD) in fees for a year-12 student. Given that this comes out of after-tax income, even successful professionals earning a 250,000AUD (195,000USD) pre-tax income will struggle to pay fees for their three or four children and maintain the lifestyle they have come to expect. The current economic downturn, combined with the large mortgages people take to live in Jewish centres of population, means that applications for fee assistance are being made by people who, 5 years ago, would not have needed to ask for help. In fact, all Jewish school fees include an element of subsidisation, with the money allocated to needier families built into fee schedules. Thus parents, already struggling to pay, carry the burden of others' fee remissions. The concern is that the middle band of families, those falling between the wealthy and those who qualify for support, will be pushed out of the system. In fact, the UJEB manager, Yossi Aron,[8] believes there is evidence of families in Melbourne opting out of Jewish day school education. In 2007, 927 students accessed religious education classes in government primary schools. In 2008, 1,010 were enrolled and for 2009 figures show a further increase. Many of these students will never enter a Jewish day school.[9]

While there is widespread agreement that one of the priorities of communal funding should be to make Jewish education more affordable, there are differing views regarding how this should be done. Johnny Baker (2006), a past president of Mount Scopus College argues for an amalgamation of Melbourne's four coeducational Jewish secondary schools which, he believes, would save on infrastructure and staffing. He also argues that the sale of some of these schools' real estate holdings would realise sufficient money for a communal fund, the size of which could encourage philanthropists to donate additional money towards fee assistance. However, Jeffrey Mahemoff,[10] a past president of Bialik College, argues that upon closer examination costs don't diminish significantly when schools are merged to create a mega-school. He also predicts that there is a risk that parents, denied their preferred ideological choice of Jewish school, would send their children to a non-Jewish private or government school. Mahemoff's proposal is that philanthropists

---

[8]Interviewed 18 November 2008

[9]Transfers from the day schools often occur at grades 2 and 3 when a family's second child may begin school and parents decide that paying the fees is beyond their means. There is a tendency for quite a number of parents to send their children to very good government primary schools, using the money they save during these years to send their children to Jewish secondary schools. For many years the trend was to favour Jewish primary day school education, but social reasons have played an important role in influencing parents to give priority to Jewish secondary schooling.

[10]Interviewed 25 November 2008

with significant wealth should create a substantial endowment, say 250 million AUD, the interest from which would cover the shortfall in the fees collected every year by Jewish schools. But this also requires strategic and centralised communal planning, an area in which Melbourne lags far behind Sydney.

In Sydney, where the JCA has initiated moves to coordinate resources between schools so that funding is not spent on purchasing commodities that can be shared, the schools are transparent in their budgeting so that existing projects are not duplicated. The JCA also designates funds to schools to subsidise students whose families cannot afford fees and additional costs. It is interesting that in 2003–2004 there was a move to amalgamate Mount Sinai College, a modern Orthodox primary school, with the Emanuel School, a Progressive K-12 school. However, the amalgamation did not go ahead because the Mount Sinai leadership wanted Emanuel to adopt all of Mount Sinai's Orthodox norms rather than the community-inclusive norms it had adopted. Many Mount Sinai families also maintained that Emanuel was not "Jewish enough" and demonstrated a strong sense of historic loyalty to their school's ongoing existence in its own right. Indeed, much of the encouragement for the merger came from the JCA which saw this as an opportunity to rationalise resources when student numbers in both schools had been falling.

Demographics

Any number of the first and second post-World War II generations made sacrifices to support their children through a Jewish school. Current and future generations did not arrive in Australia having suffered for their Jewish identity. They did not have to succeed in spite of adversity as did their grandparents and great-grandparents, and as a post-Holocaust generation, they may not have the same understanding about the importance of Judaism. Consequently, their motivation, commitment and passion for Jewish education cannot be assumed as a given. Indeed, a potential threat to the maintenance of strong enrolments are parents who can afford to pay for private schooling but choose to send their children to a non-Jewish private school. For those for whom Jewish education might mean sacrificing a luxury holiday or a larger home, if they have to choose between a good government school and a great Jewish day school, then good could become good enough. Added to all this is the fact that beyond the ultra-Orthodox community, young people marry later and have fewer children. This, combined with a growing intermarriage rate, will impact on Jewish school enrolments.

Growing Jewish School Leaders, Training Jewish School Teachers

Today, day school principals cite Jewish studies teacher recruitment as their most serious and perennial issue. This is not a new phenomenon. The first generation of Jewish studies teachers in Jewish day schools was largely educated in Europe prior to World War II. Although Jewishly well educated, they were hardly able to deal with a post-Holocaust Australian school reality. The second generation included a large number of *shlichim*, "emissary" teachers from Israel employed on temporary contracts of 3–4 years' duration. However, they often found it difficult to bridge the cultural divide between the Israeli and Australian realities, and were generally not effective in the Australian classroom. Currently, the Jewish knowledge of many homegrown teachers is quite poor. Yet others, perhaps educated in a seminary or Yeshiva, do not possess the pedagogical tools for transmitting their knowledge.

Leibler Yavneh College is the only school in Melbourne that continues to employ *shlichim* teachers as a matter of course. Currently there are seven *shlichim* employed at different levels throughout the school. They inject a strong connection to the land of Israel as well as fill the very real need for Jewish studies and Hebrew teachers. But since the *shlichim* are only contracted to work for 3 years, there is a problem with continuity, apart from longstanding issues of adaptation to Australian school mores and culture.

There is no simple formula for producing good Jewish studies teachers. The Jewish community, in general, does not regard education as a prestigious career and sees no status attached to being a teacher. For many, the lack of status is reflected in relatively low teacher salaries, especially when compared to other professions. The irony is that many Jewish studies teachers struggle to send their children to Jewish schools based on the salaries they earn. At the same time there is no defined career structure or pathway for Jewish studies educators.

In Sydney, a structured programme for training Jewish studies teachers has been in place since 1990 at the University of Sydney, and in Melbourne a similar arrangement was put in place in 1996 at Monash University. Both programmes were integrated into the framework of the education programmes offered by the respective universities. Graduates with a major in Jewish studies or Hebrew could complete a teaching qualification with method training in those subject areas. In fact, many of those graduating from these two programmes have been employed by Jewish day schools. However, the overall impact of these programmes has been relatively limited owing to the very small number of students who have expressed an interest in pursuing a career in Jewish education. In an attempt to address the teacher shortage, the Australian Centre for Jewish Civilisation at Monash University is planning to introduce a "Judaic Scholars Teaching Fellowship" for high-calibre students who have completed an undergraduate program in Jewish studies. Successful candidates will undertake a 2-year programme of study combining a Graduate Diploma in Education with a Masters in Judaic Studies.

Roy Steinman, Principal of Leibler Yavneh College, moved from Sydney's Moriah College to his current position in Melbourne 2 years ago. Prior to his move he created a scheme through which promising young people, preferably university graduates, were offered generous bursaries to study in Israel for 4 or 5 years. There they would pursue rabbinical studies or some equivalent form of advanced traditional Jewish learning, and also complete a programme at a recognised quality teacher training institute. Upon returning to Sydney, they would be bonded to the school for 5 years. There are now three such educators at Moriah College. Steinman admits that this is an expensive model, but it is "an investment in the future".[11]

In addition to the problem of recruiting Jewish studies teachers, the Australian community also suffers from a shortage of quality Jewish educational leaders. Recent appointees to various school principals' positions have mostly come from overseas. Some school boards have compromised and decided to appoint non-Jewish Principals. However, since it is the school head who acts as a role model and sets the tone of the school, this raises questions about the potentially mixed messages which might be communicated to students. Succession planning for principals, heads of schools, Jewish studies directors and curriculum planners is unstructured and haphazard because of the dearth of suitable candidates. In the smaller communities, beyond the large Jewish population centres of Melbourne and Sydney, all of these issues are greatly magnified. The Australian Centre for Jewish Civilisation at Monash University is currently planning for the introduction of a Masters-level programme in Jewish educational leadership in an attempt to address this situation.

Challenges in Developing the Curriculum

Each day school is responsible for devising its own Jewish studies curriculum in accordance with its particular ideological orientation, a situation that shapes the amount of time devoted to Hebrew language and Jewish studies, and the role of *tefillah* (prayer) and ritual observance.[12] Heads of Jewish studies decide on the direction and content of the curriculum, sometimes in consultation with their principals, though in more strictly Orthodox schools the rabbis of the community are also involved. However, preoccupied as they are with the running of their departments, heads of Jewish studies do not have the time to focus their energies on curriculum development, nor do they necessarily possess the requisite skills to do so. Consequently, over time a number of schools have sought the assistance of curriculum specialists from the Hebrew University's Melton Centre for Jewish Education or the Lookstein Centre at Bar Ilan University. Mount Scopus College and Moriah College also employed their own in-house curriculum writer for an extended period. Importantly, all these initiatives have also included the provision of related professional development for Jewish studies staff. Such developments have resulted in dramatic improvements to the overall quality of the Jewish studies curriculum and its delivery in individual schools.

With the exception of particular ultra-Orthodox schools, Modern Hebrew is taught as a modern language of communication. For many years Hebrew language education was plagued by an absence of textbooks which provided a coherent and sequential programme of learning. Many teachers also lacked the necessary skills to teach Hebrew as a second language. As a result, over the past decade or so, schools

---

[11] Interviewed 17 November 2008

[12] According to Rutland (2000) most schools devote between a quarter to a third of the school day to Jewish studies. A number also allocate additional time for *tefillah*.

have invested considerable energy and resources in their quest to improve the quality of Hebrew language instruction and many have introduced the Tal Am/Tal Sela and NETA programs which appear to have succeeded in addressing the perennial problems that have plagued the teaching of Hebrew. In the case of both programmes, teachers have received intensive and regular professional development so that they fully understand the underlying principles and methodology of the respective programmes. The results of both programmes appear to be encouraging, but perhaps more importantly, they illustrate that cooperative curriculum development can meet the needs of schools of widely different ideologies.

During the late 1980s Mount Scopus College developed a bilingual programme for year 7 and 8 students with a high level of aptitude and interest in Hebrew language. For most of the subjects they undertake, the language of instruction is Hebrew. These students then continue to study Hebrew language in an accelerated track through to year 12. Bialik College also offers a bilingual programme in year 3. When the programme at Bialik began 3 years ago, 20 students chose to participate; today 50 out of 65 students in the level participate.

Zionism represents an ideological centrepiece of most day schools in Australia, this being reflected in a wide range of both formal and informal programmes and activities. Nevertheless, Israel Studies, as a formal part of the curriculum, has been piecemeal and fragmented for many years. However, a recent initiative by the Hebrew University's Melton Centre for Jewish Education and the Zionist Federation of Australia (ZFA) has seen the development of a project which focuses on the educational challenges and dilemmas of creating models for meaningful student engagement with Israel. Its purpose was to help Jewish secondary schools in Australia create new approaches to teaching about contemporary Israel and this occurred within a curriculum development framework that enabled each school to be guided by its own educational goals. Consequently, various schools across the ideological spectrum now incorporate Israel Studies in a variety of ways into their Jewish studies curricula.

However, it is beyond the classroom where schools have experienced the greatest success with Israel and Zionist education. Of particular note are the Zionist seminars which are run in a camp setting by Israeli *madrichim* (youth leaders) as a joint venture of the Youth and Hechalutz department and the ZFA. Apart from the ultra-Orthodox sector, all schools, including the supplementary systems, participate by sending students to the camps and hosting post-camp activities. Mount Scopus College and Leibler Yavneh College also bring four *Sherut Leumi* girls from Israel each year to reinforce the Israel connection in their schools. The girls assist with informal activities, Hebrew conversation, extra study groups, camps and social activities. Bialik College sources three or four post-army personnel through Masorti Olami – the conservative movement in Israel. They, too, work at a myriad of projects and their impact is enormous. Leibler Yavneh College also benefits from a group of *Hesder Yeshivah* students who study in the *Mizrachi Kollel* for a year.

A number of schools offer students the opportunity to participate in an Israel-experience programme towards the end of year 10. In Sydney, Moriah and Masada Colleges offer the 4-week Israel Study Tour organised by the Torah Department of the World Zionist Organisation. Melbourne's Mount Scopus College has offered three programmes – one of 13 weeks, one of 8 weeks and one of 6 weeks, with more than 50% of year-10 students having travelled to Israel on one of these options. Due to the 2008 downturn in the economy, the current trip is planned for 5 weeks, though sponsorship and donations make it possible for every student who wishes to travel to Israel to do so. Bialik College also offers a year-10 Israel experience with two programmes from which students can choose. However, the offer of travelling on March of the Living to Poland and then to Israel during the first semester of year 11 has impacted on the numbers travelling to Israel in year 10. Within the supplementary system, UJEB and the BJE raise funds to assist enthusiastic students who wish to participate in an Israel-experience programme. In the more orthodox schools individual students can spend time in an Israeli school; but since a year or even two in Israel, is almost a post-year-12 rite of passage, it is not surprising that these schools cannot sustain a group programme at year-10 level.

Given the demographic makeup of Australian Jewry, with its large percentage of *Shoah* survivors, the agenda and character of Jewish life in Australia was for many years largely defined by a post-Holocaust migrant community. Nevertheless, the Holocaust was "taught sporadically and unsystematically through the 1960s and 1970s" (Berman, 2001, p. 79); though beginning with Moriah College during the mid-1970s, schools began progressively to develop units of study about the Holocaust. Thus, as Berman (2001) notes, "by the mid to late 1980s, formal, compulsory study of the Holocaust had become a permanent core topic in the Jewish Studies curricula of most high schools with senior grades" (p. 86). Added to this were the annual emotion-filled *Yom Hashoa* ceremonies conducted by the schools. It is therefore not surprising that for many students, a large number of whom were children and grandchildren of Holocaust survivors, the *Shoah*, together with Israel, served as the linchpin of their Jewish identity. Yet, Fagenblat, Landua & Wolski (2006) question the wisdom of educational and communal institutions relying "heavily on this darkest of chapters in human history" (p. 11). While understanding that there "are, of course, good and justifiable reasons for this," they also wonder "about the long term consequences of an identity so firmly rooted in pain and suffering . . . By excessively dwelling on the trauma of our identity, we may perhaps unwittingly be narrowing the horizons of our Jewishness in the present" (pp. 11–12). Consequently, as a new generation of Australian Jews is redefining the experience of what it means to be Jewish in Australia, schools will need to confront the challenge of developing an educational agenda that will best prepare students for the development of a twenty-first century Australian Jewish identity.

Researching Jewish Education in Australia

Although Jewish education in Australia has flourished, relatively little research has been carried out. Much of the research undertaken is historical in its focus. In 1972 Solomon completed a doctoral thesis focusing on the development of Jewish education in Australia from 1788 until 1920. Both Rubinstein (1991) and Rutland (1997) included detailed discussions of the development of Jewish education in their general histories of the Australian Jewish community. Conyer (1998) examined the impact of social phenomena in the broader Australian community on the historical evolution of Australian Jewish education. Useful surveys incorporating both historical and contemporary aspects of Jewish education have been produced by Rutland (2000, 2008). More specific histories of individual schools and their communities appear in Patkin (1972), Kipen (1989), Aron (1995), Ruth (1997), Tofler (2000), Grinblat (2003) and Rutland (2003).

There have also been a number of more sociologically oriented studies of Jewish education in Australia. Amongst the earliest were studies which appeared in Medding's (1973) volume dealing with various aspects of Jews in Australian society. Drawing on a 1967 Jewish community survey, Solomon (1973) analysed attitudes to Jewish education. Goldlust (1973) analysed the impact of Jewish education on Australian Jewish adolescents. Later studies, examining the relationship between Jewish schooling and Jewish identification, but limited to specific schools and communities, were carried out by Chazan (1980) and Simai (1985), though Rutland (2000) notes that they "reached fairly negative conclusions about the effectiveness of mainstream Jewish day schools" (p. 95).[13] On the other hand, two major demographic surveys, Goldlust (1993) in Melbourne and Eckstein (1999) in Sydney demonstrated high levels of communal support for Jewish day school education.[14] Adopting a more specifically school-based focus, Cohen (1992) studied the role of policy and administration in the context of a Jewish community school in Melbourne. Bryfman (2001) has examined the effectiveness of Israel education for Jewish secondary school students in New South Wales.

In referring to the fairly negative conclusions which were reached during the 1980s by both Chazan and Simai regarding the effectiveness of mainstream Jewish day schools, Rutland (2000) notes that "these findings were embarrassing for the community leadership, and since 1985 there have been no academic studies of the effectiveness of Jewish education in Australia" (p. 95). However, given the scale, scope and vibrancy of Jewish education in Australia, there is an important need for rigorous, systematic and current research regarding this issue. Moreover, such research can provide important indicators for educational change and future school improvement. Indeed, the soon-to-be released results of the recent nationwide Jewish community survey conducted by Markus (2009) will be able to serve as a useful starting point for such research, as it will include data about changing attitudes to Jewish education based on survey participants' personal experiences as well as parents' expectations and preferences.

A need also exists to evaluate the effectiveness of particular educational programmes and curricular initiatives which have been adopted by various schools. For example, schools in Australia have invested heavily in the Tal Am/Tal Sela and

---

[13] A cautionary note is offered by Rubinstein (1991, Vol. 2) regarding the interpretation of such results. He argues that "if education at a Jewish day school were not ultimately valued by graduates, this would surely result in reluctance to send these graduates' own children to a Jewish school" (p. 244). His view is that the facts do not support this.

[14] See Rutland (2000) for a more detailed analysis.

NETA Hebrew language programmes. However, no research seems to have been undertaken with a view to determining the impact of these programmes on the development of Hebrew language skills by students. Much the same can be said of other Jewish studies curriculum initiatives which have been developed within schools or in partnership with other agencies such as the Melton Centre for Jewish Education, as well as programs in which a substantial investment has been made by schools, such as year-10 Israel-experience trips and various informal Jewish education programmes. Also called for is an evaluation of the impact of established university Jewish studies teacher-training programmes.

A small number of Australian studies have examined the way in which ideology manifests itself in the life of Jewish day schools. These include Bullivant (1978), who carried out an ethnographic study of life in a Chabad boys' day school; Klarberg (1983), whose research focused on the impact of ideology on the teaching of Hebrew in Jewish day schools; and Munz (2008), who undertook a comparative study of Jewish, Greek and Islamic schools. Given that Jewish schools in Australia span the full ideological spectrum, from ultra-Orthodox to secular Yiddishist, the opportunity exists to undertake a number of case studies concerning the impact of ideology on educational practices both within individual schools, and also on a comparative basis. In this connection, it would also be of interest to investigate how teacher beliefs and knowledge, as well as personal ideology, impact on the delivery of the Jewish studies curriculum within individual schools.

In view of the earlier discussion of the challenges confronting Jewish day schools, research should also be undertaken into the professional identity of Jewish studies teachers and the related question of how to enhance the status of Jewish education as a profession.

We began this chapter by describing the historical evolution of Jewish day school education in Australia and how it became the "jewel in the crown" of the Australian Jewish community. Today, however, Jewish education in Australia stands at critical crossroads, confronted as it is by various challenges, some of which mirror those facing other Jewish communities throughout the world, and others that are particular to the local situation. How the leadership of the various Jewish schools in Australia responds to these challenges, aided among other things by rigorous and effective research, will determine how far Jewish education will continue to occupy its special and privileged status within the framework of the wider Australian Jewish community.

References

Angus, M. (2003). School choice policies and their impact on public education in Australia. In D. N. Plank & G. Sykes (Ed.), *Choosing choice: School choice in international perspective*. New York, NY: Teachers College Press.

Aron, J. (1995). *One hundred years of Jewish education*. Melbourne: United Jewish Education Board.

Baker, J. (2006). The Falling Crown? The Future of Jewish Day Schools in Australia. In M. Fagenblat, M. Landau, & N. Wolski (Eds.), *New under the sun: Jewish Australians on religion, politics and culture*, Melbourne, Black Inc.

Berman, J. (2001), *Holocaust remembrance in Australian Jewish communities, 1945–2000*. Nedlands, W.A: UWA Press.
Bryfman, D. (2001). *The current state of Israel education for Jewish high school students in New South Wales*. Masters in Education thesis. Melbourne: Monash University.
Bullivant, B. M. (1978). *The way of tradition*. Melbourne: Australian Council for Educational Research.
Chazan, B. (1980). *Jewish schooling and Jewish identification in Melbourne*. Jerusalem: Hebrew University of Jerusalem.
Cohen, A. (1992). *Policy and administration in Jewish education: A case study of a Jewish community school in Melbourne, Australia*. Master of Educational Policy and Administration thesis. Melbourne: Monash University.
Conyer, B. (1998). Social phenomena in Jewish Australia and the development of Jewish education. *Australian Jewish Historical Society Journal, 14*(2), pp. 322–344.
Fagenblat, M., Landau, M., & Wolski, N. (2006). Will the centre hold? In M. Fagenblat, M. Landau, & N. Wolski. (Eds.), *New under the sun: Jewish Australians on religion, politics and culture*. Melbourne: Black Inc.
Forgasz, P. & Jones Pellach, P. (2006). Reclaiming the book: On adult Jewish education. In M. Fagenblat, M. Landau, & N. Wolski (Eds.), *New under the sun: Jewish Australians on religion, politics and culture*, Melbourne: Black Inc.
Goldlust, J. (1973). The impact of Jewish education on adolescents. In P. Medding (Ed.), *Jews in Australian society*. Melbourne: Macmillan
Goldlust, J. (1993). *The Jews of Melbourne: A community profile – a report of the findings of the Jewish community survey, 1991*. Melbourne: Jewish Welfare Society Inc.
Grinblat, I. (2003). *Nachum Zalman Gurewicz*. Melbourne: Makor Jewish Community Library.
Kipen, I. (1989). *A life to live*. Melbourne: Israel Kipen.
Klarberg, M. (1983). *The effect of ideology on language teaching: A study of Jewish day schools in Melbourne*. Ph.D. thesis. Melbourne: Monash University
Medding, P. (1968). *From assimilation to group survival*. Melbourne: F.W.Cheshire
Medding, P. (1973). *Jews in Australian society*. Melbourne: McMillan.
Munz, M. (2008). *Culture, community, connectedness*. Ed.D thesis. Melbourne: Monash University.
Patkin, B. (1972). *Heritage and tradition*. Melbourne: The Hawthorne Press.
Rubinstein, W. D. (1986). *The Jews in Australia*. Melbourne: AE Press
Rubinstein, W. D. (1991). *The Jews in Australia: A thematic history. Volume 2 – 1945 to the present*. Melbourne: Heinemann Australia.
Rutland, S. D. (1997). *Edge of the diaspora:Two centuries of Jewish settlement in Australia*. Sydney: Brandl and Schlesinger.
Rutland, S. D. (2000). The state of Jewish day school education in Australia. *Australian Journal of Jewish Studies, 14*, pp. 8–100
Rutland, S. D. (2003). *If you will it, it is no dream: The Moriah story*. Sydney: Playright Publishing
Rutland, S. D. (2008). Jewish education in Australia. In R. L. Goodman, P. A. Flexner, & L. D. Bloomberg (Eds.), *What we now know about Jewish education*. Los Angeles: Torah Aura Publications.
Ruth, J. (1997). *Jewish secular humanist education in Australia*. Ph.D. thesis Melbourne: University of Melbourne
Simai, R. (1985). *The effect of Jewish and non-Jewish day schools on Jewish identity and commitment*. Ph.D. thesis. Melbourne: Monash University.
Solomon, G. (1973). Jewish education in Australia. In P. Medding (Ed.), *Jews in Australian society*. Melbourne: Macmillan
Solomon, G. (1978). Jewish education in Australia. In J. Cleverly (Ed.), *Half a million children: Studies on non-government education in Australia*. Melbourne: Longman Cheshire
Tofler, O. B. (2000). *Forty years on: A history of G. Korsunski Carmel School*. Perth: Sponsored publication.

Canada: Jewish Education in Canada

Michael Brown

Had this chapter been written a few months earlier, it might have begun with the assertion that Canadian Jewry is unequalled in its dedication to Jewish education. To corroborate the assertion, the author would have pointed to an almost unparalleled variety of day and supplementary schools in the largest communities, a substantial financial commitment, which, while insufficient to meet all the needs, still compares favorably to that of most other communities, a high percentage of children receiving some kind of Jewish education, although not the highest in the world, a high percentage of children enrolled in day schools, especially compared with communities in the United States, a record of innovation and research, world-renowned professional educators, two unique university-based programs of Jewish teacher education, and significant, highly professional coordinating agencies in the larger communities.

Recent developments, most especially in Toronto, the home of Canada's largest Jewish community by far, call that self-satisfaction into question. To be sure the achievements, especially of the post-World-War II years, are impressive and, for the most part, remain in place. In April 2009, however, UJA/Federation of Greater Toronto precipitously and without explanation closed its central educational agency, the Centre for Enhancement of Jewish Education (the Mercaz, formerly the Board of Jewish Education), headed by Dr. Seymour Epstein, one of the leading figures of the Jewish educational establishment in North America and beyond. The closing came without consultation with the lay board of the Centre, without prior notice to the schools serviced by the Mercaz, and despite a record of superior service and research. The closing came, moreover, less than two years after the restructuring of the agency in response to the recommendations of a high-level task force convened by UJA/Federation itself.

The precursor of the Mercaz, the Bureau of Jewish Education (later renamed the Board of Jewish Education) had been established in 1949 following a study by Dr. Uriah Z. Engelman, the director of the Department of Research, Publications and Information of the American Association for Jewish Education and the author of *Hebrew Education in America: Problems and Solutions*. From its inception,

---

M. Brown (✉)
Centre for Jewish Studies, York University, Toronto, ON, Canada
e-mail: michaelb@yorku.edu

the Mercaz and its predecessors served as "the community's central planning and coordinating educational agency and claimed credit for raising the educational standards of [its] affiliated schools" (Kurtz & Epstein, 2008). Educators, school volunteers, and communal professionals have attested to the high quality of Mercaz services (see Worth, 2003, for example), although its guidance was seen by some as the usurpation of the autonomy of constituent schools. Assurances by David Koschitzky, then chairman of the board of UJA/Federation of Greater Toronto, that the closure was not related to budget constraints (Koschitzky, 2009, and many other sources), made it all the more threatening to parents, children, and educators, wondering what further cuts to community support for education lay ahead. In the late summer of 2009, an interim caretaker was appointed to ensure that some of the ongoing activities of the Mercaz would continue and seemed to suggest that the Centre might be reconstituted in some form. That the caretaker had little experience beyond running a supplementary school, however, was cause for further disquiet, although Ted Sokolsky, the CEO and president of UJA/Federation, continued to boast of the organization's financial commitment to Toronto's Jewish schools (Csillag, 2009b). And in December, the Federation vice-president for strategic communications, claimed that, "'Virtually' all Mercaz services [remained] intact" and would continue in the future, although some might be contracted out (quoted in Kraft, 2009b).

But this is getting ahead of the story. The purpose of this chapter is to define the challenges for Jewish education in Canada and its successes, especially those specific to the Canadian context historically and at present. As well, there are comments about research that has taken place and that may be undertaken in the future.

The Context and the Challenges

From the British conquest of French Canada in 1759, the country was *de facto* a binational, bicultural, bilingual, bireligious polity; from 1867, when the quasi-constitutional British North America Act came into force, the country's duality was official. Some Canadians, most of them in Quebec or Lower Canada, were Francophone, French by culture, Roman Catholic by religion, and descended from colonists who had come from France. Others were English speaking, British by culture, and Protestant by religion (except for Catholics of Irish origin). Most members of the latter group could trace their ancestry to the British Isles.

The educational implications of the duality were considerable, especially with regard to religion. In Quebec, "public" schools were Francophone and Catholic; there was a parallel system of "separate" schools, which were Anglophone and Protestant. In Ontario or Lower Canada, the "public" schools were Protestant, and the parallel "separate" school system was Catholic. In both Ontario systems, instruction was in English. Elsewhere in the country, variations of these arrangements came into being. Perhaps the most complex school system was in the least populous province, Newfoundland, which joined the Canadian federation only in 1949. There until the 1990s, education was offered by four separate, faith-based systems:

Pentecostal, Roman Catholic, Seventh Day Adventist, and Interdenominational (Anglican, Salvation Army, and United Church). Jews, along with others who were not Christian, had no official place in the mix in most of the country.

In Ontario and elsewhere, the Protestant schools became *de facto* public schools, and the role of the Protestant churches diminished over the years. In Montreal, until the 1960s home to Canada's largest Jewish community, Jewish children were more or less reluctantly admitted to the Protestant schools. But acceptance in both Ontario and Quebec, and elsewhere was often grudging and not by right. According to a report in the London *Jewish Chronicle* (7 February 1862), Jewish parents in Victoria, British Columbia withdrew their children from the public schools in 1862, when teachers who belonged to the Church of England, tried "to seduce them from the religion of their fathers." (quoted in Leonoff, 2008, p. 135) In Toronto until well after World War II, efforts were made to concentrate Jewish children in certain schools; Jews were not hired as teachers except in schools where most pupils were Jewish; and education had definite Christian overtones.

In Montreal, the situation was even more convoluted. An 1870 law gave Quebec Jews the right to choose either Protestant or Catholic schools for their children, and they were to pay their taxes accordingly. Until 1886, almost all Jewish children attended Protestant schools. In that year, a dispute between the Protestant School Board of Montreal and the Spanish and Portuguese Congregation resulted in the synagogue establishing its own Jewish school under the aegis of the Catholic Board. Friction mounted, as the Protestant Board complained that most Jewish children were enrolled in their schools, while Jewish tax money was being paid to the Catholic Board. No account was taken of Jewish renters, whose rent helped to pay their landlords' taxes. In 1890, the Jewish community opened a second school specifically for immigrant Jewish children, the Baron de Hirsch School, under the auspices of the Protestant Board. This further heightened the tension.

Eventually a compromise was reached: the Spanish and Portuguese Congregation closed its school, and Jewish children and tax money returned to the Protestant system. But it was an uneasy and demeaning compromise. Jews could not stand for election to the Protestant Board, nor could they even vote in school board elections. In 1903, the Protestant School Board of Montreal refused to grant a high school scholarship to a Jewish boy, Jacob Pinsler, whose grades would have earned him such a scholarship had he been Protestant. A lawsuit was brought on Pinsler's behalf, but it was not successful. The ultimate result was a new Quebec school act, which declared Jews to be "Protestants for school purposes." This act accorded Jews some rights, although at the cost of their identity. They remained barred from school board office and from voting in school board elections. Although by 1914 Jews constituted almost half the "Protestant" children in Montreal, they remained largely without rights in the schools. Only in the 1950s, did Montreal Jews gain the right to vote in Protestant School Board elections and to serve on the Board.[1]

---

[1] For a somewhat fuller account of these events, see Brown (1999) and Tulchinsky (1998, pp. 63–86), and the sources cited in both.

Jews' difficulties with the educational system in Canada's two largest cities were emblematic of their anomalous position in the country. On the one hand, they fared rather well in Canada, as elsewhere in the English-speaking world. On the other hand, Canada's duality allowed them no secure space, even in theory. It is also the case that anti-Semitism has always been stronger in Canada than in the United States, and in some respects than in the mother country (Cohn, 1979; News in brief, 2009, and other sources). One result has been that Zionism, Jewish nationalism, has been consistently and almost universally popular among Canadian Jews, since its inception in the late nineteenth century (Brown, 1982, 1984). Another result has been strong support for separate Jewish schools outside the "public" system, especially in the post-World-War II years.

With the exception of the two short-lived Montreal schools mentioned above, however, and the Yiddish-language I.L. Peretz Folks Shule (first called, the Jewish Radical School) in Winnipeg, the establishment of day schools only began in the 1940s, when Jews had achieved a measure of economic prosperity and could support their own schools. In 1941, the Jewish People's School in Montreal (JPPS, the Jewish People's and Peretz Schools, as it was called after it merged with the I.L. Peretz School) became a day school, almost three decades after its founding as a supplementary school[2]; the next year, the Associated Hebrew Schools and Eitz Chaim School in Toronto, which had offered after-school programs for many years, opened day schools; in 1944, an English-language day school, the Talmud Torah, opened in Winnipeg; and in 1948, the Vancouver Talmud Torah became an all-day school (Leonoff, 2008, pp. 143–144). It should be noted that not everyone in the Jewish community welcomed separate Jewish schools. Some, especially among the acculturated element of the community, believed that Jews should endeavor to make their way in the public schools no matter how unwelcome they were.[3]

The impetus for developing a vibrant, cohesive Jewish community in Canada was, to a considerable degree, then, negative before World War II: the inability of Jews to fit into the social and political structure of Canada. After the war, however, and in no small part because of embarrassment over Canada's failure to open its doors to Jewish refugees from Nazi Europe,[4] a marked shift occurred in Canadians' attitudes to immigrants who were not of British or French origin. Over time, the country moved away from its traditional binational structure and toward a more multicultural understanding of itself. The new paradigm was the mosaic, in which each tile was distinct, but all together formed a coherent whole.

Immigrants once considered "non-preferred," a peculiar Canadian euphemism for "undesirable," were increasingly welcomed. By 1971, multiculturalism had become official, enacted into law. Now all groups were encouraged to retain their

---

[2] On the early years of the Jewish People's and Peretz Schools, see Butovsky and Garfinkle (2004).

[3] On the early history of Canadian Jewish schools, see, among other sources, Tulchinsky (1993), especially pp. 138–139, pp. 257–263, p. 273.

[4] The classic work on this subject is Abella & Troper (1982).

heritage, learn the language of their ancestors, and promote their old cultures and religions in their new country. To be sure, the official languages of Canada remained English and French and newcomers were expected to learn at least one of those languages. But government support was now available for the teaching of "heritage languages," for ethnic cultural events such as book fairs and arts festivals, for the establishment of university chairs of ethnic studies (a Canadian-Jewish Studies chair shared by York University in Toronto and Concordia University in Montreal, for example), and other activities. One impetus for change was the desire of politicians to blunt the demands for French Canadian autonomy. The influence of the American Black Power movement was another, and the desire for a different, less racist, more tolerant Canada was yet another. The Constitution of 1982, Canada's first formal constitution, enshrined in the country's fundamental law the notion of a multicultural, ethnically and religiously diverse Canada.

Now playing the ethnic card was the Canadian thing to do. And this provided positive reinforcement to Jews (and others) who sought to preserve their collective identity through a vibrant, distinct community with its own cultural institutions, among them, Jewish schools and educational camps. Once such schools had been seen as an alternative to "public" schools that were hostile to Jews. Now they were "the Canadian way." Morton Weinfeld (2001, pp. 227–228) points out, however, that no Canadian religious or ethnic group other than the Roman Catholics has the kind of extensive network of formal and informal educational institutions that Jews have developed, although Muslims and Evangelical Christians are catching up. In Canada, unlike the United States, the growth in day-school enrollment is not seen as related to a deterioration of public education (compare, Himmelfarb, 1991).

In 2009, there were Jewish day schools in Toronto, Montreal, and Winnipeg, as well as in Vancouver on the west coast, in Calgary and Edmonton, Alberta, and in London, Hamilton, Ottawa, and Kitchener, Ontario. In all provinces except Ontario, where the majority of the Canadian-Jewish population lives, Jewish schools receive some sort of government support. Here it may be noted that Canada's traditional understanding of the country as binational and bireligious worked in Jews' favor. Unlike the United States, Canadians have not seen the state as necessarily barred from supporting religious institutions, especially schools. Together with Christian and Muslim groups, the Jewish community in Ontario has vigorously lobbied the provincial government for support for their "separate" schools. An appeal to the United Nations Human Rights Commission resulted in a ruling that the province was discriminating against minorities in funding only Catholic schools. A law suit brought by the Ontario Jewish Association for Equity in Education and the Alliance of Christian Schools against the province, however, was ultimately unsuccessful in the Supreme Court of Canada. The Court ruled that the province was indeed guilty of discriminatory behavior, but that its policies were based on a constitutional provision and therefore permissible (Weinfeld, 2001, p. 229, and other sources). A 2001 decision by the Ontario provincial government, then controlled by the Conservative Party, to offer tax credits for educational expenses was reversed retroactively when the Liberal Party came to power two years later (see Braustein, 2001, and many other sources). In fact, support for faith-based schools was a major factor in the defeat of the Conservative incumbents, and it remains unpopular. Opponents of funding faith-based schools often invoke anti-Jewish stereotypes (exclusiveness and clannishness, for example), although they make their peace with funding Catholic education, a constitutional privilege, as noted earlier. Many suspect the motives of opponents of faith-based education who often advocate strongly for equity in all areas of Canadian life, but balk at funding Jewish (and other) schools. At this writing, Jewish community efforts are focused on securing aid for children with disabilities (Walfish, 2009).

According to some studies, about three times more children proportionately have been enrolled in day schools in Canada than in the United States in the last three decades. On the other hand, in South Africa, the UK, Australia, and Argentina, the percentage of Jewish children in day schools is much higher than in Canada. Within Canada, moreover, the proportion of children getting any Jewish education at all varies widely from 57% in Montreal and 48% in Toronto to 31% in Ottawa and Vancouver, and 28% in Calgary (Levine & Epstein, 2005). In 1999–2000, Toronto day schools had 10,031 pupils, almost two-thirds of all children receiving a Jewish education there, and in 2008, about the same number (The levelling off of growth reflects the lack of population increase, the high cost, and the recession that began in 2008.) In 1999–2000, Montreal schools had 8,455 pupils, over 94% of all children receiving a Jewish education in that city (Bronfman Jewish Education Centre & Association of Jewish Day Schools, 2000, 5,45).[5] There, because of the provincial subvention to Jewish and other ethnic and religious schools, the cost of tuition is considerably less than in Toronto. But even in some Montreal schools, close to half the children receive tuition subsidies from the community. In 1999–2000, UJA Federation in Toronto provided over $7 million in tuition subsidies while Federation CJA in Montreal provided $1.75 million (Bronfman Jewish Education Centre & Association of Jewish Day Schools, 2000, p. 45). As in the United States, most Canadian day schools are under Orthodox auspices, although many of those schools cater to families that are not Orthodox in their observance, which sometimes results in problems both for the school and for the parent body.[6] In both Montreal and Toronto and elsewhere across the country, many children were enrolled in supplementary schools and informal youth programs, as well as educational summer camps.

In addition to the success of day schools, the establishment in Canadian public universities of two programs for the training of teachers for Jewish schools should be seen as directly related to the Canadian multicultural context. By the 1970s, it had become clear to the Jewish community that its rapidly growing schools were not being staffed by appropriately qualified teachers. In response to the perceived need,

---

[5]Dubb (1983) claims that in the early 1980s, some 92% of Winnipeg children getting a Jewish education were enrolled in day schools, although some of those were surely enrolled in the special programs established within a few Winnipeg public schools. On more recent developments in Toronto, see Kraft (2009a) and Feldman (2009).

[6]An older article which discusses the dissonance is Grysman (1989). Grysman was then vice-principal of the Joseph Wolinsky Collegiate, Winnipeg, and he writes from his own experience.

programs were established at McGill University in Montreal and York University in Toronto for the training of a cadre of Canadian teachers who would serve not only as instructors but as role models for their pupils. Both programs were established with financial assistance from the local Jewish communities, which realized that community continuity and effective identity reinforcement were not likely to occur if teachers did not have accepted credentials and if most were of immigrant background. Although a few programs with similar goals have subsequently opened in the United States, they tend to be offered in private universities, because of American sensibilities about church-state relations.[7]

If some of the challenges facing Jewish education in Canada have to do with the particularities of the Canadian context, others relate to societal shifts that are worldwide. One of these is the alienation of increasing numbers of Jews from Judaism, Jewish life, and Jewish institutions, including schools. The distancing is especially marked among new immigrants, particularly those from the former Soviet Union and Israel, and those living an alternative life style, such as intermarried and gays and lesbians. But the alienation is surely also a reflection of the general weakening of faith in the Western world; (perhaps it would be more accurate to speak of the polarization of Western society regarding faith, with the emergence of a militant hard core among Christians, Muslims, and Jews, and an increasingly apathetic and larger periphery). Developments among Conservative Jews are illustrative. Synagogue membership has declined in Canada as well as in the United States. Enrollment in Toronto Conservative supplementary schools has declined radically, by 42% from 1992 to 2000. To some extent the decline is a result of children having switched to day schools, but researchers are convinced that the root causes are competition with more enjoyable leisure activities, parents who prefer their children to devote time to secular studies, the bother of commuting, and the lack of commitment of teachers and parents.[8] One way in which many parents in Canada and the United States have chosen to augment their children's Jewish education is by sending them to Jewish educational summer camps and to youth organizations in the winter. In Canada, camps under the auspices of the Reform, Conservative, and Orthodox movements, as well as others sponsored by the Labour Zionists and Young Judaea have proved increasingly popular. One of the oldest camps is the Hebrew-speaking Camp Masad located in the Laurentian Mountains not far from Montreal.

These developments are in many ways common to all North-American Jews, and seem to indicate a movement in Canada toward American patterns of Jewish life. Increasingly in the last decade Canadian society has been moving away from

---

[7] On the goals of the two programs, see Brown (1977) and Epstein (1977). These presentations were part of a panel discussion at the Congress plenary earlier that year. Another panel participant was Sidney Midanik, Q.C., former chair of the Toronto Board of Education and the Metropolitan Toronto School Board, who was instrumental in establishing the York University program for Jewish teacher training. On the York program, see Pomson, Brown, and Eisen (2000). On the development of university level Jewish Studies in Canada, see Menkis (1998).

[8] Much has been written on this subject. Some sources with particular relevance to this study are Schoenfeld & Pomson (2000), *Pan Echuti* (2004) and Pomson & Schnoor (2008).

the mosaic, multicultural paradigm toward that of an open society, where, as in the United States (in theory, at least), individuals are free to find their place in society without reference to a "community," or at least not an ethnic or religious community. For many Canadians now, ethnicity and religion are aspects of one's heritage, but not of an identity that needs to be nurtured. One sign of the change is the growing difficulty that Jewish organizations have in attracting volunteers; another is falling synagogue membership; and yet another is declining overall enrollment in Jewish schools. Thus day-school enrollment has grown (the hard core of believers or communally committed), while supplementary school enrollment has dropped (presumably, the uncommitted periphery, although the high cost of day-school education is surely a deterrent, even to committed parents).[9]

An educational challenge not at all related to the Canadian context, but one very creatively met in Canada, especially in Toronto, is the education of children with disabilities. Although Jewish schools for children with special needs were established in a few American communities somewhat earlier, the Ezra-Kadima supplementary school, founded in 1961 at Beth Emeth Bais Yehuda Synagogue in Toronto by Rabbi Joseph Kelman, is regarded as a pioneer institution in the field, certainly in Canada (Csillag, 2009a; www.beby.org/index.html). Ezra-Kadima was the first supplementary school in Toronto to offer special classes for the learning challenged. The school spawned the Reena Foundation, which maintains group homes and counselling services for the Jewish learning challenged, and for a time, ran a summer camp. In 1971, She'arim (later the Abraham Shore She'arim Day School), a day school for special-needs Jewish children, was established by Rabbi Kelman and his associates. That school sought to send on to mainstream schools as many of its pupils as possible. In 2008, She'arim closed, largely because of high costs and deficits and alleged pedagogical deficiencies. Other Jewish schools agreed to mount special-needs classes, although there are doubts about the viability of that arrangement (Ben Dat, 2009; Csillag, 2009b). Another Toronto school for children with special needs is Zareinu, "a Jewish Day School and Treatment Centre, which provides special education and individualized therapies to children with a wide range of physical and developmental challenges" (www.zareinu.org/aboutus.html).

Other educational initiatives in Toronto and Montreal that respond to contemporary needs that are not uniquely Canadian are programs for women. Separate schools for *haredi* girls have existed for some time in both cities. In Toronto, there is a school for girls whose families do not have a television in their homes, another for girls from families with television sets, and others with different requirements and restrictions. More interesting are programs for adult Jewish women, such as the Mekorot Institute of Torah Study for Women in Toronto, which strives "to make a full range of Jewish texts available [in]...an [Orthodox] atmosphere of spiritual and intellectual growth" (www.mekorot.org). Toronto is also home to private initiatives in Jewish education for women, most especially the seminars led by Dr. Rachel Turkienicz and Dr. Shoshana Zolty. An initiative for men is Torah MiTzion, a

---

[9]This author has explored the issue with regard to women's participation in Jewish life (Brown, 2005).

resident program for young Israeli yeshiva scholars who study and teach in Montreal and Toronto.

Also worthy of mention is a Toronto initiative for liberal Jewish learning, which appeals to younger Jews many of whom are otherwise unaffiliated with the Jewish community. Kolel, the Adult Centre for Liberal Jewish Learning, was founded in 1991 by Rabbi Elyse Goldstein, the first woman rabbi at Holy Blossom Temple, the city's largest and oldest Reform congregation, as an outreach project of the Reform Movement in Toronto. Kolel "encourages students to experience, learn, and understand traditional Jewish thought and practices and apply them in our modern world" (www.jewishtorontoonline.act/home.do). For a time, Kolel occupied its own building; then it was located in the Bathurst Jewish Community Centre, and now it offers mostly online courses and programs.

Research and Development

Research projects related to Jewish education in Canada are more numerous than might be assumed, because much of what is written about Jewish education in the United States also deals with Canada. Here, however, only works written in Canada or dealing specifically with the Canadian context will be mentioned. At the outset it should be said, that one of the reasons for concern about the closing of the Centre for Enhancement of Jewish Education in Toronto (Mercaz) is that both the Mercaz and the Bronfman Jewish Education Centre (BJEC), the central education planning agency in Montreal, have sparked or sponsored a number of valuable research projects, which have enabled educators to engage in long-term planning and have led to curricular innovation and development. While some of these studies consisted largely of market research, like the study of Israeli educational needs in Toronto, even market research can reveal a great deal about the community.

One of the most significant research and development projects ever undertaken in Canada is the Tal Am programs for teaching Hebrew (Tal Sela) and other subjects. Developed in Montreal by Tova Shimon with the help of her husband, Shlomo Shimon, the long-time former head of the BJEC, these pathbreaking programs have attracted the support of Multiculturalism Canada, a federal agency, of the American Avi Chai Foundation, and of other individuals and foundations in Canada and the United States. Now a cottage industry in Montreal, the Tal Am programs were being used in 413 schools on six continents in 2009 (Lazarus, 2008).

Perhaps the most significant "pure" research project in Canadian-Jewish education undertaken to date is the study of the Paul Penna Downtown Jewish Day School in Toronto by Alex Pomson and Randal F. Schnoor (2008). *Back to School: Jewish Day School in the Lives of Adult Jews* examines the role of a day school in Toronto whose parent body consists largely of people outside the mainstream of the Toronto Jewish community and mostly lacking other kinds of affiliation with the community. The book shows how the school serves as a surrogate synagogue and educates parents as well as their children. It should prove to be a catalyst for further research on non-standard ports of entry to Jewish life in the twenty-first century. One can hope that the researchers will return in 10 years to examine the long-term effects of the school on both parents and children. The researchers are hoping to expand the scope of their study by looking at CHAT, the Community Hebrew Academy of Toronto, the largest Toronto Jewish high school, a non-denominational school with two locations and a number of learning tracks.

Another book-length study of Jewish education in Toronto is the unpublished doctoral dissertation of Harvey A. Raben (1992) "History of the Board of Jewish Education of Toronto, 1949–1975: A Study of Autonomy and Control". That work is of particular relevance in light of recent developments related to the Toronto Mercaz, but also for Montreal, where there have been shifts in personnel and program at the BJEC, which in 2009 was headed by someone who was not a professional educator.

In his position as holder of the Koschitzky Chair in Jewish Education at York University, Alex Pomson was particularly active in educational research relating to Canada but usually with application to other places, as well. One of these projects pioneers the use of teacher narratives – most of them from Toronto schools – as a way of investigating the successes and failures of Jewish education. An initial publication resulting from that study is "Interrogating the Rhetoric of Jewish Teacher Professionalization by Drawing on Jewish Teacher Narratives" (Pomson, 1999). Pomson's (2004) article "Jewish Day School Growth in Toronto: Freeing Policy and Research from the Constraints of Conventional Sociological Wisdom," shows that the reasons usually given for day-school growth in the United States (dissatisfaction with public education, rising ability to pay, concern for continuity, and others) may not be operative in Toronto and perhaps not elsewhere either. Most growth, he found when examining enrollment figures, has occurred because the schools have been able to retain their pupils longer, not because they have been attracting new pupils.

With Stuart Schoenfeld of York University, another active researcher on topics related to Canadian-Jewish education, Pomson wrote the "United Synagogue Task Force on Congregational Schools Consultants' Report" in 2001, which reflects some of the apathy encountered by Jewish educators in the changing world of the twenty-first century (Schoenfeld & Pomson, 2000). Another study of Schoenfeld's is his (1999) "Jewish Education and Jewish Continuity in the United States and Canada: A Political Culture Perspective."

Esther Geva of the Ontario Institute for Studies in Education at the University of Toronto studies issues related to language acquisition and second language learning. Much of her work focuses on Hebrew language. Some of her research has been done in Toronto Jewish schools, although its applicability to those schools is uncertain.

As noted above, considerable research has been initiated over the years by the Bronfman Jewish Education Centre in Montreal and the Toronto Board of Jewish Education (later, the Mercaz), something that individual schools are unable to do. "Focus on Jewish Day Schools," a report by the Bronfman Center and the Association of Jewish Day Schools (2000) to the executive of Montreal's Federation CJA is an invaluable compendium of education data. Charles Shahar has completed a number of research projects, among them, "The Jewish High School Experience: Its Implications for the Evolution of Jewish Identity in Young Adults" (Shahar, 1998). He shows the effects of high school Jewish education on the behavior of young adults. "A Proposal for Meeting the Needs of School Age Jewish Children with Learning, Cognitive and Behavioural Difficulties" by Karin Gazith (no date) with the assistance of Tina Roth and Miriam Home is another project commissioned by the Bronfman Centre.

Research on Jewish education in Toronto began with the initial study by Uriah Engelman that resulted in the establishment of the Bureau of Jewish Education. Recent initiatives in addition to those already mentioned are those of Randal Schnoor, the co-author of *Back to School*, who did a study for the Board of parents' reasons for choosing day-school education for their children (Schnoor, 2004). In 2007, he examined the availability of special-needs resources in Jewish day schools (Schnoor, 2007). "A Characterization of Perceptions and Needs of the Israeli Community in Toronto: A Qualitative Study" by the "Pan Echuti" Research Institute (2004), was commissioned by the Board and provides valuable information not only on educational issues but on the attitudes and expectations of immigrants to Canada from Israel, in general. Another study commissioned by the Board, Shay Aba's (2001) Estimating the Demand for CHAT [Community Hebrew Academy of Toronto] Using an Econometric Model", seems less useful.

We return, then, to our starting point, the Centre for Enhancement of Jewish Education in Toronto (Mercaz), which is now closed and perhaps under reconstruction. With regard to research, there is cause for concern, as there is with regard to planning, coordination, and oversight for a school population about the size of that of a small city. As noted at the outset, steps are being taken to reconstitute some sort of central coordinating agency. But the process promises to be a long one, and there is little indication at this writing what its functions will be and to what extent it will be subordinate to professionals and volunteers whose main concern is not education. From the initial pronouncements, moreover, it appears that research will not be one of the future mandates of such an agency (Shaviv, 2009; UJA Federation of Greater Toronto, 2009).

The achievements of Canadian Jews in the field of Jewish education are many and significant. Most of them are related directly to the larger Canadian context, but most also provide insight into educational issues beyond the borders of Canada. But significant as those achievements are, the future is neither clear nor secure. Historian Jonathan Sarna has pointed out the extent to which cutbacks during the Great Depression of the 1930s inflicted permanent damage to the Jewish education system of the United States (Sarna, 2009, pp. 5–6). Vigilance will be needed to protect and enhance Jewish education in Canada.

References

Aba, S. (2001). *Estimating the demand for CHAT [community Hebrew academy of Toronto] using an econometric model*. Toronto: UJA Federation of Great Toronto: Board of Jewish Education.

Abella, I., & Troper, H. (1982). *None is too many: Canada and the Jews of Europe, 1933–1948*. Toronto: Lester & Orpen Dennys.

Ben Dat, M. (2009). Saying farewell. *Canadian Jewish News*, 9 July. 4.

Braustein, E. (2001). Ontario offering tax credits for Jewish day schooling. *Forward*, 8 June.
Bronfman Jewish education centre & association of Jewish day schools. (2000). *Focus on Jewish Day Schools*. Report to Federation CJA Executive [Montreal].
Brown, M. (1977). Presentation to Canadian Jewish congress plenary, Canadian Jewish congress central region. *Education and Culture Review, 6*, 5–12
Brown, M. (1982). Divergent paths: Early Zionism in Canada and the United States. *Jewish Social Studies, 44* 159–183
Brown, M. (1984). The Americanization of Canadian Zionism. In G. Wigoder, (Ed), *Contemporary Jewry: Studies in honor of Moshe Davis* (pp. 129 158). Jerusalem: Institute of Contemporary Jewry, Hebrew University
Brown, M. (1999). Good fences do not necessarily make good neighbors: Jews and Judaism in Canada's schools and universities. *Jewish Political Studies, 11*, 97–113
Brown, M. (2005). From gender bender to Lieutenant general: Jewish women in Canada 1738–2005. Toronto: *York University Centre for Jewish Studies Annual, 7*, 3–29
Butovsky, M., & Ode Garfinkle, O., (2004). *The journals of yaacov zipper: The struggle of yiddishkeit*. (Eds. and Trans.), Montreal and Kingston: McGill-Queens University Press.
Cohn, W. (1979). English and French Canadian public opinion on Jews and Israel: Some poll data. *Canadian Ethnic Studies, 11*, 31–48
Csillag, R. (2009a). Highly respected, eighth generation rabbi dedicated his life to helping people with special needs. *Globe and Mail*, 13 July.
Csillag, R. (2009b). Toronto day schools a model. *JTA*. August 21. Obtained from, http://jta.org/news/article/2009/08/21/1007388/toronto-day-schools-a-mod
Dubb, A. A. (1983). *First census of Jewish schools in the Diaspora, 1981/2–1982/3: Canada*. Jerusalem: Hebrew University Institute of Contemporary Jewry and JESNA Project for Jewish Statistics.
Epstein, S. (1977). Presentation to Canadian Jewish congress plenary, Canadian Jewish congress central region. *Education and Culture Review, 6*, 5–12
Feldman, S. S. (2009). Tuition fees rise at most day schools. *Canadian Jewish News*, 3 September. 17.
Gazith, K. (no date). *A proposal for meeting the needs of school age Jewish children with learning, cognitive and behavioural difficulties (with the assistance of T.Roth and M.Home)*. Montreal: Bronfman Jewish Education Centre.
Grysman, C. (1989). The orthodox day school and its non-observant population. *Jewish Education, 57*, 37–38
Himmelfarb, H. S. (1991). The American Jewish day school: The third generation. In P. A. Bauch (Ed.), *Private education and the public interest: Research and policy issues* Westport, CT: Greenwood Press.
Koschitzky, D. (2009). Streamlining *Mercaz* frees up cash for education. *Canadian Jewish News*, 2 April. 19.
Kraft, F. (2009a). Economy down, tuition subsidy requests up. *Canadian Jewish News*, 3 September.
Kraft, F. (2009b). 'Virtually' all Mercaz services intact: Federation. *Canadian Jewish News*, 10 December.
Kurtz, J., & Epstein, S. (2008). *Board of Jewish education: A retrospective, 1949–2000*. Toronto, ON: UJA Federation of Greater Toronto.
Lazarus, D. (2008). Hebrew teaching program gets new home. *Canadian Jewish News*, 31 January. 6 M.
Leonoff, C. E. (2008). The rise of Jewish life and religion in British Columbia, 1858–1948. *The Scribe, 28*.
Levine, J. & Epstein, S. (2005). Jewish education in Canada. *Encyclopedia Judaica* (electronic edition).
Menkis, R. (1998). A threefold transformation: Jewish studies, Canadian universities, and the Canadian Jewish community. In M. Brown (Ed.), *A Guide to the study of Jewish civilization*

in Canadian universities (pp. 43–69). Jerusalem and Toronto: The International Center for University Teaching of Jewish Civilization of the Hebrew University and the Centre for Jewish Studies at York University

News in brief. (2009). Canadians less tolerant than thought: Poll. *Canadian Jewish News*, 18 June 2.

Pan Echuti Research Institute (2004). A Characterization of perceptions and needs of the Israeli community in Toronto: A qualitative study. Unpublished report for UJA federation of greater Toronto, board of Jewish education.

Pomson, A. D. M. (1999). Interrogating the rhetoric of Jewish teacher professionalization by drawing on Jewish teacher narratives. *Journal of Jewish Education, 65*(1&2), 16–24.

Pomson, A. D. M. (2004). Jewish day school growth in Toronto: Freeing policy and research from the constraints of conventional sociological wisdom. *Canadian Journal of Education, 27*(3), 321–340.

Pomson, A., Brown, M., & Eisen, S. (2000). *Teaching teachers*. Toronto, ON: Centre for Jewish Studies, York University.

Pomson, A., & Schnoor, R. F. (2008). *Back to school: Jewish day school in the lives of adult Jews*. Detroit, MN: Wayne State University Press.

Raben, H. (1992). History of the board of Jewish education of Toronto, 1949–1975: A study of autonomy and control. Unpublished doctoral dissertation. University of Toronto.

Sarna, J. (2009). The American Jewish community in crisis and transformation: The perspective of history. *Contact, 11*, 5–6

Schnoor, R. F. (2004). *Which school is right for my child?: Educational choices of Jewish parents*. Toronto, ON: UJA Federation of Greater Toronto, Board of Jewish Education.

Schnoor, R. F. (2007). *An examination of services provided for Jewish day school students with social, emotional and behavioural challenges*. Toronto, ON: The Centre for Enhancement of Jewish Education.

Schoenfeld, S. (1999). Jewish education and Jewish continuity in the United States and Canada: A political culture perspective. *Journal of Jewish Education, 65*(1&2), 60–71.

Schoenfeld, S., & Pomson, A. (2000). United synagogue task force on congregational schools – consultants' report.

Shahar, C. (1998). *The Jewish high school experience: Its implications for the evolution of Jewish identity in young adults*. Montreal, QC: The Jewish Education Council of Greater Montreal/Federation CJA.

Shaviv, P. (2009). *Letter to community leaders*. 16 June. Letter to community leaders.

Tulchinsky, G. (1993). *Taking root: The origins of the Canadian Jewish community*. Hanover, NH and London: Brandeis University Press.

Tulchinsky, G. (1998). *Branching out: The transformation of the Canadian Jewish community*. Toronto, ON: Stoddart.

UJA Federation of Greater Toronto. (2009). Jewish education services: Questions and answers. *Canadian Jewish News*, 19 March. 22.

Walfish, I. (2009). *Letter to the community*. 5 May. Unpublished letter to community leaders.

Weinfeld, M. (2001). *Like everyone else but different: The paradoxical success of Canadian Jews*. Toronto, ON: McClelland & Stewart.

Worth, S. (2003). Downtown Jewish day school: Paying the price for education. *Jewish Education News (spring).*, 82.

Europe: Education of Adult Jewish Leaders in a Pan-European Perspective

Barbara Lerner Spectre

What has been termed "the renewal of Jewish culture in Europe" is a mixed and nuanced phenomenon. Although much of adult Jewish education in Europe retains the forms and substance of similar efforts throughout the Diaspora and in Israel, Jewish education in Europe for adults is to a great extent a reflection of the specificity of this Jewish renewal and is worthy of examination. Beyond descriptively profiling these developments, this chapter claims that what is currently taking place in Jewish education has importance not only for Jewish life in Europe, but also has far-reaching implications for education in the rest of the Jewish world.

A profile of contemporary Europe and Jewish life therein must commence with the caveat that the concept "Europe" is a construct, a geographical notion that, given the variety of cultures, languages, and histories, encompasses a great number of divergent realities. Together with all that, however, the emergence of the European Union has done much to give substance to the notion of a unified entity. Sweeping developments, including the fall of the Berlin Wall, the dissolution of the Soviet Union, the formation of a single European market, and the opening of borders of previously intact nation-states, have affected all citizens of Europe, and Jews among them. The trajectory of transformation that has been embarked upon, if successful, will lead to a pluralistic Europe composed of a mosaic of cultures that both maintain their own identities and yet participate in the common agora. Jewish life is part of that transformation. Jonathan Webber points out, "in today's new Europe the Jews have the opportunity, as do all other European citizens, to participate in the future political and economic reconstruction of the continent – and the question for them is to determine what their own social and political philosophy might be in these new circumstances."[1]

Jeremy Cohen emphasizes that the new context of the breakdown of nation-state identities towards multiethnic mosaics entails great challenges for contemporary

---

B.L. Spectre (✉)
Paedeia, Stockholm, Sweden
e-mail: barbara.spectre@paideia-eu.org

[1] Jonathan Webber, Jewish Identities in the New Europe, Jonathan Webber ed., The Littman Library of Jewish Civilization, London, 1994, p. 10

patterns of European Jewish identity: "While nineteenth and twentieth century Jews understood (rightly or otherwise) that the price of admission into the 'established' societies and cultures of Europe amounted to at least a partial repression of their Jewish identity, today's multiculturalism has rendered calls for conformity unfashionable, impractical, and politically incorrect..... Once again, the Jews of Europe must exert themselves to determine precisely where they stand within the larger non-Jewish world around them."[2]

Cohen further underscores the complexity: European Jews must now chisel out their identities "not only in relation to an ever more amorphous and nondescript European majority, but also alongside many other increasingly outspoken ethnic and religious minorities...."[3]

This amorphous and fluid state has given rise to a variety of contemporary European Jewish identity patterns. This chapter presents a case study with the purpose of illustrating some of these emerging patterns in the context of a "new Europe." I claim that there are components of Jewish identity and education in this new Europe that could be of critical interest not only in a parochial sense, but also to the Jewish educational community throughout the world. One of the factors that render it of such interest is that it encompasses a phenomenon that has transpired in Central and Eastern Europe since the fall of communism: a recurring narrative of recovered identities. The stories are rampant, and the pattern reiterates itself: in Central Europe a grandparent reveals that he or she is Jewish, a fact that has sometimes been unknown even to the rest of the nuclear family for all of the grandparent's life. His or her Jewish identity had understandably been repressed as a result of the trauma of the Holocaust and further suppressed during the Communist regime (in Eastern Europe the stories vary somewhat: often there was an awareness of Jewish identity because it was stamped into the personal papers, but the term "Jewish" was vacuous, and often onerous). A significant number of the generation of grandchildren who undergo this moment of disclosure regarding their Jewish ancestry subsequently have chosen to identify as Jews.[4]

---

[2]Jonathan Cohen, Rethinking European Jewish History, Jeremy Cohen & Moshe Rosman, eds., The Littman Library of Jewish Civilization, London, 2009, p. 5

[3]Ibid, p. 4

[4]I am unaware of any comprehensive studies that have been conducted with regard to the statistical numbers involved in this phenomenon. Obviously absolute numbers might well be moot since, by definition, those who do not acknowledge their identity might never reveal themselves to the researcher. A number that might be of interest to future researchers is one that was related to me orally by Professor Michael Berenbaum, the Holocaust scholar, who estimates that perhaps 20,000 Jewish babies were born in Poland between 1942–1945 and who were secretively given to Central European families. What percentage of these babies, now the age of grandparents, were told of their origins, or how many of those who were told subsequently revealed their identities to a member of their families is unknown. What is apparent is the significant number of grandchildren who choose to identify as Jews, as reflected in large numbers of applicants to Paideia from Central Europe with this reiterative narrative.

The phenomenon of recovered identities,[5] although acknowledged as occurring in other locations, warrants specific reflection in Europe. Perhaps, even a new term should be suggested, since its implications for Jewish life and Jewish education are manifold; the term I would suggest is "dis-assimilation," for the persons involved are those who have truly reversed the processes of assimilation. A number of defining factors in Europe indicate this reversal: first and foremost there apparently is no currency of social profit for these reclaimants, in that they know full well what non-Jews feel about Jews[6] (as opposed to the forces of assimilation that act as a pressure for shedding the burden of being different). Second, there is no social coercion, since previously no one had known them as Jewish, thus nullifying, in these cases, the claim of Jean-Paul Sartre that it is the non-Jew who makes a person a Jew.[7] Third, the people who make this decision have no childhood memories of being Jewish, and no childhood Jewish education.

It might appear that the last factor, the lack of any childhood Jewish education, establishes a deficit that is almost insurmountable. However, I would like to make the rather radical claim that, in my experience, this very point provides an educational opportunity that is both intriguing and tantalizing in its implications for Jewish education: given the lack of a childish rendition, Jewish life and thought can be presented on a high intellectual level for people who have chosen to identify themselves as Jews. It can be truly "adult" – not just because the participants are adult, but because the educator need not yield to childhood impressions, of which there are none in their cases. And, further – the education is not unidirectional, from the Jewish educator to the educational recipient, for these "dis-assimilators" can function as informants regarding what they see as giving substance and grounding to their choice. The educator can become truly educated in what these dis-assimilators find so compelling that they choose to identify as Jews.

My observations are based upon the educational experience of the past 8 years of founding and directing Paideia, the European Institute for Jewish Studies in Sweden. Paideia is the only pan-European institute of Jewish studies with a 1-year program dedicated solely to Jewish studies. It was formulated specifically with these "dis-assimilators" in mind, although persons that fit this profile are not the only participants. It brings 25 post-graduate fellows, average age 29, to Stockholm for a full year of academic study based upon intensive encounter with Jewish text. The majority of these fellows come from Central and Eastern Europe, although the spread is

---

[5] As anecdotally recorded in Barbara Kessler's "Suddenly Jewish: Jews raised as Gentiles Discover their Jewish Roots," (Brandeis University Press, Waltham, Mass. 2000).

[6] This is under the presumption, well circulated in Jewish spheres, that the general population in central Europe is anti-Semitic.

[7] They negate what Sartre claims is the essence of Jewish identity: "It is neither their past, their religion, nor their soil that unites the sons of Israel. If they have a common bond, if all of them deserve the name of Jew, it is because they have in common the situation of a Jew, that is, they live in a community which takes them for Jews." Jean Paul Sartre, Anti-Semite and Jew (Schocken, 1965), p. 67

wide – by the end of 2010 the institute will have graduated 200 fellows from 32 European countries. The curriculum is built upon 14 semester-equivalent courses (taught in 2-week concentrated blocs, in addition to 2-year courses in Talmud and hermeneutics) with the objective of granting literacy in Jewish sources and empowering Jewish activism.

Many of the claims of this chapter are based upon the experience of directing this institute, now in its ninth year. Although the actual number of graduates is 200, nevertheless interviewing and processing applicants has involved well over 1,000 persons.

The mandate that the institute declared to the Swedish government when it was founded,[8] was that it would serve as an educational instrument for the reclaiming of Jewish culture and life in Europe. With that presumptuous objective in mind, the questions regarding the target audience, framework, and most importantly, the curriculum were manifold and daunting.

The image of the "dis-assimilator," as related above, stood at the center of the conception of the institute, and this imagined entity became the target audience. What could not have been anticipated was how well based in reality this phenomenon was. The plethora of stories that surfaced through interviewing Paideia applicants affirmed the assumption that dis-assimilation was indeed a phenomenon taking place all over Europe, but most particularly in Central Europe. Some applicants related events of Jewish discovery that were almost completely tangential: one related how her mother went to a dentist's office, where the assistant asked whether she was aware that a Jewish community center was opening in their city. Her mother was astounded that the assistant had assumed that she was Jewish, and upon denying that that was the case, asked why the assistant had made that conjecture. The assistant replied that the mother's last name was Jewish. Only upon returning home, and by reconstructing the gaps in her father-in-law's life did that assumption become plausible. Indeed the family, out of curiosity, went to the newly formed community, resulting in their affiliation and ultimately conversion to Judaism. Other stories were more psychologically complex: a Hungarian high school student, in the heat of a competitive ball game, shouted out at one of the players on the opposing team: "Dirty Jew!" He was subsequently chastised by his coach, and when the parents heard of the incident they too chastised him, concluding with the fact that not only was it improper to call someone a "Dirty Jew," but that indeed the boy himself was Jewish.

These are only a sampling of the stories revealed during the interview process. As a group, these applicants to an institute dedicated to renewing European

---

[8] A major founding grant was given by the Swedish government to establish the institute in 2000, and it became operative in September 2001. The grant was the consequence of a commission of inquiry that the Swedish government established to investigate its role in the Holocaust, and which determined that although there was no legal culpability, nevertheless there was a sense of moral responsibility that resulted in three major steps: the convening of the Stockholm Forum in February 2000, the establishment of "Levande Historia" for education toward tolerance, and a grant toward the founding of Paideia.

Jewish culture challenge traditional affiliation patterns. Many of them, such as those described above, are Jews solely by the definition of the Law of Return of the State of Israel, the law that allows that citizenship is the right not only of a person born of Jewish mother or who has converted to Judaism – the traditional halachic (Jewish law) definition – but that the rights of citizenship are also vested in a child and a grandchild of a Jew, the spouse of a Jew, the spouse of a child of a Jew and the spouse of a grandchild of a Jew. Many of these European dis-assimilators do not formally convert because of the stringency of the conversion process that is administered solely by Orthodox religious authorities who would require them as converts to declare their intent to become fully observant Jews by orthodox standards. Regardless of the issues of "Who is a Jew" – which will not occupy the attention of this chapter – these dis-assimilators might represent an emerging new identity profile. As a group they are well-educated, often speaking multiple languages and knowledgeable of the literatures of those languages. They are anxious to engage as adults in serious Jewish education, are creative in cultural spheres, and frequently play key roles in Jewish life in areas where the remnant of the Jewish community was decimated by the Holocaust and the Soviet repression of identities. This then would be the core of the target audience: people such as those enumerated above, who choose to reclaim their Jewish identity. They often identify themselves as "cultural Jews." What they mean by that notion of "cultural Jew," and what can satisfy their educational quest is part of the subject of the following portrayal.

The decision regarding the curriculum at Paideia was critical and perplexing: what could serve as the basis for the rather bombastic vision that had been formulated for the Swedish government – to create an institute that would act as an instrument in the regeneration of European Jewish culture? It would appear that this mandate would necessitate a determination of one of the most controversial issues in the Jewish world: a definition of Judaism. What lies at the heart of Jewish civilization? To employ traditional categories – is it the Jewish people ("Am Yisrael"), Jewish practice and Halachah ("Torat Yisrael"), Jewish nationhood ("Eretz Yisrael")? A determination in any of these directions would obviously eliminate participation on the part of some sectors of European Jewry.

The question, once alternatively formulated, became more promising: What could give the participants the tools by which they themselves would be enabled to regenerate Jewish culture and make their own determinations regarding the nature of Jewish civilization? What could possibly empower them such that they themselves could become entrepreneurs of Jewish culture, and thus ultimately make their own verdicts concerning the definition of Jewish life? Is there any common and uniting aspect of Jewish life that could serve as the base curriculum that would not eliminate any of the possible future directions that the participants themselves might possibly make?

Inspiration was drawn from Moshe Halbertal[9] in his book *People of the Book*: "Rather than searching for the essence of Judaism in shared beliefs and practices

---

[9]Professor Moshe Halbertal serves as the Chairman of the Academic Committee of *Paideia*.

that remain constant though they take superficially diverse forms, I have chosen to focus on the shared commitment to certain texts and their role in shaping many aspects of Jewish life and endowing the tradition with coherence."[10] Based upon Halbertal's claim that one of the major uniting features of Jewish life has been text and a text-centered community, it was determined that the first basic element of the curriculum would be literacy of the texts and sources that have been at the center of Jewish life. Thus the program of study was laid out in a way in which a participant would significantly encounter the major works of the Jewish bookshelf (800 class hours). This also determined the minimal length of the program, since anything less than 1 year could not adequately address this central feature of the course of study. (Since the program was formulated with post-graduate activists in mind, it was also determined that the program – in that it is not degree granting – could not be much longer than a year.)

The response of the first year participants (2001–2002) to this feature of the curriculum was awaited with bated breath. I often found myself standing in the corridor outside the lecture room, out of sight, listening and trying to judge the reactions of that first cohort of fellows who had come for the 1-year course. Their reaction to text as curriculum was epitomized by one participant, Sorana, a fellow from Romania, who one day burst into my office exclaiming, "I feel like I have found my native language!"

Subsequent years have shown that Sorana's words regarding language were neither casual nor trivial, for within the European context the link between culture, language, and literature is inextricable. For example, many students in university major in "Philology," meaning the literature and language of their culture. In acquiring a culture, it is well understood that one must become fluent in the literary sources of the culture. Thus, the choice of text and literature as curriculum resonates well with the European understanding of what it is to gain competence and a sense of authenticity in a culture.

The equivalency between language, culture, and literature also served as a rationale for naming the new institute "Paideia." As Elias Bickerman claimed in his seminal work of Hellenistic culture, the concept of Paideia, which was brought from Greece to the Ancient Middle East by Alexander and his conquering army, was a revolutionary one, for it meant that one could acquire a culture through the study of its texts (in the Greek case, this meant mastering Homer). Previously this possibility had been unknown in the ancient world – one was born into one's identity. According to Bickerman, in the second century B.C.E. this model of Paideia was appropriated by Ben Sira who influenced the formation of the first academies of adult Jewish learning – the "Beit Midrash." Until then, learning was an activity only for priests and jurists, who needed learning in order to perform rituals and judge disputes, and for children – "v'shinantem l'vanecha."[11] Since the contemporary

---

[10] Moshe Halbertal, *People of the Book, Canon, Meaning, and Authority* (Harvard U. Press, Cambridge, Mass., 1997), p. 1

[11] Elias Bickerman, *The Jews in the Greek Age*, (Harvard University Press, 1990) pp. 166–174.

institute would be based upon a serious encounter with text (the equivalent of 14 semester courses) as a way of espousing Jewish culture, it was envisioned that through this literature one could also appropriate Jewish identity.

The second feature of the curriculum would be to empower the legitimacy of the interpretation of sources and texts.[12] These two elements, text-centeredness and interpretation, became the signature of the curriculum, whose objective was to create, in a contemporary European context, a *text-centered interpretive community*. The weight of establishing this second feature, interpretation, was to fall upon two elements. First, to employ the traditional methodology of text study, *chevruta*, whereby a text was to be explored and discussed in study-pairs prior to the lecture of the faculty-member, allowing for an empowerment of the interpretation of the student-pairs. Second, there was an attempt to infuse the curriculum with the interpretive urge by encouraging the participation of artists and creative personae.

Using chevruta methodology to ignite the interpretive mode among European participants was both more difficult than the textual curriculum element, and more surprising. It was difficult because in Paideia's experience, the learning climates in many Eastern European societies mandate against student expressiveness. The fellows from these societies often initially objected to the chevruta methodology, claiming that they were educated in more "formal" study traditions, and they deemed it unscientific to attempt to interpret a text until one had reached a level of competency in the subject. Thus, chevruta sessions at the beginning of the year were often greeted with silence, bordering on disdain by these participants.

Yet chevruta methodology during the study year became remarkably creative and vibrant, for in the context of a pan-European institute, with participants from so many different cultures (thus far participants have come from 32 European countries, and in any given year there are 12–15 languages spoken), sitting with a chevruta partner was often an act of radical discrepancy. And therein lay the surprise. As the year progressed what was uncovered was that, given the equivalency described above between culture, language, and literature, the "difference" from one's study partner was transposed into a plethora of literary references from a variety of languages. The outcome was that the more one differed from one's chevruta partner, the richer the text became. The chevruta experience was transformed into a paradigmatic example of the positive value of difference. An interesting dynamic was thus established: the text became the commonality between the group members, and yet richness of the text was a function of the differences within the group. The process became a strong experience of group cohesion through difference.

Thus chevruta became a signature of the studies at Paideia. As for the use of the arts to revitalize the interpretive process,[13] this was done on a variety of levels:

---

[12] Halbertal, "Jewish culture evolved through the interpretation of the canon." Ibid, p. 7

[13] Kreitzer among others has written on the use of the arts to inject the student into the hermeneutical flow. See L.J. Kreitzer, *The Old Testament in Fiction and Film: On Reversing the Hermeneutical Flow*, Sheffield Academic Press, Sheffield, 1994.

the invitation to a number of faculty who were also artists who could invigorate sessions with a wide array of interpretation; the exposure to creative efforts in a format called "Month of the Arts" in which artists from all over Europe and Israel were invited to perform; the inclusion of an arts track to attract artists as fellows.

The importance of the arts in the curriculum took on additional importance because of the educational challenge brought about through the creation of the European Union: the breakdown of monolithic, homogeneous nation-states into heterogeneous societies on the premise that a plurality of cultures can contribute to the common good. The arts took on additional importance at Paideia because many of the participants were engaged in various forms of cultural activities as a way of communicating both the distinctiveness of Jewish culture and also its ability to be in conversation with other cultures: fully a third of the graduates of Paideia to date work within cultural and artistic spheres.

Among the Paideia participants (200 graduates from 32 countries), establishing a text-centered interpretive curriculum has received a resounding ratification. Testimony upon testimony is recorded at Paideia that validate the desire and need for the study of text on a high intellectual level, as in academic studies in universities, but, unlike universities, the desire is that the textual studies not be detached from the living entity of Judaism.

What appeals to the adult, mature minds of these "dis-assimilators" is of course of great import for the entire Jewish world, and Paideia is an indication of an educational endeavor designed to address their needs. However, much further investigation and experimentation is needed with regard to the educational challenges facing the emerging European Jewish community. This chapter can designate but a few of the more critical educational issues in the section that follows.

Issue I: Cultural Identity

An overwhelming majority of participants in Paideia's 1-year program, when asked to classify how they identify themselves as Jews would respond "cultural." On the one hand this classification of identity holds great educational potential because of the readiness that it produces for a curriculum rich in literature, as indicated above. On the other hand, the notion of cultural identity, at least as understood within the American context, is often a synonym for "secular," and is suspect of not having sustainability, lacking the tools for being transmitted from one generation to another, such as ritual practices. However, within the context of European societies, many of which are strongly secular – Professor Lars Dencik terms, for example, the population in Denmark as being "secular Lutherans"[14] – the notion of a cultural rather than a religious identity is acceptable and perhaps even normative.

---

[14]Lars Dencik"The Paradox of Secularism in Denmark: From Emancipation to Ethnocentrism" in *Secularism and Secularity: Contemporary International Perspectives*, Barry A. Kosmin & Ariela Keysor, eds. Institute for the Study of Secularism in Society, December 2007, p. 131.

The question of the durability of this identity – especially given the possibility of literature as the transmitting agent – is tantalizing, and is one of the issues worthy of research as this new European Jewish identity takes shape and form. In theory there is nothing to prevent literary-cultural identity patterns from flourishing in other centers of Jewish life, although, as noted above, the European conditions form a particularly nourishing climate for their growth.

Issue II: The "Jewishness" of Jewish Studies in Europe

In 1999, Diana Pinto, a leading Jewish intellectual, wrote an article entitled "The Third Pillar"[15] wherein she defined what she termed "The Jewish Space."

> One of the results of the European sea change and above all, of the Holocaust's "coming home" to Europe's historical consciousness has been a major interest for Jewish themes in the non-Jewish world. This interest has grown exponentially in recent years. The result has been a plethora of publications on Jewish themes, novels and films written by non-Jews with Jewish characters in them (the most notable being of course, Roberto Benigni's La vita è bella), memoirs and histories, Jewish traditions ranging from the Torah to cuisine, Jewish jokes, Jewish museums, memorials, exhibits. Every corner of Europe is busy exhibiting the slightest Jewish traces in its past, whether they go back to more than two millennia as in Italy or to a "mere" two centuries as in Sweden. This interest in Jewish "things" which has no historical precedent in European history constitutes the greatest challenge of all for a European Jewish identity. First of all for a banal objective reason. There are not enough Jews across the continent to fill by themselves this growing Jewish space. Unlike Israel which is its own vast Jewish- Jewish space or America in which the Jewish space is filled by the Jews themselves in what can be called a sociological and cultural triumph, Jews in Europe are only one part of the Jewish space. Inside Jewish study programs at the universities, inside museums, in the realm of publishing as well as in every other Jewish manifestation (except for religion) non-Jews will constitute the majority of the "users" and even implementers of this space. Rather than perceiving this reality as an impoverishment, Jews should consider this structural condition as a major positive challenge, indeed as a challenge unique to Europe. For it is only here that Jews must confront historically charged "others," whose ancestors were very much present, if not always responsible, during the Holocaust and before that during the centuries of European anti-Semitism.
>
> Yet if Jews now live in Europe in a voluntary manner it means that they share a series of complex affinities with these "others" and it is this link which must be deepened and turned into a creative dialogue....[16]

Nowhere is this "Jewish Space" more evident than in the Departments of Jewish Studies throughout Europe, where the majority of faculty is preponderantly non-Jewish.[17] It is not surprising, therefore, that Jewish studies in Europe are for the most

---

[15] Diana Pinto "The Third Pillar? Toward an European Jewish Identity Text of a Lecture given at the Central European University, Budapest, Jewish Studies Public Lecture Series, March 1999

[16] Diana Pinto "The Third Pillar? Toward an European Jewish Identity Text of a Lecture given at the Central European University, Budapest, Jewish Studies Public Lecture Series, March 1999

[17] See Liliane Weissberg, "Jewish Studies or Gentile Studies? A Discipline in Search of its Subject" in *The New German Jewry and the European Context: The Return of the European Jewish Diaspora*, Y. Michal Bodemann, ed., MacMillan, U.K., 2008, pp. 101–110: "Jewish Studies has

part cut off from Jewish life itself. Questions yet to be addressed and researched, are whether programs such as Paideia can help to connect non-Jewish faculty (a number of non-Jewish academicians are accepted as fellows to Paideia) to areas and activities that can help inform not only Jewish studies, but also Jewish communities and Jewish life; what will be the nature of Jewish life in which non-Jewish participants play a significant role?; and what will be the definition of "who is a Jew" when non-Jews, who might not convert because of being avowedly secular, nevertheless make significant contributions to Jewish life? The definitions not only of "who is a Jew" but also of "what is Jewish" are yet to be determined within Europe. These are challenges that Jewish education must begin to address.

Issue III: Relationship with Israel

The attitudes toward Israel among European Jews are complex: on the one hand, undoubtedly, the existence of the State alters inexorably the dark recesses of memory of Europe as a place without exit; many if not most have family in Israel; the proximity makes travel to Israel entirely feasible and comfortable. On the other hand, European Jews in some countries are called upon to defend Israel in politically hostile situations. In a Pew Global Attitudes survey published in 2006, it was shown that far more Europeans sympathized with the Palestinians than with Israel.[18] Undoubtedly the New European Jews are living and functioning in political and social climates that are much more nuanced and much more compromised than Jews in other Diaspora communities.

The operative educational question becomes how, and on what basis, should ties be forged between Israel and emerging Jewish life in Europe? The issue needs to be dealt with delicately; certainly the Zionist and post-Zionist polemic is one that can produce a polarity that the new European Jewish entity can little afford.[19]

At the time of the creation of Paideia it was determined to forge strong academic and intellectual ties by inviting Israeli faculty to teach the intensive textual courses, a policy that has continued until the present day. The rationale behind this policy was that the relationship with Israeli scholars in the field of Jewish textual studies would forge an academic, intellectual, and non-political bond between the emerging European leadership and the Jewish state. Israel as such is not part of the curriculum. The message has been implicit that the presence of Israel-based scholars would forge a bond and make participants feel connected to Israel. Altogether, education for, in, and about Israel is a nuanced challenge, and research into the policies governing various educational institutions in this area awaits further attention.

---

completed a shift from a field that should be able to give the answers as to *who one is* – thus defining a person's Jewish identity via historical reflection – to a study of *subject matter*, p. 103

[18] "To Israel with Hate and Guilt" *The Economist,* August 17, 2006

[19] See for example, Shlomo Sharan (ed.), Israel & the Post-Zionists: A Nation at Risk, Sussex Academic Press, 2003

Issue IV: The Nature of Communities

Because of the tragically depleted numbers as a result of the Holocaust, many Jewish communities throughout Europe appear not to have the critical mass required for the viable functioning of a local community. Forged out of this necessity, or perhaps seizing the opportunity of enhanced methods of communication, there nevertheless seem to be emerging what could be called episodic, or event-driven communities, such as cultural festivals and the proliferation of *Limmud*, the open study festival that originated in the UK and has now spread throughout Europe. There are presently Limmud yearly events in the Baltics, Bulgaria, France, Germany, Hungary, the Netherlands, Poland, Romania, Russia, Sweden, Turkey, and the former Yugoslavia. These are certainly phenomena that deserve attention, and perhaps the European experience in this area will yet bear fruit for other episodic, non-denominational frameworks throughout the Jewish world.

Issue V: The European Union and Jewish Culture

Despite all the regional discrepancies in Europe, the formation of the European Union has established a united sociological agenda: to transform homogeneous nation-states into heterogeneous multicultural societies where diversity is celebrated and it is possible to harbor multiple identities. In the twentieth century it was the characteristic of Jews as bearers of hyphenated identities that stigmatized them with the suspicion of disloyalty (e.g., German-Jew, Italian-Jew). Ironically it is presently just this characteristic, the ability to live with divided loyalties that puts the Jew in a unique position, now assuming the role of the paradigm for European societies rather than the pariah. As Zygmunt Bauman has written, "Unlike in the modern era, with its ambitions of homogeneity, differences are no longer seen as temporary nuisances bound to get rid of tomorrow; variety and plurality of forms of life are here to stay, and the human essence seems to consist in the universally shared ability to establish and protect what Paul Ricoeur called *l'ipseite* – the identity distinct from other identities."[20]

On the level of identity patterns, the European agenda would call upon its citizens to form what could be termed "hyphenated-identities," and it is just this agenda that has struck a responsive chord in the population that has applied to Paideia. Simultaneous with the desire to be Europeans as Jews, reflected in the great success of Jewish cultural events, is the increasing aspiration to be Jews as Europeans. Not only Paideia, but pan-European frameworks such as the European Union of Jewish Students have gained strength, and increasingly European rather than Israeli or American personnel are being sought for professional positions.

---

[20]Zygmunt Bauman, "Allosemitism: Premodern, Modern, Postmodern" in Modernity, Culture and 'the Jew', Bryan Cheyette & Laura Marcus, eds., Stanford U. Press, Stanford, CA, p. 155, 1998.

In sum, Jewish education in Europe must respond to the challenges presented by new societal opportunities for Jews, to literate and cultured young adults who are choosing to recover Jewish life, to new patterns of identity, and to complex relationships with Israel. Certain paths seem particularly promising, among them the use of Jewish text understood as literature as the basis of a European cultural identity. However the yet undetermined future of Jewish culture in Europe awaits substantive educational nourishment, for which proper research would be an invaluable tool.

References

Bickerman, E. (1990). *The Jews in the Greek age*. Cambridge: Harvard University Press.
Bauman, Z. (1998). Modern, Postmodern". In "Allosemitism: Pre-modern. In B. Cheyette, & L. Marcus, (Eds.), *Modernity, culture and 'the Jew'*. Stanford, CA: Stanford University Press.
Cohen, J. (2009). In J. Cohen, & M. Rosman, (Eds.), *Rethinking European Jewish history*. London: The Littman Library of Jewish Civilization.
Dencik, L. (2007, December). The paradox of secularism in Denmark: From emancipation to ethnocentrism. In B. A. Kosmin, & A. Keysar, (Eds), *Secularism and secularity: contemporary international perspectives*. Hartford, CT: Institute for the Study of Secularism in Society.
Halbertal, M. (1997). *People of the book, canon, meaning, and authority*. Cambridge, MA: Harvard University Press.
Kessler, B. (2000). *Suddenly Jewish: Jews raised as gentiles discover their Jewish roots*. Waltham, MA: Brandeis University Press.
Kreitzer, L. J. (1994). *The Old testament in fiction and film: On reversing the hermeneutical flow*. Sheffield: Sheffield Academic Press.
Pinto, D. (1999)."The Third Pillar? Toward an European Jewish identity text of a lecture given at the Central European University, Budapest, Jewish studies public lecture series, 1999, March
Sartre, J. P. (1965). *Anti-Semite and Jew*. New York, NY: Schocken.
Sharan, S., (Ed), (2003). *Israel & the post-Zionists: A nation at risk*. East Sussex, UK: Sussex Academic Press.
To Israel with hate and guilt (2006). *The Economist,* August 17, 2006
Webber, J. (1994). In J. Webber, (Ed.), *Jewish identities in the new Europe*. (p. 10). London: The Littman Library of Jewish Civilization.
Weissberg, L. (2008). Jewish studies or gentile studies? A discipline in Search of its subject. In Y. Michal Bodemann, (Ed.), *The New German Jewry and the European context: The return of the European Jewish diaspora*. New York, NY: MacMillan.

Europe: Something from (Almost) Nothing – The Challenges of Education in European Communities – A Personal Perspective

Steve Israel

Introducing Myself and My Issues

I have been involved in informal Diaspora Jewish education in Israel for some 25 years. I do a lot of Jewish identity development and Jewish leadership training in the widest sense drawing especially on my subject areas of Jewish history, Jewish culture and literature and Israel studies. The majority of my work has been done with participants from the west – English speakers – youth movement *madrichim* (counsellors), students and teachers.

However, over the last 3 years, I have spent much time abroad in Europe and have had Jewish experiences that have opened up my eyes as an educator. These experiences have broadened my perspective on Jewish education and the wider Jewish world in a number of ways. It is these ideas and perspectives that I wish to offer through this essay to an audience of wider Jewish educators. Since these perspectives have been gained by my immersion in a number of specific projects I will spend some time now in describing the projects and my involvement in them and filter the issues that I wish to raise through the contexts of the projects in which I have been involved.

The Contexts

My involvement has taken me to many countries but I want to focus on the three main projects in which I have been involved on an ongoing basis: the international Jewish camp in Hungary, the community in Sofia, Bulgaria and (a little further away – and at least partly in Europe) the community in Istanbul, Turkey.

S. Israel (✉)
Informal Diaspora Jewish educator, Jerusalem, Israel
e-mail: dands@netvision.net.il

A. The Szarvas International Jewish Camp in Hungary

General Context: Almost 20 years ago, at the beginning of the 1990s, three bodies – the Joint Distribution Committee, the Lauder Foundation and the Jewish Agency – combined to initiate an international Jewish camp in Szarvas, a small town in south-eastern Hungary. With time the Agency dropped away and the arrangement today is that the Lauder Foundation is in charge of the site and the infrastructure while the camp itself is the sole responsibility of the JDC. The initiative behind the camp resulted from the assessment that for the tens of thousands of young Jews in East and East Central Europe, their identity as Jews could best be developed within the context of an intensive Jewish camping experience. The virtues of an immersion experience in a camp environment had been recognized decades earlier and this was part of a wider set of initiatives in the Jewish world that sought to exploit the new freedom of ex-Communist Europe to try and develop Jews and Jewish communities.

In the summer of 2008, the camp celebrated its 18th year. Each year, in recent years, up to 2,000 youngsters come to the camp for an intensive experience in four 2-week sessions. The major communities that send participants are the host community Hungary and Russia: other European communities that regularly send participants are all of the former Yugoslavian states, some of the former Soviet Union states (such as Lithuania, the Baltic states and Belorussia), Rumania, Poland, Bulgaria, the Czech Republic and Slovakia. In addition, other further-flung states also send groups – Turkey, India, the US and Israel. Each year, the camp takes a specific Jewish subject as its major theme and arranges many different activities, in small groups, country groups and on an international camp level on these themes. In recent years the themes have included "The Jewish bookshelf", "Jewish continuity" and "Living a Jewish life". I mention these details because it is important to point out that the themes are ambitious and place the camp firmly in the company of those other Jewish camps around the world which attempt to create a serious (but fun) educational environment in which it is hoped that a Jewish education can be partly obtained and a Jewish identity strengthened.

Specific Challenges: In recent years the camp has had to adjust to two major developments. One of these was initiated consciously and the other is a new situation to which the camp has been forced to react. Both of these developments are in my eyes, positive.

1. In the early years of the camp, the central staffing was done almost exclusively by a team of Israeli educators who would arrive at the camp at the beginning of the summer with the programme largely prepared and would run the camp with the help of some local educators especially at the level of the group *madrichim*. This was a logical strategy. The communities had very few Jewish educators who had either enough knowledge or experience to provide the basis of an educational staff. A few years ago, the policy was changed. It was realized that an entire generation of participants had grown up in the camp and had progressed from *chanichim* (younger participants) to *madrichim* and were ready to assume

increasing responsibility for the running of the staff. Thus began a gradual process of decreasing the influence of the Israeli educators in the central staff of the camp. The leadership and the educational direction of the camp were passed exclusively to the younger generation of local educators. Collectively, it was decided that the day-to-day work of the camp would be the responsibility of a group of some two to three dozen unit heads and coordinators who would work with teams of the younger *madrichim* to run the camp. This is the situation now. The younger *madrichim* come from each of the communities that send participants. The unit heads and coordinators are drawn from many, but not all, of the countries. They include Israelis as a sub-group of the unit head staff but not as the dominant group.

2. When the Szarvas camp started there were very few other Jewish camping or indeed educational opportunities in many of the communities. In the intervening years, many communities have started their own camps. There is now for example a Jewish community camp in Lithuania, Bulgaria, Rumania and Poland to name but four communities, as well as a whole network of camps in Russia, some of which are run by different community organisations while others are run by outside organisations such as the *Sochnut* (the Jewish Agency), the Reform movement or Chabad. This of course is a positive development in and of itself but it means that Szarvas has to compete with a whole series of camps that it inspired to a large extent and for which it served as model. There are many participants who are happy to go to their own community camps and then come on to the international camp at Szarvas but that cannot be taken for granted. In addition, the camping phenomenon has developed in Central and Eastern Europe as part of the development of commercial leisure activities. Language camps or sports camps among others have developed strongly and provide competition for the minds and pockets of potential participants and their parents. This means that Szarvas has to be able to compete in a rapidly expanding market. It also has to redefine its raison d'etre in order to explain – to itself and to others – why potential participants should choose to come all the way to Hungary in order to attend "another Jewish camp".

These two new factors formed the background to my involvement in the camp. The challenge was to help the team evolve into a high functioning, more Jewishly literate group of educational professionals (for the time that they are in the camp) and to assist the camp's central team in going forward into their new era.

B. The Sofia Jewish Community in Bulgaria

General Context: The demographics in all of the Jewish communities in former Communist countries are very complex and it is extremely difficult to be specific in regard to the numbers of Jewish population in any country. In all of these countries, many hid their Judaism during Nazi or communist times due to societal and political pressures and there was little to no community life. The Bulgarian community is one of the small communities. There are some 2,000–3,000 Jews (not necessarily according to *halacha* – the Jewish legal tradition – but according to subjective criteria) who are potentially active in the community. The vast majority are in Sofia, the capital city, while there are a few other smaller communities in the provinces. There are a couple of small Zionist youth movements and one Jewish school, all of which have started since the end of communism. Much of the educational activity in the community has been organised with the help, or at the initiative of the JDC. which has been a major factor in community development throughout the ex-Communist world of central and eastern Europe over the last two decades. They have done extraordinary work in turning a small community into quite a vibrant community, with youth and student activities, seminars and a community camp and more recently, adult educational activities. Among other things they have created a small group of students or ex-students (salaried) which coordinates and organises the educational activities of the communities.

Specific Challenges: Here the community is facing a major problem which has necessitated the increasing professionalisation of its own educational staff. This is especially important because in the last few years the initial feeling of animated enthusiasm which characterised so many of the activities in the ex-Communist communities in the early 1990s has given way to a more blasé feeling on the part of many of the potential consumers of community activities. Since there is little novelty value in community activities, the standard has to be higher. Once again, the expansion of leisure activities in the general society, while a positive development in general, has led to a new series of challenges for those involved in Jewish education. The young generation has most of the same activities/technological opportunities that characterise western youth. Jewish education has to compete with this throughout the world: the same is true for countries like Bulgaria. In addition the level of Jewish knowledge among the majority of the community staff is fairly low.

My task here has been to try and help the community workers professionalise their work and to increase the Jewish knowledge of the workers and of the *madrichim* in the community.

C. The Istanbul Jewish Community in Turkey

General Context: The Turkish community is, in many ways, a community very different from the others. It is bigger than that of Bulgaria and smaller than that of Hungary. In non-Western terms it would count as a medium-sized community. Official numbers are inflated but the current internal assessment talks of some 17,000 Jews (we can talk for the most part of *halachic* Jews). This is a community that has experienced a continuous history of many generations, but it has undergone considerable attrition due either to *Aliyah*, emigration or assimilation. The major problem of the community is of course the fact that it sits in a predominantly Moslem – and increasingly Islamic – society and has already received its share of murderous terrorist acts. They are intensely aware of the security threat and entrance to the community facilities (including synagogues) is extremely difficult to outsiders without prior arrangement or personal escort. This feeling of threat became particularly noticeable during the Gaza operation of 2008–2009.

Specific Challenges: In addition to the direct security problems, the community experiences many other challenges which are not dissimilar to the problems that face many western communities. There is assimilation among the young, both (perhaps unexpectedly) in terms of the number of mixed marriages with members of the majority Moslem community and in the general sense of apathy and self-distancing from the community. The community is largely westernised and the general taking on of a ubiquitous western identity is common among the young. In addition, there seems to be a problem of Jewish education and Jewish knowledge inside the community. There are a number of educational institutional frameworks but the number of Jews with a good Jewish education (whatever that means) is comparatively small. One ray of light is provided by the youth movements and clubs for youth, students and young adults. Some of these do very good work and have created some potentially powerful young leaders in the community. However, as is the case in many other countries, there is a strong discontinuity between the youth organisations and the adult community: youth leaders typically rise to the top of their own organisations but then disappear from the community radar, certainly in terms of any leadership roles, before some of them reappear within the community as young parents many years later. The community leadership, which is composed almost completely of unpaid volunteers, does a lot of good work, but is seen by the younger generation as largely inaccessible.

I was asked to help create a young leadership framework which would start closing the gap and provide a smoother transition between the involved young people in the community and the older leadership.

Reflections on Issues

My involvement in these frameworks over the past few years has caused me to develop a number of perspectives that I now try to articulate. I focus on six issues. Each of them provides questions and challenges for the Jewish educator. Two of them, the last two brought here, provide real dilemmas.

1. The Fear Factor: A Perspective

It is almost impossible for those of us in the West to understand the amount of fear that can sometimes underlie Jewish identity and the extent of the anxiety that can accompany emergent identity into a recognisably Jewish framework. In the early years of post-Communism, this was extremely common in the Eastern European arena. In the context, it is not only easy to comprehend but in some ways it is hard to understand how this could possibly be different. One of my first encounters with the phenomenon was a conversation that I had with a Hungarian Jewish woman who I met years ago in a leadership seminar in Israel. I re-encountered her years later when

I was on a visit to Hungary to examine and start learning about the community in the context of a Jewish Agency project, several years before my proper entry into the world that I have described. I wrote down my impressions of the conversation not long after my return and I reproduce them here.

Conversation at the Community House

I met her at the community building, Beit Balint. It is a very pleasant building, brimming with activities most days of the week and almost every evening. I met her on a Sunday morning. We had both come to the local Jewish history group. I actually got there late. Most of the people had already gone but I was told that there had been some 30 or so people there. Most of them would have been old but there were some younger people as well. She was middle-aged, a social worker, and I understand that she was a good one. She'd got a number of prizes from the Budapest Social Services Department for her work in different frameworks. But it clearly wasn't enough. She seemed very upset when we talked. They had just found her out. She didn't know how they knew. She herself had been very careful to hide the fact. But a few weeks before we talked, she had felt that some of her colleagues were giving her strange looks. Some stopped greeting her. It was then that she knew that they knew. She knew now that it was only a matter of time before they stripped her of some of her privileges. She knew that they wouldn't tell her why. Or at least, they wouldn't give her the real reason. They would say that she was inefficient. Or they would say that they were reorganising the department. They would never tell her the real reason. That they had found her out. That they knew. That she was Jewish.

This was an educated woman, who had "come out" as a Jew several years before to the extent that she had come to Israel for Jewish leadership training. And here she was, quaking with fear and frustration. It is a reality which none of us who come from stabler Jewish backgrounds can fully comprehend. For some people in these countries, even those who have made the decision to accept their Judaism, the emergence into the Jewish world can be a very frightening thing, something which, rightly or wrongly, in their perception, can cost them a lot. This is perhaps more true of the older generation and less true of the younger one. But this is something which educators must try and understand although we tend to come from a school which believes that "of course" Jews should celebrate their Judaism and their identity as Jews. We are against the phenomenon of what might be called modern *Marrano* Judaism, in which people know that they are Jewish but hesitate or refuse to acknowledge it publicly. Yet such a perspective ill equips us to understand the complex inner world of the Jews of Eastern and East Central Europe.

Judaism has brought one problem after another to the Jews of these lands. The twentieth century saw blow upon blow descend on the heads of Jewish families who have unquestionably paid an enormous price for being Jewish. Nazism, Communism and other forms of anti-Semitism have been their almost constant companions for the majority of the last century. And it continues in one form or another even in the free democratic states (at least in theory) which have replaced the fallen Communist regimes. Emerging as a Jew can demand a price from the individual. In such a situation, it is hardly surprising that so many would-be Jews would ask these questions: What is in it for me (or my children) if we identify as Jews? What do I stand to gain or to lose by my identification with Jewish life and community? This is a question one encounters less among the younger generation and perhaps one encounters it today to a lesser extent even among the older generation. They have already made their choice. Some have chosen to identify but many have not. The assumption is that there are far more unidentified and totally uninvolved Jews in these communities than there are those who have positively identified and who have chosen to involve themselves in some kind of activity within the (very loose) framework of the community. This explains the constant attempts at outreach activities. To a large extent outreach in this context means something very different from what it means in the West. In the West it tends to mean reaching out to the Jew who is not positively identified and resists involvement in the community. In these lands it tends to mean reaching out to those who have never accepted that they are Jewish and, in many cases, to those who have never confessed to or informed their families.

We have to understand that we are dealing with people with "broken" identities who are not part of the organic Jewish chain with which most of us identify. This is a challenge for us. This whole phenomenon is made more serious and becomes a greater educational challenge when some additional factors are added to the picture.

2. *The Lack of Jewish Family Life: A Perspective*

In the West and in stable communities where some kind of Jewish communal continuity has been the norm for generations, it has – at least until recently – been taken as normative that the family is the primary framework in which an individual learns and experiences Judaism and Jewish life on the initial level. After that, an effective Jewish experience in day school or supplementary school, camp or youth framework can enhance that experience, cause, as it were, the spark to burn more strongly and in many cases allow individuals to pass the level of knowledge, experience and identity that they have received from their parents. Sometimes, that might be funnelled back into the original family framework, enhancing the experience of the whole family. Whatever the specifics, it seems that as a generalisation it is true to a large extent that the primary model is still that of the family providing the initial spark and experience for Jewish identity.

However, the situation in the post-Communist communities is very different. Here, in the vast majority of cases, there is no Jewish home life to speak of. The community does not enhance the experience at home. It has to replace that experience, or rather to create the Jewish experience anew. The first time I understood this was during the same early Hungarian trip that I mentioned earlier. It happened on a Friday night when I went to a service in a back room at the great Dohany synagogue in Budapest. This was my subsequent account.

A Meeting at the Synagogue

This is a very strange scene. There are well over 100 people here, young and old. There are even a few young children brought by their parents. They sit in an upstairs room in the synagogue building, around tables with modest food and drink, listening to the speaker. The truth is that this synagogue is housed in a part of the building that belongs to the small rabbinical seminary, now called the Jewish university. Just a few minutes ago I was looking for a seat in the small cozy synagogue, and singing loudly with all the others as the old chazan led the prayers. What an enthusiastic Lecha Dodi Everyone sang along with the organ and the chazan. Tremendous spirit. And then I was invited to the Oneg Shabbat. I expected that people would stay for a few minutes and then go home for Friday night dinner. But they have been here for an hour already. The woman sitting next to me explains that most of the people don't have a Shabbat meal. Many are married to non-Jews and many have not quite mastered the art of making Shabbat for themselves yet. The whole thing is so new to them. The speaker talks on. Everyone listens. That doesn't surprise. The issue is the resurgence of anti-Semitism. It is once again on everybody's mind. People discuss what to do about it. More and more public figures are coming out with remarks against the Jews. People are frightened. But at least here, in this upstairs room, with the memory of the service not yet faded, they can discuss freely. They are among their own.

The community has become for many a vehicle for the Jewish life that many individuals simply don't have at home. It doesn't augment: it replaces. Just last year, this was brought home to me again in a conversation that I had with my Bulgarian team of student educational activists. I met them soon after Pesach and they were exhausted! When I asked why, they explained that they had been going around the different frameworks of the community doing *seder* after *seder* (the major ritual celebration of Pesach). They were tired out. In the course of the conversation I asked them whether at least their own family *seder* had given them a break or whether they had had to run those as well. They looked at me without comprehension and then it dawned on me. Not one of them had had a home *seder*. Such things didn't exist for them. The community *sedarim*, which they ran, were "their own" *seder*. They explained that almost no one ever has a home *seder*. The community provides their experience. Even for these activists, so far ahead of the rest of the members of the community that they themselves lead all the others, the community functioned as the exclusive vehicle for their Jewish experience.

Let me give an additional example from Bulgaria, one that surprised and to a certain extent shocked me. The decision of the local education team that runs a community summer camp at a place called Kovechevtsi to which some 150 youngsters go each year, was this year, 2009, both interesting and challenging. They decided that the theme of the camp this year would be the *chagim* (holidays) and their values. It is in my opinion an impressive choice because they not only wanted to educate about the details of the *chagim* (clearly necessary) but also to go one step past that and link each *chag* with a particular value so that in the course of the camp they would not only have passed through some 10 or so different *chagim* (including *Shabbat*) but also would have explored a whole series of educational and personal values with their *chanichim*. As always, in order to prepare the *madrichim* with the necessary tools to create activities for the *chanichim*, a series of *madrichim* seminars were organised and it was decided that at the first content seminar, I would present three of the *chagim* in order to start the preparation process off. The three "*chagim*" that were chosen were *Shabbat*, *Rosh HaShanah* and *Yom Kippur*. As far as *Shabbat* and *Yom Kippur* are concerned, there were no major surprises. All of the *madrichim* had some knowledge of the main aspects of the days and while all of them gained more detail and more perspective, this was grafted on to their existing knowledge. However, the session on *Rosh HaShanah* was a real eye opener. In response to the question regarding what they had done the previous year on *Rosh HaShanah*, three or four (out of just under 30 who were present) said that they had gone to *Beit Knesset* (synagogue) and another three or four mentioned the fact that they had had a family meal. In terms of the themes or motifs of the *chag*, very few knew more than the fact that there was a connection with apples and honey. When it was pointed out to them that *Rosh HaShanah* was one of the biggest and most important of the *chagim* throughout the Jewish world, they were totally amazed. For them, the big *chagim* were (in addition to Yom Kippur which has somehow proved more resilient than *Rosh HaShanah*) are *Pesach*, *Chanukah* and perhaps, *Purim*. The common denominator to all of these is that there are communal parties and celebrations. But *Rosh HaShanah*, apart from a tasting of honey and apples in the school or in the youth groups at the community, had simply got lost. Once again, to a large extent, for the majority of the Jews in the community, whatever does not filter down within a community framework simply doesn't exist. For many Jews in the West, *Rosh HaShanah* is one of the few times they attend synagogue. For these Jews, however, attending synagogue isn't part of their Jewish experience, and so if the community doesn't mark the holiday in some way, they simply will not experience it.

The challenge for educators is clear. We need a model of education which is not based on the family as a first step but rather tries to involve the families further down the line. This has started to occur in a number of different locations as family camps and seminars have been organised. Often these are organised as summer experiences at different resorts with the educational activities available for all those who want them. The Bulgarian experience is instructive in this regard. For some years, the community has organised a resort event for families in the period before the *Yamim Noraim* (*Rosh HaShanah* and *Yom Kippur*). Gradually the number of participants has gone up and the demand for more intensive education at the family events has increased. Last year some 600 people participated – in a community reckoned to be only 2,000–3,000 in number. This year as a direct result of the demand, a winter seminar is being organised for the first time. There is an additional interesting side to these activities. Many of the educators at these camps are young people whose parents attend the event as participants and see their children teaching Jewish subjects or leading Jewish activities.[1]

---

[1] It should be noted that these generalisations are clearly not true for the small orthodox (meaning, on the whole, Haredi) communities which exist next to many of the larger community structures, but with very little real interaction.

3. The Weakness of the Communities: A Perspective

A short time prior to writing this chapter I received a rather different lesson. I was sitting with the rest of the small central staff of the Szarvas camp, here in Jerusalem and we were planning the schedule of this year's summer camp which is on the subject of Jewish community. The idea was to start by talking about the idea of community and the need for community, to walk the campers through some historical Jewish communities and the challenges and dilemmas that the inhabitants of those communities had to confront and then to move on to their own communities and examine their challenges and dilemmas. I was spouting away enthusiastically on this structure when one of the members of the team brought me up short: "But the kids don't know what their community is. They might know that they go to this youth club or to that activity but they don't identify it as a "community activity". The others agreed. They told me that even many of the *madrichim* won't be able to talk of their community other than in terms of their youth framework. In the end we started to think of using the *madrichim* from those countries which do have a strong concept of a Jewish community (USA, Turkey, India etc.) as a resource. The specifics aren't important but the general lesson is, I think. The communities are so weak in many places that they don't fully affect the consciousness even of many of those who participate in community activities!

It reminded me of an exercise that was run a few years back at one of the Szarvas unit head seminars. The participants, young activists in their early twenties from many different countries, were participating in a programme on the idea of the four children of Pesach and we asked them to create their own artistic version of the four children in terms of their own community. One mixed country group created a splendid and extremely informative poster in which educators, accompanied by children ("*Chacham*" – the wise child), or children unaccompanied by educators ("*Tam*" – the innocent or simple child – and "*Sh'aino yodea lishol*" – the child that doesn't know how to ask) featured prominently and clearly. But it was difficult to figure out who they had chosen for their "*Rasha*" – the so-called wicked child. They had a rather unpleasant looking gentleman behind a large desk with a dollar sign over his head. When they presented it, it was a revelation (at least for me – not interestingly enough, for most of the others present). He represented the community leaders, interested in money, managing the community property, most of which had been reclaimed after the fall of Communism. To the activists there it was clear: the community leaders were the personification of the *Rasha*!

Was that fair? I have no idea. I have met several community leaders and have no opinion of them as a group. I hope that the representation was unfair and that these individuals do indeed work in their own way for the good of the communities. But the important thing here is the negative picture that existed in the minds of these very motivated community activists.

Such is the confused situation of many of the communities today. Communities that are the principal vehicle for effective education and identity development are seen in such ignorant, ambivalent or even negative terms by so many of those who come into contact with them. This is a challenge for many of us who work in Jewish education. We have to completely unlearn those conceptions of community that we have gleaned from our own reality and begin to rebuild our understanding anew from the bottom up.

4. Community Life: Who's in and Who's Out: A Perspective

One major challenge for educators working in this field is the Eastern European version of the perennial question of "Who is a Jew". One of the important things to understand about potential Jewish identity development in the area is the fact that for the vast majority of the possible "clients" religious identity is not a major option. There are, of course, exceptions to this generalisation (there is, for example, an Orthodox *Yeshiva* (academy of higher Torah studies) in Berlin which caters almost exclusively to students from all over Central and Eastern Europe who are looking for a religious and textual education) but on the whole, religion as a worldview is not a likely selling point for identity development to young people in the ex-Communist world. Perhaps it is the influence of the fiercely enforced secularisation of the Communist regimes which took its toll and perhaps it is the force of the secular modernisation which has steamrolled over religious sensibilities in so many parts of the world as a whole, but culture, history or tradition are buzzwords more likely to enthuse young people than religion. In my experience, religious educators can have impact if their approach is sufficiently broad and inclusive but even their influence is likelier to be felt in broad cultural terms rather than "narrower" religious ones.

One additional reason for this might well be the perceived narrowness of many of the orthodox rabbis in charge of the religious life of the communities. From dozens of conversations over the years I can say fairly conclusively that for large numbers of young people in Central and East Central Europe, rabbis are seen as an alienating force rather than a force for "*kiruv levavot*" – drawing people nearer to religion. This, incidentally, unquestionably has an influence on the popularity of the Chabad framework, whose rabbis are often seen as the acceptable face of religion, although, once again, in Central and East Central Europe, even Chabad is often seen as an unattractive – and divisive – force by many members of the indigenous community.

Now, in this context, a comparison with the West is likely to prove instructive. Throughout the West, in almost every community we find a wide range of "rabbinic possibilities" for those seeking personal or spiritual guidance. There exists a virtual potpourri of options with someone to fit every taste and to sanction many possibilities of Jewish life and behaviour. In Central and East Central Europe that is simply not the case. Not only are the more liberal forms of Judaism weak or nonexistent, but in many places, the individual rabbis represent a particularly narrow and rather unattractive (to many) kind of orthodoxy which is not calculated to attract those whose worldview is cultural-atheistic rather than spiritual-religious.

However, in the areas which we discuss here, there is an additional problem. Among those who are drawn to an examination of Jewish life by cultural or personal curiosity, there are very large numbers who are the products of mixed marriages. The reality of life under the Communist regimes was that Jewish identity played such a marginal role that for many there was no barrier to intermarriage. Many perhaps welcomed the chance to leave the "accursed" Jewish heritage, at least on a subconscious level, since as I have suggested, it was seen by many as something which brought only trouble. In any case, the fact is that tens or hundreds of thousands married out and among those who have been prepared to examine coming back to Jewish life, there are very large numbers indeed who are the products of mixed marriages. Of these, there seem to be at least as many for whom the Jewish parent is the father as the mother. The former, are not Jewish from a *halachic p*oint of view. The tendency of many of the orthodox rabbis working in these communities is to view such products of mixed marriages as "beyond the pale" and to discourage them from participation in synagogue and community life unless perhaps, they are prepared to interest themselves in the possibilities of *halachic* conversion.[2] But the fact is that in order to be sufficiently interested to discuss conversion, they have to be drawn into the community. An a priori demand for interest in conversion runs contrary to all educational logic yet that is exactly the reality with which many young people find themselves confronted.

This presents a major potential challenge for Jewish educators. The pluralistic educator finds herself or himself in a rather strange position, encouraging the involvement in the community of many young people who feel alienated from the official community and unacceptable to the rabbinic leaders of the communities, the official arbiters of Jewish identity. Thus the educational message often contradicts the larger community message.

The group of Bulgarian *madrichim* who were mentioned in the last section provide a case in point. About 80% of the *madrichim* who are involved as educators in the Bulgarian community camp – educating the children of the community in Jewish customs and values – are themselves the products of mixed marriages, with only chance dictating whether the mother or the father is the Jewish partner. This is an additional reason why the home is unlikely to provide a strong and stable building brick in the identity of many young people. Where most of the families are mixed, it is difficult to expect that Jewish rituals will be a regular feature of family life.

I suggested above that the message of the educator might well contradict the official community message as represented by the community rabbis. But it might be suggested that the problem goes deeper. In some cases, educators might well find themselves involved in "special pleading" for a wider Judaism than the participants might have had the chance to experience within their own community framework. In the West educators often find their role in enhancing the work of rabbis in one way or other; here it seems that educators are called on almost to undo the work of the rabbis and to provide an acceptable face of Judaism.

---

[2] It is worth pointing out that Chabad rabbis who are active in many of these communities tend to take a different approach, inviting non-Halachic Jews into an engagement with Jewish life and only subsequently bringing up discussion of conversion. Unquestionably, this is part of the appeal of Chabad rabbis for many non-Halachic Jews in these communities.

5. *The Aliyah Issue: A Dilemma*

One of the biggest problems for Diaspora educators of a Zionist persuasion comes in relation to the whole attitude to be taken towards the issue of *Aliyah*.

My focus in this section is Turkey. As I have explained, my work in Turkey is to try to encourage young Jewish leaders or potential leaders to think of a long-term goal of working within the adult community. The Turkish community is large enough to have the potential for a long-term future. It has some excellent youth and young adults and a strong tradition of voluntarism within the community. But, as far as I can see, that future is not assured. The potential has to be actualised and the best resources of the community have to be mustered in order for the community to have bright prospects in the future, not taking into account the possibilities for increasing difficulties with the surrounding Islamic community.

It has often been suggested that no leader is irreplaceable and I have long accepted that as a general truism. However, recently, I have begun to question it as several of the top young people that I have met in the Young Leadership courses, have started to talk of Aliyah. I find myself extremely conflicted over the issue. I have no question that on the personal level, which is the one that they talk on, they could find more personal Jewish fulfilment living in Israel. It is not so simple to live as a Jew in Turkey. Many things have to be done in secret. Everything has to be done at a low profile. It is the only country I have ever been in where I have been told categorically by my hosts that I must on no account walk the streets with a *kippah* on my head on Shabbat. To do so is to invite potential violence.

But at what point do you weigh the community needs against individual needs? Just as I know that these particular individuals will be likely to be able to live a much richer Jewish life in Israel, I also know fully that the community will suffer. This is the best of Jewish youth. I am not convinced that they are replaceable. The community is not so big that it can afford for all of its best, brightest and most Jewishly committed to leave it even for a more fulfilling personal Jewish life, in Israel.

This is a very different situation from the situation in the big Western Diaspora communities. There, the numbers are so large that one can be fairly confident that potential replacements for potential *Olim* (immigrants) will eventually be found. There might not be a bottomless pool but even in the worst cases it would seem that we are talking ponds, not puddles.

This is a problem of the small communities. Successful Jewish education suggests to many of the most seriously committed and idealistic among the younger generation that their own prospects in their own Jewish community are severely limited. The conclusion that many of them draw is that they need to relocate to a larger and more promising community where they have the scope for the sort of life that their education has suggested to them that it is worthwhile leading. Israel is a logical choice for many.

I applaud their idealism and their determination and I can only be pleased and proud as an Israeli that they wish to come. But at the same time I am painfully aware of the price that their own community will pay for the loss of its young leadership, precisely that leadership which is needed in order to help steer the community towards a better future. Very often these young people are better educated in things Jewish than their own community leaders. They have had, in many cases, chances that the present generation of adult community leaders have not had. And they want to leave. Rarely have I felt myself so torn over a Jewish issue. In this case, I have absolutely no idea what the right educational response is.

6. Investment in Jewish Community: When Do You Cut Your Losses? A Whole Set of Dilemmas

This brings me to the last of these six issues. As someone who has been brought in to help develop the educational potential of Diaspora communities, one of the questions that hits me in the face continually is the ultimate value of the work that I and other educators are doing. To put the question at its bluntest, how long can each community continue to last? I am not convinced as I once was by the concept of "*Shlilat HaGalut*" – the classic Zionist notion of "the negation of the Diaspora": I want to believe that the Diaspora communities have value. I want to believe that they can continue to sustain themselves, at least with a little help from their more powerful friends in the West and in Israel. I do whatever I can in my small way to shore up the communities to help them improve their educational standards and their Jewish knowledge and understanding. But when all things are considered soberly, do they all have a future? Should they be encouraged to stay or should the Jewish world cut its losses? These are real dilemmas with important practical implications.

Sometimes, the answer is simple. A couple of years ago I found myself in Macedonia, part of former Yugoslavia. Macedonia as a state has an overall population of just over two million. Before World War II there were over 10,000 Jews living there, almost all in the two largest cities of Skopje and Bitola. Most were destroyed in the Holocaust and many of the survivors made *Aliyah* to Israel in the early years of the state. Today there are about 200 Jews there, almost all of whom live in Skopje. Some of the most promising young Jews have moved away to other cities or to Israel. It seems clear that there is no future for the community. The only option for those who are interested in a long-term Jewish future is indeed to move out. It is regrettable to talk in these terms of an area with a Jewish history of at least 1,600 years but it would, it seems, be foolish to talk otherwise.

But what about Bulgaria? It is very small but showing great signs of life. As mentioned earlier there is an annual meeting of up to 600 Jews in a family gathering before *Rosh HaShanah* and a winter seminar for adults and families. There is an annual summer camp with a Jewish theme and a serious emphasis on learning. There are youth and student groups and a new community centre. All these are the results of substantial external investment especially by the JDC. It seems unlikely that the community will be able to continue for long without some kind of external help but that help has been instrumental in helping develop the internal resources of the community. Is the case of Bulgaria like the case of Macedonia? In the short run, the answer is clearly no. But what of the long-term prospects?

To take an example from another part of the Jewish world with which I have been involved, India is another similar small community. There are about 5,000 Jews in India out of a total population of some 1,150,000,000. Once again with the help of agencies like the JDC and Ort, the community lives a vibrant Jewish life for a small community. There are many activities in the community centre of the main community in Mumbai. But can one honestly suggest that there is any long-term future for the community? However, if one abandons that hope and refuses to work for such a future, one gives the kiss of death to one of the most colourful and fascinating communities in the whole Jewish mosaic. Already parts of the community have all but vanished. The 1,000-year-old Cochini community has disappeared to all intents and purposes (its remnants surviving in different places, mostly in Israel), and much effort has been put into the surviving community based predominantly in Mumbai. Is the investment in vain? At what point does one give up on a community and tell them that its future lies elsewhere?

And what about Turkey with its approximately 17,000 Jews and a magnificent history especially in the years of the Ottoman Empire when communities such as Istanbul, Izmir and Bursa were bywords for Jewish life? I have already sketched out my own dilemma with regard to the *Aliyah* question there. But the question is, of course, a larger one. What is the responsibility of the Jewish world to a community that is suffering both from internal attrition and external pressure? What should be the message of educators? Are we wrong when we try to encourage a new generation of local leaders? Should we instead try and influence them to understand the potential hopelessness of their situation and encourage them to move elsewhere? Should we encourage the Zionist inclinations of the youth and try and fan them into a stronger flame?

And Hungary? Here is a community with a much larger potential – some speak of over a hundred thousand Jews – although it seems clear in a realistic assessment that the sober numbers are at best about 20,000 or so. What should the policy be in regards to such a community? What should the policy be of an educator like myself, invited into the community from the outside? Should I try and spread clandestine Zionist messages in the hope that some get the message?

The questions, in my mind, are clear. Up to what point does one continue to invest in a Jewish community from an educational and community building point of view? At what point does one say that it is time to cut one's losses and to encourage the locals to "head for the hills"? Yes, the questions are fairly simple and easily defined. It is the answers which I think are much more problematic.

Closing Time

From one point of view this is a personal essay. It comes out of my own personal experiences. But the "I" is used here as a vehicle to discuss wider issues. My importance in this process is only to give voice to the sort of thoughts that any experienced Jewish educator would encounter if he/she were in my position.

In my various working travels in western communities (not so very many), I have rarely discovered totally new things. Most of what I saw tended to confirm – although certainly to deepen – the things that I had already learned from my work in Israel with groups from the West. Not so this latest phase of my work in Europe and Turkey. I have found myself constantly stretched and tested: new insights and understandings of the Jewish world have been constantly before my eyes. I hope that I have managed to convey a sense of my new perspectives and questions in this chapter. It is not really about me. It is really about us all.

Former Soviet Union: Jewish Education

Olga Markus and Michael Farbman

Introduction

Reviewing Jewish education in the Former Soviet Union (FSU) is a challenging task. This is partly because it has to be viewed in the larger context of social, political, historical, cultural, and even economic conditions in which Jews found themselves in the countries of the FSU.

The FSU is not a country, but this is a common way to collectively describe this vast region that stretches across 11 time zones and contains 15 different countries.[1] Jews of these lands have different origins and cultural backgrounds, yet share nearly a century of common history – one where religious expression of Judaism was not an option. It is through the prism of these shared experiences that we intend to approach the task at hand.

Any attempt to analyze and evaluate an endeavor requires criteria of success. It is tempting to use the familiar, established ways of evaluation in the professional world of Jewish education. To an extent, we must rely on the knowledge and experience of Jewish education around the world, as this is our professional common ground, but we believe that we have to evaluate Jewish education in the FSU somewhat differently.

A major goal of Jewish education worldwide is the creation and nurturing of positive Jewish identity and commitment. While difficult to measure, there are ways to assess our success as educators, such as counting former students who remain committed Jews, belong to synagogues, practice Judaism at home, and eventually send their children to Jewish schools. Such research is continuously conducted in the West and serves as a basis for ongoing evaluation and open discussion of Jewish education. In the FSU, no comprehensive research into outcomes of Jewish

---

O. Markus (✉)
Freelance educator, Orange, CT, USA
e-mail: olam95@gmail.com

[1]Former republics of the USSR: Russia, Belarus, Estonia, Latvia, Lithuania, Moldova, Ukraine, Armenia, Azerbaijan, Georgia, Kazakhstan, Kyrgyzstan, Tajikistan, Turkmenistan, Uzbekistan. Twelve former Soviet Republics (with exception of three Baltic States) form a Commonwealth of Independent States, known as CIS. Both terms (FSU and CIS) are often used interchangeably.

education is available. Even if we had quantitative research, it most likely would be confusing. Declining numbers of students at Jewish schools[2] do not necessarily indicate failing schools – they may reflect Jewish migration, from smaller communities to capital cities within the FSU and emigration to Israel and elsewhere. On the other hand, stable or even growing numbers of students may raise a question about the proportion of Jewish students at various institutions.[3] Whatever numbers we look at, they would be telling us only part of the story, potentially invalidating any serious research.

Last but not least, we are dealing with a brand new field of Jewish education, emerging out of the "desert." As Zvi Gitelman puts it, we are talking about those "who started little over a decade ago, with no financial or educational resources of their own..." (Gitelman, 2007, p. 391).

To sum up, one should look at the question in all its complexity, using standard means of evaluation where applicable, while acknowledging the uniqueness and limitations of the data available.

This chapter will focus both on the challenges currently facing Jewish education in the FSU, through the prism of its history and current situation, and on ways in which these challenges are being addressed.

History of Jewish Education in the FSU

Jewish Religious Schools, as well as Hebrew schools, were outlawed at the end of the Russian Civil War (1918–1920[4]) and replaced with a network of Soviet Jewish schools where Soviet morale and principles of internationalism were taught in Yiddish. Most students and teachers were Jewish; Yiddish was the language of instruction; Hebrew was not taught; and Judaism as a religion was referred to only for critique. According to Gitelman, in 1931 there were about 1,100 Soviet Yiddish schools enrolling 130,000 students. "Nearly half the Jewish children in Belorussia and Ukraine, in the former Pale of Settlement, who attended school at all were enrolled in Yiddish schools" (Gitelman, 2007, p. 377). This reflected the early Soviet doctrine of National Rights, allowing education for all people in their native languages. These schools were never designed to maintain or deepen their students' Jewish identity. They were nothing but Soviet Schools in Yiddish, which was recognized as the official language of the Jewish people, allowing instruction in schools, publication of written materials, Yiddish theatre, and so on. A brief period of Jewish

---

[2] Such numbers are, in fact, available, albeit limited.

[3] This statement is in no way designed to raise the question of the Jewish status (who is a Jew), but simply to point out an area of tension arising out of the requirement for State-sponsored schools to admit non-Jewish students.

[4] According to Encyclopedia Britannica. Other sources provide a variety of dates for the Russian Civil War, ranging from 1917 to 1923.

renewal under Communism ended by 1939–1940[5] when the last Jewish schools and synagogues were shut down. A few "token" synagogues were kept open in the Soviet Union as a showcase of tolerance, but no educational activity was allowed there, especially aimed at the young – it was considered a form of indoctrination. A radical change of policy toward Jews that began in the late 1930s and continued after World War II (1939–1945) meant that no Jewish schools were re-opened after the war. Soviet Yiddish schools were established and funded by the state as part of a nationwide attempt to provide basic education to wide masses (*Likbez*).[6] Once the state lost its interest in maintaining such schools, they were doomed. Jewish schooling also limited integration into Soviet society. Russian-language schools guaranteed better chances of secondary and higher education. Although national language-based education remained available to most ethnic groups in the Soviet Union, official anti-Semitic policies of post-war USSR ended Jewish schools once and for all.[7]

After decades of oppression, resurgence of Jewish life followed *perestroika* (late 1980s) and with the collapse of the Soviet Union in 1991 proliferation of Jewish schools and institutions began in the early 1990s, with Sunday schools and summer/winter camps leading the way. The first Jewish day school in Riga and a Jewish preschool in Vilnius opened in 1989, heralding a new era in Jewish education. The collapse of the Iron Curtain opened the doors to *aliya* (immigration to Israel) and other emigration from the Soviet Union, and the opportunity for Jewish communities from the West to openly support Jewish activities, including education, in the Soviet Union. With Western support, the enthusiasm of "Russian" Jews resulted in an explosion of Jewish activity throughout the country. In 1990 day schools opened in Tallinn and Leningrad and by the beginning of 1991 there were over 20 Jewish schools in the Soviet Union. The 1993/1994 census of Jewish Schools in the FSU published by Hebrew University of Jerusalem (DellaPergola, Bassan, Rebhun, & Sagi, 1997) provides a snapshot of rapid development. It does not reflect quality or content of the education provided, but creates a comprehensive quantitative profile of Jewish schools in the FSU. The census covered 218 schools in the FSU at the time, including 58 (27%) day schools and 169 (73%) supplementary schools[8] with

---

[5] William Korey (1972, p. 83) states that "as late as 1940... there were some 85,000–90,000 Jewish children studying in schools where Yiddish was the language of instruction. This constituted 20% of the Jewish student population."

[6] *Likbez*, from a Russian abbreviation for *likvidatsiya bezgramotnosti*, was a campaign of eradication of illiteracy in Soviet Russia in the 1920s and 1930s. The campaign was generally successful. In 1917, only 40% of all adults in Russia were literate. According to the 1939 Soviet Census, literate people were 89.7%.

[7] Levenberg (1972, p. 39) had thus described the situation: "It is the official policy of the USSR to provide children with instruction in the native language, but not a single school in the Soviet Union teaches Hebrew, Yiddish, or any other Jewish dialect, whereas the R.S.F.S.R alone has forty-five different languages of instruction and a total of fifty-nine languages is used in the schools of USSR. Jewish history and literature are also not taught in Russian or any other language."

[8] A 1995 report of the Joint Distribution Committee (JDC) has somewhat conflicting numbers, with 41 day schools and 190 Sunday/supplementary schools reported. Number of students is similar in

17,809 students and 2,041 teachers. "The most impressive finding in our census of the Former Soviet Union's Jewish education system is its very existence... Considering the fact that scarcely a half-decade earlier formal religious activity was forbidden and the few Jewish schools that existed were underground, the achievement is indeed extraordinary. Furthermore, our data comparing 1993/1994 with the same schools in the previous school year suggest a remarkable growth of 45% in just 1 year" (DellaPergola et al., 1997, p. 26). Note the ideological orientation of these schools: 85% non-Orthodox (i.e., Reform, secular, and communal) and 15% Orthodox (Charedi and mainstream).

From the 1990s, Institutions of Higher Jewish Learning were opened throughout the FSU. The first Jewish University opened in St. Petersburg (then Leningrad) in 1989, receiving State recognition in 1992. As of 1997, it operates as St. Petersburg Judaic Institute with a 2003/2004 enrollment of 120 students. December 2010 numbers reported on official website is 97 students (http://www.pijs.ru/). In 1991 a Jewish University opened in Moscow (called the Simon Dubnov Advanced School for Humanities since 2003). Similar programs appeared in several major cities of the FSU, including Kiev (1993, International Solomon University) and Minsk. The Israel Open University (OU) was introduced in the FSU in 1993. Since 2001, it has operated with support from the Jewish Agency. In 2006–2007, OU had over 6,000 enrolled students, 16 courses available in Russian, and the option of a BA in Jewish studies.

In addition to formal educational settings, many educational outreach institutions entered the Jewish scene in the FSU. Their goal was to initiate educational, cultural, and religious programs necessary for the resurgence of Jewish life. The Steinsaltz Institute published a number of Jewish texts and resources, including a partial Russian translation of the Talmud, and created professional development opportunities for Jewish educators. Project Kesher brought together women throughout the FSU for Jewish study, personal growth, and support. These are but two examples of numerous programs that have provided Jewish education in the FSU since the early 1990s to this day.

From the early 1990s, Jewish camps and retreats provide informal education, perhaps most effective in creating a positive Jewish identity among young Jews. Most organizations operating in the FSU run their own summer and winter camp programs, with the Jewish Agency a traditional leader in the field. Chabad Lubavitch, World Union for Progressive Judaism (WUPJ), and lately Masorti all report successful nationwide camp programs for different age groups.

One can identify three pillars of educational activities in 1990s FSU: (1) religious education and upbringing (to instill religious ideology, traditional way of life, and values), (2) secular education (stressing cultural Jewish identity and serving

---

both documents. This once again shows the difficulty in conducting such research, as different data available often shows conflicting findings.

particular groups within the wider Jewish community[9]), and (3) Zionist education (promoting *aliya* and aimed to ease integration into Israeli society).

An explosion of Jewish communal, cultural, and educational programs in the 1990s was understandable. Gitelman points out a number of reasons why Jewish schools were among the first institutions to be constructed successfully. Education has always been the highest priority for Soviet Jews.[10] Other Soviet nationalities had access to ethnic education (including languages) within the context of general education in national republics – something denied to the majority of Jews. Pent-up desire to explore Judaism and their Jewish identity by former Soviet Jews, deprived for decades of such an opportunity, also clearly played a role. Last but not least, both financial and curricular support from external agencies provided the necessary resources and staff to enable and facilitate incredible growth.

Alexander Lvov (1999) notes that by 1994, after 4 years of rapid development, growth of Jewish educational programming stabilized and entered the stage of qualitative changes. "This is usually referred to as the end of the era of enthusiasts and beginning of an era of professionals." Rokhlin (2004) suggests that Jewish educational development be divided into 1989–1995 forming the foundation; 1995–1998 professionalization; 1998 onward systematization of Jewish education.

Review of Current Educational Structures

Let us look at the current educational scene in the FSU and its major participants.[11] One of the oldest and biggest networks of Jewish day schools is operated by the *Chabad-Lubavitch* movement, sponsored by the Ohr Avner Foundation. According to data from the Federation of Jewish Communities,[12] the FJC currently oversees and operates 72 day schools in 65 cities across the FSU with an enrollment of over 11,000 students. These are essentially religious day schools, offering general secular education as well as Jewish history, traditions, and language instruction. In most cities, the school is strongly connected to the local Chabad community and synagogue, providing context for the education. Most students do not come from religious families, but the quality of general education, the Jewish national component, and significant benefits (such as daily hot meals, transportation to and from school, after-school activities and camps) attract large numbers of students. Despite the best efforts of the Chabad-Lubavitch movement, graduates of these schools often do not feed into adult membership of Chabad congregations.

---

[9]This category includes, in addition to secular Jewish day and supplementary schools, Yiddish classes, secular early childhood education (including special needs programs), lectures, etc.

[10]Jews had the highest level of general education among Soviet Nationalities. According to the 1959 census, Jews who had higher education outnumbered the general population 5 to 1, with similar ratio reflected in 1970 at 4 to 1 (cf. Altshuler, 1987, pp. 108, 111).

[11]This chapter does not claim to list all educational agencies operating in the FSU. Rather, it provides a brief general overview of the field. A few individual examples of educational projects and agencies mentioned in this section help describe a particular approach, challenge, or success.

[12]See www.fjc.ru for detailed information on Chabad-sponsored activities in the FSU.

Heftziba is the partnership between local governments in the FSU, local Jewish communities, Jewish Agency for Israel, World ORT[13] (joined in 1993), and the Israeli Ministry of Education to provide formal Jewish education in Jewish schools in the FSU. This educational network started in 1992 when the first 5 schools opened (in Moscow, Leningrad, Kiev, Kishinev, and Riga). In 1992–1996, 10 more schools joined this network. Today the network includes 43 Jewish day schools and 114 Sunday schools with total enrollment of approximately 16,000 students.[14] In this partnership, the Jewish Agency sees a golden opportunity to place Israel at the center of Jewish education throughout the FSU. It bolsters Heftziba by providing teachers and specialists on the ground, professional development training to local teachers, and educational programs and resources on various aspects of Jewish- and Israel-related subjects. ORT contributes their unique expertise in computer technologies and their dedication to promoting the use of modern technologies in twenty-first century education, an ORT specialty in Israel and throughout the world. ORT's state-of-the-art computers and classroom equipment make Heftziba schools highly competitive in the current FSU school system.

In addition to its involvement in the Heftziba project, the *Jewish Agency* remains a key provider of formal and, especially, informal Jewish education in the FSU. The network of summer and winter camps for children and young adults as well as students has ensured the clear lead of the Jewish Agency in this area for almost two decades. In the early 1990s, the Jewish Agency responded to the urgent need of mass *aliya*[15] by providing, in addition to crucial advice and information on actual immigration, crash courses in modern Hebrew through its wide net of *ulpanim* (Hebrew language classes). In time, a number of programs promoting *aliya* to Israel were created. Some of the most successful programs offered an opportunity for high schools students to continue their studies in Israel, with parents following in a few years. By the early 2000s, *aliya* from most FSU communities had fallen dramatically. In an unexpected move, the Jewish Agency decided to use its professional staff and expertise to support development of local Jewish communities in the FSU. Although it all but abandoned its goal of encouraging *aliya* of all FSU Jews to Israel, through its popular educational and cultural programs, the Jewish Agency continues to help build and maintain strong Jewish identity among local Jews, while ensuring that Israel remains a crucial element of that identity.

---

[13] ORT was founded in Tsarist Russia in 1880. The name "ORT" was coined from the acronym of the Russian words *Obshestvo Remeslenogo zemledelcheskogo Truda*, meaning The Society for Trades and Agricultural Labor.

[14] So reported on JAFI website, February 2009. A November 2008 report of JAFI talks of 44 day schools and nearly 10,000 students enrolled.

[15] According to the Israeli Central Bureau of Statistics (December 2007) in 1990–1999 some 821,763 people from FSU made *aliya*. Tolts (2003) gives the following numbers: "between 1989 and 2002, more than 1,500,000 ex-Soviet Jews and their relatives emigrated to countries outside the FSU."

Since 1994, *Hillel*, a student-oriented organization supported by the Charles and Lynn Schusterman Family Foundation in partnership with Hillel: The Foundation for Jewish Campus Life and with the American Jewish Joint Distribution Committee has been offering its programs and services to thousands of students and young people in the FSU. Hillel now operates 27 centers in seven former Soviet Republics, providing approximately 10,000 young adults a year with an opportunity to learn, explore, and celebrate their Jewish heritage. In December 2006, Hillel partnered with the Jewish Agency, allowing both organizations to significantly expand their programs by combining their resources and expertise.

Although the economics of operating Jewish educational and cultural programs in the FSU mean that it is much easier for large networks to maintain their institutions, there are a few historically independent projects in the FSU. One notable example is the *Adayin Lo* center in St. Petersburg, which serves local Jewish community needs with financial support from both local funds and foreign agencies. Adayin Lo includes a chain of Jewish secular preschools, a Sunday school, educational programs for tots and teenagers, a youth club, summer and winter camps, and a preschool for physically challenged children. In 2003 Adayin Lo added a Jewish day school to its array of programs, although this project may end up being too costly and ambitious for this small, independently minded organization relying on a lot of volunteer work.

The *Novaya Evreiskaya shkola* (New Jewish school) is an informal professional organization (pedagogical club) of educators, teachers, and students. It started in 1999 in St. Petersburg and aimed at encouraging educational creativity and initiatives among those involved in Jewish education. For a number of years *Novaya Evreiskaya shkola* published a monthly educational magazine, organized teacher-training seminars, published teaching resources, collected the best and most recent creative projects and materials produced by local educators throughout the FSU, and maintained a website for educators. It appears that, due to financial and organizational challenges, *Novaya Evreiskaya Shkola* ceased to exist around 2007. A variety of their materials are still available on a number of Internet websites, but no new materials have been published recently.

The American Jewish Joint Distribution Committee (JDC) has been a major participant in reviving the Jewish community in the FSU. Although its main priority has been providing welfare to thousands of Jews in desperate need, it has also supported key educational initiatives including cross-communal teacher-training seminars, Hillel, libraries, and publishing quality educational materials in Russian. "To strengthen the capabilities of Jewish educators in the FSU, JDC established *Sefer*, the Moscow Center for University Teaching of Jewish Education. Since 1994, *Sefer* has opened its doors to Jewish educators seeking to upgrade their skills in a university setting. *Sefer* provides information on continuing education opportunities and seminars to some 2,000 academics, and its own annual conference is typically attended by over 500 educators from the FSU and abroad."[16]

---

[16] Cf. JDC Annual Report 2007, p. 46.

To the best of our knowledge, the JDC has never operated Sunday schools and similar projects directly, focusing instead on supporting local initiatives. This situation may be changing with the recent development of a network of JDC-sponsored JCCs.

The *Reform* Movement entered the FSU scene in 1989 with the establishment of its first congregation in Moscow, *Hineni*. The priority was creating Reform congregations throughout the FSU. By 1993, dozens of new congregations were formed, many operating Sunday religious schools. The Institute for Modern Jewish Studies (*Machon*) opened in 1993 to train much-needed Jewish professionals and since 1995 *Machon* graduates serve congregations throughout the FSU.

A first FSU Netzer youth summer camp was organized by the WUPJ (World Union for Progressive Judaism) in July 1993. Every year since, Netzer summer and winter camps take place in Russia, Belarus, Ukraine, and most recently, Latvia. In 2007, nearly 1,300 individuals participated in WUPJ summer camps from all over the FSU.

A more detailed description of Reform Movement educational activities in the FSU, its challenges and strategies, is provided later in this chapter.

The *Conservative* movement did not establish any synagogues in the FSU in the 1990s, focusing instead on Jewish educational activities. The Masorti, or Conservative, movement supports School No. 41 in Chernovsty, Ukraine. In the last few years, Masorti has increased its activity in the FSU. In addition to the Chernovtsy school, it now runs a number of Sunday schools (seven according to Masorti Olami Monthly Report of October 2002) and student groups, the Armon Educational and Cultural Center in Kiev, a Ramah summer camp and family camp, teacher-training seminars, and family educational programs. Movement leaders estimate that about 1,000 Ukrainian Jews take part in these activities. The Chernovtsy school has 308 students from first to eleventh grade (2007 data).

Research and its Challenges

Research on Jewish Education in the FSU is limited. In 1997, the *Journal of Jewish Education* published a census of Jewish schools in the FSU for 1993/1994 school year, conducted by Hebrew University of Jerusalem (DellaPergola et al., 1997), with a comprehensive quantitative profile of Jewish schools in the FSU. Gitelman's works offer the most extensive research to date. His 2007 article "Do Jewish schools make a difference in the Former Soviet Union?" provides a broad picture of Jewish education in the FSU, with quantitative and qualitative data as well as serious analyses of the current situation and challenges. The St. Petersburg Judaic Institute published a number of books and articles on the subject in 1996–1998, as well as a *Reference Book of Jewish Educational Establishments* (ed. Elyashevich, 2001) in CIS and Baltic States in 2001. *Novaya Evreiskaya Shkola* (New Jewish School), a professional pedagogical club and a regularly published journal by the same name, published a number of research articles on the subject since its inception in 1999.

Similar to the research published by the Judaic Institute, these studies add an important dimension as they are conducted by professionals working in the field, on the ground.

Virtually all researchers lament the lack of coherent statistics, with information verifiable and updated regularly – a clear necessity for any such research. Rokhlin (2004) puts it bluntly: "The main problem here is that there is no single database on Jewish schools (at least in open access), containing the information which is totally reliable and would be updated with the required frequency. A number of Jewish organizations are attempting, with some degree of success, to create such a database; however, because of the lack of coordination of their efforts and limited resources, all available research databases have varying degrees of error." A typical example of this "degree of error" is the reference book published by the Judaic Institute in 2001, which systematically lists Jewish schools and other educational establishments throughout the FSU, provides statistics, etc. This highly respected work draws criticism from Aryeh Rotman (*Novaya Evreiskaya Shkola*, 2002) who points out that a number of schools "missing" in this updated roster have simply changed their contact details or failed to respond to requests for updated information. In other schools, a significant change in enrollment numbers resulted from use of a different calculation, most likely by the school authorities who supplied the information. Thus, the 2000 reference book listed 140 students enrolled in school #2 in Birobidjan and in 2001 the number jumped to 840! Rather than a dramatic increase in numbers, the new figure reflects all the students of the state school reported, not just those in the Jewish department of the school.

The issue is simple. Collecting data in person is highly problematic, if not impossible, although information gathered through such research is helpful and appropriate. When Gitelman quotes certain teachers and their reports made to him directly, his conclusions and statistics are worthy of attention. Once we start basing our research on information provided by other sources and agencies, we are prone to confusion as much of the information will provide conflicting numbers. Without first-hand knowledge of each and every school and preschool, the misleading information cannot be sifted from the real statistics.

Markus conducted an audit of educational activities for the Reform Movement in the FSU in 2005 to obtain practical information for formulating future educational strategy, rather than for academic research. Even working within the same Movement and not dealing with various agencies and sensitivity around denominational differences, this process was incredibly challenging. Conducting research across eight time zones, expensive and unreliable telephone communications, often unavailable email capability, especially in smaller towns, oft-changing leadership, not to mention contact information that is routinely out-of-date – this is just the tip of an iceberg. In supplementary schools, most people involved work very part time and fail to respond to pleas for updated information. This is not a singular experience – the above-mentioned reference book gives "failure to respond" as a legitimate reason for lack of data. *Novaya Evreiskaya Shkola* cites one data collection project where of 140 requests sent to schools, only 38 responded.

In researching available data for this chapter, we found a number of resources unavailable, despite our best efforts. To our regret, we have discovered that *Novaya Evreiskaya Shkola* has ceased to exist in its former capacity and attempts to contact former staff members were unsuccessful.

Having discussed the challenges of conducting research in this field, let us now concentrate on what *is* available. To analyze a complex educational schooling system, we must establish classification criteria. The criteria used in research currently available are the following:

(1) Affiliation, belonging to (under the auspices of) a religious denomination or organization. A network of schools under the auspices of Chabad-Lubavitch will all have similarities, but will be significantly different from those operated by the Jewish Agency and ORT.
(2) Ideological orientation. This criterion is closely connected to affiliation, but does not overlap entirely. It helps to divide all existing schools into religious, secular, and possibly community schools. Religious schools can further be divided into Orthodox, Chabad (and other Chassidic), Reform, and Conservative.[17]
(3) Type of school, from the point of view of organization of the educational process. Jewish day schools, Sunday schools, and preschools/kindergartens would be in different categories according to this criterion.
(4) Geographical location. In the 1993/1994 census conducted by Hebrew University, three geographical regions were identified in classifying schools: Russia, other European republics, and Asian republics. Rokhlin suggests a different geographical classification. He begins with a Central group including Russia and Ukraine. This group has a high percentage of Jewish population, wide networks of Jewish schools, high number of qualified educators, a highly developed market of Jewish educational services, and, as a result, competition. Rokhlin's second group is Periphery, both geographically and in terms of development of educational system. This group, including Belarus, Lithuania, Latvia, Moldova, and Uzbekistan, differs significantly in size from the Central group with far fewer schools, even though they are in close proximity. This results in closer ties between the schools in the region, less competition, and more monopolization of educational services. The majority of schools in this group are in capital cities with far less coverage of provincial towns. Rokhlin's third group includes countries such as Estonia, Kyrgyzstan, Kazakhstan, Georgia, and Azerbaijan, where it is difficult to talk about any kind of network, as the numbers of schools in these areas are no more than one or two per country.

---

[17] 1993/1994 census (Hebrew University) provides a slightly different division of schools according to ideological orientation: non-Orthodox 85% (Reform, secular, and communal) and Orthodox 15% (Charedi and mainstream).

(5) Funding. Some schools are fully funded by sponsoring Jewish organizations or groups (e.g., Reform supplementary schools). Other schools are funded by the State with additional funding and resources, educational and other, provided by the sponsoring Jewish organizations (the majority of Heftzibah and ORT-sponsored schools).

Gitelman also suggests four types of comprehensive schools with a Jewish component. "There are public schools 'with a national component' (e.g. Ukrainian, Jewish, Armenian) which receive 15–20% of their budgets from the state, allocated to general studies teachers' salaries and maintenance; semi-private schools sponsored by the state, though Jewish organizations take responsibility for renovated premises in the school that serve Jewish instruction; 'schools within schools' wherein a part of the premises are set aside for Jewish instruction; and private Jewish schools, almost all religious" (Gitelman, 2007, p. 381).[18]

(6) An additional criterion featured in different research is the age of the institution in question.

Rokhlin (2004) rightly suggests that all of the above classifications are valid but limited. An educational system as complex as the one that currently exists in the FSU requires a different classification system to allow for evaluation of the actual educational process and not just external factors. He suggests grouping the schools in the following manner: (1) curriculum structure, (2) content of the Jewish subjects taught, and (3) organization of methodological work. These criteria provide a more practical approach, allowing the researcher to concentrate on what happens in schools in terms of the actual educational process. Thus, the curriculum structure will classify schools according to the number of academic hours in each grade on each subject and will clearly identify precisely what is being taught in the so-called "Jewish component." Currently, different Jewish schools (or their sponsors) make their own choices with regard to what subjects are being taught as part of the Jewish studies courses (e.g., Hebrew, Jewish traditions, Jewish texts, geography of Israel, history of modern Israel, Jewish history, etc. – a wide range indeed). This is in clear contrast to the way the general educational component is structured and taught; there is a state-approved curriculum for all day schools that must be followed strictly.

Analyzing the content of Jewish subjects taught would mean classifying schools based on curriculum structure by subject, textbooks, and materials used. The last category would reflect educator creativity, interaction with educational agencies, and teachers' professionalism and relationship with school administration. All these criteria are used in some of the research currently available.

---

[18]Gitelman (2007) also points out that this classification only includes schools in Russia and Ukraine. "The three Baltic states have distanced themselves from the rest of the FSU, but the educational profiles are similar."

Challenges: Today and Tomorrow

As mentioned earlier, Jewish education has entered a new phase of development – a stage of qualitative changes and professionalization. The significant growth and development of Jewish schools in the FSU is a reality, but Jewish educational institutions continue to face many challenges. One challenge is the fact that most Jewish families do not choose Jewish schools for their children. Hannah Rotman claims that "Jewish schools here have not become schools for the Jewish masses. This is one of the biggest issues that Jewish schools are facing" (Krichevsky, 2005). There are a number of reasons for this. In many places, especially smaller towns, Jewish schools attract disadvantaged families by offering more than just education. Virtually, none of the Jewish schools charge tuition. Many provide free meals, transportation, and even dormitory accommodation and summer and winter camps. It is an important mission, especially since the local Jewish community often has no means to support these families in other settings. Nevertheless, educators point out that "failure to attract Jews from across the economic spectrum represents a challenge for the future of Jewish education in their region" (ibid). In many cities, Jewish schools find it hard to compete academically with the best local schools. Jewish parents prefer to enroll their children in schools with the best educational reputations which Jewish schools often lack. This issue has been partly addressed by increasing teachers' salaries; Jewish day schools try to pay their teachers better than the state schools. In 2002, e.g., the Avi Chai foundation made an effort to improve the general studies program in FSU day schools they support by providing 20 schools in Moscow, St. Petersburg, Kiev, and Dniepropetrovsk with salary stipends for teachers of math, physics, English, computers, and other general subjects.

They also funded new laboratory equipment and materials for marketing and recruitment efforts.[19] There is a clear and understandable shortage of highly professional teachers of Jewish subjects. This should not be a surprise; this new field has not been around long enough to generate a pool of professionals.[20]

Improving and strengthening general education will undoubtedly attract more students to Jewish day schools. On the other hand, these improvements are often at the expense of Jewish subjects. The hours dedicated to the "Jewish component" varies greatly depending on the type of school. According to Gitelman, Orach Chaim school for boys in Kiev devotes 37 h a week to Jewish subjects; in the parallel school for girls it is 19.5 h a week. "The Chabad school in the same city...divides 11.5 h a week of Judaica among prayers, Hebrew, history (1 h) and 'tradition'. Examining a third curriculum in Kiev, we see the ORT school offering 8 h a week of Hebrew, history and tradition. The Dubnov school in Riga devotes only 4 h a week to a combination of Hebrew, history and tradition... The Jerusalem school in St. Petersburg teaches Israeli music, Hebrew, history and tradition, all in 6 h a week"

---

[19]Cf. www.avi-chai.org

[20]Many of those who became involved in Jewish life in the 1990s made *aliya* to Israel or immigrated elsewhere, depleting the potential numbers.

(Gitelman, 2007, p. 388). Sunday schools try to keep up by supplementing Jewish subjects with English, computers, and other attractive activities.

Another challenge is the shortage of Jewish educational materials, especially textbooks of appropriate quality written in Russian. Age-appropriate books that acknowledge the diversity of the modern Jewish world are extremely rare. The situation is more optimistic when it comes to Hebrew textbooks; developed in Israel, there are a few curricula used in the FSU, most of acceptable quality. The lack of published materials forces many teachers to be creative and develop new lesson plans, programs, and sometimes entire curricula. *Novaya Evreiskaya Shkola* was dedicated to finding best-practice materials from all over the FSU and publishing them in the journal, in books, and on their website for other teachers to use.

Rotman and Rokhlin (2002), and other educators working in the FSU point to another challenge facing Jewish education in the FSU today – lack of clear goals. As Rynkovskaya (2000) puts it, "Despite numerous discussions, there is still no clarity in defining the goals of Jewish upbringing and education in post-Soviet Diaspora." Educators and analysts are trying to define these goals in discussions, articles, and at professional seminars and roundtables.

One thing is undeniable – there is a clear need for Jewish education in the FSU. This need is manifest in dedicated teachers and lay leaders, students, and parents; in enthusiastic professional Jewish educators and volunteers who invest their efforts in creating and maintaining Jewish educational institutions despite the lack of funds, materials, and even textbooks. There is little doubt about the reality and urgency of the educational needs of FSU Jews. Nonetheless, discussions of what the goals are (or ought to be) have not yet produced a clear result or a shared common goal.

Limited financial resources are an obvious challenge to Jewish education in the FSU. Unfortunately, despite efforts to create a self-sustaining Jewish community, an overwhelming majority of communal structures, programs, and educational institutions rely heavily, if not solely, on funding from international Jewish organizations. This challenge is not new and not likely to disappear any time soon. The inability of the FSU Jews to sustain their own communal structures was alleviated by Western agencies who undertook the support of their brothers and sisters in their quest for Jewish renewal. As a result, an unimaginable level of sophistication in Jewish communal life has been achieved in less than 20 years, something all of us can take pride in and acknowledge with excitement. The unfortunate byproduct of this reality is a mentality that has been developed among local Jews. Initially, foreign aid was needed because of a terrible economic situation and a complete inability locally to sponsor activities by direct involvement of Jewish individuals. This has turned into a total dependence on 100%-funded programs, including educational services. The challenge is thus twofold: lack of funds, a global and universal problem of the Jewish world, paired with a "receiver" mentality. For a few years now this issue has been raised, with attempts by JDC and the Jewish Agency, among others, to introduce tuition and other fees that are not just symbolic, creating a culture and an expectation that individual Jews can and should take responsibility, including financial responsibility, for their own community. In educational settings, the idea of "fees for services" is even more challenging.[21]

The most important challenge of all is the fact that most Jewish educational programs exist in a void. Regardless of ideological positions of schools and institutions, an almost universal lack of context in which acquired knowledge can be applied is the hardest challenge of all. Jewish education received at school needs a framework beyond school walls – traditions kept at home, religious observances and cultural experiences, parental knowledge, and communal affiliation. These are but a few elements that can enhance the impact of Jewish education received at school. Unfortunately, for the overwhelming majority of Jewish families in the FSU, there is very little context to give meaning and relevance to Jewish knowledge. Most Jews do not belong to any organized Jewish community, religious or secular. Children are exposed to Jewish rites and practices at school, but almost never have family or communal experience of them. The result, for most students, is Judaism that exists at school or camp, but not at home, never becoming a way of life and remaining "yet another subject." Gitelman quotes the results of a fascinating survey of students and their parents in six Moscow Jewish day schools in the late 1990s. General subjects, such as math and foreign languages, get an 80 and 95% rating of importance from students and even higher numbers, 85 and 97%, from parents. By contrast, Jewish subjects get between 24 and 67%, with the latter relating to Hebrew language that parents hope will have practical importance.[22]

In the early 1990s, many newly opened Sunday schools were attended by children and their parents together as all generations looked for basic Jewish knowledge they had been denied for so long. It was an exciting time of great enthusiasm and Jewish educational experience shared by all family members. This is no longer the case; most Sunday schools have become institutions mainly for children. Most Jewish educational institutions today struggle to involve parents and make Judaism a family experience.

Religious schools, day and supplementary, have more potential to deal with this issue. The very existence of the religious community provides those who participate with opportunities to practice Judaism; the life of a religious congregation offers a variety of such experiences. It is important to note that most Jewish religious expressions in the FSU are Orthodox: "the religious Judaism that most people see is a strain of orthodoxy that dictates practices through clear answers and authoritative texts and teachers who assert that they represent the most authentic form of Judaism" (Grant, 2008, p. 98).

---

[21] St. Petersburg's Adayin Lo offers an interesting example of addressing this very issue. A few years ago it began the process of introducing subsidized tuition fees that reflect the actual cost of their preschool services. Individual families are offered a stipend if they cannot afford to send their child to preschool. This way, the bulk of financial grants goes to supporting families, as opposed to sponsoring the institution itself and its programs. The hope is that this will help create a culture of financial support of Jewish education by the parents.

[22] For full results of this survey see Gitelman (2007).

The challenging question of Jewish status acquires a new dimension in the FSU. The Soviet official system of ethnic classification (referred to as "nationality" in Russian) was established according to patrilineality – if one's father was Russian/Belarusian/Ukrainian or Jewish, that is what the state considered one to be also. This was reflected on passports and the state strictly controlled that part of one's identity. The new freedom for FSU Jews to emigrate to Israel, as well as to create a local community, brought with it a new challenge: hundreds of thousands of people who considered themselves Jewish all their lives, who suffered oppression as a result of their identity, were now told that in fact they were not Jewish at all![23] This created a backlash toward Judaism as a religion among many former Soviet Jews, both those remaining in the FSU and especially those who made *aliya* to Israel.

Today, there is a major difference in approach between orthodox and non-orthodox (including secular) Jewish groups. Orthodox and Chassidic communities continue to operate within the *halakhic* framework (at least officially). All non-orthodox groups operate under the guidelines of the Israeli Law of Return, welcoming all who have at least one Jewish grandparent into all their programs and activities.[24] This allows most organizations to avoid the painful question of who is a Jew, although it occasionally creates difficult situations when students at Jewish day schools (or Hillel programs), for instance, have no Jewish identity whatsoever as the only Jewish grandparent passed away long before their birth. At the same time, the long-suppressed Jewish identity of many families, coupled with rates of intermarriage up to 80%, means that erring on the side of inclusivity helps reach Jews with very marginal Jewish heritage and identity who would otherwise be lost to the Jewish people.

One way of addressing some of the challenges discussed above is to conduct continuous research in the future. Collecting reliable data on a regular basis across different educational agencies should be a priority. It is definitely time to set up clear goals for Jewish Education in the FSU. In addition, it is probably time to begin asking questions about effectiveness of Jewish education in the FSU. Such professional discussion requires a set of "tools," i.e., criteria of success. Should it be "involvement in various forms of Jewish expression" (Grant, 2008), affiliation, celebration of Jewish life cycle rituals, *aliya*, Jewish education for younger siblings and future children, or even choosing a career as a Jewish professional by former and current students? These are questions for future discussion and research in the field.

---

[23] Halakhah, traditional Jewish religious Law, establishes Jewish status through matrilineality, a direct opposite of the Soviet national policy.

[24] The Reform Movement even officiates at Bar and Bat Mitzvah for children with one Jewish grandparent, considering this ceremony as a symbolic "first step" toward conversion, which can only be legally performed in Russia after the age of 16. At the same time, the marriages performed under the auspices of the Reform Movement in the FSU require both parties to be *halakhically* Jewish, either by birth or through conversion. Patrilineal Jews with strong Jewish identity are offered an "Affirmation of Jewish Status" program.

A Case Study of Reform Jewish Educational Initiative

The Reform Movement and its educational activities in the FSU have undergone major development since the establishment of the first progressive congregation "Hineni" in Moscow in 1989. Sue Fishkoff (2000) quotes the results of a 1998 survey of Russian Jews revealing "that 22% said they felt 'closest' to Reform Judaism, compared to 6.5% who said they preferred Orthodoxy or Hasidism. Given the small number of Reform congregations that existed at the time, this finding was stunning."

At first, the Reform Movement saw establishing and maintaining congregational structures as the main goal in the FSU. In 2004, Reform leadership announced education as its "number one priority." Let us take a closer look at some of the educational challenges the WUPJ faces in the FSU (both systemic and Reform Movement-specific) and ways in which they are being addressed.

In February 2005, at the request of the WUPJ, Markus conducted research on all the educational programs in the progressive congregations in the FSU. The aims of this research were to gather maximum information about educational projects, including curriculum, teachers, and educational materials; and to identify needs and challenges.

In 2005, there were 13 preschools (or kindergartens, as they are commonly called in the FSU) associated with the Reform Movement: 4 in Belarus, 3 in Russia, and 6 in Ukraine. In most of the kindergartens, in addition to general knowledge, the following subjects were taught: Hebrew, Jewish history, Jewish festivals and Shabbat (including celebrations), weekly Torah portions, traditions, English, music, arts and crafts, and dance. Most teaching personnel had teacher's qualification and/or were qualified in the subjects taught and also regularly participated in seminars for Jewish educators conducted by the JDC, Centre for Jewish Education (Kiev), or Association of the Progressive Congregations (Ukraine).

In Belarus, parents of children in Reform kindergartens were members of the local progressive communities and there was a lot of integration with congregational life. In Kiev, after graduating from kindergarten, many children enrolled in Sunday schools.

Twelve Sunday schools participated in the research: 3 in Russia, 3 in Belarus, and 6 in Ukraine. Most schools taught the following subjects: tradition, history, Torah, Hebrew, computer, Israeli dance, English, arts and crafts, music, and drama. Curriculum variations often depended on the resources available and the talents of individual teachers. Most schools operated independently and used resources from a wide range of sources including JDC, the Jewish Agency, self-created, and even Chabad. The most essential needs that were identified by most respondents are:

- teacher training for educators working in progressive kindergartens and schools;
- unified curriculum and teaching materials on Jewish subjects that would reflect the Reform Movement's ideology and values;
- educational resources, especially maps, videos, games, books, and other materials.

The research also reflected adult education, *B'nei Mitzvah* training, conversion classes, and Netzer, the WUPJ youth movement. Statistical data varied according to country, size and age of the congregation, presence of a rabbi or *Machon* graduate, etc. Challenges and needs, on the other hand, were strikingly identical.

Lack of professional Jewish educators has always been one of the major challenges in the FSU. While the general situation improved, with Jewish universities and teacher-training programs providing qualified graduates in the field of Jewish education in the FSU, this did not solve the specific challenge the Reform Movement was facing: having educators who are passionate Reform Jews and well versed in Progressive Judaism's history, ideology, and values. This challenge was first addressed in 1993 when the Institute for Jewish Studies, *Machon*, was organized in Moscow. Initially a 2-year intensive study program, *Machon*, trains professionals who serve Reform congregations throughout the FSU, with five of its graduates becoming rabbis so far and a number of others still in training at the Leo Baeck and Abraham Geiger rabbinical colleges. There are currently 10 students in their first year of this program in Moscow. The program includes a year of study in Israel as part of the now 3-year curriculum. Graduates of *Machon* serve their communities' needs, which often include running preschools and supplementary schools and teaching both children and adults.

A next step was the creation of the FSU Educational leadership team, charged with providing a vision for future development of educational programs and projects and with coordinating all educational activities in the FSU. Teacher-training seminars became regular beginning in May 2005. These twice-yearly conferences offer local educators an opportunity to learn, raise their professional level, and share best practices. Most importantly, these conferences help equip professional Jewish educators with knowledge and skills to teach the fundamentals of Progressive Judaism.

One of the challenges mentioned earlier was the lack of a clear goal for Jewish education. This absence was addressed by the Reform Movement in November 2006, with support and guidance from professional colleagues in Israel and the US, when the FSU educational team produced a mission statement to guide all the educational activities of the Reform Movement in the FSU.[25] It reads:

> *The Jewish Educational mission* of our movement is to design and deliver educational experiences that help individuals and families consciously choose a religious way of life and develop a world view shaped by Progressive Jewish values that both enrich their own lives and support and develop a strong Progressive Jewish community.

The local educators dedicated a conference to discussing this mission statement and worked out strategies needed to make this dream a reality. Based on the urgent need for a unified, Reform values-infused curriculum that was so clearly identified by the 2005 research, a number of curricula have been written and published by the Reform Movement in Russian, including an integrated preschool curriculum for ages 3–7

---

[25]This conference was first of many organized by the WUPJ with support from the Hebrew Union College and the Schusterman Foundation and led by Rabbi Alona Lisitsa and Dr. Lisa Grant.

(*Jewish Me and World Around Me*), a comprehensive 5-year curriculum for Sunday schools (*Torah Shelanu, Torah Sheli*, ages 7–12), a B'nei Mitzvah handbook, and a series of booklets on Jewish festivals. A Russian translation of the Plaut modern Torah commentary became an invaluable resource for congregational workers and educators. At the time of writing it is available online, with printed edition planned in the near future.

Limited financial resources and ongoing evaluation of its activities have prompted the World Union recently to shift its emphasis from having large numbers of smaller congregations to supporting fewer congregations in the capital cities and larger Jewish centers of the FSU. According to the 2008 annual report of the WUPJ, it currently operates 43 congregations with over 20 supplementary schools and 11 preschools in the FSU.

One of the major challenges for all educational institutions discussed earlier in this chapter is the void, the lack of context in which the Jewish knowledge acquired can be used by children. There is little doubt that this challenge also applies to the Reform schools and preschools in the FSU. Having said that, we feel there is a lot of potential in Reform educational projects which exist within the context of a congregational structure. A Hebrew lesson comes to life when a child with his/her parents comes to a Shabbat service at the synagogue. A Purim spiel prepared by a preschool group and performed at the congregational celebration after the *Megillah* reading is not merely an annual performance or educational exercise, but implementation of acquired knowledge and skills. A lesson on equality in Reform Judaism is illuminated at any Shabbat or congregational event when a child sees women wearing *tallitot* and carrying the Scroll. To be sure, Reform Judaism is not the only religious tradition using this potential. There is little doubt that involving students and their families in congregational life is still a major challenge for many Reform communities in the FSU. One thing is certain – this is an exciting challenge that can be met.

Jewish Education for FSU Jews Outside the FSU?

One of the reverberating questions in the globalized Jewish world of today is: How do we ensure the Jewish commitment among "Russian" Jews living not only in the FSU, but also in Israel, the United States, Germany, or Australia? The cultural and spiritual identity of "Russian" Jews often prevents them from actively engaging with the indigenous Jewish community. "Russian" Jews, by and large, do not feel the need to belong to an organized Jewish community, as least not in the way their Western counterparts do through formal synagogue memberships. In the United States, e.g., despite the active engagement of local Jewish communities in resettling Russian Jewish immigrants in the 1970s and 1980s, an almost insignificant percentage of those helped to settle have expressed the desire to join a congregation, belong, and participate. This is surely a challenge, as "Russian" Jews also yearn to foster a positive Jewish identity in their children but do not seem to "fit in" at American synagogues. This presents the Jewish world and Jewish education with a new challenge. Jewish schools for Russian Jewish children are operating in the United States and a number of German Jewish communities struggle with an overwhelming influx of new immigrants (up to 90% in some communities) and their needs. The Jewish Agency for Israel is beginning to turn to the West, offering the expertise it has amassed over the last two decades operating in the FSU. A major fund has been established by Russian-based Jewish businessmen with a mission to "develop Jewish identity among the former Soviet Jews" living in immigrant communities.

There are many challenges that this new initiative will face. Unlike the FSU-based activities, this may be a short-lived effort as the generation of immigrants with clear cultural and educational preferences may see their children and grandchildren feel more at home in the West. For now, however, it appears that well over a million people in Israel, Germany, the United States, and Australia may need similar educational approaches as those used in the FSU. The challenge is making sure that in adapting to their new home, these transplanted Jews find a way to connect to the Western Jewish community and culture in a meaningful way so that their children will not be lost to the Jewish people.

References

Altshuler, M. (1987). *Soviet Jewry since the Second World War*. New York: Greenwood Press.
DellaPergola, S., Bassan, E., Rebhun, U., & Sagi, D. (Winter/Spring 1997). A census of Jewish schools in the former Soviet Union for 1993/94 school year. *Journal of Jewish Education, 63*(1–2), 20–30.
Elyashevich, D. (Ed.). (2001). *Evreiskiye uchebnye zavedeniya na territorii SNG i stran Baltii. (Jewish educational institutions in the FSU and the Baltic states)*. St. Petersburg: St. Petersburg Judaic Institute.
Fishkoff, S. (2000). Perestroika miracle. *Reform Judaism, 29*(1). http://www.reformjudaismmag.net/900sf1.html
Gitelman, Z. (2007). Do Jewish schools make a difference in the former Soviet Union. *East European Jewish Affairs, 37*(3), 377–398.
Grant, L. (2008). Authenticity, autonomy, and authority: Feminist Jewish learning among Post-Soviet women. *Journal of Jewish Education, 74*, 83–102.
Korey, W. (1972). The legal position of Soviet Jewry: A historical enquiry. In L. Kochan (Ed.), *The Jews in Soviet Russia since 1917* (pp. 76–98). London: Oxford University Press.
Krichevsky, L. (2005). Russia's Jewish day schools increase but enrollment still slow. *Jewish News of Greater Phoenix, 57*(33). Accessed online at http://www.jewishaz.com/jewishnews/050415/paradox.shtml
Levenberg, S. (1972). Soviet Jewry: Some problems and perspectives. In L. Kochan (ed.), *The Jews in Soviet Russia since 1917* (pp. 29–43). London: Oxford University Press.
Lvov, A. (1999). Our "Today" in History. *Novaya Evreiskaya Shkola* 4.
Rokhlin, Z. (2004). Evreiskie srednie shkoly na postsovetskom prostranstve (Jewish day schools in the FSU). http://www.kehila.ru/article/?38 Accessed November 6, 2008.
Rokhlin, Z. (2004). Holodnaya osen 2003 (Cold fall of 2003). *Novaya Evreiskaya shkola* 13.
Rotman, A. (2002). Evreiskoe obrazovanie v zhizni i v spravochnike [Jewish education in life and in the reference book]. *Novaya Evreiskaya shkola* 11.
Rotman, H., & Rokhlin, Z. (2002). *Sostoyaniye uchebno-metodicheskogo kompleksa predmetov evreiskogo tzikla v obscheobrazovatelnykh shkolakh s etnokulturnym evreiskim komponentom*

(The state of educational and methodical segment of the Jewish subjects in State schools with the Jewish ethno-cultural component). St. Petersburg: Novaya Evreiskaya Shkola.

Rynkovskaya, N. (2000). Axiological upbringing in Sunday school. *Novaya Evreiskaya Shkola 6*.

Tolts, M. (2003). Mixed Marriage and Post-Soviet Aliyah. Brandeis archive. http://www.brandeis.edu/hbi/pubs/ToltsTextFinal.doc. Accessed April 20, 2009.

France: Jewish Education in France

Ami Bouganim

Translated by **Daniel Roseman**

Over the course of several centuries, France has been the stage for the collision between secularism and religion. In 1905, the separation of State and Church exacerbated rather than curbed the tensions between the political and religious factions. Secularism asserted itself with even more determination than in the past as the framework of the republican civil religion. Alain, the most eloquent spokesman for the 'secular religion' which later would be designated by the term 'secularism', fought the network of private schools sponsored by the Church, employing clerics and dispensing education in a religious atmosphere and according to religious norms. He was to claim, against his adversaries, 'The Republic is a philosophy before it is a regime: it is a Church, a secular Church whose dogma is free thought and whose priest is the primary school teacher' (Alain, 1986). This well-known and current quote expresses a position which largely dominated the circles of those French intellectuals who portrayed themselves as politicians of education (often in disdain for the term 'educationalist', which they considered too amateurish).

For decades, private schools did not benefit from state support, and were the responsibility of the Churches or – for the few Jewish schools which existed before the Second World War – the Consistoire [Board of Deputies of French Jews]. The authorities nevertheless ensured that they arranged two free days a week to permit those parents who wanted it to dispense a religious education – catechism for Catholics, Talmud Torah for Jews – in parishes or synagogues. After the Second World War, the debate over private schools resumed, until the adoption on 31 December 1959 of the Debré Law, which redefined relations between the State and the private educational organisations. This law, still in force today, did not so much recognise private education itself, as the plurality of school establishments. It principally recommended two types of contract between the State and private establishments that wished to benefit from its support: the 'simple contract', authorising a certain liberty in developing programmes and leaving recruitment and training of

---

A. Bouganim (✉)
Matanel Foundation, Netanya, Israel
e-mail: amib@012.net.il

teaching personnel to the school leadership; and the 'contract of association', calling for strict respect of academic programmes as in state schools, in exchange for which teachers were given the status of public employees, recruited, trained, monitored and graded by governmental academic services. The contract of association guaranteed greater backing from the State as well as not-negligible support from regional and local authorities. It was therefore not by chance that private schools balanced, and still do balance, that status. They would like to get both the pedagogical freedom vouched by the first type of contract and the material backing of the second type.

Nevertheless, the choice of a private education is not so much religious as consumerist. It is expected to give greater social protection and better educational results rather than providing specific teaching, with the exception, that is, of a strictly limited number of Catholic, Protestant, Jewish and, recently, Muslim establishments. Equally, it represents an appeal against the educational menu which limits parents' choice of state school. Often, parents make do with a private school by way of protest against the nearest state school, because of the perceived violence which is rife there, the threatening disintegration, or even a far too visible integration. The choice of Jewish school does not run counter to this general rule. It takes into account all sorts of considerations, most important of which centre around the dual concerns of extracting children from cohabitation with their non-Jewish comrades, and avoiding the violence which is endemic in certain schools in the zones known as 'unstable schooling'. It also derives from a concern to perpetuate a quasi-ghettoised way of life, in order to preserve a distinctive identity in an assimilated society. With the exception of the few rabbinical establishments which do not fulfil the required conditions to be under contract or do not wish to be, and a small number of establishments which settle for simple contracts so as not to have teachers imposed on them by the local education authority, the majority of primary and secondary Jewish establishments are under the contract of association, or are on the way to obtaining it for all their classes. The contract of association is only granted to a private school after a 5-year probationary period, except for transferral of a school or the creation of annexes. This delay of 5 years can be reduced to 1 year for the creation of organisations in new urban districts consisting of more than 300 homes. Going under contract is a progressive process, class by class.

Schools under contract therefore promise to deliver the same teaching as in the public system, to prepare their students for the same exams and to respect the same scholastic rhythms, even the same calendars. Today, it is estimated that two million pupils are educated in private establishments, making up 17% of the total number of pupils, 13% in primary education and 21% in secondary. For their part, Jewish schools educate nearly 25% of Jewish children, whose total is estimated at around 200,000. Community authorities are happy to publicise their waiting lists for the more sought-after Jewish schools. The majority of Jewish parents, therefore, continue to send their children to state schools or non-Jewish private schools, in many cases Catholic, where Jewish pupils are excused from catechism classes or are invited to participate in Jewish classes.

Recently, the wearing of the Muslim headscarf within state schools and challenges to the content of certain lessons, such as the Shoah (Holocaust), have restarted the debate on secularism. Islamist protests have reawakened old anti-clerical passions: schools were not about to authorise Crescent, scarf and Koran after having excluded Cross, cassock and breviary. On the one hand, those who held on to secularism as the civil religion of the Republic rallied together to fight all forms of sectarianism, eliminate all religious claims and plead for the promotion of a civic morality with a civic – if not positivist – inspiration. They would only agree to celebrate pragmatism, tolerance, humanism and the universalism of secularism, as well as science. They resumed the rallying cries of the grand secularists of the beginning of the century, such as 'Religions divide, science unifies' or 'The war among us is not in the trenches, it is in the schools'. On the other hand, proponents recommended secularism as a political principle for structuring the public space, without undermining the plurality of religious sensibilities, voices and liturgies. In this new phase, the debate did not centre so much on the separation of State and Church – which had been achieved in the meantime – as on the place of religion in the public space, and it was more concerned with Islam, a political religion, than with Catholicism, which had long since renounced its vague political desires. The debate was all the more passionate in that it went beyond the strict category of the separation of politics and religion and impinged on the question of French nationality which, until the Muslim demands, had been principally inspired by Christianity.

With Islam, the theological-political question was posed differently. No longer were the religious institutions under attack, as much as religion in general; this was not so much a political problem as a problem of and for society. On 15 March 2004, a law was passed forbidding 'wearing of signs or clothes by which pupils ostensibly manifest a religious importance' in public establishments. It was thought that the problem posed by the wearing of the Muslim headscarf in public establishments, if not in the civil service, had been solved; in fact, it only initiated a long legal-political debate since this law appeared to be incompatible with contemporary international texts such as the European Convention on Human Rights which stipulated the 'freedom, either alone or in community with others and in public or private, to manifest his religion or belief'.

Republican Jewishness

In his quote, Alain shows himself to be the heir of Adolphe Isaac Moïse Crémieux, Minister of Justice in the Provisional Government of 1848, founder and first president of the Alliance Israélite Universelle [Universal Jewish Alliance], who declared, 'Priest in the church, teacher in the school'. Crémieux was one of the first Jews to take his emancipation so seriously that he embarked on a brilliant career as a lawyer while campaigning against the 'More Judaico' oath that obliged Jews to swear with a hand placed on the Bible, while other lawyers and litigants were allowed simply to declare with raised hand 'I swear'. The president of the Nimes court asked him so frequently if he would swear his lawyer's oath with the More Judaico that he exclaimed, 'Am I in a synagogue? No, I am in a courtroom! Am I in Jerusalem, in Palestine? No, I am in Nimes, in France. Am I only Jewish? No, I am a French citizen as well: thus, I will take the oath of a Jewish French citizen' (Amson, 1988). This was in 1817. Ten years later, he was still denouncing the More Judaico oath. The 1815 Charter, although proclaiming Catholicism the state religion, affirmed the equality of citizens before the law, as well as freedom of religion. But the More Judaico oath contradicted these principles. Crémieux naturally presented himself as the lawyer for the whole of his co-religionists: 'I do not want to repudiate my faith, I see men growing up, amongst these Jews who have been crushed for so long, who will not spoil France which has adopted them!' At the end of the day, after many twists and turns, the More Judaico oath was abolished by a decision of the Court of Cassation [Supreme Court] on 5 March 1846. It had permitted Crémieux to become the most eloquent advocate of what was called the civil assimilation of French Jewry.

In the meantime, the Charter of 1830 had replaced the one of 1815. Catholicism was now simply the religion of the majority of French people. A law of 8 February 1831 had even put the state in charge of salaries for Jewish ministers, an eloquent recognition of the civil rights of Jews, even more so because the law was passed with a large majority. Unlike a number of Jews, among the most prestigious, who left Judaism in order to hasten their social advancement, Crémieux was no more in favour of mixed marriages than conversion. In a letter to a colleague, he presented the dilemma which preceded his marital choice in these terms: 'Obliged to choose between the daughters of Jerusalem, I had to follow education and integrity rather than money.' It was nevertheless an inter-community marriage, since a Portuguese man – Crémieux was of Portuguese ancestry – agreed to marry a German woman.

In 1830, Crémieux left Nimes for Paris, where he was to lead a brilliant career as a lawyer, politician and representative of the Jews. In 1840, he alienated the French authorities by taking up the cause of the Jews of Damascus who were accused of the ritual murder of a priest, the Superior of a Capuchin monastery, doctor and French protégé. In 1843, Crémieux was elected president of the Consistoire of French Jews. He was one of the architects of the new religious regime, officially recognised by the law of 25 May 1844, the charter of the Jewish religion which prevailed until the separation of Church and State. However, a year later, in July 1845, he had to renounce his position as the leading Jewish figure in France. His wife had secretly converted to Christianity. In addition, she had baptised her children without their father knowing. But the leading Jews of the capital still wanted him as their representative. They put him forward as President of the Paris Consistoire. Crémieux dithered before giving up. Half a century after the Revolution, emancipation may have liberated Jews, but it had also de-Judaised them.

The year 1860 was a favourable year for the birth of new institutions, such as the Red Cross, the Workers' International and the Alliance Israélite Universelle. On 17 May, 17 people met at the home of Charles Netter. Adolphe Crémieux was absent from the meeting, but was represented by Narcisse Leven. The participants shared one preoccupation: to help their co-religionists who were experiencing persecution throughout the rest of the world, in particular in Eastern Europe. They felt themselves elected to protect them, regenerate them and obtain for them the same political rights that they themselves enjoyed in France. Their Judaism was often just Hebrew remnants, ancestral memories and vague liturgical practices. Half a century after their emancipation, the best of French Jewry was making do with the faith that the revolution had attempted to substitute for traditional religions, which recommended their convergence in the universal love of God for humanity: they did not so much see themselves as philanthropists as professed, in one way or another, but as a prophetically inspired 'theophilanthropy' which cherished a messianic vocation (Salvador, 1860).

A six-member committee was put in charge of founding an association and working out its rules. The poet Eugène Manuel wrote a text. A long preamble, reconstructing the slow progression of the idea of a universal task, concluded with a manifesto which became known as the Appeal of the Alliance Israélite Universelle, and which made up one of the most eloquent pieces of 'Israelitism'. The founders of the Alliance were following in the footsteps of the Sanhedrin convened by Napoleon in 1807 to regularise the status of the Jews. Half a century later they took up its broad themes again: patriotism and love of France; scrupulous respect for the civil code; moral regeneration; apprenticeship and exercise of a trade. The Universal Jewish Alliance gave itself the mission

1. To work everywhere for the emancipation and the moral progress of Jews;
2. To lend effective support to those who are suffering because of their Jewish identity;
3. To encourage all publications helping to bring about these ends.

Starting in the summer of 1860, under the impetus of Crémieux, the Alliance engaged in its first political action in favour of the Maronite Christians being persecuted in Lebanon by the Turks. Relations were established with other organisations and contacts made with governments of countries with large Jewish communities. The AIU carried out the first demographic surveys, dwelling on legislation regulating Jews' sociopolitical status. Acting as a representative of world Jewry, the AIU denounced in the press the anti-Semitic attacks which were rife more or less everywhere. Just 4 years after its founding, Crémieux declared in front of the Alliance's general assembly.

Will we one day see all peoples forming a single people, all religions unifying in a single religion? Let this beautiful prophecy be accomplished, and when that dazzling day dawns with a pure and immense light, one of our descendants will cry 'When our elders founded the Alliance Israélite Universelle, they took the first steps towards the goal we have achieved' (Amson, 1988).

In 1860, the war between Morocco and Spain pushed the Jews of Rif, where cholera was rife, into Gibraltar. Mr Picciotto, of the British Board of Deputies, was moved by their plight. One year previously, while on a mission in Morocco, he had noted their material and moral misery. In 1861, he despaired of the European powers, which were content to address 'general remonstrances to the central government'. The town of Tetouan, in the north of Morocco, had a community totalling around 6,000 members at the time, originally from Spain and Portugal from where their ancestors had been expelled during the fifteenth and sixteenth centuries.

Impressed by Picciotto, the AIU called on the French vice-consul in the town to do everything in his power to enforce the report's conclusions: 'To encourage and help the internal reform of our co-religionists by means of public education'. Thus the AIU created its first school, which took care to combine general education with religious instruction. It was inaugurated on 23 December 1862, despite the misgivings of the rabbis, who feared ancient traditions would be watered down. The school could only accommodate a third of applicants, making up 100 pupils.

The scholastic work of the AIU was to follow without hang-ups in French colonial policy, for which Jews were among the first and most ardent proponents. The AIU intended, to quote Crémieux again, to regenerate 'hearts bastardised by contempt and humiliation'. It did not wish to provide instruction as much as education. It bet on progress and enlightenment, in which it detected quasi-messianic signs. It cultivated virtue, without mentioning this far too political word. What is more, from the beginning the AIU admitted non-Jews on the benches of its schools, almost a quarter of its pupils. Its headmasters were supposed, as was said in the protocols of the meetings of the central committee, to have 'the stoicism of Moses and the patience of Hillel to galvanise the cadavers given to them by way of pupils'.

In 1866, Crémieux visited Palestine. On his return, the central committee passed a resolution declaring it 'useful to remedy the misery of the Jews of Palestine through agriculture, and to promote the creation of schools in Jerusalem and other towns'. Charles Netter went to the region in turn. He was more resolute than the rest of his companions. It was necessary to maintain political pressure, as in Russia and Romania, emphasise educational action, as in Morocco and Iran. Jews were nevertheless on the point of great migratory movement. France could not receive them all; nor could the United States. But they had never stopped praying for a return to Palestine. They had to be able to believe in this possibility: to rip it out of the register of religious dreams, to inscribe it in reality. Netter wanted nothing less than to make Palestine a haven – an asylum – for the persecuted Jewish masses who would find their regeneration in and through working on the land. This was well before anyone had heard of Zionist visionary Theodor Herzl (1860–1904) and the State of Israel.

On 14 April 1869, Netter set off for Constantinople. In his pocket he had a letter of recommendation from Crémieux to the Grand Vizier Ali Pasha, a letter from another prominent figure to the minister of public works, David Pasha, as well as a series of letters for key personalities in the Ottoman government. In addition, he had a large sum of money available, granted partly by Salomon Goldschmidt, vice-president of the AIU, and raised partly through subscription. He wanted to create 'a Jewish establishment', whose 'good deeds would be spread over all the Porte's subjects, without religious distinction'. Thus he obtained a free grant of land destined to form an agricultural school to the south-east of Jaffa – today's city of Holon – as well as exemption from the rights of tenant farmers during the initial years, customs rules on the import of material necessary for the functioning of the school and duties on the export of its produce. He also ensured the personal patronage of the Sultan. In 1872, Netter proposed to call his school Mikveh Israel. Quickly, it became known as 'a messianic school' and in his report to his colleagues in Paris, he dared to write.

Triumphant, dominating, the new Jew ardent and firm, the new type of man which Palestine has engendered: pupils, workers, working, singing of the creative effort, saluting its resurrection. Mikveh Israel: bare hills, plains covered with pestilential marshes, a feverous nest of mosquitoes, a sacrificed land, a land destined to be covered by the dunes of the sea, which has already won in the west and the south: Jewish hands have taken it and regenerated it. Mikveh Israel, that enchanting corner of which every wealthy country will be proud. Marvellous oasis of our wealthy country.

In parallel, in 1867, in the premises of an apprentice school for the children of Eastern European immigrants sponsored by the Levens, located in Rue des Singes in the Marais area of Paris, an organisation was created to train schoolmasters for the Alliance. From the beginning, the Ecole Normale Israélite Orientale (ENIO) presented itself as a school for missionaries. It received pupils from different communities, communicated to them the love for France and its culture, gave them a teacher training and sent them out to open new classes. By 1880, ENIO was recognised as being of public utility and after having moved several times, in 1889 it installed itself at 59 Rue d'Auteuil in the 16th arrondissement, on a historic site bought thanks to the generosity of Baroness de Hirsch. This school was, until its move in 1962 to Rue Michel-Ange and its conversion into a top secondary school, then turned into a school for youngsters with educational difficulties, the crucible of the Alliance's pedagogy, and a pool of talent for its teachers. Emmanuel Lévinas was the prestigious headmaster for several decades. From its reopening in 1946, after the Second World War, it again aimed to 'create... a centre of Western Jewish spirituality which, once again, would be able to bring something new to the Judaism of the East' (Lévinas, 1946).

The AIU was never to abandon its philanthropic – not to say colonialist – vision of the Eastern Judaism which was the concern of the majority of its efforts. Its key figures, its directors and its leaders had not ceased, to quote their initial appeal, 'to moralise those who are corrupted and not to condemn them, to light up those who are corrupted and not to neglect them, to lift up those who are beaten down and not to be content with pitying them...' It went as far as recommending the teachers to extract children from the deleterious influences of their natural milieu: 'The child must be able to leave the cramped, narrow-minded and sometimes miserable environment in which it finds itself, and gain an exact and durable understanding of the universe, nature, secular culture and civilisation...' (Chouraqui, 1960) France's colonialism in North Africa was paved with good intentions: so was the educational philanthropism of the Alliance. France had not come to terms with the fall of its empire: neither had the Alliance.

On 2 September 1870, Louis Bonaparte, taken prisoner by the Prussians, surrendered his sword to their king. On 4 September, a National Defence Government was created. On 19 September, the Prussians laid siege to Paris. On 29 September, a decree organised the companies of the National Guard; another, on 2 November, ordered a mass uprising of all men aged between 18 and 40. On 12 November, a decree resolved that Crémieux, 'member of the National Defence Government, Minister of Justice, is delegated to represent the government and exercise its powers'. He immediately left for Tours where he combined the portfolios of Justice,

Interior and War, taking with him Narcisse Leven as head of his personal staff. Crémieux wanted to raise new troops to stop the Prussians. The generals and admirals declared the war lost: he was not of that opinion. At that point, Gambetta arrived in Tours in a dirigible where he was welcomed by Crémieux. Gambetta was Minister of the Interior, and took back the ministry of War. Crémieux remained at Justice with Leven as secretary-general. On 24 October 1870, the Crémieux Decree proclaimed, within the framework of the reorganisation of the government of Algeria, the collective and obligatory naturalisation of the Jews of that country.

On 26 February 1871, the Peace of Versailles was signed. The National Defence Government dissolved itself, declaring its mission completed. On 10 February 1880, Crémieux, president of the AIU since 1863 with a short interruption in 1867, died, just 10 days after his wife. Parliament decided to give him a state funeral. Leven noted that a century before, Jews had been buried at night, in the rain, without procession, so as not to provoke turmoil or scandal. Crémieux was one of those men, small in size, who was pushed by luck, audacity and a sense of opportunity into the forefront of public life. He knew of no one better than himself, and did not admire anyone more than himself. He had three passions: his wife, the Greeks and his cedar forest in the Dauphiné region, where he spent his holidays nourishing himself with the happiness of being the owner of 'millions of leaves'. That said, he put such good humour into his vanity that no one held it against him. He was an actor playing to the gallery of the palace, the assembly, the world. He did not practise Judaism any more than Christianity. He did not practise anything. The religion of France was at the heart of the mission which he gave to the AIU. In a talk in 1876 he cried.

> France, France, what beautiful examples she has given to civilisation and progress since the immortal days of 1789; if we want to see ourselves achieving, from day to day, among the civilised nations, this solemn principle of civic and political equality, extending to our Jewish brothers, objects of such cruel persecution over the centuries, we will say to ourselves with a legitimate pride: it is with the sun of our France that this divine flame was lit, whose rays light up the entire world.

His successors at the head of the institution continued to portray themselves as champions of the Judeo-French symbiosis. They had themselves achieved it in and through their integration into the French nation, which they considered the gentlest and the most moral in the world. These Jews who did not want a squalid Polish-style Judaism or a curved German one found their homeland in humanity. Still, the AIU was to attract anti-Semitic attacks: 'You could not dream of a more powerful instrument of domination', declared Drumont, 'and no wonder that it rules the world' (Drumont, 1986). The outburst of hate was to culminate in the Dreyfus Affair and, more than half a century later, the Vichy laws on Jewish status and the deportation of the most vulnerable among Jews. At the start of the 1950s, following the creation of the State of Israel, the network of the Alliance included nearly 50,000 pupils in the communities where it was present, as was currently said till these last years, 'from Khorramshahr in Iran to Mogador in Morocco'.

The New Jewish Community in France

We cannot understand the French Jewish community in the first decades of the twenty-first century without taking into consideration four important changes:

1. The betrayal of the Vichy government and the deportation of tens of thousands of Jews. Overnight, Pétain put an end to two-and- a-half centuries of emancipation, patriotism and devotion. At first, native-born Jews, unable to believe that they could be betrayed in this way, played the collaboration card with the Vichy government. The Dreyfus Affair, despite a bitter disenchantment, had had a 'happy ending': the Jewish officer's exoneration had discredited the anti-Semitic party. In contrast, the laws governing the status of Jews turned the Jewish universe upside-down. They would no longer delude themselves about the ever-possible resurgence of anti-Semitism or its murderous character.
2. The creation of the State of Israel disrupted the vision of the active participation of Jews in civil society. Jews would no longer just constitute a 'communion' as much as a community, or even a nationality.
3. The mass influx of North African Jews steeped in French colonialism increased the original dissonance between secularists and the religious. This has found one of its more entertaining expressions in the latent war between the secular leaders of the Consistoires and the rabbis working in the field.
4. The demographic evolution of France which, having long been a Christian land tolerating – or not tolerating – a Jewish minority in its midst, is in the course of becoming a multidenominational country where Jews constitute one of the smallest non-Christian communities after Muslims, Buddhists or even animists.

It is impossible not to be intrigued by the complexity of French Jewishness. The institutions are still Liberal Ashkenazi – despite the demographic decline amongst historical Israélites to a great extent due to mixed marriages – and declare themselves secular and sign up for republican legitimacy. Most of the rabbis are Orthodox Sephardi, with the exception of a handful of liberal and conservative ones. The members of communities, mostly Sephardi, are more traditionalist – in the North African vein – than Orthodox. The synagogue service is more and more Sephardi: the pomp itself remains Ashkenazi. In the institutional community (by which I mean those Jews affiliated with one of the community institutions), politics, as much focused on Israel as on the community, prevails over religion, and inter-institutional politics and small intra-community manoeuvres are more interesting than the rather desultory politico-religious arguments of a Shmuel Trigano or the rather tattered politico-cultural arguments of a Pierre Birnbaum. In the synagogues, it is not religious principles that are debated as much as the prerogatives of the great institutions and the principal community actors.

In recent decades, Jewish studies in France have experienced an unprecedented boom. A vast debate is taking place about Judaism, and it is mobilising rabbis, researchers, psychotherapists, writers, philosophers and intellectuals; listeners are left admiring the eloquence of one side and the grandiloquence of the other.

However, they retain nothing essential or new about Judaism, and it has almost no impact on real-life Judaism. The ignorance on the part of Israelis and Americans of the big names of this Judaism, such as André Néher, Léon Ashkénazi and Emmanuel Lévinas, is perhaps related to their intellectual deficiencies. Nonetheless, the fact remains that these authors are characterised neither by their Pascalian conciseness nor their Cartesian precision. Even Lévinas, from whom one could have legitimately expected a greater phenomenological rigour, willingly gives way to bombast in exhorting to who knows what quasi-Pravoslavian service of 'the other'. Their disciples take philosophical postures which visibly give thinking a stiff neck and no one really wants to take the trouble with these rather minor authors when they could take pleasure with more vigorous thinkers like Hermann Cohen, Franz Rosenzweig or Leo Strauss. The French school of Jewish thought – if there is one – has not managed, except for André Néher, Léon Ashkenazi and Emmanuel Lévinas, to conquer minds, in France or elsewhere.

In the 1950s and 1960s, the Jewish community consisted of four principal groups: native-born Jews whose parents or who themselves had escaped from the discriminatory laws of Vichy by emigrating to other countries, joining the Free French forces of General de Gaulle in London or by fighting alongside the Resistance; first- or second-generation Ashkenazis from Eastern Europe who had survived the Shoah; Jews from North Africa, whether from Algeria where they had French nationality, from Tunisia or Morocco who had chosen France rather than Israel as the land to immigrate into for linguistic or career reasons more than existential choice; and finally the nebula of Jews married to non-Jews or descended from mixed marriages from whence no one had ever tried to learn what became of them. The first group persisted, despite the betrayal of Vichy, in getting back to the civil virtues of the Republic; the second wanted to laboriously reconstruct a decimated way of life; the third were torn between their Jewishness and what Lévinas called at the time 'the sirens of assimilation' (Lévinas, 1963). They were and remained traditionalists, willingly compromising with religious law without challenging for the moment the authority of the orthodox rabbis.

The Choices of Jewish Education

In the post-war period, three choices were available for parents who wished to give their children an institutional Jewish education. These were principally aimed at (a) teaching the Hebrew alphabet to allow children to read the prayers; (b) a religious education to prepare children for their Bar Mitzvah; and (c) an involvement in the Jewish community to preserve them from mixed marriages, the anxiety of every traditionalist community. Parents could choose between three possibilities: (1) youth activities, from Jewish youth movements – classic, communitarian or Zionist – to holiday camps. These activities emphasised community or Zionist civics over Hebrew literacy or religious education. They formed veritable schools of commitment, which would find expression in engagement within the city as well as the Jewish community. Some leaders, in the community movements as much as in the Zionist ones, even considered it their duty to make this commitment a reality by achieving their emigration to Israel. (2) The Talmud Torahs – equivalent to Supplementary Schools in the United States – welcomed their pupils on Thursday (later Wednesday) and Sunday for 6 hours a week, providing the rudiments of Hebrew literacy and religious education. In general, pupils attended up to the age of Bar Mitzvah, or, later, Bat Mitzvah. (3) Lastly, there were Jewish schools, which promised to answer all of the parents' requirements. But during the 1960s, Republican spirit, encouraged by multiculturalism and multicommunitarism, which was spurred on by the waves of non-Christian immigration, continued to prompt members of the Jewish community to place their children in public establishments, and, for the most observant, to obtain all sorts of exemptions for religious constraints and commandments. There were merely a small handful of schools, including the two organisations set up at the start of the century, Lucien de Hirsch (primary) founded in 1901, which had brought together the small schools from the La Villette quarter, and the Maimonides high school, conceived in 1935 to take over from the 'little seminary' attached to the Rabbinical Seminary, kindle rabbinic vocations and link a top-level teaching in Jewish subjects with a quality secondary education. In addition, there were the establishments created straight after the war, above all the Akiva School in Strasbourg (1948) and the Yavneh School in Paris. These four institutions subscribed – and still subscribe – fairly closely to the style of Orthodoxy clarified by R. Samson Raphael Hirsch, German master of modern neo-Orthodoxy (1808–1888), whose famous *'Torah im Derech Eretz'* advocated allying Torah study with the acquisition of the knowledge required to practice a profession. Outside of these four neo-Orthodox schools, which were beginning to accept a growing number of traditionalist children of North African origin, France had a certain number of establishments categorised, for the most part, as ultra-Orthodox, such as the Yeshiva of Aix-les-Bains.

In the 1960s, community institutions were too tied up by Republican spirit to tackle the expansion of Jewish schools. The principal institution with an educational vocation, the AIU, was in decline. In Israel, it had offloaded its schools; in Morocco, it was progressively closing its network; everywhere else, it was putting the key under the doormat. Its visionaries and founders had still forbidden themselves from creating Jewish schools in France – by Republican spirit as much as from concern for secularism. They could only allow themselves to accept prospective teachers destined for the communities of the Mediterranean basin – except Algeria, of course – to train them for their tasks and their missions. In France itself, the AIU had neither schools to offer to its pupils coming from Morocco and Tunisia, nor posts to offer to its teachers. For the rest, ENIO had had to convert itself whether it liked it or not. Although it continued to recruit its pupils principally from the AIU's schools in Morocco, Lebanon and Iran, it no longer provided them with teacher training. It solely prepared them for the Baccalaureate [A-levels], nevertheless permitting sixth-formers who possessed a solid Hebrew and Jewish education to teach in the Paris region's supplementary religion schools on Thursday and Sunday mornings. Often they rivalled the community rabbis in Talmudic knowledge and in the adolescent enthusiasm which they brought to their teaching. For at least two decades, the supplementary religion schools of the Consistoire of Paris were enlivened by pupils and former pupils from ENIO. Since then, the religion schools have suffered from a chronic shortage of teachers. The rabbis are too engrossed in their priestly activities and do not always have the educational savoir-faire required to supervise children forced to give up their day off for studies which were often more repetitive than interesting. Religion schools often seem like an improvised Jewish catechism, rather than a complementary school with a curriculum. In addition, the impressive expansion of Jewish day schools has deprived the supplementary religion schools of the most Jewishly committed pupils, if not the most motivated, and those who still participate in the lessons receive the image of a community that is more anaemic than exciting. What's more, it is widely admitted that in the absence of competent teachers, religion school lessons risk putting off more than they appeal.

The Expansion of Jewish Schools

The AIU's complete carelessness had the merit of encouraging all sorts of initiatives. Initially, no longer responding to the continually growing demand, the handful of existing schools allowed itself to start selecting by level. Next, schools started growing without much planning through several networks. The ORT network, with fairly secular schools that readily included non-Jewish pupils was now putting students through the Baccalaureate after having long prepared them for the Brevet professional [GCSE]. The Otzar HaTorah network, imported from Morocco, robustly supported by American donors, joined together Orthodox schools with mainly traditionalist North African pupils. The fundamentalist Chabad network, imported from the United States, whose population, without necessarily being Lubavitch, was more Orthodox. Finally, a swarm of mainly Orthodox schools, born from the ashes of an educational network which went bankrupt in the 1980s. The AIU itself came out of its stagnation just before the year 2000 with the renovation of the school premises of Pavillons sous Bois, which was initially established without the consent or support of the AIU headquarters, the construction of the Georges Leven high school in the 12th arrondissement and the restoration of the former ENIO premises in the 16th arrondissement. One of the most beautiful odysseys of Jewish education, which had started more than a century earlier, had for a moment threatened to disintegrate in the grating of the wooden planks of its desks, the rags of its wainscoting and the rustling of its records, veritable mines of information on the communities of the Mediterranean basin, now open to researchers from all over the world.

That said, the networks are of only relative importance, since the law recognises only heads of establishments as representatives. Still, the heads are appointed by administration councils – basically figureheads – whose members are often nominated by the network leadership. Most contracted Jewish schools are within a circle of influence ranging from ultra-Orthodoxy (especially Chabad) to traditionalism (the Alliance). Throughout this circle of influence, despite the ban on admissions segregation, schools demand the parents' marriage certificate to prove the Jewishness of the mother and turn away children from mixed marriages, not to mention non-Jews; throughout, a certain separation of sexes is practised, in lessons on Jewish subjects if not between classes or even between schools; throughout, religious services remain, at least in the morning; throughout, boys are obliged to wear skull caps, within the school walls if not in the street, in Jewish lessons if not in the playground; throughout, *kashrut* is observed according to Orthodox, if not ultra-Orthodox, principles; throughout, it is the Hebrew calendar which drives the school calendar; throughout, parents pay fees meant to cover the teaching of Jewish subjects – designated as holy subjects – and general functioning expenses (administration, supervision, canteen, transport, etc.), with the granting of bursaries going as far as free places for the poorest. Only a few schools, such as the primary Ganenou school (founded in 1980), which calls itself a Jewish secular school, and the brand new Adath Shalom school, sponsored by the conservative movement, are outside this circle of influence. A small handful of schools – from *chedarim* to *yeshivot* – has chosen not to seek a contract.

The volume of the timetable for general subjects in schools under contract is such that it leaves little place for Jewish studies – 4–12 h a week. Jewish schools teach Bible, Mishnah, Talmud, and in the least Orthodox schools Jewish history, Hebrew being included in general teaching. Teachers of general subjects, often non-Jewish, benefit from a higher status than their colleagues in the so-called sacred subjects. They generally hold a CAPES (Certificat d'Aptitude au Professorat de l'Enseignement du Second Degré) or the Agrégation – the highest teaching qualification available from the State – and are monitored and graded by inspectors of the national ministry of education. Above all, they enjoy a solid guarantee of employment, unlike their colleagues in Jewish subjects who, frequently, are only employed part-time and for fixed periods. This imbalance in the volume of hours and the status of the teachers contributes largely to the dissonance between general and Jewish subjects, so much so that marks in the latter are not taken into consideration in the decision which determines whether pupils have to repeat a year, or in vocational guidance. Even more seriously, while the general subjects are meticulously planned by the ministry of education and described in very high-quality textbooks produced by the best publishing houses, the teaching of Jewish subjects is random, often left to the choice of the teacher, and suffers from a serious shortage of textbooks.

Jewish Education During Free Time

In recent decades, although France has only 140 school days a year, compared to 210 in Japan and 200 in Italy and Denmark, the school calendar has been restructured so as to impose economic considerations linked to the leisure industry, as well as pseudo-psychological considerations, onto the rhythms of education. Every 2 months or so, pupils benefit from 1 or 2 weeks of school holiday, not to mention the 2 months of summer holiday. These holiday periods allow those parents of children in state schools who wish to pass on the rudiments of Jewish life to place them in Jewish holiday or leisure centres. These stays are offered by non-profit associations who have the triple merit of being independent, of cherishing an educational vocation and of being self-financing, dependent neither on government grants or community ones. They have the advantage of aiming at children and teenagers whose parents are not affiliated to community institutions or who are from mixed marriages. The atmosphere is resolutely Jewish, made up of Hebrew songs, prayers and rituals and activities which, underneath their charm, present a Jewish style. These associations allow their members and participants to extend their network of friends – their Jewish social capital.

Paradoxically, the rearrangement of the school calendar – the four or five breaks in the course of the year – has hastened the ruin of the classic youth movements, forcing them at best to restrict their activities to the holiday periods. With the notable exception of the Eclaireuses et Eclaireurs Israélites de France [Jewish Boy and Girl Scouts of France] who have managed as best as they can to retain their members on the basis of regular activities culminating in a camp, the rest of the youth movements are now just pale vestiges of the old community movements – advocating self-fulfilment through community engagement – or the *Chalutzic* (pioneering) Movements – advocating self-fulfilment through Zionist engagement.

Founded in 1923, the Jewish Boy Scouts of France (EIF, later EEIF to include girls) quickly grew in the Jewish community. From the beginning, this scouting movement was keen to accept children and young people of different views and different backgrounds, from the most 'assimilated' to the most 'Judaised', secular and religious, liberal and orthodox. In less than 10 years, under the impetus of extraordinary characters like the poet Edmond Fleg (1874–1963) and the industrious builder of the movement Robert Gamzon (1905–1961), it established itself, with 3,000 members out of a population of 200,000 Jews, as the holding tank for a kind of educational creativity combining scouting – environmentalism before its time – with an intense Jewish experience. Gamzon pushed educational audacity as far as advocating a doctrine of Jewish scouting behind his extraordinary and premonitory notion of *Tivliut* – the word, which does not exist in Hebrew, suggests restoring responsibility, nourished by the sense of the sacred, the duty of mutual responsibility and ecological concern for the Earth or even the universe. His 'common minimum' is to this day the French Jewish community's most original and interesting educational creation. Forged in the 1920s and 1930s, this notion was almost a technical principle. It suggested – and still suggests today – creating conditions favourable to cohabitation between religious and secular, or even a Jewish Parhessia, within a meeting place or a campground if not in the public space. In its guidelines, the 'common minimum' advocates respect of the dietary laws of *kashrut*, public observance of Shabbat and a whole series of customs from table rituals (wearing a head covering, blessings before and after meals) to participation in the morning religious service, complete or abridged, with or without separation of the sexes depending on the circumstances and the leaders. No one demands adherence to a creed; people demand respect for a minimum of rules and as much politeness as needed to permit a private and public 'communion'. However technical it appears, the common minimum nevertheless represents an attempt to avoid doctrinal debates, elude the most passionate religious questions, and de-dramatise the cleavages and tensions between the movements and currents within Judaism. The common minimum is a political-religious device binding both secular people – under an obligation to respect its rules – and religious people – under the obligation to settle for them. In the end, it convinced the majority of the community, and yet today it is de rigueur in those community facilities which toy with a pluralistic vocation, from political institutions to educational organisations. It even governs the ambiance and behaviour in schools, which we can call 'para-Orthodox', in order to better restore the general balance between neo-Orthodoxy and an often imprecise and indecisive traditionalism, where parents, frequently secular, are not of the same allegiance as the teaching staff or the leadership.

The EIF was among the first to save itself from the earthly lure of Petain's government, to hide children under the covers of French scouting, and to rally resistance to form the main core of what has been called the Jewish Résistance. After the war, its leadership were among the main builders of the community. They opened and ran children's houses where they welcomed children of those who had been sent to concentration camps, and created the leadership school of Orsay (1946–1969), crucible of a Franco-North African Jewish thought which centred around key intellectual figures, the most prestigious of whom were Jacob Gordin (Dvisnk, 1896 – Lisbon, 1947), Léon Ashkenazi, known as Manitou (Oran, 1922 – Jerusalem, 1996), and a training site for community leaders.

With the notable exception of the Paris Community Centre, which has just given itself its own private Institute for Advanced Studies, the community centres imported by the Joint Committee in the 1950s and 1960s in the context of the restructuring of the Jewish community have not exercised the same influence as in the United States.

The Jewish Educational Debate

The poverty of the debate over Jewish education in France shares that of the general education debate in France. Despite the excesses of violence in certain secondary schools in the housing estates and inner cities and the measures taken to try to reduce them, state schools have not succeeded in taking up the challenge of social egalitarianism in a hierarchical society dominated by market competition and competing for jobs. The glorification of merit has its coronation in the generalised practice of selection by competition at every level: in moving from one class to another; educational counselling; access to the most sought-after universities, as well as the most coveted posts in the civil service. This meritocratic regime, favours what Bourdieu calls a 'symbolic capital' transmitted more by the socioeconomic milieu than acquired at school. Jewish students, like the rest of their compatriots, are subjected to the same pressures which do not leave them free time to attend to complementary (in this case Jewish) studies. The importance of finding a job sweeps away all other considerations. There are almost no literary tracks, not to mention art tracks, in any of the Jewish high schools across France.

Education in France is caught up in the spiral of competition and examination, devoting itself to courses leading to the most sought-after jobs, in this case engineering, commerce and communication. Despite their intellectual aura, the so-called humanist courses are in marked decline. And yet all Jewish education reprises the classical ideal of evaluating the works of the past, carried by an automatic – not to say instinctive – and mobilising – not to say vital – membership in tradition. This membership can only be transmitted from one generation to the next in so far as it is clothed in absolute authority, i.e. divine, and passed as immutable. But nowadays this transmission is undergoing a crisis, and no fundamentalist regression or post-modernist re-enchantment is able to resolve it. Individuals no longer bathe in tradition as they situate themselves in relation to it. Membership requires a choice, whether or not it is well-argued, and all sorts of religious, moral, social and emotional/cognitive considerations enter in higgledy-piggledy: 'Traditions whose essence imply the unconscious reproduction of the transmitted past', declares Gadamer, 'must have become problematic so that explicit knowledge can form the hermeneutic task of appropriating tradition' (Gadamer, 1976). The classical ideal, for an irreparably modern era, demands a more apologetic teaching method – more pragmatic for all that – than that required for science teaching. Making students rediscover the sense of the works of the past and cultivating the taste for them really demands a pedagogy of acquisition: 'In the modern world,' declares Arendt, 'the problem of education cannot flout authority or tradition, and must nevertheless be exercised in a world which is neither structured by authority nor retained by tradition' (Arendt, 1972). On one hand, it is impossible to conceive of Jewish education totally outside of tradition; on the other, the authority of that tradition is compromised by even a small amount of critical spirit. Yet from year to year, acquisition of the traditions required to find one's way in the world as a Jew is becoming more and more delicate and arduous, since no real teaching method exists for that acquisition, whether in France or elsewhere.

References

Alain. (1986). *Pédagogie enfantine*. Paris: ed. Presses universitaires de France.
Amson, D. (1988). *Adolphe Crémieux*. Paris: ed. Le Seuil.
Arendt, H. (1972). La Crise de l'Éducation. In *La Crise de la Culture*. Paris: ed. Gallimard.
Ashkenazi, L. (1999). *La parole et l'écrit*. Paris: ed. Albin Michel.
Chouraqui, A. (1960). *L'Alliance israélite universelle*. Paris: ed. Presses universitaires de France.
Drumont, E. (1986). *La France juive*. Paris: Editions du Trident.
Gadamer, H. -G. (1976). *Vérité et Méthode*. Paris: ed. Le Seuil.
Lévinas, E. (1946–1947). "La Réouverture de l'E.N.I.O." in Les Cahiers de l'Alliance, no. 11.
Lévinas, E. (1963). *Difficile Liberté*. Paris: ed. Albin Michel.
Salvador, J. (1860). *Paris, Rome, Jérusalem*. Paris: ed. Michel Lévy Frères.

Israel: State Religious Education in Israel

Zehavit Gross

Introduction

The aim of this chapter is to analyze state-religious education (SRE) in Israel. First, a chronological diachronic historical description of SRE will be given. Next, a socio-historical synchronic analysis of the SRE will be presented in relation to the development of the religious-Zionist movement as well as an analysis of SRE policy and organizational structure. Finally, the major dilemmas and main achievements of the SRE will be described.

Background: The Religious-Zionist Movement and the SRE

Until the establishment of the State of Israel, Jewish political life was organized within the framework of four streams: the General, Labor, Mizrahi (religious-Zionist), and Agudat Israel. The first two were secular, the third was modern orthodox, and the fourth was ultra-orthodox.

In 1897, Theodore Herzl established the Zionist Movement, which was secular in nature and whose aim was to strive to achieve a national-political solution for the Jewish people within the framework of a Jewish state. Initially, the religious community ignored this endeavor, as it was against their religious belief that the Jewish state be built by human beings and not by God. Since Herzl believed that there was need for consensus among all the parts of the Jewish people, he tried to convince the religious faction to join the Zionist Movement.

In 1902, when Rabbi Yitzchak Yaacov Reines, one of the leading rabbinical figures of the time, saw that the Zionist Movement planned to deal with the nature of education in the Jewish country, he took a courageous step and decided to establish a religious-Zionist party (Mizrahi, an acronym for *Merkaz Ruchani* [religious center]) within the Zionist Movement. He believed it was important for the religious community to have influence on the cultural and educational issues of the state. As

---

Z. Gross (✉)
Bar-Ilan University, Ramat-Gan, Israel
e-mail: grossz@mail.biu.ac.il

a result, in 1905, the Zionist Movement reached agreement that the new state would have two educational systems: one religious and one secular.

There were two fundamental approaches within the religious-Zionist movement that would have an impact on religious education. Rabbi Reines perceived the religious-Zionist movement as a political movement whose goal was to solve the national problems of the Jewish people who had no homeland. Rabbi Abraham Isaac Kook (the Ashkenazi Chief Rabbi of pre-state Israel), in contrast, perceived the Zionist Movement as the beginning of the Jewish messianic redemption. Whereas Rabbi Reines differentiated between the messianic redemption and political Zionism, and saw integration within the secular Zionistic Movement as a pragmatic need with no religious meaning, Rabbi Kook saw integration into the Zionist Movement as a means to bringing about the redemption. Rabbi Kook's approach became dominant within the school curriculum especially after 1967, as will be described below, and has had a strong impact upon the SRE curriculum to this day.

The four existing streams (General, Labor, Mizrahi, and Agudat Israel) had different ideological convictions (left – socialist, right – liberal), pedagogical approaches (the Labor stream favored Dewey's progressive approach whereas the General stream adopted the traditional European educational approach to learning and instruction), and separate administrative organizations that supplied services (such as employment and absorption).

With the establishment of the state, and its adoption of a melting pot ideology, David Ben Gurion, Israel's first prime minister, decided to cancel and unify the streams. In 1953, all the educational frameworks were nationalized and institutionalized under the umbrella of the state, and all were committed to the state's educational law. However, state-religious education (SRE) was granted cultural autonomy; it could teach a unique curriculum, yet remain under the auspices of the state. The 1953 State Education Law defined SRE institutions as religious according to their way of life, curriculum, teachers, and inspectors. SRE was granted full autonomy to construct its curriculum according to its religious conviction, making SRE schools "faith-based" or parochial schools, as such institutions are more commonly known in other national settings.

Lamm (1990) posits that the Israeli educational system provides three types of education: (i) apolitical (neutral education – "*klali*" schools), with most schools being in this category, as they are not supposed to be involved in politics or discuss any specific ideology; (ii) ideological, and (iii) political. (Lamm uses the term political to indicate a system that perceives socialization as a rational product of choosing ideology as opposed to socialization that imposes a specific ideology upon its students. In his mind, this is the true meaning of state education (*mamlachti*), which exposes its students to the different options available to them and asks them, after socialization and deliberation, to choose.) According to Lamm, ideological education (which includes secular kibbutz education and SRE) is obliged to enhance a specific ideology through the curriculum, school climate, and the ideological orientation of the teachers who are perceived as agents of this ideology. The aim of such education is to socialize its students to this specific ideology.

In 1998, the State Education Law was rewritten. The new law redefined SRE as educating "in the spirit of religious Zionism." This ideological amendment had far-reaching implications for the structure of SRE schools and their educational vision. The amendment was needed in order to specify the unique essence of the SRE. The national-orthodox circles (*Hardal*) in the state tried to impose national-orthodox education and it was important for SRE leadership to indicate by law that state-religious education is modern (implied by the word Zionist) orthodox education so that the contents, structure, and staff be modern Zionist rather than orthodox.

In order to understand SRE, there is a need to understand the convictions of religious Zionism and its socio-historical background. Religious Zionism is a national religious movement obligated to a combination of traditionalism and modernity. It preserves Jewish law yet is open to modernity; it utilizes new opportunities in terms of technology and conceptualization, while maintaining a religious way of life. SRE policy is not organized as a systematic philosophy and it has no mandatory practical application (Goldschmidt, 1984). Its principles were forged and developed in accordance with changing circumstances and practical needs. Other Jewish-religious schools are orthodox and are officially obliged to enhance and perpetuate traditional rather than modern values. SRE encourages its graduates to serve in the army (boys) and national service (girls), whereas in the orthodox system, this is unacceptable as boys are expected to study in a yeshiva (in higher religious studies) and girls are expected to get married.

The theoretical and practical principles behind SRE are based on a combination of the values of the traditional, religious yeshiva education and its general focus on teaching religious studies only, together with modern Jewish education as it developed primarily in Germany under the influence of the Jewish *Haskalah* [Enlightenment] movement (Feiner, 2002; Schweid, 2002) and the *Torah im Derech Eretz* movement of Rabbi Samson Raphael Hirsch (Ayalon & Yogev, 1998; Breuer, 1996; Kleinberger, 1969), which combined religious commitment to religious practice and study of the religious literature with an integration within secular life. This ideology of *Tora im Derech Eretz* was interpreted in SRE to undergird the integration of religious and secular studies.

The SRE system is based on three main tenets (Kiel, 1977) which are as follows:

1. *Religious education* – A traditional, Jewish-religious education that includes teaching belief in God, the performance of *mitzvoth*, "commandments," the advanced study of sacred texts, such as Bible, Mishna, Jewish law, Gemara, and writings of the rabbis and Jewish thinkers who have shaped the spiritual heritage of the Jewish people for generations.
2. *Modern education* – Teaching the basic skills students need to function as citizens and to conduct constructive lives as required of all members of a modern society in general and a secular, democratic state in particular. Therefore, the SRE system has created a mandatory curriculum that incorporates secular contents and subject matter (math, physics, English, etc.) that will enable its pupils to pass the national matriculation examinations and allow them, upon completion

of their education, to either continue with their studies or find a job by which they can support themselves and contribute to the society.
3. *Nationalist education* – Education with a Zionist quality in order to preserve the unity of all sectors of the Jewish people (both secular and religious, as well as Jews living in the Diaspora), to intensify students' feeling of identification with and contribution toward the Land of Israel (which is perceived as a territory with religious significance), and to reinforce their sense of loyalty and belonging to the State of Israel and its laws (whose establishment is seen as the first step of the Jewish redemption). SRE promotes the founding of settlements throughout the entire country and encourages contributing to the homeland through army service in elite military units. Furthermore, the SRE system requires identification with the state on national holidays, such as Independence Day and Jerusalem Day (in contrast with the ultra-orthodox sectors who do not celebrate these special holidays).

The Socio-historic Background of Religious-Zionist Education

The history of religious-Zionist education can be periodized by way of analogy to the theoretical approach of Livesly and Mackenzie (1983) in psychotherapy (Gross, 2003b). Adapting their approach to a social context, a social system might be defined through the roles and patterns of interaction that exist within it. In these terms, four primary roles are required: (a) the social role – feeling responsible for the unity of the group; (b) the task-oriented role – feeling responsible for focusing and achieving the group's goals; (c) the scapegoat – being responsible for all of the society's ills, in order to distract the society from its real problems; and (d) the oppositional role – opposing society and what is taking place by emphasizing individuality and thus defining society's boundaries. This role-based method of classification will serve as a basis for describing the stages of development of the religious-Zionist sector. Periodization of religious-Zionist education includes four main historical periods, which parallel the four roles described above.

1902–1967 (the social role): From the founding of the Mizrahi Movement (the religious party in the Zionist Movement) in 1902 and until the Six-Day war, religious society and religious education assumed the social role. During this entire period, religious schools accepted all the pupils of parents who desired religious education for their children, based on an acknowledged policy of "religious education for all." This policy, from as early as the 1940s, prompted parents from economically stable religious families and generally of western European origin to establish private, alternative religious high schools for their sons, which were influenced by the western European religious-education system, so as to provide them with a superior religious education (Bar-Lev, 1977). These schools (for boys only), which were private, selective, and charged relatively high fees, were known as "yeshiva high schools." Later on, parallel institutions were also established for girls, called "Ulpanas" (Katz, 1999). And thus, through the yeshiva and Ulpana framework, a correlation was introduced between a desire for religious excellence, a high socio-economic level, and sectarianism. This process was the start of the religious-Zionist elite.

1967–1981 (the task-oriented role): Beginning in 1967, a significant change took place in Israeli society in general and in the status of religious society in particular. Rather than remaining on the sidelines, the religious-Zionist public was now perceived as pioneers and leaders. Religious-Zionists took upon themselves the role of preserving the charismatic dimension (Weber, 1979) of the ideological aspect of society, in order to defend Israeli society against the inevitable processes of institutionalization and routinization that threatened to erode the Zionist efforts and rock its foundations. The curriculum and teaching practices were imbued with nationalist motifs, for example, encouraging students to settle on the West Bank and the Gaza Strip as the highest priority of school socialization. To settle in those areas was considered a sign of religiousness (Gross, 2003a).

1982–1996 (the scapegoat role): One of the greatest crises endured by the religious-Zionist movement was the withdrawal from the Sinai Peninsula in 1982 and the return to Egypt of Jewish settlements in the Yamit region. The sights and sounds of the evacuation of Sinai and Yamit left a void, and even introduced into the Israeli public discourse new, militant behavior and speech patterns that had been previously unknown. Beginning with this period, the public legitimacy given to the religious-Zionist sector began to erode, because of its anti-government demonstrations and policies. Following the evacuation of the Sinai region, a drive toward legal and illegal settlements (including SRE students who, in some institutions, were encouraged by their teachers to actively participate, in the name of legitimate democratic protest) began flourishing on the West Bank, and a series of militant protest activities were initiated against the peace process and against the government, which turned the religious-Zionist public into a scapegoat. As a result, the religious-Zionist sector was accused of jeopardizing the country's economy and its security.

1997–The present (the role of the other): In March 1997, a circular was distributed by the religious administration, which presents the official position of the state-religious education authority. This circular aimed officially to shake off the role of the scapegoat, by referring to the contribution of graduates from the SRE system to Israeli society. It also demanded that intervention programs be developed to prevent fundamentalist and extremist phenomena in the SRE system's schools. Since this time, circulars coming from the religious administration have dealt with questions of the boundaries of religious Zionism and of the relationship between the religious-Zionist society and the sovereignty of the state, democracy, and the status of the country's laws. Furthermore, clarifications were undertaken regarding the character and nature of the link between Judaism and democracy, and the question of which came first.

Curriculum

In his analysis of the basic principles of curriculum, Tyler (1949) asserts that curriculum planning must take into account the society's cultural characteristics, the learners' needs, and the character of the subject matter. Curriculum development is, therefore, an ideological rather than a pedagogical decision. According to Tyler, the values of society determine what will be taught in the school: which subjects and which periods will be taught, which written material will be included and which will be excluded.

As an integral part of the state-educational system, SRE schools are obliged to teach the official state curriculum in terms of general studies; the schools have the same inspectorate and their students take the official state matriculation examinations (*Bagrut*). However, the SRE is granted pedagogical autonomy regarding the religious curriculum and has a separate religious inspectorate for history, civic education, literature, and all religious studies. Because there may be a conflict between the contents of general studies and religious-Zionist values, in general studies, a special curriculum adapted to the needs of SRE was devised (e.g., relating to the theory of evolution or maps of the state of Israel and its biblical and actual borders) (Schwartzwald, 1990, pp. 23–25).

Jewish studies are considered necessary cultural capital in religious society (Yogev, 1998, p. 60). The prestige of different bodies of subject matters is connected to the ideological value given to them by society. The prestige of religious studies (which in the secular schools are categorized as part of humanities studies, and thus less prestigious than science and math) is higher, for example, than in the secular sector, and more hours are dedicated to these subjects. This is a fundamental difference between the religious and secular systems. It causes what Yogev calls "curricular inequality" (p. 55) and is the result of the autonomy that SRE is granted by the state. The SRE director is not under the authority of the Minister of Education and thus can function according to the particularistic needs of religious-Zionist society where she/he can adapt the general studies curriculum according to the religious needs of her/his religious community, provided she/he acts within the spirit of the state education law. State-religious schools are not monolithic; they include different types that place a different emphasis on the three components mentioned above: religious, modern, and nationalist education. In practice, there are different ways of balancing these three components. There are schools in the SRE system that mainly emphasize religious studies (*Talmudei Torah*). In some of these schools, secular matriculation exams are optional. The ideal graduate of this type of school and the ideal teacher for boys is the scholar (*Talmid Hacham*); for girls, the ideal teacher is a woman who enables her husband to become a scholar. There are other schools that emphasize the national component (especially in the settlements on the West Bank). In these schools, the curriculum mainly emphasizes the connection to biblical Israel and the fact that the national components, such as active protest against the evacuation of the land of Israel, army service for boys, and national service for girls, are necessary for the future survival of the Jewish people. The ideal graduate of this school and the ideal teacher are people who settle the biblical parts of the country (the West Bank, East Jerusalem, etc.) and whose entire being is channeled toward the implementation of their interpretation of the national aspiration of Judaism.

However, there are also schools (especially in the large cities like Tel Aviv, Haifa, and Jerusalem) that emphasize a modern educational orientation. In these schools, the ideal graduate and teacher is someone who is integrated into the Israeli economy, in industry or science, and who has broad knowledge and skills in general studies alongside their religious devotion. Most of the schools in the SRE integrate those three components (the religious, the modern, and the national) with one or two components dominating, depending on the school population.

The ideal graduate of the SRE school system is one who's every activity in the private and public spheres is shaped and informed by intensive Jewish study. This is then translated into behavior and lifestyle in accordance with Jewish law, while becoming integrated into the modern way of life and applying the general secular knowledge acquired during schooling (Dagan, 1999). This integration between tradition and modernity becomes even more challenging and complicated in the context of the civic responsibility required of SRE graduates, who are taught to view the founding of the state of Israel as the beginning of the Jewish redemption, and thus their religious and civic obligations are intertwined and sometimes conflicting. If the state is perceived as the beginning of the redemption, then army service is considered a religious obligation and not only a civic obligation. When a religious soldier has to perform a special army operation on the Sabbath, for example, he can disobey the religious law in order to fulfill his army obligation.

Organizational Structure

The organizational structure of SRE, led by an executive committee and the head of the system, reflects its unique religious identity and educational priorities. The executive committee represents the spiritual leadership of the system. Its role is "to define, articulate, defend and evaluate the agenda for the school system which is based on principles established by the modern orthodox religious Zionist community that the schools are there to serve" (McGettrick, 2005, p. 106). This includes ideals, values, and attitudes deriving from religious Zionism. The head of the SRE system is the highest authority regarding all pedagogical religious issues. He leads a board consisting of seven members, two deputies (one for pedagogical aspects and one for administrative aspects), and national inspectors for the different levels (kindergarten, elementary, junior high, and high schools). There are inspectors for religious and general studies and there are seven regional inspectors throughout the country. These inspectors represent an advisory framework on all practical and strategic decisions. The school inspectors (who are rabbis) and the inspector of religious studies are considered the senior leadership in the system.

SRE is committed to a modern orthodox religious ideology that is interpreted through a pedagogical philosophy that strives to combine religious life with an occupation that is suitable to the secular modern world. This demands an adaptive mechanism and "negotiation" between secular and religious studies within the curriculum. Two basic approaches can be found in SRE which are represented by two distinct leadership orientations: conservative and liberal. Conservatives emphasize the superiority of religious studies and view secular studies as a "necessary evil," which needs to be taught for instrumental reasons. They have a selective approach toward the secular components of the curriculum and wish to include only those subjects that do not contradict religious values. The liberal approach holds that even if they contradict certain religious values all secular studies should be included in the curriculum (including, for example, the theory of evolution, secular ideas against God that appear in works of literature, or critical analysis of the scriptures). This group believes that including such studies proves the superiority of religious thinking over the secular and shows that it is open enough to contain it (Schremer, 1985; Yogev, 1998). From this perspective, confronting "challenging" content, while adopting and adapting it, strengthens the reliability and validity of the religious corpus. The pedagogical autonomy granted to SRE has enabled this process of curriculum adaptation.

Ultimately, the SRE leadership adopted a "golden way" that integrated religious studies into secular studies in a conservative manner so that SRE graduates would be able to fully integrate professionally into civic society in Israel.[1] However, in the matter of appointing supervisors of curriculum, since religious studies are considered more important than secular studies, the inspectors of religious studies who are nominated are usually strictly religious (in terms of Jewish practice) yet consider themselves to be modern (in terms of worldviews and attitudes and the inclination to adapt to modernity). These personalities are viewed by the entire religious-Zionist society and by religious political circles to be a meaningful reference group and are positioned at the summit of the hierarchal leadership.

State education allocates a special budget for the unique demands of SRE. This pays for additional hours for religious studies, employing rabbis who are spiritual leaders in each school, infrastructure (e.g., synagogues in the schools) and separation between boys and girls in school. Moreover, there are special requests for unique religious outreach and informal education programs.

The Accomplishments of the State-Religious Education System

The accomplishments of the religious-Zionist education system can be found in four main spheres as follows:

1. *In the social sphere* – SRE graduates have integrated into key roles in all spheres of endeavor in Israel, while publicly maintaining and preserving their religious way of life. SRE graduates can be found in all walks of life and the state's modern activities: economics, industry, science, technology, security, law. Similarly, SRE has become one of Israel's official and important institutions for absorbing new immigrants. Because of its "open to everyone" policies, SRE has absorbed many new immigrants over the years, most of whom came from deprived socio-economic backgrounds. The absorption and nurturing in the schools of Jewish immigrants from Muslim countries during the 1950s, and

---

[1] Interestingly, in the time of the Mishna and the Talmud, the same dilemmas arose: rabbis considered the question of whether studying Greek knowledge and culture was permissible. Initially, this was rejected; then it was agreed that only the elites could study Greek, and later, it was allowed for the sake of bread winning (Lieberman, 1984).

Jewish immigrants from Ethiopia and the FSU in the 1980s and 1990s and their successful integration into Israeli society should be studied and imitated.

2. *In the scholastic field* – State-religious education can be proud of the high percentage (66%) of its graduates eligible for matriculation. The success on matriculation exams can be seen in general subjects (math, English, etc.) as well as in Judaic Studies. State-religious education is particularly noteworthy for its high success rate among those pupils designated as disadvantaged from schools considered to be failures. In 1995, the then director of the state-religious education division, Mr. Mati Dagan, made a courageous decision to cancel all vocational study tracks (which did not train pupils for the regular official matriculation exams) in the comprehensive religious schools and to convert all the SRE schools into academic schools that would train pupils to receive a full matriculation certificate. As a result, the scholastic and educational status of the high schools in the periphery has improved, and the success rates on matriculation examinations among this weaker population are continually improving.

3. *In the religious sphere* – Most of the SRE graduates (some 70%) remain religious to varying degrees of observance after they complete the school socialization process (Leslau & Rich, 1999) even when they encounter the secular world for the first time in the army or national service. Moreover, the yeshiva high schools and academic yeshivas established to house graduates of the SRE schools have provided a basis for the revival of religious and Jewish centers in Israel following the destruction and devastation during the Holocaust of the centers of Jewish-religious life in Europe (Gross, 2003b). Jewish-religious revival in Israel, as part of a secular, liberal, democratic state, has constituted a new pattern of religiosity which integrates aspects of modernity and sovereignty; this approach is a new, religious creation that demands further study and research.

4. *In the feminist-educational sphere* – SRE has constructed a modern educational system that socializes women and fully integrates them in the civic public sphere. This is little short of a revolution. The exposure of religious women to knowledge that was once accessible only to men, and the openness that enables women to function equally in the realm of modernity and in the corpus of religious canonical literature, has turned SRE into one of the major socialization agents of the feminist revolution within religious society in particular and in secular Israeli society in general.

The Major Dilemmas of the State-Religious Education System

State-religious education in Israel is currently tackling five major dilemmas (Gross, 2003a):

1. *The status of secular studies in the religious-education system* – One of the innovations initiated by the SRE system since its establishment has been the introduction of secular studies as a legitimate component of the official religious-education system and as an integral part of its ideology and educational

orientation. As explained above, this orientation was inspired by the educational approach of the *Torah im Derech Eretz* movement founded by Rabbi Samson Rafael Hirsch in the nineteenth century. The main objective of this approach has been to enable complete integration of SRE graduates into any field of endeavor in society. Indeed, the SRE schools ponder such issues as what is the proper quantity of secular studies relative to Judaic studies, when these subjects should be studied (in the morning, when the children are more awake, or in the afternoon), and what are the resources that should be allocated to each one of the spheres (Ayalon & Yogev, 1998). This dilemma relates to the contradictory aspirations of the SRE system to be open to the modern world, on the one hand, and to shut itself up within the world of religion and halacha (Jewish law), on the other. Furthermore, this question is connected to the problem of how to cope with the values and lifestyles of the Western world and its culture while carefully trying to maintain a full religious way of life (Dagan, 1999).

2. *The educational ideal* – A different dilemma has involved asking whether the religious-education system should develop the image of an ideal graduate with a clear and unequivocal perspective (Schremer, 1985) whose religious properties are based on an Ashkenazic-European point of view or whether it is possible to develop several alternative, and equally legitimate, religious-educational ideals? Should the educational ideal continue to be the traditional "*talmid chacham*" (religious scholar), or perhaps the modern "pioneer" or the Jewish-religious engineer, pilot, or scientist (see also Rosenak, 1996)? This question is closely related to the matter of whether the educational ideal proposed by SRE prepares its graduates to leave the hothouse environment of the school and successfully enter military and civilian life. Can SRE pupils and graduates realistically live with the monumental educational ideal presented to them in school, or in reality are they actually working against this educational ideal (Gross, 2002)?

3. *Religious selectivity versus education for all* – One of the dilemmas facing the SRE system is whether it should be open to everyone, or whether it should be religiously selective (Gross, 2003a). As stated above, the consumers of SRE are religiously pluralistic and represent a broad range of religious behavior, from those who are very careful to observe all the commandments prescribed by halacha, to those who are satisfied with a partial or even symbolic observance of Jewish law but who want their children to be part of a religious framework. Therefore, there is the question of how the SRE system can maintain its uniqueness as a coherent religious setting, on the one hand, while, on the other hand, remaining loyal to its state-mandated objectives and obligations, which support equality and integration. On a practical level, one can ask whether SRE can continue to function in the long term in the anomalous social reality where in some parts of the country the economically weakest sectors constitute a majority of the students in the system even though many of them do not come from a religious background (Adler, 2002).

4. *Attitude toward the state and its institutions* – A critical question for the SRE today is how the system should regard the State of Israel, its secular-democratic regime, and the laws founded on secular legitimacy. This dilemma is complex

because the *Torah* and halacha (Jewish law), according to which religious Jews act, deal with how people should behave in their private or communal lives, but not their political lives (Adler, 2002; Dagan, 1999). The halachic literature does not discuss issues concerning foreign relations, economics, or running a country with a secular, democratic Jewish regime because historically the Jewish people lived under foreign rule and their civilian experience had no significance in the religious-Jewish context throughout its long history. Only with the establishment of Jewish sovereignty in the land of Israel has full participation in political life meant accepting shared responsibility and granting legitimacy to public decisions that are secular in nature, even when they may contradict Jewish law. For example, the state celebrates Independence Day in a month that is considered, according to Jewish tradition, a period of mourning due to the death of 12,000 of Rabbi Akiva's disciples. In this period, Jews are required to observe customs of semi-mourning (no marriages take place, no listening to lively music, no dancing). So how can one celebrate a national-civic independence day, which is secular in nature, which contradicts explicit Jewish law? Religious Zionism perceived the establishment of the state as the beginning of redemption; to denote and celebrate it, Jewish law was "renewed," making this a day of celebration including distinct Jewish thanksgiving prayers. This constitutes a major controversy between the orthodox and religious-Zionist movements. Under these circumstances, the SRE has come to perceive the State of Israel, Zionism, and Jewish nationality as phases in the development of the redemption, and "the religious education system has been charged with the task of demonstrating that it is possible to live as a Jew in a democratic country" (Adler, 2002). All the same, the practical partnership with the secular elements in Israel constitutes a serious theological and ideological problem (see also Silberman-Keller, 2000). For example, in 2005, the disengagement plan to evacuate the Gaza Strip was accepted by law by the Israeli government. However, SRE students and graduates actively resisted this decision. This militant resistance was perceived as religious theological resistance rather than simple civic disobedience (see Gross, 2006a).

5. *Organizational structure* – A last question that flows from those reviewed above asks whether the SRE system should remain under secular state-organizational sponsorship, or establish a separate educational-organizational framework with a religious character. In practice, despite the State Education Law (1953), the secular education system does not always take the special needs of the SRE into consideration (for example, the need for additional job slots because of gender separation for religious reasons in SRE schools). The desire of the state education system for equality and uniformity (in resource allocation, for example) is sometimes carried out by hurting minority groups. It should be noted that the decision to remain under state sponsorship was, and always has been, ideological rather than organizational-procedural, because of the religious significance with which the religious-education system relates to the principle of state sovereignty. In practical terms, all of these dilemmas are related to the central question that has occupied religious-Zionism from the moment of its inception to this very

day, that is, the question of the Jewish nature and character of the State of Israel; or to put it differently, to what extent must the State of Israel possess particularistic Jewish characteristics (as a Jewish state) or a universal civilian character (as a state of all its citizens)? Solutions to this dilemma have a direct impact on the policies and activities of the SRE system.

This last question is also connected with the method by which the religious person and establishment copes with the phenomenon of secularization. According to SRE ideology, since the *Haskalah* (Jewish Enlightenment) period of the eighteenth century, the foremost enemy of the Jewish people has been secularization. The appearance of modern Zionism is to a large extent connected to this phenomenon (Gross, 2003a), because this process denotes the liberation of humanity from the generalized perception of the sovereignty of God and emphasizes individuals' responsibility for their own actions. Secular Zionism presumes the liberation of the Jew from the idea of national redemption by God, to a reality of national redemption wrought by humans and under their full responsibility (Don-Yehiya, 1998).

The innovation of the religious-Zionist approach, in contrast with the ultra-orthodox approach, was that it accommodated secularization (Sagi, 2000; Schwartz, 1999, 2002) and perceived it as a "necessary evil" and a temporary reality that was a precondition for fulfilling and realizing the complete Jewish redemption. In discussing these matters, Liebman (1982) proposed four main approaches to modernity: assimilation, isolation, compartmentalization, and expansion. He claimed that religious-Zionism adopted the strategy of expansion, and the practical interpretation of this was to sanctify the entire process of modernization and secularization which are, as previously stated, a necessary precondition, according to this approach, to the full Jewish redemption. In this way, the entire secular aspect of political sovereignty and the state's institutions were given religious significance and validity. Furthermore, these dilemmas reflect the ideological status of the religious-Zionist movement which, from its inception, has straddled two dichotomous worlds within Jewish society: the secular-Zionist leadership that rejected both Jewish tradition and religion as part of the process of creating a new national Zionist identity; and the traditional, orthodox, and ultra-orthodox world, which perceived the Zionist Movement and the creation of a Jewish national identity as heresy. The unique position of the religious-Zionist movement has been from its establishment until today the source of both its strength and its weakness; it hoped to become an integral part of both worlds (the secular and ultra-orthodox), while simultaneously not being part of either one of them (Gross, 2003b). Understanding the basis for this dialectic is important for understanding the dilemmas and difficulties in which the state-religious education system functions.

Last Thoughts and Next Steps

Despite the increasing secularization of Israeli society, on the one hand, and the isolationist tendencies of religious extremism, on the other, the SRE system has succeeded in maintaining a stable number of pupils and has conducted an extensive system of institutions, from preschools to teacher training institutes, comprising approximately 20% of all the pupils in the Israeli state education system. These numbers are noteworthy, particularly in consideration of the fact that the process of joining the SRE system is not inevitable by virtue of the Compulsory Education Law; rather it is part of a conscious decision and an informed choice made voluntarily by parents and pupils in favor of a religious-Zionist education as their preferred education system. The success of this education system, despite all of the difficulties, apparently derives from the careful preservation of several fundamental religious principles as well as tremendous flexibility and openness to the changing needs of the modern and pluralistic world in which we live.

When parents send their children to orthodox schools, they know what to expect in terms of curriculum, dress code, etc. However, in modern orthodox schools, there is a constant debate about the ethos of the school, something that is undefined and open to discussion. Modern orthodox schools all over the world (which are generally religious-Zionist) are frequently considered problematic, in terms of the way they define themselves to their target populations. In Brussels, Paris and Geneva, Toronto and Montreal, Melbourne and Sydney, and in the USA, both ultra-orthodox and secular schools are very clear in terms of their school ethos. Whereas ultra-orthodox schools have a definite vision of what they would like to be, which is described in absolute language, secular schools know what they would *not* like to be. However, discussions concerning the modern orthodox school ethos are currently conducted in vague and obscure language which usually juggles an attempt to enjoy the advantages and disadvantages of both secular and orthodox life.

Future research on SRE should concentrate on the foundations of the SRE ethos and its attitude to modernity. In modern orthodox schools, questions of ethos are a major source of controversy between parents, board members, stakeholders, and policy makers (see Gross, 2006). The above-mentioned dilemmas should be at the core of this research, then, and might inform five main questions. A first question for investigation is, what is the status of secular studies in the religious-education system? This question is connected to considering whether secular studies are a legitimate or illegitimate component of the official SRE system, and an integral part of its ideology and educational orientation. Another fundamental question concerns the educational ideal of SRE; this should involve a major survey of whether the religious-education system should develop the image of an ideal graduate with a clear and unequivocal perspective whose religious properties are based on an Ashkenazic-European point of view or whether it is possible to develop several alternative, and equally legitimate, religious-educational ideals. For example, should the educational ideal continue to be the traditional "*talmid chacham*" (religious scholar), or perhaps the modern "pioneer," or perhaps the Jewish-religious engineer, pilot, or scientist? Another important question that threatens the coherence of SRE is whether it should be open to everyone, or whether it should be religiously selective. A no less critical question for the SRE today is how the system should regard the State of Israel, its secular-democratic regime, and the laws founded on secular legitimacy. A last question for investigation, which is directly connected to school ethos, is whether the SRE system should remain under secular state-organizational sponsorship, or should establish a separate educational/organizational framework with a religious character.

These questions should be investigated both theoretically and empirically using qualitative and quantitative research methods. The empirical investigation should be conducted among students, teachers, parents, principals, stakeholders, and policy makers. The answers to these questions will make it possible to open up future discussions concerning the SRE ethos and its raison d'être. Such research, and discussion of the main dilemmas, questions, and challenges of SRE raised in this chapter, can perhaps be utilized as the basis for further comparative research in other Jewish educational sites that face the constant challenge of accommodation between traditional convictions and modern aspirations and options.

References

Adler, S. (2002). *Challenges in 2003. Circular for the religious principal*. Jerusalem: Ministry of Education and Culture, Religious Division (Hebrew).

Ayalon, H., & Yogev, A. (1998). Torah with secular studies (*torah im derekh eretz*): The alternative perspective for state-religious high school education. In H. Ayalon (Ed.), *Curricula as social reconstruction* (pp. 33–54). Tel Aviv: Ramot (Hebrew).

Bar-Lev, M. (1977). Graduates of the yeshiva high schools in Israel: Between tradition and renewal. Unpublished doctoral dissertation, Bar-Ilan University, Ramat Gan (Hebrew).

Breuer, M. (1996). The historical roots of the yeshiva high school. In M. Bar-Lev (Ed.), *Celebrating the jubilee* (pp. 127–141). Tel Aviv: Friends of the Midrashia (Hebrew).

Dagan, M. (1999). State-religious education. In A. Peled (Ed.), *50th anniversary of the education system in Israel* (pp. 1011–1024). Jerusalem: Ministry of Education, Culture and Sport (Hebrew).

Don-Yehiya, E. (1998). Religious fundamentalism and political radicalism: The nationalist Yeshivot in Israel. In A. Shapira (Ed.), *Atzmaut: Fifty years of statehood* (pp. 431–470). Jerusalem: Zalman Shazar Center (Hebrew).

Feiner, S. (2002). *The enlightenment revolution: The Jewish haskalah movement in the 18th century*. Jerusalem: Zalman Shazar Center (Hebrew).

Goldschmidt, J. (1984). State-religious education in Israel. In A. Wasserteil (Ed.), *Philosophy and education: Letters of Joseph Goldschmidt*. Jerusalem: Ministry of Education and Culture (Hebrew).

Gross, Z. (2002). The world of Zionist religious women in Israel: Between charisma and rationalization. Research Report. Ramat Gan: Bar-Ilan University, Institute for the Research and Advancement of Religious Education (Hebrew).

Gross, Z. (2003a). The social roles of the religious Zionist education. In A. Sagi & D. Schwartz (Eds.), *A hundred years of religious Zionism* (Vol. 3, pp. 129–186). Ramat Gan: Bar-Ilan University Press (Hebrew).

Gross, Z. (2003b). State-religious education in Israel: Between tradition and modernity. *Prospects, 33*(2), 149–164.

Gross, Z. (2006). Power, identity and organizational structure as reflected in schools for minority groups: A case study of Jewish schools in Paris, Brussels and Geneva. *Comparative Education Review, 50*(4), 603–624.

Gross, Z. (2006a). Voices among the religious Zionist in Israel regarding the peace process and the disengagement plan. In Y. Iram, H. Wahrman, & Z. Gross (Eds.), *Educating toward a culture of peace* (pp. 259–279). Greenwich, CT: Information Age Publishing.

Katz, Y. (1999). The Yeshiva high schools and Ulpanas for girls in the secondary school system. In A. Peled (Ed.), *50th anniversary of the education system in Israel* (pp. 1025–1034). Jerusalem: Ministry of Education, Culture and Sport (Hebrew).

Kiel, Y. (1977). *State-religious education: Its roots, history and problems.* Jerusalem: Ministry of Education and Culture, Religious Education Division (Hebrew).

Kleinberger, A. F. (1969). *Society, school and progress in Israel.* London: Pergamon Press.

Lamm, Z. (1990). Types of ideological education in the Israeli school. In D. Bar-Tal & A. Klingman (Eds.), *Selected issues in psychology and counseling of education* (pp. 7–17). Jerusalem: Ministry of Education (Hebrew).

Leslau, A., & Rich, Y. (1999). *Survey of 12th-grade pupils on state-religious examinations.* Ramat Gan: Bar-Ilan University, The Eliezer Stern Center for the Study and Advancement of Religious Education (Hebrew).

Lieberman, S. (1984). *Greek and Hellenism in Eretz Yisrael.* Jerusalem: Mosad Bialik (Hebrew).

Liebman, Y. (1982). Neo-traditional development among orthodox Jews in Israel. *Megamot (Trends), 27,* 231–250 (Hebrew).

Lively, W. J., & Mackenzie, K. R. (1983). Social roles in psychotherapy groups. In R. R. Dies & K. R. Mackenzie (Eds.), *Advances in group psychotherapy, monograph I* (pp. 117–135). New York: International Universities Press.

McGettrick, B. (2005). Perceptions and practices of Christian schools. In J. Cairns, R. Gardner, & D. Lawton (Eds.), *Faith schools: Consensus or conflict?* (pp. 105–112). New York: RoutledgeFalmer.

Rosenak, M. (1996). Educating the person: A Jewish ideal and modern culture. In M. Bar-Lev (Ed.), *Celebrating the jubilee* (pp. 142–150). Tel Aviv: Friends of the Midrashia (Hebrew).

Sagi, A. (2000). Religious Zionism: Between acceptance and reticence. In A. Sagi, D. Schwartz, & Y. Stern (Eds.), *Internal and external Judaism: A dialogue between two worlds* (pp. 124–168). Jerusalem: Magnes Press (Hebrew).

Schremer, E. (1985). State-religious education: Between fundamental commitment and operative criteria. In V. Ackerman, A. Carmon, & D. Zucker (Eds.), *Education in an evolving society* (pp. 349–373). Tel Aviv: Hebrew.

Schwartz, D. (1999). *Religious Zionism: Between logic and messianism.* Tel Aviv: Am Oved (Hebrew).

Schwartz, D. (2002). *Faith at the crossroads: A theological profile of religious Zionism.* Leiden: Brill.

Schwartzwald, Y. (1990). *State-religious education: Reality and research.* Ramat Gan: Bar-Ilan University Press (Hebrew).

Schweid, A. (2002). *History of the philosophy of the Jewish religion in modern times.* Part I: The Haskalah period – A new agenda for philosophically coping with religion. Jerusalem: Am Oved Publishers and the Shechter Institute for Judaic Studies (Hebrew).

Silberman-Keller, D. (2000). Education in a multi-cultural society: The case of state-religious education. In M. Bar-Lev (Ed.), *Teaching culture in a multi-cultural society: Issues for teacher in-service training* (pp. 139–158). Jerusalem: Hebrew University (Hebrew).

Tyler, R. W. (1949). *Basic principles of curriculum and instruction.* Chicago: University of Chicago Press.

Weber, M. (1979). *On charisma and building institutions.* Jerusalem: Magnes Press, Hebrew University.

Yogev, A. (1998). Cultural capital and professional prestige: The curricular stratification of teachers in Israel. In H. Ayalon (Ed.), *Curricula as social reconstruction* (pp. 55–78). Tel Aviv: Ramot (Hebrew).

Israel: Innovations in Secular Schooling in Israel

Yehuda Bar Shalom and Tamar Ascher Shai

Israeli society is still a society in formation. Within the Jewish majority, most children in the classroom are either immigrants or the children of immigrants. Public education has always been perceived, as in many other countries, as a means for creating a unified myth and ethos. However, almost immediately following the birth of the State of Israel, in the 1950s, political pressures enabled the creation of separate public school systems: the Jewish secular, the Jewish – national Orthodox, and the Arab schools. The ultra-Orthodox communities opted to create their own independent and semi-private tracks, and some private schools decided to go their own separate ways, and continue to do so until this day.

Despite a sharp decline in numbers over the past 20 years, the secular public schools were and still are the largest section in Israeli society. The percentage of Jewish students attending secular schools moved from 74% in 1980 down to 54% in 2008.[1] If we add the Arab students into the equation, then we assume that in the near future Jewish-secular education will be in the minority. Over the past 50 years secular education has faced many challenges that resulted, among other things, in the creation of innovations and alternatives within the school system. Educators and parents, dissatisfied with the philosophies, educational outcomes, and school culture in general, have chosen to create options within the school system that offer a solution for some or most of the challenges that schools face in Israel's societal context.

One reason for changes in the school system is the growing awareness of educators of the multicultural society that has developed in Israel. Ethnic, religious, and class diversity in Israel is not surprising, given the country's character as an immigrant state. This phenomenon appears also in many other Western societies and many researchers and educators over the past two decades have strongly recommended promoting a positive approach to multiculturalism as well as the

---

Y.B. Shalom (✉)
David Yellin College, Jerusalem, Israel
e-mail: yehudabar2@yahoo.com

[1] Information derived from Israel's Central Bureau of Statistics on September 9, 2009, from: http://www.cbs.gov.il/reader/cw_usr_view_SHTML?ID=668

nurturing of tolerance in teacher training programs (Banks & Banks, 1989; Bennett, 1990; Sleeter & Grant, 1988; Wurzel, 1988). In Israel, researchers have examined educational issues in their cultural context, suggesting possible directions for the creation of deeper cultural understanding and intercultural bridging (Saber & Gur, 2001; Gottlieb, 2000; Bar Shalom, 2006). Many educators and thinkers who support the empowerment of excluded and disadvantaged sectors of society support an approach that empowers students by their endorsement of the students in recognizing their own narratives and that of their communities, and raising serious questions regarding the unjust distribution of resources, power, and dignity in society (Diab, 2002; Yona & Zalmenson Levy, 2004; Zalmenson Levy, 2004).

The lack of serious attention given in the past to questions of identity, and the disrespectful attitude toward the founding myths of excluded communities, has caused great frustration for members of such communities (Shabbtai, 2001). Suleiman (2004) discusses the twofold marginalization, civil and national, experienced by Palestinian citizens of Israel. Karnieli (2004) looks at the next generations of the Mizrahi immigrants of the 1950s, and offers a convincing illustration of how the educational failure of their schools inadvertently caused the creation of a culture of discrimination, ultimately preventing their chances of social and economical integration. The mass immigration from the former Soviet Union also led to extensive misunderstandings in the cultural sphere, due to the contrast between the attitudes of the immigrants and those of native Israelis regarding values, proper government, democracy, and pluralism (see Gommel, 2006). Another factor that has encouraged the creation of innovative schools is the emerging ethos of choice. Many Western thinkers have defined "choice" and "innovation" as synonymous, often borrowing from economic theory (Flaherty, 1995; Friedman, 1962, 2007; Perelman, 1993). An example of how this has worked in the United States would be the charter school movement. The positive attitude toward charter schools stems largely from the idea that greater choice will encourage innovation (Lubienski, 2003). Flaherty claims that this thought was exactly what led the legislators to approve the charter system (Flaherty, 1995). But to simplify matters, we will argue that the schools that are presented here are innovative because they basically present something new (Good & Braden, 2000). They offer options that plainly did not exist before in Israeli schooling (Bar Shalom, 2006).

In this chapter, we will show how individual schools strive to create a model for the restoration and healing of Israeli society, each within its special cultural context. The Kedma School focuses on empowering the marginalized Mizrahi student group, the Bialik School restores respect for and gives social legitimacy to migrant workers and other excluded groups, the Mofet School answers to the needs of Soviet immigrant students, the Keshet School seeks to repair the secular/religious rift in Israel, and Neve Shalom aims at bridging between Jewish and Arab identities. In this chapter, we will show how different communities have decided to approach the challenges they meet in innovative and creative ways. As we will see, these innovations are creating change in the structures and meaning of Jewish secular education in Israel.[2]

Hegemonic Culture Versus Excluded and Marginalized Groups: The Case of Mizrahi Education

The dominant Ashkenazi Zionist group, in its initial phase of State and nation building, saw the public secular education system as a means to create and generate the "new Jew:" secular, modern, optimistic, and rational (Bar Shalom, 2006). The approximately one million immigrants to Israel from Asian, African, and mostly Arab countries were perceived by the establishment as a primitive lump, labeled as "Mizrahi;" and the hope was that the Mizrahi would eventually blend in with the dominant culture. Until the 1970s the Mizrahi population was separated geographically and they studied in their own communities, often in low-quality schools (Swirsky, 1995). To modify this segregation policy, a middle school system was created. The thought behind creating the middle schools was that this way children from different backgrounds and cultures would blend and mix, thus giving a fair chance for all to succeed in the system (Bar Shalom, 2006). It seems that while some Mizrahi children profited from the experience of integration, there were many who performed poorly, possibly because of the fact that they simply did not find their own culture reflected in the school (Bairey Ben-Ishay, 1998; Bar Shalom, 2006; Shalom Chetrit, 2004).

The Kedma School

The ideology of Mizrahi resistance, found in academia and in the arts, also made its way eventually into the primary and secondary school system (Dahan & Levy, 2000). The Kedma School in Jerusalem was founded in 1994 by a group of teachers and parents who felt that the educational system was not giving their communities a fair chance to succeed. The first of the changes they inspired was in the curriculum. Clara, the principal comments:

> We don't follow the classic division into literature, language and expression. We have developed our own draft reader—we chose the texts and the children like them a lot. We divided each class into three groups. The children learn in small groups of eight students. The students really enjoy these classes.

This is an interdisciplinary learning model that enables students to search for their own personal voice through a dynamic encounter with the text. Some of the texts are of Western origin, while others address issues relating to Mizrahi and Arab culture.

---

[2]The main data (besides the literature review) presented in this chapter have been generated from observations and interviews with principals, teachers, parents, and students at the Bialik, Kedma, Keshet, Neve Shalom, and Mofet Schools, between the years 2000 and 2008.

Furthermore the school sets out to promote their students' exploration of their identity and the formation of their personality, while encouraging them to ask critical questions, such as "in our society, who has the power and why? Is power distributed equally? What can be done about this?" Still, the aim of the school is not to create a separate, segregated, and possibly antagonistic Mizrahi identity; rather, it attempts to create a multicultural identity in which students feel comfortable with both their indigenous identity and with that of the hegemony's group. After all, Mizrahi intellectuals themselves admit that they gained their power, position, and social status by understanding and operating well within Western academia (Bar Shalom, 2006).

Ariela Barey Ben Ishai, one of the advisors of the Kedma School, comments:

> Yesterday we had an argument ... how to make the students "multilingual," in the sense that they can consciously and freely move from "high" language to "low" language according to context, without feeling either inferior or patronizing.[3] When they learn a richer and more intellectual language, they look for ways to keep their own identity and hold on to the language of the neighborhood as part of their identity. Some people gave Dr. Meir Buzaglo [of the Hebrew University] as an example of someone they admire. When he lectures on philosophy in the university, he uses the language of the neighborhood – he does not disguise himself or change his style. Others were disturbed by precisely this approach, and disliked the fact that when he lectures, he speaks like a "bro from the hood." Someone commented, "I don't like that pose." Rafi (One of the teachers) said: "I'm an existentialist; I don't want to compromise and lower my language. In the neighborhood I speak like people do in the neighborhood. I'm multicultural."

On a visit to the school, one of us (Bar Shalom) wrote in his field notes:

> I observe Rafi's lesson. At first, some of the students find it difficult to relate to the subject of the lesson. Slowly, however, they are attracted by his skillful and interesting presentation of "Plato's Dinner." The students find similarities between the dinner and their own world. One girl seems worried. Rafi explains to me later that Plato's thoughts on love have an effect on her due to her own doubts about her relationship with her current boyfriend. Several students respond to Rafi's challenge and bring concrete examples from their own lives.

After class, I questioned Rafi about the role and presence of Eastern/Arab philosophy in a school such as Kedma, which aims to foster Mizrahi consciousness. In his words:

> I don't have to teach Eastern/Arab philosophy just because I am Mizrahi, although this year I have included some attention to the philosophy of Abarbanel. I think that Plato and Socrates are universal rather than Western or Eastern. I'm not going to stop liking Plato just because I'm Mizrahi.

The staff members at Kedma, understanding that many of their students come from homes devastated by economic conditions, created a tutoring system in which each student has the opportunity to discuss problems in their studies and in life

---

[3]Delpin (1995) proposes that children should be taught to speak according to the appropriate cultural context in each given situation. For example, "public language" may be practiced through roleplaying, drama, simulated newscasts, etc. In this way, the students learn that different languages are appropriate for different situations (Delpin, p. 53).

in general with one of the school's educators (Ayalon, 2007). The teachers take a psychosocial approach, and they have come to recognize that in order for the children to achieve success cognitively, they must create a "holding" environment, in which the affective domain is taken into consideration (Ayalon, 2007; Bar Shalom, 2007).

Again, from our field notes:

> Rafi (teacher) discusses the difficulties faced by some of the students whom he supervises. The role of the "supervisor" in Kedma is holistic, combining aspects of the teacher, parent, psychologist and friend. He tells me about H., a student who was sometimes disruptive during the lesson I observed, but who also contributed some valuable comments to the discussion: "H. tells me that when he gets bored, he goes out to steal motorcycle helmets. He comes from a very problematic background. I listen to him, and then try to work together with him to identify the disadvantages of the choices he makes. Recently I have begun to see some changes in him."

The strategy of combining cultural recognition and affective responsiveness has been proven to promote higher-academic achievement (Bar Shalom, 2006; Capps, 2003). Students belonging to marginalized groups in Israel are notorious for not doing well in the matriculation exams. At Kedma, however, the success rate of the students is above the national average in Israel (55%). Also, the school strives to be in contact with its graduates, some of whom sit on the school's management board. The school also offers discounted courses to prepare its graduates for the college- and university-level matriculation exams.

The Kedma School has drawn a lot of attention from among intellectuals, academics, and educators. Its emphasis on cultural representation follows Taylor's (1994) idea regarding the need of minorities for recognition. Many Israeli educators have used examples from the Kedma School that have been published in various sources (Ayalon, 2007; Bairey Ben-Ishay, 1998; Bar Shalom & Krumer Navo, 2007; Bar Shalom, 2006) in order to try to create a more multicultural classroom in which each child may feel represented. The following section will give an example of a multicultural school that integrates children from around the world.

A Pluralistic Multicultural Approach

The relative ease with which people can move from one country to another in search of better living conditions, adventure, work, or professional training means that many people now experience cross-cultural encounters. Cross-cultural contact does not automatically lead to greater understanding of the other. Different sides need to become acquainted with one another from a place of equality. In situations of cross-cultural encounters between a hegemonic culture and a traditional culture, institutions tend to reinforce the mechanisms of inequality between different groups. Moreover, members of dominant groups tend, sometimes unconsciously, to believe that the values of the hegemonic culture are the best and the most effective for the entire population. In the case of Israel, dissatisfaction over the lack of integration in the education system may be due in part to the sense that ultimately only one group has been represented in the country's hegemonic educational ideology, and in an attempt to create a balance, this has led to the founding of schools such as the Kedma School.

Another response seen increasingly in the Israeli secular-education system, and that also stands in contrast to the classical mainstream model of education, is for schools to declare themselves as multicultural. The schools strive to create a positive cross-cultural encounter while empowering each cultural group. This response is seen in the example of the Bialik School in Tel Aviv.

The Bialik School

The Bialik School was founded in 1934 as a classical Zionist educational primary school. It was named after the famous Israeli author Chaim Nachman Bialik, soon after his death. The school is situated in the center of Tel Aviv (Lewinski Street), an area that houses the old central bus station. The area is filled with abandoned and dilapidated buildings, smog and decay, and which like many other poor urban areas in the Western world, houses hordes of migrant workers. Israel had almost no migrant workers in the first 40 years of its existence, but the first intifada, with Palestinian workers no longer on the market, brought a shortage of cheap labor. This shortage caused an influx of migrant workers from Asia, Africa, and South America. This is how Bialik became a school for the children of migrant laborers. Amira Yahalom, the ex-principal, who served in that capacity between 1992 and 2003, reports that the increase in migrant workers started in the early 1990s and that by 1997 the migrant workers became a majority at the school, with many of the children having experienced the crisis of migration, either themselves or through their parents[4]. This of course created the need for serious changes in the teaching and the curriculum of the school. For some of the teachers, the process of change was personal and painful. Not a single teacher was dismissed, manifesting the belief that every educator can learn to teach and work differently. As a result, the school took on the view that change must come from within.

Individuals and human societies generally function best in conditions of stability. The only stable factor at the Bialik School is the willingness of the staff to cope with a world that is uncertain, different, and constantly changing. The curriculum at Bialik was adapted to meet the needs of a population that is different from that toward which the standard curriculum was oriented.

The Bialik School has succeeded in pooling resources, in particular those of the neighborhood community center. In return the community center enjoyed the filling of its empty and lifeless spaces, becoming more active and meaningful for its community. With all the children from the Bialik School continuing their day at the community center, inadvertently they had created what was later to become

---

[4]Supplementary interview, with Amira Yahalom, April 8, 2009.

an official "long school day." The school is regarded as part of the broader communal system, and places the child at its center, acknowledging that the students are affected both directly and indirectly by the social processes occurring around them. Disadvantaged populations are sometimes unable to help their children, not because of a lack of resources in the community, but because they lack the knowledge regarding how best to take advantage of these resources. The Bialik School has quite successfully found ways for bridging this knowledge gap, the problem being mainly caused by the population's fear of exposure to the establishment (Bar Shalom, 2006). By signing all children up for subsidized activities in the community center, Yahalom proved to the parents that their fears were unfounded in this case.

As Yahalom explains,

> When someone gets stuck on an iceberg, they have to take the decision to act. An iceberg can be a problem, but it can also become an opportunity. The same is true of diversity. This kind of multiculturalism and poverty can be a basis for progress or it can turn into a quagmire. Our success is that Israel's "fig leaf" has been turned into an advantage. The State of Israel cannot allow its "fig leaf" to be anything other than presentable.

Many of the questions addressed by the school relate to issues of socialization. The public education system in Israel strives – with varying levels of success – to "educate" citizens to identify with the State and with the Zionist ideal, to support the idea of democracy and to become acquainted with the canonical texts of the Jewish people (Shenhav, 2006). The Bible is viewed as the book that binds the Jewish people to its heritage – not necessarily a book related to faith, but one that raises the questions, themes, and dilemmas that characterize an emerging society.

At the Bialik School, the study of canonical texts such as the Bible has undergone a revolution. The reason for this is not a sudden passion for postmodernist insights among the teachers, but rather a reaction to the intuitive realization that the "regular" pattern of Bible studies is inappropriate for a school that includes so many traditions, some of which are mutually contradictory.[5] The teachers find themselves in a situation in which they cannot function as agents of socialization who seek to replicate "good Jewish citizens," and accordingly they use their knowledge of other cultures to transform Bible studies into the comparative study of cultural myths. From agents of socialization they have now become cultural mediators (Bar Shalom, 2006; Resnik, 2006). Such an approach would create difficulties among those whose views tend toward more particularistic and iconographic identities and attitudes (see Shilhav, 2006).

However, at Bialik the teachers examine the school subjects from a more interdisciplinary perspective than is usual in Israeli schools. The teachers realize that they are teaching "great stories." The multiplicity of cultures represented in the school leads them to develop a relativistic approach to culture in general, and to Israeli Jewish culture in particular.

---

[5] Interview with Yahalom and teachers.

A Multicultural Learning Environment

The children at the Bialik School enjoy a certain cultural advantage. An ethnocentric approach might have made these children ashamed of their own culture and heritage and would likely have forced them to adopt the dominant culture. The only alternative for children in such a situation is to cling to their original culture, and antagonistically reject the hegemonic culture. As mentioned before, in its formative decades the State of Israel attempted to create "new Israelis" who acted and behaved in keeping with the secular Zionist ethos of socialist European Jews. In recent years, Israeli society in general and the educational world in particular have seen an awakening of groups that feel that their voice went unnoticed in this socialization process.

At the Bialik School, the demographic change in the student population and the ideological change among the teachers determined the multicultural ethos and the special quality of contacts between teachers and students. It goes without saying that these students cannot and will not undergo a process of socialization to Zionism or "Israeliness," since a national Israeli conscience divorced from Judaism has not yet emerged. Accordingly, each student is proud of his or her own heritage. The teachers respect each heritage, and are grateful to the students for giving them the opportunity to learn about other cultures. No single culture is perceived at the school as better than any other.

The Bialik School serves as a model for multicultural education in Israel (Bar Shalom, 2006; Resnik, 2006). As more immigrants become part of Israeli society, this model is likely to become more widespread.[6]

Incorporating Jews from the Former Soviet Union

The mass immigration of Soviet Jewry to Israel has influenced Israeli society on many levels. This particular population, in contrast to the Mizrahi immigration back in the 1950s, came to Israel with a strong sense of agency. Soviet Jews arrived with a feeling that they had much to contribute to Israeli society in the fields of politics, culture, the arts, and education. They can be seen as an autonomous community that does not consider itself inferior (Shamai & Ilatov, 2005). The Shevach Mofet School in Tel Aviv evolved in the early 1990s from a discredited low-level school, catering to mostly Mizrahi students from lower socio-economic backgrounds, into what became the flagship of adaptation to the cultural and educational needs of immigrants from the FSU. This evolution succeeded when the school opened its doors to two educational entrepreneurs, Dr. Ina Levinov and Yaakov Mazguenov (Resnik, 2006). Mazguenov was especially interested in recreating what he had experienced as an educator in Russia, a school environment that emphasizes excellence in the sciences (Marom & Miller, 2008). Today, parents who immigrated

---

[6]The Kadoori School, for example, which is similar to the Bialik School, started as a classical Zionist institution, and seems now to follow a quite similar ideology (Gaphney & Hameiri, 2008).

from the FSU are willing to make tremendous efforts in order to send their children to this particular school.

The Shevach Mofet School in Tel Aviv succeeds at teaching classes with a majority of children of immigrants from the former Soviet Union, taking into account the parents' expectations of what schooling "should be." The school greatly emphasizes the sciences, as well as general academic achievements.

From an interview with the principal, Dov Orbach:

> I don't say that I can totally identify with the parents, but they do see the act of sending their children to Mofet as one that protects their children from all the maladies of Israeli education that they feel exist in the regular system. But they make tremendous efforts, they send their children from far away, places like Kfar Sabah, so that they will study in what they perceive to be a decent science program.

In other words, Mofet does not represent a segregated approach to the newcomers; instead it can be seen as a protest against the failure of the public school system to meet the needs of this particular immigrant population (Epstein & Kheimets, 2000).

The teaching style is a blend of the more formal "old school" approach brought by people like Mazguenov from the FSU, and the more liberal approach of veteran Israeli educators who see themselves as agents of "Israelisation." The dialogue between veterans, and newcomers, with all its ambiguity, enriches both sides and creates a new blend of education that suits the needs of this large-immigrant population very well (Marom & Miller, 2008).

With regard to the formation of a Jewish identity, the school succeeds at assisting in the negotiation between the immigrant identity and the needs of the teenage immigrants to fit in with their Israeli peer group. The veteran teachers try to maintain a non-judgmental approach, very different from the paternalistic approach typical to the teachers who operated in the Israeli school system of the 1950s.[7]

S.A., a veteran Israeli who teaches Bible comments:

> Teaching Bible studies is a tricky issue. Some of them find it a waste of time, since they are more interested in what the parents push them towards: academic success in studies. Still, I make every effort possible to make it fun and meaningful to their lives, to show them that the moral dilemmas of the Bible are relevant to their lives today. Some are concerned about the whole Judaic studies aspect because they are dealing with issues around the validation of their own Jewish identity.

In another interview, this same teacher commented that she indeed sees herself as an agent for socialization toward the larger Israeli identity. She tries to instill, through Bible studies, a sense of belonging and love for the country, and she tries to convince children who ask for her opinion, that they should indeed let themselves be drafted into the IDF.

Dov Orbach, the current school principal, is very much worried about the issue of the salience of Israeli identity among the students. He believes that while the school has to work toward academic excellence, it also needs to instill a strong sense of belonging. Otherwise, Orbach believes that the many temptations of the

---

[7] Interview with a veteran Israeli teacher and Soviet immigrant teacher, June 2007.

global world and economy, which could lead the average student to travel abroad for a few years to work as a high tech engineer, could possibly leave the student rootless and homeless. He sees it as the school's responsibility to make an effort to socialize students in a way that even if they do leave the country, they will still remember that Israel is where their roots are.[8]

To magnify the effect that the school has as an agent of socialization to the greater Zionist Israel, the school encourages its students to participate in activities such as a trip to Jerusalem on "Jerusalem Day," where they visit combat landmarks from 1967 and the Western Wall. There is also a large investment in the commemoration of national holidays such as Yom Hashoah and Yom Hazikaron. According to the principal, ceremonies around Yom Hazikaron, the Memorial Day for fallen soldiers and victims of terror attacks, serve as an additional tool for bringing the students closer to their decision to serve in the IDF (Marom & Miller, 2008). This effort by the school can be seen as a balancing act against the trend in the larger FSU immigrant Community to maintain its unique separate identity, something which is relatively easy in a globalized world. In general, it seems that many FSU immigrants feel that they have a great deal to contribute to the Israeli society, which they have perceived as very provincial in many ways. It seems that the Shevach Mofet experience allows them to negotiate their safe entrance into the Israeli mainstream, while still preserving many of their educational values.

Bilingual Education in Israel: Religion – Politics – Symbols and the Challenge of "the Other"

An interesting trend in secular education in Israel is the emergence of bilingual educational models. The school of Neve Shalom/Wahat El Salam was initially founded in order to accommodate the needs of the children of this particular bi-national village. Later the school began incorporating into its student body children from the neighboring villages, Arabs and Jews alike. An attempt is being made to create some degree of balance and symmetry between religious and national subject matters, language, staff members, and the number of children from each group.

According to Boaz, the Jewish co-principal of the Neve Shalom School,

> We are involved in the search for and development of identity. People believe that when someone has a clear perception of his or her identity, they will be less threatened by the differing identities of others. The same applies to the case when people use words with national connotations, such as Arab or Jew or proud Palestinian. We don't avoid the word "Arab" here. A comment such as "the Arab children are on vacation today" does not raise any problems for us. It's part of life, just like saying "boys to the right, girls to the left." That's how we learn to deal with things. It's part of our identity, without any great trauma. Respect, acceptance and the place given to the national identity of each child and of the other enable the children to grow up confident and proud of their own identity.

---

[8] From an interview with the principal, Dov Orbach.

In Jewish society, the word "Arab" is a curse. Not here. At our school the children have to look for other, more effective curses.

> When the school was established, it was intended to meet the needs of the children from the village. We emphasize the three religions and the festivals of each national culture. We don't talk about it – we live it. It isn't a matter of "you should be nice to..." or "treat equally" – but a matter of living together. As someone who was born on a kibbutz, I am aware that when you speak about equality you raise expectations, and this can sometimes lead to disillusionment. It's a fascinating dilemma. But Neve Shalom is a place where we have really been trying to maintain equality for a long time.

The internal process of the individual and the group in Neve Shalom is based on the basic conditions of equality on all levels. This is an equal encounter within the confines of an unequal society. What happens in Neve Shalom is not a sanitized effort to be nice to one another. The school community allows its members to live with the conflict, with all its complexity. The participants are invited to experience mutual and parallel processes through which they gain a deeper understanding of both the other and of themselves.

The school makes an effort to socialize children toward mutual tolerance and provides a great exposure to the beliefs and customs of the "other." This raises many dilemmas, such as how to celebrate different and sometimes conflicting national holidays and religious festivities, as well as how to teach subject matter in two different languages. Conflict arises when the two national narratives, the Jewish and the Palestinian, contradict each other, and teachers and parents are faced with the challenge of finding ways to accommodate these differences (Bar Shalom, 2006).

Diana, the Palestinian co-principal of the Neve Shalom School, reports:

> Sometimes five or six of our children's friends visit their homes. When they come, they do not think "Now I'm going to an Arab home or a Jewish home." It is all so natural and automatic. Since the 1970s I have had to work so hard on myself in order to realize that the Jew is not an enemy, but rather a person who thinks and feels and believes in things – sometimes contrary to what I believe in, but I accept the complexities of my own people and of their people. Everyone has their own ideas and thoughts. If I accept myself, why shouldn't I accept them? Everyone in this country thinks that their side is OK, their thoughts and actions are legitimate, but that those of the other side are unacceptable.
>
> ... The children here live the Arab-Jewish conflict. How can you cope with this complexity in a way that turns it into an advantage? Take the vacations as an example. One Jewish girl postponed her birthday party because the Arabs were on their winter vacation, although her mother wanted to go ahead with the party. At another occasion one of the Arab girls said, 'Why don't we have the party in class after the Jews come back?" For the children, both sides are positive.

Diana and Boaz, the co-principals, often observe, document, and engage in reflection relating to the behavior of the children in the "peace laboratory" in which they live. Their stories are created in the community and in the school, and there is an evident connection between the two that is not devoid of problems. Through the children, it becomes apparent just how artificial and dissolvable the archeological strata of hatred and barriers are. The community and the school engage in socialization for peace and conflict resolution. They transform the "other" into a living, real person. When the girl cancelled her birthday party, she emphasized the difference in attitudes. For her mother, "the Arabs" were an abstract, distant concept. The daughter, meanwhile, thought of friends who were so meaningful that it would be pointless to hold the event without them. Clearly, the school makes a very real contribution to interpersonal rapprochement, understanding, and acceptance.

In educational terms, this is an example of pre-figurative learning (Mead, 1974). The children cannot learn proper models for conflict-solving behavior from the adults. On the other hand, the adults learn through the children that there is a chance for a better future.

Teachers find this work very complex, and they often go through a process of self-discovery and the heightening of self-consciousness, as they face these matters. Another issue is the sense of the unequal status between the Hebrew and the Arabic languages. With Hebrew being the dominant language, the staff is required to create a balance which is very difficult to achieve within this context.[9]

Neve Shalom represents a radical shift from the classic Zionist approach of educational socialization to an approach based on the acceptance of the "other." While Bar-on (2005) claims that classical Zionism was based on the negation of the "other" (including the Arab), here we see the acknowledgment by the Jewish majority of the existence of a sizable minority. It seems that in many ways, the Neve Shalom School has influenced the newer Yad-be-Yad Schools (two in the North of Israel and one in Jerusalem), which also emphasize Hebrew/Arabic bilingual education, dialogue, and co-existence (see http://www.handinhandk12.org/).[10] These schools seem to face similar complexities and paradoxes (see Bekerman, 2003, 2005). Therefore, Neve Shalom/Wahat Al Salam and Yad-be-Yad schools can be seen as bridges between identities in a society characterized by a lack of social tolerance and cyclical trends of ethnocentrism.

The Keshet School

Serving a religious as well as a secular population, the Keshet (Hebrew for "rainbow") School incorporates into its student body both secular and religious students, striving to maintain an exact structural and numerical balance between children and staff members alike. Keshet puts forth an ideal of creating an environment in which secular and Orthodox children strengthen their own identity while co-existing respectfully and learning from one another (Weil & Roer-Strier, 2000).

The Keshet School was established in 1995 in Jerusalem with a mission to overcome, or at least soften, the chasm between secular and religious Jews in the State of Israel. Typically, Israeli children study in separate education systems and the two populations have differing opinions regarding the Jewish character of the State, the place of religion within a democratic government, and the question of "Who is a

---

[9]From an interview with the principals and with the teachers.
[10]Yad-be-Yad Schools have increased their student body from merely 50 in 1998 to almost 1,000 today (2009).

Jew?" In addition, differences emerge on broader political issues: the national religious stream is strongly identified with the establishment of Jewish settlements in Judea, Samaria, and the Gaza Strip. Many secular Israelis do not distinguish between the ultra-Orthodox and the national religious, viewing all religious Jews as an obstacle to the building of a progressive and enlightened society in Israel (Bar Shalom, 2006).

Ruti Lehavi, who conceived of and founded the Keshet School in 1995, often comments on how Israel made a mistake in the 1950s when it was decided to establish two separate educational tracks, State and State-religious. She decided to design a school that would "attract parents interested in a good education for their children," regardless of their religious or secular identity. It was important for her to define what constituted a "good" school; part of the school ethos was to be manifested in the possibility of reaching "a common definition that does not relate to our way of life, while nonetheless bringing our lifestyles to the school"[11] (Bar Shalom, 2006).

Similar to the approach at Neve Shalom, the assumption is that a properly mediated encounter may help children from both sides to develop their own identity, while respecting and understanding the identity of the other. While at Neve Shalom there is no real likelihood for students to change their national identity, in the Keshet School the "other" is a Jewish other, and at least in theory, every student could possibly abandon his or her identity in favor of that of the "other side." The school does not encourage this option, but the children enjoy freedom of thought and determination. Thus, the school attempts to engage in the clarification of differences while maintaining them.[12]

Despite the efforts made to reinforce the students' diverse identities, while accepting and understanding the other, the Keshet School nevertheless appears to create a more complex identity that internalizes behaviors that make their categorization as either "secular" or "religious" very difficult. In order to prevent confusion, the school is careful to remind both religious and secular students of their group affiliation. Students may visit the assembly or prayer service of one or the other group, but no more than once a week, reflecting the desire to avoid confusion and identity problems among the students.

It should be noted though that many of the religious parents at the school do not appear to be "regular Orthodox" Israelis and do not belong to the mainstream of the national religious movement. Many of these parents have a strong commitment to democratic values, hold a political outlook that is more left-wing than is usual among religious Jews, are open to the secular world and even identify with parts of it. These parents seek interaction with secular Jews as part of the socialization process of their children.

The daily school schedule is arranged in accordance with the consideration that the religious side must pursue its traditions, while the secular side creates alternative

---

[11] Interview with Ruth Lehavi.
[12] Interview with Ruth Lehavi and senior teachers.

traditions and content. In practice, through the encounter with the religious side, the secular side creates what could almost be described as a new "religion" – a religion that focuses on the class assembly, in which each student must take part, speak his or her mind, and listen to others, feel part of the collective and seek spiritual content.[13] This brand of secularism favors poetry, dialogue, intellect, and a rich emotional language. It could be termed a "spiritual" brand of secularism. The participants are involved in a joint search for "meaning" as defined by Frankl (1963), and they develop tools for discourse, self-expression, and attentiveness. In real-world encounters between religious and secular Jews, the secular side feels exempt from the obligations incumbent on the religious. Contrary to this, the school does not leave room for a secularity based on exemptions. The religious students have to pray, and their secular peers have to attend the assembly. The morning ceremonies, followed by a half-hour discussion by the whole class, remind each student – frequently but informally – of their place as members of a community with a high level of cohesion, giving the students a sense of belonging that is rarely found to the same degree in most educational frameworks.

The ideological approach of the Keshet School may suggest the potential for the emergence of a new type of Judaism, one that is complex, pluralistic, and critical, and that could develop from a network of schools offering a tolerant encounter between both the secular and the religious.[14] Many parents and students clearly display readiness for such a process.

As more positive social conditions allow for the encounter between religious and secular Jews, the Keshet School with its unique ethos may provide a positive model for a society that could emerge in Israel. This could serve as an example for a future-educational approach fitting an era of peace which would include the clear separation of religion and State. It may be assumed that Israelis, once freed of the fundamental problems of survival, will be more inclined to devote serious thought to the complex task of creating new forms of Jewish identity.

What Does It All Mean?

At the start of this chapter we looked critically at the challenges faced by a country characterized by immigration, a force that has the capacity of bringing great change to society. The founding of the Shevach Mofet School, for example, presented

---

[13] Ethnographic observations of several encounters in grades 5, 6, and 7.

[14] Since Keshet was founded, many other schools have adopted a similar pluralistic approach. It is of no surprise then that the Knesset (the Israeli parliament) has recently approved a law that allows the creation of a whole new stream in the State's education system, the "Integrative Model," which (like Keshet and Reut in Jerusalem, the "pioneers") basically allows Orthodox children to study side by side with secular children. Knesset member Michael Melchior, who represents a great force behind this effort, reports that there were no less than 300 schools who wanted to join the new approach, but that only eight schools were allowed to be part of the program in its first year (2008), hoping to create a successful pilot.

an interesting case of how innovative educators and thinkers found an effective response to the varying needs of the wave of immigrants from the FSU.

Immigration issues are only one part of what the Israeli society and education system must deal with, and they are included in the broader realm of multicultural challenges that Israel has faced in the past and is still facing today. What has been identified as a growing need for religious, cultural, and social tolerance has found its expression in the schools that have been described in this chapter. In order to make room for more tolerance, more acceptance, and a more multicultural approach to society, it is essential to instigate serious changes in social and educational attitudes.

All the schools described in this chapter see themselves, tacitly or explicitly, as agents working to change the classic, monolithic, Zionist educational ethos. If classical Zionism was largely based on the negation of the other (Bar-On, 2005), the schools presented here usually invite the "other" in through the front door. At times, these schools strive to empower groups that were seen as "others," and make an honest effort at making room for them to connect to a salient identity which can operate well within their special contexts. This way we can appreciate Kedma's effort to support a significant Mizrahi identity, while striving for equal opportunity for its students; we see Mofet's effort to celebrate a mixed Russian–Israeli identity that allows them to excel academically and integrate successfully into Israeli society; and the Bialik School's effort to create an adaptive, multicultural identity that will allow children to operate well within their perhaps temporary status within Israeli society (Resnik, 2006). Neve Shalom and the Yad-be-Yad schools can be seen as attempting to re-examine the classic Zionist perception of the Arab other, and the Keshet School operates within the realm of the re-evaluation of the old dichotomies in Israeli society regarding religion and religious education.

The re-definition of identity seems to be the main focus of all the above schools. Postmodern identities are becoming more and more difficult to define. We witness a fluidity of identities in which they are re-designed by individuals using multiple cultural resources (Kalantzis & Cope, 2000). Recent research has shown that when Jews in Israel fill out questionnaires dealing with Jewish identity, when they are required to define themselves as secular, conservative, traditional, orthodox, etc., there is an ever increasing trend of people who prefer to label themselves as "other" (religious secular, secular believer, free Jew, etc.)[15]. It appears that more and more people are dissatisfied with the rigid identity constructs from the past, and accordingly, they search for or create institutions in which new identities can be explored and celebrated.

It is clear that these schools are associated to other institutions that operate within Israeli society who develop alternative identities. We can see a clear and logical connection between Keshet's mission and operation and that of organizations such as Elul that strives to have secular and religious adults engage in joint Jewish text study (see http://elul.org.il/e-babout.shtml). Elul is just one example of many other similar

---

[15] From Hagit Hacohen Wolf's presentation (2009).

institutions and organization. Neve Shalom and the bilingual schools can be seen as the schooling venue for the effort of other formal and informal organizations that deal with the Arab/Jewish divide. See, for example, the Re'ut Sadaka Arab/Jewish youth movement (http://www.bkluth.de/reut/MAIN.html) and the peace organization IPCRI (http://www.ipcri.org). Kedma's mission is in line with the Mizrahi Democratic Rainbow Coalition's effort to help Mizrahi and other excluded groups implement values of democracy, human rights, social justice, equality, and multiculturalism in Israel (see http://www.ha-keshet.org.il/english/english_index.html). The public recognition of the Bialik School's efforts in helping migrant children may very well have helped current organizations that try to help refugees from Darphour in Israel in 2009 (see http://www.plitim.co.il/). The Shevach Mofet School's effort to cater to the FSU students and parents can be seen as one of many efforts of this particular community to find ways to integrate and at the same time build countless institutions that may help them keep some of their distinctive identities (Gommel, 2006).

We can see that most of these schools operate within the context of immigration and/or needs of specific ethnic groups and individuals for self-representation and recognition. It seems that these schools could not have operated in the early days of the State, since, then, the ethos was one of socialization for classical Zionism (Bar-On, 2005). The above schools represent, as stated before, a softer kind of Zionism, one that acknowledges that different groups may have different ideas on culture, values, and ideologies. Still, we see that schools that are closer to mainstream Zionism, such as Keshet, seem to have much higher demand and we see an increase in the numbers of similar schools. Schools (like Kedma and Neve Shalom) that change the classical Zionist concept, or challenge it altogether, seem to be growing in numbers, but on a much smaller scale.

Some thinkers (for example, Ohana, 1998) are concerned that the emergence of schools and institutions that celebrate identities of difference endanger the Zionist ethos by creating cultural ghettos and tribes which broaden the gap between the different groups.[16] Others believe that classical Zionism with its education system, created severe injustice and misrecognition (see Shenhav, 2006).

We believe that the truth may be somewhere in the middle. Zionism seems to be alive and well, as a major uniting force for most of the Jewish majority. The schools described in this chapter deal not necessarily with the destruction of Zionist Jewish identity, but rather, they offer different colors and emphasis for each particular context. It is most important to note that all the schools have a critical approach and they have an interest in producing what Westheimer and Kahne (2004) frame as justice-oriented citizens. We can only wait for the future to show us whether these innovative schools will in fact have an actual influence as agents of change toward transforming Israeli society.

---

[16] See also interview with Eli Amir, in Bar Shalom (2007).

References

Ayalon, A. (2007). A model for teacher mentoring of poor and minority children: A case study of an urban Israeli school mentoring program. *Mentoring and Tutoring*, *15*(1), 5–23.

Bairey Ben-Ishay, A. (1998) Teacher burnout and consciousness-complexity: An analysis of the mentors at Kedma (An Alternative Israeli High School). Harvard University Doctoral dissertation.

Banks, J. A., & Banks, C. M. (1989). *Multicultural education: Issues and perspectives*. Needham Heights, MA: Simon & Schuster.

Bar-On, D. (2005). *The "other" within us: Changes in the Israeli identity from a psychosocial perspective: An enlarged edition*. Jerusalem: Mossad Bialik and Ben Gurion University (in Hebrew).

Bar Shalom, Y. (2006). *Educating Israel: Educational entrepreneurship in Israel's multicultural society*. New York: Palgrave-McMillan.

Bar Shalom, Y., & Krumer Navo, M. (2007). The usage of qualitative methods as means to empower disadvantaged groups: The example of the Kedma School in Jerusalem. *The International Journal of Interdisciplinary Social Sciences*, *2*(1), 237–244.

Bar Shalom, Y. (2007). *Lova Eliav's pedagogical poem*. Jerusalem: Carmel (Hebrew).

Bekerman, Z. (2003). Reshaping conflict through school ceremonial events in Israeli Palestinian-Jewish co-education. *Anthropology and Education*, *34*(2), 205–224.

Bekerman, Z. (2005). Complex contexts and ideologies: Bilingual education in conflict-ridden areas. *Journal of Language Identity and Education*, *4*(1), 21–44.

Bennett, C. (1990). *Comprehensive multicultural education*. Boston: Allyn & Bacon.

Capps, M. A. (2003). Characteristics of a sense of belonging and its relationship to academic achievement of students in selected middle schools in Region IV and VI Education Service Centers, Texas. Doctoral dissertation, Texas A&M University.

Dahan, Y., & Levy, G. (2000). Multicultural education in the Zionist state – The Mizrahi challenge. *Studies in Philosophy and Education*, *19*(5), 423–444.

Delpin, L. (1995). *Other people's children: Cultural conflict in the classroom*. New York: New Press.

Diab, H. (2002). The missing narrative: A self-search. In A. Shai & Y. Bar Shalom (Eds.), *Qualitative research in the study of education*. Jerusalem: David Yellin College Press (Hebrew).

Epstein, A. D., & Kheimets, N. G. (2000). Cultural clash and educational diversity: Immigrant teachers' effort to rescue the education of immigrant children in Israel. *International Studies in Sociology of Education*, *10*(2), 191–210.

Flaherty, J. F. (1995). Innovations: What are the schools doing? In: R. G. Corwin & J. F. Flaherty (Eds.), *Freedom and innovation in California's charter schools* (pp. 63–73). Los Alamitos, CA: Southwest Regional Laboratory.

Frankl, V. E. (1963). *Man's search for meaning*. New York: Washington Square Press, Simon and Schuster.

Friedman, M. (1962). *Capitalism and freedom*. Chicago: University of Chicago Press.

Friedman Foundation. (2007). *The ABCs of school choice* (2006–2007 ed.). Indianapolis, IN: Friedman Foundation.

Gaphney, T., & Hameiri, M. (2008). *Multiculturalism as a way of life: The case of the Kadoori School*. Jerusalem: Ministry of Education (Hebrew).

Good, T. L., & Braden, J. S. (2000). *The great school debate: Choice, vouchers, and charters*. Mahwah, NJ: L. Erlbaum Associates.

Gomel, I. (2006). *The pilgrim soul: Being a Russian in Israel*. Tel Aviv: Kinneret Zmora-Bitan (Hebrew).

Gottlieb, T. (2000). Thoughts following group art work with immigrants. In: A. Shai & Y. Bar Shalom (Eds.), *Qualitative research in the study of education*. Jerusalem: David Yellin College (Hebrew).

Hacohen Wolf, H. (2009). "Identity Spaces" Lecture at the multiple identities in Jewish education conference. Oranim, January 7, 2009. The 5th International Conference of the Israel Association of Research in Jewish Education.

Karnieli, M. (2004). *Miss, don't call us screwballs*. Tel Aviv: Kalil (Hebrew).

Kalantzis, M., & Cope, B. (2000). Changing the role of schools. In: B. Cope & M. Kalantzis (Eds.), *Multiliteracies: Literacy learning and the design of social futures*. London/New York: Routledge.

Lubienski, C. (2003). Innovation in education markets: Theory and evidence on the impact of competition and choice in charter schools. *American Educational Research Journal, 4*(2), 395–443.

Marom, D., & Miller, M. (2008). *Dialogue from the heart of confusion: Intercultural encounter at the Shevach-Mofet School*. Jerusalem: Keter (Hebrew).

Mead, M. (1974). *Culture and commitment*. Garden City, NY: Doubleday.

Ohana, D. (1998). *The last Israelis*. Bnei Brak: Hakibbutz Hameuchad (Hebrew).

Perelman, L. J. (1993). *School's out: Hyperlearning, the new technology, and the end of education*. New York: Avon.

Resnik, J. (2006). Alternative identities in multicultural schools in Israel: Emancipatory identity, mixed identity and transnational identity. *British Journal of Sociology of Education, 27*(50), 585–601.

Saber, R., & Gur, Y. (2001). Contact lenses: Intercultural bridging in a youth village with a large number of Ethiopian youngsters. *Encounter for Social Educational Work, 15*, 163–191 (Hebrew).

Shabbtai, M. (2001). *Between reggae and rap: the affiliation challenge of Ethiopian youth*. Tel Aviv: Cherikover (Hebrew).

Shalom Chetrit, S. (2004). *Mizrahi struggle in Israel: 1948–2003*. Tel Aviv: Am Oved (Hebrew).

Shamai, S., & Ilatov, Z. (2005). Acculturation models of immigrant adolescents in Israel. *Adolescence, 40*(159), 629–644.

Shenhav, Y. (2006). *The Arab Jews: A postcolonial reading of nationalism, religion, and ethnicity*. Stanford CA: Stanford University Press.

Shilhav, Y. (2006). The educational dilemma in a globalized world. *The International Journal of Interdisciplinary Social Sciences, 1*(2), 15–22.

Sleeter, C. E., & Grant, C. A. (1988). *Making choices for multicultural education. Five approaches to race, class, and gender*. Columbus, OH: Merrill Publishing Company.

Suleiman, R. (2004). On the national and civil identity of the Palestinian citizens of Israel. In: D. Golan Agnon (Ed.), *Inequality in education*. Tel Aviv: Bavel (Hebrew).

Swirsky, S. (1995). *Seeds of inequality*. Tel Aviv: Breirot (Hebrew).

Taylor, C. (1994). *The politics of recognition*. In A. Gutmann (Ed.), *Multiculturalism: Examining the politics of recognition*. Princeton, NJ: Princeton University Press.

Weil, S., & Roer-Strier, D. (2000). *The religious secular encounter at school: The case of the Keshet School in Jerusalem*. Jerusalem: NCJW Research Institute for Innovation in Education, School of Education, Hebrew University (Hebrew).

Wurzel, J. S. (1988). Introduction: Multiculturalism and multicultural education. In: J. S. Wurzel (Ed.), *Toward Multiculturalism* (pp. 1–13). Yarmouth Maine: Intercultural Press.

Westheimer, J., & Kahne, J. (2004). What kind of citizen? The politics of educating for democracy. *American Educational Research Journal, 41*(2), 237–269.

Yona, A., & Zalmenson Levy, G. (2004). This and that – The curricula at Kedma. In: D. Golan Agnon (Ed.), *Inequality in education*. Tel Aviv: Bavel (Hebrew).

Zalmenson Levy, G. (2004). Exclusion and disconnection of youth from the education system – Things could be different. In: A. Golan (Ed.), *Inequality in education*. Tel Aviv: Bavel (Hebrew).

Latin America – Jewish Education in Latin America: Challenges, Trends and Processes

Yossi Goldstein and Drori Ganiel

Translated by **Kaeren Fish**

The Current Challenges Facing Jewish Education

The concept of "challenge" is an equivocal one: on the one hand, it hints at problems, while, on the other hand, it points to crossroads and new opportunities. From this point of view, Jewish education in Latin America presents challenges that concern problematic issues, but at the same time raises possibilities for new and positive developments. Some of the challenges facing Jewish education in Latin America in the coming years may be defined as follows:

1. Maintaining growth – or at least stability – in the number of students enrolled in the formal education system, despite the merging of some schools, particularly in Argentina and Brazil, for mostly financial reasons.
2. Maintaining a vision of Jewish education that identifies with the State of Israel under governments which, in some cases, oppose Israel's policy towards the Palestinians.
3. Maintaining Zionist perceptions and values in a post-modern era where firm ideologies have no special meaning or influence, and in which Israel's old image as a pioneering, innovative society has given way to an image of a normal society that adopts an aggressive approach to its enemies, cares only for itself, and is out of touch with diaspora Jewry, or is too secular and materialistic, imitating the US.
4. A trend towards ultra-Orthodoxy and a growing number of students enrolled in ultra-Orthodox schools.
5. A waning of the hegemony of Zionist parties in communal life and in Jewish education, and a deepening integration and acculturation into national societies.
6. Changes in the nature and status of the classic Zionist youth movements, along with the increasing importance of Jewish sports clubs in informal education.

Y. Goldstein (✉)
Hebrew University, Jerusalem, Israel
e-mail: yosi.goldstein@gmail.com

Below we address some of these challenges, and we focus on the formal education system, since it represents a prominent and distinguishing feature of Jewish education on this continent and is the source for various studies conducted over the years.

Jewish education on this continent is an excellent example of the pendulum of communal life. In some countries, we see enormous achievements in the sphere of Hebrew language acquisition, in the development of "integral" – as they are officially called all over Latin America – day schools which succeed in combining Jewish and general studies, and in informal education systems – whether in the framework of sports and cultural clubs such as Macabi, and Hebraica or in the form of Zionist youth movements. Elsewhere, there are countries in which the Jewish education system is shrinking and showing clear signs of crisis.

Almost no research has been done on the informal education frameworks even though they represent a strong element in communal life: The Hebraica organizations (in Argentina, Brazil, and Venezuela, for instance), Macabi (throughout the continent), sports centers (such as the Centro Deportivo Israelita in Mexico and the Estadio Israelita in Chile), attract tens of thousands of Latin American Jews and unquestionably represent the most popular organizations attracting Jewish youth and families. According to a demographic study conducted in 2005 by the Joint Distribution Committee (JDC) among the Jews of Buenos Aires and environs, 61% of respondents were not members of any Jewish institution. Of the Jews who belong to Jewish organizations, 64% are members of community sports clubs (Jmelnizky & Erdei, 2005, pp. 45–50). In this context, there should also be mention of the organized – and ultimately field-leading – activity of the Zionist youth movements, such as HaBonim Dror, HaShomer HaTza'ir, HaNo'ar HaTzioni, and HeHalutz LaMerhav, which involve several thousand youth, especially from the lower socioeconomic strata, and also youngsters who are active in other educational frameworks such as community schools (Even-Shoshan, 1987; Bar-Gil, 2007). These movements serve as an energizing factor and as a source of communal leadership, while at the same time providing waves of *aliya* to Israel. It is difficult to estimate in numbers the scope of informal education activity at present since, as noted, there has been no orderly research in this area. Nevertheless, it is clear that this is still an important and vibrant phenomenon.

There are a total of 80 Jewish day schools in Latin America.[1] In the Argentine capital of Buenos Aires and its environs there are 28 day schools that combine secular studies, following the official state curriculum, with Jewish studies. Another five such schools are maintained in difficult conditions in the country's interior, in the cities of Córdoba, Rosario, Santa Fé, Tucumán, and Mendoza. These, however, are diminishing numbers. In the 1980s, about 22,000 students were enrolled in the Jewish school system in Argentina in some 50-day schools. By the mid-1990s

---

[1] This figure is not final or static, and does not include supplementary schools and informal educational frameworks. Some of these schools such the Einstein School in Quito, Ecuador, include a large majority of non-Jews, because of the small size of the Jewish community.

the number had dropped to about 15,000; today there are about 18,000. In the last decade, increases have occurred in the number of children at kindergartens and elementary schools run by ultra-Orthodox institutions, with a decline in enrollment at Zionist educational institutions.[2]

In Mexico City – with a Jewish population of over 38,000 – there are no less than 15 Jewish schools within the same relatively small geographical area (the northwestern part of the city), with perpetual institutional building and an interesting growth pattern that contrasts with the situation in other countries and communities. The number of students has risen by about 16% in recent years. Analysis of these figures by ethnic sector or ideological stream shows a growth of 55% in the Orthodox schools, where 30% of the overall number are concentrated. The two largest ethnic schools – Magen David (Aleppo) and Monte Sinai (Damascus) – include 33% of this total, while the two Ashkenazi schools, with only 11%, are in continual decline. In addition there are two small community schools in the cities of Monterrey and Guadalajara. In total, the Jewish school system in Mexico caters to some 10,000 students, representing about 90% of Jewish children of school age – a remarkable achievement that may have no parallel in any other country in the world.[3]

Brazil is a continent all on its own, with its own language and culture. This multiracial country hallows the present and is constantly looking to the future. The strong federal structure results in a significant separation between each of the states comprising Brazil, with three main geographical centers: Sao Paulo, Rio de Janeiro, and Porto Alegre. There are 15 day schools, of which 8 are in Sao Paulo and 3 in Rio de Janeiro. Their combined enrollment is about 8,000, out of a Brazilian Jewish community numbering about 96,000.

The Jews of Brazil are concentrated mostly in the cities of Sao Paulo (about 47,000, with 4,000 students at Jewish schools) and Rio de Janeiro (28,000, with 3,500 students). There is also a smaller community (about 10,000) in Porto Alegre, in the south of the country, with a relatively large Jewish school numbering about 650 students.[4] Here, too, we see some interesting sociological trends such as a move to ultra-Orthodoxy (with growth in ultra-Orthodox schools and kindergartens), and trends towards integrating and combining different schools, especially among the secular or Zionist sector. A study by Marta Topel shows that the trend towards ultra-Orthodoxy in communal life is most prominent in Sao Paulo (Topel, 2005). In this city there is a developing trend of renewal in school education, reflected in the unification of the Renaissance and Bialik schools, and in the establishment of a large

---

[2]Data based on publications by the Central Education Committee and a discussion with Batia Nemirovsky, director of the Central Education Committee in Argentina, in 2009, as well as on a report on "Project Mifné" (Y. Rubel, 2009). See Rubel's analysis as coordinator of the project, pp. 5–7.

[3]Data based on research by Dr. Daniel Feinstein, rector of the Hebraica University in Mexico, and reports by the Education Committee in Mexico.

[4]Data based on a report by the Sao Paulo representative of the Jewish Agency Department of Education, and for the city of Sao Paulo – and based also on correspondence with the director of the Jewish Federation, Alberto Milkevitch.

new day school in 2008. In Rio, the Liessin and Eliezer Steinberg day schools are the largest; they continue the tradition of a cultural and pluralistic Judaism that encourages the preservation of Jewish identity along with integration into Brazilian society. From this perspective Brazil represents an interesting laboratory for evaluating changes in Jewish education in the era of globalization (Goldstein, 2008).

One of the important challenges at this time is the need to address the popular waves of anti-semitism sometimes disguised as anti-Zionism or opposition to the existence of the State of Israel. The severance of diplomatic ties with Israel by Venezuela and Bolivia, during the recent Gaza War (January 2009) was accompanied by demonstrations and graffiti that blurred the distinction between Israel and world Jewry (for example, equating the Star of David with a swastika) – a phenomenon that has become common even in countries with large Jewish populations, such as Argentina and Brazil. From a geo-political perspective, this challenge goes hand in hand with the amplified Iranian influence on revolutionary regimes in socialist countries such as Venezuela, Bolivia, and Nicaragua. There are some 12,000 Jews living in Venezuela, and the capital city – Caracas – is home to the Herzl-Bialik school, located in the community center, which also houses a Hebraica club with informal educational activities. The great challenge here is to maintain the educational systems in the shadow of establishment anti-semitism[5] (which encourages a merging of hatred for Jews and anti-Zionism or hatred for the State of Israel), anti-semitic attacks in various forms (graffiti painted in front of community institutions, police searches for weapons in the major community center, or an attack on the Sephardic synagogue and desecration of religious items at the end of January 2009). Even if the external anti-semitic threat is not of decisive weight in terms of Jewish education, indirect damage has been caused by the severance of diplomatic ties with Israel and the banishment of Israeli educators. The practical outcome has been the removal of the "*shlichim*" teachers who worked at the Jewish school.

The global era and the move, during the 1990s, to a neo-liberal economy likewise contributed to instability in communal life. On the continental level, a major challenge was presented by the appearance of a previously unknown stratum of "newly poor", the impoverishment of broad strata that had until then belonged to the middle class, and increasing dependence on external bodies to fund membership fees in various frameworks, including Jewish education – which is private education for all intents and purposes (Kliksberg, 2002).

The classic Zionist model of Jewish education, which had been expressed both in the establishment of schools identified with various Zionist parties and in the existence of pioneer youth movements involving many thousands of children, has been severely undermined in recent decades. The Zionist model was based, inter alia, on a connection with the State of Israel and sometimes with a Zionist Israeli party, with the Jewish Agency, and with the Hebrew language. A country such as Brazil, which had been characterized by attempts at Hebraization in the schools and a massive

---

[5]Not necessarily directly initiated by the government, it may be seen as "xenophobic expressions made by extremists of the margins of the mass movement". See L. Roniger, 2009, p. 36.

Israeli cultural "conquest" during the 1950s, today no longer relies on "*shlichim*" educators, save for isolated exceptions, mostly in the Orthodox schools (national religious, such as the Bar-Ilan school in Rio). Argentina has ceased its dependence on "*shlichim*" altogether, the working assumption being that the necessary educational personnel are being trained locally. However, even at this level of training teachers and educational personnel, a grave crisis (mainly financial in character, and also due to generational changes in personnel) became apparent during the 1990s, leading to the closure of the Shazar College in Buenos Aries as well as pedagogic tracks at various high schools in Argentina, Chile, Uruguay, and Brazil.

This crisis in the training of educational personnel for Hebrew and Jewish studies instruction has led to renewed efforts in recent years, in light of a real shortage of staff for communal schools. Manifestations of this new trend include the establishment of the Hebraica University in Mexico City, towards the mid-1990s, and of the *Melamed* Institute for training community teachers in Argentina, in 2006. These initiatives not only expressed a strong desire to respond to local or regional needs, but also reflected the importance of the connection with the State of Israel and of the educational input represented by the academic patronage of an Israeli university. At the same time, the drawing power of the young, newly graduated teachers continues to be small, and there is no solution to the low status associated with teachers and educators involved in Jewish education. Moreover, Jewish studies at the academic level are not widespread in Latin America, other than in university centers in some cities, such as Santiago de Chile, Sao Paulo, and the "Ort" university in Montevideo. The failure and closure of the Bar-Ilan Jewish University in Buenos Aires, towards the end of the 1990s, is a further symptom of weakness with ramifications for Jewish education.

As noted, the decline of the major ideologies and the appearance of new spiritual responses have placed a question mark over the classical Zionist model of Jewish education and raised new alternatives. The classical model, which reached its peak in the 1960s, was based on Zionist education with emphasis on the Hebrew language, appreciation for the pioneering image of the young state as projected by Israel's first prime minister, Ben-Gurion, and Israel's role as a refuge for persecuted Jews, something that implicitly pointed to the Arab world's hatred, of the dangers of anti-semitism, and a sense of instability in various Latin American countries. In keeping with this model, Jewish education was based on general Jewish and Zionist values, although the goal of the schools was not at all to encourage *aliya*.

In the global era it is more difficult to maintain education towards values and to preserve the ideological anchor which, in the past, had characterized so many different schools throughout Latin America. The collapse of social networks, including community networks, and the abandonment of the schools to their fate, with each institution facing new challenges alone, has forced a reevaluation of the day school and its place in Jewish community life.

On the macro-social level, most Latin American countries have adopted more multi-cultural and pluralistic views towards minorities or special groups. In Brazil and Argentina, the public discourse is today more open towards the integration of

Jews as a special community with a particular identity – despite some important differences in the political regimes and the fact that the political leadership in these countries is not identified with a similar ideological world-view.

Throughout the twentieth century, Jewish day schools served as "cities of refuge" and as islands of belonging, minimizing assimilation into the surroundings and providing protection against anti-semitic attacks. The schools also served as a solid foundation for socializing towards national Jewish values or political values supporting Jewish identity, especially of the various Zionist streams, and also others such as the "Bund" – the Jewish Yiddish socialist party, and Jewish communists. In the era of globalization, this objective – of socializing towards Jewish values according to clear streams and ideologies – has been partly lost, and is now identified mainly with the Orthodox schools. As mentioned before, globalization processes brought ideological deterioration and much more emphasis on personal or career achievements, which for Jewish schools meant a reduction in Jewish and Hebrew studies and an increase in English and Computers studies. Moreover, this transformation of the Jewish-educational system required some adjustments to new realities, beyond the curricular structure of schools.

This process has led to three types of responses in Jewish education in Latin America, with competing models of Jewish education and community vision. These may be set forth as follows:

a. *Adaptation and adoption of a pragmatic approach*: Here, emphasis is placed on inculcating knowledge and tools for success in professional life – such as success in entrance examinations to prestigious universities, or guidance towards career tracks that promise high status and earnings. This has become a prominent approach, inspired by a market economy model that is open to international corporations and multi-national companies. As might be expected, this trend has led to a decrease in the number of hours devoted to Hebrew and Jewish studies. The clearest examples of these processes are seen in the two "Ort" schools in Buenos Aires, whose joint enrollment stands at more than 4,000 students, the vast majority of whom are Jewish. The "Ort" schools are an outstanding example of the trend towards adaptation since they are oriented mainly to careers in science and technology, and the number of hours set aside for Hebrew and Jewish studies is relatively low in relation to other Jewish high schools (5 weekly hours compared to 8–10). This trend is also reflected in a wave of school mergers, such as the unification of the Renaissance and Bialik schools in Sao Paulo, and the establishment of schools that adopt English as a first language alongside Spanish, including even instruction in Jewish studies –as is the case at the A. Fern School in Buenos Aires, and the *Atid* School in Mexico City. In Rio de Janeiro, Liessin and Eliezer Steinberg are the largest Jewish schools and they continue the tradition of cultural, pluralistic Judaism that encourages preservation of Jewish identity while integrating into Brazilian society – a trend which expresses well the ability of Jewish schools in Brazil to adapt to historical and sociological processes that are characteristic of Brazilian society.

b. *Spiritual renewal*: This trend began to spread over the Latin American continent in the 1960s. It proposed a new world-view of traditionalism that sits well with modernity and does not rule out involvement in the life of the countries in which Jews are living. An outstanding example is the Bet El community and school in Buenos Aires. We may also cite the various initiatives of the traditional-Conservative movement throughout the continent (Goldstein, 2009).

The era of globalization produced a spiritual crisis which in turn led to the appearance and expansion of the traditional-Conservative movement in Latin America – a wave which commenced with the arrival of Rabbi Marshall T. Meyer (a close disciple of Rabbi Abraham Joshua Heschel) in Argentina in 1959 and the establishment of the Latin American Rabbinical Seminary in Buenos Aires in 1962. This model represented a synthesis between a Zionist and a humanist world-view orientated towards the surrounding society and social justice. The success of the traditional model, as manifested in the growing numbers of communities throughout Latin America led by rabbis who are graduates of this rabbinical seminary – communities which in many cases are established on the foundations of empty Orthodox synagogues or waning Jewish schools – has contributed to real change in Latin American Jewry which, until the 1970s, had been defined as culturally Zionist or secular. The success of this stream has also proved that it is possible to provide education with values, addressing the ramifications of globalization but not leading to the negation of modernity or to insularity.

The rallying cry of renewal spoke of nurturing Jewish moral commitment in an "amoral" world, or a world of pragmatic and egoistic values. It is therefore no wonder that the Bet El school and community define themselves as an "educational community of Jewish renewal, committed to the present and to social justice", maintaining a Zionist and Argentine synthesis inspired by Marshall Meyer's vision.[6]

Another example of the "renewal" response is the *Fundación Judaica* coalition of communities under the direction of Rabbi Sergio Bergman, which includes the Arlene Fern School. This organization defines itself as a "network that connects social organizations, institutions, and programs, on the basis of a view of Judaism as a religious and cultural civilization.[7] This network deliberately blurs the boundaries of identification with a stream: formally it belongs to Reform Judaism, but in practice it is based upon the leadership of progressive Conservative rabbis. The Arlene Fern school was founded in 1996 and defines itself as "an educational community based upon Jewish values", with the inculcation of "creative Judaism, perceived as a broad world-view that is directed towards integration in Argentine society and the integration of all children, including those with different abilities". This school promotes an innovative idea

---

[6]See the website: www.betel.edu.ar
[7]See the website: www.fundacionjudaica.net

that was once perceived as blasphemy in Jewish education in Argentina: Hebrew language instruction is not mandatory but elective, and Jewish studies are taught in English.[8]

The Jewish schools in Brazil present themselves as being directed towards the future and change, founded upon the values of equality and justice, integration into Brazilian society, fighting religious and racial discrimination, and living in a democratic and pluralistic society. These messages transcend boundaries and streams, and are also emphasized by the Modern-Orthodox Bar-Ilan School in Rio de Janeiro, and by the Yavneh School in Sao Paulo. The cooperation among the various schools led, in 2006, to an attempt to market jointly the registration to community schools representing different streams. The joint view was unique to the city of Sao Paulo, with a common goal of deepening Jewish elements and drawing students to the community schools.[9]

The "renewal" model clearly projects a message of blurring the boundaries of the collective, of openness towards the surrounding society, of civil equality and human rights. In view of this perspective there is also openness among the liberal religious streams towards mixed-faith couples and the children of mixed marriages.

c. *Insularity and ultra-Orthodoxy*: One of the responses to the threat of globalization and the blurring of particular identity has been the growth of many educational institutions identified with ultra-Orthodox streams, such as Habad-Lubavitch. The growth of ultra-Orthodox schools throughout the continent represents a challenge both in the positive sense and in the sense of an existential problem or danger – depending on one's perspective – of seeking a strong and absolute spiritual anchor in an age of relativism and uncertainty. Examples of this phenomenon are the Chabad *Ohalei Hinukh* School in Buenos Aires and the *Keter Torah* School of the Halabi (Aleppo) *Magen David* community in Mexico City.

The ultra-Orthodox model takes the same direction of spiritual renewal, but its path is one of return to Jewish roots and absolute identity. This model is based on insularity and a return to deeply rooted Judaism in accordance with the self-definition of each stream, including observance of the commandments. In quantitative terms, this response has unquestionably been the success story of the past decade throughout the continent. Movements such as Chabad and Aish ha-Torah, and Sephardic rabbis identified in Israel and elsewhere in the world with the Shas party in Israel, have entered the vacuum created by the crisis of the Zionist model, and have attracted thousands of youth who had been identified with the secular Jewish public or as assimilated Jews, far removed from any Jewish framework. In Argentina there are varying estimates as to the scope of this trend. According to Yaakov Rubel's

---

[8] See the website www.fundacionjudaica.net
[9] Río: www.liessin.com.br/. www.eliezermax.com.br/. www.tthbar-ilan.com.br/. See for Sao Paulo: www.renascenca.br/colegionovo/. www.peretz.com.br/. www.bialik.g12.br/. www.iavne. com.br/. For the joint effort of Jewish Schools in Sao Paulo in 2006–2007 see: www.escolasjudaicas.com.br

study, this model encompasses close to a third of the Jewish schools (Rubel, 2009). The education offered by this model is conservative, on the one hand, reflecting obligation to an accepted, closed world-view, in accordance with the halakhic interpretation of a certain rabbi or stream, but highly innovative, on the other. The innovation has been manifested in a warm emotional embrace and the inculcation of a genuine sense of community and solidarity. Many young people have viewed this model as a new and firm anchor that can stand up to the challenges of globalization.

The ultra-Orthodox model is perceived as a success not only on the quantitative level, but also because of its ability to raise resources and to develop extensive institutional infrastructure (including the purchase of community centers or schools that are empty or in financial bankruptcy). They also provide nurturing-determined spiritual leadership that conveys messages that are perceived as consistent and possessed of strong values-related, educational content. For example, on February 18, 2008 the directorates and leaders of the Orthodox schools in Buenos Aires announced the supremacy of the Orthodox model (ultra-Orthodox and national religious jointly) in relation to the secular model (broadly generalized) which, to their view, has come to the end of the road, reflecting ethical and moral emptiness.[10] The secret to the success of this model is its assurance of connection and cyclical continuity among variables such as the ability to combine institution building with determined and visionary leadership, in contrast to a system that appears mired in general crisis. The rallying of the Orthodox camp in the AMIA community elections in April 2008 brought about the victory of the joint front of the Orthodox parties and the appointment of Guillermo Borger, a member of this camp, as president of the community, commencing his term of office in June 2008.[11]

Case Study: Addressing the Challenges of Jewish Education in an Era of Change

For the purposes of understanding the way in which communities have addressed the various challenges, we shall present a case study: the establishment in 2001 of Bamah, the House of the Jewish Educator in Argentina.[12]

Jewish education in Argentina – and especially the school education system, headed by a powerful and influential Education Committee – served as a kind of communal cement up until the 1990s. During the 1990s the community suffered a number of crises, including the bombing of the Israeli embassy in Buenos Aires in March 1992, the terror attack on the community center (AMIA) in July 1994,

---

[10] Itón Gadol, Agencia Judía de Noticias, "Las escuelas judías ortodoxas, cada vez con más alumnos en Argentina", 19 February 2008.

[11] Itón Gadol, Agencia Judía de Noticias, 21 April 2008, and 5 May 2008.

[12] This section was written mostly by Dr. Drori Ganiel, who was the representative of the Jewish Agency Department of Education in South America during the years 1999–2003; he initiated the establishment of Bamah and served as the institution's first director.

and the collapse of the large Jewish banks in 1998. All of these brought difficulties, and one of the results was a regression in Jewish education, manifested inter alia in the closure of the community's pedagogic center and central library, the closure of institutions training teachers for schools and kindergartens, and the disbanding of the Education Committee, with a significant decline in financial support for educational institutions, the expiration of small, outlying communities, and the closure of the Bar-Ilan Jewish university. Along with these challenges, there was a significant rise in the crime level, and an acute crisis in leadership.

In 2000, the Jewish Agency proposed, via its chief emissary for education on the Latin American continent, to establish Bamah (The House of the Jewish Educator) as an innovative and communal (not agency-related) center of education intended to serve all educators, of all streams and frameworks, based on the basic assumption that the figure of the educator is at the center of educational activity. The Jewish Agency believed that this place, with its holistic outlook, would be a genuine professional support and laboratory for an educational revival that would inspire the educational system – and thereby the community as a whole. The expected side effect of this process would be the restoration of the educational system in Argentina to its central status in Latin America.

The local community institutions, the presidency of AMIA, its Education Committee, and other senior members of the community, did not believe in the idea and chose, initially, to ignore the proposed initiative.

The founders of Bamah faced a number of dilemmas as follows:

1. Involvement vs. interference – or, in other words, colonization from the outside vs. empowerment of community forces.
2. In view of the lack of cooperation of the community establishment, would it be appropriate to build Bamah alone or with other bodies?
3. What was the proper relationship between support for school education and informal education?
4. Would the appropriate approach be to initiate or to wait and respond?

The decision, taken at the beginning of 2001, to establish Bamah turned out quite dramatically, a year later, to have been correct, since Bamah was already operating when the colossal economic crisis erupted in Argentina in December 2001.

Bamah was established (in the Y.L. Peretz Jewish School building, which had stood empty for several years, located in the heart of the old Jewish quarter *ONCE*) with Jewish Agency funding and the support of an academic advisory council including the best "Jewish minds" in Argentina. Initial projects housed in the building included a library and resource center, a center for educational programs in Israel, a center for ongoing training, and a school for informal education counselors. A short time afterwards, and as part of the overall plan, ten supplementary schools, called "Lomdim", were established in outlying towns for 7th–12th grade students. Within 2 or 3 years this number grew to 25 centers under the supervision and direction of Bamah. All of the Bamah personnel were local educators; only the director was a Jewish Agency representative who had established the institution.

When the major crisis of December 2001 hit, Bamah established an emergency team to deal with the education system, creating partnerships with the Keren ha-Yesod, AMIA, the Jewish Agency, and the JDC (the "Joint"). This decision was taken in light of the immediate results of the crisis, such as the collapse of some schools and an accelerated exodus (dropout) of students, thousands of new poor who created a new and needy social stratum, dismissal of teachers, etc. The emergency team, which within a short time became an educational coalition for crisis, set itself a number of objectives from within the Bamah infrastructure:

1. Preventing dropouts and bringing dropouts back to the schools or to alternative frameworks.
2. Stabilization of schools, wherever possible.
3. Setting up the scaffolding for new and different educational leadership.

To deal professionally with this major challenge, Bamah appointed a strategic planning unit comprising lawyers, accountants, and educational planning personnel. A sum of $2.5 million was raised for the purposes of supporting the schools, providing discounted education vouchers for needy students, merging some schools, and closing others.

Soon after the crisis began, educational frameworks in the form of supplementary schools, called "Halomot", were established for elementary-school-age students, paralleling the "Lomdim" schools for high-school students. In order to exploit this process to build a better future, and in keeping with the vision, the Bamah organization was founded, and an educator and local rabbi placed at its head. Likewise, a Jewish Education Council was created as a supreme body, comprising all of the above elements, which took it upon itself to manage the education system in Argentina, with the participation of AMIA, the Joint, and the Jewish Agency.

The desired results of the establishment of Bamah have been achieved to a significant degree:

The dropout of students from the community schools has been halted, and nearly 2,000 new students have been absorbed into the system through the supplementary schools, along with hundreds of families who have returned to the circle of community life. This has halted severe assimilation in outlying towns and even in the capital. The education system has been stabilized and the schools have continued to function – now with much improved economic efficiency. The number of participants in youth movement activities has grown, and the first branch of Hillel, the international organization of Jewish students has opened (preceded by a preparatory study by Bamah).

Bamah has become a central point of knowledge and guidance for educators for all ages, from all sectors and areas, in formal and informal education, in all the surrounding countries. This entity, originally perceived as an externally imposed caprice, had within two or three years become a significant and essential body without which it would be difficult to imagine Jewish education in Argentina and in South America altogether.

The challenge remains to transfer overall responsibility for Bamah, its budgets, and its activities to a local community body, in an age of budget cuts in the institutions of the Jewish Agency and a crisis in world Jewish philanthropy.

There are diverse reasons for the success of the process of establishing Bamah, despite difficult circumstances in the life of Argentina in general and the Jewish community in particular.

1. The vacuum created in education highlighted the need for central educational services which had ceased.
2. Spreading news of a new and innovative institution that brought together all the educational services that had existed along with the addition of new service that had never existed in Latin America.
3. Obtaining the support of the Jewish Agency, and through it of world Jewry, for the Jewish community of Argentina and for its educational system.
4. Obtaining a budget (from the Jewish Agency to the New York Federation) for the establishment and operation of the center, with a pooling of existing resources.
5. A professional, community-wide, and objective approach by the leaders of the process towards school (formal) education, informal education, the state and religious institutions in the capital and in the outlying towns.
6. Establishment of a committee of senior Jewish (non-institutional) academics and thinkers and representatives of school principals, which accompanied the establishment and operation of Bamah.
7. The initiator and first director of Bamah was perceived by the community and its leaders as a professional who not only founded this project, but also, following the crisis of the presidential change and the strikes in the country, initiated the establishment of the emergency educational coalition, which was the basis for the educational coalition that operates to this day.

Successes in Jewish Education in Latin America: A Continental Perspective

An accepted yardstick for measuring the success of Jewish education throughout the world is the percentage of Jewish students who are enrolled in Jewish schools. According to data from the Jewish People Policy Planning Institute, the level of participation by children and youth in day schools in Latin America is impressively high – especially relative to the Jewish world in general.[13] In Brazil, according to the Institute's annual report, the level is relatively high – 71% – although in practice, and according to reports by the community institutions and the representative of the Jewish Agency department of education, the actual level is lower. The discrepancy arises from the absence of systematic studies and access to nation-wide data for Brazil. In Argentina, the rate of enrollment in Jewish schools is between 50 and 55%. These figures should be reevaluated on the basis of empirical and demographic studies. Obviously, enrollment data alone give us no possibility for evaluating the

---

[13]The Jewish People Policy Planning Institute, Annual Assessment 2008, Executive Report No. 5, p. 17: http://www.jpppi.org.il/

quality of the Jewish studies and the sociological structure of these schools. One of the prominent distinguishing features of the system in Argentina is the weight of the Hebrew language in the curriculum. In Brazil the Hebrew influence is weaker, and is significantly lessened with the transition from elementary school to high school. However, in recent years and as part of the processes of adaptation to the era of globalization, Hebrew is losing its influence throughout the continent – as reflected in a reduction in the hours devoted to Hebrew instruction, and in an undermining of its status as a second language as a result of parents and students alike questioning the benefits of its acquisition. For example, up until the 1970s, Hebrew study in the supplementary schools in Argentina covered an entire block of time – i.e., 4 h daily, totaling 16 or 20 study hours per week. The transition to the day-school system and the crisis of globalization in the 1990s brought about not only the collapse of the supplementary schools (until the establishment of the new frameworks of Lomdim and Halomot, providing 4–6 h of study per week), but also a significant reduction of Hebrew language study, as in the Ort schools (overall, Jewish studies were reduced from 8 h per week in 1990 to a maximum of 5 h per week at present, for all Jewish studies combined, including Hebrew language). In Brazil, too – where in 1950 there was an attempt at "Hebraization" by bringing *shlichim* from Israel – there are now almost no *shlichim* teachers, and the place of Hebrew in the schools and in informal education is low to non-existent.

The schools symbolized the pinnacle of achievement on the level of continued communal life. The existence of networks that connect the community schools throughout the continent is a sign of the success of the formal education system. An example is the "Reshet I.L." (network for Israel) project, which connects some 30 schools around subjects related to the State of Israel, and trains school coordinators to spearhead innovative curricula revolving around Israel. A further example of success is the "Manhim" (guides or leading educators) project at Bamah in Buenos Aires which connects 28 principals, Jewish studies coordinators, school and kindergarten teachers who are leading new initiatives in educational institutions in Argentina, Uruguay, Brazil, and Chile. The project guarantees systematic training, led by the Jewish Agency and the Melton Center for Jewish Education at the Hebrew University. It includes intensive seminars, three distance-learning courses, and a 3-week seminar in Israel. In addition, each educator develops a personal school project, under the supervision of Israeli experts and local advisors.

Research

Scholars such as Raanan Rein of Tel Aviv and Jeffrey Lesser of Ivory University in the United States highlight the new multi-cultural reality in Latin America, and examine the Jewish reality through the eyes of Latin American society and culture, from a perspective of ethnic studies (Lesser & Rein, 2006; 2008; Rein, 2008). Other scholars prefer to examine the Jewish reality through Jewish community eyes, with a view from the inside, deliberating the continuation of Jewish existence.

In recent years, research on Jewish education in the southern region of the American continent has been relatively inactive, largely as a result of the absence of research institutes encouraging this direction of study, both in Israel and on the American continent in its entirety.[14] Two books by Haim Avni laid the foundations for the research of Jewish education in Argentina: "Argentine Jewry, its Social Status and Organizational Image" [Heb.] (1972), and "Emancipation and Jewish Education: The 100 years' Experience of Argentine Jewry, 1884–1984" [Heb.] (1985). While Avni's attention to the education system is relatively limited (ten pages), it presents an interesting socio-historical view. The central thesis of his analysis relates to processes of "division vs. unification". The main conclusion is that, up until the beginning of the 1970s, there was an organized system of Jewish education, with strong super-organizations highlighting its centralized structure.

Avni addresses, among other sources, the reviews of the Central Education Committee, and also takes into account various reports that were published at the time. Prominent among these is an analysis by Simha Sneh, published in 1968. In this study, Sneh defines the processes taking place within the "network of Jewish education in Argentina" such as its secular and Zionist foundations, its connection with the State of Israel, the growth of the Hebrew language at the expense of Yiddish, the importance of the generous subsidies awarded by AMIA, and more. Another important foundation is the existence of a stratum of "negotiators", or voluntary school leadership, rooted in the generation of immigrants from Europe but rejuvenated by the involvement of young activists. Sneh highlights the moral and material support of Argentine Jewry for the State of Israel during the Six-Day War, in the context of worldwide Jewish solidarity. To his view, this support was made possible in Argentina thanks to the centrality of the community schools (pp. 132–133). A further trend emphasized by Sneh, and explained at length in Avni's work from 1985, is the transition from supplementary schools to the integral schools, which took place from 1967 onwards.

Sneh views the transition to integral schools as a positive process, "The sole possible solution to the danger threatening Jewish education" – i.e., state day schools with their Catholic, conservative orientation (p. 138). At the same time, in his view there is also need for reform in teacher training, a genuine integration of general studies with Jewish studies, fair salaries for educators, and more serious recruitment of resources to ensure the integration of children from relatively less well-off families. The clear conclusion is a call for joint planning and centralized effort – a difficult test for the Central Education Committee.

In 1968, the Brazilian sociologist Henrique Ratner published his pioneering work on Brazilian Jewry, "Nos Caminhos da Diaspora", but it gave no attention to the educational dimension. Ratner's studies in the 1970s likewise did not address Jewish education as a research subject in its own right. David Schers published a pioneering

---

[14] In 2009, the "Liwerant Center for the Study of Latin America and its Jews" was established at the Hebrew University – an academic research center that adopts an inter-disciplinary approach to examine the reality of Latin American and Latin American Jewry.

work in 1980 on the Jewish education system in the city of Rio de Janeiro, under the auspices of the David Horowitz Institute for the Study of Developing Nations, which published various studies on Latin American Jewry during the 1970s. In Brazil, too, it is noticeable that there were no continuing studies in this area, such as Goldstein's study on Jewish education in Brazil from the establishment of the State of Israel up until 1957 – published in 1993 (Goldstein, 1993).

The Education Committees in Brazil and in Argentina did admittedly try to conduct quantitative studies of schools, but it is doubtful whether these made an impression on educational policy or on the organizational structure of the Jewish schools. An example is the study of the schools in Rio de Janeiro published in 1997. Another example is the report by the AMIA Committee for Strategic Planning in Buenos Aires, with the patronage of the Pincus Fund for Jewish Education, which was published in 1993 and led to a process of unification of Jewish schools in Buenos Aires (Goldstein, 2001).

Another study that contributed to a comparative sociological examination of Jewish education in Latin America was published in 1987 in a collection edited by Judith Laikin-Elkin and Gilbert Merkx, in which Daniel Levy reviews what he defines as the region's "unique success in maintaining group identity". Here, too, the study highlighted the centrality of the school and the importance of the central, secular stream – as in the studies by Sneh and by Avni. Levy focuses on two major issues within the school system:

1. The level of Jewish autonomy vis-à-vis political necessities created by hegemonic groups and the state.
2. Group identity vs. assimilation: how the community addresses the challenges of identity within the framework of political freedom; what are the processes of socialization of an observable minority subject to processes of upward social mobility?

If we try to translate these tensions into today's terms we might state that the former has dissipated and is almost non-existent; at any rate it does not represent an important issue on the communal agenda. Communities and Jewish education systems have adopted the language of multi-culturalism, heterogeneity, and pluralism. The latter tension does exist even today, but here too we are no longer speaking of a serious challenge in an age in which democracy is well established in most Latin American countries and where the rights of religious-ethnic groups to nurture self-awareness and a unique identity are widely recognized. This trend finds expression in the studies of Efraim Zadoff (1994, 2007).

The last significant study on Jewish education in the schools in Argentina was published in 1998 by Iaakov Rubel: "The Jewish Schools in Argentina (1985–1995)". Rubel's major thesis is that Jewish education in Argentina lacks strategic planning, it has insufficient quality oversight, and the distance between the personnel actively involved in education and those with political decision-making ability in education policy planning is very great (p. XV). His conclusion is that there is disparity between the level of reflection and the level of execution. Rubel rightly points to the negative ramifications of the terror attack on the AMIA building with regards to continued research and systematic follow-up on formal Jewish education.

Ultimately, the Jewish schools are miniature communities, and the crisis of community is manifest in them, too. The Zionist model and the traditional model are today projecting weakness, both on the level of institution building and on the level of leadership, despite the growth of the traditional-Conservative model in the 1970s and 1980s. In an age of multiple identities and cultures, and Judaism's entry into the public sphere, it is no wonder that various streams are making themselves heard and are demanding not only legitimacy, but also a place of honor in communal life. The system of Jewish education in Argentina was bound, in the past, to a centralized, networked perception. This fact stands out prominently in the studies cited above (such as those of Avni and of Sneh). The most obvious identifying feature, since the 1990s, has been a shattering of this perception and the individual struggle for existence by each educational institution, with only weak ties connecting them to one another. The question of dividing vs. uniting, mentioned by Avni at the beginning of the 1970s, exists in no small measure today, too, but the pendulum is clearly swinging in the direction of division and disintegration. Specifically Brazil, with its federal structure, has been characterized by a splintered Jewish education system that sanctifies the independence of each school. Because of the uniquely multi-ethnic cultural context, too, it was easier for Brazilian Jewry to adopt the approach of communal building from the grass roots, without a strong centralizing force. This approach also explains the great openness on the part of the schools in Brazil towards the surrounding culture, and their self-representation as islands of pluralism and heterogeneity. In other words, the structure of Jewish education in Argentina today is approaching the model that has existed successfully for many years in Brazil, and represents most faithfully the influences of globalization on Jewish education.

Agenda for Future Research

Research on Jewish education in Latin America is still in its infancy, owing to the weakness of Jewish studies on this continent and the lack of resources for academic research, arising from a lack of awareness on the part of the community leadership about the importance of research.

Future research must therefore address not only the number of Jewish schools and students in the formal education system, but also qualitative phenomena such as curricula, teachers, and educators employed in the schools, new challenges – including the creation of networks or coalitions on the basis of common interests or values, innovative projects and their influence on the quality of instruction, ebbing of the influence of the Hebrew language and of the State of Israel on the community schools, etc. In our view, future research must also focus on case studies, and on qualitative studies dealing with internal institutional processes, such as Goldstein's study on the Bet El day school in Buenos Aires (2009).

An additional challenge is presented around the study of informal education, representing an important link in Jewish education on this continent. It is concentrated around major sports and cultural centers such as Macabi, Hebraica, and Ha-Koaj, and around youth organizations that develop alongside older movements such as the Zionist movement and the Pioneer youth movements, or around new movements such as the Noam–Marom organization affiliated with the Conservative movement. In this context it is important to study the influence of summer camps on the youth organizations and movements: these camps draw thousands of Jewish youth, a great many of whom (it is believed) do not attend Jewish schools.

Conclusion

Jewish education in Latin America is a dynamic phenomenon that has been shaped by a wide set of variables over recent decades. Of course, the situation in each country is unique, with factors at play in the largest Jewish communities – Argentina, Brazil, and Mexico – that are far from identical. Nevertheless, all communities (large and small) face shared challenges produced by processes of democratization and globalization that have swept the entire continent since the 1980s. The variables that shape Jewish education are structural, ideological, and even curricular. But more than anything else, they are linked to the political and economic instability with which all Latin American countries have had to wrestle and which have shaped the very existence of Jewish and communal life across the continent.

Jewish-educational research in Latin America has not until now reflected the complexity and diversity we have tried to highlight in this chapter. The lack of investment in research into communal life is most problematic. It is, for example, of critical importance that we study the impact of globalization on Jewish education in case studies that can explore these matters through the prism of particular communities. The Bamah case, we tried to show, is indicative of what can be learned from such cases in its demonstration of the problems and possibilities latent in the changed circumstances of Jewish communal life in Latin America. In conceptual terms, too, we have tried to indicate how the response of Jewish education to new realities can be better understood through the three models we presented of pragmatic change, spiritual renewal, and insularity. In this respect, Jewish education in Latin America is one piece of a larger global mosaic.

References

Avni, H. (1972). *Argentine Jewry, its social status and organizational image* (In Hebrew). Jerusalem: Ministry of Education and Culture.

Avni, H. (1985). *Emancipation and Jewish education: A century of Argentinean Jewry's experience 1884–1994* (In Hebrew). Jerusalem: Zalman Shazar Center and Melton Center for Jewish Education at the Hebrew University.

Bar-Gil, S. (2007). *Youth – Vision and reality: From Deror and Gordoniya until Ihud HaBonim in Argentina: 1934–1973 (Hebrew)*. Tel Aviv: Yad Tabenkin.

Even-Shoshan, I. (1987). Informal Jewish education in Argentina. In J. Laikin Elkin & G. W. Merkx (Eds.), *The Jewish presence in Latin America* (pp. 271–284). Boston: Allen and Unwin.

Goldstein, Y. J. (1993). The Zionist Movement and Jewish Education in Brazil: 1948–1955 (Hebrew). *Yahadut Zemanenu – Shenaton le-Iyyun u-le-Mehkar,* Institute for Contemporary Jewry at the Hebrew University, 8 (1993), 39–66.

Goldstein, Y. J. (2001). Comunidad voluntaria y educación privada: Tendencias en el seno del Judaísmo argentino en los años 1990–1995. *Judaica Latinoamericana, IV,* 157–181.

Goldstein, Y. (2008). Jewish communal life in Argentina and Brazil at the end of the 20th century and the beginning of the 21st: A sociological perspective. In J. B. Liwerant, E. Ben-Rafael, Y. Gorny, & R. Rein (Eds.), *Identities in an era of globalization and multiculturalism – Latin America in the Jewish world* (pp. 151–169). Leiden and Boston: Brill.

Goldstein, Y. J. (2009). Community school versus school as community: The case of Bet El community in Buenos Aires. In A. Pomson & H. Deitcher (Eds.), *Jewish day schools, Jewish communities: A reconsideration* (pp. 72–92). Oxford: The Littman Library for Jewish Civilization.

Jmelnizky, A., & Erdei, E. (2005). *The Jewish population in Buenos Aires – Sociodemographic survey.* Buenos Aires: Joint DC & AMIA.

Kliksberg, B. (2002). *Jewish communities in distress: The Jews of Argentina and Latin America face an uncertain future.* Jerusalem: World Jewish Congress.

Lesser, J., & Rein, R. (2006). Challenging particularity – Jews as a lens on Latin American ethnicity. *Latin American and Caribbean Ethnic Studies, 1*(2), 249–263.

Lesser, J., & Rein, R. (Eds.). (2008). *Rethinking Jewish-Latin Americans.* Albuquerque: University of New Mexico Press.

Levy, D. C. (1987). Jewish education in Latin America. In J. Laikin Elkin & G. W. Merkx (Eds.), *The Jewish presence in Latin America* (pp. 157–184). Boston: Allen and Unwin.

Rein, R. (2008). Waning essentialism: Latin American Jewish studies in Israel. In J. B. Liwerant, E. Ben-Rafael, Y. Gorny, & R. Rein (Eds.), *Identities in an era of globalization and multiculturalism – Latin America in the Jewish world* (pp. 109–124). Leiden and Boston: Brill.

Roniger, L. (2009). *Antisemitism, real or imagined? Chavez, Iran Israel and the Jews.* Jerusalem: The Vidal Sassoon International Center, Hebrew University, ACTA no. 33.

Rubel, I. (1998). *Las Escuelas judías argentinas (1985–1995): Procesos de evolución y de involución.* Buenos Aires: Editorial Milá.

Rubel, Y. (2009). *Proyecto Mifné – Del Estudio a la Acción.* Buenos Aires: Fondo Pincus para la Educación Judía.

Sneh, S. (1968). La red escolar judía en la República Argentina. In *Comunidades Judías de América Latina.* Buenos Aires: Congreso Judío Latinoamericano.

Topel, M. F. (2005). *Jerusalém & Sao Paulo – A nova ortodoxia judaica em cena.* Río de Janeiro: Topbooks Editora.

Zadoff, E. (1994). *Historia de la Educación Judía en Buenos Aires 1935–1957.* Buenos Aires: Editorial Milá.

Zadoff, E. (2007). La Educación Judía en Argentina como paradigma del proceso de pluralización y privatización de la sociedad argentina en una era de globalización. *Índice,* 37/24, 127–144.

Netherlands – Social Integration and Religious Identity

Henny van het Hoofd

Introduction

Amsterdam *Oud-Zuid* (Old South), built in the early twentieth century, is one of the prettiest quarters in town, close by the Vondelpark and main museums. Arriving from the south, the eye is caught by an impressive row of buildings along the Reijnier Vinkeleskade. A monastery, a chapel and a variety of schools indicate the self-awareness of the Catholic minority at that time. The Jewish community showed its presence in this new city extension with a hospital and a monumental synagogue. Inaugurated in 1928, the latter was meant to be 'a sound and solid stronghold against thorough assimilation' (Weekblad voor Israëlietische Huisgezinnen 11-5-1928). So it is surprising that no school was included in the synagogue property, and furthermore not a single Jewish school was built anywhere else in the neighbourhood.

This seems puzzling, especially as 1928 was a high point for Dutch Jewry. In Amsterdam alone, two new community synagogues were built. But a Jewish day school does not even seem to have been considered, even though the circumstances were ideal. After a long struggle by religious political parties, an Education Act was passed by the Dutch government in 1920, which guaranteed state subsidy for denominational schools. The Catholics made good use of this new law, and so did the Protestants. Then why did not the Jews do the same? This question will be the focus of this chapter. The answer is complex and sheds light on developments in Jewish education in the Netherlands whose influence can be felt even today. Because of the abundance of source material, the discussion in this chapter had to be limited to schools, and therefore, adult education and youth movements will not be discussed.

Thirty years before the inauguration of the new synagogue, the Ashkenazi Chief Rabbi of Amsterdam, Dr. Josef Hirsch Dünner, sent out an urgent appeal. His circular letter caused great turmoil, and not only within the Jewish community. Several meetings of the city council were dedicated to it, and articles appeared in the national press. Jews and non-Jews alike were astonished by the words of the Chief Rabbi: 'One more generation raised in this way and the Jewish spirit will have disappeared from our midst as well. May the Almighty avert such catastrophe! And this will come true only if we, from our side, shall use all our strength to establish, or at least to prepare the establishment, of Jewish day schools that will ensure our renewal' (Gans, 1978, p. 380). Coming from the Chief Rabbi, a request for Jewish schools seems completely natural. So why did his 1898 appeal cause such commotion? The key to the answer can be found in the Dutch governmental policy towards the Jewish community.

Jewish Nation

Although small groups of Ashkenazi Jews lived in the country from the thirteenth century onwards, the real history of Dutch Jewry begins around 1,600. After Antwerp was conquered by the Spaniards in 1585, large groups of people fled to the newly founded Republic of the United Netherlands. Among the refugees were Jews who had managed to escape the Inquisition in Portugal and Spain.[1] Some 30 years later, they were joined by Ashkenazi Jews who had fled the pogroms in Germany and Poland. They mainly settled in Amsterdam, where the urban government was tolerant towards religious minorities, i.e. non-Protestants.

This policy was partly based upon conviction, as the 1579 charter of the Republic stated that 'Each and every person will be allowed to practise his religion in freedom, and no-one will be liable to neither prosecution nor interrogation because of religion' (Gans, 1978, p. 7). In addition, self-interest played a role. Many refugees were qualified craftsmen, introducing professions such as cartography and printing, or merchants bringing substantial capital in addition to an extended international network. These were assets most welcome in a city striving to become a world trade centre.

The Ashkenazi and Portuguese Jews were known to the authorities as the *Joodsche Natie* (Jewish Nation), a name indicating that they were perceived more as an ethnic group than as a religious community. Except for their religion, they had nothing in common. In Spain and Portugal, many Jews had belonged to the upper class or even nobility. They were well integrated into society, spoke the vernacular in addition to other languages and had a broad secular knowledge. Ashkenazi Jews were mainly poor and had separated themselves from the often hostile general society, focusing on their own religion and culture. The differences between the two communities were clearly noticeable in their educational systems. In the schools of the Ashkenazi community, the language of instruction was Yiddish. Education was based upon the traditional method, emphasising memorised study of the Talmud from an early age on. In essence, only religious studies were taught. The Portuguese

---

[1] Despite the fact that Jews came from Portugal and Spain, the Sephardi Jewish Community in the Netherlands is known as the Portuguese Community since Holland was at war with Spain at the time of the immigration.

community had no such educational tradition to build on. Due to their background, knowledge of their religion had been very limited for generations.

They soon discovered that the Judaism they encountered was quite different from what they had assumed from loose traditions and close study of *Tanach* (Jewish Bible). For many this meant an enormous enrichment, motivating them to give their offspring the best Jewish education available. For others, the inconsistency between their own conceptions and reality led to an inner struggle, causing unrest within the community and giving the leaders an additional reason to set up a sound educational system (Gans, 1978, p. 92). Study of Tanach was emphasised, together with a thorough knowledge of the Hebrew language and grammar. Bible commentators such as Rashi were studied, as were the codices of Maimonides and other Jewish scholars. In addition, Hebrew poetry and several modern languages, the vernacular among them, were part of the curriculum. The schools of the Portuguese community and their comprehensive library were described by foreign visitors, such as Rabbi Shabtai Sheftel Hurwitz, who visited Amsterdam in 1649 while travelling from Frankfort to Poland. Among his many praises, he mentions that 'Rabbis and teachers are appointed and paid for by the community. In this way, they can give equal attention to each and every child, regardless whether its parents are rich or poor' (Gans, 1978, p. 107).

During the eighteenth century economic crises led to impoverishment. The recession weighed down heavily especially upon the Jewish community with its already large percentage of persons reduced to charity or even beggary, their poverty forcing them to have their children absorbed into employment from an early age on. Figures show that in Amsterdam by the end of the eighteenth century around 1,000 children out of a total Jewish population estimated at 30,000 went to school. This seems to prove that the large majority of poor children were indeed deprived of education (Michman, Beem, & Michman, 1992, p. 72).

Political Emancipation

The Enlightenment at the end of the eighteenth century and its ideas about the equality of mankind was a turning point in the history of Western Europe. Attitudes changed. Jews were no longer seen as a separate ethnic group, but as a religious community. The ideas of the Enlightenment were turned into official policy in France. When the Republic of the United Netherlands was occupied by the Napoleonic troops, citizenship was almost immediately granted to Jews with the Emancipation decree of 1796. This implied that Jews henceforth were ruled no longer by their own leaders, but by the state. As a result, the Jewish leaders lost their powerful position, as they could no longer turn to the local authorities to enforce their will upon recalcitrant members.

After the French left and national sovereignty was restored in 1813, an enlightened Jewish vanguard endeavoured to continue the new policy, while others sought to restore the old situation. The government of the now Kingdom of the Netherlands indeed returned leadership to the Jewish leaders as far as religious matters were concerned, but all other issues were delegated to a Supreme Council for Israelite Affairs. Jewish representatives, appointed by the authorities, included both Ashkenazi and Portuguese members, some traditional but most enlightened. The Portuguese, who were considered role models for integration, were overrepresented. The main task of the Supreme Council was advising the government on matters relating to the Jewish community. As religion had become the only difference between Jewish and non-Jewish Dutch citizens, all national Jewish features had to be given up. It was up to the Supreme Council to decide what was national, and what should be considered religion, thus falling under the authority of the religious Jewish leaders. In addition, the Supreme Council was to control whether the regulations set by the authorities were indeed executed by the local Jewish communities (Wallet, 2007, p. 10).

It was not the Jewish community alone that was streamlined, but the whole of Dutch society, the aim being to turn the Kingdom of the Netherlands into a unity with a shared language and nationality. An important role was reserved for education, as schools were considered an ideal means to create a national Dutch identity. The national school system took shape in the 1806 Education Act. Two types of schools were authorised: state schools founded and subsidised by the authorities and private schools, established at personal initiative and financed by a trust or by means of tuition. Both schools were to teach children 'all social and Christian virtues' while religious education had to be acceptable to all denominations (Meijer, 2004, p. 34). Dogmatic religious education was not allowed, as this would cause segregation between children instead of the desired unity. All schools had to teach at least reading, writing and arithmetic in addition to the Dutch language (Meijer, 2004, p. 39).

For the Jewish community, at the time the only non-Christian denomination, an exception was made. Jewish private schools did receive state subsidy, on condition that the language of instruction was Dutch and that the same general curriculum was taught as at the state schools. Both the Ministry and the Supreme Council realised that the problems with Jewish schools would only grow worse if these conditions would have to be met from day one, so they opted for a transitional stage. The use of Yiddish as the language of instruction was tolerated until teachers had been trained and new school books had been written in the Dutch language (Wallet, 2007, p. 137). Between 1817 and 1860, a respectable number of 79 state subsidised books were published for use at Jewish schools (Coppenhagen, 1988, p. 55). More than half (45) deal with Hebrew language and grammar, 22 are dedicated to Judaism and the remaining 12 to Jewish history or the geography of the Holy Land. Judging by their titles, such as 'Israelite Religious and Ethical Schoolbook' or 'Foundations of the Religious and Moral Obligations of the Israelites', teaching moral and social virtues indeed had a central position in Jewish schools.

Social Emancipation

Until 1800, most Jews lived in the larger cities, the majority of them in Amsterdam. But in the first half of the nineteenth century, many families moved to the countryside. As a consequence, Jewish state schools were set up all over the

Netherlands. Not all Jewish children attended those schools. Especially in the larger cities, well to do families sent their offspring to private teachers. For example, young Abraham Carel Wertheim (1832–1897), who was to become member of the Provincial States as well as president of the Jewish community of Amsterdam, or Netje Asser (1807–1893), whose diaries give a fascinating view of the life of a young girl from the Jewish bourgeoisie. Netje learned Dutch, French, English and arithmetic, supplemented with piano lessons, dancing and embroidery (Groften, 2007, p. 1). The lives of Abraham and Netje were not very different from those of their non-Jewish peers. In their families, Jewish holidays were no longer celebrated. Even though both Netje and Abraham married Jewish spouses, it is not surprising that the assimilation rate was growing fast within their social circles. But it was not families like the Wertheims or the Assers Chief Rabbi Dünner was referring to.

Born in Poland, Josef Hirsch Dünner (1833–1911) studied in Germany where he obtained rabbinical ordination and a doctorate in Philosophy. Rabbi Dr. Dünner thus combined thorough Jewish scholarship with an academic background. In 1874 Dünner was appointed Chief Rabbi of Amsterdam with the strong support of Abraham Carel Wertheim. Due to his University degree, Dr. Dünner was acceptable to leaders like Wertheim, while the orthodox members saw in Rabbi Dünner's thorough Jewish scholarship a safeguard for the continuation of traditional Judaism (Rijxman, 1961, p. 228). Wertheim, who used to say that 'the Jewish community should be orthodox or not be at all' (Rijxman, 1961, p. 224) was representative of the Jewish community leaders of his time. Even though many had broken with the religious tradition themselves, they did not want Judaism to be lost to the community as a whole. In their vision, it was the poor who had to preserve the orthodox character of the community. As leaders, they could make these demands explicit, because half of the Jewish population depended on poor relief during the greatest part of the nineteenth century. Many Jewish charitable organisations expected not only gratitude and impeccable behaviour, but also a certain level of orthodoxy.

The constitutional separation of Church and State in 1848 meant the end of the Ministry of Religious Affairs – and of the Supreme Council. After a long period of discussion, the Council was transformed only in 1870 into two religious communities: the *NPIK* (Dutch Portuguese Israelite Community) for the Portuguese community and the *NIK* (Dutch Israelite Community) for Ashkenazi Jews. The 1857 Education Act permitted the establishment of private denominational schools teaching religious doctrine, but these did not qualify for subsidy in contrast to state schools. Under the new law, Jewish state schools were no longer possible. If Jewish state schools wanted to continue as Jewish schools, they would have to become private denominational schools and lose their subsidy. Within a few years, almost all Jewish day schools disappeared and were replaced by *Talmud Torah* schools where children could obtain religious education after regular school hours on a voluntary basis. Meanwhile, Protestants and Catholics continued their fight for what the Jewish community had just given up: state subsidised denominational schools. As seen in the introduction, this so-called 'School Struggle' would last another 60 years.

Jewish Denomination

Around 1900, the Jewish community had grown rapidly to 104,000. Many Jews were completely integrated into Dutch society, mainly due to the Liberal and Socialist political movements (Wallet, 2007, p. 9). Still, almost everyone belonged to a Jewish community. For most this was a way of expressing their connection to the Jewish people, and had little or nothing to do with religious feelings or traditional observance. At the time, Dutch society was characterised by strong compartmentalisation based upon ideology or denomination in all spheres of social life. The dividing lines between the groups, called 'pillars', were strong and resulted in Protestant, Catholic, Liberal and Socialist newspapers, shops, housing corporations, youth movements, sporting clubs and much more. Unlike the Protestants or Catholics, Jews did not have their own 'pillar', but were represented by either the Liberals or Socialists. Both political movements were against state subsidy for denominational schools, as opposed to the Protestant and Catholic parties. The topic frequently returned to the political agenda, leading to heated debates. Around the beginning of the twentieth century, when compulsory education was about to be introduced, the School Struggle was raging fiercely. The fact that the unofficial leader of Dutch Jewry seemed to take sides with the Protestant and Catholic 'pillars' fighting for state subsidised denominational education explains the fierce reactions of both Jews and non-Jews against the Chief Rabbi's appeal.

Rabbi Dünner expressed his concerns about the influence of socialist and other anti-religious teachers at state schools frequented by children of the Jewish proletariat. His appeal, endorsed by the Chief Rabbi of the Portuguese community resulted in a trust called *Kennis en Godsvrucht* (Knowledge and Piety). In 1905 one of the very last private schools was turned into a Jewish day school called Herman Elteschool after its founder and principal, which started with 85 pupils (Dodde, 2009, p. 145). In addition, a Jewish school for poor children was established in the basement of a synagogue.

At that time, most children obtained their Jewish education during after school hours in one of the Talmud Torah schools run by the local Jewish communities. In 1908 there were 106 such schools all over the country, supported by a yearly state subsidy of Fl. 11,300 distributed by the NIK (HPC, 1908–1909). Communities too small to afford a teacher could apply to a special fund for a subsidy to send children to the Talmud Torah classes of the nearby community. In 1908, 12 such communities were subsidised by the NIK, a number that would almost double to 22 in 1938 (HPC, 1938–1939).

Criticising Education

In 1893 the teachers union *Achawah* (brotherhood) was founded (NIW, 11-8-1893). In its monthly magazine, also called Achawah, educational topics were among those discussed. While in the first issues teachers outdid themselves by translating difficult

Hebrew words and inventing complicated grammatical questions, the attention soon focused on the teaching of Hebrew. One of the younger teachers dropped a bombshell: '... because of the old-fashioned, adult language of the outdated manual, it does not matter if the children are droning Dutch or Hebrew: they don't understand it anyhow. No wonder our pupils become bored. In order to stay in control in the classroom, a teacher is forced to take measures of punishment belonging to the former century' (Achawah November, 1894). While some teachers gave suggestions for improving the lessons, others admitted that 'the dry, dull and boring, half unconscious droning of blessings and prayers fosters aversion and indifference' (Achawah March, 1895).

In the first decades of the twentieth century, the number of children attending Talmud Torah classes dropped rapidly, especially in the larger cities. In their magazine, teachers discussed the reasons why. Some blamed the children: They skip school because they prefer piano lessons or other activities, or pretend to be too tired after their regular school day. Some teachers saw in the parents' apathy 'the final blow for our schools' (Achawah March, 1895). Others mentioned 'the lack of a national curriculum and modern schoolbooks' (Achawah March, 1899). But some, albeit few, blamed themselves: '... so often do we act contrary to the basic principles of psychology and pedagogy, while only rarely succeeding in really catching the attention of the children' (Achawah August, 1895).

The same remarks could be heard in other schools. Teachers, especially those in working class districts, started criticising the educational system. For example, Jan Ligthart condemned the 'sit-and-listen' schools and had his pupils cooperating in projects like churning butter, brick-making and school gardening. His ideas of self-motivation, group work and focus on the child's habitat were shared by many (Bakker, Noordman, & Rietveld-van Wingerden, 2006, p. 508). In the first decades of the twentieth century, education in the Netherlands was reformed according to modern pedagogical insights. But the schools run by the Jewish communities did not follow suit, even though modern educational ideas from time to time appear in the Achawah magazine: 'When your pupils enter a classroom where not a single picture or drawing can be found, where no bright flower or plant decorates the room, with rags for curtains, stovepipes brown with rust and desks lacking paint, can you blame them for immediately drawing an unfavourable conclusion when they compare it to the spacious, cosy classroom of their primary school?' (Achawah April, 1921). Clara Asscher-Pinkhof, an inspired and beloved educator, described in her biography the situation of Jewish education around 1920. 'The way teachers sinned against the soul of the children hurt my teacher's heart. The methods used are at least a 100 years old. It is the custom that the Chief Rabbi writes the curriculum, but often he has never been a teacher himself, and maybe he does not even know what a child is. No Rabbi ever had the idea of listening to the teachers using their ideas for improving Jewish education.' Her conclusion is shocking: 'The system for Jewish education has done everything to chase young people away from Judaism' (Asscher-Pinkhof, 1981, p. 58). Similar remarks blaming the lack of a national curriculum, outdated material and dilapidated classrooms were also made by other educators.

Jewish Day Schools

The 1920 Education Act, which granted equal state subsidy to denominational schools and neutral (non-denominational) schools, stimulated the establishment of two more Jewish primary schools in 1929 and 1934, and enabled the day school for poor children to move to a modern building in the eastern part of the city. Two Jewish secondary schools were founded in 1927 and 1928. At these schools, 3–5 h per week were available for Jewish lessons in addition to the programme of the non-denominational schools. Both secular and Jewish lessons were given by the same teacher as an integral part of the school curriculum. Relative to the Jewish population of the city which was estimated at 70,000 at the time, the schools had only a limited number of pupils. In 1928, the number of children enrolled in Jewish day schools was 254 for the Herman Elteschool and 79 for the two secondary schools (Michman et al., 1992, 136), while 1,950 children attended the after-school Talmud Torah classes (Weekblad, 2-3-1928).

The only other city where a Jewish day school was founded was The Hague, where the city council suggested constructing one large modern building to be shared by three neutral primary schools. One of them would have an adjusted schedule, enabling it to close down on Shabbat and Jewish holidays, while compulsory Jewish lessons would be included in the curriculum. This new type of school became known as the *Haagse Stelsel* (The Hague System) (van Creveld, 2003, p. 120). The school was supported by the local Jewish community and the Chief Rabbi immediately volunteered to be a teacher (Weekblad, 24-2-1928). Even though the 'Haagse Stelsel school' was successful, it was not introduced in other cities. In Amsterdam, the city council allowed neutral schools with over 50% of Jewish pupils to close on Shabbat and holidays, while the Jewish community obtained permission to use their facilities for Talmud Torah classes during after school hours. This was an improvement, not only because of the well-equipped modern classrooms, but also because many families had left the old Jewish quarter for the new neighbourhoods.

One of the frequently heard arguments at the time against Jewish day schools is that children who associated almost exclusively with other Jews would feel uncomfortable towards the gentile society in which they were supposed to live and work. The fact that in pre-war Amsterdam not one of the Jewish community leaders sent his children to a Jewish day school proves that this view was shared by many (Dahan, 1989, p. 9).

The spirit of the times is noticeable in a report of a meeting held in the Transvaalbuurt, a new quarter in the eastern part of Amsterdam. In 1928 over 12,500 Jews lived there and in the adjacent neighbourhoods, which were to a large extent built by socialist housing corporations. The meeting was organised as a protest against the establishment of a Jewish day school and was attended by both supporters and opponents, almost all of them Jewish. While the presentation by a neutral school teacher is described as 'very interesting and refreshing', the representative of the Jewish denominational school is depicted as tedious and boring. According to the reporter, those in favour of a Jewish school are assimilators. 'Why do they need denominational schools? Because the *goyim* have them?' (Weekblad, 2-3-1928).

Between 1920 and 1940, several Jewish schoolbooks were published. While they look attractive and are in agreement with pedagogical ideas of the time, there is something peculiar about them. The idea behind the Hebrew primer 'A present for the Israelite Youth' is original. It teaches children to read Hebrew using Dutch words written in Hebrew script. When correctly read in Ashkenazi pronunciation, it turns out to be a Dutch children's story resembling those in a popular Dutch reader. The stories about children playing are nice enough, but there is nothing Jewish about them. Similarly, the Hebrew method Ha-Méliets has stories and exercises written in biblical Hebrew dealing with the daily life of Dutch children. Jewish themes can be found in it, but only rarely. One story, illustrated with a typically Dutch setting with a flag, tells about the birthday of 'the beloved Queen', which is not the first thing one expects in a Hebrew schoolbook.

The attractive Hebrew *leesplankje* (hornbook, a board showing pictures with words underneath) was designed after a very popular tool in general education. Not one of the 19 pictures shown has a Jewish theme. The 'book' on the picture opens from left to right and the word 'light' is not illustrated by *Shabbat* candles but by sconce which in the 1930s must already have been an old-fashioned object. Exactly the opposite was happening at Catholic schools, where children learned how to read 'in a Catholic spirit, with words and stories from a familiar environment' (Ghonem, 2007, p. 2). As no extensive research has been done so far in the field of Jewish curricula and schoolbooks, only some first superficial remarks can be made. Protestant and Catholic schools were put on the same footing with neutral schools after a long struggle, and they emphasised the differences between denominational and neutral education, while for the Jewish schools the neutral school was both their competitor and their role model. Both Catholic and Protestant 'pillars' had a longstanding tradition of developing material and the Catholics had a large group of religious educators at their disposal eager to teach and develop material for free.

But there might be another reason why official Jewish educational materials emphasised Dutch nationality to such a degree. The ideas of Zionism and the renewal of Hebrew as a spoken language were well known at the time. The Rabbinate, even though some of its members belonged to the *Mizrachi* (religious Zionist) movement, officially distanced itself from Zionism. It is very possible that this rabbinical point of view can be seen in the Hebrew pedagogic methods published around 1930, with their strong emphasis on Ashkenazi pronunciation and Dutch nationality. In contrast, the influence of Zionism was reflected in the Achawah magazine. 'Many youngsters want to learn and understand Hebrew, the means of communication between our tribesmen, the language of our holy books and scholars, and also of our brothers in Palestine. We teachers are the ones who master this language. Show your students that not only do you know five synonyms for "burning wrath", but that you can also tell them the Hebrew word for slate, desk and picture. Use these words to create child friendly exercises. Your lessons will become interesting, yes, even Jewish' (Achawah January, 1929). The same edition of Achawah mentioned a school in Amsterdam South, which in contrast to all the other Talmud Torah classes, is growing rapidly and attracts children from all over the city. The reason why can be found in another source: 'The classes, meeting on Wednesday afternoons and Sunday mornings, were organised and financed by Zionist oriented families. The lessons were given by young teachers, all members of the religious Zionist *Zichron Jaäkow* movement. They imparted to us a warm love for Judaism and Zionism' (Boas, 2002, p. 63). Among the first principals of this school, that surely must have 'ensured Jewish renewal', was a grandson of Rabbi Dünner (Fuks, 2007, p. 66). Even though no Jewish day school was to be found in the whole neighbourhood, the children of Amsterdam South probably got the best Jewish education in town.

Another very successful way to reach out to Jewish children was the weekly *De Joodsche Jeugdkrant* (The Jewish Youth Magazine), founded by Rabbi Dr. De Hond in 1928. In addition to Torah, Prayers, Biblical History, Hebrew and Jewish knowledge, there are Jewish songs, riddles, stories and even serials. Several teachers were involved in this unique project. The correspondence between Rabbi De Hond and children from all over the Netherlands provides an insight into their lives and reveals much about Jewish life especially in smaller communities. A longing for more Jewish education is reflected in the magazine, as illustrated in a letter from Betsy from the town of Zierikzee in the remote province of Zeeland, whose greatest wish for *Chanukah* is 'a teacher to tell us all about Judaism' (De Joodsche Jeugdkrant, 31-12-1931).

In the 1930s, the number of children attending Jewish day schools rose due to the influx of refugees from Germany. In 1938, the four primary schools in Amsterdam together had 1,010 pupils, while another 236 attended the secondary schools (Dodde, 2009, p. 146). A total of 1,514 children attended the after-school *Talmud Torah* classes given in 13 locations all over the city (Michman et al., 1992, p. 153). But nevertheless, the large majority of Amsterdam children attended a neutral school for ideological reasons. Such schools offered the opportunity to be together with children of other religions and so were held to promote tolerance and respect (Van Wingerden, 2008, p. 186).

In May 1940, the Netherlands was attacked and occupied by Nazi Germany. By October 1941 over 14,000 pupils were evicted from their schools and forced to enrol in special schools for Jewish children with Jewish teachers. In 36 cities all over the country 111 such institutions were founded (Michman et al., 1992, p. 185). Amsterdam had 25 schools for Jewish children attended by 6,940 pupils (Stigter, 2005, p. 38). When the last of them closed down in September 1943, no Jewish children could be found anymore in the country, except for those in hiding. Out of a Jewish community estimated at 140,000 in 1940, over 110,000 Jews perished in the concentration camps, among them Betsy and more than 13,000 other children.[2] Their fate is described in a poem by the Jewish poet Ida Vos:

---

[2]Born in 1930 or later. Information provided by Herinneringscentrum Westerbork.

Geography
She had a bad mark
for Geography
that last day.
But knew a week later
exactly where Treblinka was.
For just one moment (Vos, 1983, p. 11).

Traumatic Restoration

Four months after liberation, just before *Rosh Hashanah* 1945, the monumental synagogue in Amsterdam Old South was used again for the first time. The Rabbi cited Ezra 3:12 'Many that had seen the first house, when the foundation of this house was laid before their eyes, wept with a loud voice.' He expressed his deep sorrow 'at the loss of so many well-known persons from this neighbourhood, whose places are now unoccupied, of the Rabbis and cantor who shall be sorely missed' (NIW, 14-9-1945).

The end of Second World War found the Jewish community of the Netherlands in a dramatically changed situation. Only about 25,000 had survived the Nazi horrors, the majority by going into hiding or due to mixed marriages. In addition to the enormous human losses, the structure of the community had, of course, also been severely damaged. Most synagogues and Jewish institutions were in ruins or expropriated. Very few of the Rabbis, teachers and community leaders had survived. The almost impossible task of rebuilding the community rested on the shoulders of a small group of people, who all had undergone traumatic experiences and suffered heavy personal losses.

Young people were considered of extreme importance in the rebuilding of Jewish community life, and setting up a Jewish educational system therefore had priority. But according to the temporary board of the Jewish community of Amsterdam, it was to be different from pre-war focus: 'Judaism without *Erets Jisrael* (the Land of Israel) is impossible. Therefore, Erets will be in the centre of Jewish education. The old fashioned religious classes as they used to be, a terror for many, taught with outdated methods will be altered completely. The emphasis will be on modern Hebrew, Jewish history and Jewish customs' (NIW 26-10-1945). In 1947, the Jewish community organised classes run along these lines in three locations in the city, attended by 90 children between 6 and 14 years old (NIW, 28-11-1947). The 'emphasis on modern Hebrew' was striking. According to many, the future of the remnant of Dutch Jewry was no longer in the Netherlands but in the new Jewish state to be. This is illustrated by an advertisement in the Jewish press: 'Learn Hebrew – the language of your future, the language of your children' (NIW, 6-3-1947). The last sentence of the first post-war Hebrew primer is 'When I grow up, I will to go to Erets Jisrael'.

In November 1946 the Herman Elte school, re-named Rosj Pina, opened its doors again. It started with 70 pupils, and by the end of the school year there were over 200. Five hours per week were available for Jewish studies, taught during the regular school hours by the class teachers, while additional classes were provided after school hours (NIW, 11-7-1947). The secondary school called 'Joodse HBS' re-opened in December 1947 (NIW, 15-12-1950). Both schools were and are governed by *JBO* (Foundation for Jewish schools).

It was not easy to convince parents to send their children to the JBO schools. Many associated Judaism only with the tragedy that had befallen their families. The principal of the primary school alluded to these sentiments: 'at a Jewish school, the Jewish child feels at home. We, who were not at home for several years, all know the difference between being at home and not being at home. During the occupation time children perforce lived an abnormal life, let us therefore bring them back into their element, which in the *galuth* (diaspora) is the Jewish day school. Thousands of children have been snatched away from us. Without children the continuation of the Jewish people is impossible. So let us see to it that our few remaining children will grow up to be self-aware Jews' (NIW, 6-6-1947). During the 1950s, the unwillingness of well-to-do and intellectual families to enrol their children in a Jewish day school lessened. At their request, in 1958 the Joodse HBS was turned into a comprehensive school where all types of secondary education were given. The school was re-named 'Maimonides' (Dahan, 1989, p. 7).

Meanwhile, the NIK began the heavy task of re-organising Jewish education outside Amsterdam. Out of the 150 Jewish communities existing in 1940, the majority (90) no longer had an organised structure, while only 12 of the remaining communities were able to provide Jewish classes on their own. A Central Education Committee was founded, its slogan being 'Jewish education for every Jewish child, wherever it may live' (HCC, 29-11-1960). As early as 1946 a written course on Jewish life was published. 'Dear boys and girls, today we will go for a walk to the synagogue. Children from larger towns may have been there before, while those of you living in villages probably have never seen one. So let me explain to you on the way...' The author, David Hausdorff, is sensitive towards the children's background. After 'parents' he adds 'or the uncle and aunt taking care of you'. In the early 1950s, additional courses on Jewish History, Hebrew and Torah were published, while a national curriculum based upon weekly lessons of 1 h was completed in 1956. The focus of Jewish education was no longer religion only, but 'raising children to love the Jewish people, the Jewish culture and Hakadosh Baruch Hu (God)' [Leerplan (1956), p. 3].

By 1952, the Committee had four full-time and eight part-time 'travelling teachers' at their disposal, teaching 278 pupils living in 44 towns and villages (HPC, 1952–1953). Their teachers were 'travelling' indeed. In 1959 Levi Israëls from Amsterdam went on Sundays to Tilburg, on Mondays to Oss, on Tuesdays to Zutphen, on Wednesdays to Oss again while on Thursdays he could be found in Eindhoven. All together, he was teaching 12 h per week, while travelling time by public transport took up another 16 h (HPC, 1959).

Due to the limited number of children living in many locations all over the country, the system of centrally organised Jewish education grew inefficient and costly over the years (HPC, 1962), as confirmed in a report written in 1974 by Joop Sanders, the newly appointed secretary-general of the NIK. He advised undertaking a re-organisation and suggested introducing audiovisual means such as slides, tape-recorders and videos to supplement the lessons (HPC, 1974).

His report pointed out something even more alarming. Except for one, all of the teachers were 65 years or older. One generation after the war, the Jewish community had reached a turning point. While in the first decades after the war the focus had been on individual surviving and basic reconstruction of the community, people were now beginning to understand the long-term consequences of the Shoa for the future of the Jewish community. Those who had run the Jewish organisations after 1945 were getting older, and there was no one to take their place because there were so few of the next generation, children having been so especially vulnerable during the war. A whole generation was missing, causing a lack of teachers, rabbis and community leaders (HPC, 1974). Several Jewish communities, especially those in remote districts became inactive.

A New Generation

Although hundreds of young people had immigrated to Israel (Blom, Fuks-Mansfeld, & Schöffer, 1995, p. 366), it became clear that not everyone would follow suit. Contrary to the expectations in the first post-war years, a Jewish community was going to remain in the Netherlands and the next generation was prepared to invest in its future. The eagerness of these young parents to pass on the Jewish tradition to their offspring led to several initiatives in Jewish education.

Already before the war there had been Reform Jewish communities in Amsterdam and The Hague, most of their members being refugees from Germany joined by a few Dutch families. A Reform synagogue was inaugurated in Amsterdam in 1937 (Brasz, 2006, p. 67), and 60 children attended the Talmud Torah classes there (Brasz, 2006, p. 69). During the Shoa, the *LJG* (Reform Jewish Community) had shared the same fate as all other Jews in the Netherlands, and after liberation the small community had to start again from scratch. The Jewish lessons attracted young Dutch families, and gradually the image of the LJG changed from that of a small group of German refugees to a community rooted in the Netherlands (Brasz, 2006, p. 122). In 1966, a newly built synagogue and a community centre were inaugurated in Amsterdam. Some of those joining the LJG had been members of the NIK, but many newcomers had been unaffiliated.

Further initiatives were taken in the Jewish Community, such as the establishment of three new Jewish day schools. In 1974 a new Jewish Kindergarten called 'the Cheider' began with five children at a private home in Amsterdam. The emphasis was on Jewish studies taught in Yiddish, making it the kind of school Dutch Jewry had not seen in 150 years. The school was founded by ultra-orthodox parents because 'Rosj Pina has become more of a gathering of Jewish children than a Jewish school' (NIW, 25-10-1974). The next year the Cheider began a primary school 'with a ridiculously low number of 4 children' (NIW, 28-2-1975). But even though it was illegal, housed in a squatted building and financed by donations, the school continued to grow and became officially recognised by the Ministry of Education. By

1993 the Cheider, then consisting of both a primary and a secondary school, moved into its own premises. Some of its pupils came from the JBO schools, but most were children of the large families of Rabbis and teachers from abroad appointed as religious leaders by NIK communities from the late 1980s onwards.

Another Jewish day school was established near Amsterdam in 1982 by the LJG, the main reason being the admittance policy of JBO. The Leo Baeck school welcomed children of 'all parents wishing to educate their children in a Reform Jewish way' (NIW, 27-8-1982). Due to a serious conflict among teachers the number of pupils decreased from 60 to 20, forcing the school to close down in 1990 (NIW, 16-11-1990). According to Rabbi David Lilienthal, 'It was the largest frustration and disappointment in my life at that period. We had more than enough pupils, an excellent curriculum, the necessary money and educational materials, but it failed due to unexpected reasons' (Brasz, 2006, p. 270).

A day school was established in Rotterdam, because 'the lessons provided by the Jewish community are not bad, but too few. And Amsterdam is too far away' (NIW, 9-10-1987). Beth Sefer Etgar opened its doors in 1988 with six pupils, aiming 'to strengthen Jewish identity by teaching Jewish history and customs' [NIK archive 31.55]. Due to the limited number of pupils (19) and 'bad luck with teachers' the school closed down in 1992 (NIW, 4-9-1992). Looking back, one of the founding parents commented: 'the project fell apart because honestly said, we were enthusiastic but did not know enough about education. But at least we tried' (van Trigt, 2007, p. 67).

In addition to the day schools, attended by a small minority, both NIK and LJG provided Talmud Torah classes all over the Netherlands. After the professional teachers had retired, these were mainly run by volunteers. Both organisations tried to train their teachers. The LJG even established a special Teacher Training Course in 1982. But most candidates were interested only in furthering their own Jewish knowledge and not in becoming teachers, a problem also encountered by the NIK. Those who did become teachers had to work without a curriculum, choosing their own teaching material which often was developed in Israel. Neither the language nor the contents were suitable for Diaspora children.

At the Jewish primary school Rosj Pina, the class teachers who could teach both secular and Jewish studies retired. After that, children got three different teachers: one for the secular curriculum, a second for Hebrew language and a third for Jewish studies. Especially in the case of Jewish studies teachers, attracting professional teachers who speak Dutch was and continues to be a key problem.

With respect to the education of children outside the framework of the day schools, changes came in 1989 when the NIK appointed a professional educator as its national director for Jewish Education.[3] She began her job by visiting the volunteer teachers to investigate their wishes. They knew exactly what they wanted: 'Ready to use attractive worksheets in the Dutch language with activities on different levels. Something more challenging than a wrinkled old colouring plate' (HPC,

---

[3] In fact the author of this chapter.

1989). By the next year, a series of worksheets on the Jewish holidays had been developed, while teachers were invited to a computer seminar, introducing Jewish software translated into Dutch (HPC, 1990). When the basic material was there, the time had come to develop a curriculum including all of the necessary teaching materials and software. As this type of curriculum was non-existent, it would have to be developed from scratch, turning it into a long-term and expensive project. But with a secretary-general highly involved in Jewish education and new media, and a president who was also the principal of the Maimonides school, the NIK ranked Jewish education as its top priority and gave the green light. The Jewish community of Amsterdam joined the effort and a supporting group was founded, consisting of board members, Rabbis and professional educators, all of them experienced teachers. Looking back, they had something else in common. All were born after 1945 – the new generation of leaders was taking up its position within the Jewish community.

The main aim of the curriculum was set as: 'making a child feel at home in a Jewish setting' (HPC, 1992). Activity booklets on the Jewish holidays and other topics were written for different levels, each introducing the topic from a new angle, while the Israeli books for spoken Hebrew were replaced by methods based upon Jewish keywords and basic texts from the liturgy and other Jewish sources. In 1997 the new curriculum was nationally introduced, used by 178 children (HPC, 1997), growing to 268 in 2003 (Dodde, 2009, p. 223) and to over 300 in 2009.

In 2000 translated versions of the NIK curriculum were introduced in Switzerland, and then in Finland (2001) and Germany (2006), enabling international cooperation in Jewish education. In 2004 the trilingual (Dutch, German and Finnish) website JELED.net went online. The site supports the curriculum with extra material and is a source of educational ideas and exchange for children, parents and teachers living in different European countries. Meanwhile, the LJG, nowadays called Unity for Progressive Judaism, began producing Dutch versions of children's books on Jewish topics and has launched the educational website 'Rimon'.

In 2007, in the still remote province of Zeeland the first child educated with the new NIK curriculum became a teacher herself. Sometimes, miracles do happen.

Cultural Minority

In the 1990s the focus in Jewish self-awareness shifted from the Shoa as the defining Jewish experience to a more general approach to Jewish culture, sparking several initiatives. A new attitude could be seen: 'I will decide for myself whether I am Jewish or not' (van Solinge & de Vries, 2001, p. 112). New communities were established, especially by those who could meet neither the NIK nor the LJG standards for admittance. These developments were made easier by large sums of money made available to the Jewish community by the government and banks as compensation for the financial losses during the Shoa.

In 2009, three Jewish day schools existed in Amsterdam: the two JBO schools Rosj Pina and Maimonides, and the Cheider, consisting of both a primary and a secondary school. All schools have financial problems, mainly due to the limited number of pupils. They very much depend on governmental subsidy, with the comprehensive schools being exceptional in the general school system, because they do not meet the statutory minimum number of pupils.

In addition, Rosj Pina has an identity problem due to the fact that there are three very different groups of parents: first, secular Dutch Jewish parents who want their children to be with other Jewish children, but who are not very interested in either Jewish studies or Hebrew (50%); second, secular Israelis who want their children to learn Hebrew, but not religious subjects (40%); third, the remaining 10% are religious Jewish parents who want the school to stress religious subjects, even in Hebrew language classes. For these traditionally Dutch Jewish parents the Cheider is in many cases not an option because of its separation from the secular world and its emphasis on Eastern European Jewish traditions.

Contrary to the situation at Rosj Pina, Maimonides has always had a Jewish principal who himself has a modern orthodox lifestyle. This has created continuity in the school's approach to Jewish education and has prevented many of the identity problems faced by Rosj Pina. Both Maimonides and the Cheider now offer the possibility of official final examinations in both Modern and Biblical Hebrew, recognised as such by the Ministry of Education, as well as secular matriculation subjects.

In 2009, out of a Jewish population of Amsterdam and surroundings estimated at 25,000, around 770 pupils are enrolled in a Jewish day school (570 at JBO and 200 at the Cheider). Compared with 1938, the percentage of children attending a Jewish school has risen slightly, with the large majority still preferring a non-Jewish school. The reasons people give for not sending children to Jewish schools are the secularisation of Dutch society from the 1960s onwards, as well as the traumatic experiences during the Shoa. The difference with neighbouring Belgium is striking. In Belgium, secularisation is at a similar level, while the Jewish community experienced the same traumas. Nevertheless, almost 90% of the Jewish children in Antwerp, religious or not, attend Jewish day schools. It can be assumed that the former integration policy of the Dutch government and the Jewish community leaders still exerts its influence.

In the twenty-first century, Jews are no longer the only minority and their numbers are insignificant compared to the Muslims. Current government policy is to supervise Muslim schools closely in order to guard against anti-integration tendencies. This policy also affects Jewish schools.

Outside the framework of the day schools, the Talmud Torah classes, provided by NIK, LJG and others, are attended by a mere 200 children in Amsterdam and another 350 all over the country. Although this number is growing, in terms of percentage it is significantly lower than it was in 1938. This low attendance rate of Talmud Torah classes fits in with the fact that out of a total Jewish population estimated at 52,000, only 8,000 are affiliated with a Jewish community (5,000 with NIK and 3,000 with LJG). Reaching out to this large group of unaffiliated Jews will be the greatest challenge for Jewish organisations in the Netherlands in the coming decades. It will be necessary to join efforts across the board, both nationally and internationally, wherever cooperation is possible, building together a twenty-first century 'sound and solid stronghold against thorough assimilation'.

References

Achawah – Maandblad van de Bond van Israëlietische Godsdienstonderwijzers van Nederland
Asscher-Pinkhof, C. (1981). *Danseres zonder benen's*. Gravenhage: Leopold.
Bakker, N., Noordman, J., & Rietveld-van Wingerden, M. (2006). *Vijf eeuwen opvoeden in Nederland*. Assen: Van Gorcum.
Blom, J. C. H., Fuks-Mansfeld, R. G., &Schöffer, I. (Eds.). (1995). *Geschiedenis van de Joden in Nederland*. Amsterdam: Balans.
Boas, H. (2002). *Terug in de Den Texstraat*. Kampen: Kok.
Brasz, C. (2006). *In de tenten van Jaäkov. Impressies van 75 jaar Progressief Jodendom in Nederland 1931–2006*. Amsterdam: Stichting Sja'ar.
Coppenhagen, J. H. (1988). *De Israëlitische 'kerk' en de Staat der Nederlanden*. Amsterdam: NIK.
Dahan, B. (Ed.). (1989). *Van Joodsche Hogere Burgerschool tot Joodse Scholengemeenschap Maimonides*. Amsterdam: JSG Maimonides.
De Joodsche Jeugdkrant (translation: The Jewish Youth Magazine).
Dodde, N. L. (2009). *Joods onderwijs – een geschiedenis over het tijdvak 1200 tot 2000*. 's-Gravenhage: Own Publication.
Fuks-Mansfelt, R. (Ed.). (2007). *Joden in Nederland in de twintigste eeuw – een biografisch woordenboek*. Amsterdam: Winkler Prins.
Gans, M. H. (1978). *Memorboek – platenatlas van het leven der joden in Nederland van de middeleeuwen tot 1940*. Baarn: Bosch & Keuning.
Ghonem-Woest, K. (2007). Voor de roomse jeugd. Geschiedenis van de jeugdboekenfondsen van Zwijsen en Malmberg': Lessen 04
Groften, D. (2007). Asser, Netje. Digitaal vrouwenlexicon van Nederland. http://www.inghist.nl/onderzoek/projecten/DVN/lemmata/data/Asser. Accessed 8 March 2007.
HCC Handelingen van de Centrale Commissie tot de Algemene Zaken van het Nederlands-Israëlitisch Kerkgenootschap (reports).
HPC Handelingen van de Permanente Commissie tot de Algemene Zaken van het Nederlands-Israëlitisch Kerkgenootschap (reports)
Leerplan voor het Joods Onderwijs in Nederland. (1956). Amsterdam: NIK.
Meijer, M. L. J. (2004). *Onderwijs in Amersfoort 1850–1920*. Amersfoort: Bekking.
Michman, J., Beem, H., & Michman, D. (1992). *Pinkas – geschiedenis van de joodse gemeenschap in Nederland*. Ede: Kluwer and Amsterdam: NIK.
NIW Nieuw Israeliëtisch Weekblad (weekly magazine)
Rietveld-van Wingerden, M. (2008). Jewish education and identity formation in The Netherlands after the Shoa. *Journal of Beliefs and Values, 29*(2), 185–194.
Rijxman, A. S. (1961). *A.C. Wertheim – een bijdrage tot zijn levensgeschiedens*. Amsterdam: Keesing.
Stigter, B. (2005). *De bezette stad. Plattegrond van Amsterdam 1940–1945*. Amsterdam: Athenaeum – Polak & van Gennep.
van Creveld, I. B. (2003). *Jong geleerd – drie eeuwen joodse jeugd in Den Haag*. Den Haag: De Nieuwe Haagsche.
van Solinge, H., & de Vries, M. (2001). *De joden in Nederland anno 2000*. Amsterdam: Aksant.
van Trigt, P. (2007). *Een kleine kehilla met de jeroesje van een grote – de geschiedenis van de Nederlands Israëlitische Gemeente te Rotterdam*. Rotterdam: Stichting Historische Publicaties Roterodamum.
Vos, I. (1983). *Vijfendertig tranen*. 's-Gravenhage: Nijgh & Van Ditmar.
Wallet, B. (2007). *Nieuwe Nederlanders – de integratie van de joden in Nederland 1814–1851*. Amsterdam: Bert Bakker.
Weekblad voor Israëlietische Huisgezinnen.

Author Index

A

Ackerman, W., 121, 129–130, 134, 717, 720, 940–942, 1098
Alderman, G., 32, 85, 1107–1108, 1111
Allport, G., 171
Alter, R., 381
Amkraut, B., 597–612
Amson, D., 1206–1207
Anderson, C., 611
Anderson, R., 339, 343–344, 347, 353
Arendt, H., 1218
Argyris, C., 843
Arnett, J. J., 835
Aron, I., 260–261, 325, 543, 651–652, 675, 691–711, 834, 836, 849–851, 855, 908, 914, 1044, 1047, 1049, 1099
Aron, J., 1138
Ashmore, R. D., 192, 194
Ashton, D., 126–127, 549
Asscher-Pinhkoff, C., 1277
Association for Jewish Studies, 132, 659, 660, 665
Astor, C., 1022
Avni, H., 1266–1268

B

Backenroth, O., 337, 355–370, 722, 929
Bailyn, B., 118, 121, 123
Ball, D. L., 920–922, 924, 926–927, 930, 962–964, 968, 975
Ball, D., 952, 977
Bar-Lev, M., 1222
Barton, K., 448, 457
Bateson, G., 50
Batson, D., 171
Bauman, Z., 53, 873, 1165
Bayit, S., 786, 788–789
Beck, P., 204, 515, 753
Bellah, R., 393–394

Ben-Avie, M., 599, 722, 749–764, 769, 775, 948, 960, 1049, 1058, 1100
Benderly, S., 84, 119–120, 124, 133, 379, 384, 940–942, 944, 946–947
Ben-Rafael, E., 195, 422
Benstein, J., 395–396
Berger, D., 566
Berger, J., 344
Berger, P., 272, 543
Berlin, I., 221, 273, 285–287, 297–298
Berryman, J., 302, 309
Bickerman, E., 1160
Bildner, E. S., 817–819, 822
Billig, M., 1017
Bloomberg, L. D., 2, 47, 66, 455
Blum-Kulka, S., 425, 427
Board of Jewish Education (Mercaz), 763, 1131, 1141, 1150–1151
Bolman, L. G., 252–253, 256, 718
Borrowman, M., 937, 944
Boyd, J., 865–867, 869–871
Bransford, J., 955
Brewer, M. B., 192, 194
Britzman, D., 25, 466
Bronfenbrenner, U., 901–902
Bronfman Jewish Education Centre, 1146, 1149–1150
Bronfman, C., 811–812, 814–816, 819
Brosh-Weitz, S., 420
Brown, L. M., 788, 790, 795, 797
Brown, S., 411
Buber, M., 219–220, 226–233, 240, 289, 295–296, 302, 305, 493, 498, 517
Bullivant, B., 271, 274, 1139

C

Cantle, T., 31
Caplan, K., 733, 1064, 1067, 1069, 1074–1076
Carson, R., 397

Chamo, N., 984–985, 992–993
Charmé, S., 8, 163–198
Chazan, B., 8, 11–26, 131, 165, 169, 204, 233, 340, 441–442, 449, 452, 457, 479, 481, 526–527, 615, 674, 693, 713, 768–770, 772, 774–775, 806–807, 810–811, 814–817, 821, 871, 875, 929, 983, 985, 988, 1095, 1098, 1138
Chertok, F., 188, 190, 205, 503, 680, 715, 722, 825, 828
Chouraqui, A., 1209
Cochran-Smith, M., 798, 880, 883, 885, 889–890, 892–893, 918–919, 924
Cohen, D., 755
Cohen, E. H., 189, 499, 515, 519, 615–627, 716, 769
Cohen, E., 335–336, 415, 509
Cohen, G., 132, 447
Cohen, J., 8, 130, 220–224, 226–228, 230, 232, 249, 251, 260, 573, 879, 1155–1156
Cohen, S. M., 165, 170, 174, 185, 187–192, 195, 203–216, 479, 502–503, 542–543, 604, 670, 674–675, 680, 695, 698, 721, 769, 903–904, 906, 910, 912
Cohen, S., 8, 23, 47–49, 55, 95, 825–826, 831
Coles, R., 302, 314–315
Comer, J. P., 750, 755–756, 758–759, 764
Conyer, B., 10, 267–282, 720, 1126–1129, 1138
Cope, B., 1249
Cordal, S., 1017
Cowan, P., 467, 471
Crawford, K. A., 469, 472
Cremieux, A., 1205–1210
Crenshaw, J. L., 373
Csikszentmihalyi, M., 358, 774
Cytryn, J., 953

D

Dahill, L., 1006
Darling-Hammond, L., 953, 955, 959, 962, 965, 969, 975, 1051, 1054–1055
Dashefsky, A., 189–190, 203
Dawidowicz, L., 462, 464
DCSF, 29–30, 33, 37, 39
De Hond, M., 1280
Deal, T. E., 252, 718, 907
Deaux, K., 192–193
Deborah, D. M., 123, 521
Deitcher, H., 541–557, 720, 736
DellaPergola, S., 1185–1186, 1190
Dencik, L., 1162
Denton, M. L., 831, 836, 907

Derrida, J., 285, 291–292, 295
Dewey, J., 31, 72, 88, 238, 268, 271, 287, 290, 325, 331, 356–357, 368, 381, 398, 401, 451, 543, 755–756, 774, 846, 874–875, 918, 942, 945, 961, 964, 982, 985, 1220
DfES, 33–35
Don-Yehiya, E., 1230
Dorph, G. Z., 67, 381–382, 384, 555, 651, 655, 722, 925–926, 938, 959–978
Duman, J., 377–378
Dunner, J. H., 1271, 1275
Dushkin, A., 118–120, 716, 939, 946–947

E

Edwards, D., 1017
Eisner, E., 358
Elkind, D., 172
El-Or, T., 103, 1069, 1073–1074
Elyashevich, D., 1190
Emilia, R., 72, 756
Epstein, A. D., 1243
Epstein, J. N., 581
Epstein, S., 360, 385, 1142, 1146–1147
Erikson, E. H., 22, 104–105, 173, 550, 621

F

Feiman-Nemser, S., 410, 651, 655, 880, 882, 908, 924, 927, 937–956, 959, 963, 969, 981, 985, 993, 1048, 1053, 1056–1058
Felman, S., 465
Ferziger, A. S., 288, 732, 734–735
Feuerman, C., 277
Fishbane, M., 373, 385
Fishman, S. B., 165, 170, 185–187, 203–204, 518, 699, 775, 826, 831, 833, 904–907, 909–911
Fishman, S., 50, 775, 785
Fleishman, J., 806, 814, 822
Flexner, P. A., 2, 901, 1098
Flusser, D., 567
Foster, C. R., 852, 1006, 1011–1013, 1015, 1017
Foster, S. J., 469, 472
Foucault, M., 285, 290–292
Fowler, J., 301–304, 307, 738, 755
Fox, S., 2, 19, 132, 170, 219, 277, 319, 320, 324–325, 331, 356, 360, 379, 769, 809, 864, 917, 924
Fredriksen, P., 565, 567
Freeman, S., 368
Friedman, M., 1063, 1065, 1067, 1069, 1074–1075, 1236
Fullan, M., 256, 258, 260, 821, 845, 849

G

Gamoran, A., 694, 722, 762, 960, 965, 1045–1047, 1049
Gane, M., 1017
Garber, Z., 662
Gardner, H., 358–359, 364
Gardner, W., 194
Gartner, L., 117–118, 120–122, 691, 715
Gitelman, Z., 621, 1184, 1187, 1190–1191, 1193–1196
Gladwell, M., 768, 770
Glickman, C. D., 879, 882–883, 889, 891, 893
Goldberg, M. R., 365
Golden, J., 451
Goldman, R., 172–173, 301
Goldstein, S., 810, 883
Goldstein, Y., 723
Goodman, R. L., 2, 722, 749–764, 769, 775, 901, 1044–1047, 1050, 1098, 1100
Goodman, R., 694, 751
Gordin, J., 1217
Goren, A., 120, 122–123
Gottfried, L., 1005, 1012
Gramsci, A., 289, 392–393, 395
Grant, L. D., 1–4, 128, 159, 170, 203, 279, 485, 507, 535, 546, 549–550, 622–623, 651, 654, 669–687, 698, 904, 929, 982–985, 987, 989–990, 997, 1001–1019, 1196–1197, 1199
Gratz, R., 126
Greenberg, I., 19, 85, 219, 270, 272–273, 275, 662
Gringras, R., 337, 339–353, 485, 929, 981, 988
Grishaver, J., 381, 599
Gross, Z., 1219–1232
Grossman, P., 952, 967–968
Gurock, J., 123–127, 133
Guttmann, J., 220–225

H

Hacohen Wolf, H., 183–198, 1249
Halbertal, M., 375, 410, 1071, 1159–1160
Hall, G. S., 786
Hall, S., 167
Hartman, D., 272, 275, 277–278
Hausdorff, D., 1282
Hay, D., 302, 307–308
Hayman, P., 581
Hegel, G. W. F., 287
Heifetz, R., 253–254, 256
Heilman, S., 51, 131, 366, 710, 769, 929, 1063, 1071, 1075
Helmreich, W., 124, 131, 1070

Herman, S., 22, 170, 173, 193, 625
Heschel, A. J., 78, 219, 287, 396, 402, 566, 754, 956, 1259
Hochstein, A., 501–503
Holtz, B. W., 225, 336–337, 368, 373–385, 552, 555, 710, 718, 762, 926, 959, 965, 967, 981–982, 984
Holzer, E., 375, 407–415, 583–584, 595, 927
Horenczyk, G., 8, 183–198, 621
Horowitz, B., 95, 165, 168, 170, 172
Husserl, E., 295
Hyman Zelkowicz, T., 8, 163–198

I

Ilatov, Z., 1242
Inbar, O., 426
Inbari, A., 340–341, 343
Ingall, C., 91, 93
Isaacs, L., 248, 651, 655, 847, 853, 1041–1060

J

Jackson, R., 2, 564, 571, 573, 1113
Jacobs, H. H., 88, 93
Janowsky, O., 940, 946
Jensen, E., 313, 358
Jick, L., 661
Jones Pellach, P., 1131
Joselit, J. W., 128, 131
Jung, W. S., 717, 1028
Juzwik, M., 465
JWI (Jewish Women International), 789, 790

K

Kahane, R., 624
Kalantzis, M., 1249
Kaminetsky, E., 1023–1024
Kanarek, J., 337, 581–595
Kaplan, M., 119, 124, 133–134, 220, 240, 287, 349, 359, 429, 486, 517–518, 520–521, 691, 730, 753, 762, 794, 910, 939, 941–943, 945, 955, 1066, 1094
Katz, B. D., 671–672, 676, 685, 714, 909
Katzman, A., 324
Kaufman, D., 124, 133, 174, 586, 941–943
Kelman, A. Y., 206–207, 261, 479
Kelner, S., 47–49, 65, 131, 170, 178, 504, 508, 623, 674, 681, 769, 775, 785, 813, 825, 906, 910, 929, 981, 1046–1048, 1051, 1100
Kent, O., 407–415, 927–928
Kesher, 704–705, 709, 835, 1092, 1186
Kessler, R., 737
Keysar, A., 204, 546, 769, 775, 827, 831, 833
Kheimets, N. G., 1243
Kirschenblatt-Gimblett, B., 453

Klapper, M., 127–129, 135
Kleinfeld, J., 585, 590
Kliksberg, B., 1256
Knapp, M. S., 962–965, 975
Knowles, M. S., 872, 988, 991
Kochhar, C. A., 1025
Kohlberg, L., 143, 151–152, 304, 307
Kolel, 675, 1149
Kopelowitz, E., 487, 518–521, 607, 619, 718, 983
Korczak, J., 9, 143–144, 146–157, 159, 302, 308
Koschitzky, D., 1142, 1150
Kosmin, B. A., 204, 546, 552–553, 769, 775, 827, 831, 833, 1162
Krasner, J., 9, 117–135, 170, 379, 446, 449, 457, 938, 1098
Kreitzer, L. J., 1161
Kress, J., 47, 170, 172, 190–191, 581, 599, 651, 654, 694, 697, 948, 1049, 1058, 1100

L

Lamm, Z., 883–884, 890, 892–893, 895, 1220
Lampert, M., 919, 922, 925, 930, 968
Lave, J., 51, 57
Lawton, C., 1116
Lehman, M., 581–595
Leibowitz, N., 382
Leibowitz, Y., 568
Lesko, N., 787, 794
Leven, N., 1206, 1210
Levin, T., 426
Levinas, E., 8, 220–226, 286, 295–296, 566, 618–619, 1209, 1212
Levine, C., 599
Levisohn, J., 95, 938
Levi-Strauss, C., 54
Levstik, L., 448, 457
Levy, D., 1267
Leyser, Y., 1034
Lickona, T., 156
Liebman, Y., 1230
Lifton, R. J., 609
Linsky, M., 253–254, 256, 744
Lippman Kanfer Institute, 259, 854
Lord, B., 967
Lynn-Sachs, M., 696
Lyotard, J. -F., 285, 291–292
Lytle, S. L., 880, 883, 889–893, 918–919, 924–925, 981

M

MacCannell, D., 616, 621
MacIntyre, A., 298, 341

Maitles, H., 467, 471
Malkus, M., 9, 83–95, 411, 555, 718, 722
Marom, D., 2, 19, 170, 219, 277, 320, 324–326, 360, 717, 864, 995, 1242–1244
Martin, E. W., 1024
Martin, R., 1024
Ma'yan, 792–793, 799
Mcdermott, R., 53, 57, 59
McGettrick, B., 1225
McGill University, 1147
McLaughlin-Volpe, T., 192
McLennan, G., 268, 273
McTighe, J., 65, 75
Mead, M., 54, 1246
Mendelsson, D., 9, 1082, 1105–1121
Mendes Flohr, P., 83
Mendlowitz, S. F., 125–126
Meyer, M. A., 441, 446, 598, 661, 664, 752, 994
Mezirow, J., 868, 870–872
Midgley, M., 399
Milgrom, J., 346, 361, 368
Miller, H., 1–4, 8–10, 29–44, 85, 338, 361, 368, 564, 655, 716, 1085, 1108, 1120
Mintz, A., 133, 429, 940, 942, 946
Mintzberg, H., 248
Mittelberg, D., 131, 204, 335–336, 515–537, 619–620, 625, 769
Moore, D. D., 123, 127, 131, 521–522, 719
Mordecai, K., 110, 119, 133, 240, 349, 517–518, 691, 941, 1094
Morris, B., 484
Moving Traditions, 792–794, 796
Muszkat-Barkan, M., 654–655, 879–896, 1001–1018

N

Nemser, S. F., 19, 410, 651, 655, 880, 882, 908, 924, 927, 937–956, 963, 969, 981, 983, 985, 993, 1048, 1053, 1056–1058
Nicholls, J., 865–867, 869–870
Nietzsche, F., 285, 289–290
Nisan, M., 19, 328, 467, 879, 883–884, 896, 982–983, 993, 1002, 1006, 1010, 1017
NJPS, 249, 523, 680, 699, 805, 825, 908, 1042–1043
Nussbaum, M., 325, 348, 350, 582, 594
Nye, R., 302, 307–308

O

Oakeshott, M., 8, 286, 296–298, 331
Oeschlaeger, M., 393
Ofek, A., 76–77, 434
Orr, D., 390

Oser, F., 301, 304
Osgood, R. L., 1022
Osler, A., 37

P

Pajack, E., 883
Parker, M., 672, 909
Parker-Jenkins, M., 35, 44, 1111, 1113
Parsons, G., 1115–1116
Patkin, B., 1127, 1138
Patton, M. Q., 259
Pekarsky, D., 7, 19, 64, 277, 279, 319–332
Peters, R. S., 11, 18
Phillips, A., 365
Phillips, B. A., 825–827
Phillips, B., 479, 697, 710, 825, 828, 903–904, 908
Phinney, J. S., 173, 184, 193
Pilch, J., 122, 135, 939, 948
Piper, D., 868, 870–872
Plaskow, J., 99, 112, 168
Pollack, W. S., 785
Pomson, A., 1–4, 48, 86, 90, 94, 446, 450, 535, 555, 651–652, 713–724, 736, 901, 907, 909–910, 929, 938, 983, 989, 1090, 1147, 1149–1150
Porat, D., 443, 457
Prager, Y., 716, 721, 805, 814
Prell, R. -E., 47, 128, 131, 165, 170, 174, 719, 904–906, 908, 911, 1088

R

Raider-Roth, M., 411
Ratner, H., 1266
Raz-Krakotzkin, A., 484
Reimer, J., 16, 20, 121, 134, 260, 554, 652, 708, 710, 720, 769, 773–774, 778, 805–822, 849, 1050, 1053, 1058
Rein, R., 1265
Reisman, B., 615, 769, 773, 809–810, 983
Resnik, J., 1241–1242, 1249
Rinaldi, C., 72
Ritterband, P., 132–133, 657–659, 662, 667
Rodman, P., 431–433
Rokhlin, Z., 1187, 1191–1193, 1195
Rosenak, M., 7, 16, 19, 219, 233, 237–246, 278, 324, 336, 349, 355, 498, 510, 516, 552, 864
Rosenzweig, F., 220, 566, 683, 1212
Rosov, W., 847, 853, 969
Rotman, H., 1194–1195
Rubel, Y., 189, 1255
Rubin, N., 546, 555

Rubinstein, W. D., 1125–1128, 1130–1131, 1137–1138
Rushkoff, C., 605
Rutland, S., 270, 1125–1131, 1135, 1137–1138

S

Sacks, J. R., 270, 275–276, 298, 373, 562, 735, 1114, 1117
Sacks, K. B., 51
Sales, A. L., 65, 166, 170, 204, 249, 619–620, 769–770, 775–776, 778, 849, 869, 976, 1043, 1094, 1100
Salvador, J., 1207
Sampson, E. E., 53, 56
Sanders, J., 1282
Sarna, J., 48, 83–85, 117, 129–131, 133, 135, 165, 380, 454, 487, 543, 670, 715–716, 723, 807–808, 954, 1151
Sartre, K. P., 1157
Sasson, T., 204–205, 479, 503–504, 527, 619, 680, 953, 981, 983
Saxe, L., 65, 131, 166, 170, 204–205, 479, 499, 503, 526–527, 615, 619–620, 674, 680, 769–770, 775–776, 785, 811, 814–817, 825, 828, 829, 929, 981, 983, 1046, 1048, 1051, 1094–1095, 1100
Schaap, E., 66, 722, 749–763, 827–828, 1044–1045, 1050, 1100
Schachter, L., 76–77, 434
Schama, S., 394
Scharfstein, Z., 120
Schatzker, C., 462
Scheffler, I., 2, 12–19, 23, 25, 87, 219, 277, 295, 320–321, 328–329, 360, 864, 943
Schein, E., 94, 326, 703
Schein, J., 325, 546, 1011
Schick, M., 131, 692, 714, 716, 721, 730, 735, 743, 1024, 1068, 1088, 1092, 1094
Schiff, A. I., 125, 185–188, 429, 713
Schneirer, S., 102, 1073
Schnoor, R. F., 719–720, 901, 907, 1090, 1147, 1149, 1151
Schoenfeld, S., 187, 190, 545, 547–548, 550, 552, 693, 698, 1147, 1150
Schon, D., 257, 982
Schonfeld, S., 1109, 1119
Schuster, D. T., 170, 203, 669–687, 698, 904, 983, 985, 1097
Schwab, J. J., 925
Schwab, J., 18–19, 220, 325, 331, 375, 380–381
Schwartz, D., 1230
Schwartzwald, O., 1224

Schweber, S., 336, 461–476, 1072
Segal, A., 410, 442, 449
Senge, P., 326, 843–846, 849–850, 856–857
Shalom, Y. B., 620, 625–626, 1235–1250
Shamai, S., 268, 469, 1242
Sharon, F. -N., 19, 655, 937–956, 1048
Shenhav, Y., 1241, 1250
Shepherd, K., 1025
Shevitz, S., 69, 251, 257–258, 262–261, 270–271, 280, 651, 694, 696–697, 721, 843–858, 1100
Shire, M., 8, 32, 301–332
Shirky, C., 600–601, 603, 606, 780
Shkedi, A., 722, 879–880, 883–884, 895
Shohamy, E., 421, 424, 426, 428–429, 431
Short, G., 50, 58, 464, 467, 473, 564, 1115
Shulman, J., 583
Shulman, L. S., 375, 382, 582–584, 919, 961, 964, 967
Shulman, L., 506, 617, 952, 955
Silvera-Sasson, R., 680, 953
Silverman, J., 818–821
Simon, B., 1106
Sjostrom, L., 786, 796
Smith, C., 830–831, 833, 836
Smith, M. K., 33, 40, 507, 771–772, 867, 869, 871
Sneh, S., 1266–1268
Solomon, B., 17, 84–85, 302, 450, 555–556
Solomon, G., 1127, 1138
Soloveitchik, H., 124
Soloveitchik, J. B., 90, 125, 219–220, 226–229, 232, 287, 394, 566, 568
Soltis, J., 8, 11–15, 25
Sonntag, S., 348
Sparks, D., 962, 1050, 1052, 1054–1055, 1057
Spolsky, B., 424, 426
Starkey, H., 37
Steiner-Adair, C., 786, 796
Stern, M. H., 102, 124, 126, 130, 808
Stodolsky, S. S., 959–960, 966–967, 969, 972, 975, 981–983
Strauss, L., 110, 227–229

T
Tal Am, 68, 76, 1136, 1138, 1149
Tamir, E., 953
Tanchel, S., 384, 718, 925–926
Taymans, J. M., 1025
Tenenbaum, S., 660, 662
Terman, D. L., 1024
Timothy, D., 615, 622
Tolentino, B. W., 1006
Topel, M., 1255
Totten, S., 462–464

Tucker, J., 368
Turner, V., 541, 546
Tyler, R. W., 64–65, 1223–1224

U
Urry, J., 621

V
Valins, O., 50, 721, 1107, 1110–1111, 1113
Van Gennep, A., 541
Varenne, H., 59
Vos, I., 1280–1281
Vygotsky, L., 72

W
Walzer, M., 269, 271, 510
Wasserman, S., 583, 590, 592
Waxman, C., 732–736
Weber, M., 1223
Wechsler, H., 132, 134, 657–659, 662
Wei, R. C., 962, 1054–1055
Weinfeld, M., 1145
Wenger, E., 51, 54, 57
Wertheim, A. C., 1275
Wertheimer, J., 66, 80, 83, 125, 133, 135, 170, 190–191, 261, 356, 357, 556, 604, 692, 694, 710, 716, 721, 729, 738, 775, 825, 854, 856, 901, 904–905, 909, 933, 1043, 1082, 1084, 1087–1101
West, L. L., 1025
Westerhoff, J., 543, 695
Westley, F., 259
Wiggins, G., 65, 75
Wineburg, S., 442, 456–457, 473, 967
Winzer, M. A., 1021–1022
Witkin, R., 351
World Union of Jewish Studies, 665
Wyschograd, M., 394–395

Y
Yerushalmi, Y. H., 443–445, 447–448, 1042
York University, 126, 449, 758, 854, 1145, 1147, 1150
Yuval, I., 562

Z
Zadoff, E., 1267
Zakovitch, Y., 381, 885, 890
Zeichner, K. M., 798, 879, 883, 918–919, 923, 925
Zeldin, M., 84, 86, 91, 135, 555, 715, 717–718, 949–950, 1042
Zielenziger, R., 379–381, 384
Zimmerman, B., 259
Zunz, L., 657

Subject Index

A

Academic
  education programs, impact on, 797–798, 969, 972
  Hebrew, 424, 426, 428, 430, 435, 941, 943–944
  identity formation, 177, 184–185, 188–189, 442, 653
  North American, 657–667, 671, 813, 1043
  religion and ethnicity, 132–133, 149, 315, 376, 380–382, 445, 626, 709, 714–716, 794, 849–850, 1002–1004, 1009, 1074, 1114, 1116, 1119–1120, 1204, 1227, 1239

Academic Jewish Studies, 657–667

Adolescence, 127, 164, 169, 172–173, 191, 211, 216, 225, 306, 436, 453, 547, 786, 826–829, 835

Adolescents, 91, 129, 173, 184–185, 190, 205, 211, 224–225, 304, 312, 467–468, 502, 516, 547–548, 554–555, 654, 669, 709, 738, 785–799, 825–827, 829–830, 833–838, 1030, 1138, 1213

Adult education, 77, 79, 131, 170, 267, 319, 491, 499, 544, 573, 654, 672, 674, 676, 683, 685–686, 698, 862, 868, 871–872, 904, 908, 912, 929, 932, 1083, 1087, 1170, 1199, 1271

Adult Jewish
  educators, 679, 686
  identity, 24, 165, 170, 189–190, 203–216, 249
  learners, 671, 673–674
  learning marketplace, 679–687
  learning programs, 669–670, 674–679, 685, 687

Advocacy, 135, 151, 327–328, 396, 452, 491, 663, 715, 736, 741, 752, 762, 811, 1012, 1024–1027, 1032, 1034, 1060, 1091

Aesthetics, 220, 242, 348

Agudath Israel, 732, 734, 739

Alliance israelite universelle, 1083, 1205–1207

American Orthodoxy, 731–732, 735, 738, 741–742

Analytic philosophy of education, 11–26, 238–241

Anti-semitism, 134, 289, 292, 464, 468–469, 473, 475, 485, 543, 561, 633, 648–649, 657, 715, 902, 1042, 1127, 1144, 1163, 1172, 1174, 1211, 1256–1257

Anti-semitism and Anti-zionism, 1256

Anxiety, 37, 176, 224, 337, 547, 583, 585, 590, 592, 594–595, 738–739, 1101, 1171, 1212

Argumentation, 414, 461, 583, 585

Arts
  -based school, 355, 362–365, 367, 369–370
  in education, 356–358, 363
  -infused school, 355, 362–365
  integration, 362
  Midrash, 367–368
  skills, 364–365, 369

Assimilation, 41, 55, 58, 121, 123, 127, 157, 163, 429, 444, 481, 484–485, 696, 805, 818, 948, 1042, 1083, 1113, 1125, 1157–1158, 1170–1171, 1206, 1212, 1230, 1258, 1263, 1267, 1271, 1275, 1286

Attentive travel, 506–508

Authenticity, 60, 150, 158, 166–169, 177, 220, 227, 297, 485, 487, 505, 568, 616, 621, 1006, 1160

Autonomy, 69, 87, 93, 189, 240, 244, 269, 286–287, 290, 293–298, 573, 735, 838, 874, 886, 890, 1052, 1058, 1107, 1111, 1121, 1142, 1145, 1150, 1220, 1224, 1226, 1267

B

Baby Boomers and Jewish education, 658
Babylonian Talmud, 1, 109, 374, 507, 581, 583, 594, 997, 1022–1023
Bamah (The House for the Jewish Educator in Buenos Aires, Argentina), 1261–1264, 1269
Bar/bat mitzvah (bnei mitzvah), 203, 542, 545–554, 693–694, 707, 709, 825–828, 830, 833, 837, 839, 904, 906, 910–911, 913, 1046
Bava Metzia 33a, 582, 586, 591–594
Beauty, 109–111, 223, 309, 343, 345, 350, 355, 776, 834
Beit Midrash, 102–103, 107, 114, 374, 407–413, 529, 678, 706, 927, 949, 951, 993, 1004, 1019, 1071–1074, 1160
Beth Jacob, 948, 1073, 1076
Bialik School, 1236, 1240–1242, 1249–1250, 1255–1256, 1258
Bible, 19, 36, 49, 63, 99–100, 104, 106, 111, 128, 229–232, 243, 268, 288–291, 295, 309–310, 314, 319, 336–337, 356, 360–361, 365, 367–368, 370, 373–385, 390–392, 407, 419, 424, 441, 444, 446, 453, 480, 491, 493, 505, 545, 552, 556, 570, 658, 683, 850, 886, 925–926, 928, 930, 933, 940, 942–943, 946, 960–961, 967, 975, 989, 1069–1070, 1072, 1074, 1098, 1108, 1121, 1205, 1215, 1221, 1241, 1243, 1273
Birthright Israel, 22, 170, 205, 250, 256, 499, 503, 508, 526–527, 673, 770, 775, 805, 814–816, 1084, 1094, 1100
Body Image, 653, 788, 795–796, 798
British Columbia, 1143
Bulgarian Jewish community, 1169–1170, 1178
Bureaus of Jewish education (central agencies), 691, 693, 940, 942, 1055, 1101

C

Camping, 130–131, 208, 250, 306, 508, 770, 806, 817–819, 822, 912, 953, 1019, 1084, 1094–1095, 1101, 1168–1169
Canada, 267, 449, 457, 505, 659, 661, 691, 713, 845, 1081, 1084, 1141–1151
Case Studies, 30, 131, 260, 263, 279, 325, 551, 582, 584–585, 594–595, 626, 635, 652, 655, 710, 722, 781, 798, 886, 968, 1139, 1268–1269
Category formation, 270–271
Central Education committee, 1255, 1266, 1282

Central Europe, 129, 634, 657, 713, 1129, 1156–1158, 1163, 1168, 1172, 1177
Challenge, 29–44, 74, 79–80, 326–331, 425–427, 500–501, 590–591, 626–627, 666, 707, 713–724, 735–741, 776, 901–903, 960–961, 1074–1076, 1131, 1135, 1142–1149, 1167–1182, 1190, 1196–1198, 1244–1246, 1253–1269
Challenges and dilemmas in teaching and learning, 1136
Change
 cultural, 327, 394, 822, 1042
 educational, 175, 248, 258–260, 328, 834, 849, 920, 924, 1045, 1100, 1138
 systemic, 601, 794–798
Character education, 128, 379–381
Charedi (Haredi Jewish school), 30, 1107–1109, 1111–1113, 1119–1120, 1186
Chavrusa, 51
Chevruta, 352, 988, 1161
Child development associates (CDA) degree, 753, 763
Childhood, 203–216, 301–316, 749–764
Children, 307–314, 905–910
Choice, 791, 1087–1101, 1212–1214
Christianity, 34, 85, 107, 112, 147, 287, 302, 310, 563–576, 603, 643, 1116–1118, 1205–1206, 1210
Citizenship, 30–31, 33, 41, 83, 90, 113, 153, 287, 336, 442, 448, 450–452, 454–455, 462, 464, 469, 475, 521–522, 582, 644, 947, 1030, 1159, 1273
The Classical Jewish Text Model, 484, 490
The Classical Zionist model, 484–485, 490, 1257
Climate change, 389, 399
Coaching, 879, 881–882, 907, 963, 1005, 1029, 1052, 1055
Code, 49, 102, 215, 330, 343–346, 350, 565, 595, 602, 788, 1207, 1231
Collaborative team teaching, 1031
Collective identity, 183–187, 192, 194, 449, 523, 549, 768–769, 1145
Collective memory, 336, 445, 449, 471, 635–638, 640–641, 643–644, 992
"Committed core" of adult Jewish learners, 675–676
Communal funding, 663, 665, 1121, 1132
Communication, 254, 256, 309, 322, 365, 408, 410, 422, 428, 430, 433–434, 451–452, 466, 469, 497, 529, 551, 562, 597, 599–603, 610, 617, 624, 660, 694–695,

Subject Index

697, 757, 789, 791, 819, 914, 965, 973, 975, 1043, 1076–1077, 1118, 1135, 1142, 1165, 1191, 1218, 1279
Community
    cohesion, 30–39, 41–43, 564
    engagement, 29–44, 564, 1216
    of learners, 254, 797, 851, 1056
    Schools, 84, 131, 279, 451, 743, 948, 1027, 1106, 1138, 1192, 1254–1255, 1260, 1263, 1265–1266, 1268
The Comparative Model, 484, 489–490
Competition, 41, 119, 392, 522, 526, 606, 610, 695, 717, 732–744, 792, 817, 906, 1129, 1147, 1169, 1192, 1217
Complementary schooling, 1042, 1214
Complexity theory, 254, 256, 259
Congregational religious schools, 833, 1042
Congregational (supplementary) schools, 1088–1090
Conservative Judaism, 276, 671, 686, 702, 1012, 1092
Constructivism, 70–72, 756
Consultant teacher/push-in, 1032
Contextual orientation, 383–384, 926
Continuity, 47–51, 56, 58, 92, 100, 120, 196–197, 248, 261, 296, 319, 338, 403, 427, 429, 442, 444, 448, 457, 464, 486, 501–502, 515, 582, 604–605, 607, 669, 699–700, 735–741, 743–744, 754, 758, 806, 809–811, 818–819, 825, 830, 834, 838, 847, 893, 906, 947, 983, 985, 1023, 1030, 1065, 1090, 1119, 1134, 1147, 1150, 1168, 1171, 1173, 1261, 1286
Contract, 78, 135, 295, 517, 680, 971, 976, 994, 1088, 1134, 1142, 1203–1204, 1214–1215
Core concepts, 14, 91–92, 952
Cost, 15, 43, 69–70, 105, 331, 356, 551, 568, 589, 598, 661, 721, 741, 743, 760, 818, 905, 912, 922, 1026, 1029–1030, 1033, 1051, 1075, 1100–1101, 1106–1107, 1111, 1131–1133, 1143, 1146, 1148, 1172, 1189, 1196, 1282
Costs of Jewish Living, 1101
Costs of schooling, *see* Cost
Counter-enlightenment, 285, 287–289
Critical thinking, 9, 330, 337, 364, 369, 392, 411, 442, 453, 456, 470, 583, 585, 590, 592–594, 682, 718, 736, 1006, 1016
Critique, 16–18, 87, 104, 108, 110, 124, 175, 192, 224, 248, 270, 276, 278, 280, 285–288, 292–295, 297–298, 301, 305,

315, 320, 393, 402, 442, 447, 474, 483–486, 492–493, 521, 566–567, 572, 594–595, 753, 846, 851–852, 866, 884–885, 889, 891–892, 894, 919, 923–925, 1027, 1113, 1117, 1184
Cross-communal, 653, 862–865, 875, 1189
Cultural analysis, 48, 54–58
Cultural change, 327, 394, 822, 1042
Cultural competence, 343, 509
Cultural education, 9, 47–60, 144, 150, 394, 986, 1114–1115, 1242
Culture, 47–60, 93–94, 145, 175–176, 340–341, 641–642, 1165–1166, 1237
Curricula, 63–81, 83–95, 432–433, 472–475, 573–577, 788–791, 1097–1099
Curriculum
    analysis, 571, 920
    integration, 83–95, 275, 454, 556

D

Dance, 330–331, 346, 355–357, 359–361, 368, 856, 942, 1094, 1198
Day schools, 83–95, 355–370, 713–724, 729–744, 946–949, 1107–1111, 1126–1133, 1278–1281
DCSF, 29–30, 33, 37, 39
Definitions of education
    descriptive, 13
    programmatic, 13
    stipulative, 13
DeLeT (Day School Leadership Through Teaching) Program, 948–951, 954–955
Democracy, 88, 144, 151, 268–269, 451, 464, 472, 498, 756, 869, 947, 1075, 1223, 1236, 1241, 1250, 1267
Democratic learning, 86, 451, 950
Demography, 38, 486, 500, 599, 610
Dialogue, 41, 50, 54, 56, 58–59, 71, 73, 76, 79, 144, 167, 230–233, 276, 295, 327, 395, 398, 402, 415, 427, 466, 503–504, 517–518, 522, 536–537, 568, 571, 592, 598, 635, 637–638, 643–644, 673, 787–789, 792, 795–799, 817, 820–822, 882, 886, 888–890, 914, 987, 1163, 1243, 1246, 1248
Dialogue between educators and philanthropists, 821–822
Diaspora, 419–438, 527, 534, 618–619, 633–649
Digital, 338, 423, 428, 597–612, 671, 676
Dis-assimilation, 1083, 1157–1158
Disciplines of knowledge, 88–89
Discourse, 275–277, 516–522, 951–952

Diversity, 2–3, 30–31, 33, 42, 44, 57, 86, 114, 189, 191, 197, 269–271, 273, 276–277, 291–292, 368, 391, 393, 470, 509, 520, 566, 573, 658, 661, 663, 666, 721, 732–744, 768, 785, 797, 863–865, 875, 906, 1022, 1026–1027, 1084, 1092–1093, 1110, 1112–1113, 1116, 1120, 1128, 1165, 1195, 1235, 1241, 1269
Diversity of student body, 720

E
Early childhood, 65–66, 68, 70–72, 306, 433, 653, 681, 749–764
Early childhood education, 2, 653, 681, 749–764, 1043, 1046, 1071–1072, 1187
Education, 11–26, 47–60, 65–66, 77–79, 87–89, 99–115, 117–135, 143–198, 203–205, 219–234, 237–246, 247–263, 267–282, 285–298, 319–332, 355–370, 389–403, 428–431, 443–448, 461–476, 479–495, 497–511, 525–528, 536, 541–557, 561–578, 616, 709, 749–764, 767–782, 787–788, 794–798, 805–822, 825–839, 846–851, 879–896, 903–911, 917–933, 944–945, 951–954, 959–978, 984, 1021–1035, 1041–1060, 1063–1077, 1087–1101, 1105–1121, 1125–1139, 1141–1151, 1155–1166, 1167–1201, 1203–1218, 1219–1232, 1237, 1244–1246, 1253–1269, 1276–1277
Educational challenges, 106, 114, 390, 541, 977, 1075, 1136, 1148, 1162, 1173, 1198
Educational choices, 190, 654, 833, 905–906, 1090, 1119
Educational decision making, 905
Educational leadership development, 679, 1006
Educational professionalism, 118–121, 938, 1041, 1170
Educational slogans, 13, 23
Education and Inspections Act 2006, 30, 33, 37, 564
Educators in Jewish Schools Study (EJSS), 1042–1047, 1051–1054
Elite religion, 548
Emancipation, 55, 164, 245, 287–289, 441, 444, 713, 1162, 1205–1207, 1211, 1266, 1273–1275
Empowerment, 550, 606, 787, 790, 797, 799, 830, 865–867, 873, 875, 1161, 1236, 1262

Emunah, 296, 305
Enclave culture, 1064
Enculturation (in contrast to instruction), 543, 696
Enculturation and instruction, 696
Engagement of families in Jewish life, 750, 760
Enlightenment, 83, 164, 245, 285–298, 377, 420, 441, 444, 566, 604, 616, 657, 713–714, 871, 1066, 1208, 1221, 1230, 1273
Enrollment
    day schools, 131, 721, 947, 1082, 1145, 1148
    supplementary schools, 1148
Environmental crisis, 389–392, 395
Ethics, 11, 18, 49, 78, 145, 168, 224, 226, 228, 270, 286, 295, 331, 484, 489, 498, 567, 791, 942, 1070
Ethnic identity, 124, 169, 173, 183–184, 192–193, 195, 427, 546, 646, 717, 1108, 1110
Ethnicity, 38, 43, 145, 158, 173, 184, 517, 609, 626, 1110, 1148
Ethos, 33–36, 51, 90, 143–144, 150–151, 153, 156–158, 225–226, 229, 279, 391, 485, 497, 866, 870, 940, 1087, 1106–1107, 1231, 1235–1236, 1242, 1247–1250
Evaluation, 9, 21, 35, 71, 80, 159, 164, 168, 175, 190, 248, 250, 259, 271, 297–298, 315, 322, 324–325, 329, 331, 408, 430, 437, 495, 502, 520, 527–528, 555, 565, 621, 777, 780, 848–849, 851, 853–855, 882, 922, 929–931, 969–970, 973, 975, 1043, 1055–1056, 1058, 1066, 1139, 1183–1184, 1193, 1200, 1249, 1257
Experiential learning, 509, 511, 651, 681, 773, 775, 807, 850
Experimentation, 173, 176, 178, 253, 262, 603, 700, 710–711, 845, 849, 943, 954, 1058, 1084, 1162

F
Facebook, 25, 681
Faith based school, 33–34, 44, 564, 1145–1146
Faith development, 177, 301–302, 304–305, 756
Faith schools, 30, 33, 35, 37–38, 40, 42–43, 1113–1114, 1120
Feminist theory, 102–105
First language, 393, 419–427, 435–437, 1258
Foreign language, 68, 77, 421–423, 425–429, 435, 1196

Subject Index

Former Soviet Union, 185, 423, 426, 432, 435, 665, 730, 1084, 1147, 1168, 1183–1201, 1236, 1242–1244
Foundation for Jewish Camp, 249, 788, 796, 817–820, 1091, 1094, 1189
Foundations, 443–448, 817–820, 981–982
Four frames, 253, 256
FSU, 1085, 1183–1191, 1193–1201, 1227, 1242–1244, 1249–1250
Functional vs. visionary congregations, 708
Funding, 9, 23, 29–30, 41–43, 66, 69, 80, 135, 190, 250, 499, 508, 659, 663, 664–665, 667, 676, 691, 698–699, 701, 736, 743–744, 808, 810–811, 819, 848, 853, 856, 933, 949, 974, 1024, 1026, 1033, 1058, 1067–1068, 1093–1094, 1099–1101, 1105–1121, 1130, 1132–1133, 1145–1146, 1193, 1195, 1262

G

Gateway to Jewish life, 847
Gender
    difference, 173–174, 585, 617
    issue, 653, 785–799
    separation, 733–734, 1111, 1229
Globalization, 419–420, 422, 425, 437–438, 597, 846, 1084, 1256, 1258–1261, 1265, 1268–1269
Glocal relationship, 520
Godly play, 309
Governance, 285, 759, 764, 907–908
Grammar of (congregational) schooling, 696–697
Grammar of congregations, 696
Grammar schools, 1106, 1108–1111, 1114, 1126

H

Haredi, 378, 408, 627, 652, 729–735, 737–741, 1025, 1063–1077, 1099, 1130, 1148, 1175
Hassidism, 350, 547, 608, 1109
Havruta
    learners, 409–414
    learning, 407–415
    practices, 412–413
Hebraization, 1256, 1265
Hebrew in Diaspora, 428–432
Hebrew for immigrants, 419, 421, 425–427, 437
Hebrew language study, 618, 661, 1265
Hebrew for minority groups, 419, 421
Hebrew for native speakers, 421

Hebrew Teachers Colleges, 655, 938–942, 944, 955
Hebrew University, Melton Centre for Jewish Education, 19, 431, 485, 491, 573, 933, 1135–1136, 1139
Hegemony, 51, 59–60, 290, 391–393, 420, 442, 562, 604, 1238, 1253
Hevruta, 78–79, 352, 890–891, 894–895, 927–928, 951, 970, 988, 1072, 1161
Historical inquiry, 446–448, 456
Historiography, 9, 117–135, 444, 446
History
    education, 336, 441–458
    Jewish, 22, 60, 105, 121, 129, 134–135, 166, 173, 222, 288, 292, 336, 356, 377–378, 390, 441–458, 484, 491, 516, 524, 562, 566, 576, 639–640, 647, 658, 660, 662, 675, 940, 942, 1069, 1108, 1156, 1172, 1180, 1185, 1187, 1193, 1198, 1215, 1274, 1281–1282, 1284
History of
    spoken Hebrew, 379, 420, 431, 438, 943, 1098, 1285
    written Hebrew, 420, 1098
Holocaust
    -based trips, 471
    education, 39, 41, 129, 336, 461–476
Human Authority, 585, 590–594
Humanization, 144, 149–152
Hungary, 469, 666, 1054, 1063, 1165, 1167–1170, 1172, 1181

I

Identification, 8, 22, 53–54, 123, 144, 156–159, 170, 173, 184–195, 197–198, 213, 238, 244, 253, 277, 303–304, 327–328, 429, 442, 445–450, 452, 456–457, 467–468, 473, 486, 505, 511, 516, 527, 550, 607–608, 620, 662, 667, 697, 722, 723, 729–731, 741–743, 755, 827, 861, 884–885, 887, 889, 891–894, 992–993, 1012, 1025, 1082, 1138, 1173, 1222, 1259
Identity
    national, 157, 159, 399, 484, 644–645, 1089, 1230, 1244, 1247
    religious, 29, 52, 157, 169, 302, 304, 568, 603, 607, 626, 736, 833, 990, 1006, 1091, 1162, 1177, 1225, 1271–1286
Ideological education, 1219–1232
Ideological orientation/Ideologies, 174, 470, 879–880, 883, 895, 1135, 1186, 1192, 1220

Ideology, 25, 60, 197, 206, 239–240, 250, 268–269, 271, 277, 289–290, 292–293, 392, 398, 425, 429, 444, 481–482, 490, 493–495, 502, 516, 520–521, 536, 562, 635–636, 654, 713, 735–738, 884–885, 887, 889–895, 906, 940, 989, 1017, 1065, 1074, 1076, 1139, 1186, 1198–1199, 1220–1221, 1225, 1227, 1230–1231, 1237, 1240, 1276

Impact on Jewish identity, 621

Implicit religion (religiosity), 144–149

Independent schools, 30, 361, 704, 1048, 1082, 1106, 1110–1111, 1116–1117, 1119, 1126

Indian Jewish community, 620, 1176, 1181

Influence, 4, 7–9, 13, 18–19, 43, 65, 94, 107, 123, 127, 133, 150, 164, 178, 184, 186–191, 193, 201, 203, 205, 209–210, 213, 215–216, 230, 251, 274, 276, 280, 287–288, 290, 294, 297, 325, 330–331, 342, 347, 352, 374–375, 380–382, 395, 398, 422, 437, 473, 532, 551, 562–563, 572, 576, 597–598, 657, 673, 707, 714, 738, 740, 759, 775, 806, 815–816, 827–828, 833–835, 837–838, 844, 855, 864, 895–896, 903, 905–906, 908, 911–913, 932, 984–986, 988–989, 991, 993, 1011, 1042, 1044, 1052, 1054, 1056, 1059–1060, 1101, 1121, 1145, 1169, 1219–1221, 1256, 1265, 1268, 1276, 1279

Informal
education, 3, 16–17, 20, 22, 41, 120, 185, 190–191, 241, 280, 316, 319, 441, 466, 470
Jewish education, 20, 65, 131, 145, 149, 191, 208, 211, 479, 608, 622, 652, 719, 767–774, 778, 785, 789, 805–822, 826–827, 850, 912, 1045, 1083, 1094, 1096, 1131, 1139, 1188

Infrastructures, 40, 322, 326, 390, 425, 525, 527, 750, 976, 1058, 1065, 1100, 1132, 1168, 1226, 1261, 1263

In-marriage, 206–211, 214–215

Innovations in Israeli Schools, 156, 424, 529–530, 533–534, 576, 597, 619, 1005, 1083, 1137, 1236, 1241, 1243

Inquiry, 12, 50, 54–55, 72–73, 89, 91, 113–114, 117, 123, 126–128, 220, 239, 241, 290, 316, 328–331, 336–337, 375, 381, 409, 441–442, 446–448, 451, 453, 456, 466, 471, 595, 687, 716, 723, 743, 757, 797–798, 850, 857, 894, 913, 918, 924, 966, 970, 974–975, 1002, 1018, 1035, 1048, 1055, 1158

Inspiration, 18, 63, 105, 111, 133, 341, 508, 511, 573, 637–638, 718, 815, 928, 984, 988–989, 991, 993, 1159, 1205

Institute for Informal Jewish Education, 812–814

Instrument, 23, 94, 125, 151, 171, 203–204, 216, 240, 295, 314, 345, 356, 391, 393–394, 421, 431, 485, 494, 528, 537, 555, 624, 645, 693, 713, 771, 776–777, 781, 816, 844, 875, 945, 982–984, 988–989, 991, 993, 995, 1147, 1158–1159, 1180, 1210, 1225

Integration, 9, 17, 30–32, 40–41, 47, 83–95, 121–122, 124, 129, 144–145, 156, 166, 189, 192, 195, 198, 228, 236–237, 275, 419, 427–428, 448, 454–455, 547–548, 551, 555–556, 652, 666, 672, 713–714, 717–719, 723, 762, 798, 1013–1014, 1021, 1023, 1109, 1111, 1113–1114, 1125, 1127–1128, 1137, 1139, 1185, 1187, 1198, 1204, 1210, 1220–1221

Intellect, 40, 51, 78, 83, 86, 101–102, 125, 132–133, 149, 151, 158, 168, 174–175, 186, 188, 221–222, 224, 227, 239, 258, 271, 280–281, 285–286, 289, 326, 328–331, 336–337, 346, 357, 361, 376, 379–380, 393, 396, 411, 442, 445–448, 455–456, 468, 519–521, 574, 593–595, 600, 606, 626, 660, 666, 673, 675, 679, 682–683, 716–717, 723, 735, 816, 834, 865, 874, 883, 920–921, 924, 937, 951–952, 955, 970, 984, 988–989, 991–992, 1010, 1016, 1027, 1043, 1052–1053, 1055, 1065, 1073–1074, 1148, 1157, 1162–1163, 1203, 1211, 1238–1239, 1248, 1282

Intelligence, 153, 254, 358–359, 821, 944–945

Interdependence, 33, 194, 274, 398–400, 411, 519, 536, 822, 1006

Interfaith families, 177, 551, 681, 825–839

Islam, 2, 34, 147, 287–288, 376, 561–563, 565, 569–571, 576–577, 1113, 1115, 1117–1118, 1139, 1170, 1179, 1205

Israel
Education Design, 491–492
Education Studies, 491

Israel engagement, 350, 484–486, 490, 498, 503, 505, 508–511, 981, 983

The Israel Engagement Model, 484–486, 490

Israelite, 34, 107, 231, 311, 373, 441, 622, 1083, 1205–1207, 1209, 1211, 1216, 1274–1275, 1279
Israel studies, 129, 491, 660, 665–666, 775, 1136, 1167
Israel trip, 24, 203, 207, 483, 491, 526, 655, 669, 672–673, 678, 698–699, 720, 769, 812, 817, 926, 929, 972–973, 983–984, 987, 1082, 1094
Italy, 72, 178, 666, 1021, 1163, 1215
Ivrit b'Ivrit, 379, 384, 737, 941

J

JELED, 1285
"The Jerusalem School", 19, 1194
Jesus, 107, 313, 465, 471, 509, 561, 566–569, 574–575, 608
Jewish
    Arab Encounter, 1245
    citizenship, 450–452, 454, 521–522
    culture, 47–48, 50, 57, 106, 117, 120, 130, 145, 176, 186, 188–189, 196, 324, 330, 340–342, 382, 395, 400, 402, 427, 433, 442, 485, 487, 489, 565, 608, 642, 665, 684, 695, 716–717, 808, 861, 884, 887, 889–890, 892, 906, 909, 945, 1011–1013, 1064, 1096–1097, 1128, 1155, 1158–1159, 1161–1162, 1165–1166, 1241, 1282, 1285
    environmental education, 337, 394–398, 400–403
    friendships, 8, 204–205, 209, 215–216, 818
Jewish day school
    community, 718, 951
    conservative, 717, 721, 736
    reform, 556, 717, 1015
Jewish history, 441–458, 468, 484, 491, 524, 535, 562, 566, 576, 618, 635, 639–640, 647, 658, 660, 662, 675, 736, 940, 942, 1069, 1172, 1180, 1187, 1198, 1215, 1274, 1281–1282
Jewish identity
    authenticity, 60, 166–169, 177
    complexity, 197, 473, 607
    components, 158, 183, 185–186
    developmental approaches, 1049
    dissonance and, 166–167, 176–178, 990
    educational cultures, 167, 174–176
    ethnicity and, 173, 1110
    Jewish survivalism, 22, 164–165
    levels, 164
    measurement, 56, 164, 197
    measuring, 164, 186
    pedagogical approaches, 174–175
    space, 183–198
    spirituality, 168–169
    tradition, 168–169
Jewish journey, 639–640, 649, 706, 761, 772, 868–869, 875, 910
Jewish life, 1–3, 7, 20, 23, 40, 48, 59, 63–64, 67, 70–71, 74–76, 79, 83–85, 108, 113–114, 145, 159, 163–166, 170, 174, 177, 188, 216, 240, 243–246, 249–250, 278–279, 286–287, 289–293, 298, 306, 319–322, 324, 326–327, 329–332, 335, 340, 342, 359, 378, 385, 395, 400, 429, 441–442, 447, 449, 451, 454, 475, 480, 482–486, 488–490, 495, 497–498, 501, 503, 505, 507–511, 516, 518, 530, 541–557, 576, 596–598, 602–605, 607, 610, 612, 633, 638, 669–670, 673–674, 676, 679, 684, 705–706, 717, 754, 759–762, 808, 826–827, 834, 847, 938, 1010, 1013, 1082, 1090, 1093–1096, 1099, 1147, 1155, 1157, 1159–1160, 1164, 1173–1175, 1178, 1194, 1197, 1215, 1280, 1282
Jewish literacy, 70, 78, 102, 163, 177, 536, 669–670, 673–676, 682, 716, 945–946, 950, 1099
Jewish Movements, 657, 1063
Jewish Peoplehood, 335–336, 449, 484, 486, 490, 515–537, 620, 635, 863, 989, 993
The Jewish Peoplehood Model, 484, 486, 490
Jewish philanthropists, 651, 658, 806, 811, 817–818, 821–822
Jewish setting, 74, 129, 178, 243, 466, 473, 505, 553, 686, 769, 780, 1034, 1047, 1285
Jewish social networks, 8, 187, 204–216, 669, 672
Jewish studies (higher education), 132–134, 653, 657, 666, 1057
Jewish summer camps, 22, 24, 170, 255, 485, 616, 618, 620, 622–623, 625, 769–770, 772, 776, 807, 810, 817–818, 822, 853, 909, 912
Jewish Texts, 1, 41, 49, 51, 67, 76, 90, 100–102, 105, 128, 164, 173, 230, 341, 365, 368, 407, 411, 413, 415, 430, 436, 488–490, 494, 567, 574, 582, 584, 603, 661, 682, 714–716, 718, 789, 791, 794, 797, 849, 891, 950–951, 1011, 1035, 1042, 1096, 1148, 1157, 1164, 1186, 1193, 1249

Jewish travel, 306, 335, 500, 507–508, 618–619, 625–626, 633–649, 769
Joint Distribution Committee, 1096, 1168, 1185, 1189, 1254
Judaism, 122–124, 163, 221, 223–227, 243–246, 395, 401–402, 517, 543, 565–566, 570, 582, 603–605, 619, 681, 698, 705, 719, 791–792, 887, 941, 948, 991, 1015, 1063–1064, 1071–1073, 1076–1077, 1117–1119, 1130, 1133, 1147, 1159, 1196–1197, 1200, 1209, 1259–1260, 1281–1282, 1285
Justice
 education, 144, 156
 social, 33, 167, 452, 509–510, 605, 706, 1019, 1052, 1250, 1259

K

Kedma School, 1236–1240
Keshet School, 1236, 1246–1248
Kipen, Israel, 1128

L

Landlord, 986, 988–990, 996, 1143
Language and literature, 505, 510, 658, 661, 940, 1160–1161
Leadership development and adult Jewish learning, 670, 684–685
Learning
 and development outcomes, 751
 organization, 651, 843–858
Liberal Judaism, 224
Liberal and radical feminism, 113
Literary criticism orientation, 383
Literature
 education, 84, 410, 442, 462, 465 472
 jewish, 312–314, 336, 510, 595, 1099
Liturgy, 147, 309, 548, 704, 857, 942–943, 991, 1285
LJG (Reform Jewish Community, Netherlands), 1283–1286
Lost objects, 586–587, 591–592, 594

M

Maimonides Jewish comprehensive school, 457
Management, 35, 60, 759, 764, 866, 904, 945, 950, 955, 1016–1017, 1032, 1239
Market conditions, 744
Marketing perspective, 815, 817
Maturity, 222–224, 226, 309, 425, 502
Meaning
 jewish, 95, 165, 495, 503, 543, 807, 993

 personal, 169, 171, 280, 358, 368, 409, 542, 669, 673, 682, 836, 893, 947, 993, 1117
Media, 44, 357, 385, 420, 423, 427, 435, 472, 482, 491, 569, 598, 600, 602–603, 605, 671, 674, 676, 767, 770, 779–780, 787, 791, 921–922, 1098, 1285
Melton Bible Curriculum, 380–381
Mentoring, 69, 369, 654, 685, 739, 862, 879–896, 1010, 1051, 1053, 1055, 1057–1058
Midrash, 1, 102–103, 107, 114, 174, 280, 288, 291, 311–312, 346, 367–368, 374, 376–377, 385, 402, 407–415, 451, 488, 529, 595, 684, 706, 926–927, 951, 991, 993, 1004, 1019, 1071–1074, 1160
Mifgash/encounter, 526–527
Migrant workers, 1236, 1240
Mimetic vs. transformative education, 374, 961
Miracles, 78, 229–232, 438, 638, 946, 1285
Mitnagdim, 1066–1067
Modern Orthodox, 84, 87, 102, 106, 123–125, 287–288, 568, 608, 692, 730–741, 791, 953, 1084, 1129, 1133, 1219, 1225, 1231, 1260, 1286
Montreal, 811, 1084, 1143–1150, 1231
Moral education, 16, 144–145, 152–156, 241, 718
Moral inclination, 312
Motivation to learn, 551
Multicultural education, 394, 1114–1115, 1242
Multiculturalism, 57, 268, 427, 562, 564, 646, 716, 1110–1112, 1114, 1116, 1120, 1129, 1144, 1149, 1156, 1213, 1235, 1241, 1250
Multidimensional model, 195, 197
Multidisciplinary, 88, 337
Multiple Identity, 518, 609
Multiple intelligences, 358
Music, 39–40, 130, 186, 188, 257, 306, 310, 340–342, 346, 355–361, 363–367, 422, 454, 480, 491, 644, 684, 733, 755, 869, 942–943, 990, 1026, 1067, 1194, 1198, 1229
Muslim schools, 1112–1114, 1286

N

NAA, 779, 810–812
National Curriculum, 33, 37, 39, 301, 304, 468–469, 1113, 1115, 1117, 1277, 1282
Nationality, 517, 522–523, 527, 609, 615, 617, 621–622, 1197, 1205, 1211–1212, 1229, 1274, 1279

Subject Index

National Jewish Population Study, 207, 522, 670, 673, 675, 695, 699, 740, 947, 1090
National sovereignty, 286, 293, 297–298, 510, 1273
Network
  Jewish, 189, 203–216
  social, 8, 32, 186–188, 204–216, 261, 474, 518, 524, 551, 605, 607, 669, 672, 675, 681, 780, 867, 1257
Neve Shalom, 1236–1237, 1244–1247, 1249–1250
NIK (Dutch Israelite community), 1275–1276, 1282–1286
Normative philosophy of education, 238–240
Norms, 4, 17, 32, 95, 107, 127, 154, 166, 176, 228, 233, 238–239, 242, 269, 392, 394, 411, 414, 420–421, 434, 444, 543, 548, 552, 562, 573, 602–603, 720, 733, 739, 786, 812, 902, 906, 908, 913, 928, 965–967, 1043, 1069, 1081, 1133, 1203
North Africa, 286–287, 441, 469, 619, 1209, 1211–1214
NPIK (Dutch Portuguese Israelite Community), 1275

O

Observer, 122, 206, 319, 471, 529, 622, 735, 739–740, 869, 876, 929, 937, 946, 986–988, 996, 1101
Ontario, 845, 1142–1143, 1145, 1150
Organizational change, 718, 759
Organizational structure, 687, 1219, 1225–1226, 1229, 1267
Organized anarchies, 251, 256
Orientations
  ideological, 174, 470, 879–880, 883, 895, 1135, 1186, 1192, 1220
  mentoring, 887, 889–895
Orthodox Jewish education, 23, 1084, 1106
Orthodox Judaism, 85, 275–277, 288, 864
Orthodoxy, 102, 114, 123, 125, 286–289, 291, 296, 652, 731–739, 741–742, 744, 1074–1075, 1108, 1127, 1177, 1196, 1198, 1213–1214, 1217, 1253, 1255, 1260, 1275
Outcomes
  developmental, 751, 754, 761, 763
  educational, 183–187, 195, 332, 888, 1051, 1235
  identity, 8, 174, 203, 205–207, 215
  student, 70, 135, 655, 965, 975, 1030, 1032, 1054, 1056–1060

P

Paideia, 1083, 1156–1162, 1164–1165
Paraprofessionals, 673, 1032–1033
Parental expectations, 914, 1090
Parenting, 589, 606, 673, 681, 740–741, 904, 908, 1064
Parent school involvement, 908, 913, 1034
Parshanut, 381
Particularistic, 57, 268–269, 278, 304, 390, 563, 649, 659, 664, 1224, 1230, 1241
Patriarchal cultures, 101, 105, 107
Pedagogical content knowledge, 337, 883, 891, 895, 919–920, 928, 961, 964–965, 967, 972–974
Pedagogies
  of contextualization, 1007, 1011–1013, 1015, 1017
  of formation, 1006, 1013–1015
  of interpretation, 1006–1007, 1015–1016
  of performance, 1007, 1016
PEJE, 249, 852, 854, 1022, 1024, 1026, 1091
PELIE, 700–701, 705, 1091
Pendulum Theory, 981, 1254, 1268
Peoplehood, 166–167, 191, 220, 335–336, 484, 486–487, 490, 501, 515–537, 607, 634–647, 863, 989, 993
Personal autonomy, 269, 287, 298, 735
Personalism, 222–223
Personnel in Jewish Education, 1041–1060, 1088
Phenomenology of religion, 572, 575
Philanthropy, 20, 543, 551, 664, 670, 673, 776, 805–822, 853, 1090, 1101, 1207, 1263
Philosophy of Israel Education, 491
Pilgrim, 507, 987, 990–992, 995–996
Pilgrimage, 178, 470, 488, 507, 511, 615, 617–620, 622, 642, 776, 990–992
Place, 357–358, 399–400, 431–432, 543–544, 639, 965, 985–987
Planning, 92–93, 247–263, 551, 1029
Plato, 238, 294, 296, 328, 1238
Pluralism, 267–282, 562–563, 1012–1013, 1087–1101
Policy, 551, 976–977, 1056–1059
Posek, 890–891, 893–895
Post bar/bat mitzvah, 551, 707, 709, 825–828, 830, 833, 837, 839
Post-communist communities, 1173
Post-enlightenment, 286, 295–298, 657
Post-Zionism, 292, 463

Practice, 11–26, 29–44, 47–60, 63–81, 83–95, 99–115, 117–135, 143–159, 163–178, 183–198, 203–216, 219–234, 237–246, 247–263, 267–282, 285–298, 301–316, 319–332, 350–351, 483–492, 503, 520–521, 843–858, 968
Practitioner Enquiry, 654, 917–933
Praxis, 10, 18, 59, 247–263, 267, 279, 798–799
"Praxis" planning, 8, 257–263
Pre-kindergarten, 750–751, 763
Pre-service, 381, 436, 471, 474, 654, 880, 1028, 1047–1048, 1050–1051, 1053, 1059
Private Jewish foundations, 809
Private school, 42, 95, 125, 261, 716, 721, 754, 905, 1035, 1068, 1082, 1126, 1130, 1132–1133, 1193, 1203–1204, 1235, 1274, 1276
Professional development, 68–69, 777–779, 794–795, 880–885, 922–923, 959–978, 981–997, 1053–1056
Professional identity, 655, 1001–1003, 1005–1008, 1010, 1012–1013, 1017–1018, 1139
Professional learning community, 951, 985, 1058
Professional preparation, 930, 937, 944–945, 952, 955, 960, 1002–1003, 1007–1008
Progressive education, 84, 124, 129, 415, 756
Protestant schools, 1143
Psychoanalytic, 465–466
Public school, 84, 118, 121, 123–124, 188–189, 356, 358, 421, 450–451, 461, 471, 552–553, 563, 693–694, 696, 710, 715–717, 719, 721, 751, 758, 786, 830, 846, 886, 905–906, 913, 940, 944, 949, 1001, 1004, 1014, 1019, 1025, 1034, 1045, 1048, 1050, 1052–1054, 1126, 1142–1146, 1235, 1243

Q
Quality indicators, 752–753
Quebec, 1142–1143

R
Rabbi-educator, 655, 1001–1018
Rabbinic commentary, 111, 377, 380
Rational planning, 248, 251–253, 256–257
Rav-U-Moreh, 890–895
Readiness, 222, 226, 262, 410, 751, 895, 1162, 1248
Reciprocal relationship, 525
Recruit/Recruitment, 50, 132, 232, 247, 249, 254, 380, 501–502, 551, 617, 623, 625, 654–655, 707, 714, 720, 741, 751, 812, 814, 816, 849, 866, 937, 942, 949, 951–953, 1041, 1044, 1046, 1048–1052, 1057, 1059, 1087, 1091, 1099, 1100, 1133, 1135, 1194, 1203–1204, 1213, 1266
Reflection, 8, 19, 48, 55, 89, 111, 147, 156, 222–223, 228, 237, 242–244, 257, 260, 304, 308, 320, 367, 475, 504, 532–533, 585, 598, 601, 609, 634–635, 675, 738, 751, 756–757, 767, 774, 791–792, 795, 797–799, 835–836, 850, 854–855, 880, 896, 914, 921, 923–924, 926, 928, 930, 948, 955, 966, 990, 993, 996, 1005–1006, 1016, 1076, 1097, 1147, 1155, 1157, 1164, 1171–1181
Reflective practitioner, 257, 501, 505, 919, 923, 1016
Reform Judaism, 68–69, 74, 76, 276, 671, 673, 675, 697, 702, 717, 785, 788, 826, 827, 836, 854, 1198, 1200, 1259
Reggio Emilia, 72, 756
Relationships, 29, 31–33, 41, 59, 72, 86, 91, 93, 100, 105, 113–114, 144, 147, 151–152, 155–156, 174, 184, 193, 195, 206, 216, 243, 252, 259, 270, 276, 411, 414, 437, 463, 474, 505, 520–522, 524–525, 528–529, 532–533, 536–537, 591, 598, 608, 638, 663, 667, 722, 755, 757–759, 764, 786, 788–792, 794–795, 798–799, 806, 810, 829, 831, 833–837, 844, 866–867, 871, 881–882, 890, 894, 901–903, 906, 918, 963, 966, 985–986
Relativism, 272, 283, 329, 1260
Religious development, 301–302, 304, 315–316, 447, 550, 638
Religious education, 563–565, 571–573, 1105–1121, 1219–1232
Religious experience, 172, 223, 226, 228, 306, 603, 926
Religious selectivity, 1228
Religious Zionism, 288, 491, 736–737, 1121, 1223, 1225, 1229–1230
Republic, 666, 723, 1168, 1203, 1205, 1212, 1272–1273
Research, 80–81, 131, 183–198, 279–281, 323–326, 358–359, 369–370, 410–415, 437, 456–458, 503–504, 544–548, 687, 710–711, 721–724, 781–782, 799, 838–839, 875–876, 896, 994–996, 1002–1004, 1033–1035, 1149–1151, 1190–1193, 1265–1269
Resilient youth, 654, 838–839

Subject Index 1305

Resource room, 741, 1026, 1030–1031
Responsibility, 33, 63, 67, 110, 115, 119, 135, 143, 175, 188, 224, 226, 253, 267–269, 296, 298, 306, 312, 359, 398–399, 412, 435, 463, 466, 469, 472, 491, 509–511, 520, 522, 543, 545, 548, 551, 561, 637, 643–644, 666, 669, 707, 719, 736–737, 751, 754, 785, 790, 830, 866, 875, 882, 889, 892, 906, 909, 921, 938, 950, 991–994, 1013, 1018, 1023, 1028, 1031, 1042, 1069, 1101, 1118, 1126, 1158, 1168–1169, 1181, 1193, 1195–1196, 1203, 1216, 1225, 1229–1230
Restructuring the religious school, 1217
Retention, 70, 358, 365, 654, 826–829, 948, 953, 1044–1045, 1049, 1050–1053, 1055, 1057, 1059, 1100
Revolution, 14, 50, 83, 100, 102, 132, 150, 192, 286, 296, 379, 381, 390, 510, 597–612, 691, 713, 723, 1022, 1043, 1160, 1206–1207, 1227, 1241, 1246
Rewrite ceremonies, 107, 552
At-Risk Youth, 787
Rituals, 57, 101, 106, 112, 125, 146, 149, 164, 167, 169, 174, 177, 186, 203, 206, 211, 215, 269, 304, 306–307, 312, 314, 400, 430, 471, 507–508, 541–557, 572, 611, 666, 679, 681–682, 735, 777, 786, 861, 902, 909–912, 991, 1072, 1110, 1115, 1135, 1162, 1174, 1206
The Romantic/Realist Model, 225, 484, 487, 490
Rosj Pinah Jewish primary school, 1284

S
Scheduling, 92–93, 254, 356, 454
Scheffler, Israel, 5, 8, 11–17, 19, 23, 25, 87, 170, 219, 277, 295, 320–321, 328–329, 360, 864, 943
Schein, Jeffrey, 671, 681, 683, 685–686, 703, 1005, 1011
School(s)
 choice, 716, 721, 751, 906
 culture, 74, 77, 89, 93–94, 280, 448, 537, 741, 880, 966, 1011, 1030, 1049, 1056–1058, 1235
School Twinning Partnership, 528–529, 531–532
Science and religion, 397–398
Second language, 76, 365, 392–394, 419, 421, 425–427, 434–435, 437, 1135, 1150, 1265

Secular, 1, 19, 29, 32, 43–44, 83–85, 90, 100, 102, 123, 125, 131, 164, 166–167, 206, 219, 273, 280, 286–287, 289, 291, 306, 340, 345, 356, 377–378, 391, 394, 397, 408, 445–446, 454–455, 480, 488, 491, 493, 500, 518, 564, 576, 607–608, 620, 623, 653, 657, 662, 698, 705, 717–718, 736, 738, 740, 758, 763, 818, 888, 893, 905, 908, 939, 943, 946–948, 988–989, 1004–1005, 1012, 1019, 1021–1022, 1042, 1066–1067, 1083, 1109, 1126, 1128, 1131, 1139, 1147, 1186–1187, 1192, 1197, 1209, 1211, 1214–1217, 1219–1222, 1224–1250, 1253–1255, 1259–1261, 1266–1267, 1272, 1278, 1284, 1286
Secularisation, 1177, 1286
Secularism, 563–564, 1115, 1162, 1203, 1205, 1213, 1248
Secularization, 422, 562–563, 1042, 1230
Secular studies, 43, 83–84, 102, 391, 714, 939, 1047, 1147, 1221, 1225–1228, 1231, 1247, 1254
Selection criteria for schools, 760
Self-directed learning, 872, 991
Self study, 556, 918–920, 922
Seminaries
 Hebrew Union College, 133, 664, 778, 835, 849, 948–949, 954, 1003
 Jewish Theological Seminary, 19, 65, 133, 379, 411, 556, 655, 778, 795, 798, 834–835, 928–929, 939–944, 975, 1003, 1058
 Yeshiva University, 102, 126, 133, 272, 734–735, 742, 788, 791, 809, 940, 1021
Separate-sex education, 787–788, 791
Sex Education, 787–788, 791
Sexuality, 9, 110, 653, 785, 787–789, 797–798, 863, 1069
Shabbat Community, 703–704, 707
Shared vision, 31–32, 528, 844, 849, 852, 952
Shevach Mofet School, 1242–1243, 1248, 1250
Shoah/Holocaust, 40, 463, 467–470, 473–475, 616–620, 625, 713, 1081, 1085, 1137, 1205, 1212, 1244
Shortage of teachers and educators, 709–710
Skepticism, 250, 286, 289, 291, 585, 594, 925, 937, 946
Social capital, 31–33, 40, 518, 520, 525, 536, 866–867, 1216
Social criticism, wonder, 289, 396, 402
Social innovation, 259

Social pedagogy, 152
Social psychology, 21, 192
Socrates, 328–329, 582, 594, 1238
Spiritual development, 301–307, 316, 573, 956
Spiritual guidance, 994, 1011–1012, 1177
Spirituality, 8, 168–169, 177, 186, 220–221, 223–225, 233–234, 301–302, 304–311, 315–316, 356, 360, 364, 367, 369–370, 408, 542, 549, 572, 608, 620, 680, 684, 719, 736–737, 861, 904, 990, 1011, 1014–1015, 1018, 1035, 1118, 1209
Spiritual Renewal, 314, 1084, 1259–1260, 1269
Spontaneity, 223, 225, 309
Sputnik, 88, 379
State Religious Education, 1083, 1219–1232
Student enrollments, 132, 1045
Successful schools, 835
Supervision, 362, 812, 852, 879, 881–882, 885, 941, 1009–1010, 1029, 1032, 1057, 1083, 1113, 1215, 1262, 1265
Supplementary schools
 congregational schools, 65–66, 69–70, 461, 468, 485, 544, 691–699, 701, 707–708, 772, 791, 846–847, 852, 929, 948, 960, 971, 983, 1004, 1042–1045, 1047–1050, 1054–1055, 1060, 1088, 1150
 Khayders, 119
 Sunday schools, 60, 120, 127, 189, 379, 696, 1042, 1185, 1188, 1190, 1192, 1195–1196, 1198, 1200
 Talmud Torahs, 119, 123–124, 655, 691, 694, 938–941, 1213
Supreme Council for Israelite affairs, 1274
Symbols, 252, 291, 296, 303–304, 392, 429, 546, 622, 642, 644, 1244–1246
Synagogue, 22, 34, 38–40, 74, 111–112, 124, 130, 164, 171, 186–187, 191, 196, 206, 208–214, 250–252, 254–256, 260–261, 269, 287, 306, 341, 429, 491, 532, 537, 542, 546–548, 550–553, 604, 607, 609, 611, 634, 639, 641–645, 647, 654, 669–671, 675–679, 681, 684, 686, 691, 693–696, 698–711, 719–720, 741, 790, 794–795, 799, 809, 826, 828, 832, 834, 836–837, 839, 847, 852, 856–857, 863–864, 905, 908, 911, 932, 962, 973, 975, 1032, 1042–1043, 1055, 1064, 1084, 1088–1089, 1092–1093, 1096–1097, 1101, 1107–1108, 1111, 1113, 1143, 1147–1150, 1170, 1173–1175, 1178, 1183, 1185, 1187, 1190, 1200, 1203, 1206, 1211, 1226, 1256, 1259, 1271, 1276, 1281–1283
Synagogue and/or religious school transformation, 74, 254, 710
Systematic change, 242, 685, 923
Systems thinking, 844, 852
Szarvas international Jewish camp, 1168–1169

T
Talmudic prohibition, 101
Talmud Torah, 22, 63, 84, 119, 121, 123–124, 208, 378, 655, 691, 694, 696, 708, 938–941, 954, 1025, 1072, 1144, 1203, 1213, 1275–1278, 1280, 1283–1284, 1286
Teacher
 education, 379, 383, 385, 412, 506, 584, 595, 794–798, 922, 927, 937–939, 941, 944–946, 948–949, 951–956, 960, 1041–1060
 efficacy, 1028–1029
 training, 19–20, 39, 103, 134, 435, 469, 475, 529, 652, 696, 700, 739–741, 879, 881, 896, 938–940, 943, 1029, 1044, 1057–1058, 1064, 1074, 1076, 1100, 1134, 1139, 1147, 1189–1190, 1198–1199, 1209, 1213, 1231, 1236, 1266, 1284
Teachers Institute, Jewish Theological Seminary, 133, 655, 939–944
Teachers' professional development, 879–880, 889, 891, 896
Teaching
 Hebrew, 76–77, 365–366, 424–427, 430–437, 707, 939, 946, 967, 1149
 Jewish history, 336, 442–443, 456, 576, 1284
 and learning, 1, 3, 9–10, 19, 79, 86–87, 335–649, 655, 772, 851, 855, 857, 883, 928, 949, 951, 953, 955, 961–964, 966–967, 969–971, 974–975, 981, 1013, 1041, 1056–1058
 team, 91–92, 363, 686, 1031–1032
Technical and adaptive challenges, 253
Technology, 3, 41, 50, 67, 70, 86–87, 227–228, 244, 251–252, 337, 378–379, 408, 422, 438, 474, 509, 526, 575, 597–612, 683, 740, 780, 843, 921–922, 928, 930, 1026, 1033–1034, 1050, 1058, 1221, 1226, 1258
Technology in adult Jewish education, 77–79, 684

Teenagers, 41, 76, 469, 551, 610, 635, 739–740, 825–839, 910, 926, 929, 1189, 1216
Textbooks, 67, 103, 120, 128–129, 346–347, 357, 379, 384, 442, 446, 450, 463, 472, 474, 476, 576–577, 662, 1088, 1098, 1121, 1135, 1193, 1195, 1215
Text-centered, 124–125, 1160–1162
Textual Authority, 585–590
Theme-based learning, 89–91
Theology, 112, 177, 220, 228, 271, 305, 309–310, 314–315, 444, 552, 675, 928, 930, 1002, 1065–1066
Theology of childhood, 310, 314–315
Theories of change, 845
Torah, 1, 22, 34, 65, 74–76, 85, 90, 100–102, 104–105, 108, 119, 121, 123–126, 133, 164, 208, 225, 245, 268, 272, 309, 311, 314, 324, 341, 352, 360, 368, 373–378, 395, 420, 428, 444, 454, 488, 497, 550, 565, 567, 570, 586–587, 589, 616, 655, 682–684, 691, 693–694, 696–699, 706, 708, 717, 735, 785, 791, 826, 834, 838, 862, 892, 938–943, 948, 950, 988, 1008, 1022–1023, 1025, 1063–1066, 1068–1070, 1072–1074, 1077, 1098, 1109, 1111, 1113, 1136, 1144, 1148, 1163, 1177, 1198, 1200, 1203, 1213, 1221, 1224, 1228–1229, 1260, 1275–1278, 1280, 1282–1284, 1286
Torah Im Derech Eretz, 1213, 1221, 1228
Torah U'mesorah, 67, 126, 544, 729, 731, 733, 739, 948, 1068
Toronto, 451, 457, 675, 721, 862, 1084, 1141–1151, 1231
Tourism, 177, 470, 497–498, 501–502, 504, 507, 615–616, 618, 620–621, 623–627, 634–635, 655, 983–984, 990
Tradition
 Hebraist, 713
 Islamic, 577
 Jewish, 1, 76, 103, 105, 107–108, 167–169, 175, 196, 220, 226, 230, 251, 278, 287, 337, 341, 344, 352, 377, 394–395, 402, 482, 489, 516, 566, 581–582, 584, 594–595, 601, 674, 777, 791, 829, 847, 855, 888, 1010, 1015, 1163, 1193, 1229–1230, 1283, 1286
 Mimetic, 374, 961
 Peshat, 381

Rabbinic, 290, 311, 337, 381, 567, 595
Schwab, 381, 383
Socialist, 713
Training Educational Personnel, 501, 1101, 1257
Transformative learning, 509, 817, 850, 861–876, 962
Translation, 64, 67, 111, 115, 154, 220, 226–233, 321, 325, 344, 383, 422, 429, 487, 555, 587, 982, 1005, 1011, 1186, 1200
Transnational relationship, 525, 537
Travel, 22, 73, 170, 177, 306, 328, 335–336, 482, 497–511, 530, 615–627, 633–667, 673, 719, 769, 772, 811, 868, 924, 990, 1137, 1164, 1244
Tuition subsidies, 1146
Turkish jewish community, 1170, 1179

U
UK, 30, 32–43, 341, 347, 469, 633, 653, 665, 671, 862, 864–865, 876, 923, 987, 1081–1082, 1114, 1118, 1146, 1165
Ultra-Orthodoxy, 286–288, 291, 296, 1214, 1253, 1255, 1260
Underlying operating system, 761–762
Understanding by Design, 65, 68, 74–76, 80
Universalistic, 282, 305, 462, 474
Universities, 4, 12, 20, 70, 132–134, 391, 421, 430–431, 453, 470, 506, 509, 581, 653, 657–659, 661–662, 664–666, 685, 715, 769, 853, 937, 949, 953, 1043, 1071, 1096, 1100, 1106, 1134, 1146–1147, 1162–1163, 1199, 1217, 1258

V
Values, 18, 509–510, 573, 788–789, 791, 863–875, 967–968
Vancouver, 1144–1146
Virtue, 155, 216, 224–225, 242–243, 305, 313, 324, 434, 518, 536, 567, 684, 867, 1168, 1208, 1212, 1231, 1274
Vision, 3, 7–332, 526, 700, 777, 1010, 1053
Vision-Guided Jewish education, 7
Visual art, 343, 355–356, 359, 361, 364, 367, 602
Voluntary aided denominational schools, 1120
Volunteerism, 865–867
Vouchers, 1075, 1101, 1263

W
Well-qualified, 722, 1041–1060
Western world/perspectives/paradigm, 51, 57–58, 143, 569, 1147, 1228, 1240

Winnipeg, 1144–1146
Wissenschaft des Judentums, donors, 445, 657
World religions, 34, 572, 575, 1112, 1115

Y

Yeshiva, 102, 124–126, 133, 272, 407, 410–412, 421, 618, 733–735, 742, 788, 791, 809, 939–940, 947, 1033, 1066–1068, 1070–1073, 1075–1076, 1094, 1127–1129, 1134, 1149, 1177, 1213, 1221–1222, 1227
Yeshivas (and Bais Yaakov), 126
Yiddish, 120, 131, 378, 421, 423, 429, 645, 661, 1068, 1096, 1127–1128, 1144, 1184–1185, 1187, 1258, 1266, 1272, 1274, 1283

Youth, 129–131, 433, 491, 739, 790, 810–811, 831, 833, 1004, 1095–1096, 1116, 1136, 1279–1280

Z

Zechut banim, 311
Zionism, 122, 167, 255, 285–289, 292, 294, 349, 366, 377, 399, 441, 453, 463, 480, 482, 484–488, 490–494, 521, 622, 736–737, 808, 939, 942, 1015, 1125, 1136, 1144, 1220–1221, 1223, 1225, 1229–1230, 1242, 1246, 1249–1250, 1256, 1279–1280
Zionism/history of Israel, 487
Zionist movement, 377, 485, 492–493, 498, 1109, 1219–1223, 1229–1230, 1269, 1279
Zionist Youth Movements, 23, 185, 500, 1121, 1131, 1170, 1253–1254